Four in One

Thinking, Reading, Writing, Researching

Edward A. Dornan
Orange Coast College

Robert Dees
Orange Coast College

Allyn and Bacon
BOSTON LONDON TORONTO SYDNEY TOKYO SINGAPORE

Vice President, Humanities: Joseph Opiela
Editorial Assistant: Mary Beth Varney
Senior Marketing Manager: Lisa Kimball
Editorial-Production Administrator: Donna Simons
Editorial-Production Service: Susan Freese, Communicáto, Ltd.; Omegatype Typography, Inc.
Text Design: Carol Somberg/Omegatype Typography, Inc.
Electronic Composition: Omegatype Typography, Inc.
Photo Researcher: Laurie Frankenthaler
Manufacturing Buyer: Suzanne Lareau
Cover Administrator: Linda Knowles
Cover Designer: Susan Paradise

Between the time website information is gathered and then published, it is not
unusual for some sites to have closed. Also, the transcription of URLs can result
in unintended typographical errors. The publisher would appreciate being notified
of any problems with URLs so that they may be corrected in subsequent editions.

Library of Congress Cataloging-in-Publication Data
Dornan, Edward A.
    Four in one : thinking, reading, writing, researching / Edward A.
Dornan, Robert Dees.
        p.   cm.
    Includes index.
    ISBN 0-205-15280-5 (alk. paper)
    1. English language—Rhetoric.   2. Critical thinking—Problems,
exercises, etc.   3. Report writing—Problems, exercises, etc.
4. English language—Grammar.   5. College readers.   I. Dees,
Robert.   II. Title.
    PE1408.D674   1999
    808'.0427—dc21   98-42007
                                                                      CIP

*Photo and text permissions credits appear on page 734, which constitutes a
continuation of this copyright page.*

Printed in the United States of America
10   9   8   7   6   5   4   3   2   1   RRDV   03   02   01   00   99   98

Contents

PART IV
The Research Essay   305

CHAPTER 20

Finding and Researching
a Topic   307

CHAPTER 21

Researching on
the Internet   334

PART VII
Handbook   641

Sentence Errors   643

Punctuation   679

Mechanics   702

Author Biographies   717

Indexes

Preface

Four in One started as an idea in the mid-1990s, a time at which selecting textbooks had become a major chore. Our freshman writing program had become so complex that not a single book fit our needs; rather, we needed specific sections from several books. In the process of choosing these books, our office floor had become a maze of texts stacked three feet high, each waiting to be considered for adoption. There were stacks of rhetorics, stacks of handbooks, stacks of readers, and stacks of research and critical-thinking guides.

We were not the only faculty members to feel frustration. One day, a second-year teacher walked into our office and held up four books bound with rubber bands. He said, "Here, this is the perfect text," and then he dropped the bundle on the desk.

We decided he was right and set about writing *Four in One*. Our overall goal was to integrate thinking, writing, reading, and research instruction in a single text—one that would meet all the curriculum requirements of freshman composition. More specifically, we developed the following set of objectives to guide the development of *Four in One*:

- To be user friendly, a book students could take up on their own and learn from
- To emphasize thinking—random, reflective, and critical thinking—and to integrate concepts about thinking throughout the text
- To offer plenty of examples and a mixture of professional and student writing, thus creating realistic portrayals of experienced and inexperienced writers at work
- To be flexible so the text could support a variety of teaching styles
- To provide authentic collaborative learning activities so students could work effectively in groups
- To include a variety of writing assignments so as to launch students into their own writing projects
- To outline the most recent guidelines for documenting research essays in both the Modern Language Association (MLA) and the American Psychological Association (APA) styles
- To provide a complete guide to conducting research on the Internet
- To showcase important information
- To give editing and revising tips that are clear and succinct

The result of our efforts is *Four in One*. We believe we achieved our goal and objectives in writing it. We hope you agree and find this book supports your teaching style as well as it does ours.

ORGANIZATION AND FEATURES

Part I, Thinking Clearly (Chapters 1–3), introduces students to different modes of thinking and presents concepts that are used throughout the text. Because reading, writing, and discussion engage the mind at several levels, we emphasize the importance of using different modes of thought for different purposes. Through anecdotes and examples, we *show* students, not just explain, how thinking works. Individual and collaborative activities, found at the each of each chapter in Part I, help students put what they've learned to work.

Chapter 1, Effective Thinking, covers three kinds of thinking. Students learn that *random thinking* is spontaneous, allowing fugitive thoughts to bubble into consciousness; that *reflective thinking* is associative, making it the closest to what most people think of as creative thinking; and that *critical thinking* is analytical and based on definable principles of thinking. The discussion identifies characteristics of each mode of thinking and how all three modes work together in daily life as well as in writing, reading, and discussion.

Chapter 2, Critical Thinking, teaches students that to think critically is *not* to find fault. Students are introduced to the profile of an effective critical thinker and read Mike Royko's "Endorsements: Just a Shell Game" to see a critical thinker in action. This chapter also explains key critical-thinking skills, such as distinguishing fact from opinion, identifying assumptions, and evaluating information by five criteria. One chapter-ending activity asks students to read Gary Soto's "Like Mexicans" and analyze the perceptions of the key figures in the essay.

Chapter 3, Critical Thinking and Working with Others, presents three ways that groups organize themselves and the roles individual group members play. Students learn the Rogerian method of conflict resolution and concept clarification. There is also an ample discussion of reasoning processes and advice on how to avoid the pitfalls of group work, such as succumbing to groupthink, being misdirected by emotional appeals, and getting swept away by persuasive techniques. The chapter closes with a collaborative activity that encourages students to work together to solve a survival problem.

Part II, Writing College Essays (Chapters 4–10), reviews the writing process by following the development of a single student essay. Readers then apply what they've learned at each stage by completing activities at the end of each chapter. The discussion in this part emphasizes the interplay of reflective and critical thinking in the composing process. Information related to composing on a computer is also integrated.

Chapter 4, Preparing to Write an Essay, lays the foundation by emphasizing the relationship between thinking and writing. Students learn cognitive levels of thinking as they relate to writing assignments. This chapter also introduces guidelines for assessing a writing situation, including the importance of picturing a reader. The chapter closes with a discussion of common essay conventions and an activity for students to test their knowledge of them.

Chapter 5, The Composing Process: Prewriting and Informal Planning, begins tracing the development of one student's college essay. While emphasizing the role of reflective thinking, this chapter covers a variety of prewriting techniques and shows students how to identify and limit a subject. The chapter also shows students how to write an effective purpose statement, which will guide the early stages of essay development.

Chapter 5 also introduces a teaching strategy we are particularly proud of: A finished student essay, which is fully annotated with marginal comments, is presented at the beginning of the chapter. That essay is then referred to throughout the chapter in discussing specific aspects of its development. Our goal is first to establish what the final draft of a student essay will look like and then to look back and capture the evolution of the essay. In doing so, we aim to demonstrate to students that writing is recursive. We use this strategy in all the subsequent chapters of Part II.

Chapter 6, Writing a Thesis Statement and a Formal Plan, shows how a thesis statement evolves from a purpose statement and prewriting activities. Here, the emphasis shifts from reflective thinking to critical thinking as it relates to the composing process. Students learn how to analyze and evaluate information generated through reflective thinking so they can begin to shape an essay.

Chapter 7, Writing Paragraphs for the Rough Draft, presents paragraphs as cohesive units of the essay, not as discrete blocks of information. Students continue to follow the evolution of a student essay while learning a variety of paragraph arrangements that provide several options for writing introduction, discussion, and closing paragraphs.

Chapter 8, Responses to a Rough Draft: Instructor and Peer Comments, offers guidelines for both giving and receiving comments on rough drafts of essays. The discussion also emphasizes the importance of working in peer groups and suggests ways for students to offer meaningful comments during peer-review sessions.

Chapter 9, Revising a Rough Draft: Structure, Paragraphs, and Sentences, provides specific guidelines for revision along with plenty of examples for illustration. Students are shown how to revise in stages, beginning with the whole essay and working down to paragraphs, sentences, and words. They learn how to sharpen their sentences by making them clear and concise, applying such skills as using specific words, revising passive voice, and reworking sexist language.

The last chapter in the essay-writing sequence is Chapter 10, Preparing to Submit an Essay. It gives tips on proofreading the final draft to ensure it contains consistent diction and sentence variety and to correct those nagging errors that seem to appear magically, even when the computer is turned off. This chapter also shows students the standard format for a manuscript.

After completing Part II, students will have encountered every stage of the writing process, from prewriting to proofreading. They will also have learned the importance of shifting their thought process from reflective to critical thinking as they move from prewriting to analyzing and evaluating information for the final draft of the essay.

Part III, Development Patterns, is composed of nine chapters (11–19), each of which is devoted to a single rhetorical pattern: description, narration, examples, comparison, cause and effect, process analysis, classification and division, definition, and argument (respectively). Each chapter emphasizes the composing process, as reflected in the chapters in Part II, and follows the same arrangement:

1. A detailed explanation of the development pattern under discussion
2. An annotated student essay that reflects the pattern and specific commentary on it
3. A specific discussion of how to write an essay using the pattern, illustrated with paragraphs from the student essay and from the work of professional writers and ending with reminders about using transitions effectively
4. Tips on revising, using a sample paragraph from the student essay for demonstration
5. A list of guidelines for writing an essay using the pattern
6. Extensive suggestions for writing activities, including one that asks students to respond to a photograph

The coverage of Chapter 19, Argument: Convincing a Reader, is even more extensive than that of the other chapters in Part III. In addition to the sections just outlined, it includes a discussion of evidence, logical arrangement, and structuring an argument for a reader. This chapter recalls from Chapters 2 and 3 the full discussion of logical fallacies, induction, and deduction. Moreover, it provides a clear explanation of Toulmin's method of building and analyzing an argument.

We have used the same teaching strategy throughout Part III that we introduced in Part II: that is, presenting a student model early in each chapter and then referring to it throughout the discussion of each development pattern, again reinforcing the recursive nature of the writing process. We decided not to include full-length professional essays in Part III for two reasons:

1. We didn't want to create the impression that all essays fit neatly into one development pattern or another. In fact, writers typically use several patterns when developing their thoughts in essays. We do emphasize, however, that most essays have a dominant pattern of development but few embody only one pattern.
2. We wanted to offer a collection of essays for the purpose of emphasizing critical reading as well as writing. Arranging professional essays rhetorically and placing them at ends of appropriate chapters would have focused the reading on patterns exclusively, thus limiting their value in most classrooms. Instead, as we'll discuss shortly, we arranged a body of professional essays in alphabetical order in Part VI. We have included a *rhetorical* index for those instructors and students who want to concentrate more intensely on development patterns and a *thematic* index for those who like to discuss themes.

Part IV, The Research Essay, presents a comprehensive four-chapter sequence on writing a research essay:

- Chapter 20, Finding and Researching a Topic
- Chapter 21, Researching on the Internet
- Chapter 22, Writing Your Research Essay: From Planning to Typing the Final Draft
- Chapter 23, Documenting Sources in Your Research Essay

Part IV has several outstanding features. One is the comprehensive coverage of researching on the Internet provided in Chapter 21—from accessing the Internet to using search engines and evaluating sources. A reliability checklist for Internet sources is provided as well, encouraging students to be critical readers of all sources, electronic and otherwise. In addition, Chapter 22 applies the strategy used elsewhere of demonstrating how a student essay is developed and then presents the completed essay at the end of the chapter, with detailed annotations. Finally, Chapter 23 provides complete and current guidelines for both MLA- and APA-style documentation along with ample illustrations.

The three chapters in Part V, Writing for Other Purposes, give students a taste of practical writing. Chapter 24, Writing about Literature, offers practical information about writing in response to a piece of writing; it also includes a sample student essay about A. E. Housman's "To an Athlete Dying Young." Chapter 25, Writing for an Essay Exam, aims to take the discomfort out of writing in class; the discussion is direct and simple, concentrating on the practical application of writing technique. And Chapter 26, Writing for Business, is packed with practical information about the kinds of writing that occur in the workplace: letters, resumes, memos, FAXes, and e-mail.

Part VI, Readings for Writers, begins with a discussion of how to read critically in both first and second readings. Students then practice these critical-reading skills by analyzing Willard Gaylin's "What You See Is the Real You." A section of Selected Readings, mentioned earlier, includes a variety of essays, ranging from the tried and true—such as Jonathan Swift's "A Modest Proposal," George Orwell's "A Hanging," and E. B. White's "Once More to the Lake"—to the outrageously contemporary—such as David James Duncan's "Toxins in the Mother Tongue," a chronicle of a novelist's encounter with small-town censors; Andrew Klavan's "The Shrieking of the Lambs," an energetic defense of violence in fiction; and Michael Medved's "Denial Behavior," an argument against violence in the media. The essays also vary in length and complexity. Some are short and direct, such as Judy Brady's "I Want a Wife"; others are long and complex, such as Klavan's "The Shrieking of the Lambs." Their common trait is that all of them will engage students and stimulate discussion.

Note that none of the essays in this section is prefaced by comments about its content or author. Other than the title and the name of the author, the only information given about each essay is the year in which it was written or, in some cases, published. Our rationale for eliminating the usual introductory material is that it's more effective for students to come to an essay with open minds. We feel they should find their own way through a reading, tracing the thread of discussion and bringing fresh responses to the reading experience. We do, however, guide students after they have read each essay by having them complete a variety of activities: journal-writing assignments, rereading activities, collaborative work and group discussion, and writing assignments based on responses students generated during the reading process.

Part VII is a straightforward handbook supplement that covers the most commonly committed errors in writing. It also has an extensive section designed for ESL students who have had some writing experience but may still make common second-language errors. In order to make referencing errors easy, a correction chart is provided inside the back cover of the book. Each symbol in the chart identifies an error and the page number on which it's discussed. Exercises are also provided at key points throughout the handbook section.

ACKNOWLEDGMENTS

We owe an enormous debt to the teachers and students who have contributed their insights and time to the development of *Four in One*. We were also fortunate to have had a committed team of reviewers who not only scrutinized the manuscript but also contributed their years of teaching experience to help make *Four in One* a more writer-friendly textbook:

William K. Buckley, Indiana University, Northwest

John Covolo, Lakeland Community College

M. Jean Jones, Columbia State University

Rodney Keller, Ricks College

Bill Lalicker, West Chester University, Pennsylvania

Bill Lamb, Johnson County Community College

Joyce Miller, Collin County Community College

Kathryn Mincey, Morehead State University

Edna Troiano, Charles County Community College

Stephen Wilhoit, University of Dayton

We owe a special debt to Professors Michael Finnegan and Don Pierstorff of Orange Coast College for their extensive contributions to Part VI, Readings for Writers. We also wish to acknowledge our debt to Sue Freese, of Communicáto, Ltd., whose keen eye and sensitive suggestions helped refine the final publication.

Without the patience, persistence, endurance, and, whenever it was required, the blind trust of Allyn and Bacon's professional staff, *Four in One* would still be in our imaginations, not on your desk. Our gratitude goes out to Production Director Judy Fiske and Production Administrator Donna Simons for guiding *Four in One* through production in record time. Our deepest appreciation goes to Joe Opiela, Allyn and Bacon's Vice President of Humanities. It was his trust, insight, and determination that fueled *Four in One* from conception to completion.

Thinking Clearly

Effective Thinking

Let us tell you a story about thinking—*effective* thinking.

Recently, a student named Sarah reminded us of the mind's mysterious ways. Quite by chance, an anatomy lecture helped her understand *Hamlet, Prince of Denmark,* perhaps Shakespeare's most enigmatic play.

Sarah's anatomy professor, a deep-voiced, ruddy-faced man in owlish glasses and with a mischievous sparkle in his eyes, was lecturing on the human nervous system. He described it as an "intricate watershed for pain and joy that all collects—" he paused dramatically, tapping a finger against his skull, "here, behind a half-inch of bone!"

Then from a black box, his eyes flashing in delight, he lifted a jar in which floated a human brain. "This lump of flesh," he continued, "is the reservoir of human experience." Light was streaming through the laboratory windows. He tilted the jar overhead, as if he were making a sacrificial offering. "Mystical, isn't it? Pleasure and pain, each thought, each vision, intuition, or dream— every single human sensation—must flow through the nervous system's tributaries to pool *here* in the brain. An entire universe swims in this mysterious organ's chemistry."

This was the first brain Sarah had seen. "A real brain!" she said, her voice full of awe.

Two weeks later, Sarah's literature class was discussing *Hamlet.* The discussion centered on Hamlet's sense of despair and the feeling of being disconnected from everyone around him because of his father's suspicious death. The discussion had bogged down over a comment Hamlet makes to two friends, in which he compares the world to a prison. One of his friends suggests that Hamlet's ambition to be King of Denmark must make the world seem like a prison. Hamlet scoffs, "Oh God," he says, "I could be bounded in a nutshell and count myself a king of infinite space, were it not that I have bad dreams."

What does Shakespeare mean? The class struggled with an interpretation. Finally, they agreed: Hamlet's comment means he does not have any raging ambition. Moreover, he feels agitated because of his dark attitude toward humankind.

Sarah remembered the brain she had seen two weeks before. Even though she was usually shy, Sarah spoke up anyway. "I think Shakespeare means something else. Don't we all live in our individual nutshells?"

Several students laughed politely; others listened thoughtfully. "What do you mean?" one finally asked.

So Sarah explained. "Think about a brain. What is it shaped like? What does its surface look like?"

"Like half a walnut, a walnut shell!" one student said.

"We *are* all 'bounded' in a nutshell. We live in our brains."

"Yet from that small space, we can all contemplate infinity . . . like kings of 'infinite space.' "

"And the world around us is like a dream we create in our own little nutshell minds."

"And since Hamlet sees the world so darkly, his 'dreams' are dark, just like our feelings shape the way we look at life."

Sarah's group reread other parts of the play, testing to see if Shakespeare's observation fit with other imagery. In the end, they decided Shakespeare's metaphor is apt, both for the play and for human experience. Figuratively speaking, we *are* each bounded in a nutshell—the human brain.

How does this story illustrate effective thinking? That's a fair question. The interpretation of Hamlet developed through three kinds of thinking—*random thinking, reflective thinking,* and *critical thinking*—all of which work together in our daily lives.

USE RANDOM THINKING TO RELEASE THOUGHTS

Have you ever noticed your mind drifting? Maybe you're bored. Maybe you've been concentrating too long. Or, as happens with many of us, maybe you're just closing your eyes to get a good night's sleep. At these moments, full consciousness begins to fade, and you enter a twilight state, in which spontaneous thoughts come unbidden—an aimless flow of images, disconnected memories, and unrecognized feelings that seem to be hovering at the edge of consciousness. We'll call this spontaneous kind of thinking *random thinking.*

When you think randomly, logic falls away. For no apparent reason, fragments from a song might float into your memory. Mysteriously, your mind then leaps ahead to a weekend event you've planned—a dance, a ball game, a trip home. You construct it in your imagination, perhaps putting yourself at the center of the activity. You linger there a while and then slip into childhood memories—your first day at school, the time you tumbled from a tree, a raucous family gathering. All this twilight travel might even give you a vague sense of well-being or anxiety, depending on what feelings are associated with the events drifting through your memory. These thoughts come spontaneously. If there is an unconscious connection among them, trying to figure it out will probably leave you scratching your head, puzzled.

Sometimes, spontaneous thoughts are too strong to resist. They demand attention, possibly even setting the imagination ablaze. "Ah ha!" "Eureka!" an important discovery. You emerge from this twilight state and begin to think with a conscious purpose. In other words, you begin to direct your thoughts—that is, you begin to reflect.

USE REFLECTIVE THINKING
TO GENERATE INFORMATION

Having a conscious purpose is what distinguishes the three kinds of thinking. Random thinking is spontaneous; it lacks direction. Reflective and critical thinking are purposeful; they have direction.

Reflective thinking is the conscious effort to discover unexpected connections among diverse experiences and information. Have a problem? Use reflective thinking to generate a list of possible solutions. Want to find the meaning of an event? Reflect on its possible causes and effects or relate it to other events to discover their similarities and differences. At the heart of reflective thinking is *association:* a process that generates information, insights, and ideas from memory.

In one respect, reflective thinking is similar to random thinking: Once you've developed a clear purpose, you let your thoughts drift, hoping to recall experiences related to your purpose—experiences such as casual observations, unexplainable hunches, startling ideas, fragments from conversations, details from lectures, even snippets from reading. This activity is similar to what's done in random thinking, but it has a purpose.

USE CRITICAL THINKING TO ANALYZE
AND EVALUATE INFORMATION

Now the going gets tough. Remember, all thoughts aren't equal. In fact, it's easier to think foolishly than wisely. To think wisely, you must use *critical thinking* to sift through the bits of information reflective thinking generates. You ask yourself: Are the connections clear? Is this the best approach? Is this information logical? At the heart of critical thinking is *evaluation*—that is, does *it* work? Is *it* right? Reasonable?

When thinking critically, you test possibilities, explore assertions, reveal implicit assumptions, trace logical relationships, and apply standards of reasoning—all of which are highly defined activities in the critical thinker's repertoire. At the highest level, critical thinking helps you select diverse information, shape it into coherent form, and evaluate it. At the lowest level, critical thinking helps you figure out where you left the car keys.

For example, imagine that you face a problem—nothing complex, just a little annoyance that must be solved. You and your roommate have a class at 11:00 a.m. The class syllabus states that four absences will result in being dropped for nonattendance. You each have three absences already.

It's now 10:15.

It's a 30-minute drive to campus, hitting all green lights.

It's 10° below zero outside, the first big winter freeze brought on by a heavy wind blowing across the lake.

Now the noose tightens: Your roommate rushes through the door, saying, "The car won't start. Dead battery! Stone dead. Ohmygod! What'll we do?"

You're at a crossroads. You could think randomly about the problem—that is, you wait for a solution to appear spontaneously. In this case, you might play your favorite compact disk, stretch out on the sofa, and let your mind drift. The fact is, random thinking will not be very productive, given the time pressure, but it is still a possibility.

More than likely, you would reflect on the problem by mentally compiling a list of possible solutions:

- Call a friend?
- Borrow the neighbor's car?
- Catch the bus?
- Bike?
- Walk?

As you compile this mental list, you evaluate each item by a single standard: Will it work?

- Your friends have early morning classes—they've left.
- The neighbor's car is at the mechanic's—it's gone.
- The next bus won't arrive for 40 minutes—too late.
- It's too cold to bike or walk.

"Maybe we won't be dropped," you begin to speculate. After all, the weather is bad. Other students will miss class, too.

Unfortunately, this instructor is a first-semester TA. His syllabus spells out the rules *in detail.* He clings to the syllabus as if it were the only map showing the way through enemy territory to safety.

You clutch your temples, trying to squeeze out a solution. "Think! Think! Think!" And then you remember a newspaper advertisement: "Call a cab. No more than a 10-minute wait anywhere in town! 432-RIDE!"

Will it work? You bet!

The whole process probably took no more than two or three minutes. After all, the problem isn't much more complicated than "Where are the keys?"

Now, back to Hamlet, a king of infinite space—definitely a more complex problem.

It was Sarah's hunch, a random thought, that initiated a deeper class discussion of Hamlet's comment. Sarah spontaneously associated it to a past experience: an anatomy lecture. Her classmates picked up the thread of her thought by offering their own associations. In what might be called a *brain-*

storming session, they generated an interpretation and evaluated it within the logic of the entire play—that is, they evaluated the interpretation.

To be human is to think. Thinking is as natural to all of us as swimming is to fish. How *effectively* we think is another matter, though. It just isn't natural to think effectively. You must learn how to do it, which is no simple task.

You must begin by viewing effective thinking as a purposeful activity that you can direct but maybe not control. Second, you must learn what makes for effective thinking, especially critical thinking, one of the three types of thinking processes that philosophers have scrutinized in depth. Third, you must orchestrate all the elements of effective thinking within your own thinking process, so that you know the right time to use reflection and the right time to use evaluation.

Activities

■ **RECORDING REFLECTIONS**

The following photograph is unnamed. Your task is to name it. How? First, reflect on the photograph, speculating about each of its elements: What does the physical structure suggest? What consistent patterns do you discern? What is similar and what is different among the elements? What associations do you have with the image? Make notes as you speculate about the photograph. When you've finished speculating, review your notes, looking for any relationships among them that suggest a title. Finally, compose a title that captures the dominant impression the photograph creates.

Next, think critically about the photograph. Write a 100- to 150-word analysis that explains what *specific elements* in the photograph helped you decide on a title. Remember, identify specific elements, not random speculations, in the photograph.

GROUP WORK

In work groups, present your titles and compare your reasons for composing them. Be sure each title is justified by specific details in the photograph. Among group members, try to agree on the most appropriate title—the one that captures a dominant impression and guides viewers to particular details that support it.

Critical Thinking

In popular culture, random and reflective thinking often are categorized as *creative thinking,* thus linking them to the *creative process.* The intuitive, spontaneous, and associative characteristics of these types of thinking are important to creativity, but to emphasize them while ignoring the significant role critical thinking plays in the creative process leads to a common stereotype.

In the popular media, such as film and television, artists and scientists are frequently portrayed as wild-eyed mavericks whose imaginations are fueled by emotion, not by reason. Think of the Hollywood image of the crazed painter, slashing a brush across a canvas, or the mad doctor in the lab, waiting for lightning to strike. Artists and scientists, according to the stereotype, live in a world of imagination, where inspiration supplants reason.

Like most stereotypes, this image only paints part of the picture. As we indicated in Chapter 1, the different kinds of thinking processes—that is, random, reflective, and critical thinking—work together. Just as artists and scientists must rely on intuition, spontaneity, and association to explore their unique insights, they must also rely on critical thinking to shape and evaluate the outcome, whether it's a painting or a scientific theory.

THINKING CRITICALLY IS NOT FAULT FINDING

Perhaps the word *critical* creates confusion. In common usage, it means "taking a negative view" or "searching for mistakes." We've all heard misleading comments like "They criticize my every imperfection," when the speaker probably meant *ridicule,* not *criticize.*

Being *critical* is more accurately associated with *interpreting, analyzing,* and *evaluating,* which are all very complex intellectual activities. In fact, an initial step toward becoming a critical thinker might be to avoid using the word *critical* to describe any sort of fault finding. It's better to use the word appropriately, as in "We must avoid emotionalism and think critically about arguments against gun control." Using *critical* accurately will help you keep the purpose of critical thinking clearly in mind.

SURVIVING THE INFORMATION ONSLAUGHT

Random thinking happens spontaneously. Reflective thinking is more purposeful, often employing such informal idea generating practices as *brainstorming*, *clustering*, and *free association*. In contrast, critical thinking is downright calculated, often employing highly defined concepts and skills to examine personal and cultural experiences.

So-called conventional wisdom tells us that the traditional institutions of family, school, and church used to be the dominant influences in most people's lives. For better or worse, parents, teachers, and clergy members shaped personal and cultural perceptions through presenting a set of consistent values. Now, the mass media—television, radio, music, motion pictures, newspapers, magazines, and books—have more influence in shaping personal and cultural perceptions than traditional institutions—or so conventional wisdom claims. Of course, such wisdom also once claimed that black-skinned people were property, that a woman's place was in the home, and that Asian countries would tumble into communism like falling dominos if the U.S. military withdrew from Vietnam. All these claims were wrong then. So how do we know what's right now?

The pervasive onslaught of the mass media is relatively recent. Consider that Johannes Gutenberg invented the printing press with moveable type in the fifteenth century. And with this invention, print was established as the primary means of mass communication for the next 550 years.

Today, there are over 1,650 newspapers around the world, publishing roughly 65 million copies each day. There are also approximately 10,000 magazines published every month and close to 50,000 new books published every year. In addition, over 1,400 television stations send programs to 93 million American homes, and approximately 10,000 radio stations broadcast to almost 500 million radios. Plus, there are nearly 25,000 movie houses operating on the average of eight hours a day. And now we have the World Wide Web, with its infinite possibilities for dispensing information and images.

Is conventional wisdom on target? Does the mass media dominate daily life in the United States? There is no escaping the fact that the media saturates our culture. Advertisers, celebrities, talk show hosts, and politicians float through all of our lives, trying to convince us to buy or support uncritically their products or ideas. In an interview, psychologist Eric Fromm summed up the threat of the mass media, saying that it influences our values by encouraging people to "acquire more and more, not to become more and more."

What defense do you have against the onslaught of mass media values? You must learn to think defensively by processing information critically.

PROFILE OF A CRITICAL THINKER

What is a critical thinker? Is it a rare creature or just one that's exceptionally stealthful? It's not difficult to spot a critical thinker if you know what to look for when you see one in action. Generally, he or she can come from any walk of life and has what those mesmerized by the mass media would call an *attitude*—that is, the desire to think beyond the obvious. To see what we mean, read the following essay by the late Mike Royko, who was a *Chicago Tribune* newspaper columnist. Follow his reasoning as he humorously digs beneath the surface of his own experience.

Endorsements: Just a Shell Game

The man from an advertising agency had an unusual proposition. 1

His agency does the TV commercials for a well-known chain of Mexican restaurants in Chicago. 2

"You may have seen our commercials," he said. "They include a cameo appearance by Lee Smith and Leon Durham of the Cubs. It shows them crunching into a tortilla." 3

No, I somehow missed seeing that. 4

"Well, anyway, we'd like to have you in a commercial." 5

Doing what? 6

"Crunching into a tortilla." 7

I thought tortillas were soft. I may be wrong, but I don't think you can crunch into a tortilla. Maybe you mean a taco. 8

"Well, you'd be biting into some kind of Mexican food." 9

What else would I do? 10

"That's it. It would be a cameo appearance. You'd be seen for about four seconds. You wouldn't have to say anything." 11

I'd just bite into a piece of Mexican food? 12

"Right. For a fee, of course." 13

How big a fee? 14

He named a figure. It was not a king's ransom, but it was more than walking-around money. 15

"It would take about 45 minutes to film," he said. 16

Amazing. In my first newspaper job almost 30 years ago, I had to work 12 weeks to earn the figure he had mentioned. 17

It was a small, twice-a-week paper, and I was the only police reporter, the only sports reporter, the only investigative reporter, the assistant political writer, and on Saturday I would edit the stories going into the entertainment page. The publisher believed in a day's work for an hour's pay. 18

Now I could make the same amount just for spending 45 minutes biting into a taco in front of a TV camera. 19

"Well, what do you think?" he asked. 20

I told him that I would think about it and get back to him. 21

So I asked Slats Grobnik, who has sound judgment, what he thought of the deal. 22

"That's a lot of money just to bite a taco on TV. For that kind of scratch, I'd bite a dog. Grab the deal." 23

But there is a question of ethics. 24

"Ethics? What's the ethics in biting a taco?" Millions of people bite tacos every day.   25
Mexicans have been biting them for hundreds of years. Are you saying that Mexicans
are unethical? Careful, some of my best friends are Mexicans."

No, I'm not saying that at all. I like Mexicans, too, although I'm opposed to bull-   26
fighting.

"Then what's unethical?"   27

The truth is, I can't stand tacos.   28

"What has that got to do with it? I can't stand work, but I do it for the money."   29

It has everything to do with it. If I go on TV and bite into a taco, won't I be en-   30
dorsing that taco?

"So what? You've endorsed politicians and I've never met a politician that I liked   31
better than a taco."

But endorsing a taco I didn't like would be dishonest.   32

"Hey, that's the American way. Turn on your TV and look at all the people who en-   33
dorse junk. Do you think they really believe what they're saying?"

Then it's wrong. Nobody should endorse a taco if they don't like a taco.   34

"Then tell them you'll bite something else. A tortilla or an enchilada."   35

But I don't like them, either. The truth is, I can't stand most Mexican food. The only   36
thing I really like is the salt on the edge of a margarita glass.

"Can't you just bite the taco and spit it out when the camera is turned off?"   37

That would be a sham. Besides, even if I liked tacos or tortillas, what does it mat-   38
ter? Why should somebody eat in a restaurant because they see me biting into the
restaurant's taco? Am I a taco expert? What are my credentials to tell millions of people what taco they should eat? I'm not even Mexican.

"You're as Mexican as Jane Byrne [former Chicago mayor], and she's doing it."   39

To get the Hispanic vote, she would go on TV and eat a cactus.   40

"Well, you're a sucker to turn it down. Why, it's almost un-American. Do you think   41
that in Russia any newsman would ever have an opportunity to make that much
money by biting into a pirogi?"

That may be so.   42

But maybe someday a food product will come along that I can lend my name to,   43
something I can truly believe in.

"I doubt it. Not unless they start letting taverns advertise shots and beers on TV."   44

Royko, tongue in cheek, displays several characteristics of critical thinkers.
First, he is a *cultural interrogator*. Critical thinkers relentlessly interrogate the
dominate values of their culture, or what we referred to earlier as *conventional
wisdom*. Every culture's conventional wisdom usually embraces what is considered "normal"—that is, a habitual way of looking at life. But what is normal?
It varies from age to age and from culture to culture. For example, it was once
normal to believe that by understanding astrology, you could reveal how someone's life would unfold. Once, the earth was believed to be the center of the

universe and its surface was thought to be flat, like a table top. It was once normal for children to work in fields and factories from dawn to dusk. And it was once normal to pay men more than women for the same work (and still seems to be, in some professions!).

Royko confronts the conventional wisdom that celebrities should capitalize on their status. He decides that it would be unethical for him to endorse tacos, since he not only doesn't like tacos but doesn't like Mexican food in general. Moreover, he challenges the ethics of celebrity endorsement altogether, wondering why anyone would visit a restaurant after seeing a well-known person bite into one of its tacos on television. He also questions the economic justice of paying him (or anyone, for that matter) such a substantial amount of money for so little work—as much money as he used to make for twelve weeks of hard labor as a reporter.

Royko is also *self-analytical*. Critical thinkers look into themselves to discover what they do and don't believe. When faced with temptation, they re-examine their values and then alter or stick by them, as appropriate. They also know that powerful experiences might have two levels of meaning: the *manifest* meaning, which they can understand intellectually, and the *latent* meaning, which influences them emotionally. In any case, self-analysis helps them through difficult decisions.

Royko no doubt feels the subconscious pull of the endorsement offer, but he sticks by his values. As his buddy pressures him to accept the money and endorse the restaurant, Royko reveals how he truly feels. It would be dishonest—worse, a sham—for him to endorse anything he doesn't truly believe in.

Even so, Royko keeps an *open mind*. Critical thinkers are willing to consider information that opposes their position. They remain objective while trying to understand why they react to a person or an experience in a certain way. They accept that their first reactions are tentative. A critical thinker might ask: Have I been influenced by a friend? A celebrity? A politician? An unexamined value? Or perhaps by the emotional seduction of advertising or political rhetoric? Critical thinkers are always open to change. That is, they are willing to modify a decision, if new information and analysis warrants modification, or leave a question open, sometimes holding in mind two opposing points of view as viable possibilities.

As an effective critical thinker, Royko actively listens to the advertising agency's offer and then seeks out a friend's opinion. He listens to his friend's reasoning and weighs it while exploring his own reasons for rejecting the offer. Royko clearly resists influence. His friend approves of celebrity endorsement. By lending their names to products, celebrity figures like athletes and even the Chicago mayor also approve. In the end, Royko stands up for his personal values yet humorously keeps an open mind about accepting such an offer in the future, saying, "But maybe someday [something] will come along that I can . . . truly believe in."

Critical thinkers have two other characteristics, although they are not obvious in Royko's essay. First of all, critical thinkers are *consensus builders*. They make an effort "to walk in the other person's shoes"—that is, they work at understanding other people's points of view. Although they might disagree with someone's beliefs, they don't concentrate on the disagreements. Instead, they attempt to keep communication open and identify common ground, on which they can build agreement. Furthermore, critical thinkers are *intellectually daring*. They pursue knowledge, especially knowledge that will help them clarify experience. They understand that to think critically not only requires self-understanding but also having accurate information and the intellectual skills necessary to analyze experience.

In sum, there are five characteristics of critical thinkers:

1. *Culturally interrogating:* They relentlessly question their culture's dominant values.
2. *Self-analyzing:* They look into themselves to examine their own values.
3. *Open minded:* They consider information that opposes their position.
4. *Consensus building:* They keep communication open to build agreement.
5. *Intellectually daring:* They pursue knowledge to help them clarify experience.

BECOMING A CRITICAL THINKER

Interpret Experience

An ancient wise man once said, "A student should pursue truth like a man whose hair is aflame pursues water." Ultimately, the pursuit of truth will not lead you to water. Rather, it will lead to a puzzling question: *What constitutes truth?* Facts or people's perceptions of facts? Over 25 centuries ago, two Greek philosopher/historians wrestled with this question. Thucydides decided that truth should be based on facts. Herodotus took the opposite view, believing that people's self-images, folklore, and even delusions—everything that makes up their perceptions—are as important as hard facts.

The question of what constitutes truth always comes up when people from strikingly different backgrounds examine their experience. For example, in Los Angeles, on the night of March 3, 1991, an event took place that would rock the city. A videotape of the event showed a band of police beating an African American named Rodney King. The tape was played on television sets around the world. It galvanized public opinion by creating a sense that viewers were actually witnessing the beating. But did the videotape reveal the facts? *All* the facts? *Enough* of them? *Whose* facts?

The infamous tape had been edited for television. It did not show the high-speed, 7-mile chase that led up to the event. It did not show King—over 6 feet tall and muscular from working out for hours in weight rooms—appear virtually psychotic from drugs, according to police. It did not show that two jolts from a stun gun had no effect on him or that he threw off several officers who tried to subdue him. It did not even show King charging an officer who had hit him with a baton.

Nonetheless, this single video depicted two conflicting facts: To many viewers, it showed the police subduing a criminal resisting arrest, but to others, it showed Anglo police officers brutally clubbing an African American man. A year later, when a jury acquitted the three officers of using excessive force in arresting King, those conflicting perceptions triggered a riot. Fifty-four people died. Two thousand were injured. Over eight hundred buildings were burned.

So, which is the basis of truth: fact or perception? The two must work together to create an *interpretation*. An interpretation pulls together facts and opinions and tries to make some sense of them. It is speculative, an attempt to think beyond the obvious to find a deeper truth. Personal experience, literary works, cultural phenomena, and historical events are often the bases of interpretation.

In public events, such as the Rodney King beating, facts that may seem clear are often clouded and fuel conflicting interpretations. For example, conspiracy theorists have claimed for years that President Franklin D. Roosevelt knew that the Japanese military was going to launch a surprise attack on Pearl Harbor yet did not warn the U.S. military. According to most historians, that attack is what brought the United States into World War II. The accusation against Roosevelt is based mainly on the interpretation of one suspicious fact: Before Pearl Harbor was attacked, the United States had cracked Japan's top-secret diplomatic code, which enabled intelligence agencies to monitor messages to and from Tokyo. This fact is accurate, but another fact, overlooked by conspiracy theorists, is that U.S. government leaders didn't know of the attack because Japan didn't send messages about the plan to attack Pearl Harbor.

The validity of an interpretation is usually difficult to verify, as the conflicting interpretations of the Rodney King video show. Often, even careful analysis won't reveal the truth, but as a critical thinker, you will have to begin an interpretation by separating fact from perception—or as we refer to it, *opinion*.

Distinguish Fact from Opinion

Before you can evaluate what someone claims, you need to know if it is fact or opinion. A *fact* is any statement that can be verified through research, experiment, or observation. Here are some examples:

President John F. Kennedy was shot in Dallas, Texas, on November 22, 1963.

American astronauts landed on the moon during the summer of 1969.

Rock climbers run the risk that a rope will break.

As a critical thinker, you might question how a fact was established. You might consider its accuracy or the method used to determine its truth. You might doubt, for instance, that Lee Harvey Oswald shot President John F. Kennedy. You could then research official reports of the Kennedy assassination to determine the statement's accuracy.

You should always question the validity of facts when someone has something to gain from them. For decades, tobacco companies claimed that smoking was not unhealthful. Tests proved that claim to be a fact, they maintained. But tobacco money was paying for the research that supported the claim. Years later, objective research proved the opposite—that smoking *is* a serious health hazard. Always determine who is behind a factual claim. If it's a self-interested party, then the claim is suspect.

An *opinion* is a statement of interpretation and judgment. Opinions are not simply true or false in the way that factual statements are. You must determine if an opinion is accurate based on how well it is supported by evidence. Consider these examples:

> The assassination of President John F. Kennedy is the most tragic event of this century.

> The moon landing changed the way Americans view technology.

> Rock climbers must have the patience of chess players.

These opinions may be accurate, but they cannot be verified the way facts can. Opinions can, however, be supported with evidence that might be convincing.

One way to distinguish fact from opinion is to think beyond the obvious. For example, "The Pope has more influence than the president" is an opinion that sounds factual. But is it factual? What is meant by *influence?* And with whom does the Pope have influence: Catholics or world leaders whose decisions directly affect millions of people? Asking these questions points out that this statement is really quite subjective.

Identify Assumptions Buried in Information

Assumptions are beliefs that often go unnoticed. When you closely examine an opinion, you will find that it usually rests on one or more assumptions. Consider the following statement, for instance:

> AIDS is nature's way of punishing gay men for their sexual orientation.

Several assumptions are at work in this brief statement. First, it assumes that *nature* is a conscious entity and dispenses punishment. It also assumes that gay men are guilty in some respect and deserve to be punished. Finally, it assumes that sexual orientation is a choice, not a genetic given. Once the assumptions behind this statement are revealed, it loses its power.

Evaluate Information by Five Criteria

In any examination of experience, you or someone else will bring essential information to the discussion. Generally, the information will consist of examples from personal observations, facts, statistics, or expert opinions. When considering the value of the information, keep these five criteria in mind:

1. Information should be relevant and fairly represented. Facts should be accurate, and statistics should be current and come from reliable sources.

2. Information should be representative and embody the full range of experience and opinion. Expert opinions and personal observations should be typical, not exceptional.

3. Information should be sufficient. Generally, the more information, the better. At least enough should be provided to facilitate a complete examination of the subject.

4. Information should be qualified. Avoid using words like *all, always,* and *never.* Instead, qualify information with words like *most, many, often, frequently, probably, infrequently,* and *seldom.*

5. Information must be accurate. Inaccurate information is worse than useless; it's misleading. Always present information carefully, without distortion.

Identify Logical Fallacies Embedded in Information

Logical fallacies are common mistakes in thinking. The word *fallacy* means "a deception" or "a fault in reasoning." Information tainted by logical fallacies is ineffective. As a critical thinker, recognizing common fallacies will help you avoid misdirection. We'll look at specific types of fallacies in the following sections.

Hasty Generalization. Writers and speakers commit hasty generalization when they draw conclusions from insufficient or unrepresentative evidence. Consider this conclusion:

> In recent years, almost every major college athletic program has been investigated by the NCAA for recruitment violations. Every year, at least one team is placed on probation as a result of these investigations. Clearly, those in charge of college athletics must be immoral.

The person who's drawn this conclusion has done so from insufficient evidence. Are *all* violations of complex regulations a matter of immorality? Perhaps some violations are inadvertent or technical. As for the investigations and penalties, they could indicate rigorous enforcement of the rules, rather than widespread immorality.

Next, look at this conclusion:

> During the last year, three of five award-winning films concentrated on family violence. An examination of family violence was just broadcast on national television. No doubt, these events indicate that family violence is on the rise.

Three films and a television program do not represent a trend. The conclusion that family violence is rising should be substantiated with statistics and reports from such authorities as psychologists, sociologists, and law enforcement officials.

And what about this conclusion?

Politicians, whether currently in office or not, should not be allowed to sit on the boards of nonprofit organizations, such as charities, foundations, and educational institutions. We all know that to win an election, a person must always compromise common standards of ethics. Politicians are notorious for representing the individual interests of their supporters and then seeking their financial support in the next election. All of us should fight to keep nonprofit organizations free from this kind of corrupt behavior.

This opinion is based on a common hasty generalization called a *stereotype*. A stereotype is a conclusion—usually, negative—drawn from limited information about a particular group of people. Stereotypes have power because many people accept them uncritically and they are often confirmed in the media. For example, if you already believe that politicians are corrupt, your stereotype will be reinforced by what's reported about political scandals in newspapers and on television. Yet the reality is that only a few politicians of the thousands holding office in city, county, state, and federal governments are ever involved in corruption.

Oversimplification.   People oversimplify when they ignore the essential information a conclusion is based on. Too often, people are eager to offer a simple explanation for a complicated problem. For example:

Getting a good grade in a composition class may involve a lot of your time, but there is nothing difficult about it. All you have to do is meet the required word length and avoid errors in grammar and punctuation.

As you doubtless know by now, getting a good grade in composition also requires clear thinking, organizational skills, and a good deal of effort and practice at writing.

Faulty Either/Or Reasoning.   Many writers and speakers commit the *either/or* fallacy by assuming there are only two alternatives when, in fact, there are many. The slogan "America, love it or leave it" implies that love of country must be unqualified, which has the effect of excluding constructive criticism.
Look for the *either/or* fallacy in this statement:

Drug use is destroying the social order of American cities. The drug problem is so monumental that no one can afford to be neutral. Are we going to do nothing and let criminals rule our cities? Or are we going to give our police more power so that they can control drug traffickers, dealers, and users?

Of course, other actions may relieve the situation: initiating public education, funding rehabilitation for drug users, developing agreements with other countries to curtail drug traffic, and so on. The choices are not just between doing nothing and increasing police power.

Post Hoc Argument.   Assuming that one event *causes* a second, simply because the second follows the first, is committing the *post hoc, ergo propter hoc* ("after this, therefore because of this") fallacy. Here's an example:

> Some people think that microwave ovens are a health threat. I disagree. Our family purchased a microwave oven two years ago. Since then, none of us has seen a doctor.

As stated, the only relation between the purchase of a microwave oven and the good health of this family is that one followed the other. Time sequence alone cannot prove the existence of a cause-and-effect relationship.

Non Sequitur.   The Latin phrase *non sequitur* means "it does not follow." People often commit this fallacy when their conclusions do not logically follow from their premises, as in this statement:

> Ryan Beach has the highest per capita income in the state, but it has the lowest-paid police force, city employees, and schoolteachers. These facts are revealing. They show that those with money know how to keep government expenses under control.

Many factors contribute to per capita income. Perhaps in a small beach town, a few wealthy landowners drive up the average income. Moreover, individuals don't directly pay for city government and schools; they're paid by tax dollars that may come from state or local government. And finally, elected city and school officials—none of whom, in this specific case, may be wealthy—determine employee salaries. Clearly, this writer's conclusion does not follow from the premises.

False Analogy.   A false analogy assumes that if two things are similar in one or more characteristics, then they are similar in other characteristics. For example:

> The European experience in World War II is clear. The lessons should not be ignored. You cannot ignore the rise of a dictator, and you cannot successfully negotiate with one to avoid a war. The best solution is to attack an enemy before he or she attacks.

Conditions today are not the same as they were before World War II. To compare pre–World War II conditions to those in the world today is to fall into the trap of false analogy.

Ad Hominem Argument.   The Latin phrase *ad hominem* means "to the man." Writers and speakers use the *ad hominem* argument when they attack the person connected with an issue, rather than the issue itself. Here's an example:

> The senator has made an interesting case for eliminating the inheritance tax. No wonder! When his father dies, he will inherit millions!

In this statement, the writer ignores the senator's arguments for abolishing the inheritance tax and focuses on his personal situation. The following statement makes the same mistake:

> Do not believe film critics. They are all frustrated actors or directors who could not succeed in the film industry.

The statement attacks the film critics, rather than discuss any inaccuracies or bias in their reviews.

Begging the Question. Another error that people frequently make is begging the question, or using circular reasoning. In its most fundamental form, a circular argument ends up where it began: merely restructuring the original assumption without introducing actual information. For instance:

> Welfare recipients are lazy because they don't like to work. Have you heard about someone on welfare who likes to work? That's because welfare recipients are lazy.

The argument travels in a circle, confirming the assumption it makes in the opening assertion.

Activities

■ **ON YOUR OWN**

  1. Begin by identifying the logical fallacies in these brief statements. Be prepared to discuss your choices.

   a. I think Ms. Sawyer is the best history teacher at our school. She is a strong conservative.

   b. We must reject gun control laws or sacrifice a sacred right granted to us by the Constitution.

   c. Glenview College always has a winning football team because its coach believes in team spirit.

   d. The least-promising students achieve the greatest success as adults. Winston Churchill's teacher predicted he would be a failure, and William Faulkner, who won the Nobel Prize for literature, never even earned a college degree.

   e. Ancient religious leaders were responsible for the sun's rising because they went to high ground every morning and prayed for the sun god to return.

   f. Ann is intelligent and hard working. There is no doubt she will rise to the top of her field.

   g. A brain absorbs information just as a sponge absorbs water. But eventually, a sponge becomes saturated; it cannot hold any more water. Students, too, reach a saturation point, and then it is foolish to expect them to soak up more information.

h. If I had not gone out of my way to pick up Mia this morning, the car would not have broken down.

i. I don't see how young people can enjoy his music; he has been arrested several times, and his wife left him because he was cruel.

j. Lola Allure—star of stage, screen, and television—starts every day with Skinny Wafers. Don't you think you should, too?

2. Reread Royko's "Endorsements: Just a Shell Game" on pages 11–12. Identify and record the fallacies at work in his or his friend's thinking.

3. In "Like Mexicans," an autobiographical essay set in rural California, Gary Soto reveals how thinking can be limited by a so-called cultural perspective. He opens the essay with his grandmother giving him advice on employment and marriage. And as the essay unfolds, the narrator tries to understand the advice he's been given. He seeks opinions from his brother, friend, and mother. Finally, he visits the home of the young woman he plans to marry. During the visit, he realizes the meaning behind the advice he has been receiving from family and friends. For this reading, concentrate on what Soto reveals about his family's and friend's perceptions of the world. Identify and record specific reasoning errors you spot.

Like Mexicans

My grandmother gave me bad advice and good advice when I was in my early teens. 1
For the bad advice, she said that I should become a barber because they made good money and listened to the radio all day. "Honey, they don't work como burros," she would say every time I visited her. She made the sound of donkeys braying. "Like that, honey!" For the good advice, she said that I should marry a Mexican girl. "No Okies, hijo"—she would say—"Look, my son. He marry one and they fight every day about I don't know what and I don't know what." For her, everyone who wasn't Mexican, black or Asian were Okies. The French were Okies, the Italians in suits were Okies. When I asked about Jews, who I had read about, she asked for a picture. I rode home on my bicycle and returned with a calendar depicting the important races of the world. "Pues si, son Okies tambien!" she said, nodding her head. She waved the calendar away and we went to the living room where she lectured me on the virtues of the Mexican girl: first, she could cook and, second, she acted like a woman, not a man, in her husband's home. She said she would tell me about a third when I got a little older.

I asked my mother about it—becoming a barber and marrying Mexican. She was in 2
the kitchen. Steam curled from a pot of boiling beans, the radio was on, looking as squat as a loaf of bread. "Well, if you want to be a barber—they say they make good money." She slapped a round steak with a knife, her glasses slipping down with each strike. She stopped and looked up. "If you find a good Mexican girl, marry her of course." She returned to slapping the meat and I went to the backyard where my brother and David King were sitting on the lawn feeling the inside of their cheeks.

"That is what girls feel like," my brother said, rubbing the inside of his cheek. David put three fingers inside his mouth and scratched. I ignored them and climbed the back fence to see my best friend, Scott, a second-generation Okie. I called him and his mother pointed to the side of the house where his bedroom was a small aluminum trailer, the kind you gawk at when they're flipped over on the freeway, wheels spinning in the air. I went around to find Scott pitching horseshoes.

I picked up a set of rusty ones and joined him. While we played, we talked about school and friends and record albums. The horseshoes scuffed up dirt, sometimes ringing the iron that threw out a meager shadow like a sundial. After three argued-over games, we pulled two oranges apiece from his tree and started down the alley still talking school and friends and record albums. We pulled more oranges from the alley and talked about who we would marry. "No offense, Scott," I said with an orange slice in my mouth, "but I would never marry an Okie." We walked in step, almost touching, with a sled of shadows dragging behind us. "No offense, Gary," Scott said, "but I would *never* marry a Mexican." I looked at him: a fang of orange slice showed from his munching mouth. I didn't think anything of it. He had his girl and I had mine. But our seventh-grade vision was the same: to marry, get jobs, buy cars and maybe a house if we had money left over.

We talked about our future lives until, to our surprise, we were on the downtown mall, two miles from home. We bought a bag of popcorn at Penneys and sat on a bench near the fountain watching Mexican and Oakie girls pass. "That one's mine," I pointed with my chin when a girl with eyebrows arched into black rainbows ambled by. "She's cute," Scott said about a girl with yellow hair and a mouthful of gum. We dreamed aloud, our chins busy pointing out girls. We agreed that we couldn't wait to become men and lift them onto our laps.

But the woman I married was not Mexican but Japanese. It was a surprise to me. For years, I went about wide-eyed in my search for the brown girl in a white dress at a dance. I searched the playground at the baseball diamond. When the girls raced for grounders, their hair bounced like something that couldn't be caught. When they sat together in the lunchroom, heads pressed together, I knew they were talking about us Mexican guys. I saw them and dreamed them. I threw my face into my pillow, making up sentences that were good as in the movies.

But when I was twenty, I fell in love with this other girl who worried my mother, who had my grandmother asking once again to see the calendar of the Important Races of the World. I told her I had thrown it away years before. I took a much-glanced-at snapshot from my wallet. We looked at it together, in silence. Then grandma reclined in her chair, lit a cigarette, and said, "Es pretty." She blew and asked with all her worry pushed up to her forehead: "Chinese?"

I was in love and there was no looking back. She was the one. I told my mother who was slapping hamburger into patties. "Well, sure if you want to marry her," she said. But the more I talked, the more concerned she became. Later I began to worry. Was it all a mistake? "Marry a Mexican girl," I heard my mother say in my mind. I heard it at breakfast. I heard it over math problems, between Western Civilization and cultural geography. But then one afternoon while I was hitchhiking home from school, it struck me like a baseball in the back: my mother wanted me to marry someone of my own social class—a poor girl. I considered my fiancee, Carolyn, and she didn't look poor, though I knew she came from a family of farm workers and pull-yourself-up-by-your-bootstraps ranchers. I asked my brother, who was marrying Mexican poor that fall, if I should marry a poor girl. He screamed "Yeah" above his terrible guitar playing in his bedroom. I considered my sister who had married Mexican. Cousins were dating Mexican. Uncles were remarrying poor women. I asked Scott, who was still my best friend, and he said, "She's too good for you, so you better not."

I worried about it until Carolyn took me home to meet her parents. We drove in her Plymouth until the houses gave way to farms and ranches and finally her house fifty feet from the highway. When we pulled into the drive, I panicked and begged Carolyn to make a U-turn and go back so we could talk about it over a soda. She pinched my cheek, called me a "silly boy." I felt better, though, when I got out of the car and saw the house: the chipped paint, a cracked window, boards for a walk to the back door. There were rusting cars near the barn. A tractor with a net of spiderwebs under a mulberry. A field. A bale of barbed wire like children's scribbling leaning against an empty chicken coop. Carolyn took my hand and pulled me to my future mother-in-law who was coming out to greet us. 9

We had lunch: sandwiches, potato chips, and iced tea. Carolyn and her mother talked mostly about neighbors and the congregation at the Japanese Methodist Church in West Fresno. Her father, who was in khaki work clothes, excused himself with a wave that was almost a salute and went outside. I heard a truck start, a dog bark, and then the truck rattle away. 10

Carolyn's mother offered another sandwich, but I declined with a shake of my head and a smile. I looked around when I could, when I was not saying over and over that I was a college student, hinting that I could take care of her daughter. I shifted my chair. I saw newpapers piled in corners, dusty cereal boxes and vinegar bottles in corners. The wallpaper was bubbled from rain that had come in from a bad roof. Dust. Dust lay on lamp shades and window sills. These people are just like Mexicans, I thought. Poor people. 11

Carolyn's mother asked me through Carolyn if I would like a *sushi.* A plate of black and white things were held in front of me. I took one, wide-eyed, and turned it over like a foreign coin. I was biting into one when I saw a kitten crawl up the window screen over the sink. I chewed and the kitten opened its mouth of terror as she crawled higher, wanting in to paw the leftovers from our plates. I looked at Carolyn who said that the cat was just showing off. I looked up in time to see it fall. It crawled up, then fell again. 12

We talked for an hour and had apple pie and coffee, slowly. Finally, we got up with Carolyn taking my hand. Slightly embarrassed, I tried to pull away but her grip held me. I let her have her way as she led me down the hallway with her mother right be- 13 hind me. When I opened the door, I was startled by a kitten clinging to the screen door, its mouth screaming "cat food, dog biscuits, *sushi*. . . ." I opened the door and the kitten, still holding on, whined in the language of hungry animals. When I got into Carolyn's car, I look back: the cat was still clinging. I asked Carolyn if it were possibly hungry, but she said the cat was being silly. She started the car, waved to her mother, and bounced us over the rain-poked drive, patting my thigh for being her lover baby. Carolyn waved again. I looked back, waving, then gawking at a window screen where there were now three kittens clawing and screaming to get in. Like Mexicans, I thought. I remembered the Molinas and how the cats clung to their screens—cats they shot down with squirt guns. On the highway, I felt happy, pleased by it all. I patted Carolyn's thigh. Her people were like Mexicans, only different.

RECORDING REFLECTIONS

After reading "Like Mexicans," use your Reflection Log to record any experiences you might have had with people who think like Soto's family and friends. What were the assumptions behind their beliefs? How did their assumptions manifest themselves in conversation? What were the reasons for their beliefs?

ACTIVITIES FOR REREADING

1. On what is Soto's grandmother's advice based? What do you imagine would be her third point, the one she will hold back until he's older?

2. What fallacies do you see in Soto's grandmother's reasoning? What assumptions are behind them?

3. What reasoning errors do you see in the thinking of Soto's mother and his friend Scott's mother?

4. What specifically leads to Soto feeling comfortable with his decision to marry Carolyn? What specifically makes them "like Mexicans"?

GROUP WORK

Personal Responses: Share your experiences with people who have strong social and racial biases. What do they have in common in terms of background and experience? What steps can be taken to change someone's biases? Or is such change possible?

Objective Responses: Discuss the influence that might have shaped Soto's values. Which influences seem the most important, and which seem the least important? How can such influences be changed?

WRITING ASSIGNMENT

Write a brief report—no more than one typed, double-spaced page—that identifies the reasoning errors in "Like Mexicans." First, name the error; then, follow with an example from the essay.

CHAPTER 3

Critical Thinking and Working with Others

Whether it's myth or reality, the United States is viewed as the land of opportunity—a place where anyone can apply his or her natural talent and rise above the crowd. Indeed, American culture celebrates and dramatically rewards individual achievement. Sports figures, business magnates, entertainers, and political leaders are the kinds of people who appear on the covers of *Time* and *Newsweek*. They're the ones profiled in *Vanity Fair, People,* and *Vogue*. They're the ones who chat with Barbara Walters, Oprah Winfrey, and Jay Leno, revealing the details of what it's like to be rich and famous.

But beyond their symbolic significance as icons of what can be achieved, how much do such figures as Michael Jordan, Bill Gates, Kim Basinger, and Bill Clinton affect your life? Probably not much at all. Most of the decisions that affect our everyday lives are made by anonymous people working together in government, business, education, and entertainment. The laws you follow daily, the choices you have in the marketplace, the courses you take in college, and the programs you watch on television all come from people working collaboratively—not single individuals with unique vision or talent.

Yes, you will make many important decisions on your own or with someone significant to you, but most of your daily interactions will probably be in relationship with others in a group of some kind. Michael Jordan is clearly a great basketball player, but how successful would he be on the court without his four team members? Likewise, could Bill Gates build a billion-dollar business empire alone? Could Kim Basinger make a movie alone? Could any president run the country alone? Of course not. Only teamwork—people collaborating in a group to achieve a common purpose—makes things happen.

People can work together in a number of ways:

- *Social groups* include families, roommates, clubs, and athletic teams. Throughout your life, there will be structured times when you engage in social interaction with others. Social groups allow people to become part of something beyond themselves. These groups can be sources of affection and self-esteem.

- *Work groups* come about when there are specific tasks to be achieved. These groups are typically formed in classrooms, businesses, and civic agencies—for example, a project is due and a team of students, employees, or neighbors collaborate to get the job done. In social groups, interaction is the purpose; in work groups, creating a product is the purpose.

- *Decision-making groups* form to build a consensus, solve a problem, and develop a plan. Unlike a work group, a decision-making group does not produce a tangible product. Often, a decision-making group will concentrate on problem solving—finding the best solution to a particular problem and developing ways to put that solution into practice.

- *Brainstorming groups* form to develop pools of ideas. Participants in a brainstorming group often develop individual idea lists before meeting. Each participant contributes his or her observations until the task has been fully explored. Sometimes, the process ends here, but other times, the group will seek an outcome. The group list will then be evaluated to determine what will and what will not be useful in resolving the task.

WORKING IN GROUPS

An ideal small group is made up of three to six members. As more people are added to a group, the chance for each person to communicate decreases. In fact, as the size of a group increases, a person may turn to a neighbor and start a whispered conversation, creating cross-talk, while other group members are concentrating on someone else. This kind of breakdown occurs because people want to be involved. The bigger the group, the less individual involvement.

Establish a Clear Organization

Group *organization* starts with something as simple as arranging chairs. In small-group discussion, especially work groups in college settings, sitting in a well-ordered circle enhances communication. A circle arrangement encourages interaction and group relationship, clearly positioning each participant to take part in the process and to see the other group members.

Group work usually implies group *leadership,* as well. Unfortunately, many people think of leadership in terms of a single person directing the group. But in groups that function effectively, leadership is better understood as participation that influences the group but doesn't direct it. Furthermore, influence shifts. At times, one participant will influence one part of a group discussion, but at other times, other participants will influence the discussion, depending on their experience and expertise.

Leadership styles will vary among participants:

- *Authoritarian* leadership is characterized by one person dominating the group and the other members accepting it. A single group member can have complete influence over the group, and the group goes along with it.

- *Democratic* leadership is the kind most Western cultures value because it utilizes group resources and gives everyone a chance to participate.

- *Laissez-faire* leadership is characterized by a hands-off style. It offers minimal direction, allowing the group to find its own way.

- *Abadacratic* leadership is characterized by total breakdown. No one is able to influence the group, and any attempt that is made is quickly rejected. Group disintegration is quick to follow.

It may be productive for our purposes here to talk in terms of *facilitating*, rather than *leading*. A *group facilitator* keeps the process moving, not through the use of power but by clarifying, refocusing, summarizing, and redirecting the group when it strays from the task. The facilitator smoothes the way for the group to work effectively—to accomplish something. When a group is able to concentrate its creative energy, to work hard, and to accomplish its task in a positive and constructive fashion, everyone participating in the process feels better about themselves and each other.

Sometimes, it is effective to assign the task of facilitator to a group member. Other times, a facilitator emerges; this is usually someone who remains neutral, is able to involve everyone in the discussion, and has the patience to honor all points of view.

A good facilitator has these qualities:

- Does not prematurely evaluate ideas
- Concentrates group energy of the task
- Suggests alternatives
- Protects individual members and their ideas from attack
- Encourages participation
- Helps the group find solutions

Another key figure in the group process is the *recorder*. Unlike that of facilitator, the role of recorder is always assigned, usually to a volunteer. The recorder's job is to write down—if possible, in full view of group members—a record of the main points of what is said, using the words of the group members. At the end of the group's work, everyone will be able to refer to the record to remind themselves of what transpired. Members can also correct the record, as necessary.

Group sessions should unfold in an orderly fashion. Once the chairs have been arranged in a circle, the facilitator and recorder have been identified, any needed introductions have been made (i.e., of new members or among all members of new groups), it's time to begin. Each session should have a clear *pur-*

pose, which should be stated and understood by every group member. Next, a timeline or agenda should be set for the meeting, so everyone can pace the discussion accordingly. Then, the process begins.

Use the Rogerian Approach to Resolve Conflicts

Although an effective group process moves toward harmonious agreement, reaching that point might involve some conflict. No doubt, you will encounter people with views that dissent from yours. You may find yourself arguing with another group member or even reach a point where you believe an issue cannot be resolved without one of you being a loser and the other a winner. Psychologist Carl Rogers believes that the goal of argument is to reduce conflict, not enflame it. He maintains that there should not be any winners or losers; there should only be consensual resolution.

But is that always possible? Some people feel so strongly about their opinions that they are deeply threatened by any challenge to them. What's a typical response to such a challenge? Most people become defensive. They swallow hard, cross their arms, and become intransigent—that is, so immovable their feet might as well be nailed to the floor. When presented with contradictory, irrefutable evidence, they ignore it. Keep in mind that emotion, not logic, is involved at this point.

If you were to ask Carl Rogers for advice, he would recommend another strategy, one that avoids confrontation. You should adopt a respectful, even conciliatory attitude. Then actively listen to someone with an opposing viewpoint. After you have heard out the other person, restate in your own words what you believe the person said, which is a technique called *reflective listening*. Then ask the person if you paraphrased his or her points accurately. If so, then find common points of agreement, not just points of disagreement, before stating your position. Continue this process until everyone clearly understands the similarities and differences of the two arguments. Doing so will make it easier to reach consensus—that is, a synthesis of every position that the group can agree on.

To apply the Rogerian approach to consensus building, you should do the following:

- Make an effort to understand the opposing viewpoint. Try to "walk a mile in the other person's shoes." Concentrate on what he or she is saying, not on how you can counter it.

- In an unbiased fashion, restate what the other person has said. Giving an objective description will show that you are open minded.

- Acknowledge the value of some of the other person's points. This will show you are fair and balanced and seeking the appropriate resolution, not one that has a winner and a loser.

- Identify areas of common ground—not just points expressed in the disagreement but general areas, such as values, beliefs, and goals.
- Reasonably present your position with supporting evidence. By now, your opposition will realize that this is not a win/lose situation. Now's the time for him or her to consider your viewpoint.

THINKING CRITICALLY DURING GROUP WORK

In 1961, the U.S. government secretly financed and trained Cuban expatriates to invade their homeland. The action became known as the Bay of Pigs invasion. It failed miserably and nearly brought the United States to nuclear confrontation with the former Soviet Union, Cuba's main ally. Historians who have studied this event have revealed that the group planning the invasion did not meet its fundamental obligation: to examine all the evidence in support of and in opposition to launching the invasion.

John F. Kennedy, who was president at the time, had a small group of advisors who relied on inaccurate information and an unrealistic belief in their own superiority. None of the group wanted to appear weak when facing a communist threat in their backyard. The sense of invincibility and the pressure of time prevented the group from engaging one another in open dialogue, so plans were neither creatively formed nor critically evaluated.

The final decision to launch the invasion resulted from *groupthink:* the pressure to abandon the critical process and conform to the prevailing opinion, no matter how unsound it might be. Clearly, peer pressure affects adults as well as children—even well-educated and responsible adults like lawyers, teachers, government officials, physicians, and religious leaders.

Avoid Groupthink

You must rely on *critical thinking* to evaluate what you hear when processing information in a group session, just as you would when reading, writing, listening to the news, or engaging in conversation. As we pointed out in Chapter 2, you must distinguish fact from opinion, identify assumptions buried in information, and determine if interpretations of experience are logically consistent. Remember, any information put forth as evidence in a discussion should be subjected to careful evaluation.

Ask these five questions when evaluating evidence:

1. Is it relevant?
2. Is it representative?
3. Is it sufficient?
4. Is it qualified?
5. Is it accurate?

Examine Emotional Appeals Critically

Groupthink takes over when group members surrender to emotion, rather than exercise intellect. People can be easily swayed by common emotional appeals, often without even being conscious of it. The use of emotional appeal is so pervasive in culture, especially in advertising, that many people believe this is an illegitimate way to present information.

Is it necessary to point out that someone is appealing to emotion, rather than reason? Not necessarily, but it is important that you be able to recognize emotional appeals. Here are some common types:

1. *Glittering generalities* are sweeping statements that appeal to such emotions as love, generosity, and patriotism. Speakers who employ glittering generalities frequently use such words as *truth, freedom, honor,* and *love* to trigger related emotions.
2. *Name calling* is an obvious but surprisingly effective emotional tactic that is designed to belittle or arouse contempt for a person or idea. Name calling is often used in conjunction with an ad hominem argument (see Chapter 2).
3. A *testimonial* involves pointing out that a popular or respected person supports a particular cause, idea, or position. The person giving the testimonial need not be an expert; in fact, he or she may know nothing at all about the subject, but having prestige lends credibility to the information.
4. The *plain folks* approach is the opposite of the testimonial: The appeal comes from relating to ordinary people with ordinary backgrounds, as opposed to those who are rich and famous.
5. The *bandwagon* tactic appeals to people's strong desire to be one of the crowd, especially their peer group. Speakers who employ the bandwagon tactic refer to how many people support their position.

Be Aware of Persuasive Techniques

Certain persuasive techniques, often associated with sales, are sometimes applied in group work. As with emotional appeals, you must critically scrutinize these persuasive techniques or risk falling into a verbal trap. Consider the following:

1. The *all-or-nothing* technique involves insisting that the group accept everything included in a given viewpoint. Someone using this approach would insist either the group take the plan in its entirety or forget it.
2. The *like one/like 'em all* approach links the new with the old to convince listeners to go along with a viewpoint. Someone using this tactic might argue for a position by telling the group that the plan he or she created last week worked, so his or her new plan will also work.
3. The *"I call 'em like I see 'em"* technique is more subtle, in that it tries to convince a group through candor and honesty. Someone using this tactic must appear trustworthy in order to be successful.

4. *Card stacking* involves telling the group only the facts that the persuader wants them to hear, selectively omitting others that would give both sides of an issue. The viewpoint usually seems right until the group hears the other side.

EVALUATE A GROUP'S LOGICAL THINKING

Two elements are always active in group work: the process the group engages in and the content the group concentrates on. In this sense, the group experience can be compared to chewing gum: The act of chewing is the process, and the chunk of gum is the content.

Most of a group's energy is devoted to examining the content of a discussion; consequently, how the process unfolds is often ignored. The process is important, nonetheless. One implicit aspect of any group process is the way individual members and the group as a whole think logically.

Logic, sometimes defined as "clear thinking," is at the center of the group process, especially in a decision-making group. Learning to think logically will help you and other group members to be more effective communicators. Generally, logicians—people who study the reasoning process—divide logical thinking into two categories: *inductive reasoning* and *deductive reasoning.*

Inductive Reasoning

Inductive reasoning begins with a series of specific, concrete experiences or *evidence,* often generated through brainstorming techniques. After critically examining this evidence, the group reaches a conclusion based on the information it has gathered. This conclusion is usually a *generalization;* that is, a statement that explains all the specified evidence and makes a general statement about the subject.

In fact, we all learned to use induction while growing up. It's natural to thinking. For example, a child bites into a hard green apple and discovers that it tastes bitter. When the child tastes a hard green pear, it, too, is bitter. At another time, the child bites into a hard green plum and an apricot. Both are bitter. By induction, the child makes a generalization: Hard green fruit is bitter and should not be eaten.

Gathering the Evidence. An inductive discussion follows a similar pattern. For example, imagine that your group is concentrating on the environmental practices of a city named Glenwood. Your group would begin by generating information, such as this:

Glenwood has curbside recycling for glass, newspaper, aluminum, and plastics.

Glenwood has a system to dispose of household toxic waste, such as solvents and paint.

Glenwood has laws prohibiting release of ozone-depleting chlorofluorocarbons
from air conditioners.

Glenwood has a refuse landfill designed to protect groundwater from toxic
pollution and to generate methane gas.

Glenwood plans to develop a wetlands bird habitat to be preserved as open space.

Making a Generalization.   From this information, the group might logically
conclude the following:

Glenwood is an environmentally responsible city.

The group has made this generalization based on five pieces of evidence, all
generated from group members. But is it a *valid* conclusion?

Something is valid if it is reasonable and justifiable. In order to reach a
valid conclusion about Glenwood's environmental practices, you would have to
engage in an even more specific critical analysis. For instance, you could examine how effectively Glenwood implements its environmental policies. A
closer examination might reveal the following:

The curbside recycling is in the experimental stage. It has been implemented in
the northern quarter of the city, and only a few residents actually recycle.

Household toxic waste disposal is only available once a year.

The law prohibiting the release of ozone-depleting agents is not enforced.

Although the landfill design is state of the art, there is no groundwater
threatened by pollution.

The wetlands development is still waiting to be funded.

Now, the conclusion that Glenwood is environmentally responsible must be reconsidered, more than likely resulting in a new generalization:

Although Glenwood has environmentally responsible policies, they have not
effectively been implemented.

Conclusions drawn through inductive reasoning are usually referred to as
probable conclusions, or *inferences,* rather than valid conclusions, because they
are reached with incomplete evidence and subject to revision once new evidence comes in. Remember the child sampling green fruit and concluding that
such fruit is always bitter? Well, the child would have to revise that conclusion
after tasting a ripe avocado.

Having one, two, or three pieces of evidence cannot lead to drawing a valid
conclusion. A generalization based on only a few pieces of evidence is, in fact,
a *hasty generalization* (see pp. 17–18). Since the evidence resulting from induc-

tive reasoning cannot prove that the generalization is valid, accepting the generalization is often referred to as making an *inductive leap.*

In sum, to evaluate an inductive discussion, consider these questions:

1. What is the conclusion?
2. What evidence is the conclusion based on? Is there enough evidence?
3. What is the source of the evidence? Is the source reliable?
4. Does the generalization explain all the evidence, or is it contradicted by some of the evidence?
5. Does the discussion contain any fallacies?

Deductive Reasoning

Deductive reasoning is harder to follow than inductive reasoning. Remember, inductive reasoning moves from the particulars to a generalization that explains the particulars. The reasoning trail is strewn with evidence, so reviewing the evidence that leads to a generalization is easy.

In contrast, deductive reasoning moves from a broad assumption to a particular instance. In other words, deductive reasoning begins with a generalization, applies the generalization to a particular example, and arrives at a conclusion. For example:

GENERALIZATION	Natural events are beyond influence.
SPECIFIC EXAMPLE	Earthquakes are natural events.
CONCLUSION	Earthquakes are beyond influence.

In formal logic, this pattern is called a *syllogism* and the reasoning process is called *syllogistic reasoning.* In a syllogism, the general assumptions are called *premises.* Each syllogism has a *major premise* and a *minor premise* that leads to a *conclusion,* which is the logical result of the major and minor premises.

The classic example of syllogistic form comes from the Greek philosopher Aristotle:

MAJOR PREMISE	All humans are mortal.
MINOR PREMISE	Socrates is human.
CONCLUSION	Therefore, Socrates is mortal.

Simple, right? Not necessarily. Syllogisms can be tricky. First, you need to understand what makes a valid syllogism. The conclusion of a syllogism is *always* drawn from the major and minor premises, both of which must be accurate for the conclusion to be accurate. If the premises are composed of relevant, sufficient, and representative evidence—the same criteria used to evaluate sound conclusions in inductive reasoning—the conclusion of a syllogism will probably be accurate.

But syllogisms can be illogical. For example, consider the following:

GENERALIZATION   Natural events are beyond influence.

SPECIFIC EXAMPLE   Humankind is a natural event.

CONCLUSION   Humankind is beyond influence.

Although it may often appear that humankind is beyond influence (especially people in our immediate lives), plenty of evidence shows that people can be influenced.

Here are examples of several other ways that syllogistic reasoning can go awry:

1. *An inaccurate major premise may make the syllogism illogical.* For instance:

MAJOR PREMISE   Professional gamblers carry large quantities of cash and drive expensive cars.

MINOR PREMISE   John Murphy is a professional gambler.

CONCLUSION   Therefore, John Murphy must carry large quantities of cash and drive an expensive car.

The major premise is inaccurate. Certainly, not all professional gamblers are successful enough to win a lot of money, let alone choose to carry around cash and drive expensive cars. Because this major premise is inaccurate, the conclusion is also inaccurate.

2. *The language of the syllogism is deceptive.* Look at this example:

MAJOR PREMISE   Every good American accepts the provisions of the U.S. Constitution.

MINOR PREMISE   Martin Luther King, Jr., did not accept the provisions of the U.S. Constitution because he worked to change it.

CONCLUSION   Therefore, Martin Luther King, Jr., was not a good American.

Consider how the terms *good American, accept,* and *change* are used in this flawed syllogism. *Good American* is too vague to describe a class of people accurately. And what do *accept* and *change* mean in this context? The U.S. Constitution allows for change. In fact, it has been amended many times. So, anyone who accepts the Constitution accepts the possibility of changing it. Because language is used deceptively in the premises, the conclusion is meaningless.

3. *A syllogism is illogical when constructed improperly.* Examine this properly constructed syllogism, step by step:

MAJOR PREMISE   All artists rely on intuition.

In a properly constructed syllogism, the subject of the major premise—in this example, *artists*—must appear in the minor premise and be narrowed.

MINOR PREMISE   John is an artist.

The conclusion then follows necessarily from the major and minor premises:

CONCLUSION   Therefore, John relies on intuition.

The preceding syllogism is properly constructed as well as valid. Now examine the following invalid syllogism:

MAJOR PREMISE   All artists rely on intuition.
MINOR PREMISE   All psychics rely on intuition.
CONCLUSION   Therefore, all psychics are artists.

This syllogism is improperly constructed because the minor premise does not repeat the subject of the major premise. The conclusion, therefore, is invalid.

Like inductive reasoning, deductive reasoning can help organize discussion. But remember, deduction is never quite as simple as the skeletal form of syllogisms we use to illustrate it. A premise might not be expressed completely based on the assumption that the listener will supply it mentally. Aristotle called this partial syllogism an *enthymeme,* and he pointed out that in discussion, speakers often omit premises or conclusions, assuming listeners will fill them in for themselves. Doing so often leads to faulty conclusions. For example, consider the following enthymeme:

Migrating Canada geese are disappearing from the marshes where they forage each winter, so we must restrict access to the marshes during migration.

At first glance, the conclusion makes sense because most of us would fill in the missing minor premise:

People frighten Canada geese.

What we might *not* do is evaluate the missing minor premise carefully. If the minor premise had been stated, then a discussion might have raised three key questions:

Do many people visit the marshes during winter months?

Are fewer geese migrating south?

Have the geese found better foraging sites?

These questions might reveal that geese are disappearing for other than the assumed reason.

Some scholars have argued that Latin American history would be dramatically different today if President Kennedy and his circle of advisors had fully examined the missing premise that launched the 1961 Bay of Pigs invasion. Stripped to its basics, their argument went something like this:

Communist governments are unacceptable in our hemisphere, so Fidel Castro's government must be overthrown.

At the time, the missing premise—*Fidel Castro's government is communist*—seems never to have been fully examined. Some would have argued that Castro's government was not communist. Indeed, it had strong socialistic values and a working relationship with the Soviet Union. It only became aggressively communist following the U.S. attempt to overthrow it.

In sum, to evaluate a deductive discussion, ask these questions:

1. What are the premises? Are they completely identified?
2. Are the premises true? How can you tell?
3. What is the conclusion?
4. Does the conclusion follow logically from the premises?
5. Has the conclusion been reached because of emotional appeals?

Activities

ON YOUR OWN

You experience emotional appeals most frequently in advertising. They are imbedded in the text, in the images, and, if televised, in the music. Select three advertisements from magazines, and write a brief summary of the emotional appeals you uncover. Then select a television advertisement; write a four- to six-sentence description of it, and then identify the emotional appeals it uses.

GROUP WORK

In your work group, share your ads and identify the emotional appeals you discovered in the magazine and television advertisements. Identify the underlying assumptions in each ad.

ON YOUR OWN

Study each of the following items, and determine the reasoning pattern imbedded in it. If the reasoning is incomplete—that is, if it is an enthymeme—state the missing element in your own words. Then state what logical conclusions you might draw from the argument.

1. After hundreds of driving tests of American and imported automobiles, including subcompact, compact, midsize, and full-size vehicles, a consumer agency claims that full-size vehicles are the safest of all the categories and subcompact cars are the least safe.

2. An important skill in becoming a successful economist is the ability to interpret statistical information from a variety of sources. Sometimes, that information comes from the far reaches of the world—from undeveloped countries as well as highly developed countries. Phyllis Murphy worked for the Economic Study Institute, a nonprofit institution, while she was a graduate student. Her job required that she analyze statistical information in key production areas.

3. You doubt that this city is dangerous. Check out the statistics. They show that there has been an increase in muggings and other violent crimes in the public transportation system as well as in parks, schools, and shopping malls. Moreover, the statistics show that home break-ins are on the increase. To protect law-abiding citizens, we must put more police on the streets and in the neighborhoods, for a city that can't protect its citizens is not worth living in. We just can't seem to protect our citizens, so I'm looking for property in Seattle.

4. Only a person who hated the victim could have committed such a brutal crime. Killers always leave clues to their identity, though. Now I have examined all the evidence: the details from the original crime scene, including photographs, the bloody but blurred shoeprint, the unidentifiable smudged thumbprint, the pistol, and the angle at which the bullet entered the head. It all points to murder, not suicide. That leaves us only one suspect: Bill Rimes, with whom the victim had a love/hate relationship. I have no doubt we will find that one of his shoes has blood on the sole.

5. You keep on jumping from lover to lover like that, and you'll end up alone in life.

GROUP WORK

Discuss your analysis of the above items in a work group. Try to arrange any syllogistic reasoning imbedded in each item in the form of a syllogism. Are the conclusions valid?

RECORDING REFLECTIONS

Suppose your spaceship has just crash-landed on the moon. You were scheduled to rendezvous with a mother ship 200 miles away on the lighted surface of the moon, but the rough landing has ruined your ship and destroyed all the equipment on board, except for the 15 items listed below.

Your crew's survival depends on reaching the mother ship, so you must choose the most critical items available for the 200-mile trip. Your task is to rank the 15 items in terms of their importance for your survival. List them in your reflection log, and briefly state the reason for each item's ranking. If you are unsure of the value of an item, place it in a second list without explanation.

Consider these items:

1. Box of matches
2. Food concentrate
3. 50 feet of nylon rope
4. Parachute silk
5. Solar-powered portable heating unit
6. Two .45-caliber pistols

7. One case of dehydrated milk

8. Two 100-pound tanks of oxygen

9. Stellar map (of the moon's constellation)

10. Self-inflating life raft

11. Magnetic compass

12. Five gallons of water

13. Signal flares

14. First aid kit containing injection needles

15. Solar-powered FM receiver/transmitter

GROUP WORK

As a group, develop a master list that ranks the above items; include the reasons for each item's rank. To facilitate the process, decide as a group how to proceed. Remember, the fate of the crew may depend on the ranking.

Writing College Essays

Preparing to Write an Essay

We live in the Age of Communication. Telephones, cellular phones, and beepers all make it easy to "reach out and touch someone." Link a television to a dish; soon, a satellite will bring you voices and faces from around the world. Connect a personal computer to the Internet, and you'll be "chatting through your fingers" in no time. So, why should you learn to write?

WRITING AND THINKING

Writing Sharpens Critical Thinking

We *do* live in the Age of Communication, but much of that communication is really thoughtless jabber, speculation, or high-level gossiping—of which we may be the passive recipients. Call it the *Oprah Winfrey Effect*. Basically, it all boils down to what student writer Michelle Bennett, the author of "Hype, Heighten, and Hit Hard," calls "Info'n'Motion for OUTertainment." What does she mean? She explains this way:

> I see friends passively sitting in front of the tube. Yes, maybe they're watching the news, but the news is entertainment. Think about it: Reports of murders, automobile crashes, kidnappings, driveby shootings--all presented in dramatic film footage and breathless narration. This is information in motion, or "Info'n'Motion," but to no purpose other than to titillate. I call it all "OUTertainment" because it deals solely with the outside world, not the inner world of the self, which I call "INNERtainment." All this might sound like an odd way of thinking about television, but it's my way. I figured it out for myself. Some CNN Expert Guest didn't figure it out for me.

Figuring it out for yourself is at the heart of writing. But reality is much different. Most of the communication flooding into our lives is received without critical evaluation. Even in classrooms, you probably set aside your critical perspective. During lectures, for example, you seldom have the opportunity to question professors who dispense information that could be as easily read or broadcast on video. Even in a heated group discussion, only two or three participants are actively engaged. Moreover, in a discussion, it's easy to state a position and then sit back while others respond. No one is held intellectually accountable for what he or she says. Spoken words, it seems, quickly evaporate once uttered. Furthermore, speech frequently mirrors the mind's disorderly nature. Often undisciplined, it reflects the flow of information as it occurs in undisciplined thinking—random, spontaneous, and discursive.

In contrast, writing forces systematic thought. When writing, you must hold up your knowledge and experience to critical scrutiny. Writing, unlike unedited speech, is bound by principles of logic, transition, and clarity. You must linger over a piece of writing, thinking through your opinions, detailing the reasons you hold them, and carefully delineating them in words. Simply stated, when you write, you're engaged in active, not passive, learning. Sure, you might be sitting at a desk, but your mind is alive. You are figuring things out for yourself.

Writing Provides a Record of Thinking

Most of your college papers will be *essays*, which are relatively brief, nonfiction compositions. They usually concentrate on a limited aspect of a subject. Essays sometimes integrate research, especially in college writing, but even then, they tend to embody the writer's personal perspective—his or her unique understanding of the subject. Keep in mind, however, that even though an essay might embody a writer's perspective, it is not necessarily *about* the writer. Instead, an essay gains its personal character from the individual writer's insights, values, and reasoning power.

Most importantly, an essay provides a visible record of your knowledge as well as your ability to apply it. Objective tests can effectively measure how well you've memorized facts and information, but only through writing can teachers evaluate your performance in all its complexity. Written works can effectively demonstrate how well you use facts and information at higher levels of thinking; that is, your writing can specifically show if you can apply information, interpret its significance, analyze its parts, synthesize its diverse elements, and maybe even evaluate the results.

Levels of Thinking

Moving from the most complex to the least, the levels of thinking range from evaluation to knowledge. Each successive level involves aspects of the preceding levels. In other words, intellectual behavior becomes increasingly complex.

- *Evaluation* involves decision making or judging based on a set of criteria.
- *Synthesis* involves combining elements to form a new entity.
- *Analysis* involves separating a complex whole into its parts until the relationship among the elements is clear.
- *Application* involves using information in a situation that is different from the one in which it was originally learned.
- *Comprehension* involves interpreting, translating, summarizing, or paraphrasing given information.
- *Knowledge* involves recognizing and recalling facts and specifics.

To recall a text—knowledge—is a minor intellectual achievement; to evaluate a text—evaluation—is a major intellectual achievement.

ASSESS THE WRITING SITUATION

Assessing the writing situation is a call for you to be *realistic*. Figure out what it will take to finish a writing project. Before you begin writing, you should systematically assess the writing situation, keeping in mind the key elements it embodies:

1. Length and time limit of the assignment
2. Purpose of the assignment
3. Available information sources
4. The audience

Determine an Assignment's Length and Time Limit

In most college assignments, the professor will assign an approximate length for a paper and set a due date. The length of a paper and the time you have to write it will obviously impact the writing situation. For example, you will need to limit the scope of your subject more for a 500-word essay than for a 1,500-word essay. If you have two weeks to finish the paper, you will not have much time for research, and if you are writing in class, you will not have much time to plan. In any case, you must accurately assess the length of the paper and the time you have to write it. Then adjust your writing behavior realistically.

Avoid the mistake made by many beginning writers, who don't start until the deadline approaches with the speed of a threatening steam engine. This approach is just plain unrealistic. You won't do good work facing a relentless deadline you ignored until the last minute.

Clarify the Purpose of the Assignment

In college, you are usually assigned a subject, which may, at first glance, seem to make writing easy. It doesn't. It just provides a little more direction.

Some assignments are open ended, merely providing you with a simple prompt. For example:

> Discuss one of the following general subjects: family, films, friends, career, work, authority, marriage, or responsibility.

But even with such an open-ended assignment, you still must understand what your instructor expects. There are usually cues in an assignment's wording.

The preceding assignment, for instance, offers two cues: the word *discuss* and the phrase *general subjects. Discuss* means you should consider as many elements of the subject as possible, keeping to the assignment constraints, such as length and time. *General subjects* tells you the instructor wants to see if you can limit, or more narrowly *focus,* the scope of a subject. To limit a subject means to make it specific and avoid overgeneralizing or writing a series of abstract observations. For example, *work* is general; *summer jobs* is more specific; *summer jobs have taught me four important principles* is even more specific; and *Working last summer at Mesa Riding Stables taught me the value of being responsible for my own horse* is very specific.

Other assignments are closed, providing you with very specific directions. For example:

> In a 500- to 750-word essay, explain the three chief reasons arsonists give for their destructive behavior and compare/contrast them with the reasons psychologists give.

This assignment from an abnormal psychology class could not be much clearer. The instructor provides the content: the arsonist's reasons and the psychologists' reasons. The structure is also clear: comparison and contrast. The key word *explain* tells you to show that you understand or can interpret key concepts. This kind of an assignment sends a clear message from an instructor: "Show me what you know!"

Learn to recognize key words and determine what levels of thinking they indicate. Here are some examples of key words you should know, including what they mean, what levels of thinking they indicate (in parentheses), and how they might by used:

- *Analyze:* To distinguish the parts of something and discuss their relationship. (Analysis)

  Analyze the reasoning in Andrew Marvel's "To His Coy Mistress."

- *Apply:* To use material from one area of knowledge and relate it to another. (Application)

  Apply the principles of dramatic structure to selected commercials.

- *Assess:* To determine the success or failure of something. (Evaluation)

  Assess President Clinton's first year in office.

■ *Clarify:* To make a complex subject clear, which may involve defining words and concepts. (Comprehension)

Clarify the phrase "liberty and justice for all."

■ *Compose:* To create from diverse sources. (Synthesis)

Compose an argument that justifies lower taxes.

■ *Criticize:* To analyze the strengths and weaknesses of a subject. (Analysis and Evaluation)

Respond critically to the president's "Blueprint for Learning."

■ *Discuss:* To consider as many elements of a subject as possible. (Comprehension)

Discuss the results of inner-city unemployment.

■ *Evaluate:* To give your opinion, or judge, the value of a subject. (Evaluation)

Evaluate the use of airbags in automobiles.

■ *Explain:* To clarify a subject that needs to be understood. (Comprehension)

Explain the relationship between high-intensity populations and livable cities.

■ *Interpret:* To offer what you believe a subject means. (Comprehension and Application)

Interpret the symbol of fire in Frost's poem "Fire and Ice."

■ *Justify:* To argue that something is valid or correct. (Evaluation)

Justify the assertion that election laws were violated.

■ *Relate:* To show the connections between subjects. (Knowledge and Application)

Relate SAT scores to success in college.

■ *Review:* To re-examine, summarize, or paraphrase a subject. (Knowledge)

Review the reasons for Operation Jump Start's success.

■ *Summarize:* To relate the major points of a subject. (Knowledge)

Summarize Joan Didion's "On Morality."

■ *Support:* To argue for or justify something. (Synthesis)

Support the position that there is life after death.

Use Common Information Sources

No matter how open or closed an assignment, the facts, details, and examples you provide to make your point must come from somewhere. Use any of the following common information sources to help generate material for an assignment:

- *Personal experience* is often the best source for a subject or subjects. You might write about how your neighborhood has changed over the years or how a certain event has changed your vision of the world—all based on your individual experience. An effective way to uncover an interesting personal experience subject is to make a list, no entry more than a line or two, of random events from your past. Once you've developed 15 to 20 items, select one to write about without regard for correctness. The goal is to go through the list until you uncover some aspect of an experience worth writing about.

- *Direct observation* sends you into the world as an observer. Here, you can put on a social anthropologist's hat, examining commonplace human behavior that often goes unnoticed. For instance, you might observe and then write about the behavior of strangers gathered in confined places, such as elevators, lunch counters, and crowded public transportation. You might observe and then write about a television program, a film, or a series of advertisements. The possibilities are almost endless: children interacting in a playground, college students at a cigar party, family members at any social function, and so on.

- *Reading* is the basis of your college education. Many writing situations are based on the careful reading of a text, whether a book, essay, short story, or poem. In these situations, be careful not to let your paper become an extended summary; instead, concentrate on interpreting the work and support your interpretation with details and examples from the text. Another possibility is to select criteria a writer uses to analyze a situation, and then use those criteria to examine a situation in your own life.

- *Questionnaires and interviews* can also serve as rich sources of information for essays. A questionnaire can help you gather information for an essay on student attitudes toward such subjects as work, family values, childrearing, and marriage. For a law course, you might interview several legal authorities—such as a judge, defense attorney, prosecuting attorney, and police officer—and then use the information you collect in an essay.

Picture a Reader

Imagine yourself blindfolded. You're led into a crowded room. You can sense people waiting, a little restlessly, shuffling in their chairs, coughing, laughing, and whispering. After a moment, someone taps a glass to draw people's attention. The room becomes quiet. You realize you are expected to speak.

In this situation, your mind would whir into action. You would zero in on a few clues to help you picture the audience. For instance, it's late in the evening; they must be adults. Their muffled voices sound like men, not children or women. The tinkling of glass and the tapping of silverware suggest you're at a banquet. So now you think, "But what do I say to them?"

A speaker would never want to deliver a speech blindfolded, but sometimes inexperienced writers write blindly, never figuring out who they're writing for. Don't make that mistake. You should write with a particular audience in mind.

In much of college writing, figuring out your audience is easy. It is usually a professor reading to evaluate your performance. Is your knowledge accurate? Are your assertions justified? Is your reasoning valid?

In writing classes, however, having your professor as your audience can sometimes be tricky. Often, writing professors serve two roles: coach and judge. On the one hand, they are evaluating *what* you write, as do most professors from other fields. On the other hand, they are evaluating *how* you write in order to improve your writing skills.

Some writing professors specify an audience as part of an assignment, such as an opinionated group who lack knowledge of the subject or a well-informed environmental group who want to save the local wetlands. Other times, you might be writing as a member of a student writing group; in these situations, your audience will be composed of fellow students. But more frequently, a writing professor will expect you to imagine an audience appropriate to your subject.

Your audience will often be too diverse to be categorized. This is the *universal audience*. When writing for such an audience, you might have to seek characteristics that everyone in the audience shares. A typical universal audience might be composed of consumers, males, females, students, teenagers, or senior citizens. Once you have a sense of your universal audience, you can address them indirectly in your essay:

All consumers are targets . . . suggests an audience of consumers.

No matter how many semesters you've completed here . . . suggests an audience of students.

For those of you over 55 . . . suggests an audience of senior citizens.

Even though you have been smoking for a lifetime . . . suggests an audience of long-time smokers.

This tactic serves two purposes: It establishes the perspective from which your reader should read the essay, and it also keeps the reader clearly established in your mind.

Here's a practical tip: Even though you are writing for a universal audience or group, imagine that you are writing for one person. To do so, create a mental construct of him or her. Choose someone you know who would symbolize the general group. Then plan your essay as if you were writing for that person. Imagine the questions he or she would ask. Imagine what would hold your ideal reader's interest. Imagine that your ideal reader is looking over your shoulder.

Consider these questions for audience analysis:

1. Is my reader part of a group or an individual?
2. What is my relationship to my reader?
3. How much does my reader know about the subject?
4. Should I consider my reader's age, gender, education, political bias, or social values?
5. Is reading ability a consideration? Can my reader follow a complex discussion? Do I need to simplify the discussion?

EMPLOY COMMON ESSAY CONVENTIONS

When composing an essay, imagine that you are participating in a relationship between you and your reader. Every relationship has its obligations. In the writer/reader relationship, your obligation is to meet the reader's expectation that you will use common essay conventions to guide him or her through the reading process. Two of these conventions involve purpose and strategy in both essay and paragraph construction.

Have a Dominant Purpose

Readers adjust how they read to fit an essay's dominant purpose. For instance, most readers approach descriptive writing much differently than persuasive writing. Description involves the senses, so readers reconstruct experiences as they read. Persuasion involves the intellect, so readers trace the key points and counterpoints throughout a discussion.

Generally, the purposes of essays can be categorized according to the four different ways you can approach a subject:

1. A *narrative* essay tells a story by relating a sequence of events. You might write a narrative essay on the criminal justice system by tracing the chronology of a typical day in the life of a district attorney.
2. A *descriptive* essay uses details and images to depict a scene, event, person, object, or setting. You might write a descriptive essay that re-creates a courtroom scene for its emotional impact.
3. An *expository* essay explains, informs, analyzes, or interprets. You might explain the causes of a particular crime, inform your readers about several approaches to ending street crime, analyze the effects of crime on a community, or interpret what crime suggests about a community.
4. An *argument* essay attempts to persuade readers to take some action or to accept your position on a debatable issue. You might try to persuade your readers to join a crime alert program or argue against police harassment of teenagers.

These purposes are not rigid. You might, for example, use descriptive or narrative techniques in writing an argument. You might supply useful and interesting information in a narrative. But keep in mind that readers will expect an essay to have a dominant purpose, one that allows them to adjust their reading style appropriately.

Use a Consistent Essay Strategy

Narrative and descriptive essays are more fluid than expository and argument essays. They are more exploratory, sometimes concentrating on the writer's personal experience and the insight that comes from having lived it. As a result of their fluid nature, narrative and descriptive essay patterns are often unique. They embody a flow of experience, not an analytical interpretation of experience.

In sharp contrast, expository and argument essays usually follow a pattern instructors have come to expect college students to use: the *thesis/support pattern.*

College thesis/support essays are composed of several paragraphs. They are typically 500 to 1,500 words in length and follow a general pattern that has three main parts:

1. The *introduction,* usually one or two paragraphs, presents the thesis statement and any background information that readers might need to understand the discussion, which follows. An effective introduction also arouses reader interest and limits the discussion to come.
2. The *discussion* (or *body*) usually contains several paragraphs, each organized by a topic sentence that relates to the thesis statement. The discussion paragraphs develop the ideas expressed in the thesis statement in a detailed, thorough manner.
3. The *conclusion,* usually no more than a single paragraph, gives a sense of completion to the essay. Often, though not always, the conclusion restates the thesis statement and touches on the essay's subpoints.

In short, here is the general pattern of a thesis/support essay:

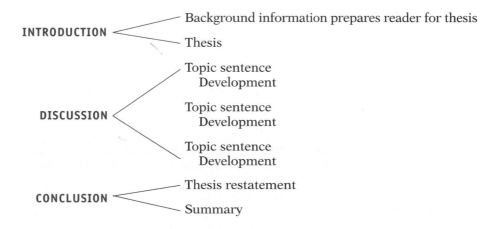

INTRODUCTION — Background information prepares reader for thesis
— Thesis

DISCUSSION
— Topic sentence Development
— Topic sentence Development
— Topic sentence Development

CONCLUSION — Thesis restatement
— Summary

Within this overall pattern, an essay should demonstrate three other characteristics:

1. *Unity:* The topic sentences must clearly relate to the idea expressed in the thesis statement, and the information in individual paragraphs must clearly relate to the idea expressed in the topic sentence.
2. *Coherence:* The thoughts expressed in sentences should be connected by transitional techniques, such as repeating key words and phrases, rephrasing key ideas, and using transitional words and phrases.
3. *Adequate development:* There should be thorough supporting explanation and detail.

Use Consistent Paragraph Strategies

Just as readers expect essays to follow clear patterns, they expect the paragraphs in essays to be effectively arranged (see Develop Paragraphs, pp. 94–95) and to reflect recognizable modes of thought or development strategies (see Chapters 11 to 19), such as the following:

- *Examples and details* includes typical and specific illustrations and concrete descriptions to develop a point.
- *Comparison and contrast* presents the similarities and differences between two subjects.
- *Analogy* explains a complicated or abstract idea by comparing it to something familiar.
- *Process* explains how to do something or how something works.
- *Cause and effect* explains why something happened or the results of something that happened.
- *Classification* organizes a subject into distinct categories.
- *Definition* differentiates a concept from others.

Since most essays are composed of several paragraphs, they might contain a variety of paragraph strategies; they will usually be dominated by one, however. Think of these paragraph development strategies as a repertoire to draw from. The sooner you master them, the sooner you will be able to control your writing.

Activities

- **ON YOUR OWN**
  1. Identify the information sources that you could use to develop each of the following subjects. Then identify who the audience might be.
     a. The rising cost of tuition
     b. An insight that altered your understanding of life

     c. The uses of technology in political campaigns

     d. Nannies who can't be trusted

     e. Chess masters as strategists

     f. The impact of sports on high school athletes

     g. Parochial education

     h. Life in the tropics

     i. Surfing the Internet

2. Study "Sorcerers of Desire," which follows, and respond to the following:

     a. Review pages 65–66, and then write a purpose statement for "Sorcerers of Desire."

     b. Identify the introduction, discussion, and conclusion, and write a brief explanation of what each achieves.

     c. Analyze the essay's overall pattern:

- Study pages 75–79, and then record the thesis statement.
- Study pages 90–94, and then record the topic sentences.
- Study pages 95–96, and then identify key words that help create unity.
- Study pages 96–100, and then identify words and phrases that help create coherence.

     d. Review pages 97–98, and then identify paragraph arrangements you recognize.

     e. Based on information in this chapter and your responses to the prompts above, write a one-page critique of "Sorcerers of Desire." Is it an effective or ineffective essay? Why? Be specific.

Sorcerers of Desire

     Magic involves the art of creating illusions. It embodies mystery, employs spells, and secret rites. The dark side of magic is sorcery; that is magic used for manipulative ends. When I think of magic and sorcery, I think of bearded men in pointy hats and purple robes decorated with crescent moons, ringed planets, and silver stars. These sorcerers hide out in caves or dense forests far from the nearest village. In reality, today's sorcerers wear designer clothes and hide out in high-rent offices. They are advertisers. Advertisers, our modern-day sorcerers, can use words and images to create the illusion that their products will fulfill our deepest desires.   1

     Perhaps the advertisers for Marlboro are the master sorcerers. They have transferred a desire for the rugged life to smoking Marlboros. Always set in the American West—the copywriter's idea of Marlboro land—Marlboro advertisements feature a rugged cowboy riding the range or sitting near a campfire or working in a corral. More often than not snow-capped mountains rise in the distance with a prairie spreading toward them. The sky is clear. The air is supposedly fresh. The life is robust and healthy. One recent advertisement in *Time* successfully captures Marlboro Land. It features a cowboy attempting to rope a bucking horse. He is in jeans, chaps, and Stetson, his back to the viewer, swinging a lariat cowhand fashion. The horse is rearing up on   2 its hind legs, its mane whipping, its neck and head stretching upward and its front hooves churning in the air. They are in the wide-open spaces framed against a blue western sky. "Smoke Marlboros," the image suggests, "and you too can be seen as leading the rugged life in Marlboro land where cowboys still work the range."

The desire for personal freedom by being close to nature must have a magical influence on consumers. In a recent issue of *Men's Health,* several advertisers associate their products with the freedom that nature promises. For instance, a Polo Sport advertisement features a young man and woman isolated in a mountain cabin. They are dressed in Polo and gaze longingly past the pine trees at a snow covered mountain range. The written text is peppered with words that suggest freedom, such as "searching," "spirit," "independence." An Evian advertisement shows a runner juxtaposed with a photo of the French Alps. He is portrayed as thinking, "In me lives a wildcat who chases the moon and races the wind and who has never measured his life in quarterly earnings." Nissan Motor Corporation shows a man on an isolated plain and a snow-capped mountain bathed in moonlight. He is in a sleeping bag, surrounded by camping equipment and lying by a blazing campfire. An Infiniti off-road vehicle is parked nearby, the truck that took this adventurous spirit beyond the borders of civilization. Obviously Nissan wants consumers to associate its off-road vehicle with the freedom of wide-open spaces.

Alcohol advertisers seem to have turned in the other direction. Instead of personal freedom, they emphasize the desire to fit into society and the value of tradition. For instance, a liquor advertisement in *Vanity Fair* shows a laughing threesome socializing in a restaurant and drinking Margaritas topped with Grand Marnier. An advertisement for Johnnie Walker Black Label, a high-end Scotch whisky, states, "If the world's biggest problem is a lack of communication, might we suggest a corner table and a fine scotch." Of course, they might . . . and they do. An advertisement for Johnnie Walker Red Label suggests that drinking Red Label is not merely the socially correct thing to do, but the right thing to do, "Politically Correct? Here's to being just right." Other liquor advertisements emphasize the desire to be part of tradition. For instance, Jack Daniels claims to be "The same since the sixties—that would be the 1860s." Gallo winery associates its current chardonney release as part of "a great wine-making tradition."

Cuervo, a producer of tequila, associates its products with both the desire for tradition and for social acceptance. One advertisement for 1800, an exclusive tequila label, identifies with tradition, "Like fine art, fine tequila is a window into a nation's soul." The 1800 family of tequila is a distinctive expression of culture and history of Mexico. In contrast, a recent advertisement for Cuervo Gold, a popular Tequila label, features a party scene with over fifteen people raising their glasses to toast the viewer. They seem to be saying, "Welcome to the Cuervo Party where you'll never be lonely."

Are these modern-day sorcerers performing magic? Do we rush into stores to buy these products? Of course not, but each of us, in the backs of our minds, must carry the memory of these products each time we gaze at the mountains, ponder tradition, or want to join a party. Then maybe—just maybe—when we make a purchase our hand reaches for the product with the most effective advertising.

COMPOSING ON COMPUTER

Get access to a computer—now! Effective writing is the result of rewriting. A computer makes rewriting easy. Think about it. No more than 15 years ago, writers had to completely rewrite pages to make corrections. Now, they can call up pages on a screen; make a few keystrokes, entering corrections or adding more information; press the "Print" key; and seconds later, they have clean pages. But a computer not only will make correcting copy and adding information easy, it will also help perform a variety of writing tasks, such as these:

- Generate ideas quickly
- Create outlines easily
- Produce drafts and save them in a file to be reworked
- Perform electronic spelling checks
- Revise, revise, and revise without the tedium of retyping

The bottom line is that a computer is a writer's best friend.

The Composing Process: Prewriting and Informal Planning

Acollege essay begins with an assignment and ends with a final draft. In between, a lot takes place—a process, the *composing process*. It's not always neat and orderly. In fact, it's often intellectually chaotic. Sometimes, it demands super persistence, the raw determination to keep going even though you want to toss up your hands in surrender.

When the composing process breaks down, writers have trouble. Maybe you've experienced this. Have you ever slumped at the keyboard, stumped about what to write next? Your fingers feel paralyzed. Your mind travels in circles, ideas circling through your imagination like horses on a merry-go-round. *Brain death, writer's block, mental constipation*—these are a few of the phrases writers use to identify this frustrating experience.

What can you do? One writing teacher we know used to tell students to merely type *The* at the beginning of the first line and then plunge ahead, writing on to the end. Actually, that's not very helpful advice. Not many writers can compose an effective essay straight through, from beginning to end. Writing is a recursive process, and that's a fact you must accept. This means that writers work and rework their material—again and again and again. They move ahead in creative spurts, falter, return to a passage they wrote earlier, revise it, and pick up speed and race toward completion. The process can take hours or even weeks, months, or years, but it is always there—the intellectual journey that leads to the final paper.

So, understanding and following your own composing process is the first major step toward effective college writing. Try thinking of the composing process this way: It employs reflective and critical thinking to help writers discover what they know and need to learn about a subject and to help them shape their knowledge into final written form.

How does the composing process work? That's hard to explain. We can identify the common activities writers go through. Keep in mind, though, that writers approach the process in different ways based on their assessment of the writing situation at hand.

A STUDENT'S COMPOSING PROCESS

For the next few chapters, we will follow the composing process of student writer Michelle Bennett. By studying one writer's process, you may discover your own. In these chapters, three activities will be going on at once: You will track the development of Bennett's essay, "Hype, Heighten, and Hit Hard"; learn essay conventions; and write your own essay. To work through these chapters will take patience and concentration, but the result will be worth the effort. You will learn to compose your own essay.

American writer Edgar Allan Poe maintained that the best way for him to write a story was to write the ending first. He would then know where he was headed. We're going to apply Poe's advice to this situation.

We will begin at the end with Michelle Bennett's final draft, the one she submitted for evaluation. In order to understand how an essay has evolved, we must first study the final draft and then go back to the beginning to trace its development.

Let's start by reading what Bennett says about her writing process and this particular assignment:

I've always been one of those perfectionist writers. I try to write the perfect paper in a single draft. Once or twice it worked, but those were simple assignments, and my thinking was very superficial. I deserved the weak grades I received.

This essay wasn't so simple. First, I had to think beyond the five-paragraph essay structure I learned in high school. Okay. I knew I could do that.

Second, I had to build this essay from class notes, personal experience, and observation.

Third, I made a commitment to work every day for two weeks until the essay was done. This was absolutely new for me. I'd always been a "binge" writer.

Now, study Bennett's essay. After reading it through once, reread it along with the margin notes, which point out some of the strategies she uses.

Title comes
from last line
of conclusion.

Hype, Heighten, and Hit Hard

The Justice Department just announced that violent crime in the   1
United States has dropped 10% when compared to last year. The drop
continues a trend downward that has lasted several years. But the

Introduction provides background information to prepare readers for thesis statement.

Thesis statement clearly promises to show that *News at Eleven* both showcases and dramatizes violent stories.

Topic sentence 1 announces this paragraph will show violent stories dominate *News at Eleven*. Sets up three examples that represent kinds of stories on the news any night.

Third example is most dramatic; detailed description brings reader up close.

Topic sentence 2 announces that paragraph will emphasize how stories are hyped.

Background information sets up series of brief examples.

Contrasting examples show hyping

producers of our local News at Eleven must not have heard of the downward trend. Frequently, News at Eleven portrays a world as violent as any in television thrillers. For instance, News at Eleven regularly features hard-hitting stories that have lots of blood and mayhem, but have very little significance for the entire community. Such stories appear to meet a single guideline: "If it bleeds, it leads!" Moreover, News at Eleven not only showcases violent stories, it also unnecessarily dramatizes them.

Typically, violent stories dominate News at Eleven even though they may affect only a few people. For example, last Monday night's broadcast opened with a gang-shooting story. A reporter stood on the porch at the crime scene while a detective pointed out bullet holes. The reporter then said that two people had been brutally murdered. The camera cut to victims in body bags being wheeled away on gurneys. Another night opened with a story of a failed carjacking. The driver had been violently "pistol whipped" when she refused to give up her Explorer. Last week's most violent lead story was captured on videotape. Two men attempted to rob a convenience store. Surveillance cameras videotaped the robbers as they strode toward the check-out counter. News at Eleven played the tape for its viewers. It showed one man take a pistol from his coat. In response, a clerk lifted a shotgun and blasted away, hitting one robber in the chest while the other ran. There is plenty of mayhem in these stories, but where is the news value? The events affect only a handful of people, yet local news producers put them at the top of the program.

News at Eleven producers also shamelessly hype their violent stories to heighten the dramatic impact. During commercial breaks throughout the evening, stern-faced commentators relentlessly pitch the "hot" stories to be broadcast at eleven. Usually the hype has something to do with fear, perhaps a violent threat lurking in everyday experience. For example, last week one commentator breathlessly announced, "At eleven, see firemen risking their lives to stop a coed from leaping to her death." On another evening, a commentator asked, "Does your overgrown shrubbery hide a rapist? At eleven, see how one woman saved herself from a hidden tormentor." Sometimes the dramatic hype backfires. For example, a commentator recently announced, "A man-eating, twenty-five-foot shark was spotted cruising for food in a harbor near docked boats." When eleven rolled around, the story turned out to be a flop. The shark had been spotted in Hong Kong Harbor, not in nearby Dana Point Harbor as the announcement suggested. But whether or not a threatening story is a dud doesn't matter. Local news producers seem interested only in shamelessly hooking viewer emotion. If the story has no actual relevance to viewers, well, that's not a consideration.

Effective paragraph close.

Topic sentence 3 emphasizes dramatic tactics.

Besides teasing viewers into watching their program, News at Eleven   4 producers use two other dramatic tactics to heighten violent stories. Newspaper reporters are taught objectivity. They are trained in a strict journalistic code: Stick to "what," "where," "when," "why," and "how." In contrast, like actors, News at Eleven reporters adjust their speech rhythm, tone, and vocabulary and their facial expressions to dramatize a story. Calculated camera work also heightens the events. News footage is edited for dramatic impact. Rather than merely focusing on a reporter who sticks to the facts at a crime scene, for example, the camera will cut to the grisly results of the event: victims writhing in pain, sobbing parents, a pool of blood. By focusing on these graphic details, the violent event is further dramatized.

Background information sets up analysis that follows in next paragraph.

Topic sentence 4 emphasizes use of sympathy in violent stories.

A tactic all television thriller directors use is to heighten the drama   5 of a hard-hitting story while creating sympathy for victims. News at Eleven producers employ the same tactic to dramatize their violent stories. For example, News at Eleven recently reported a dog attack. The story opened with dramatic tape of a barking pit bull, its vice-sized jaws snapping as it charged toward a chain-link fence. A reporter in a tough narration used such words as "vicious," "brutal," "dangerous," and "murderous" as he explained how pit bulls are bred for violence. The camera then zoomed in on the bloodstained sidewalk where the attack happened. Next, the story cut to the hospital. An eight-year-old child was asleep. One leg, an arm, and his face were wrapped in bandages. In a sympathetic narration, the reporter whispered that the child had undergone "three hours of reconstructive surgery," that it took over "two-hundred stitches to close the wounds," and that the child was in shock from the attack--"deep shock!" The story then cut to an interview with the victim's distraught parents who praised their son's courage.

Specific example is analyzed in depth; notice how analysis is based on information from previous paragraph.

Topic sentence 5 raises question Why?

Clearly, the report had been manipulated to create sympathy for   6
the victim. Was it necessary? No, it was not. Even without the dramatic
narration, camera work, and emotional interview, viewers would
sympathize with the victim of a vicious pit bull attack. But there is still
Writer offers in-terpretation of reasoning behind dramatizing violent stories.
a larger question to ask, "Why did News at Eleven lead the wrap-up of
the day's news with this story?" Are pit bulls terrorizing the community?
Is there a plague of rabies? If so, indeed the news should be reported
because of the community threat. But this story affected only the child,
his family, and the pit-bull owner. Why, then, did it open the eleven
Very effective close—it cuts to the point.
o'clock news? For one simple reason, it would emotionally grip viewers:
"The child bled, so the story led!"

Conclusion opens with question, pro-vides brief reminder of essay's content, and makes point that news producers are cynical for how they manipulate viewers.

Are local News at Eleven producers as cynical as this view suggests?   7
There is no way to know except by looking at what they showcase--and
it isn't pretty. Violent stories--murders, robberies, and vicious attacks--
usually head the news hour. Given the emphasis on violence, News at
Eleven reporters seem to have abandoned objective journalism to embrace
a new journalistic code--Hype it! Heighten it! Hit Hard with it!

Michelle Bennett's essay follows the conventions of the college thesis/
support structure: She establishes a strong purpose and expresses it in a clear
thesis statement that comes at the end of the *introduction* paragraph. She develops an ample *discussion* section by arranging her information in paragraphs
organized by topic sentences, each of which is related to the thesis. And her
conclusion successfully closes the essay, creating a sense that she kept an implicit promise to cover the territory her thesis laid out.

Assessment of the Writing Situation

Before beginning to write, Bennett assessed the writing situation, as follows:

- *Length and time:* This was simple. The instructor stated the length in the
assignment—750 to 1,000 words—and wrote the due date on the board—
October 12, just two weeks away.

- *The assignment:* It was a relatively open-ended assignment. The instructor
wrote it out in detail but with plenty of room for each student to shape the content and approach:

    For this assignment, assume that the following information is accurate. Last Friday,
    the Justice Department announced that violent crime in the United States decreased

by 10 percent when compared to the previous year. Moreover, violent crime has been decreasing each year for the last several years.

In an essay of 750 to 1,000 words, analyze how one category of television programming treats violence. I suggest you concentrate on one series within a single category of television broadcasting, such as situation comedy, sports, drama, children's cartoons, or news.

Bennett began by clarifying the assignment in her own mind. She wrote:

The heart of this assignment is in the second paragraph. The first paragraph merely provides a starting place, which meant I didn't have to document a decline in crime. It was a given for this assignment. Obviously, I had a length restriction, and I knew I had two weeks to write the essay. I had a general subject, violence, which indicated that my instructor wanted to see if I could make it more specific. In fact, by giving me a direction, television programming, and some general categories, she was actually helping me find a more specific subject.

Finally, the key word analyze told me that I had to distinguish certain elements from others. What those elements would be, I wasn't sure. Finally, this assignment would take time, so I decided to start right away.

Assessing the assignment doesn't stop here. It continues through much of the composing process. You will probably find yourself shaping and reshaping your interpretation of an assignment to accommodate your working material, just as you will shape and reshape the working material to accommodate the assignment.

■ *Information sources:* Bennett quickly realized that she could draw on her own experiences, especially from a journalism course she had taken. She also realized that she would have to watch several hours of television.

■ *The audience:* Clearly, she would be writing for television viewers. But if she were to write about violence in cartoons, she might imagine children reading her essay or perhaps parents or psychologists. She knew her sense of audience would have to develop as she worked on the subject.

We'll return to Michelle Bennett's writing process later in this chapter, when we look at how she used prewriting techniques to generate material for her essay. But first, we'll review those techniques to give you an idea of how many ways you can approach prewriting.

USE PREWRITING TECHNIQUES
TO EXPLORE AN ASSIGNMENT

Once you've assessed the writing situation, it's time to find a specific subject. Start with prewriting activities, which will help you uncover a limited subject at the heart of the more general subject.

Remember the discussion in Chapter 1 on reflective and critical thinking? Reflective thinking is closest to *intuition*. It generates ideas, events, and metaphors—the intuitive skills that make fresh, interesting writing. In contrast, critical thinking is closest to *logic*. It emphasizes judgment, organization, and reason—the intellectual skills that make accurate, coherent writing. Intuition fuels the reflective process; logic guides it. Through the reflective process, you invent material; through the critical process, you evaluate and organize it.

Both reflective and critical thinking are needed to write successfully. Reflective thinking, however, is far less self-conscious than critical thinking. As a consequence, prewriting activities emphasize reflective thinking while restraining critical thinking.

When prewriting, free your mind to follow its own thought patterns, associating one thought with another without worrying whether the connections are logical. When you use association techniques, resist the urge to analyze what comes up. Instead, encourage the reflective exploration of your imagination.

Listing

Listing, sometimes called *brainstorming*, is a quick way to get ideas on paper. Begin by simply listing your thoughts and associations in whatever order they come to you. Here is a list developed for the subject *poverty:*

"Summer, oh summer," who wrote that? My summer flew by. What did I do?

-- Worked: steamed milk, expressos, lattes--must have made a thousand of them, two thousand. $6.00 an hour plus tips.

-- Art class: draw, draw, draw. Three hours a day, four days a week. Charcoal, pencil, pastels--a stuffed bird.

-- Movies: The Strand--classic films. Maltese Falcon, Bringing up Baby (Cary Grant searching for a fossil; I'm searching for a subject).

-- Art Museum, Kienholtz exhibit--dramatic.

-- The river, hot, hot, hot; the lake, drifting.

-- Safari Land, fascinating, lions, tigers and bears, oh boy! (Wizard of Oz?). Animals fascinated me--only the monkeys and apes were kept separate.

Zebras, giraffes, lions all running freely through the park. Why don't the lions feed on them? They're not hungry. A full stomach makes them vacationers; an empty stomach makes them hunters.

-- Hunger can organize a life. Change your view of life. Wasted food--feeding soybeans to cattle instead of starving humans. The hungry child poster.

-- Abundant supermarkets. Run out of food, drive to Ralph's, fill a cart, fill a refrigerator. My friends and I take this convenience for granted. But most people in the world have never been inside a supermarket! Many have to beg for food. Many are starving.

-- Earthquake on TV. Central America. People roaming the streets, hungry.

The entries in this list are very rough, but that doesn't matter; only the writer will see them. What's important is that this list helps lead the writer to a topic for his or her paper.

Freewriting

Freewriting is valuable during any phase of the writing process. Simply set aside a block of time, reflect on the assignment or problem, and write nonstop. Associate one idea with another. Don't judge your ideas or shut them out. Often, the unexpected will present itself—ideas connecting to ideas in ways you could not have planned. Don't be concerned with the technical aspects of writing: grammar, punctuation, sentence structure, and logic. They will all come later. Immerse yourself in your own creative flow while holding in check the critical process. Keep in mind that this draft is for your eyes only.

Clustering

Listing and freewriting usually generate a hodgepodge of material, but once a subject emerges, you can begin to make connections among key ideas. In this sense, *clustering* brings order to chaos.

Begin a cluster in a simple fashion. Write what you have determined to be your tentative subject in the center of the page, and draw a circle around it (see the sample on p. 62). As you carefully reread the items from your listing or freewriting, arrange major ideas around the tentative subject in orbits connected by lines. Also circle the major ideas. As you discover or develop ideas related to these major ideas, create another orbiting system.

Do all of this using single words and brief phrases. Remember, you can always return to the prewritten draft to examine the full entry. Through this process, you are simply dividing and subdividing your working material, becoming more specific as you isolate facts, opinions, examples, and specific details, all of which might become part of your essay.

Look more closely at the sample cluster below, which was developed for a descriptive essay that dramatizes a personal insight. This cluster has come from the list generated earlier. Notice how the writer focuses on one aspect of the list and abandons the rest. Why? There is no reason to try to include everything that a prewriting activity generates. In fact, it only takes a single idea to trigger an essay.

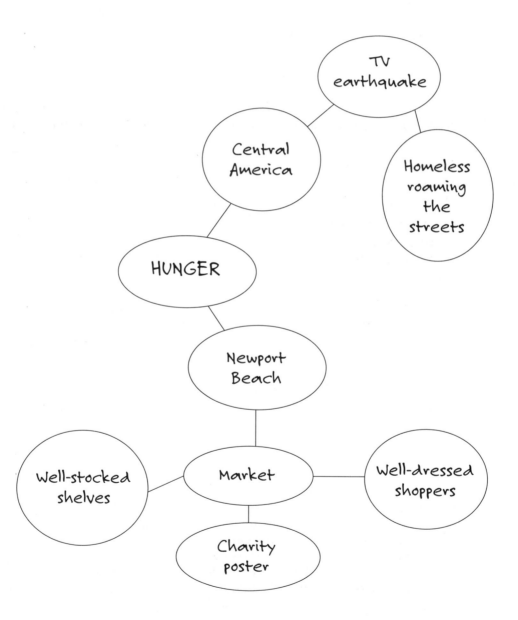

Here's a tip: Be prepared to create more than one cluster. Clustering, like freewriting, often generates even more material. We also suggest that you cluster on a large piece of drawing paper, or at least be prepared to tape several sheets of notebook paper together to accommodate all the material you will generate.

Asking Questions

Another useful prewriting technique is to *ask questions* about a subject. These are sometimes referred to as *reporter's questions:* Who? What? When? Where? Why? and sometimes How?

Of course, not every question will be appropriate for your particular subject, but using the ones that are can ignite an associative chain that will help you view your subject from different perspectives. For example, the subject *rude behavior* could be approached through asking the following questions:

What is rude behavior?

Who is rude?

Who is affected by rudeness?

Who can change rude behavior?

What causes rudeness?

What is my attitude toward rudeness?

When did I first become interested in rudeness?

Where have I seen rude behavior?

Why are people rude?

How can rude behavior be corrected?

Asking questions will get you started on most general assignments. Keep in mind, though, that you might have to tailor questions for more specialized assignments.

Consulting

Writers often describe the writing process as lonely. At some point, they must sit down alone to write. But before sitting down at the keyboard, writers often find that discussing or brainstorming their projects with other people helps them generate ideas and material.

You may become part of a writing group that discusses class assignments. You may also consult a writing buddy—another student or a friend who is more experienced with writing than you are. You can also engage your instructor in a discussion to test your ideas against another point of view. Whenever you discuss an assignment, take notes or use a tape recorder. Don't risk letting good ideas slip away.

Discussing an assignment with others will help you generate ideas and perhaps refine them, but *you* must also commit them to paper. Ultimately, this responsibility is yours.

IDENTIFY AND LIMIT A SUBJECT

The goal of prewriting activities is to identify a specific subject. Most assignments provide general subjects that are much too broad to cover in a typical college-length essay. Unless the writer narrows a general subject, he or she will risk writing a defuse, rambling essay composed of generalizations.

When you limit a subject, you move from the general to the particular. It might help to think of this process as an inverted triangle, which is broad across the top and gets more and more narrow until you reach the point. Look at the figure below, which starts with the very general topic of *television* and gets progressively more specific, resulting in the topic *Mulder's mysticism*. This is a workable topic for an essay.

Trust your composing activities. They will usually lead you from a general subject to a more particular subject.

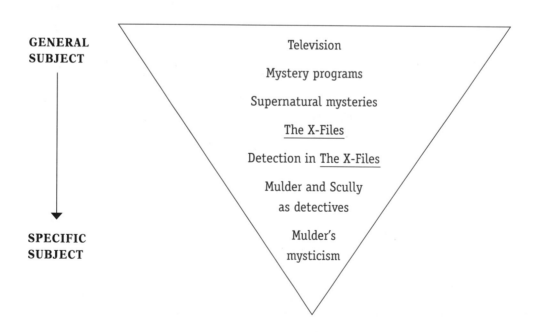

GENERAL
SUBJECT

SPECIFIC
SUBJECT

Television

Mystery programs

Supernatural mysteries

The X-Files

Detection in The X-Files

Mulder and Scully
as detectives

Mulder's
mysticism

COMPOSE A PURPOSE STATEMENT

Composing a purpose statement is particularly important for open-ended assignments, which give you a great deal of freedom. A *purpose statement* should do two things:

1. Identify a specific subject.
2. Express how you will develop the subject.

For informal essays, such as character profiles or personal narratives, the purpose statement can serve as a general guiding statement, not only for the composing process but also for the final essay. For thesis/support essays, the purpose statement will be the starting point for a more formal thesis statement, which you will write later in the composing process.

An effective purpose statement can usually be phrased in a single sentence. It should use key words that indicate your overall approach to the subject. For example, read the following purpose statement for a brief personal insight essay, the one we used earlier to illustrate listing:

I plan to tell the story of how a television news report of an earthquake and a visit to the market made me aware of how lucky I am not to be poor.

The phrase *to tell the story* says the essay will be a narrative. Since narrative essays tend to be informal, this purpose statement will work as a general guiding statement for the final draft.

The following purpose statement was written for a thesis/support essay and will lead to a more formal thesis statement:

I plan to define propaganda, identify several propaganda devices, and analyze how advertisement writers use them.

The key words *define, identify,* and *analyze* indicate the writer's approach to the subject. This purpose statement is absolutely clear.

In contrast, the following purpose statement is ambiguous:

I plan to write about Batman and Superman.

It does not clearly indicate an approach. *To write about* is too vague. But if the writer used more accurate words, then the approach would be nailed down:

I plan to argue that Batman's personality is more complex than Superman's.

Often, merely changing a word or two will give a purpose statement a clear direction. Look at these examples:

I plan to ~~talk about~~ *explain* how active community involvement reduces neighborhood crime.

I plan to ~~explore how~~ *argue that* television cartoons influence children.

I plan ~~on telling~~ *to narrate* how living through a natural catastrophe can change a person's view of the world.

A STUDENT'S PREWRITING ACTIVITIES

Now, let's look at the initial stages of Michelle Bennett's prewriting activities. At the end of this phase of the process, she will frame her purpose statement for "Hype, Heighten, and Hit Hard" and develop an informal plan.

Prewriting Activities at Work

Bennett used several prewriting activities to generate material for "Hype, Heighten, and Hit Hard." She began by freewriting:

> What an assignment! I have to analyze how television programming treats violence. There's enough violence on TV to keep me writing for years. Does this include films shown on TV? I saw "Silence of the Lambs" last weekend--violence resulted from the actions of a madman. Okay, but what about the "psychological" violence Lecter puts the Foster character through?
>
> Stop. Too, too, subtle. Keep the big picture. Professor Duncan says violence has decreased after years of increasing. But I don't need to go there. That's a given. I have to "analyze" how violence appears in programming, not discuss violence in general.

Bennett continued to freewrite in this fashion for another page; then she stopped, realizing she was drifting too far, and began clustering her ideas to put herself back on track.

> Stop, stop, stop! Drifting again, what do I know in simple terms? Draw a picture:

Bennett concluded by deciding on a general area and subject: *violence on the news.* She finished this phase of the composing process by returning to prewriting:

Not much for me to write about. I hate films made for TV, just too slow. I've never watched Saturday morning cartoons. Football, forget it. I do watch Seinfeld reruns, but that's it. NYPD Blue, okay, once in awhile. X Files, always.

ER, yes. The news, frequently. There is plenty of violence on the news. Also the news is neatly packaged, easier to deal with than an ongoing series with complicated relationships. Next step: Spend some time watching news reports.

About the actual composing activities, Bennett wrote:

> At first I was reluctant to begin. It seemed like a "programmed" activity and I doubted that anything would come of it. What a shock! I got into it. It felt very much like talking to myself, kind of making an inner conversation public, or at least keeping a record of it so I could refer back to it.
>
> Also I found that this "talking to myself" was very reassuring. It relaxed me. I didn't rush it. I would pause, let my mind drift, and then return to writing. Usually, I have about a hundred ideas going on in my head at one time. But I found myself being drawn into this single activity. I was in control.

After a couple of days of watching the news, both local and national, Bennett decided to concentrate only on the local news. Street violence was seldom covered on national news, so pursuing it would be a waste of time. But local news reporters seemed to revel in violent stories. In fact, on the evening news— *News at Eleven* in Bennett's hometown—violent stories seemed to be given top priority, even though they affected the lives of only a few people.

Bennett spent several days watching *News at Eleven*. The experience shocked her. She realized she just hadn't noticed the coverage of violent stories before. Each night, she took notes and recorded the material on VCR for later reference. She created headings for the stories, and listed details under each heading. Here are some of her notes:

Dog bites people--Two stories:
1. Pit bull attacks child. Shots of attack scene, including blood stains; child in hospital; interview with parents. Dramatic footage of dog charging fence.
2. Brief report about a dog (unidentified) crawling through a "doggy door" and chewing off a comatose woman's foot! Can you believe it? Only a shot of the house, doggy door, and neighborhood. A reporter's commentary.

Shootouts--Four stories:
1. Videotape of robbery and shooting. Convenience store, two gunmen, clerk with shotgun. Clerk shoots one gunman; the other flees.
2. Carjacking. Woman pistol whipped when she would not give up the car.
3. High-speed chase. Gun fight at the end. Police fired "bean bags," which stunned the car thieves.

4. Gang shooting. Very detailed and graphic. Reporter using a dramatic voice (they all use dramatic voices); police detective pointing out bullet holes; victims on stretchers.

Car accidents--Two massive freeway accidents:

1. Victims shown lying on stretchers, blood on asphalt, twisted metal.
2. Gory description by reporter. Jaws of life. All very grisly.

Finally, in the last phase of prewriting activities, Bennett used freewriting once more to respond to the programs she recorded:

Observations

I can't see any purpose for the violent segments other than to play on viewer emotion. The relentless bombardment of violent stories must make people feel that the world is a dangerous place, but they haven't much news value in themselves.

Titillation?

Curiosity?

Fulfill a viewer desire for blood?

Blood: What's that line from Up Close and Personal, the Redford movie about TV news--"If it bleeds, it leads!" This seems to be the rule people who run News at Eleven follow. They dramatize violence, not glorify it, but create drama.

How? Isn't news supposed to be objective? Who, What, Where, When, and so on? Yes, but . . .

The people who produce news actually do "produce" it, because there isn't much news value in these reports.

Okay. What do they do?

1. Play on fear.
2. Offer previews of coming attractions like films, in the form of announcements--they "hype" the news.
3. Give "dramatic" presentations of the news. Shocking language; facial expressions; voice tone.
4. They create lots of sympathy for victims.
5. Choose hard-hitting stories with plenty of visual value.

Behind this level of reporting is a cynical attitude: It might go something like this--If you want to control someone, feed him what he eats! Well, maybe they just want to feed the public what it eats: Superficial drama laced with violence that constantly renews itself.

Bennett's use of several prewriting activities is not unusual. Our advice is to stay flexible. Once you begin to use reflective thinking, you might find yourself—like Bennett did—first freewriting, then clustering, then observing and taking notes, making lists, and finally freewriting again. No single activity is appropriate for all writing situations. Use one or a combination of several to explore an assignment and discover a subject.

Formulating a Purpose Statement

Prewriting activities can be chaotic. Reflective thinking usually leads writers in a variety of directions—some toward the goal and some astray. That's why critical thinking dominates the next phase of the composing process.

You must begin by evaluating your prewriting material. Delete useless observations, odd digressions, cliched thinking, stalled musings, and dead-end ideas. Search for a fresh perspective—interesting ideas and observations that can be developed in examples.

This phase of the process will lead you to the finished essay. You will discover what else you need to know to do so. You'll be able to return to information sources to fill in the blank spaces: reading, class notes, discussions with friends, teachers, relatives, films, television—whatever will help you generate enough detail to meet the assignment's requirements. Once you've evaluated the information that composing activities have generated, you'll be ready to write a purpose statement that puts the goal in focus. Remember, in a single sentence, the purpose statement should identify a subject and how you plan to develop it.

After thoroughly exploring her assignment through prewriting activities, Michelle Bennett wrote the following purpose statement:

I plan to demonstrate that <u>News at Eleven</u> features stories that emphasize violence and mayhem, even though they directly affect only a few people, and to analyze how they have been dramatized.

Bennett will use this purpose statement to guide her through the planning process.

Developing an Informal Plan

To sort and group information, writers often arrange the major ideas related to their purpose under broad headings in an informal plan. The plan may include only the broadest headings, or it may include broad headings followed by more specific points, even phrases that capture specific details. The complexity of the plan depends on the subject and how you like to work. For instance:

- Some writers use a computer to create several drafts of informal plans, each becoming more specific. After several drafts, the essay slowly emerges.

- Other writers like to scribble their informal plans on notepads. They also use scissors and glue to rearrange elements of their plans. Here's a tip: Rather than spend a great deal of time rewriting your plan, photocopy it and then cut and paste sections until you have a plan that works.

- Other writers plan on 3" × 5" file cards. They write each major point on one card, and then add supporting details.

You can adopt any method to fit your own composing process. We suggest, however, that you always write your purpose at the top of the plan to keep you pointed toward your goal.

The following is Michelle Bennett's informal plan for "Hype, Heighten, and Hit Hard." She used a computer to develop several drafts before deciding on this one. Notice that she has arranged the information according to the structure she plans to use:

Introduction

I plan to demonstrate that <u>News at Eleven</u> showcases stories that emphasize violence and mayhem, even though they directly affect only a few people, and to analyze how they have been dramatized.

Discussion

Violent Stories: If it bleeds . . .

-- Gang shootings: reporter, detective, bullet holes and bodies

-- Carjacking: owner pistol whipped

-- Convenience store robbery: videotape, two robbers, one clerk, pistol and shotgun blast

-- Dog attack: images of pit bull; child in hospital; interview with parents

Dramatic Tactics

-- The tease/story hype: firemen, suicide attempt; shrubbery, rapist; shark threat, a dud

-- Dramatic commentary

   Reporter's voice, facial expressions, words

   Camera work, close-up details

   Creates sympathy: dog details placed against boy in hospital bed and
      parents

Conclusion

Why does this all happen? Cynical attitude? Objective journalism abandoned--who, what, where, when, why, and how. It's been replaced by hype and drama and stories that affect only a few people.

About developing this informal plan, Bennett wrote:

> Writing a rough plan is what really began to make the essay work for me. After tinkering with it, I began to see the structure I wanted. Even though the plan is skimpy, I had a clear sense of the kinds of details I would include. I also began to get a little angry. I hated to see a child's plight dramatized for no other reason than to feed the public thirst for violent stories. That's when I thought of the phrase "The child bled, so the story led." This also helped me realize how far our local news had drifted from an objective code . . . just the facts, please, no longer applied.

Bennett's observations about developing an informal plan show that even though you might think you are completing a fairly straightforward task, insights may come at any time in the composing process. Jot them down. They might be useful later.

Activities

■ **ON YOUR OWN**

In an essay of 750 to 1,000 words, address one of the writing prompts listed below or one your instructor assigns. Follow the process presented in this chapter:

- Assess the writing situation.
- Use prewriting techniques to generate material.
- Limit the scope of the subject.
- Create a purpose statement.
- Develop an informal plan.

1. The prosperous 1990s have been a hotbed for trends in fashion, film, music, publishing, and lifestyle.

   Write an essay that identifies and briefly explains several specific trends of the nineties; then project into the future and identify three trends you predict will develop within the next five years.

2. Most of us who watch television know about what commentators call "the creative cultural changes" that lie immediately ahead of us due to the impact of the information superhighway. Most people seem optimistic about these predicted changes. They maintain that once everyone owns a high-capacity computer and can tap into the Internet, culture will become decentralized and soulless governments, elitism, and mass culture will come to an end. But others see the changes that lie ahead as negative. The sky really is falling, they claim, and civilization is wandering into a cultural catastrophe.

Write an essay that agrees with one of these positions, or propose a third option, perhaps agreeing with parts of both positions. Explain in specific detail what cultural changes you believe we will face in the near future.

3. Advertisers are pursuing what has been called "liberation marketing." It's goal is not just to promote toothpaste that will get your teeth whiter but to promote toothpaste that will liberate you. Likewise, advertisers sell soft drinks that will bring freedom and sports cars that will set you free. These advertisers are not selling actual products, they are selling abstractions—liberation, freedom, communication, love, and family—that target human yearnings. Liberation advertisers promise avenues for escape from the drudgery of daily life.

Write an essay that analyzes several advertisements that promise more than the products can actually deliver, including such abstractions as social acceptance, success, freedom, and individuality.

4. Decide what characteristics you feel are important to becoming a successful person. Then identify several public figures you admire from a variety of fields—such as film, television, politics, sports, and music—who embody one or more of these characteristics.

Write an essay using the public figures to illustrate the characteristics you identified. No single public figure must have all the characteristics. Support your assertions with specific examples associated with each public figure.

5. Everyone has prejudices—strong feelings on some subject, for or against, that exist without much thought or reason. Identify at least three prejudices held by people you know. Ask each person for an explanation of his or her particular point of view.

Write an essay that explains and evaluates the validity of these three commonly held prejudices.

6. Examine some local custom—a campus tradition, a dating practice, a strong interest in some kind of activity—and determine its sources and purpose.

Write an essay that describes the custom and identifies why it exists.

7. What improvement do you think is most needed in the neighborhood you live in? Take stock of things. Identify and list the specific areas that need attention.

Write an essay that identifies and explains neighborhood problems and offers solutions to them.

8. Anxiety and fear are both emotional reactions to danger, yet there is a difference between the two. Fear is a reaction that is proportionate to real danger; anxiety is a disproportionate reaction to danger or even a reaction to imaginary danger. People may have anxiety without knowing it. In fact, anxiety may be the determining factor in people's lives without their being conscious of it.

Write an essay that explains the difference between fear and anxiety. Identify the role each plays as you or others have experienced them or as they are represented in film or television characters.

9. The phrase *poker face* describes someone who doesn't let his or her emotions show in a card game or in any social context where it's preferable not to reveal one's true feelings. Sociologists would refer to this behavior as *impression management,* through which people try to mask their own feelings to create a positive impression on others—for example, beauty pageant contestants or job applicants smiling to mask their exhaustion or anxiety.

Write an essay that identifies and examines at least four impression management strategies you've seen used by your friends and relatives. Interpret what is being masked and how successful or unsuccessful the masking is.

10. *Artifactual communication* includes all those elements a person adds to his or her body, such as earrings, watches, necklaces, eyeglasses, hairpieces, makeup, fragrance, and other cosmetic enhancements. Other artifacts that can act as extensions of oneself include cars, interior decoration, and designer clothes. All these extensions serve as nonverbal identifiers.

Write an essay that analyzes several artifactual communication enhancements. Describe them, associate them with people you know or know of, and explain what they communicate about the people wearing them.

PREWRITING ON COMPUTER

Begin by assessing the writing situation:

- Write out the assignment in your own words.
- Create a schedule reflecting your estimate of how long the assignment will take.
- List your information sources, and identify how they might be used.
- Identify your readers and describe them—age, education, gender, and so on. Include everything that's important.

Then explore the assignment. Here's where the computer's lightning-quick speed comes into play. No matter what freewriting technique you use, the computer can help you think reflectively. Try not to read or otherwise judge what you're typing. Just type! Don't worry about spelling, either. When you finish prewriting, merely push the "Spellcheck" key and make the corrections.

Warning: Protect your work. Hit the "Save" key often.

PLANNING ON COMPUTER

Because writing on a computer is so easy, you can pursue all your hunches—saving each one and comparing them all later. You can shape purpose statements, limiting their scope and refining them while keeping a record of the process. Then you can select and reassemble elements from your prewriting material. Eventually, an informal plan will emerge. You can print out the informal plan, make revisions by hand, and then type in the revisions and print out the plan again for re-evaluation.

Writing a Thesis Statement and a Formal Plan

If uncertainty makes you feel anxious, by this point, you've probably discovered that the writing process is tough. It isn't neat. It requires patience. It's unpredictable. Think about it this way: An essay mysteriously evolves, often changing shape as you reveal new connections among details in the working material. But if you trust the process, you will gradually see the final essay in your mind's eye. More than likely, this will happen when you compose a thesis statement.

WRITE AN EFFECTIVE THESIS STATEMENT

A *thesis statement*, usually written in a single sentence, serves as the intellectual center of an essay. The language of an effective thesis should be just broad enough to anticipate an essay's entire discussion and just limited enough to be developed within the assignment's required length. In other words, if your essay were a tract of land, the thesis statement would identify its boundary lines.

Thesis and purpose statements are similar but have different uses. A purpose statement is for a writer's eyes only. It serves as a pointer, focusing an essay's subject and purpose in your mind as you organize the working material. A thesis statement usually evolves from a purpose statement, but a thesis is useful to *both* the writer and reader. For the writer, an effective thesis statement precisely articulates the essay's central purpose and serves as a touchstone to keep discussion paragraphs unified. An effective thesis statement also helps the writer decide what to include and exclude from the final draft. If you have trouble developing a thesis statement, then that's a signal that you should return to prewriting activities or information sources.

For the reader, the thesis statement indicates where an essay is headed. It helps the reader put discussion paragraphs in perspective. Imagine how confused your reader will be if you fail to clarify the relationship among several paragraphs. A thesis statement will show that relationship.

Sometimes, beginning writers mistake titles, factual statements, and purpose statements for thesis statements. For example, consider the following:

TITLE
Sesame Street: The Hidden Message

A title may arouse reader interest, but it does not give a specific sense of the discussion that will follow.

FACTUAL STATEMENT
Sesame Street is a successful children's education program.

A factual statement leaves no room for development. It is a dead end. Who would disagree that *Sesame Street* is successful? No one. It's a fact. An essay based on a factual statement usually restates commonly accepted information and does not invite discussion.

PURPOSE STATEMENT
I plan to argue that *Sesame Street* emphasizes entertainment over education.

Purpose statements inserted into essays are usually stylistically intrusive and sound more like announcements than carefully crafted sentences.

THESIS STATEMENT
Sesame Street communicates the message that entertainment is more important than education.

A thesis statement, as we have already indicated, is a refinement of a purpose statement. It does not blatantly announce a writer's plan and approach; it is integrated into the introduction of the essay.

There is no exact time when you should begin to compose a thesis statement. At some point, after you've become satisfied with your informal plan, you'll find yourself mulling over what to do next. This is the time to turn to writing a thesis.

Make a Promise

An effective thesis statement always makes a promise—one that you, the writer, must keep. A good thesis promises the reader that you will fulfill the essay's purpose, as you conceive it.

Study these examples to see the evolution from purpose statement to thesis statement and the implicit promise:

PURPOSE STATEMENT
I plan to convince readers that the death penalty should be abolished, even though murder is a horrible crime.

THESIS STATEMENT

Although murder is humankind's most repugnant crime, the death penalty should be abolished.

PROMISE

To argue that capital punishment should be abolished.

PURPOSE STATEMENT

I plan to identify different kinds of action films and classify them in groups.

THESIS STATEMENT

Action films, which lack clear definition, can be divided into four categories.

PROMISE

To define action films and to identify categories for grouping them.

PURPOSE STATEMENT

I plan to illustrate how guns in the home lead to trouble.

THESIS STATEMENT

The presence of handguns in households with children frequently leads to fatal accidents, suicides, and murders.

PROMISE

To explain how pistols kept in the home can be dangerous in the hands of children.

Because a thesis statement evolves from a purpose statement, it takes into account the working material arranged in an informal plan. Its scope, however, is more limited, and its language is more precise than that of a purpose statement. In other words, the promise the thesis makes becomes more specific than the general intent expressed in a purpose statement.

Use Precise Language

You can limit the scope of your thesis statement by using precise language. For example, a simple thesis statement can be developed from the following purpose statement:

PURPOSE STATEMENT

I plan to argue that Batman's personality is more complex than Superman's.

THESIS STATEMENT

Batman's personality is more complex than Superman's.

For a brief essay, this thesis statement promises too much. What does it tell a reader to expect? A discussion of Batman and Superman as they appear in an early television series from the 1950s and 1960s? Or as they appear in films? Or as they appear in comic books? Would the discussion include the personalities of Bruce Wayne and Clark Kent, too? The scope of the thesis is too broad; it needs further limiting. Here's another try:

> In the early editions of *Batman* and *Superman* comics, Batman's personality is more complex than Superman's.

Now, the writer promises only to discuss Batman's and Superman's personalities in early comic books. This revised thesis is limited but not limited enough. Let's try again:

> In the early editions of *Batman* and *Superman* comics, Bruce Wayne's personality is more complex than Clark Kent's.

Now, the thesis promises a discussion of Bruce Wayne's and Clark Kent's personalities, not those of their superhero alter egos. But this thesis can be limited even more:

> In the early editions of *Batman* and *Superman* comics, Bruce Wayne is more pessimistic than Clark Kent.

At this point, the thesis is effectively limited. It pinpoints what the writer will discuss: Bruce Wayne's pessimism and, by implication, Clark Kent's optimism.

Imply a Method of Development

Sometimes, the way a thesis statement is written implies how the writer will develop the discussion. For example, the previous example implies comparison and contrast:

> In the early editions of *Batman* and *Superman* comics, Bruce Wayne is more pessimistic than Clark Kent.

If implying a development method in a thesis statement isn't intrusive, it can be an effective strategy for keeping a reader focused. Usually, you can make the implication in a word or two. For instance:

EXAMPLES
Three former boxing champions *show signs* of brain damage.

CAUSE AND EFFECT
Cellular phones, video cameras, and faxes are three *reasons* Czechoslovakia's student rebellion succeeded.

PROCESS ANALYSIS
The psychoanalytic *process* requires as much intuition as training.

CLASSIFICATION
Pro football linebackers fall into one of three *groups:* mean, meaner, and meanest.

DEFINITION

The phrase *family values* has different *meanings* for different political groups.

But if you have to twist a thesis statement into an announcement, then don't attempt to imply a development method.

Forecast a Development Pattern

Sometimes, a thesis embodies a concise forecast of an essay's development pattern. The discussion subpoints are summarized in grammatically parallel words, phrases, and clauses and then written as part of the thesis. For example:

Cigarette advertisers manipulate smokers by using *bandwagon, transfer, and plain folks.*

or

Cigarette advertisers use *bandwagon, transfer, and plainfolks* to manipulate smokers.

or

Cigarette advertisers use three key propaganda devices to manipulate smokers: *bandwagon, transfer, and plain folks.*

When the points can't be summarized briefly, then add a sentence after the thesis statement to forecast the pattern:

Once, our local parks provided a safe retreat where families could relax, but now they are dangerous for anyone who visits them. It seems *that rival gangs treat the parks as their territory, that random violence frequently erupts,* and *that the police ignore the danger to law abiding citizens.*

Astute readers would immediately know what pattern would be followed in the essay's discussion section.

When should you include an essay's development pattern in your thesis statement? That depends on how you assess the writing situation. Perhaps this tactic is most effectively used for inclass essay assignments. Such assignments are usually brief, so you won't have many points to represent in the thesis. In addition, these assignments are written under pressure, so announcing the development pattern in the thesis will help you stay focused. Finally, instructors tend to read inclass assignments in batches, which means their concentration might waver from time to time. By announcing your key points early, you will quickly show an instructor that you will adequately address the assignment.

One caution: Forecasts of development patterns often read like announcements and may seem intrusive. While you may justify their use in inclass essay assignments, use forecasts cautiously whenever you have time to consider more subtle strategies to introduce a discussion.

DEVELOP A FORMAL PLAN

We discussed informal planning in Chapter 5, identifying the various approaches different writers use and examining the approach followed by student writer Michelle Bennett. We're going to use Bennett's work as an example again in this chapter, as we discuss formal planning—the next stage in the writing process.

Plan with a Reader in Mind

Have you been thinking of a reader? Usually, the reader is a minor character in the composing process until it takes you to the thesis statement and formal planning stage. If you haven't done so already, now is the time to ask: Who, exactly, is my audience?

In speaking, you adjust to an audience quite easily. If you were to make separate spoken reports of an accident to a friend, your parents, a police officer, an insurance agent, and as a witness in court, you would automatically select different details and words for each occasion. In writing, however, you have to give this adjustment some thought. For instance, if you were writing an inclass essay for an instructor, you would want to show the full range of your understanding of the subject. If writing for fellow students, you would select examples that would relate to their experience. If writing for a universal audience, you would select examples that reflect broad experience.

In writing "Hype, Heighten, and Hit Hard," Michelle Bennett was responding to a Freshman composition assignment; even so, she decided to direct the paper to a wide audience of local television viewers. In making this decision, she realized she would have to select common examples and explain her ideas in ways that many people would understand. This decision and the formulation of a thesis meant that she was ready to develop a more formal plan for her essay.

Formal Outlines

One planning method is to write a *formal outline* that identifies the thesis and lists the essay's supporting points. For a long essay, a formal outline is needed to provide a detailed view of the essay's final arrangement. For short essays, however, a less formal, *scratch outline* may be effective. Here's an example of a scratch outline for a brief insight essay:

> I want to contrast my affluent world with the impoverished world
> of Central American earthquake victims.
> 1. Earthquake in Central America on TV
>   • Buildings in rubble
>   • Dead bodies in heaps to be burned

- Military men with rifles
- Children roaming the streets
2. Supermarket in Newport Beach
   - Clean and orderly
   - Well-stocked shelves
   - Well-dressed people
3. Poster of starving child
   - Thin
   - An extended hand

A formal outline includes the thesis statement as well as the subpoints of the discussion and a certain level of detail, depending on the subject's complexity. A formal outline can be written in topic or sentence form. The main items are identified by roman numerals, the first sublevel of items by capital letters, the second sublevel by arabic numerals, the third sublevel by lowercase letters, the fourth sublevel by arabic numerals enclosed in parentheses, and the fifth sublevel by lowercase letters enclosed in parentheses. All letters and numbers at the same level are indented to fall directly under one another, as shown here:

FORMAL OUTLINE STRUCTURE

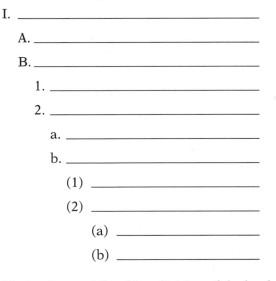

I. _____

   A. _____

   B. _____

      1. _____

      2. _____

         a. _____

         b. _____

            (1) _____

            (2) _____

               (a) _____

               (b) _____

Notice that each level is a division of the level above it. This means that there must be at least two items at every level because logically, a topic cannot be divided into one subitem. So in outlining, you can't have an A without a B or a 1 without a 2, for example. All items at the same level of the outline must be expressed in parallel structure, and the first word of each item must be capitalized. You will rarely need six levels in an outline, especially for writing college essays.

A Student's Outlining Process

Study the following example of a formal topic outline for Bennett's essay "Hype, Heighten, and Hit Hard":

Thesis: <u>News at Eleven</u> showcases and dramatizes violent stories that only affect a few people.

I. Typical violent stories
   A. Gang shooting
      1. Detective pointing out bullet holes
      2. Victims in body bags
   B. Carjacking and pistol whipping
   C. Convenience store robbery attempt
      1. Videotape
      2. Shootout between robber and clerk

II. Hyping "hot" stories
   A. Gang shooting
   B. Carjacking
   C. Convenience store robbery

III. Dramatizing violent stories
   A. Reporting style
      1. Language
      2. Facial expressions
   B. Camera work
      1. Editing
      2. Grisly details
   C. Creating sympathy
      1. Dog attack
         a. Tough and sympathetic narration
         b. Stirring imagery
         c. Emotional interview
      2. Appealing to emotion
         a. Affect only a few
         b. Child bled; story led

IV. Cynicism in <u>News at Eleven</u>
   A. Violent stories lead
   B. Loss of objective reporting

By composing a formal outline, you will be forced to think in terms of your reader—that imaginary person standing at your shoulder. You'll ask yourself: What would the reader already know? What should I develop in detail? Throughout the process, you'll probably refer to your informal plan and to material you generated in prewriting activities. Finally, if you discover holes in your outline, you can revisit information sources to fill them.

Michelle Bennett explained her approach to outlining as follows:

> I used my working material, which included the notes I'd taken while watching the news, my informal plan, and my thesis.
>
> I laid it all out on a table, going through everything and trying out different arrangements. In my mind I selected someone to be my reader, someone I knew was a news groupie but didn't reflect on what he watched--my uncle. He takes a lot of convincing, so I decided to use plenty of examples and to dramatize them with details. I doubt if he has ever thought about the process of selecting stories; he just watches them and comments on how law and order is breaking down.
>
> I also decided to arrange my material with the "dog attack" last because it was the most dramatic. I wanted to bring my reader along slowly with a barrage of brief examples, and then analyze one example in detail to show some of the very dramatic tactics at work.
>
> I found a simple way to work. I grouped my notes by subpoints and paper clipped them together. For example, I put the working material on "typical violent stories" into a separate group, which meant I had to use the scissors again, and so on for each subpoint. I had already done some of this grouping and sorting for my informal plan, but I narrowed it even further. I was struck by how much I was excluding--especially random notes on a variety of crimes other than violent crimes.

Too often, inexperienced writers want to skip formal planning, which is a huge mistake—one they'll pay for later. Formal planning is an important phase of the composing process; it forces you to figure out the final arrangement of your material.

Activities

ON YOUR OWN

1. Read the following thesis statement. Then unscramble the list that follows and recast it in a formal topic outline.

Thesis: Advertisers use propaganda devices to trick consumers into buying their products.

Transfer associates products with good feelings

Michael Jackson for soft drink

Dentist for toothpaste

Bandwagon says join the crowd

Cowboys represent the healthy life

Today's business woman on her own

Plain folks features common people

Yesterday's housewife serving a man

Marlboro cigarettes and the outdoors

Michael Jordan for shoes

A party crowded in a minivan

Good and bad propaganda

Twenty-somethings toasting Cuervo Gold

Testimonial features celebrities

An all-star list

1940s movie star June Allyson for adult diapers

1970s pro quarterback Joe Namath for panty hose

Advertisers and propaganda

Propaganda appeals to emotion not reason

1950s comedienne Martha Raye for denture cleaner

Advertising works

Neighbor for coffee

Cuervo Gold and Dennis Miller

Smoking and roping a horse

Mom pitching Solgar Vitamin Supplements

2. Return to the working material and purpose statement you developed for the exercise in Chapter 5, and then do the following:

   a. Rough out an effective thesis statement, keeping the following in mind:

      • *An effective thesis statement makes a promise.* Remember, you're not keeping a secret from your reader. You want to build expectation for what follows.

      • *An effective thesis statement is written in precise language.* Vague language might misdirect a reader. Express your thesis directly and clearly.

      • *An effective thesis statement limits discussion.* Use the thesis statement to narrow the scope of the discussion that follows and direct your reader's concentration.

      • *An effective thesis statement implies a method of development.* The development method can usually be implied in one or two key words.

- *An effective thesis statement may forecast a development pattern.* If you choose to forecast a development pattern, either integrate the key discussion points into the thesis statement or present them in a second sentence.

b. Now, develop a formal outline, keeping the following in mind:

- *Write the thesis at the top of your outline.* The thesis and its implicit promise will keep you on track as you sift through your working material.
- *Identify a reader.* The reader you imagine will affect what kind of information you include in your outline. Imagine the reader is looking over your shoulder.
- *Select appropriate information from prewriting.* You might have to continue the prewriting process to generate more information or add new information. The selection process will show the weak spots in your working material.
- *Include enough information in your outline to meet the assignment.* It's better to have too much, rather than not enough, information. It's also easier to cut extra information than to come up short and have to generate more later in the process.
- *Review the outline.* Be sure that the entries are parallel and that the information is arranged in the appropriate levels.

WRITING A THESIS AND OUTLINE ON COMPUTER

Generate plenty of versions of a thesis statement, since it's so easy to do on the computer. Play with them until you frame the one you think will work best.

Then revisit your informal outline on the screen and in printed form (from Chapter 5). Make sure the material fits the thesis statement. If your computer has a split-screen function, use it. Keep the informal outline in the upper half, and type the thesis statement in the lower half. Then, under the thesis statement, develop a formal outline by referring to the informal outline.

When you have a draft of the formal outline, consider its arrangement. Use the "Cut and Paste" feature to rearrange the order of your key points and subpoints, if necessary.

CHAPTER 7

Writing Paragraphs
for the Rough Draft

At this point in the composing process, no matter how hard you try, you just won't be able to write a perfect first draft. Rest assured, you're not alone. It's impossible even for professional writers. If you try for perfectionism in writing your rough draft, you will develop a writer virus. The symptoms are clear: reluctance to sit still; unreasonable urges to seek more information; mild confusion; clock watching; fear, panic, and, finally, paralysis.

So, sit back and remember this: When you begin a rough draft—that is, a working draft—you will probably write several more drafts before you complete the final essay. Instead of being concerned with perfection now, try to keep writing by concentrating on content and structure. If you get stuck, leave some space and write yourself a reminder to return later. Chances are that by the time you finish, you will have solved the difficulty. So, don't hesitate. Pick up a pen or switch on the computer and get started—now!

We'll consider the work of student writer Michelle Bennett in this chapter, as we have in Chapters 5 and 6. Later, we'll look at the introduction, discussion, and conclusion paragraphs she wrote as well as how she pulled them all together into the rough draft of her essay. Here's what Bennett wrote about getting started on that draft:

> I had my working notes, my thesis, my outline. What else did I need? Trust in the process. I told myself that whatever I wrote at this point would be for my eyes only. It would be a working draft. I wouldn't be judged by it. It wouldn't be graded. Still, I had trouble starting, so my instructor said to write "This will stink, but I'm writing it anyway" at the top of the page. That helped.
>
> Having a well-detailed outline also helped. I hadn't read the outline for a day, so I was surprised; it was like being given a map before taking a road trip.

With a good outline in hand you can start at any point. However, we suggest that you start with the introduction.

WRITE THE INTRODUCTION

In a college essay, the introduction almost unvaryingly presents the thesis statement that will be supported in the discussion. The prevalence of this pattern is the reason such essays are often called *thesis/support essays.* Sometimes, the thesis will begin the introduction, especially in a short essay that doesn't require much background information. But usually, the thesis will come at the end of the introduction. By closing the introduction with the thesis, you are placing it at the point of greatest emphasis, thus using paragraph structure to tell your reader that this sentence is important. It embodies your promise.

An introduction doesn't have to be long; in fact, it should never be longer than one-fifth of the essay's entire length. Regardless of length, it should be meaningful—as meaningful as any other part of the essay. Too often, inexperienced writers waste the opportunity an introduction offers. They merely write a few general, aimless sentences and tack on an ill-phrased thesis at the end. An *effective* introduction does much more:

1. The sentences that lead to the thesis statement should place the subject in context and give any background information a reader will need to move from the thesis through the discussion.
2. The introduction offers a chance for you to grab—or "hook," as professional writers say—reader interest.
3. The introduction lets you implicitly establish who you perceive the reader to be.
4. The introduction lets you implicitly establish your own voice and authority.

For example, consider the following introduction. It sets the stage for the thesis by introducing the general subject (*attitude*) early and by leading to the thesis, which limits the scope of the discussion: . . . *you can acquire [attitude] if you follow five simple rules.* It also suggests a reader: young and steeped in popular culture. Finally, it suggests a writer: like the reader, young and steeped in pop culture. See what you think:

> "Attitude" is in. I don't mean a good attitude; I mean bad, real bad, attitude. You're probably attracted to it, and your parents, like mine, probably hate it. It's a combination of arrogance, anger, and dark humor. Raw comedians have attitude. Cool actors have attitude. Sullen rock stars have attitude. Dennis Leary, Will Smith, and Axl Rose—all are soaked in attitude. Is it strictly a male trait? Hardly—Whoopi Goldberg, Sigourney Weaver, and the Spice Girls all have serious attitude. *Attitude doesn't come easily, but you can acquire it if you follow five simple rules.*

This writer has written an effective introduction: He showcases the subject, presents a limited thesis, provides a context, and creates senses of the reader and himself. Does he hook reader interest? He certainly attempts to by teasing the reader with the mysterious power of attitude.

Unfortunately, you can't rely on a single strategy to always hook reader interest. But you can draw from several effective strategies. Which one you use depends on how you assess the assignment. Consider the following strategies and examples:

1. *Use vivid details to capture the reader's imagination.*

Members of my generation have grown up during a time when the majority of Americans have lived in relative comfort. Nevertheless, we have all seen photographs of the Great Depression of the 1930s: images of anonymous men in dark suits and tweed caps selling apples on street corners; hollow-cheeked women cuddling infants in front of clapboard shacks; crowds milling before factory gates; hoboes gathered around campfires and eating from tin cans; Model T Fords loaded with chairs, tables, mattresses, and boxes of clothes crawling along desert highways toward the Pacific. These dreadful memories, preserved in history books, are grim. But besides the dreadful memories, *there are positive aspects of the Depression that haven't been preserved in history books. These memories are carried by people who suffered yet lived through the thirties.*

2. *Show a change taking place or a chronology of events unfolding.*

There is a dramatic change in the life cycle. Puberty arrives earlier by several years than it did at the turn of the century. Adolescence is now prolonged until the late twenties. Adulthood often does not start until the thirties. Middle age does not seem to begin until the late forties and old age, well, as the saying goes, you are as young as you feel. *Today's description of the life cycle contrasts sharply with the life cycle that psychologists described over 75 years ago.*

3. *Present statistics that relate to the thesis.*

Midway is a typical urban school with a typical student body. It has over 20,000 registered students. The student body is composed of four major ethnic groups: Anglo, Asian, Hispanic, and African American. The average student-family income is between $45,000 and $50,000, but if a student is under 20 years of age, the chances are that he or she will earn only minimum wage and live at home. Most of these students do work and take reduced academic loads. Most want to transfer to a four-year college. *None of these statistics are too surprising, but when a survey revealed student attitudes toward sexual relationships, the picture changed.*

4. *Use dramatic quotations to arouse reader curiosity.*

"I'm right; you're wrong." "You don't have a clue about war; you weren't in the Marines." "How can she comment on families? She's divorced." "Smart, how can you say he's smart? He likes the president." Personal attacks disguised as argumentative points are expected from radio talk show hosts, but these are comments from a recent discussion in political science. Unfortunately, they are all too common in classes across campus. After three years on this campus, I've concluded *personal attacks, non sequiturs, and guilt by association seem to have replaced reasoned discussion.*

5. *Open with a question that catches reader attention.*

What do you buy when you buy an airline ticket? What does it entitle you to, and what are the airline's legal obligations to you? What's their responsibility if they cause you to miss a connection or a hotel reservation? Next time you're sitting in an airport, waiting for your delayed flight to get off the ground, try passing the time by reading the fine print on your ticket. *A page titled "Conditions of Contract" could serve as a syllabus for a course in travel education.*

6. *Use a dramatic narrative to hook readers.*

It was Bill Washington's first backpacking trip, one he had planned for over a year. His son Tommy was with him, and it was their second day in the woods. They were breaking camp and packing up for a six-hour hike to the next campsite. Tommy was folding up the tent, and Bill was dismantling the tiny backpacker stove. He tugged at the fuel cartridge to disconnect it, but it was stuck. He pulled harder; butane began to hiss and then exploded loudly. Bill was knocked to the ground, shocked by the blast. Tommy turned to look at him as Bill's clothes burst into flames. It turned out that the stove's shut-off valve was defective and Bill's clothes had not been treated with a fire retardant. Bill learned a lesson the hard way: *The gravest danger a hiker faces comes from the manufacturers of camping equipment and apparel.*

7. *Draw readers into an essay by defining a key word or concept.*

The ancient Irish held a beautiful notion of friendship. In their religion, someone who was a teacher or trustworthy companion was referred to as an *anam cara*, Irish for "soul friend." If you lived in Ireland then, your soul friend would be the person with whom you shared your life's confidential experiences, your deepest thoughts, and dreams. You and this person would have a special intimacy. It would transcend all barriers of social convention, morality, and religion. Your soul friend would understand your deepest motives and be able to place your life in perspective whenever you began to drift from your path. What is today's equivalent to an *anam cara*? Clergy members? Family members? Brothers or sisters? Probably not. *The closest most us will come to having a soul friend will be to consult with a trained psychologist.*

Any one of these strategies can be effective in introducing a thesis. But keep in mind that at this point you are writing a rough draft—an approximate draft—not a final draft. Still, when you block out the rough draft of your introduction, start with a clear strategy in mind—one of the strategies in the preceding list or one that fits the demands of an assignment more directly. And then start writing!

A Student Roughs Out an Introduction

Bennett decided to start the first draft of her introduction with a shocking statement. Here's how she explained that decision:

> I liked the phrase "If it bleeds, it leads," so I decided to start with it and then move quickly to my thesis. I felt it really capsulized what was driving

news decisions. I also thought it would hook my designated reader. My first attempt read like this:

> "If it bleeds, it leads" seems to be the single guideline News at Eleven uses to decide what stories they should feature each night. Just last week, every news broadcast opened with violent, sometimes even bloody stories. News at Eleven showcases these stories even though they affect only a handful of people; maybe none are even viewers. Worse yet, they do not just present the facts, they create minidramas out of them.

I wasn't happy with this introduction. My reader wouldn't know why I was writing it. Maybe violence is so rampant every news show should open with the day's violent acts. Also, I didn't create a sense of how extreme I felt the stories were.

What makes News at Eleven programming especially shocking is that crime has been dropping. I decided to take that idea from the assignment and add it to my introduction. Of course, doing so led to other changes:

> The government just announced that violent crime has been reduced 10% when compared to last year. But News at Eleven must not have heard of this new trend. They feature dramatic stories that have lots of blood and mayhem but do not affect many people. Their guideline for programming seems to say, "If it bleeds, it leads." News at Eleven not only showcases violent stories, they also unnecessarily dramatize them.

Better, I thought. Now I was on the right track.

WRITE THE DISCUSSION

The discussion section of an essay is usually composed of several paragraphs. These paragraphs are usually organized by topic sentences. Each topic sentence should develop a subpoint of the thesis statement. If you have written a thorough formal outline, you will see the relationship between the thesis statement and the subpoints.

Organize Discussion Paragraphs

Different writing situations call for different kinds of discussion paragraphs. In one paragraph, you might give readers more background information to set up the discussion. In another, you might summarize the evidence in an argument or the dramatic high points in a narration. You might have to write a transition paragraph to show the relationship between major parts of an essay. You might even write dialogue using paragraphing to indicate changes in the speaker. But in most college essays, you will write discussion paragraphs that advance your reader's understanding of the thesis.

A well-organized discussion paragraph develops a single subpoint of the thesis. Regardless of differences in plan and content, a successful, fully developed paragraph has the following qualities:

1. *A topic sentence:* One or two sentences that introduce the paragraph's main point.
2. *Adequate development:* Enough information is provided to develop the idea in a reasonably thorough manner.
3. *Unity:* All of the sentences contribute to the main point.
4. *Coherence:* The discussion proceeds logically from sentence to sentence.

By studying the following paragraph, you can see how Olivia Vlahos, author of *Human Beginnings,* applies the principles of good paragraph structure. Vlahos develops a single point—in this case, that all living creatures communicate in some form. She maintains unity by making every sentence relate to this single point. She achieves coherence by repeating similar sentence structures, only varying these structures in the closing two sentences. She adequately develops her subject, the third characteristic of an effective discussion paragraph, by listing examples of animal communication. Consider this paragraph:

> *Nearly all living creatures manage some form of communication.* The dance patterns of bees in their hive help to point the way to distant flower fields or announce successful foraging. Male stickleback fish regularly swim upside-down to indicate outrage in a courtship contest. Male deer and lemurs mark territorial ownership by rubbing their own body secretions on boundary stones or trees. Everyone has seen a frightened dog put his tail between his legs and run in panic. We, too, use gestures, expressions, postures, and movement to give our words point.

Use Topic Sentences.   Topic sentences announce paragraph content. In the last paragraph example, the topic sentence is a clearly phrased, direct statement that begins the paragraph:

Nearly all living creatures manage some form of communication.

Most topic sentences are direct statements, as these examples show:

The college needs a portable cellular phone policy to define their use in public.

Doomsayers base their turn-of-the-century predictions on four sources.

In fashion, several corporate logos seem magical, but many more seemed cursed.

Social trend spotting has become a specialty among political scientists.

A growing mass of evidence shows that self-generated sounds—chants, mantras, raps, and the like—can be potent emotional and physical healers.

An effective topic sentence has three dominant characteristics:

1. It has a subject and a controlling idea.
2. It is limited enough to be developed in one paragraph.
3. It lends itself to debatable discussion.

Consider the following topic sentence:

In casual conversation, emotional meaning is often communicated unconsciously through nonverbal messages.

This topic sentence has these three characteristics. It has a subject—*emotional meaning*—and a controlling idea—*is often communicated subconsciously in nonverbal messages*. It is reasonably limited in scope, because the writer has not staked out the entire territory of *meaning* as expressed in all communication. She has limited it to *emotional meaning* that is revealed in *casual conversation* and to *nonverbal messages*, thus excluding spoken messages. She has also limited the discussion by using the qualifying word *often*, thus avoiding the impossible task of proving that her assertion is always true. Finally, the sentence lends itself to discussion. The writer could easily follow with examples of such nonverbal messages and interpret them for the reader. That, in fact, is what the reader will probably expect.

For contrast, consider the following topic sentence:

Nonverbal language is interesting.

This topic sentence is less focused, and, therefore, it is less clear just what information should follow. Besides that, the direction has changed. The first sentence promises discussion; the second merely states an attitude. The reader doesn't know what's coming and may be thinking, "Oh, yeah! I think it's a hoax!"

Consider the next topic sentence:

The guinea pig is a member of the rat family.

Clearly, this sentence does not meet all the characteristics of an effective topic sentence. It does not lend itself to debatable discussion. It might be a useful fact to know and it could be followed by other facts about guinea pigs, but where is the language that leads to discussion?

As you write topic sentences, ask yourself if they have the three characteristics we have been discussing. For example:

TOPIC SENTENCE

Dumping waste in Long Beach Harbor is threatening the shoreline's ecology.

Subject?

Dumping waste in Long Beach Harbor

Controlling Idea?

Threatens the local ecology

Limited?

Yes

Development?

Explanation of how dumping waste threatens the local ecology

TOPIC SENTENCE

Temporary workers, often referred to as *disposable workers,* have legitimate reasons to be angry.

Subject?

Temporary workers

Controlling Idea?

Have legitimate reasons to be angry

Limited?

Yes

Development?

Presentation of reasons for temporary workers being angry

TOPIC SENTENCE

Journal writing is a deeply personal process, full of mystery and surprise.

Subject?

Journal writing

Controlling Idea?

Is a deeply personal process, full of mystery and surprise

Limited?

Yes

Development?

Description of the writing process from a personal perspective that emphasizes mystery and surprise

TOPIC SENTENCE

Although Anne Rice and Joan Didion are contemporary women fiction writers, the experiences they capture are startlingly different.

Subject?

Anne Rice and Joan Didion as contemporary women fiction writers

Controlling Idea?

The experiences they capture are startlingly different

Limited?

Yes

Development?
Contrast Rice's content with Didion's

TOPIC SENTENCE
Students interested in a career in landscape architecture often visit the Randolph Nursery to see the miniature replicas of the world's most famous gardens.

Subject?
Students interested in a career in landscape architecture

Controlling Idea?
Often visit Randolph Nursery to see the miniature replicas of the world's most famous gardens

Limited?
Yes

Development?
The writer will have trouble here. The controlling idea—*often visit*—does not lend itself to debatable discussion. It seems to require a list of the times visited, which is not very interesting content. The writer probably intends to describe the miniature gardens. If so, the sentence should be rephrased to make the *gardens* the subject.

TOPIC SENTENCE REPHRASED
Randolph Nursery's miniature replicas of the world's most famous gardens are a valuable resource for landscape architecture students.

Development?
Now, the miniature garden replicas serve as the paragraph's subject. Their value as a resource for landscape architecture students serves as the controlling idea. The development can include description and a discussion of what can be learned by visiting the gardens.

Most writers find their own methods of working out their topic sentences for their rough drafts. They might write each topic sentence as they come to each discussion paragraph, or they might first approximate the topic sentence of each discussion paragraph before developing the individual paragraph. A lot of such "rough drafting" activities rely on a writer's instinct. But no matter what your instinct tells you to do, you will still have a single goal: to produce a polished final draft, ready to submit for evaluation.

Develop Paragraphs.   How long should a paragraph be? Paragraph length depends on many things: the complexity of the idea; the method of development; the length of adjacent paragraphs; and the age, knowledge, interest, and educational background of its intended audience. Most importantly, a paragraph should be developed enough to do justice to the idea expressed in the topic sentence.

Short paragraphs are easier to read than long ones, but a paper consisting entirely of two- or three-sentence paragraphs may make the entire effort seem immature and underdeveloped. Long paragraphs seem more intellectual and weighty, but too many of them may discourage a reader and make the subject appear more difficult and intricate than it actually is.

The best approach, really, is not to worry much about paragraph length. Instead, concentrate on fully developing the controlling idea in your topic sentence by including enough specific supporting information to avoid skimpy, immature paragraphs, such as this one:

> A number of curious experiences occur at the onset of sleep. A person just about to go to sleep may experience an odd physical sensation, the most common of which is the sense of floating or falling. A nearly universal occurrence at the beginning of sleep (although not everyone recalls it) is a sudden jerk of the body. The onset of sleep is not gradual at all. It happens in an instant.

Obviously, the above paragraph is underdeveloped. The writer needs to add more specific information and concrete details to develop the topic sentence adequately.

Now, study the original paragraph, as Peter Farb wrote it. Notice how the addition of information and specific details turns an underdeveloped paragraph into a fully developed one:

> A number of curious experiences occur at the onset of sleep. A person just about to go to sleep *may experience an electric shock, a flash of light, or a crash of thunder—* but the most common sensation is that of floating or falling, *which is why "falling asleep" is a scientifically valid description.* A nearly universal occurrence at the beginning of sleep (although not everyone recalls it) is a sudden, *uncoordinated* jerk of the *head, the limbs, or even the entire* body. *Most people tend to think of going to sleep as a slow slippage into oblivion, but* the onset of sleep is not gradual at all. It happens in an instant. *One moment the individual is awake, the next moment not.*

Achieve Unity. A paragraph is *unified* when all the sentences clearly relate to the controlling idea expressed in the topic sentence. Read the following paragraph by Lael Morgan, from "Let the Eskimos Hunt," to see how the supporting information and details relate to the idea that many people oppose hunting even where animal populations are dangerously large:

> (1) *Many Americans mindlessly oppose hunting, even in cases where animal populations are dangerously high.* (2) In some areas of Alaska, wolves have become so prolific they are running out of hunting ground and prey heavily on moose, deer, and occasionally dogs. (3) Wolves run in packs and hunt with more cunning than any other predator in North America. (4) In the past, game managers curbed wolf populations by trapping and aerial hunting without wiping out the species. (5) Still, whenever they propose to do this nowadays, they receive tens of thousands of letters

in protest. (6) Growing deer populations in parts of California threaten to starve themselves out. (7) No doubt images of Bambi rise up in the minds of hunting opponents. (8) Sea-otter colonies, burgeoning along the Pacific coast, are fast running out of fodder, too, as well as putting commercial fishermen out of business. (9) Because otters are so cute, ecologists have rushed to their aid.

Sentences 3, 7, and 9 do not relate directly to the controlling idea expressed in the topic sentence. They disrupt the paragraph's unity and should either be integrated into other sentences or deleted.

Now read Lael Morgan's paragraph from "Let the Eskimos Hunt" as it was actually written. See how all the supporting information and details relate to the topic sentence's controlling idea:

> *Many Americans mindlessly oppose hunting, even in cases where animal populations are dangerously high.* In some areas of Alaska, wolves have become so prolific they are running out of hunting ground and prey heavily on moose, deer, and occasionally dogs. In the past, game managers curbed wolf populations by trapping and aerial hunting without wiping out the species. Still, whenever they propose to do this nowadays, they receive tens of thousands of letters in protest. Growing deer populations in parts of California threaten to starve themselves out. Sea-otter colonies, burgeoning along the Pacific coast, are fast running out of fodder, too, as well as putting commercial fishermen out of business.

By deleting the three extraneous sentences, Morgan makes the paragraph unified and keeps the reader's attention on the key point—*Many Americans mindlessly oppose hunting*—by giving a series of on-target examples.

Maintain Coherence.   While writing the rough draft of an essay, keep in mind that you should strive to be coherent. When an essay is *coherent,* it means that the writer's thought progresses smoothly and logically from sentence to sentence. When coherence breaks down, then the sentences are not working together. They seem disconnected, and the writer's thought does not unfold smoothly from sentence to sentence.

The following paragraph lacks coherence. As you read it, notice how the line of thought seems disrupted, skipping from sentence to sentence:

> Dunlap paints holiday scenes with a touch of menace. "Picnic," one of her early paintings of a family on vacation, suggests approaching danger. In "Picnic" a family sits on the beach. The sea is edged with whitecaps. Two children stand facing the sea and a line of sailboats leaning into the wind, heading for safe harbor. A third child stares back at a man and woman sitting on the sand, a fearful expression on the child's face. The couple she stares at are the focus of the canvas, taking up a third of the space. Near them is a watermelon with a butcher knife leaning against it, the knife tip in the sand. Dunlap only represents the back of the man's head and just a slice of his profile. He seems to be staring beyond the children at an impending squall. The woman is staring at him, a slightly fearful expression on her face, and she appears to have the faint trace of a bruise on her neck. At the top of the canvas, clouds are gathering as if ready to erupt with rain.

The lack of coherence in the preceding paragraph can be corrected in two ways: (1) by sequencing the descriptive detail more effectively and (2) by using overt transitional phrases that will serve to guide reader attention.

Next, reread Tyler Freidenrich's revised version of the earlier paragraph. Notice how the detail has been reordered to move from far to near (in this case, from the top of a painting to the bottom). The rearrangement also places the most dramatic details in the closing sentences, the most climatic position in the paragraph. Freidenrich also adds overt transitions—such as, *At the top of "Picnic," in the upper middle ground,* and *On shore, in the middle foreground*—to lead the reader in an orderly fashion from the beginning to the end of the paragraph. Here's the revision:

> Dunlap paints holiday scenes with a touch of menace. "Picnic," one of her early paintings of a family on vacation, suggests approaching danger. At the top of "Picnic," clouds are gathering as if ready to erupt with rain. Between the sky and shore, in the upper middle ground, the sea is edged with whitecaps and a line of sailboats lean into the wind, heading for safe harbor. On shore, in the middle foreground, two children stand facing the sea and a third stares back at a man and woman sitting on the sand, a fearful expression on the child's face. The couple she stares at are the focus of the canvas, taking up a third of the lower foreground. Dunlap only represents the back of the man's head and just a slice of his profile. He seems to be staring beyond the children at the impending squall. The woman is staring at him, a slightly fearful expression on her face, and she appears to have the faint trace of a bruise on her cheek. Behind her, in the lower left corner, is a watermelon with a butcher knife leaning against it, the knife tip in the sand.

Two common ways that writers keep paragraphs coherent is through the logical arrangement of information and by using overt transitions.

Arrange Information Logically.　　When appropriate, writers tend to order their material in one of five possible ways:

1. *Order of climax:* Some paragraphs lend themselves to an arrangement of details or examples according to increasing importance. In sum, save the most dramatic material for last.
2. *General to specific or specific to general:* Most paragraphs begin with a general comment—usually contained in the topic sentence—and follow with specific details, reasons, or examples that support the generalization. Some paragraphs, however, reverse this order by beginning with specifics and ending with a general observation that serves as the topic sentence.
3. *Time order:* Narrative paragraphs—those that tell a story or present a series of incidents—usually follow the order in which the events occurred.
4. *Spatial order:* Descriptive paragraphs lend themselves quite easily to a spatial arrangement: that is, the details are presented from left to right, from right to left, from near to far, from the center outward, from top to bottom, and so on.

These ordering methods are useful in some situations, but the most suitable arrangement for any given paragraph will depend on your particular purpose and content. The purpose of establishing a clear paragraph order is to lead a reader through the progression of sentences as they unfold from the beginning to the end of the paragraph.

Use Overt Transitions.   *Overt transitions* are mechanical techniques employed to keep readers on track. They serve as guideposts, marking the way from the beginning to the end of a paragraph.

When you give directions, develop illustrations, explain difficult concepts, or shift into a new pattern, you should take some care in drawing your reader along. At these times, signal your reader with a transitional word or phrase. For example, study the use of overt transitions in this paragraph from Tom Paradis's "A Child's Other World":

> In addition to causing viewers to lose touch with society, television has had negative effects on viewers' imagination. Before the days of television, people were entertained by exciting radio shows such as *Superman, Batman,* and *War of the Worlds.* Of course, the listener was required to pay careful attention to the story if all details were to be comprehended. Better yet, while listening to the stories, listeners would form their own images of the actions taking place. When the broadcaster would give brief descriptions of the Martian space ships invading earth, for example, every member of the audience would imagine a different space ship. In contrast, television's version of *The War of the Worlds* will not stir the imagination at all, for everyone can clearly see the actions taking place. All viewers see the same space ship with the same features. Each aspect is clearly defined, and therefore, no one will imagine anything different from what is seen. Thus, television cannot be considered an effective tool for stimulating the imagination.

Overt transitional words and phrases, such as the ones Paradis uses, connect the thoughts as the writer moves from sentence to sentence. A wide range of transitional words are available to show the relationship of one sentence to another or one thought to another. Here are some familiar examples:

TO SHOW SIMILARITY
likewise, similarly, in the same way

TO SHOW DIFFERENCES OR CONTRAST
but, however, still, yet, nevertheless, on the one hand/on the other hand, on the contrary, in contrast

TO SHOW ADDITION
moreover, and, in addition, equally important, next, first, second, third, again, also, too, besides, furthermore, moreover

TO SHOW TIME AND PROCESS
soon, in the meantime, afterward, later, meanwhile, while, earlier, finally, simultaneously, next, the next step

TO SHOW DIRECTION

here, there, over there, beyond, nearby, opposite, under, above, to the left, to the right, in the distance, up, down

TO ANNOUNCE AN END

in conclusion, to summarize, finally, on the whole, at last

TO ANNOUNCE A RESTATEMENT

in short, in other words, in brief, to put it differently

TO INDICATE A RESULT

therefore, then, as a result, consequently, accordingly, thus, thereupon

Repeat Key Words and Phrases.   You can also maintain coherence by repeating key words and phrases to emphasize how your ideas are being carried forward from sentence to sentence. For example, in a paragraph from "The Artist as Housewife," Erica Jong repeats a key word to create coherence. The paragraph's controlling idea deals with a poet's problem of creating a personal voice in her work. Jong associates the idea with *authenticity* in the second sentence, and she then repeats or rephrases this key word throughout the paragraph:

> The main problem of the poet is to raise a voice. We can suffer all kinds of kinks and flaws in a poet's work except lack of authenticity. Authenticity is a difficult thing to define, but roughly it has to do with our sense of the poet as a mensch, a human being, an author (with the accent on authority). Poets arrive at authenticity in very different ways. Each poet finds her own road by walking it—sometimes backward, sometimes at a trot. To achieve authenticity you have to know who you are and approximately why. You have to know yourself not only as defined by roles you play but also as a creature with an inner life, a creature built around an inner darkness. Because women are always encouraged to see themselves as role players and helpers ("help-mate" as a synonym for "wife" is illuminating here), rather than as separate beings, they find it hard to grasp this authentic sense of self. They have too many easy cop-outs.

Pronouns referring to clearly established antecedents function in the same way as the repetition of key words or phrases. For example, conservationist Cleveland Amory repeats the key noun *coyote* and uses pronouns to refer back to it, thus creating coherence throughout the following paragraph:

> The coyote's only hope lies in his cleverness. And stories of coyotes outwitting hunters are legion. Coyotes will work in teams, alternately resting and running to escape dogs set upon them. They have even been known to jump on automobiles and flat cars to escape dogs. And they have also successfully resisted bombing. Lewis Nordyke reports that once when a favorite coyote haunt in Texas became a practice range for bombing, the coyotes left—temporarily. Soon they were back to

investigate and found that the bombing kept people out. They decided to stay. Meanwhile, they learned the bombing schedule and avoided bombs.

Use Parallel Structure.   By repeating a particular structure in successive sentences, writers can create a parallel form that indicates the relationship among sentences. *Parallelism* is effective because of the repeated tempo and sounds that help reinforce the connections in thought and because of the emphasis on key words that are often repeated in the structure. For example, in the following paragraph, William G. Carleton creates a strong tempo by opening repeated sentences with a subject/verb arrangement and by repeating *books* for emphasis:

> As sources of ideas, professors simply cannot compete with books. Books can be found to fit almost every need, temper, or interest. Books can be read when you are in the mood; they do not have to be taken in periodic doses. Books are both more personal and more impersonal than professors. Books have an inner confidence which individuals seldom show; they rarely have to be on the defensive. Books can afford to be bold and courageous and exploratory; they do not have to be so careful of boards of trustees, colleagues, and community opinion. Books are infinitely diverse; they run the gamut of human activity. Books can be found to express every point of view; if you want a different point of view, you can read a different book. . . . Even your professors are at their best when they write books and articles; the teaching performance rarely equals the written effort.

Stylistically, parallelism in a paragraph is dramatic. Used effectively, it can rivet reader attention. When you use parallel structure, make sure the content justifies the dramatic emphasis that parallelism brings to the page.

A Student Roughs Out Discussion Paragraphs

Once Michelle Bennett roughed out a thesis and an introduction, she decided to compose her topic sentences before developing the discussion paragraphs themselves. She felt her topic sentences would serve as touchstones and mark the way through the essay. Bennett wrote:

> I like to know where I'm headed. I guess that's why I spent a lot of time outlining. Once I completed the thesis statement and introduction for the rough draft, I wanted to develop a better sense of where I was headed. I roughed out topic sentences--not perfect ones but ones that could take the outline's subpoints and recast them as paragraph openings.
>
> I knew my conclusion would emphasize the cynicism I sensed behind news story selection. But I'd deal with that later.

Bennett began by re-examining her thesis statement to keep what she was promising the reader in mind. The re-examination helped her decide how to approach the topic sentences:

BENNETT'S WORKING THESIS

<u>News at Eleven</u> not only showcases violent stories, it also unnecessarily dramatizes them.

She recognized that the reader would expect three promises to be fulfilled: She would have to give examples showing how *News at Eleven* emphasized violent stories. She would have to analyze how *News at Eleven* dramatized the stories. And she would have to assert that the actual violent events affected very few people, even though they often led the news.

Next, Bennett began to recast the outline's subpoints as topic sentences:

BENNETT'S OUTLINED SUBPOINTS

 I. Typical violent stories

 II. Hyping hot stories

 III. Dramatizing violent stories

 IV. Creating sympathy

BENNETT'S SUBPOINTS ROUGHED OUT AS TOPIC SENTENCES

 I. Stories of violence and mayhem dominate <u>News at Eleven</u>.

 II. <u>News at Eleven</u> hypes violent stories for dramatic effect.

 III. To dramatize violent stories, <u>News at Eleven</u> uses two tactics.

 IV. <u>News at Eleven</u> also attempts to create sympathy.

Bennett then recast each main item in her outline as a topic sentence. Each topic sentence supported a promise in the thesis statement and would be developed in a discussion paragraph. The details under the main items would then become separate examples that develop the topic sentences. Although worded differently, Bennett's roughed-out topic sentences reflected the topic sentences in her final draft.

Bennett then went on to rough out the entire discussion section one paragraph at a time. As she explained it:

> I used my working notes to flesh out each paragraph. I began with the first discussion paragraph. I followed the arrangement in the outline, using three very dramatic examples to develop the topic sentence. I arranged them climatically--that is, saved the most dramatic example for last and developed it in more detail.
>
> After I roughed out the paragraph, I rewrote the topic sentence to better reflect what I had to say, emphasizing that these events had very little significance for the vast majority of viewers.

The rough draft of the first discussion paragraph, with the revised topic sentence, reads as follows. It was based on the following items in the formal outline:

I. Typical violent stories
   A. Gang shooting
      1. Detective pointing out bullet holes
      2. Victims in body bags
   B. Carjacking pistol whipping
   C. Convenience store robbery
      1. Videotape
      2. Shootout between robber and clerk

Now, read the roughed-out paragraph and notice how it reflects the outline:

Stories of violence and mayhem dominate News at Eleven even though only a few people are affected. For example, last Monday I saw a broadcast that opened with a gang-shooting story. A reporter stood on the porch at the crime scene asking a detective questions. The detective answered the questions and pointed out bullet holes. Two people had been brutally murdered. The camera cut to the bodies being wheeled away on gurneys. Another night opened with a story of a carjacking. The driver had been beaten when she wouldn't give up her Explorer. Last week's most violent lead story was seen on videotape. Two men tried to rob a store. Video cameras taped the robbers as they walked toward the check-out counter. News at Eleven played the tape for its viewers. It showed one man with a pistol and a clerk with a shotgun. He blasted away, hitting one robber in the chest while the other robber ran. There is plenty of mayhem in these stories, but where is the news value?

Notice that the paragraph still needs work; that will come during the revision process. But in this rough draft, Bennett did block out the general structure and add plenty of detail. She continued the process for the entire discussion:

Through the process, I kept referring to my working notes for details. My outline and topic sentences kept me on track, but the details in the working notes gave me plenty of material to develop the paragraphs.

EXERCISE

Continue to develop the essay you began in Chapter 6. Use your thesis statement and outline to rough out the discussion section, organizing each paragraph with a topic sentence. To begin, try roughing out each topic sentence. Then develop each paragraph, keeping in mind the characteristics of effective paragraphs. Remember, this is a rough draft. You're not striving for perfection, only to complete a solid rough draft that you will revise and edit in another stage of the composing process.

Even so, you should still write paragraphs that approximate effective discussion paragraphs:

1. Develop a single aspect of the thesis.
2. Open with a topic sentence.
3. Develop the idea adequately.
4. Maintain unity.
5. Retain coherence.

WRITE THE CONCLUSION

Like introductions, conclusions have a variety of styles and purposes; no single one fits all essays. Your only obligation is to design a conclusion that naturally follows from the entire paper and clearly ends it. Avoid writing a conclusion that seems tacked on, and *never* write one that raises a new question or apologizes for how you've covered the subject.

The samples that follow are just a few of the many methods writers use to end essays. Notice how methods tend to overlap. One has a quotation, but the quotation is a definition. Another holds an anecdote, but the anecdote includes a quotation. Several use questions. The label placed on a method isn't important. What is important is to write a conclusion that echoes the entire essay.

1. Give a brief summary. In college writing, the most common practice is to restate the thesis statement and then summarize the subpoints to reinforce what has come before. Too often, this summary method seems mechanical, but it can be effective if handled in an interesting way. A summary conclusion does have one strong advantage: It is clearly linked to the rest of the essay.

2. Draw an inference. You can use the conclusion to deepen the dimension of an essay. One student ended a paper on being robbed and threatened at pistol point by shifting from the external details of the experience to an implicit psychological fact. Notice how she uses questions to put the reader in a reflective mood:

> What does it mean when somebody holds you up? Just the loss of a few dollars? Or just the loss of a wallet and some mementos—a few peeling photographs, worn identification cards, tattered ticket stubs? Yes, it means that. And it means more. It means you have become part of that chosen group that no longer feels safe after dark to walk the neighborhood streets.

Although the writer draws a fresh inference from the whole paper, she does not raise a new issue. She has, instead, highlighted an implicit aspect that ran beneath the surface of the entire essay.

3. *Use an anecdote.* You can also conclude an essay with an anecdote: a brief story that puts the central idea in clear perspective. Tom Worth closes an essay on the threat of hate groups on civil rights with an anecdote:

> A supremacist group tried to remove a gay group's name from a commemorative plaque. They met with resistance from Mayor Larry Agran, who said, "The rules were that for 100 bucks you got your name on the plaque. And they, God bless 'em, are following the rules. . . . This is America. You can't change the rules after the fact, or you may as well tear the plaque down." Yet hate groups are trying to change the rules every day.

4. *Link the subject to the reader.* A writer may conclude by drawing a lesson that links the subject to the reader's condition. In "Kennedy without End, Amen," Tom Wicker explores the significance of John Kennedy's brief term as president. Wicker adds a new dimension to his essay by linking the lessons Kennedy learned to the reader's learning process:

> "In his life," I wrote those many years ago, "he had had his dreams and realized them," but he learned also the hard lessons of power and its limitations. After his death, the rest of us began to learn those lessons, too. The shots ringing out in Dealey Plaza marked the beginning of the end of innocence.

5. *Close with a quotation.* You can conclude with a quotation that deepens the meaning of an essay. One student who wrote a description of her creative process used a quotation from Joseph Campbell to bring her discussion to a close:

> At best, my artistic process seems haphazard, a kind of inner blindman's bluff that finds its expression in chaotic collages. My groping and stumbling used to bother me until I came across a passage in Joseph Campbell's "The Inspiration of Oriental Art." He writes, "There is an important Chinese term, *wu wei, not doing,* the meaning of which is not *doing nothing,* but *not forcing.* Things will open up of themselves, according to their nature."

Each essay you write will lead to its own proper conclusion. So don't force it to an unnatural end. It's best to let the conclusion grow naturally from the composing process. Remember, too, that at this point in the composing process, you will merely be blocking out a rough conclusion. You will refine it later.

A Student Roughs Out a Conclusion

Michelle began her conclusion with an idea she already had in mind. Early in the process, she decided that a deep cynicism drove *News at Eleven*'s treatment of violent stories. In thinking about her conclusion, she wrote:

I decided to rough out my conclusion around an inference I made early on in the composing process. It had to do with a cynical attitude that led these news people to tug at the public's fears and emotions. They featured violent stories and dramatized them just to manipulate viewers. What was my evidence for this inference? I saw them do it several nights in a row.

Bennett's rough draft of her conclusion reads as follows. Notice that she gets right to the point in the first sentence:

News at Eleven programmers have a cynical attitude toward their viewers. Stories of murders, robberies, and vicious attacks usually lead the news hour. They emphasize violence at the expense of the traditional journalistic code that demands that they present news objectively. Instead of being objective, they hype violent stories and dramatize them, even though they may only affect a few people.

EXERCISE

Write a conclusion for your essay. Keep in mind that a conclusion should echo the entire essay. Use one of these traditional strategies:

1. Give a brief summary.
2. Draw an inference.
3. Use an anecdote.
4. Link the subject to the reader.
5. Close with a quotation.

CREATE THE TITLE

A title should not be an afterthought—a phrase hastily typed at the top of the page before rushing to class. The title actually begins the essay. Think about it: the title will be read before the first sentence of the introduction.

Creating a title has a lot to do with intuition, which is why you should start the reflective process early. By creating a title *after* composing the rough draft, you will have it in mind during the revising and editing process, and like the rough draft, you will refine it.

The title should suggest the general subject and serve as an invitation to read the essay that follows. It should be brief but interesting. It can be taken directly from the essay. Often, however, it will pick up a thought that runs through the essay. A title can be a representative phrase taken from the text, such as *"Three Kinds of Discipline,"* or it can be provocative, such as *"The Killing Game."* A effective title can suggest irony, such as *"A Modest Proposal,"* or humor, such as *"I Want a Wife."* Often an effective title will echo another well-known title, such as *"The Shrieking of the Lambs."*

Whatever you do, do not title a college essay something like *"Essay 2"* or *"Assignment 3."* The title should suggest the essay's content, not its sequence in the course. Also do not underline or put your title within quotation marks—unless you happen to use another title as part of your title. Then underline or put that title within quotation marks, as appropriate.

A Student Creates a Title

"I hate thinking of a title," Bennett wrote, "but for this essay, I decided to spend extra time capturing the essence of my essay in a few words."

She started with *"If It Bleeds, It Leads"* but felt it did not encompass the entire essay. Then she wrote *"Hype and Heighten: Violence on the News."* She knew this would not be the final title, but at least she was on the right track. She felt comfortable moving on, knowing she would sharpen the title later.

EXERCISE

Begin to think of a title for your essay. Compose one or two, keeping in mind that you can change it later. Remember, a title is an integral part of any essay. It embodies the first words that readers encounter. Don't waste them. Instead, use them to invite readers into the essay.

COMBINE THE SECTIONS OF THE ROUGH DRAFT

Few writers actually compose a rough draft as a single document. They tend to move randomly from paragraph to paragraph. Sometimes, they complete a paragraph and then return to add information that came to mind while writing another paragraph. All this is part of the recursive nature of the composing process.

At some point in the process, however, you will be ready to shape the entire rough draft in sequence. By way of review, a thesis/support essay is arranged as follows:

Introduction: Usually one, sometimes two paragraphs with the thesis statement placed at the end for emphasis.

Discussion: Several paragraphs usually organized by topic sentences, each of which expresses a single promise embedded in the thesis. The paragraphs can be developed through a variety of strategies, depending on the content.

Conclusion: Usually a single paragraph that provides a sense of completion to the essay. A common practice in college writing is to restate the thesis and summarize the key points.

A Student Completes a Rough Draft

After Bennett finished the three main sections of her rough draft, she had to fit them together in a unified whole that flowed smoothly from beginning to end. She wrote:

Actually, writing the first complete rough draft was more a typing problem than a writing problem. Most of the sections were well detailed and developed. I did change some words to create better coherence, but for the most part, I just wanted to have a complete draft in hand to begin the revising and editing phase.

But even as I fit the parts together, I saw places where I needed to add information or smooth out the language.

Now review Bennett's complete rough draft. Analyze its structure. Figure out how the parts work together. Then reread the essay along with the observations in the margin.

Hype and Heighten: Violence on the News

Title announces subject: *violence on news.*

Introduction raises question: Why does *News at Eleven* dramatize violence when crime rates are falling? Thesis prepares readers for discussion.

Topic sentence sets up first discussion paragraph. Vivid examples substantiate that violent stories dominate *News at Eleven.* Bennett effectively links examples with transitions.

1   The government just announced that violent crime has been reduced 10% when compared to last year. But News at Eleven must not have heard of this new trend. They feature dramatic stories that have lots of blood and mayhem but do not affect many people. Their guideline for programming seems to say, "If it bleeds, it leads." News at Eleven not only showcases violent stories, they also unnecessarily dramatize them.

2   Stories of violence and mayhem dominate News at Eleven even though only a few people are affected. For example, last Monday I saw a broadcast that opened with a gang-shooting story. A reporter stood on the porch at the crime scene asking a detective questions. The detective answered the questions and pointed out bullet holes. Two people had been brutally murdered. The camera cut to the bodies being wheeled away on gurneys. Another night, I saw a story of a carjacking. The driver had been beaten when she wouldn't give up her Explorer. Last week's most violent lead story I saw was on videotape. Two men tried to rob a store. Video cameras taped the robbers as they walked toward the check-out counter. News at Eleven played the tape for its viewers. It showed one man with a pistol and a clerk with a shotgun. He blasted away, hitting one robber in the chest while the other robber

ran. There is plenty of mayhem in these stories, but where is the news value?

Paragraph 3 dis-
cusses how *News at
Eleven* dramatizes
violence. "Hot" sto-
ries are hyped, of-
ten in misleading
ways. Notice that
Bennett uses spe-
cific examples to
support point.

News at Eleven hypes their violent stories to heighten the dramatic   3
effect. During commercial breaks throughout the evening, stern-faced
commentators announce the "hot" stories to be broadcast at eleven.
Usually the stories have something to do with fear. Often a violent
threat lurking in the city. Last week, one commentator announced,
"At eleven, see firemen risking their lives to stop a coed from leaping
to her death." On another evening, a commentator asked, "Does your
overgrown shrubbery hide a rapist? At eleven, see how one woman
saved herself from a hidden tormentor." Sometimes it backfires. A
commentator recently announced, "A man-eating, twenty-five-foot
shark was spotted cruising for food in a harbor near docked boats." The
story turned out to be a flop. The shark was in Hong Kong Harbor, not
in nearby Dana Point Harbor, as the announcement suggested. But
whether or not a threatening story is a dud doesn't matter. Local news
producers seem interested only in hooking viewer emotion. If the story
has no actual relevance to viewers, well, that's not a consideration.

Paragraph 4 shows
two ways *News at
Eleven* dramatizes
violence: through
(1) nonverbal be-
havior and (2) dra-
matic editing.

To dramatize violent stories, News at Eleven uses two tactics to   4
dramatically heighten violent events. They are trained in a strict
journalistic code: Stick to "what," "where," "when," "why," and "how."
But News at Eleven reporters adjust their language and facial expressions
to dramatize a story. News footage is edited for dramatic impact. Rather
than merely focusing on a reporter who sticks to the facts at a crime
scene, for example, the camera will cut to the grisly results of the event.
By focusing on these graphic details, the violent event is further
dramatized.

Paragraph 5 shows
how *News at Eleven*
creates sympathy
for victims to fur-
ther dramatize vio-
lence. One highly
emotional example
supports her topic
sentence. Bennett
closes by again rais-
ing question "why"
and then gives
ironic answer.

A tactic News at Eleven uses is to create sympathy for victims. For   5
example, News at Eleven recently reported a dog attack. The story
opened with a pit bull. A reporter explained how pit bulls are bred for
violence. The camera then focused on the bloodstained sidewalk where
the attack happened. Next, the story went to the hospital. An eight-
year-old child was asleep. He was wrapped in bandages. The reporter
whispered that the child had undergone "three hours of reconstructive
surgery." It took over "two-hundred stitches to close the wounds." The
child was in shock from the attack. The story then showed an interview

with the victim's distraught parents. They praised their son's courage. Clearly, the report had been manipulated to create sympathy for the victim. But this story affected only the child, his family, and the dog owner. Why, then, did it open the eleven o'clock news?

Conclusion brings key elements together. Bennett draws obvious conclusion: News programmers are cynically manipulating viewers.

News at Eleven programmers have a cynical attitude toward their viewers. Stories of murders, robberies, and vicious attacks usually lead the news hour. They emphasize violence at the expense of the traditional journalistic code that demands that they present news objectively. Instead of being objective, they hype violent stories and dramatize them, even though they may only affect a few people.

6

"At first I felt straight-jacketed by the process," Bennett wrote, "but my instructor told me I would always have room for my imagination to enter the process."

By the time she completed the final draft of her essay, the goal of the composing process, she had developed her unique perspective on violence in the news. She selected the details, the words, and the tone—all of which make her writing different from anyone else's.

Activities

ON YOUR OWN

Combine the parts of your rough draft into a unified whole. Begin at the beginning, and work through to the end. Revise for clarity and coherence as you make your way to the conclusion. If possible, skip extra spaces between the lines so you will have plenty of room for the next phase: revising and editing.

WRITING A ROUGH DRAFT ON COMPUTER

If you can type your rough draft on computer, you'll save a lot of time. But not everyone can or wants to do so immediately. Most writers-in-training like to start with pen and paper and then move to the computer, first roughing out sentences and paragraphs by hand then keyboarding them later. Remember that the purpose of the first draft is to get it written as quickly as possible. So even if your typing skills are weak, working on a computer may still increase your speed. All your mistakes can be easily corrected later. Keep in mind that your rough draft will be on disk, easy to access for revision.

CHAPTER 8

Responses to a Rough Draft: Instructor and Peer Comments

I t can be helpful to have others review your work before you complete a final draft. We all have blind spots, which are usually revealed when several sets of eyes examine our essays.

Many instructors like to give developing writers comments on rough drafts written early in the semester—whether their own comments or those of peers. Such commentary generally concentrates on the larger elements of writing, rather than the fine points. This is, after all, a rough draft, not a polished essay. You should expect to hear whether the thesis is limited, whether the structure is effective, whether the discussion is unified, and whether the conclusion works. You shouldn't expect solutions to any problems that might be identified, but you should expect suggestions to consider.

INSTRUCTOR COMMENTS

As you've no doubt experienced so far in your education, instructors have different teaching styles. Writing instructors are no different. Some will simply collect a rough draft, make notes in the margin, and return it to the student. Others will write or type extensive notes they attach to the draft before returning it. Others will meet each student for an individual conference to discuss the draft. Sometimes, instructors will offer both written and oral comments; other times, they will offer only oral comments. A growing number of instructors are evaluating essays through e-mail or FAX. Students submit their drafts electronically, and the instructor responds in the same way.

No matter what method your instructor uses to give you feedback, read the comments with care. If the instructor uses correction symbols, refer to a correction chart to be sure you understand what each symbol means. If you meet an instructor in conference, be sure to take notes on his or her oral comments.

Keep in mind that a writing instructor is not only trying to help you improve a particular paper but is also laying the foundation for your future success as a writer.

PEER COMMENTS

Some writing instructors organize formal peer-review sessions; that is, they require their writers to submit early drafts of their essays to other class members for comments. Peer review is often done in established writers groups, whose members work together throughout the semester. Other times, instructors form new writers groups every few weeks to give everyone in class a chance to work together.

In either case, writing instructors usually set aside some classtime for the groups to complete their reviews. In addition, instructors generally provide peer-review guidelines based on the particular requirements of the assignment, thus establishing clear directions for the evaluation process.

If your instructor does not require formal peer review, you and other classmates may wish to set up an informal writers group to help you revise your rough drafts. Or you may wish to work with another class member to review one another's work. But no matter if you work in a formal or an informal writing group or in pairs, your goal will be the same: to see your work through another reader's eyes. You will be surprised to see how often a passage—or even an entire essay—that may be perfectly clear to you is confusing to a reader who has intellectual and emotional distance from the material.

Peer-Review Responsibilities

You have two main responsibilities during the peer-review process: to receive and to give informed advice in a collegial manner.

Receiving Advice.   Writing isn't easy, and unfortunately, it's sometimes the flawed piece of writing that receives the writer's most focused emotional energy. So when someone criticizes, the natural tendency is to become combative and defend each paragraph, each sentence, each word against what's perceived as an attack. Of course, when writers look at responses to their work unemotionally, it's easy to see that reviewer comments are offered as suggestions for improvement, not challenges. So, relax when receiving advice. Judge the observations by what you are trying to accomplish.

Once someone has reviewed your work, read all the written responses with care. Although they may be brief, they may still be valuable. Moreover, you can follow up written responses to a draft by asking the reviewer questions to help clarify or amplify any written advice.

Be sure to consider all oral responses, too. Jot down the advice you feel will help improve your draft. If a group member asks you a question, answer it, but don't feel you have to justify any decisions you made during the composing process. Most importantly, *don't become defensive.* Always remember that your reviewers are evaluating the effectiveness of a piece of your writing, not your character.

Should you incorporate reviewer suggestions while revising? That's your decision. Reviewers' responses sometimes conflict, often reflecting one or more reviewers' inexperience or misunderstanding. Other times, reviewers' responses agree, giving you a clear direction for revision. Remember, only you can decide which responses are appropriate and inappropriate for your paper. The responsibility for the final draft lies solely with you, not your group or your partner.

Giving Advice.   When reviewing another writer's work, keep in mind that your task is not to rewrite the draft but to respond as an informed reader and offer advice for improvement. It's up to the writer to write the next draft.

What kind of advice should you offer?

1. *Know the assignment.* Each draft you read will be written in response to a writing assignment. To respond intelligently, you must be familiar with the assignment. Chances are, you will be writing an essay for the same assignment, but if not, then it's your job to know what the assignment calls for. Keep those requirements in mind when reviewing a writer's early draft.

2. *Apply your knowledge.* You will likely have studied the same strategies as the writer whose rough draft you are reading. Use that knowledge. Applying these strategies will help you make accurate observations and give you the specialized vocabulary to describe your observations in a way the writer will understand.

3. *Offer specific advice.* Identify the strengths and weaknesses of a draft as specifically as you can. Vague and general observations don't help much. Consider the following ineffective response:

> Good work. I like the way it reads, even though it isn't always clear. Also good use of words. Keep it up.

Clearly, this is an ineffective response. Perhaps the reviewer fears hurting the writer's feelings, or perhaps he's just plain lazy. The fact remains: The student offers only vague, feel-good responses that avoid giving specific advice.

Here's a much more specific and thus effective response:

> Discussion paragraph 2 is particularly strong. Using a question as a topic sentence followed by an answer clearly sets the pattern that follows and establishes the classification categories. But the three categories--comedy, sitcom, and musical--overlap. Several examples overlap, too.
>
> One problem is unity. You seldom refer to your thesis in topic sentences. To fix it wouldn't take much. I suggest you add a key word to the thesis, such as

dysfunctional and use it, or use its synonyms, in the topic sentences. For example, The dysfunctional family lurks behind all the antics of "I Love Lucy." Whatever you do, you'll need to improve the unity somehow.

Another strong point is your active verbs: shrieked, maul, cavort, and so on. They add specific detail and color to the whole essay.

This reviewer's response is effective. She identifies strengths and weaknesses in specific language. Where she can, she gives advice to help the writer revise. She does all this specifically and clearly.

4. *Don't be distracted by surface errors.* Don't spend time correcting grammar, punctuation, and mechanics. Tell the writer that the errors exist, but remember that it's the writer's job to proofread carefully and eliminate surface errors from the final draft. As a reviewer, you should concentrate on the larger elements.

General Questions to Guide a Peer Review.   In order to stay on track, use the following five questions to guide the peer-review process:

1. Does the draft meet the requirements of the assignment?
2. What is the dominant purpose, and does the organization logically reflect that purpose?
3. At what points is the draft confusing?
4. Is the draft adequately developed, or does it need more information and examples?
5. What are the draft's main strength and weakness?

The first step in the review process is usually done in writing. After the writer reads the review, the reviewer and the writer will discuss the comments.

Guidelines to Discuss a Peer Review.   Above all else, always respond sensitively. Most beginning writers have little or no experience submitting their work for peer review. They may misconstrue genuine advice for negative criticism. To avoid sounding negative, make objectively descriptive comments instead of subjectively evaluative comments. Keep in mind that your responsibility is to help other writers improve their work, not to criticize them for making mistakes.

When discussing your responses with a writer, keep in mind the following guidelines:

1. Use the review session to hold a dialogue, not a debate.
2. Ask questions that might help you develop a clear understanding of the writer's goals.
3. Take notes while reading, and use them to discuss the draft's strengths and weaknesses. Emphasize the strengths, but remember that the writer needs to know about the weaknesses, too.
4. Make suggestions for improvement related to the writer's purpose.
5. Close your response by summarizing ways the writer can improve the draft.

Remember, the emphasis is on *improvement*—both for the writer as a writer and for the reviewer as a reader.

Activities

■ **GROUP WORK**

If your instructor doesn't establish a process for rough-draft review, you and other classmates can hold your own peer-review sessions:

1. Identify students interested in peer commentary.

2. Have everyone review the sections on receiving and giving advice (pp. 111–113).

3. Meet as a group, read the papers, write comments, and discuss them. Remember, concentrate on the large elements: thesis, structure, discussion, and conclusion. Making refinements will come later in the composing process.

Revising a Rough Draft: Structure, Paragraphs, and Sentences

By now, you've nudged, pulled, trimmed, tucked, and rearranged your rough draft for hours. You think, "There isn't anything else I can do. It's as good as it can get." You may even think this essay is better than any you've ever written. So at this point in the composing process, you might be wondering, "Why are we *still* talking about the rough draft?"

Trust us. It still needs work.

True, roughing out a draft made you add and delete information. And yes, you probably rearranged the paragraphs, shaped the sentences, and selected accurate words. But you were concentrating on the big picture—your promise to cover the territory your thesis defined. You weren't thinking about refining your essay.

That's the word to keep in mind during this part of the composing process: *refining.* It can make the difference between good writing and superior writing. Revision concentrates on refining.

Student writer Michelle Bennett, whom we've visited in earlier chapters, had this to say about refining:

> I always reach a point where I don't know what more to do. I'll be told an essay needs careful revision, but I'll look at it and ask, "Where?" The answers are always different. "These sentences need to be improved" or "This topic sentence doesn't work" or "You use too many was's and is's."
>
> So I'll read and read the essay and rearrange sentences and change words, but it doesn't get much better. It feels like being a kid and mooshing mashed potatoes around your plate because Mom said to finish your dinner.

Bennett makes an important point: You can't refine an essay if you don't know how. Learning how will be our task in this chapter.

APPROACH REVISION SYSTEMATICALLY

Different writers revise in different ways. Some are neat; some cluttered. Some revise in a single swoop; others in layers—first, the weak spots and then smaller and smaller refinements. But no matter how a writer revises, the principles he or she follows are the same. Master the principles; master the process.

To begin, we recommend one approach: Work in phases, first concentrating on the whole essay, then on the paragraphs, and finally on the sentences. Or as an economics major once said, move from the *macro* to the *micro*.

Revise the Whole Essay

We assume you have an amply developed rough draft in terms of the amount and detail of information. We also assume you've integrated or rejected any suggestions that might have come from your instructor and/or a peer-review group. If so, you're ready to revise.

When you reach this point, other writing textbooks recommend that you set your draft aside for a day or so. You'll be more objective when you come back to it, they say, and perhaps be better able to see the draft's strengths and weaknesses. While this makes sense, the reality of most writing situations is that you are forced to revise under pressure. A deadline looms ahead, probably within hours.

Revise from the Reader's Perspective

Here's where getting inside the reader's head becomes even more important. If you can read like your reader reads and think like your reader thinks, then you can approach this draft with a new pair of eyes. This is the kind of objectivity you should strive for—one where you read for all the imperfections a reader might see.

Start with a pencil in hand and a printed copy of your rough draft—one with plenty of space between the lines so there is room to make revision notes. First, read through the draft quickly. Keep in mind that there are two kinds of reading time: writer's time and reader's time. So far, you've been working in writer's time, which is much slower than reader's time. Moreover, as a writer you will tend to fill in where you have actually left out something—information or a transition, for instance.

Now, you should shift to reader's time. Read quickly without stopping to fix a sentence or change a word. Mark any place you imagine a reader would become lost or confused. You'll fix it when you return to writer's time.

After the first reading, read the draft again, this time trying to figure out ways to fix the flaws. For this reading, pay particular attention to the following:

1. Is there adequate introductory information?
2. Is the thesis clear, and do the topic sentences advance it?

3. Is the point of view consistent?
4. Is there enough content?
5. Does the conclusion effectively close the essay?

After the second reading, return to the sections that need refinement. Start by concentrating on three areas: content, organization, and point of view. Let's look at each.

Revise to Add or Delete Content

While roughing out a draft, many writers underdevelop the content, planning to expand a particular example or explanation in the final draft. We don't recommend this practice, but if you need to add content at this point, you can either return to your working material or to the prewriting process to generate more information to add to this draft.

Other writers purposefully overwrite their rough drafts, knowing they have generated excessive information. They might overdevelop a minor point or add too many examples. We recommend this practice for one reason: It is easier to trim content than to expand it.

A Student Adds Content to Her Essay. Michelle Bennett added content to her fifth paragraph. She decided that at this point in her essay, she needed to emphasize how far news producers will go to create sympathy for victims. She also wanted to emphasize that most of these kinds of stories do not affect many viewers. The pit-bull attack gave her a specific example to analyze in support of her point. In the margin of her printed draft, she penciled in the changes:

A tactic <u>News at Eleven</u> uses is to create sympathy for victims. For example,
in a tough <u>News at Eleven</u> recently reported a dog attack. The story opened with a barking ~~pit bull.~~
narration ~~dog.~~ A reporter explained how ~~some dogs~~ *pit bulls* are bred for violence. The camera
used emotional words as he
then focused on the ~~scene~~ *bloodstained sidewalk* where the attack happened. Next, the story went
to the hospital. An eight-year-old child was asleep. ~~He was~~ *One leg, an arm, and his face were* wrapped in
bandages. The reporter whispered that the child had undergone "three hours
of reconstructive surgery." It took over "two-hundred stitches to close the
wounds." The child was in shock from the attack. *--"deep shock!"* The story then showed
an interview with the victim's distraught parents. They praised their son's
courage. Clearly, the report had been manipulated to create sympathy for the
victim. But this story affected only the child, his family, and the ~~dog~~ *pit bull* owner.
Why, then, did it open the eleven o'clock news? *For one simple reason, it would emotionally grip viewers: "The child bled, so the story led!"*

Bennett explained why she revised this paragraph:

> I wanted to make my point clear here. The dog attack was dramatic and reported with a lot of emotion. It was a perfect opportunity to analyze the news producer's motivation. In other words, all my evidence was presented. It was time to draw a conclusion.

With the additions, Bennett decided to create two paragraphs out of one. The logical break was at *Clearly;* the new paragraph emphasized manipulation.

Revise the Organization for Unity

Reread the essay, this time tracing the overall organization, much like a reader would. At the most general level, this draft has a distinct introduction, discussion, and conclusion. More specifically, each discussion paragraph should be organized by a topic sentence that clearly connects to the thesis statement, thus creating unity among the key sentences of the essay.

While roughing out their drafts, writers often forget to make the direct connections from theses to topic sentences. Of course, the central idea in the thesis is carried forward in the topic sentences, but by repeating a key word or phrase from the thesis, each topic sentence then directly expresses its relationship to the thesis. Moreover, each topic sentence should flow smoothly from the preceding paragraph. Sometimes, the transition can be achieved using a single word or brief phrase. Other times, it can be achieved by using a summarizing phrase.

A Student Revises for Unity.   Bennett checked her whole essay for unity by first writing out her thesis statement and topic sentences on a separate sheet of paper. She then revised them so they would flow smoothly, one from another, referring back to the paragraphs to keep in touch with the content the sentences introduced. Bennett described her process as follows:

> Once I wrote out the thesis statement and topic sentences, I made a list of the key words and phrases that recurred in the thesis:
>
> News at Eleven
>
> violent stories
>
> dramatize
>
> I reread the topic sentences to be sure those words and phrases were expressed in each one.
>
> Then I checked to see if each topic sentence pointed to what would be discussed in the paragraph it opened. Here, I looked for key words that

would point to the content, such as <u>dominate, hype, use, tactic,</u> and
<u>manipulated</u>.

Finally, I checked for clear transitions from one paragraph to another.
Several were missing, so I added them.

Implicitly, Bennett has revealed one characteristic of topic sentences: They
point back, by referring to the thesis statement, and they point ahead, by suggesting the content of the paragraph they introduce. Always try to make your
topic sentences point back as well as ahead.

Bennett's thesis statement did not require much revision. She merely corrected a plural inconsistency—*they* to *it*, since she is referring to a single program:

THESIS

<u>News at Eleven</u> not only showcases violent stories, ~~they~~ ^{it} also unnecessarily
dramatize_s them.

Next, Bennett looked at each of her topic sentences, fine-tuning them, as
needed:

TOPIC SENTENCE 1

~~Stories of violence and mayhem~~ Typically, violent stories dominate <u>News at Eleven</u> even though only a
few people are affected.

Bennett decided to drop *mayhem* and changed *stories of violence* to *violent sto-*
ries, which reflected the thesis statement more directly. She also added *typically*
to indicate that typical examples would follow—stories that would be similar
to the violent ones broadcast on any night of the week.

TOPIC SENTENCE 2

<u>News at Eleven</u> ~~hypes~~ producers also shamelessly hype their violent stories to heighten the dramatic ~~effect.~~ impact.

Bennett added *also* as a transitional word and discovered she was attributing
behavior to a news program. *News at Eleven* couldn't *dramatize* stories, but as
the people who created the news each night, its producers could. She realized
she would have to make changes throughout her essay to be consistent.

TOPIC SENTENCE 3

Besides teasing viewers into watching their program, ~~To dramatize violent stories,~~ <u>News at Eleven</u> ~~uses~~ producers use two tactics to ~~dramatically~~ other dramatic
heighten violent events.

"This is a mess," Bennett thought. "I have to rewrite it." She decided to write a brief summary phrase to connect the previous paragraph to this one, using *teasing* as a key word. She also refined the language, reducing the unnecessary repetition.

TOPIC SENTENCE 4   ~News at Eleven~ producers employ
           all television thriller directors use   the same tactic to dramatize
A tactic ~News at Eleven uses~ is to ~create~ sympathy for victims. their violent stories.

        heighten the drama of a hard-hitting story while creating

Bennett felt topic sentence 4 needed even more work. She wrote:

It's too simple. By this point, I felt I needed to openly link my attitude toward the news with entertainment values. I, therefore, referred to television thrillers and a technique thriller directors use--that is, they create sympathy for the victims of their plots. To make this work, I had to rewrite the opening of this paragraph to make two sentences. The first set up the second, which brought entertainment in conjunction with the news.

In the final discussion paragraph—the one Bennett created after roughing out an early draft—the topic sentence is not directly stated. In fact, the paragraph is a logical extension of the preceding paragraph. But if Bennett were to write a topic sentence for this paragraph, it might read:

News at Eleven producers cynically exploit viewers.

Revise for Point of View

Reread your essay to be sure the *point of view* is consistent. In the broadest sense, writers present their material from a personal or impersonal point of view. A *personal* point of view places the writer in the experience, which is reflected by the use of personal pronouns: *I, me, my, we, us, our.* Sometimes, writers address their readers directly, which is reflected in second-person pronouns: *you, your.* An *impersonal* point of view is more objective. The writer is removed from the experience and seldom directly addresses the reader or uses personal pronouns. A personal point of view usually presents personal experience and observation, whereas an impersonal point of view usually presents reports and research.

Your material will usually dictate which point of view to use. For instance, you would not write about childhood experiences in an impersonal way, nor would you write about historical, social, or scientific research in a personal way.

When revising for point of view, ask yourself where the material came from: From research? From reports by others? From personal experience? The point of view will follow from the answer.

A Student Revises for Point of View.   In "Hype, Heighten, and Hit Hard," Michelle Bennett wrote from an impersonal point of view, even though the information came from her experiences and observations. Those experiences and observations were common enough, however, that a broad audience would recognize and relate to them. During revision, Bennett made sure the point of view was consistent. After revising the topic sentences, she revised those sentences that unnecessarily reflected the personal point of view:

> *Typically, violent stories*
> ~~Stories of violence and mayhem~~ dominate <u>News at Eleven</u> even though only
> *night's*
> a few people are affected. For example, last Monday ~~I saw a~~ broadcast ~~that~~
> opened with a gang-shooting story. A reporter stood on the porch at the crime
> scene asking a detective questions. The detective answered the questions and
> pointed out bullet holes. Two people had been brutally murdered. The camera
> *opened with*
> cut to the bodies being wheeled away on gurneys. Another night ~~I saw~~ a story
> of a carjacking. The driver had been beaten when she wouldn't give up her
> Explorer. Last week's most violent lead story ~~I saw~~ was on videotape. Two men
> tried to rob a store. Video cameras taped the robbers as they walked toward the
> check-out counter. <u>News at Eleven</u> played the tape for its viewers. It showed
> one man with a pistol and a clerk with a shotgun. He blasted away, hitting one
> robber in the chest while the other robber ran. There is plenty of mayhem in
> these stories, but where is the news value?

Since this essay is an analysis, there is no need to emphasize the first-person point of view. In fact, deleting the intrusive *I* improves the flow of the paragraph.

EXERCISE

Revise the first draft you roughed out from the Chapter 5 assignment for content, organization, and point of view:

- Reread your essay. Note points that might need more development or support. Wherever appropriate, generate more content and work it into this draft.

- Reread for organization, making sure that the discussion paragraphs reflect the thesis statement.

- Reread for point of view, making the necessary revisions to keep the point of view consistent. Revise the draft once again, if necessary.

Revise the Paragraphs

By adding and deleting content, as appropriate, when revising the whole rough draft, you were actually revising paragraphs. Next, it's time to concentrate on paragraphs as separate units of thought.

At this point, your essay is unified: The topic sentences embody aspects of your thesis statement—the promise you made to your reader. Now, you should judge whether each individual paragraph is unified and coherent, especially each of the discussion paragraphs. Read each paragraph slowly, imagining that you are the designated reader. Ask yourself the following questions:

1. Is the topic sentence clear?
2. Does the content support the assertion made in the topic sentence?
3. Is there enough detail to support the topic sentence?
4. Do the sentences flow smoothly together—that is, is each paragraph coherent?
5. Does each paragraph have a sense of closure?

A Student Revises Her Paragraphs.   While revising paragraphs, Bennett made sure that each topic sentence had a key word that embodied the main focus of each paragraph. She also checked to see if there were adequate transitions to guide her reader. Study the revisions Bennett made to her second discussion paragraph:

News at Eleven ~~hypes~~ *producers also shamelessly hype* their violent stories to heighten the dramatic ~~effect.~~ *impact*

During commercial breaks throughout the evening, stern-faced commentators ~~announce~~ *relentlessly pitch* the "hot" stories to be broadcast at eleven. Usually the ~~stories have~~ *hype has* something to do with fear. ~~Often~~ *perhaps* a violent threat lurking in the city. ~~Last~~ *For example, last* week one commentator announced, "At eleven, see firemen risking their lives to stop a coed from leaping to her death." On another evening, a commentator asked, "Does your overgrown shrubbery hide a rapist? At eleven see how one woman saved herself from a hidden tormentor." Sometimes ~~it~~ *the dramatic hype* backfires. A commentator recently announced, "A man-eating, twenty-five-foot shark was spotted cruising for food in a harbor near docked boats." *When eleven o'clock rolled around, the* ~~The~~ story turned out to be a flop. The shark was in Hong Kong Harbor, not in nearby Dana Point Harbor as the announcement suggested. But whether or not a threatening story is a dud doesn't matter. Local news producers seem interested only in hooking viewer emotion. If the story has no actual relevance to viewers, well, that's not a consideration.

The paragraph concluded well, but Bennett felt it needed more overt transitions. Moreover, she emphasized the word *hype* throughout the paragraph to draw the reader back to the main point in the topic sentence. She felt the paragraph close worked, so she didn't make any changes.

EXERCISE

Revise the paragraphs in your rough draft. Check to see if the information clearly develops the topic sentence. Also, check for adequate detail, coherence, and closure.

Revise the Sentences

Next, revise your sentences to make them more readable and interesting. Unfortunately, no one has invented a clear procedure to follow when editing and revising prose. Some writers revise as they carefully work their way through a rough draft; others swoop through the first draft and then revise during the second or third draft. Each writer, it seems, devises his or her own approach. Even so, all writers seem to follow two preliminary steps in revision: (1) They learn what makes sentences effective and (2) they pick up a pencil and go to work on their sentences. Toward that end, we offer Guidelines for Revision, which starts on page 125 of this chapter. We suggest you study this section with care before revising the sentences in your rough draft. It explains and illustrates in detail 15 general guidelines for refining sentences:

1. Cut unnecessary words (p. 125).
2. Cut intensifiers (p. 127).
3. Select specific and concrete words (p. 129).
4. Replace weak verbs with strong verbs (p. 132).
5. Make passive sentences active (p. 134).
6. Eliminate sexist language (p. 135).
7. Consider the denotations and connotations of words (p. 136).
8. Use figurative language with care (p. 136).
9. Revise sentences for proper coordination (p. 138).
10. Revise sentences for proper subordination (p. 140).
11. Place modifiers with care (p. 141).
12. Correct faulty pronoun references (p. 142).
13. Eliminate inconsistencies (p. 143).
14. Complete incomplete sentences (p. 145).
15. Maintain parallelism (p. 145).

You should revise sentences with an eye for effectiveness—for clarity, conciseness, diction, and style. Reread the essay slowly, preferably out loud. The ear often detects problems that the eye misses. As you read, make improvements directly on the page.

A Student Revises the Sentences in a Passage.   Look at this paragraph from Bennett's essay:

> A tactic all television thriller directors use is to heighten the drama of a hard-hitting story while creating sympathy for victims. <u>News at Eleven</u> producers employ the same tactic to dramatize their violent stories.

After having revised the opening sentences of this paragraph—adding more detail and the key words *heighten* and *hard-hitting*—Bennett still felt the rest of the paragraph needed work:

> This paragraph had my most dramatic example, so I wanted to make it more specific to create a picture for my reader. I wanted my reader to be able to see the example in his mind.

First, Bennett revised the opening:

A tactic <u>News at Eleven</u> uses is to create sympathy for victims.

Then, she worked through the rest of the paragraph, replacing weak verbs with strong ones, using specific language to create an up-close picture, and eliminating inconsistencies:

For example, <u>News at Eleven</u> recently reported a dog attack. The story [*dramatic tape of*] opened with a barking pit bull[,] [*its vice-size jaws snapping as it charged toward a chain-link fence.*] A reporter in a tough narration used ~~emotional~~ [*such*] words as [*"vicious," "brutal," "dangerous," and "murderous" as*] he explained how pit bulls are bred for violence. The camera then [*zoomed in*] ~~focused~~ on the bloodstained sidewalk where the attack happened. Next, the story ~~went~~ [*cut*] to the hospital. An eight-year-old child was asleep. One leg, an arm, and his face were wrapped in bandages. ~~The~~ [*In a sympathetic voice, the*] reporter whispered that the child had undergone "three hours of reconstructive surgery." ~~It~~ [*that it*] took over "two-hundred stitches to close the wounds," [*and that the*] ~~The~~ child was in shock from the attack-- "deep shock!" The story then ~~showed~~ [*cut to*] an interview with the victim's distraught parents, [*who*] ~~They~~ praised their son's courage.

After Bennett integrated the changes, her final paragraph read as follows:

> A tactic all television thriller directors use is to heighten the drama of a hard-hitting story while creating sympathy for victims. <u>News at Eleven</u>

producers employ the same tactic to dramatize their violent stories. For example, News at Eleven recently reported a dog attack. The story opened with dramatic tape of a barking pit bull, its vice-sized jaws snapping as it charged toward a chain-link fence. A reporter in a tough narration used such words as "vicious," "brutal," "dangerous," and "murderous" as he explained how pit bulls are bred for violence. The camera then zoomed in on the blood-soaked sidewalk where the attack happened. Next, the story cut to the hospital. An eight-year-old child was asleep. One leg, an arm, and his face were wrapped in bandages. In a sympathetic narration, the reporter whispered that the child had undergone "three hours of reconstructive surgery," that it took over "two-hundred stitches to close the wounds," and that the child was in shock from the attack--"deep shock!" The story then cut to an interview with the victim's distraught parents who praised their son's courage.

Once you have learned the guidelines that form the basis of revision, you will find yourself writing better drafts, which will need less revision than this early one. But first, you should master the information in Guidelines for Revision, which follows.

EXERCISE

After reviewing Guidelines for Revision, revise the sentences in your rough draft. As suggested earlier, handwrite the changes on a well-spaced copy of your paper. Then integrate all the revisions you have made throughout this phase of the composing process and reprint your paper.

GUIDELINES FOR REVISION

1. Cut Unnecessary Words

Your goal is to write in a simple, clear style. Your words should be easily understood, and your sentences should move with some speed. But some writers—either out of ignorance or a sense of self-importance—impede clarity and speed by using several words when one or two will do.

Cut Empty Words and Phrases. Writers who pad their writing with empty words and phrases muddy the verbal waters, forcing readers to strain to see what's really there. Read the following example and note how cutting the clutter improves readability:

Roland Barthes ~~is of the opinion~~ believes that culture can be understood by reading the "signs" it generates.

~~It is usually the case that diet~~ Diet usually books encourage the dieter's fantasies about being slim.

To help you revise, here's a list of commonly used empty words and phrases along with shorter, clearer ways of saying the same things:

EMPTY PHRASE	REPLACEMENT WORD/PHRASE
come to the realization	realize, see
of the opinion that	think, believe
present with	give
for the purpose of	for
in the nature of	like
along the lines of	like, similar to
prior to	before
subsequent to	after
in connection with	by, in, for
during the course of	during
for the period of a week	for a week
concerning the matter of	about
with respect to	about
with reference to	about
with regard to	about
in the amount of	for
at this point in time	now
at that point in time	then
at any point in time	whenever
on the occasion of	when
in the event that	if
in case of	if
regardless of the fact that	although, even though
with a view to	to
make contact with	call, write
it is often the case that	often
inasmuch as	since

EMPTY PHRASE	REPLACEMENT WORD/PHRASE
the fact that	that
in view of the fact that as,	since, because
for the reason that	because
for the simple reason that	because
due to the fact that	because
despite the fact that	though, although
regardless of the fact that	though, although
on the occasion of	when, on
give consideration to	consider
have need for	need
make an adjustment	adjust
give encouragement to	encourage
make inquiry	ask
comes into conflict with	conflicts
give instruction to	instruct

Cut Unnecessary **there are** *and* **there is** *Constructions.* The word *there* followed by a form of the plain verb *to be* is an *expletive*—a word used to fill out a sentence. An expletive signals that the subject of a sentence will follow the verb. This construction is unnecessarily wordy and lacks the vigor of subject/verb constructions. Consider these examples:

~~There were~~ two reasons ~~for their disagreement.~~ *(They disagreed for)*

~~There is~~ little ~~we can do~~ to save the rainforests. *(We can do)*

At times, however, *it* is needed as an expletive, as in *It is raining.*

2. Cut Intensifiers

You can almost always cut out *intensifiers*—words such as *very, really, quite, totally, completely, definitely,* and *so.* These words carry over into our writing from our speaking, when we use them with vocal stress:

The really terrible storm ripped across the bay and totally destroyed business buildings and homes when it hit shore. The result was very disastrous: so much wreckage, so many helpless people, so many lost dreams. The sight was really heartbreaking.

In writing, emphasis comes from using strong, specific words, not from using vacant intensifiers. In fact, intensifiers seem to *deintensify* by distracting from more muscular words. To see what we mean, reread the previous passage with the intensifiers cut out:

> The storm ripped across the bay and destroyed business buildings and homes when it hit shore. The result was disastrous: wreckage, helpless people, lost dreams. The sight was heartbreaking.

Once you've cut out the intensifiers, you can clearly see what you've said. Sometimes, you'll want to revise by adding more detail because you'll sense some empty spaces. But by cutting intensifiers, you'll be eliminating unnecessary clutter.

Cut Modesty and Hedging. You should also cut phrases that suggest modesty, such as *I think, I feel, I believe, in my opinion,* and *it seems to me.* What do phrases like these tell readers that they don't already know? You wrote whatever they're reading; therefore, the piece must reflect your opinion, right? So, cut the modesty.

Also cut hedging. You'll sometimes need to qualify your points; there's no doubt about that. But when you overqualify, you're hedging. Avoid using words and phrases such as *for the most part, more or less, somewhat, rather, as it were,* and *virtually.* Removing them from the following passage makes it much stronger:

> ~~In my opinion the~~ The registration procedures at this college ~~virtually~~ require more discipline to complete than the academic courses. ~~For the most part, it seems to me, each~~ Each of us is subjected to standing for hours in lines that twist from steamy registration bungalows into the cement quad beneath the blazing sun. ~~I feel the~~ The situation is not only unhealthy but also ~~somewhat~~ inhuman.

Now, the passage has more impact and reads faster. Often reading speed and power are improved by cutting clutter from your prose.

Cut Pretentious Language. Pretentious writing draws attention to itself. The vocabulary is unnecessarily complex, as though the writer has thumbed through a thesaurus, replacing simple words with difficult ones.

Always try to use simple, direct words. If you want to indicate that dogs make good pets, don't write *Domesticated canines will contribute felicity to anyone's life.*

Revise all sentences that sound pretentious, such as these:

> The earthquake killed ~~struck with a malignant force that destroyed the lives of~~ more than four thousand villagers.

> Children ~~frolicking~~ playing with their ~~companions exhibit~~ friends show these fears.

Cut Repetition and Redundancy.   Repetition of key words is often necessary for parallel structure or for emphasis, but needless repetition leads to wordy sentences:

The Pacific ~~rattlesnake~~ is California's most dangerous snake.
<small>rattler</small>

Redundancy is similar to needless repetition in that it conveys the same meaning twice, as in the phrases *visible to the eye* and *large in size*. And like needless repetition, redundancy makes sentences wordy:

By probing the ~~factual truth deeply~~ researchers found the solution.
<small>facts,</small>

Millions of ~~people who vote~~ support national health insurance.
<small>voters</small>

Revise any of the following common redundancies in your writing:

advance ~~forward~~   disappear ~~from sight~~

autobiography ~~of her life~~   expand ~~outward~~

circle ~~around~~   ~~factual~~ truth

close ~~proximity~~   ~~important~~ essential

combine ~~together~~   refer ~~back~~

consensus ~~of opinion~~   repeat ~~again~~

continue ~~to go on~~   round ~~in shape~~

3. Select Specific and Concrete Words

Definite, specific, and concrete language pulls the reader to the page, whereas general, vague, and abstract language pushes the reader from the page. As an ad writer might phrase this thought, vivid language gives an up-close feeling, and vague language gives a far-back feeling. Consider these examples:

FAR BACK

He was old when he gained success.

UP CLOSE

He had turned gray and seen his seventy-first birthday when he won the Nobel Prize.

FAR BACK

The police arrested him in an alley.

UP CLOSE

Six police officers with drawn pistols captured him in an alley.

FAR BACK

At Bernard's, the sales staff greets customers courteously.

UP CLOSE

At Bernard's, the sales staff greets customers with a smile.

FAR BACK

For me to write an essay takes patience.

UP CLOSE

For me to write an essay takes hours of pacing and pencil chewing, at least a hundred pages covered with useless scribbling, and several pots of black coffee.

Although most writing assignments required in such courses as history, geology, sociology, and psychology will lead you into making general observations, you should still use vivid language wherever possible. Sometimes, a line or two of vivid language mixed with the most general observations will bring the reader up close to the page. Compare these two versions of a paragraph:

FAR BACK

No student of human experience can deny one fact: Once we were all children. We still carry that child inside. The childhood experience has shaped our world view. It has influenced the way we relate to others and created our approach to problem solving. When we find ourselves quarreling over petty issues instead of negotiating reasonable solutions, more than likely our inner child is behind the behavior.

UP CLOSE

No student of human experience can deny one fact: Once we were all children. We still carry that child inside. The childhood experience has shaped our world view. It has influenced the way we relate to others and created our approach to problem solving. When we find ourselves quarreling over petty issues instead of negotiating reasonable solutions, more than likely we have activated the tiny tyrant who used to fall to the floor, kick, scream and cry until the adults gave in.

The revised version ends with vivid language that brings the reader closer to the experience. When you find yourself writing general observations, always work in a line or two of vivid language.

Revise Slang. *Slang* is the colorful vocabulary that arises from the experience of a group of people with common interests, such as teenagers, actors, baseball fans, street gangs, and even truck drivers. Unfettered by dictionary definitions, slang changes rapidly, reflecting the group's coded perceptions. Most slang expressions—such as *awesome, bummer,* and *rad*—appear, increase in general use, and then either become trite or shift in meaning.

When slang words such as *jazz* and *A-bomb* become part of the general vocabulary, you may use them freely in writing. But generally, in college writing, you should revise your sentences to eliminate slang because it is imprecise and may be confusing. For example:

As a type, comedians are ~~bummed out~~ *depressed* one moment and ~~flying~~ *elated* the next.

The reviewers ~~ragged on~~ *criticized* Kaufmann's poetry collection for being superficial.

Revise Euphemisms.   A *euphemism* is a word or phrase substituted for another that is considered harsh or blunt. For instance, the funeral industry substitutes *loved one* or *the deceased* for *corpse, vault* for *coffin,* and *final resting place* for *grave.*

Euphemisms often may be necessary for tactfulness. No doubt, most of us prefer to ask a stranger to guide us to the *restroom* rather than the *toilet.* Euphemisms may, however, distract us from the realities of experiences such as poverty, unemployment, and war. We have become accustomed to the euphemisms *low income, inner city,* and *correctional facility* as substitutes for *poor, slum* or *ghetto,* and *jail.*

Euphemisms are pervasive in language, especially political language. You must guard against their slipping into your finished papers. If you find euphemistic phrasing when revising your sentences, rewrite the phrase in more specific language. Here are some examples:

~~The deterioration of his economic status~~ *His money problems* began when he ~~became unemployed.~~ *lost his job.*

Military officials seem to believe that ~~misrepresenting the facts~~ *lying* is acceptable ~~behavior.~~

Use Technical Language, or **Jargon,** *with Care.*   Most occupations and special activities have their own *jargon,* or technical vocabulary. For instance, people in advertising use *storyboard, outset, keyline,* and *live tag* with ease. Ballet dancers feel equally at ease with *adagio, barre, sickle foot,* and *pointe.*

When used among members of a specialized group, jargon is acceptable. Such language is inappropriate for more general readers, however, who likely won't know the terms or what they mean. Technical language is especially insidious when taken from its proper field and used in a broader context. For instance, it is inappropriate to use technical vocabulary from psychiatry to describe the behavior of any animals other than human beings, as in this example:

The whale ~~seemed traumatized as it~~ floundered in the shallow surf, struggling to beach itself and ~~fulfill its unconscious death wish.~~ *die.*

4. Replace Weak Verbs with Strong Verbs

Verbs serve as the flywheels of your sentences. To make your writing strong and vivid, we suggest you find strong, specific verbs. For example, consider something as simple as saying how a man *walked:*

The man walked down the street.

If you wanted to tell *how* the man walked, you might write:

The man walked quickly down the street.

or

The man walked rapidly down the street.

These revisions are okay, but a strong, more specific verb would make the sentence better:

The man scurried down the street.

The man strode down the street.

The man swaggered down the street.

Each of these sentences is sharper; the verbs *scurried, strode,* and *swaggered* are all more vivid. If you stop to think for a moment, you'll realize how many words we have to describe the way a person might walk:

strut	tramp	toddle	scuff	trudge
stumble	tread	waddle	meander	stamp
promenade	pace	file	stroll	limp
saunter	step	glide	creep	stagger
stride	ramble	straggle	stalk	ambulate
clump	march	shuffle	wander	perambulate

When revising, try to replace weak verbs with strong ones. Remember to select verbs that fit what you're saying; don't pick them because they sound fancy. For instance, you won't help your prose much if you write *A drunk perambulated down the street*—unless you want to get a laugh. Instead of *perambulate,* you would probably do better with *staggered.*

Sometimes, selecting the right verb can change a fairly good passage into a really good one. Here's one student's fanciful description of an experience in a bookstore:

The crowd walked through the bookstore. Some couples talked softly with each other and others walked in silence, stopping at times to read a page or two. One woman looked up and called out, "OHMYGOD!" as a rider on a white stallion came through the door.

Now read the revised version to see how using more active and specific verbs creates a better passage:

> The crowd browsed through the bookstore. Some couples whispered to each other and some strolled in silence, pausing at times to read a page or two. One woman glanced up and blurted, "OHMYGOD!" as a rider on a white stallion clip-clopped through the door.

Browsed, whispered, strolled, and *pausing* help create the casual atmosphere you might find in a bookstore. Using *glanced* in place of *looked* is more effective because it seems more abrupt. *Blurted* works better than *called out* because it conveys shock or surprise. *Clip-clopped* works better than *came* because it generates the sound of hooves and fractures the casual mood established in the opening sentence. By substituting active and accurate verbs, the writer has sharpened the passage.

Finding strong verbs may seem easy for writing and revising description, but what about expository or argument writing? Well, it can be done. Read the following passage from C. M. Bowra's *Classical Greece:*

> The Greeks won their war with a famous ruse that military men and statesmen often try to repeat in other ways. They gave Troy a gift—a wooden horse with Greeks hidden inside. While the Trojans slept, the Greeks crept out and opened the city's gates to the rest of their army. Masters at last, the Greek soldiers saw Helen reunited with Menelaus, and everyone started for home. But one among them, the ingenious Odysseus who had devised the wooden horse trick, found the route 10 years long.

Verbs such as *won, gave, crept, opened,* and *saw* make this passage active. Use strong verbs to generate life in any writing you do.

Rewrite Hidden Verbs Disguised as Nouns.   In the following sentences, *lead, search,* and *perform* are not the real verbs. *Solve, replace,* and *analyze* are the real verbs, but they are hidden because they are disguised as nouns. The revisions make the real verbs obvious:

~~I was lead to the solution of~~ *I solved* Travanian's identity through my research.

Since John Simmons quit the committee, we must *replace him.* ~~search for a replacement.~~

To understand The Deer Hunter, we must ~~perform an analysis of~~ *analyze* its imagery.

When you edit and revise a rough draft, watch out for verbs that have been turned into nouns. Often, they can be recast as verbs and used to make your writing more direct and concise.

Avoid Overuse of **to be** *Verbs.*   Wherever possible, revise sentences and passages that overuse forms of *to be,* which often clutter your writing. Here are some examples:

(Max Ernst) ~~was~~ sixty-three ~~and~~ knew madness and death ~~were~~ before him.
At   *lay*

The sun ~~was~~ (setting.) ~~The~~ few clouds ~~that were~~ on the horizon ~~were~~ orange.
turned the

Hemingway's "The Killers" ~~is a story that is dominated by~~ (the feeling of
The

impending violence, dominates)

When you reread a passage, mark the various forms of *to be* and see if you can revise to eliminate them. Usually, you'll be able to cut out some unnecessary words and use stronger verbs.

For further illustration, study the following student example, noting the revisions:

The motorcycles ~~were sweeping~~ into the park like 1,000-pound bees.
swept

The lead rider ~~was~~ a huge man ~~and~~ was hunched over the handlebars. His

face was hidden behind a mirrored visor that ~~was reflecting~~ a miniature
reflected

and distorted image of the road ~~that was~~ stretching before him.

Rewritten with the changes, the passage will be more concise and vivid.

5. Make Passive Sentences Active

Voice is the quality in verbs that shows whether a subject is the actor or is acted upon. *The arroyos were flooded by rain* is a passive sentence because the subject, *arroyos,* is acted upon. In contrast, *Rain flooded the arroyos* is an active sentence because the subject, *rain,* is the actor. Active sentences are more concise, direct, and forceful than passive sentences. Note the improvements made in revising these sentences:

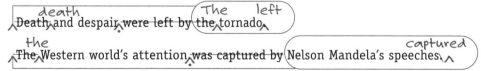

~~Death~~ and despair ~~were left by~~ (the tornado.)
death   *The*   *left*

~~The~~ Western world's attention ~~was captured by~~ (Nelson Mandela's speeches.)
the   *captured*

Although eliminating passive sentences is generally advised in revising, at times, the passive voice may be necessary. Passive sentences are appropriate when the subject is ambiguous or when you wish to emphasize the receiver of the action. In this example, the writer does not know who sent the story:

The mysterious story was received by e-mail.

In this example, the writer wishes to emphasize *self-esteem*, the thing that receives the action:

His self-esteem was damaged by years of severe criticism.

6. Eliminate Sexist Language

Changes are taking place in American English usage that reflect a growing awareness of sexism in American society. These changes affect what some social critics describe as a masculine bias embedded in our language. One striking illustration of this bias appears among masculine and feminine word pairs. Generally, female forms are created from male forms:

actor	actress
heir	heiress
hero	heroine
host	hostess
prince	princess

Although you may have a difficult time eliminating words such as these, you can avoid other words and usages that might be construed as masculine:

- Avoid using singular, masculine pronouns (*he, him, his*) to refer to both men and women when the sex of the antecedent is unknown or when the antecedent consists of both males and females. One way to eliminate sexist language in this situation is to make the subject plural:

  <u>Each manager</u> must post <u>his schedule</u>. [*Managers* written above "Each manager"; *their schedules* written above "his schedule"]

- Avoid the generic use of *man* to refer to both men and women by substituting *human* or *human beings,* terms that are generally considered inclusive and less offensive. For instance:

  <u>Man dominates</u> the natural world. [*Humans dominate* written above "Man dominates"]

- Using recent coinages will also help you avoid sounding biased. For instance, replace *chairman*, which in the recent past was used to refer to both men and women, with *chairwoman* when a woman holds the position and *chairperson* when the person's sex is unknown.

At this time there is no comprehensive set of rules for avoiding the use of language that carries a masculine bias. You, however, should be sensitive to this social issue. Whenever possible, avoid perpetuating a masculine bias in your own writing.

7. Consider the Denotations and Connotations of Words

Denotation refers to a word's literal definition, which is found in the dictionary. *Connotation* describes the emotional coloring that surrounds a word and influences how a reader might respond to it.

For instance, according to one dictionary, the word *apple* denotes "a round, firm, fleshy, edible fruit with a green, yellow, or red skin and small seeds." For some people, the word *apple* also connotes health (e.g., "An apple a day keeps the doctor away") and knowledge (e.g., the apple is often referred to as the forbidden fruit in the Garden of Eden, and the apple is traditionally the gift left on the teacher's desk).

When revising, consider both the denotations and connotations of the words you use. If you don't, you may create meanings you didn't intend. For instance:

Robert Rice, the company president, ~~maneuvered himself to~~ *sat at* the head of the table.

By using the word *maneuvered,* the writer creates the feeling that Robert Rice somehow manipulated his way into the presidency of the company. The word *sat* is much more objective.

When selecting from among several words that have nearly the same meaning, take special care. Consider the words *emulate, copy,* and *mimic.* Their denotations are similar, but they differ in connotation.

Beginning writer Jane West ~~mimics~~ *emulates* romance novelist Rosemary Rogers's style.

The connotation of *mimics* is too negative for the sense this writer wants to convey, which is that West strives to achieve a style similar to that of Rogers. *Emulates* is the best word in this case.

8. Use Figurative Language with Care

Figurative language draws a comparison between two things that are essentially different but alike in some underlying and surprising way. The two most common figures of speech are simile and metaphor.

A *simile* expresses a comparison directly by connecting two ideas with *like* or *as:*

His face was like the sky, one minute overcast, the next minute bright.
                                                                        —Joseph Conrad

The bowie knife is as American as the half-ton pickup truck.
                                                                        —Geoffrey Norman

A *metaphor* expresses a comparison indirectly, using neither *like* nor *as:*

Roads became black velvet ribbons with winking frost sequins.
                                                                        —Hal Borland

A sleeping child gives me the impression of a traveler in a very far country.
—Ralph Waldo Emerson

To be effective, a simile or metaphor must create a verbal image or clarify a writer's thought by making it understandable through the comparison. When a metaphor or simile is trite or overblown, it must be revised. Here are some poor uses of figurative language:

reflected the light.
When he smiled, his gold tooth ~~shined like a bright star.~~

Mixed metaphors create confusion by combining two or more incompatible comparisons:

circling
Thought is restless, soaring and diving before ~~coiling~~ around an idea.

Soaring and *diving* suggest a bird in flight, but *coiling* suggests a snake, leaving the metaphor mixed and in need of revision.

Revise Trite Expressions.   *Trite expressions* are phrases that have become stale from overuse. They include the following:

CLICHÉS	He ran around the neighborhood like a chicken with his head cut off.
WEDDED ADJECTIVES AND NOUNS	They made a lifelong commitment.
OVERUSED PHRASES	We all know that the rich get richer and the poor get poorer.

Trite expressions often appear in rough drafts of college essays, especially if the writing has been rushed. When revising, identify such expressions and rewrite them:

undeniably
He was guilty ~~beyond a shadow of doubt.~~

almost bankrupt.
The company was ~~sinking in a sea of red ink.~~

The
~~To make a long story short, the~~ widow married the banker.

The following is a list of commonly used trite expressions that you should remove from your writing:

a crying shame	at this point in time
a thinking person	depths of despair
after all is said and done	drop in the bucket

in this day and age	face the music
in the final analysis	flat as a pancake
in the nick of time	none the worse for wear
last but not least	pay the piper
method in his madness	quick as a flash
never a dull moment	sadder but wiser

9. Revise Sentences for Proper Coordination

Clauses that have equal importance in a sentence are *coordinate* and should be connected by a coordinating word or punctuation mark. To show the relationship between equal clauses, you need to select the proper coordinator:

COORDINATING CONJUNCTIONS

and	for	so
but	or	yet

CORRELATIVE CONJUNCTIONS

both/and	either/or	neither/nor
whether/or	not only/but also	

CONJUNCTIVE ADVERBS

consequently	however	meanwhile
furthermore	nevertheless	thus
moreover	therefore	

Different coordinators show different kinds of relations. The common kinds of relations are *addition, contrast, choice,* and *result.* Here are some examples:

ADDITION

Reviewers criticized his paintings, and collectors stopped buying them.

CONTRAST

Once novels were the primary home entertainment, but today television predominates.

CHOICE

Either we human beings will stop polluting the earth, or we will perish amid our waste.

RESULT

Advertising campaigns sell products; therefore, manufacturers are willing to pay for them.

Writers sometimes use a semicolon to connect yet give equal emphasis to independent clauses when they are closely related in meaning and structure, as in this sentence:

In Irish folklore, spirits sometimes appear as men or women; at other times, they appear as birds and beasts.

When revising sentences, correct faulty coordination that gives equal emphasis to unequal or unrelated clauses. For example:

FAULTY
John Fowles is the author of three best-sellers, and he lives in England.

The clause *he lives in England* has little connection to the clause *John Fowles is the author of three best-sellers*. These two clauses therefore should not be coordinated. Still, the writer might want to include the information about where Fowles lives, even though it does not relate directly to the main idea. Here are several revisions:

REVISED
John Fowles, who lives in England, is the author of three best-sellers.

REVISED
John Fowles, an English Writer, is the author of three best-sellers.

You should also revise to eliminate excessive coordination—that is, stringing together independent clauses for no apparent purpose. This practice can become monotonous for the reader and fails to show the proper relation between clauses. A sentence with excessive coordination must be untangled and rewritten:

FAULTY
Americans desire heroes, and they find them in films, sports, and politics, but sometimes the real-life behavior of hero figures is disappointing, and then people must find new ones.

REVISED
Americans desire heroes, whom they find in films, sports, and politics. Sometimes the real-life behavior of hero figures is disappointing, which means people must find new ones.

10. Revise Sentences for Proper Subordination

Clauses that deserve less emphasis in a sentence are *dependent* and should be introduced by a *subordinating* word. To establish the correct relation between an independent clause and a dependent clause, you must use the proper subordinating word:

COMMON SUBORDINATING CONJUNCTIONS

after	although	as	as if
as soon as	because	before	even though
if	in order that	since	so that
though	unless	until	when
whenever	where	wherever	while

RELATIVE PRONOUNS

that	what	whatever	which
whichever	who	whoever	whom
whomever	whose		

Choosing which clause to subordinate depends, of course, on your intention, but writers commonly subordinate a clause to show concession, identification, time, cause, condition, or purpose. Look at the examples:

CONCESSION: *as if, though, although*

Although the evidence clearly called for a guilty verdict, the jury found him innocent.

IDENTIFICATION: *that, when, who, whom, which*

Medical researchers, who came from around the world, gathered in San Francisco for the convention.

TIME: *before, while, as soon as*

The attacks continued as soon as the troops withdrew.

CAUSE: *because*

Because historians know how events turned out, they study the causes.

CONDITION: *if, unless*

If bombastic masculinity hides fear of inferiority, many police officers lack feelings of self-worth.

PURPOSE: *so that, in order that*

Following a catastrophe, people must accept reality so that healing can begin.

When revising your sentences, check to see if you have faulty or excessive subordination. If so, revise the sentences. For instance:

FAULTY

Professor Clark, who is noted for her work, which is in the chemistry of cells when they reproduce, has received the Louis Pasteur Award, which is highly prestigious.

REVISED

Professor Clark, who is noted for her work in the chemistry of reproducing cells, has received the highly prestigious Louis Pasteur Award.

11. Place Modifiers with Care

A writer can confuse a reader by misplacing a *modifier*. When revising your sentences, be sure to place modifiers so that a reader will be certain which words they modify.

Correct Sentences with Dangling Modifiers. A *dangling modifier* is a phrase or clause not clearly attached to any word in a sentence. To correct a dangling modifier, revise the sentence to relate it clearly to a specific word:

Running through the meadow, his breathing made steamy clouds. *[As he ran]*

To complete a screenplay, a daily schedule must be kept. *[a writer must keep]*

After six months in therapy, the psychiatrist pronounced him cured. *[he was ... by his psychiatrist]*

When a student at Reed, Ken Kesey was the student body's favorite writer. *[I was]*

Place Modifiers Close to the Words They Modify. When a modifier or modifying phrase is placed away from the word it modifies, the result is often confusing. Revise your sentences to correct problems like these:

Many beginning actors wait on tables to support themselves in Hollywood restaurants.

An aging athlete who exercises occasionally hurts himself.

Be particularly aware of where you place *limiting* modifiers, such as *only, hardly, just, nearly, almost,* and *ever.* These modifiers can function in many positions in a sentence, but they modify the expression immediately *following*

them. So as a limiting modifier changes position in a sentence, the meaning of
the sentence also changes:

I will go only if he asks me.   [Otherwise I will not go.]

Only I will go if he asks me.   [The others will not go.]

I will go if only he asks me.   [I hope he asks me.]

I will go if he asks only me.   [If he asks others, I will not go.]

Revise Lengthy Modifiers.   Sometimes, writers place lengthy modifying
phrases between important sentence elements, thus causing confusion. Note
how revising this sentence brings the main elements together:

inner   Because
~~Inner-city crime,~~ ~~because~~ of increased drug use and reduced law enforcement

budgets, is rising.

Rewrite Faulty Split Infinitives.   An *infinitive* consists of the word *to* plus the
simple form of a verb: *to dance, to moan, to study,* and so on. Usually, a split infinitive can be revised effectively by placing the modifier more accurately:

FAULTY

His inability to clearly explain the issues cost him the election.

FAULTY REVISION

His inability to explain the issues clearly cost him the election.

GOOD REVISION

His inability to explain the issues in clear language cost him the election.

12. Correct Faulty Pronoun References

The term *pronoun reference* describes the relation between a pronoun and
its *antecedent,* which is the word to which it refers. If a pronoun's reference
word is unclear, the sentence will confuse or misinform the reader. Revise sentences so that each pronoun refers clearly to one antecedent. For instance:

Shakespeare

After Duff had studied Shakespeare for a decade, he realized that ~~he~~ was a

master psychologist.

Also revise sentences that use *this, that,* or *it* to make a broad reference to
an entire sentence, rather than to a specific antecedent:

I was

While watching Friday the 13th on television, my cat howled and sprang onto

                which
my lap, ~~This~~ frightened me.

Revise sentences that use *it, they,* and *you* without specific antecedents. In conversation, these pronouns are often used to make vague reference to people and situations in general. But in writing, this practice should be avoided. Revise to correct these vague references:

During the <u>Six O'Clock News,</u> ~~it~~ gave a special report on intelligence testing.
one reporter

School policy does
~~They do~~ not allow soliciting on campus.

In law enforcement, ~~you~~ must stay alert to a community's changing values. If *they* *they* ~~you~~ do not, then ~~you~~ will fail.
police officers

Using *you* to refer to *you the reader* is perfectly appropriate in all but the most formal writing, as long as the reference to the reader is clear:

If you major in accounting, then you should find a job easily.

Revise sentences with pronouns ending in *-self* and *-selves,* which are sometimes used incorrectly in place of other personal pronouns. For example:

The philosophy professor tried to convince Robin and ~~myself~~ that Albert Camus was fundamentally an optimist.
me

A pronoun ending in *-self* or *-selves* should refer to a word within the same sentence:

To stay calm, I talked to myself.

Nick Ufre and Janet Lee tricked themselves.

13. Eliminate Inconsistencies

Revise sentences that make faulty shifts. Often, such shifts take place in pronoun references:

If you stretch your muscles before a workout, ~~a runner~~ will not face injury.
you

Faulty shifts in verb tenses can confuse time sequences:

The dancer rehearsed for six months but finally ~~masters~~ the movement and was ready to perform.
mastered

Faulty shifts in the *mood* of a verb also can be confusing:

Study the causes of World War I, and then ~~you should~~ study World War II.

A common inconsistency occurs when a writer shifts from active to passive voice, thus dropping from the sentence someone or something performing the action. Here's an example:

In the game of curling, a player slides a heavy stone over the ice toward a
                              a teammate sweeps
target, and the ice in front of the stone ~~is swept~~ to influence its path.

You should also revise sentences that shift between direct and indirect discourse. *Direct discourse* includes a direct quotation:

Dr. Jones said, "Life, my friends, is boring."

Indirect discourse rephrases a direct quotation and therefore does not require quotation marks:

Dr. Jones indicated that life is without interest.

Also consider these examples:

FAULTY SHIFT

The judge said to pay the fine and "Never return to my court again."

REVISED

The judge said to pay the fine and never return to his court again.

REVISED

The judge said, "Pay the fine and never return to my court again."

Finally, revise sentences with *faulty predication,* which occurs when the information that follows a linking verb does not rename or describe the subject of the verb. In the sentence *Dr. Brown is a full professor,* both *Dr. Brown* and *full professor* refer to the same person. And in the sentence *Dr. Brown is short, short* clearly describes *Dr. Brown.* In both sentences, the predication is logically consistent; that is, the information following the linking verb *is* clearly renames or describes the subject. When the sentence's predication is faulty, however, you should revise it:

FAULTY

The issue of gun control is an easy solution to a complicated problem.

The predication is faulty because the subject *issue* is not a *solution,* as the sentence indicates. The *issue,* however, is *complicated.* Here are two revised sentences:

REVISED

Gun control is an easy solution to a complicated problem.

REVISED

The issue of gun control is complicated.

Sometimes predication is faulty because the word *when* is misused. *When* should be used only to refer to time. For instance:

Nepotism is ~~when~~ the practice of officials ~~appoint~~ appointing relatives to desirable positions.

14. Complete Incomplete Sentences

Some sentences are incomplete because they lack certain information a reader needs to understand them. Often, comparisons are not complete, which leaves the reader hanging. Revise comparisons to make them clear and logical, as in these examples:

Dr. Casey treats students better than other professors do.

Mystery novels are easier to read than romance novels are.

The silence of the streets was more frightening than the wail of a siren.

In some sentence constructions, writers omit words that are understood. This practice is correct; a comma is often added to create a pause where the words have been omitted. For instance:

Two people control the city government: one is the mayor; the other, the mayor's husband.

But if the omitted words do not fit consistently into the structure, the omission is faulty and the sentence must be revised:

In the woods, I feel the peace of nature; now, I feel the violence of the city.

Humans have a strong belief in and desire for love.

15. Maintain Parallelism

Maintain *parallel structure* by presenting similar ideas in the same grammatical form. In a pair or a series, you must make items parallel to avoid awkward shifts in construction. A noun must be matched with a noun, a verb with a verb, a phrase with a phrase, and a clause with a clause. Revise your sentences to make coordinate ideas parallel:

She loved reading Anne Tyler's novels and ~~the~~ Anne Sexton's poetry ~~of Anne Sexton~~.

His summer activities were ~~the dances~~ dancing at Hotspur's and sleeping until noon.

Words such as *by, in, to, the,* and *that* should usually be repeated when they apply to both elements in parallel construction:

By not developing their land and by ignoring tax-reporting requirements, the family found itself bankrupt.

Also revise sentences to make ideas in comparisons and contrasts parallel:

Ms. Lauko would prefer ~~to work~~ working on her physics project rather than playing chess.

Zen masters are materially poor, but they are rich spiritually ~~in spirit~~.

Revise correlative constructions to make them parallel. The ideas joined by correlative conjunctions—such as *either/or, rather/than,* and *not only/but also*—should be parallel. For example:

The law applies not only to people but also to corporations.

Cosmo is either dreaming about the future or ~~in an examination of~~ examining the past.

Activities

▪ REVISING ON COMPUTER

Think about it: You have a complete rough draft on the computer. You can make changes and reprint it by exercising some simple keystrokes, so don't be afraid to revise.

Most writers like to revise on *hard copy*—that is, a printed version of the essay with plenty of space between the lines to accommodate handwritten changes. After reading the essay and writing out changes, these writers go back to the computer and make the changes in the text. A computer makes adding, deleting, and moving information easy, whether a word, a sentence, or even a paragraph.

You can also use the quick searching power of the computer to help you revise your draft. To check paragraph unity, use the "Find" feature to trace how frequently you use key words to keep your central purpose before the reader. Or if you want to make your essay more impersonal, use the "Find" feature to spot each use of *I;* then revise the sentence to eliminate it. If you want to avoid sexist pronoun references, search for all the uses of masculine pronouns to be sure they have clearly masculine referents; if they don't, revise to remove the gender bias.

When concentrating on sentences, you can probably revise right on the screen. Chances are you've already revised some sentences as you revised other aspects of your essay. But now is the time to evaluate each sentence as it relates to the others. Experiment with phrasing. Change words to create different effects. Even try some different sentence structures to increase reading speed.

Give yourself plenty of time to revise. Be willing to reprint your essay after each major revision. Reread the reprinted copy, and continue to make appropriate changes.

Preparing to Submit an Essay

Once you have finished making revisions in your rough draft, you should integrate them in a single, clean draft—one that is free of scribbles and notes. Now is the time to make one more attempt at refinement.

PROOFREAD YOUR REVISED DRAFT

At one level, *proofreading* a revised draft involves checking for typographical errors and other problems with punctuation and mechanics, the "nitty-gritty" of writing. But proofreading also offers you one last chance to refine your draft in significant areas: diction and sentence variety.

Proofread for Consistent Diction

Diction refers to the use of appropriate and accurate words. Using such words often has more to do with your sensitivity to the English language than with your knowledge of its rules.

Standard American English is used in literature and printed documents, is taught in schools, is written by political and business leaders, and is propagated by the mass media—television, radio, newspapers, and magazines. In most writing, standard English is appropriate. *Nonstandard English* consists of variations not found in the speech or writing of people who have been trained in standard American English.

Standard American English can be formal or informal. Informal writing is characterized by common expressions taken from spoken English. Contractions, such as *don't* and *they'd*, are common in informal writing, but in formal writing, such words are usually written out as *do not* and *they would*.

Informal English is appropriate for casual essays, diaries, personal letters or reflections, and creative works whose authors are attempting to capture the sounds and rhythms of everyday speech. But because most of the writing you will do in college and in your profession will be formal—serious essays, theses, reports, and memos—you should generally avoid writing informally.

Proofread for Sentence Flow and Variety

When proofreading, make sure your sentences flow smoothly together. You can still delete any unnecessary words that have gone unnoticed and might impede sentence flow.

You can also use this opportunity to rewrite sentences to create more variety and rhythm. One way to create varied sentences is to revise sentence beginnings. Most inexperienced writers start their sentences with a subject. Unyielding repetition of this pattern can become monotonous, but if you frequently vary your sentence beginnings, you can offset the monotony. Try these varations:

- *Begin with an adverb:*

  Suddenly, a low moan echoed through the empty mansion.

  Unexpectedly, the answer came in a dream.

- *Begin with a prepositional phrase or verbal phrase:*

  For most politicians, victory justifies any behavior.

  To be successful, a banker must speak Japanese and "computerese."

  Rubbing his hands together, Allen Bates studied the photograph.

- *Begin with a descriptive phrase:*

  His hand trembling, he picked up the pencil.

  Food, shelter, and love, these are the basics necessary for a secure childhood.

You can also vary sentences by mixing their structures. In an early draft, you might rely too heavily on one kind of structure. When you revise your sentences, try to use these different structures:

- A *simple sentence* has only one independent clause and no dependent clauses, although it may have several modifiers and modifying phrases. For example, here are two simple sentences:

  A crucial function in writing advertisements is manipulating clichés. They help involve consumers in the text.

- A *compound sentence* has two or more independent clauses but no dependent clauses. For example:

  Puns are said to be the lowest form of humor, but ad writers breathe new life into them.

broadcast at eleven. Usually the hype has something to do with fear, perhaps a violent threat lurking in everyday experience. For example, last week one commentator ~~breathlessly~~ announced, "At eleven, see firemen risking their lives to stop a coed from leaping to her death." On another evening, a commentator asked, "Does your overgrown shrubbery hide a rapist? At eleven, see how one woman saved herself from a hidden tormentor." Sometimes the ~~dramatic~~ hype backfires. For example, a commentator recently announced, "A man-eating, twenty-five-foot shark was spotted cruising for food in a harbor near docked boats." ~~When~~ ^{At} eleven ~~rolled around~~, the story ^{flopped} ~~turned out to be a flop~~. The shark had been spotted in Hong Kong Harbor, not in nearby Dana Point Harbor as the announcement suggested. But whether or not a threatening story is a dud doesn't matter. Local news producers seem interested only in ~~shamelessly~~ hooking viewer emotion. ~~If the story has no actual relevance to viewers, well, that's not a consideration.~~

Besides teasing viewers into watching their program, <u>News at Eleven</u>   4
producers use two other dramatic tactics to heighten violent events. Newspaper reporters are taught objectivity. They are trained in a strict journalistic code: Stick to "what," "where," "when," "why," and "how." In contrast, like actors, <u>News at Eleven</u> reporters adjust their speech rhythm, tone, and vocabulary and their facial expressions to dramatize a story. Calculated camera work also heightens the events ^{especially when news} ~~News~~ footage is edited for dramatic impact. Rather than merely focusing on a reporter who sticks to the facts at a crime scene, for example, the camera will cut to the grisly results of the event: victims writhing in pain, sobbing parents, a pool of blood. ~~By focusing on these~~ ^{These} graphic details, ~~the violent event is~~ further ^{dramatize the violence.} ~~dramatized.~~

A tactic ~~all television~~ thriller directors use is to heighten the drama of a   5
hard-hitting story while creating sympathy for victims. <u>News at Eleven</u> producers ~~employ~~ ^{use} the same tactic to dramatize ~~their~~ violent stories. For example, ~~News at Eleven~~ ^{they} recently reported a dog attack. The story opened with dramatic tape of a barking pit bull, its vice-sized jaws snapping as it charged toward a chain-link fence. A reporter ~~in a tough narration~~ used such words as

"vicious," "brutal," "dangerous," and "murderous" as he explained how pit bulls are bred for violence. The camera then zoomed in on the bloodstained sidewalk where the attack happened. Next, the story cut to the hospital. An eight-year-old child was asleep. One leg, an arm, and his face were wrapped in bandages. In a sympathetic narration, the reporter whispered that the child had undergone "three hours of reconstructive surgery," that it took over "two-hundred stitches to close the wounds," and that the child was in shock from the attack--"deep shock!" The story then cut to ~~an interview with~~ the victim's distraught parents who praised their son's courage.

Clearly, the report had been manipulated to create sympathy for the   6
victim. Was it necessary? No, it was not. Even without the dramatic narration, camera work, and emotional interview, viewers would sympathize with _any_ ~~the~~ victim of a vicious pit-bull attack. But there is still a larger question to ask, "Why did <u>News at Eleven</u> lead the _day's_ wrap-up ~~of the day's news~~ with this story?" Are pit bulls terrorizing the community? ~~Is there a plague of rabies?~~ If so, ~~indeed the news~~ _it_ should be reported because of the community threat. But this story affected only the child, his family, and the pit-bull owner. Why, then, did it open the eleven o'clock news? For one simple reason, it ~~would~~ _was_ emotionally _gripping:_ ~~grip viewers:~~ "The child bled, so the story led!"

Are local <u>News at Eleven</u> producers as cynical as this view _analysis_ suggests? ~~There~~   7
~~is no way to know except by looking at what~~ _What_ they showcase-- _tells the story_ ~~and it~~ isn't pretty. Violent stories--murders, robberies, and vicious attacks--usually head the news hour. Given the emphasis on violence, <u>News at Eleven</u> reporters seem to have abandoned objective journalism to embrace a new journalistic code--Hype it! Heighten it! Hit Hard with it!

In sum, Bennett wrote:

I truly thought I was done when I typed my revised draft, but while proofreading I could still find plenty to cut out and still improve how my essay read.

PREPARE THE FINAL DRAFT USING STANDARD MANUSCRIPT FORM

Following standard manuscript form is a courtesy to the reader. These standard guidelines, as set by the Modern Language Association (MLA), make a paper easy to read.

Materials

For handwritten papers, use 8½" × 11" lined white paper with neat edges, not pages torn from a spiral notebook. Write with black or blue ink, not green or red, and use only one side of the paper. Skip every other line to make reading and adding comments easier.

For typewritten and computer-printed papers, use 8½" × 11" white typing paper. Do not use onionskin because it is flimsy; do not use erasable bond because it smudges. You may use correction fluid (such as White Out) to cover any typing errors you have made. Double-space between lines, and type only on one side of the paper. Be sure that you have a fresh ribbon in the typewriter or plenty of toner or ink in the printer. Also make sure that your hands and the keys on the keyboard are clean.

Use a typestyle or font that is standard and easily readable; do not use italic or cursive type. Palatino and Times are good typefaces, and 12 point (or pitch) is a readable size. For a computer-printed manuscript, use a letter-quality printer or a dot-matrix printer in a letter-quality mode.

Unless otherwise directed, use a paper clip to hold the pages of your essay together. Many instructors do not like pages stapled together, and no instructor likes to have the upper-lefthand corners of pages "dog-eared" to hold them in place. Put your paper in a folder or binder *only* if your instructor asks you to do so.

Margins

Leave margins of 1" on all sides of the paper to avoid a crowded appearance. For handwritten essays on lined white paper, the vertical line indicates the proper lefthand margin. If you are typing your paper, you can set the left and right margins to 1" but will have to mark 1" at the top and bottom of the page and line up the paper accordingly. If you are using a computer, you can set up the page to have 1" margins all around.

On most computers, you can justify each line of type, which makes the right margin even all down the page. But doing so creates awkwardly spaced lines. Turn off the right justification feature while formatting your paper on computer.

Regardless of whether you are writing on a typewriter or computer, do not divide words at the ends of lines. You may, however, break words that already contain hyphens.

Indentation

Indent the first line of every paragraph uniformly: 1" in a handwritten manuscript, 5 spaces in a typewritten one, and ½" in a computer-printed one.

Pagination

Number pages using arabic numerals (*2*, not *II*) without periods or parentheses. Place each page number in the upper-righthand corner, ½" from the top of each page. You may omit the number on the first page, but if you choose to include it, center it at the bottom.

Identification

Include your name, your instructor's name, the course title and number, the date, and any other information your instructor requests. Place each piece of information on a separate double-spaced line, beginning in the upper-lefthand corner of the first page. Start the line that your name is on 1" from the top of the page. Also put your last name in the upper-righthand corner with the page number: *Bennett 3.*

Title

For a handwritten paper on lined paper, write the title on the first line and center it on the width of the page. Begin the first sentence two lines below the title. For a typed or computer-written paper, double-space below the date and center your title on the page. Begin the first sentence two lines below it.

Capitalize the first and last words of the title, any word that follows a colon, and all other words except articles, conjunctions, and prepositions. Do not underline the title or place quotation marks around it. However, if the title of another work or a quotation is part of your title, underline or use quotation marks, as appropriate.

A Student's Final Draft

The following is Bennett's final draft, which incorporates the changes made during proofreading.

Bennett 1

Michelle Bennett

Dr. Duncan

English 102

21 September 1998

Hype, Heighten, and Hit Hard

The Justice Department just announced that violent crime has dropped 10% when compared to last year. The drop continues a trend downward that has lasted several years. But the producers of our local News at Eleven must not have heard of the downward trend. Frequently, News at Eleven portrays a world as violent as any in television thrillers. For instance, it regularly features hard-hitting stories with lots of blood and mayhem but with very little significance for the entire community. Such stories seem to meet one guideline: "If it bleeds, it leads!" Moreover, News at Eleven not only showcases violent stories, it unnecessarily dramatizes them.

Typically, violent stories dominate News at Eleven even though they may affect only a few people. For example, last Monday night's broadcast opened with a gang-shooting story. A reporter at the crime scene said, "Two people had been brutally murdered." The camera cut to victims in body bags being wheeled away on gurneys. Another night opened with a story of a failed carjacking. The driver had been violently "pistol whipped" when she refused to give up her Explorer. Last week's most violent lead story was captured on videotape. Two men attempted to rob a convenience store. Surveillance cameras taped the robbers as they strode toward the check-out counter. The tape showed one man take a pistol from his coat. In response, a clerk lifted a shotgun and blasted away, hitting one robber in the chest while the other ran. There is plenty of mayhem in these stories, but where is the news value?

News at Eleven producers also shamelessly hype their violent stories for dramatic impact. During commercial breaks throughout the evening, stern-faced commentators pitch the "hot" stories to be broadcast at eleven. Usually the hype has something to do with fear, perhaps a violent

Bennett 2

threat lurking in everyday experience. For example, last week one
commentator announced, "At eleven, see firemen risking their lives to stop
a coed from leaping to her death." On another evening, a commentator
asked, "Does your overgrown shrubbery hide a rapist? At eleven, see how
one woman saved herself from a hidden tormentor." Sometimes the hype
backfires. For example, a commentator recently announced, "A man-
eating, twenty-five-foot shark was spotted cruising for food in a harbor
near docked boats." At eleven, the story flopped. The shark had been
spotted in Hong Kong Harbor, not in nearby Dana Point Harbor as the
announcement suggested. But whether or not a threatening story is a dud
doesn't matter. Local news producers seem interested only in hooking
viewer emotion.

    Besides teasing viewers into watching their program, News at Eleven   4
producers use two other dramatic tactics to heighten violent events.
Newspaper reporters are taught objectivity. They are trained in a strict
journalistic code: Stick to "what," "where," "when," "why," and "how." In
contrast, like actors, News at Eleven reporters adjust their speech rhythm,
tone, and vocabulary and their facial expressions to dramatize a story.
Calculated camera work also heightens the events, especially when news
footage is edited for dramatic impact. Rather than merely focusing on a
reporter who sticks to the facts at a crime scene, for example, the camera
will cut to the grisly results of the event: victims writhing in pain,
sobbing parents, a pool of blood. These graphic details further dramatize
the violence.

    A tactic thriller directors use is to heighten the drama of a hard-   5
hitting story while creating sympathy for victims. News at Eleven
producers use the same tactic to dramatize violent stories. For example,
they recently reported a dog attack. The story opened with dramatic tape
of a barking pit bull, its vice-sized jaws snapping as it charged toward a
chain-link fence. A reporter used such words as "vicious," "brutal,"
"dangerous," and "murderous" as he explained how pit bulls are bred for
violence. The camera then zoomed in on the bloodstained sidewalk where

Bennett 3

the attack happened. Next, the story cut to the hospital. An eight-year-old child was asleep. One leg, an arm, and his face were wrapped in bandages. In a sympathetic narration, the reporter whispered that the child had undergone "three hours of reconstructive surgery," that it took over "two-hundred stitches to close the wounds," and that the child was in shock from the attack--"deep shock!" The story then cut to the victim's distraught parents who praised their son's courage.

Clearly, the report had been manipulated to create sympathy for the victim. Was it necessary? No, it was not. Even without the dramatic narration, camera work, and emotional interview, viewers would sympathize with any victim of a vicious pit-bull attack. But there is still a larger question to ask, "Why did News at Eleven lead the day's wrap-up with this story?" Are pit bulls terrorizing the community? If so, it should be reported because of the community threat. But this story affected only the child, his family, and the pit-bull owner. Why, then, did it open the eleven o'clock news? For one simple reason, it was emotionally gripping: "The child bled, so the story led!"

Are local News at Eleven producers as cynical as this analysis suggests? What they showcase tells the story--and it isn't pretty. Violent stories--murders, robberies, and viscous attacks--usually head the news hour. Given the emphasis on violence, News at Eleven reporters seem to have abandoned objective journalism to embrace a new journalistic code--Hype it! Heighten it! Hit Hard with it!

6

7

Activities

■ **PRINTING THE FINAL DRAFT ON COMPUTER**

All computers have formatting commands that allow you to choose type sizes and styles, line spacing, margins, and so on. Learn to use them. If you set them up once, then each time you print out an essay, it will be perfectly formatted—or as publishers say, it will be a "fair copy."

Finally, gather up all the files of information you saved, put them into a single folder, name it, and save it on a disk. You'll then have a documented history of the writing process that led to this "fair copy" of your essay.

■ **ON YOUR OWN**

Proofread your revised draft, checking that you maintain consistent diction and have effective sentence flow and variety.

Development Patterns

CHAPTER 11

Description: Rendering Experience

THE METHOD

Random thought tends to be vague, unhinged from realistic detail, much like a surrealistic collage floating through the imagination. Even reflective thought—though more concentrated than random thought—tends to be highly generalized until it is submitted to critical examination. It is through critical thinking, whether by discussion or writing, that generalized thought becomes more specific. *Description* plays a role in the critical-thinking process.

For example, imagine that Emelda from down the street has a dog named Gypsy. She phones to tell you Gypsy is missing. On the edge of tears, she asks, "Have you seen her?"

Immediately, a generalized image of Gypsy comes to mind—a large dog with black fur marked by brown at key points, a long snout, ears pointed up, a long tail. "No," you tell your friend, "I haven't seen her."

You go on to say you will keep an eye out for Gypsy and will alert your roommates, one of whom is just walking through the front door. "Emelda's dog Gypsy is missing," you say.

"Didn't know Emelda had a dog," your roommate says. "What's it look like?"

You give the general description you have in mind.

"You mean that Doberman that chases motorcycles?"

"No," you say. "Similar color but not as sleek. Has longer hair and a long fluffy tail. Dobermans have short tails."

"I saw one yesterday but smaller than the Doberman."

"That's Brian's new puppy." Then you say that Gypsy is six or seven years old but the same kind of dog—although you don't know what they're called.

"Shepherd—a German shepherd."

And so the conversation goes, the roommate dragging descriptive details from you to flesh out the generalized picture in your memory.

To *describe* is to picture experience in words. Effective description makes the general more specific by engaging the senses. The sound of thundering surf, the smell of ripe apples, the sight of darkening clouds, the taste of chocolate cake, the feel of soapy water—each appeals to one of the senses. Because sensory experience is so powerful, descriptive writing will often snap readers to attention and pull their imaginations into a discussion.

Consider, for example, a passage from Naomi Wolf's *The Beauty Myth*. It opens a discussion of anorexia and bulimia, which are eating disorders that ravage mostly young women. To grab the reader's attention, Wolf describes these life-threatening eating disorders as a young *man's* disease; she believes society values young men more highly than young women. Here's the passage:

> There is a disease spreading. It taps on the shoulder of America's firstborn sons, its best and brightest. At its touch, they turn away from food. Their bones swell out from receding flesh. Shadows invade their faces. They walk slowly, with the effort of old men. A white spittle forms on their lips. They can swallow only pellets of bread, and a little thin milk. First tens, then hundreds, then thousands, until among the most affluent families, one young son in five is stricken. Many are hospitalized, many die.

Wolf's ironic description might stun readers at first glance. She no doubt hopes it will and make them want to read on.

Most writers embed brief descriptive passages in all but the most scientifically objective papers, bringing life to reports, explanations, arguments, and even essay exams. For example, in an argument against using fur in fashion design, a writer might stir reader awareness by vividly describing the slaughter of fox or mink.

Most often, readers associate description with imaginative literature, such as children's tales, short stories, and novels. While dramatic events give structure to most works of imaginative literature, vivid descriptive details add flesh to that structure.

A STUDENT ESSAY DEVELOPED BY DESCRIPTION

Clarita Tan wrote the following report for a contemporary art history assignment. The assignment required her to review an art exhibit by describing an artist's method of working and at least two representative works:

Descriptive Essay Assignment

This assignment will require you to attend a current art exhibit at a local gallery or museum and to do minor background research. Select a contemporary artist, currently being exhibited, as your subject. Visit the exhibit. In a 750- to 900-word report, review at least two representative works on display and describe the artist's method of working.

Remember: When you review the artist's work, create a strong impression of what the work looks like. You cannot describe every detail, but you should describe the dominant elements in each work.

Finally, in the opening of your report, be sure to identify the exhibit's location, the artist, the movement he or she is associated with, and an overall impression of the work, which will be developed in more detail in the report's discussion section.

Tan's dominant impression is actually announced in her title, "Imaginatively Chaotic Art." Throughout the essay, Tan has selected language and images that suggest a chaotic quality. We see it in the way she describes George McNeil at work and his paintings. As you read, note how Tan uses detail from the photographs and paintings to justify her responses and *to engage the reader's senses:*

Title suggests Tan's attitude toward artist's work.

Imaginatively Chaotic Art

Introduction gives background: Who? What? Where? and When?

The Fine Arts Gallery is featuring George McNeil, a figurative abstract expressionist who lived and worked his entire life in New York City. The ten canvases, drawn together from local collections, are stunning for their color and imagery. It is hard to separate color and imagery in McNeil's work. From pools of purple, orange, and yellow emerge massive faces, airplanes, bodies, and cryptic scrawls. The imagery magically emerges from the method McNeil uses to compose his canvases. The result is that the viewer's mind is pulled from the real world into an imaginatively chaotic world.   1

Closing sentence suggests how Tan will approach McNeil's work.

Tan begins the discussion. She describes McNeil's working method based on the photographs of artist at work. She starts with overall impression, then presents descriptive details.

In the foyer, the curator displayed a series of photographs showing McNeil at work. The first photograph shows him walking into his studio to begin his day. A muted gray light streams from a skylight, and McNeil stands in the doorway. At first glance, he looks like a retiree getting ready to putter in a garden. He wears heavy work boots, tattered oversized jeans that ride on his hip bones, a chambray shirt open at the neck with a T-shirt underneath, and a watch cap against the morning chill. But unlike a gardener's work clothes stained with soil and grass, McNeil's are splattered with paint. In fact, his boots are so crusted with paint they look like art objects.   2

Tan concentrates on two strong physical characteristics: hands and eyes.

Two of McNeil's physical features are dramatically riveting: his massive hands, gnarled from arthritis, which hang at the ends of long arms, and his riveting eyes, set in the eighty-five-year-old face, which   3 sparkle mischievously as if they belong to a spirited ten-year-old possessed by a humorous demon.

The next three photographs capture the first phase of McNeil's painting method. Like other abstract expressionists, such as Jackson Pollock who is noted for his drip-and-splatter paintings, McNeil begins by stapling his canvas to a plywood sheet and laying it on the studio floor. The first photograph in this sequence shows him in action. McNeil leans over the canvas, dripping paint from a Styrofoam cup taken from a nearby table covered with other Styrofoam cups running over with paint. The next photograph shows him aggressively slashing the air with a brush as if it were a weapon, paint arcing toward the canvas. The third photograph shows him whipping the brush back, lashing downward, a mischievous grin on his face, his eyes twinkling.

The final phase of McNeil's method is captured in the fifth photograph. The canvas is now raised upright on the plywood base, a practice that deviates from Pollock's and that of other abstract expressionists. Here McNeil stands with his back to the camera and faces the massive canvas. He is hunched forward with an upraised brush held like a symphony conductor's baton, and I think of composer Paul Dukas's Sorcerer's Apprentice. Indeed McNeil is performing artistic sorcery, for he is creating images that suggest themselves from the splattered configurations on the canvas.

The images themselves are startling to view, often suggesting the untainted imagination of a child who knows none of the technical restraints of someone who is "trained" to paint. Two paintings affected me the most. Kennedy Airport (1989, 78 × 64 inches) is awash in color with patches of blues, reds, purples, yellows, whites, oranges, and blacks. McNeil has created the feeling that the viewer is looking down from the sky at a flat surface. Nothing is to scale--a huge head dominates the upper-lefthand corner and a smaller head, its mouth agape, fills the lower-righthand corner. In between floats a mysterious cartoonish world--a woman in high heels and net hose, two tiny airplanes, and many spirals and circles. All is aswirl, as if the images have been whipped into the sky by an infernal wind that has brought havoc to the airport.

4

5

6

Second painting: Description reflects first: vivid and cartoonlike; the painting suggests chaos.

Diablo Disco (1986, 78 × 64 inches) is as dramatic as Kennedy Airport. It, too, is alive with clashing colors. The central figure is a lime green dancer, whose high-heeled feet touch the canvas bottom and tilted head touches the canvas top. The figure is an abstraction, the lips and eyes smeared on with thick layers of blue, red, and purple paint. The hair, a massive mop, shoots upward. It is painted in orange, red, and yellow that suggest flames. In the center of the dancer's body, McNeil has painted what appears to be a small city. The dancer herself is surrounded by other dancing figures, all much smaller but all equally bizarre, perhaps even devilish.

Tan closes paragraph by reinforcing impression of devilishness.

Tan ends by reminding readers of what's been covered and of two dominant images: artist as creative sorcerer and chaotic world he creates.

7

Every canvas in the show is powerful, offering a unique vision of contemporary life. But perhaps the most important element in the show is the opening photographs that reveal this artistic magician at work. Without an understanding of how his paintings evolve from colorful splatters and pools into chaotic figures, I would have merely been distracted by the question, "How does anyone think of these images?" No doubt, this question is the wrong one to ask when responding to art.

8

A careful reading of Tan's descriptive essay shows that she has responded to both parts of her assignment: that is, she has described McNeil's working method and reviewed two of his paintings. She uses description as her dominant development method, carefully selecting details from the photographs and paintings to support her interpretation.

Tan organizes this descriptive essay with a clear introduction that provides readers with background information they might need and indicates her purpose. Basically, she promises to write a review of contemporary artist George McNeil to show that his work is "imaginatively chaotic." She develops her purpose in a discussion of several paragraphs, devoting a separate paragraph to each important element. She ends with a conclusion that emphasizes her impression of McNeil and his work.

WRITING AN ESSAY DEVELOPED BY DESCRIPTION

Novelist Joseph Conrad said that the writer's primary task is to make the reader *see*. But seeing is only part of the task. Writers must appeal to all the senses—sight, sound, smell, taste, touch, and even the sense of motion—when the writing situation calls for it. Writing that includes more than visual images can be called *sensuous*, for it appeals to the senses through descriptive detail.

Provide Descriptive Detail

To see descriptive detail at work, consider the passage that follows. It describes two simple events: a wild stallion trying to trample a wrangler and the wrangler trying to escape. But before you read the passage, read a few of the descriptive details the writer uses to appeal to the reader's senses:

SIGHT

The stallion rearing back on its hind legs

Its hooves pawing the air

Its mane whipping around its neck

SOUND

The stallion's hooves clubbing the ground

Its whinny echoing over the ranch

SMELL

Dust filling the wrangler's nostrils

TASTE

Dust coating the wrangler's lips and teeth

TOUCH

The wrangler grabbing the fence post with his hand

His palm being raked with slivers

MOTION

The stallion rearing back

Its hooves pawing the air

Its mane whipping around its neck

The wrangler rolling toward the fence and scrambling from the corral

Now read the passage to see how the writer uses these and other descriptive details to create a sensuous picture of the action:

> The stallion reared back on its hind legs, its hooves pawing the air, its mane whipping around its neck. The wrangler rolled toward the fence, gasping for breath, dust filling his nostrils and coating his lips and teeth. The stallion's hooves clubbed the ground, and again it reared up, a whinny erupting from deep in its throat, echoing over the ranch, as the wrangler grabbed the bottom fence post, his hand raked by slivers, and scrambled from the corral before the hooves flashing sunlight pummeled him.

In this brief passage, the descriptive details—not the events themselves—create the experience. Creative writers know they must activate the senses or risk the chance that readers will become bored and set the work aside. You should take a page from the creative writer's notebook: Make your readers see, hear, smell, taste, touch, and sense movement in your descriptive passages.

Often, inexperienced writers believe that adjectives and adverbs make for sensuous writing, so they pile these descriptive words against their nouns and verbs, which can make for slack prose. Here's an example:

> The shiny red Porsche drove quickly through the wet streets. Its massive engine echoed loudly from the tall buildings that formed vertical canyons along the asphalt streets. Then a shrill siren erupted as a mud-smeared patrol car sped rapidly after the out-of-control Porsche.

For comparison, reread the wild stallion example. You'll see that the writer only uses one adjective: *bottom,* modifying *fence post,* which functions as a compound noun, like *hind legs.* The descriptive power in the wild stallion passage is carried by concrete nouns, active verbs, and verb phrases.

If you've written a descriptive passage with excessive adjectives and adverbs, you can always rewrite it by restructuring the adjectives into phrases and by finding accurate verbs to eliminate the adverbs. Doing so will make your descriptions more vigorous. For instance, read the rewritten version of the last example:

> The Porsche, sunlight glinting from its red paint, raced through the streets slick from rain. The engine's roar echoed from skyscrapers that formed canyons along the Porsche's path. Then a siren erupted in a shrill blast as a patrol car smeared in mud raced after the Porsche fishtailing out of control.

Now there are only two adjectives: *red* and *shrill.* The passage reads more quickly, the verbs are more accurate, and the descriptive detail is easier to visualize. This is an effective revision.

When description enhances an explanation, then adjectives and adverbs work effectively. For example, read the following passage from John Steinbeck's *The Log from the Sea of Cortez.* Steinbeck is providing his readers information about sea life that he and his companions collected:

> The reef was generally exposed as the tide went down, and on its flat top the tide pools were beautiful. We collected as widely and rapidly as possible, trying to take a cross section of the animals we saw. There were purple pendent gorgonians like lacy fans; a number of small spine-covered puffer fish which bloat themselves when they are attacked, erecting the spines; and many starfish, including some purple and gold cushion stars. The club-spined sea urchins were numerous in their rock niches. They seemed to move about very little, for their niches always just fit them and have the marks of constant occupation. We took a number of slim green and brown starfish and the large slim five-rayed starfish with plates bordering the ambulacral grooves.

Steinbeck's use of descriptive details makes his explanation come to life. Keep in mind, however, what your purpose is. If your primary purpose is to describe, not to explain, then reduce the use of adjectives and adverbs by recasting your sentences.

Now study a passage from Tan's "Imaginatively Chaotic Art." Note how she uses description to create an impression of artist George McNeil's work. In particular notice how Tan creates a sense of movement with the following verbs and adjectives: *awash, looking, agape, fills, floats, aswirl, whipped:*

> Two paintings affected me the most. <u>Kennedy Airport</u> (1989, 78 × 64 inches) is awash in color with patches of blues, reds, purples, yellows, whites, oranges, and blacks. McNeil has created the feeling that the viewer is looking down from the sky at a flat surface. Nothing is to scale--a huge head dominates the upper-lefthand corner and a smaller head, its mouth agape, fills the lower-righthand corner. In between floats a mysterious cartoonish world--a woman in high heels and net hose, two tiny airplanes, and many spirals and circles. All is aswirl, as if the images have been whipped into the sky by an infernal wind that has brought havoc to the airport.

Tan uses adjectives sparingly, never overloading her nouns with excessive description. Several adjectives don't describe exactly; rather, they qualify nouns, such as *mysterious, cartoonish world*, and *infernal wind*.

How much descriptive detail should you include? Enough to picture the experience. Keep in mind that in descriptive writing, your task is to create an *impression* of an experience, not to meticulously recreate the experience in words.

Distinguish Objective from Subjective Description

Descriptive writing is either objective or subjective. In *objective* description, writers concentrate on the subject, rather than their personal reactions or feelings toward it. The purpose is to create a literal picture of the subject.

Many college assignments require objective description. For instance, marine science reports often ask for precise descriptions of weather patterns or sea currents. A history project might call for a detailed description of a battle. A psychology class might require an objective description of a personality type. Newspaper reports are also written with objective distance from events, giving readers only the factual details.

Of course, it is impossible to be completely objective. After all, a writer must select the subject and the words to describe it. Nevertheless, in objective description, writers try to keep their personal reactions out of their work. For example, in the following paragraph from *The Mountains of California*, naturalist John Muir objectively presents a panoramic view of the Sierra Nevada mountain range:

> The north half of the range is mostly covered with floods of lava, and dotted with volcanoes and craters, some of them recent and perfect in form, others in various

stages of decay. The south half is composed of granite nearly from base to summit, while a considerable number of peaks, in the middle of the range, are capped with metamorphic slates, among which are Mounts Dana and Gibbs to the east of Yosemite Valley. Mount Whitney, the culminating point of the range near its southern extremity, lifts its helmet-shaped crest to a height of nearly 14,700 feet. Mount Shasta, a colossal volcanic cone, raises to a height of 14,440 feet at the northern extremity, and forms a noble landmark for all the surrounding region within a radius of a hundred miles. Residual masses of volcanic rocks occur throughout most of the granite southern portions also, and a considerable number of the old volcanoes on the flanks, especially along the eastern base of the range near Mono Lake and southward. But it is only to the northward that the entire range, from base to summit, is covered in lava.

For the most part, Muir keeps his objective distance from his subject. He presents a detailed overview of the range, describing significant peaks, their heights, and the materials that compose the Sierras. He does give the reader a peek at his feelings, though, by using the words *colossal* and *noble*, but not to the extent that the passage becomes subjective.

In *subjective* description, writers emphasize their personal reactions to or feelings toward a subject to create an impressionistic picture of it. Their goal is to get readers to share those reactions or feelings. Sometimes a writer may seem to present the material objectively but then end the passage with a subjective response. Consider, for example, the following passage from Sue Hubbell's *A Country Year: Living the Questions:*

> I've been out in the back today checking beehives. When I leaned over one of them to direct a puff of smoke from my bee smoker into the entrance to quiet the bees, a copperhead came wriggling out from under the hive. He had been frightened from his protected spot by the smoke and the commotion I was making, and when he found himself in the open, he panicked and slithered for the nearest hole he could find which was the entrance to the next beehive. I don't know what went on inside, but he came out immediately, wearing a surprised look on his face. I hadn't known that a snake could look surprised, but this one did. Then, after pausing to study the matter more carefully, he glided off to the safety of the woods.

Hubbell not only presents the objective detail of the experience, she also offers her impression of the snake, which stands in sharp contrast to objective facts—that is, snakes do not normally look surprised, but her snake does.

In the opening paragraph of "Cyclone," Peter Schjeldahl writes at the extreme of subjective description. He provides as much descriptive detail about how he feels riding the Coney Island roller coaster as he does objective description of the actual experience:

> The Cyclone is art, sex, God, the greatest. It is the most fun you can have without risking bad ethics. I rode the Cyclone seven times one afternoon last summer, and I am here to tell everybody that it is fun for fun's sake, the pure abstract heart of the human capacity for getting a kick out of anything. Yes, it may be anguishing initially. (I promise to tell the truth.) Terrifying, even, the first time or two the train is hauled upward with groans and creaks and with you in it. At the top

then—where there is sudden strange quiet but for the fluttering of two tattered flags, and you have a poignantly brief view of Brooklyn, and of ships far out on the Atlantic—you may feel very lonely and that you have made a serious mistake, cursing yourself in the last gleam of the reflective consciousness you are about, abruptly, to leave up there between the flags like an abandoned thought-balloon. To keep yourself company by screaming may help, and no one is noticing: try it. After a couple of rides, panic abates, and after four or five, you aren't even frightened, exactly, but *stimulated*, blissed, sent. The squirt of adrenaline you will never cease to have at the top as the train lumbers, wobbling slightly, into the plunge, finally fuels just happy wonderment because you can't, and never will, *believe* what is going to happen.

Schjeldahl's paragraph is packed with highly charged language: *The Cyclone is art, sex, God, the greatest; fun for fun's sake; anguishing; terrifying.* He also mixes objective detail with his impressions: *the train is hauled upward with groans and creaks; a sudden strange quiet but for the fluttering of two tattered flags; a brief view of Brooklyn and of ships far out on the Atlantic; the train lumbers, wobbling slightly, into the plunge.* To write effective subjective description, writers carefully mix objective detail with their responses.

A passage from Tan's "Imaginatively Chaotic Art" mixes objective and subjective description effectively. Tan expresses her subjective view by using a simile—that is, she compares the artist to an orchestra conductor—and an allusion—that is, she refers to the *Sorcerer's Apprentice:*

> The final phase of McNeil's method is captured in the fifth photograph. The canvas is now raised upright on the plywood base, a practice that deviates from Pollock's and that of other abstract expressionists. Here McNeil stands with his back to the camera and faces the massive canvas. He is hunched forward with an upraised brush held like a symphony conductor's baton, and I think of composer Paul Dukas's Sorcerer's Apprentice. Indeed McNeil is performing artistic sorcery, for he is creating images that suggest themselves from the splattered configurations on the canvas.

Tan's subjective response reinforces the artist-as-magician image she develops throughout her essay. And once again, she generates a sense of movement by carefully selecting verbs: *raised, stands, faces, hunched, performing,* and *creating.*

Create a Dominant Impression

Considering how much detail is available in any experience, skillful writers must be able to select descriptive details with care and shape them with precision to achieve a *dominant impression*—that is, an overall mood or feeling, such as mystery, joy, anger, security, loneliness, or terror. Writers may clearly identify or merely suggest the impression they wish to create. But no matter which approach they use, writers must decide what feelings they want to evoke and then select and shape the details to create that impression. For example, a writer might wish to write a descriptive passage of the sea that creates the dominant impression of fear. To do so, he or she could use details such as mountainous waves thrusting from the sea and crashing over a helpless yacht, wind ripping the sails, a jagged reef seething with foam as the ship drifts toward it, and so on.

Consider the following passage from Gretel Ehrlich's "A Season of Portraits." Ehrlich, a writer and Wyoming rancher, describes the 1988 fires that consumed much of the forest in Yellowstone National Park. In this passage, she concentrates on the wind, which she describes as a wind from hell, savage and ghostly:

> A breeze stiffens. Gusts are clocked at forty-five, sixty, eight-five miles per hour. Rainless thunderclouds crack above, shaking pine pollen down. *La bufera infernale*—that's what Dante calls winds that lashed at sinners in hell. I decide to go out in the infernal storm. "This is hell," a herder moving his sheep across the mountain says, grinning, then clears his parched throat and rides away. Wind carries me back and forth, twisting, punching me down.
>
> I'm alone here for much of the summer, these hot winds my only dancing partner. The sheep and their herder vanish over the ridge. I close my eyes, and the planet is auditory only: tree branches twist into tubas and saxes, are caught by large hands that press down valves, and everywhere on this ranch I hear feral music—ghostly tunes made not by animals gone wild but by grasses, sagebrush, and fence wire singing.

Ehrlich arranges the descriptive details in this passage in two parts: the world she sees and the world she hears. These parts are clearly separated when she writes, "I close my eyes." She then goes on to suggest that the wind creates ghostly music. As we'll discuss in the next section, arranging the details of a descriptive passage is as important as arranging the parts of any piece of writing.

Consider Arrangement of Details

There is no strict formula for arranging the details of a descriptive passage; nevertheless, writers often follow some general principles. In visual description, for instance, writers often follow a spatial arrangement, moving in an orderly fashion from left to right, top to bottom, front to back, near to far, or even a reverse of any of these arrangements. To describe a moving crowd, a writer might begin with the mass of people, then concentrate on a smaller group, and end by describing a couple or an individual. Or when describing an open space—say, a garden or fun zone—a writer might select the most dramatic image, such as a cascading fountain or a neon-lit Ferris wheel, and move outward to cover the whole territory.

Tan has carefully arranged detail so her readers can move easily through the essay. When describing the photographs of the artist at work, she presents the images in a step-by-step sequence, which is the logical way to proceed. But to describe the two paintings, she had to invent an arrangement, since there was no logical pattern to the chaotic imagery. For example, to describe *Kennedy Airport,* she begins with an overview that moves from large to small details. To describe *Diablo Disco,* she begins with the large central figure and then relates other figures to it.

When developing a dominant impression, skillful writers may only discover an appropriate arrangement—one that uniquely fits that particular passage—during the writing and revision process.

Use Transitions

Unless you are describing a process, descriptive writing doesn't rely on overt transitions like expository writing does. Instead, writers tend to rely on the logical arrangement of details or, as is often the case, on *parallel structure*—a practice in which similar grammatical structures are used to discuss similar material. In the following example, student writer Joyce Brown describes a typical year for a police detective. Note how she arranges the descriptive details in parallel structure by beginning most of the main clauses with *detectives will* or *they will:*

> In any year, individual detectives will spend hundreds of hours in routine work behind a government-gray desk under the glare of fluorescent lights. They will punch thousands of telephone numbers until calluses form on their fingertips. They will each get thousands of busy signals and few answers for their trouble. They will individually spend hours filling out reports and sitting in courtrooms waiting to testify in a trial. They will often see criminals they have arrested sent home by judges. In a year, they will spend endless hours driving crowded streets during a steamy summer and frigid winter. They will eat pounds of hamburger, salami, and bologna for lunches and wash it all down with enough coffee to kill 10 average kidneys. The odds are they will never be shot at, but they will probably get spit on and cursed. No doubt, some violent drunk or strung-out junkie will retch on their shoes. A dramatic life--no. Moreover, keep in mind how hard it is to stay alert, calm, and fair in the face of this kind of psychological torture.

By using parallel structure, Brown arranges diverse detail such that her readers can follow it easily. And because the parallel structure is so predictable, Brown also reflects the routine police detectives face year in and year out.

REVISING DESCRIPTIVE PARAGRAPHS

You should revise a descriptive essay with an eye on arrangement and detail. For example, after Tan reread the following passage, which appeared in an early draft, she realized it was weak. See what you think:

> Three more photographs show McNeil's painting method. Like other abstract expressionists, such as Jackson Pollock, who is known for his drip-and-splatter paintings, McNeil staples his canvas to a plywood sheet and lays it on the studio floor. Then he leans over the canvas and drips paint from a Styrofoam cup. Nearby is a table covered with other Styrofoam cups running over with paint. Mischievously, he then flips paint from a brush he swings at the canvas, all of which speckles the canvas with paint.

Tan realized she had jammed together descriptions of the photographs, instead of describing them separately. She also felt the paragraph lacked visual action and was missing the energy McNeil put into his work. As a result of her analysis, Tan made three changes:

1. She rearranged the description to emphasize the sequence of events.
2. She added more detail.
3. She used active verbs to create a sense of movement.

Now study Tan's revisions:

> ~~Three more~~ photographs ~~show~~ McNeil's painting method. Like other
> *The next three* *capture the first phase of*
>
> abstract expressionists, such as Jackson Pollock, who is known for his drip-
> and-splatter paintings, McNeil ~~staples~~ his canvas to a plywood sheet and ~~lays~~
> *begins by stapling* *laying*
> it on the studio floor. ~~Then he~~ leans over the canvas, ~~and drips paint~~
> *The first photograph in this sequence shows him in action.* *McNeil* *dripping*
> from a Styrofoam cup. ~~Nearby is a~~ table covered with other Styrofoam cups
> *taken from a nearby* *paint*
> running over with paint. ~~Mischievously, he then flips paint from a brush he~~
> *The next photograph shows him aggressively slashing the*
> ~~swings at the canvas, all of which speckles the canvas with paint.~~
> *air with a brush as if it were a weapon, paint arcing toward the canvas.*
> *The third photograph shows him whipping the brush back, lashing downward,*
> *a mischievous grin on his face, his eyes twinkling.*

After finishing the line editing, Tan retyped the paragraph, adding the changes:

> The next three photographs capture the first phase of McNeil's painting method. Like other abstract expressionists, such as Jackson Pollock who is noted for his drip-and-splatter paintings, McNeil begins by stapling his canvas

to a plywood sheet and laying it on the studio floor. The first photograph in this sequence shows him in action. McNeil leans over the canvas, dripping paint from a Styrofoam cup taken from a nearby table covered with other Styrofoam cups running over with paint. The next photograph shows him aggressively slashing the air with a brush as if it were a weapon, paint arcing toward the canvas. The third photograph shows him whipping the brush back, lashing downward, a mischievous grin on his face, his eyes twinkling.

Guidelines for Writing Descriptive Essays

1. Select a subject that lends itself to description, examine it closely, and decide whether your description should be objective or subjective.
2. Establish the dominant impression, whether you're writing a passage in an explanation or argument or a full descriptive essay.
3. Develop an extended list of descriptive details.
4. Select details from the list, and arrange them for effect.
5. Write your essay, making sure that the dominant impression is clear.

Suggestions for Descriptive Essays

1. Write a descriptive essay of at least three paragraphs that concentrates on one of the subjects below. Keep in mind that your description may be objective, subjective, or a combination of objective detail and subjective responses. While developing your description, be sure to appeal to more than two senses and also create a dominant impression.

   Choose one of these subjects:
   a. A *person,* such as a mail carrier, a professor, an elderly man or woman, a politician, a film star, or a news commentator or sportscaster.
   b. An *object,* such as a butcher knife, an unusual toy, a train, an airliner, a hot-air balloon, or a collection of souvenirs.
   c. An *experience,* such as shopping in a supermarket, hiking a nature trail, shopping in a mall, skiing down a slope, riding a wave, or swimming in a lake.

   Or create your own subject for description, using these suggestions to stimulate ideas.

2. Vividly describe a place such that you create a negative or positive impression of it. Choose from the following list, or create your own subject:
   a. A bowling alley
   b. An arcade
   c. A barroom
   d. The student lounge
   e. A science lab

3. Visit an art gallery or museum. Select two contrasting works, and describe them objectively. Close by presenting your subjective opinion of each.

4. Describe a segment of a film that leads to a dramatic moment. Don't summarize the entire film; instead, concentrate on one sequence. Close by stating why this segment is important to the film.

5. Use photographs as the basis for a descriptive essay. Perhaps you have a collection of photographs that capture important aspects of your life, such as a childhood party, a trip away from home, a graduation, a sporting event, or a close friend. Select three to five such photographs and describe them in detail, linking them in a way that shows the significance of important moments and people in your life.

6. Use advertisements as the basis for an objective descriptive essay. Select at least three advertisements for the same product type. For example, if you select cigarette advertisements, you might use ads for Marlboro, Virginia Slims, and Camel. Describe the images in the ads as if you are a reporter, concentrating on the lifestyle being associated with the product, which is open to your interpretation. Close your essay by drawing a conclusion about the effects the images are designed to have on viewers.

7. Use a wild animal as the basis for a descriptive essay you are writing for children. Begin by selecting an animal that interests you, such as a bat, hawk, turtle, alligator, wolf, or snake. Then go to the library and conduct research to determine what role the animal has played in folklore or myth. Write your description by integrating the animal's mythic image with an objective description. Keep in mind that you're writing for young readers, so adjust your prose accordingly.

8. Devote several paragraphs to the description of a carnival ride, such as a merry-go-round, Ferris wheel, bumper cars, or roller coaster. Be sure to capture the sense of movement. Your purpose is to convince someone to go on the ride.

9. Select a character from film or fiction whom you find interesting. Describe the character in a way that shows why he or she is special.

10. Describe a place from the point of view of a particular person, such as someone who is in mourning, who has fallen in love, who is angry, or who has recently graduated from college. Don't directly reveal the person's state of mind but instead reveal the emotion indirectly through descriptive detail. Describe one of the following places:
    a. A lake
    b. A busy street
    c. The view from the top of a high building
    d. Crashing waves
    e. A rushing train
    f. A meadow
    g. A doctor's office
    h. A police station

This assignment requires an act of imagination; you must get under the observer's skin, so to speak.

11. Responding to a photograph: *Woman Brushing Her Hair*

Before children speak, they see. Children look and recognize before they can form words. At an early age, we learn to respond to visual experience and interpret it. A smiling or scowling face, a closed or open hand, an erect or slumped body—all are gestures that invite our interpretation.

As we move through life, our interpretations of visual experiences become more complex. A young man walking down the street might go unnoticed. But add spiked hair, a leather coat, and torn jeans held up by a chain belt. Put a safety pin through one earlobe and thread an earring in his pierced nose, and this visual experience catches our attention. We examine the details of the young man's attire and perhaps draw conclusions about his character, lifestyle, personal values, or musical taste.

A photograph, unlike a spontaneous visual experience, arranges details for the viewer. It is not, as is often assumed, a realistic record of an experience but an arranged and reproduced moment of experience. Whenever we look at a photograph, we are being guided by the hand that held the camera. And whenever we look at a photograph, we are being invited to respond to the image—to interpret it.

At first glance, *Woman Brushing Her Hair* seems to capture a spontaneous moment in this woman's day. But on closer examination, the image seems carefully arranged, as if the hand of the photographer is reaching to pull a response from the viewer.

Using description as a dominant method of development, complete one of the following writing tasks. Before beginning your essay, reread Guidelines for Writing Descriptive Essays (p. 174) to familiarize yourself with the conventions of effective descriptive writing.

a. Write a fly-on-the-wall description, one that strictly reports the arrangement and content of *Woman Brushing Her Hair*. After studying the content of the photograph, decide how you wish to arrange your description. Throughout your essay, be sure to follow the arrangement consistently.

b. Use *Woman Brushing Her Hair* as the basis for an *objective* description that creates a dominant impression of this woman's life. Like any writer—or photographer, for that matter—you should select details, gestures, objects, and arrangements that help generate the dominant impression you wish to create. Remember, your task is not to describe everything in the photo but to use material from the photo for your purpose.

c. Use *Woman Brushing Her Hair* as the basis for a *subjective* description that creates a dominant impresson of this woman's life. Again, you should select material from the photo that leads readers to a single impression, but because you are approaching the photograph subjectively, you may color the details with your feelings.

d. Select a photograph that engages your interest. Title the photograph, and then use it as the basis for your description to complete one of the writing tasks just outlined. Be sure to include a copy of the photograph as part of your final draft.

Narration:
Connecting Events

THE METHOD

In plain terms, to *narrate* is to tell a story. Simple narratives play an important role in our everyday thinking. When talking to friends and acquaintances, we often spontaneously shape raw experience into narratives. These oral narratives help validate our personal observations. For instance, imagine you're in the following situation:

Just as your professor is passing out the week's reading assignment, you race through the door and slump into your usual seat, breathless.

You just left your old VW abandoned in the back lot after the engine sputtered, coughed, and then shuddered into silence—an ominous sign.

"That's awful," a student says. "What kind of car?"

"A '67 VW Beetle," you say. Then you moan something about having it towed to a mechanic.

"Don't go to Jack's VW," she says. "Jack doesn't fix cars; he holds them hostage."

"Hostage?" Her comment alarms you. Jack is the only VW mechanic near the campus. The other one, Value VW, is over 25 miles away, which would mean a $75 towing fee, even through the auto club.

"Pay the price. It's worth it," she says, and then she goes on to narrate the story of her experience with Jack.

It seems her VW broke down, too. "Like yours," she says, "right here in the parking lot. I found Jack's name and number from the Yellow Pages. Since he was only a block away, I called."

"Sounds simple," Jack told her over the phone, and then he promised to pick her VW up and have it repaired the next day—Tuesday.

"Okay," she said. She called Tuesday afternoon to see if it was ready.

"Sorry," Jack said, "emergencies. I'll have it Friday by 3 o'clock, no later," and he hung up before she could protest.

For the rest of the week, she had to take the bus everywhere. The worst storm in the state's history swept in, and she had to slosh from bus stop to class, getting soaked—all because Jack hadn't finished fixing her VW on time.

Friday arrived. She had a head cold by then, sneezing and coughing. She tried to call Jack to make sure the VW was repaired but couldn't reach him because his line was always busy. She needed her car for the weekend, so she walked over a mile to his shop.

She found Jack with his feet propped up on a desk, puffing on a cigar, and grunting into a cellular phone. "Big shot," she remembers thinking.

She tells you she found her VW, the engine exposed, dismantled, the parts spread on the garage floor. She was shocked.

Jack, a big guy, maybe 6'3", strolled from the office, still talking on the cellular. He clicked it off and looked down at her, apparently amused at her consternation.

"Don't worry," he told her, "it's almost ready to go. I'm waiting for a new part. They don't deliver on Fridays. It'll be here Monday, Tuesday at the latest." Then the cellular buzzed. He clicked it on and put it to his ear, ignoring her.

Wednesday rolled around; still no part. She confesses she is still waiting, two weeks later, for Jack to fix her car. "I love my car. Sometimes I feel I may never see it again." She grows silent, her face becoming soft, vulnerable. She looks as if she's going to cry. You, of course, decide to have your car towed to Value VW, even if it does cost $75.

This speaker has offered a minidrama—a dramatic rendition of her experience—to make a point. Basically, she is saying, "It's a mistake to take a car to Jack's VW for repair. To prove I'm right, let me tell you about my experience."

Like all effective narrators, she recreates the experience by concentrating only on the details that relate to her main purpose, which is, of course, to communicate the emotional distress the experience caused. The re-creation of an experience and its emotional impact is what gives narrative its peculiar power. In this case, a sensitive listener can understand and also feel the speaker's frustration and helplessness.

Like speakers, writers also use brief narratives. They can serve as dramatic examples—*narrative examples*, usually no longer than a paragraph—to help drive home a point. For instance, in the following excerpt from "What I've Learned from Men," columnist Barbara Ehrenreich uses a narrative example to emphasize how women tend to be ladylike in threatening situations that call for a more forceful response:

> After more than a decade of consciousness raising, assertiveness training, and hand-to-hand combat in the battle of the sexes, we're still too ladylike. Let me try that again—we're just too *damn* ladylike. Here is an example from my own experience, a story that I blush to recount. A few years ago, at an international conference held in an exotic and luxurious setting, a prestigious professor invited me to his room for what he said would be an intellectual discussion on matters of theoretical importance. So far, so good. I showed up promptly. But only minutes into

the conversation—held in all-too-adjacent chairs—it emerged that he was interested in something more substantial than a meeting of minds. I was disgusted, but not enough to overcome 30-odd years of programming in ladylikeness. Every time his comments took a lecherous turn, I chattered distractingly; every time his hand found its way to my knee, I returned it as if it were something he had misplaced. This went on for an unconscionable period (as much as 20 minutes); then there was a minor scuffle, a dash for the door, and I was out—with nothing violated but my self-esteem. I, a full-grown feminist, conversant with such matters as rape crisis counseling and sexual harassment at the workplace, had behaved like a ninny—or, as I now understand it, like a lady.

Ehrenreich's narrative example is certainly more dramatic than a dry explanation of how women are socially conditioned to be courteous, even when being sexually exploited. Moreover, her narrative example might also reflect another reader's experiences, thus adding emotional validity to her assertion.

Popular narratives dramatize imagined events. They are often long and complex, such as ancient tales about children wandering into forbidden forests or contemporary tales about alligators living in city sewers. They come in the forms of novels, films, and television dramas about spies in faraway lands, detectives walking down back streets, cowhands riding the prairies 100 years in the past, and spaceships traveling distant galaxies 100 years in the future. They portray love and hate, betrayal and loyalty, truth and deception.

Narrative essays, in contrast, dramatize actual events, such as news accounts, biographical and autobiographical incidents, and brief dramatic experiences. But whether dramatizing imagined or actual experiences, all narrative writers employ common conventions to tell their stories.

A STUDENT ESSAY
DEVELOPED BY NARRATION

Richard McKnight wrote the following narrative essay in response to a composition course assignment. He was to narrate a personal experience that revealed an important lesson to him. He was to avoid stating the essay's meaning directly, as he would have done in an expository essay. Instead, the assignment required him to arrange the narration in a way that would lead his readers to the lesson, thus allowing them to draw their own conclusions from the experience:

Narrative Essay Assignment

In "A Hanging," George Orwell uses first-person narrative to communicate ideas without stating them directly. His narrator might not know the meaning of the events himself, but the reader is able to interpret the meaning from the way Orwell presents them. Write a 750- to 1,000-word narrative in which you make a point without explicitly stating it. Tell a story of an incident that illustrates your point, such as (1) how a social event, such as a stylish wedding, shows that people care too much about money and appearance, (2) how a charismatic speaker shows that people are easily persuaded to believe something, or (3) how a sports event shows that being elderly doesn't mean the end of an active lifestyle.

McKnight's implicit purpose is to show that growing old doesn't necessarily mean a person can't engage in challenging physical activity. As you read the essay that follows, notice how McKnight's attitude toward the surfer changes from being skeptical about his ability to surf dangerous waves to being in awe that he does it so well. McKnight has carefully arranged the information and events in his narrative to take you along the same psychological path he traveled:

The Last Ride

McKnight establishes situation in opening paragraph: people involved, location, conflict, and possible outcome—Will surfer be washed over reef?

Last sentence suggests general purpose for narrative.

McKnight's vivid description helps readers visualize the danger.

I watched a gray-haired surfer sitting on the longest board I had ever seen, waiting for a wave in Candle Cove. He was 40 yards beyond the edge of a reef that seemed to rise and fall dangerously as the sea sucked to and from the shore. Connie stood nearby, a year-round lifeguard who patrolled the beaches in a jeep during winter. I wondered why a man his age was alone and riding such dangerous winter swells.   1

At Candle Cove, a winter swell can sometimes rise to 12 feet. Twelve feet is not a remarkable height for waves at sandy beaches, where they break slowly and leave plenty of room for surfers to maneuver. But at the Cove, waves break quickly and crash over a reef crusted with razor-sharp barnacles. Surfers must race across the wave's face to clear the reef and reach the sandy beach. Only the best surfers will risk being swept over the rocks, even for a spectacular ride. But sometimes even the best do not make it safely to the beach.   2

First flashback. Notice that McKnight introduces it with *Just two weeks earlier,* which clearly indicates narrative will move back in time. McKnight wants to dramatize danger in way last paragraph did not. He shows surfer being washed over reef, thus concretely establishing danger.

Just two weeks earlier, a hot-shot from Hawaii paddled out in the heavy surf that a Mexican storm had kicked up. He sat on his board beyond the break and waited for the big swells to roll in. Suddenly, he swung his board's nose toward shore to catch the day's biggest wave. He seemed to do everything right: He quickly leaped to his feet, cut sharply left, moved to the board's nose to gain speed as he shot ahead of the curl--but not in time. The massive wave broke over his shoulder and tossed him into the roiling foam. The breaking wave's force snapped his board in half and swept him over the reef. He survived but barely. Lifeguards raced him to an emergency ward, where doctors hovered above his body for two hours with needles and thread.   3

In this sentence, McKnight links old surfer to specific danger, echoes narrative purpose, and ends opening section. Dialogue embodies subtle conflict between narrator and lifeguard.

McKnight effectively condenses dialogue into report of what was said. Never use dialogue merely to give information; use it to suggest conflict.

Once again, McKnight emphasizes danger.

McKnight begins to build to climax.

Most dramatic moment. McKnight's vivid, carefully arranged description helps readers visualize event.

Now, the old man was in that kind of danger but with one difference--he was well past his prime, much too old to be riding in dangerous waters. 4

"Better call him in," I said. "He's going to get hurt." 5

"He won't come in," Connie said. 6

"You're in charge of the beach." 7

"Don't you know who he is?" she asked. 8

I said I didn't. She asked if I had ever seen <u>Slippery When Wet</u>. The film was made by an amateur photographer 30 years earlier and had become a surfing classic in the late 1950s. I told her I had. She said that when he was a young man, the old surfer had been featured in it. She said he was shown riding long boards on waves over 25 feet high at Sunset Beach in Hawaii and that he was even shown riding shore break at this beach. I vaguely remembered him, but there were many surfers in the film agilely maneuvering their boards as they rode waves. 9

"He's a living legend," Connie said. 10

"A living legend should know when to quit." 11

"If it's in your blood, you don't quit." 12

"Look," I said, "the living legend's going to need an ambulance." 13

The old surfer was paddling to catch a wave, the largest since I had been watching. His arms dug three, four times into the water before the wave swept him up, the reef rising dangerously close. He sprang to his feet, arched his back, and turned the board left as he raced down the wave's face. The wave broke behind him and crashed over the reef. Taking short, choppy steps, he inched his way to the board's nose to gain more speed and crouched low, avoiding the curl as it cracked behind him. Suddenly, he was out of sight. The wave had tossed forward, and the curl folded over his crouching body. 14

"He's tanked," I said, looking at the white water as it washed over the reef. "Better get him." 15

"Wait," she said. 16

"Now!" I said but didn't know why. I wasn't a lifeguard or her boss. 17

She looked at me, "Show a little courage," she said. "He is." 18

She was right. Still bent low on the front of the board, the old surfer shot out of the curl, well ahead of the white water. And then an image from the film came back to me: A young man, over 30 years 19

Second flashback shows what surfer could do in his youth and leads to resolution.

younger than this man, riding waves at this same beach. He, too, was shot out of the curl and cleared the reef on a massive wave, bigger than this one, that was crashing behind him. In the film, the beach was crowded with cheering spectators. They had seen a ride beyond their belief, but that was when surfing was new and still viewed as an astounding feat.

In resolution, McKnight returns to present and links flashback directly to this moment, thus suggesting narrative purpose. Last sentence strongly suggests purpose without stating it directly.

Now, this time as an old man with only two people watching, he 20 once again cleared the reef and guided his board toward shore. In shallow water, he stepped from the board and swung it up under his arm, striding toward the sand where we stood. He walked past us, nodding to Connie, who smiled at him. He looked ancient, his skin thick from years of sun, his hair gray and thin, his face wrinkled, and his belly growing thick. Yet his blue eyes were full of life, full of future rides. I knew that I, like that crowd in the film, had seen something special, an astounding feat, not just for someone with gray hair and wrinkled skin but for anyone, young or old.

McKnight's essay meets the requirements of the assignment. He tells the story of a single incident—an elderly surfer in dangerous water—and uses it to make an implicit message: Aging doesn't necessarily make a person incapable of meeting challenging physical feats.

McKnight effectively uses several common narrative techniques. For instance, he employs a consistent *voice,* or *point of view,* to tell the story. He uses dialogue that suggests conflict. He creates a dramatic movement that builds to a high point, the story's climax. And he closes with an observation that leads the reader to reflect on the story.

McKnight has also effectively structured his essay, carefully providing readers with background information and guiding them smoothly to the conclusion. Look at the structure:

- *Paragraph 1:* McKnight sets up the situation, identifying the people, the location, and the conflict. He raises a key question: Why is the surfer taking such a risk?

- *Paragraphs 2–3:* These paragraphs provide appropriate background information that both describes the dangers and shows that many surfers have been injured at this surfing spot, thus emphasizing the danger the surfer faces. McKnight presents a specific narrative example to further emphasize the risk surfers take to ride these waves.

- *Paragraph 4:* This paragraph serves as a transition from background information to the danger the old man faces.

- *Paragraphs 5–8:* This dialogue establishes McKnight's subtle conflict with Connie and brings up the surfer's identity.

- *Paragraph 9:* McKnight establishes the surfer's identity by summarizing key points that might have been made in dialogue.

- *Paragraphs 10–13:* McKnight uses this dialogue sequence to intensify the dramatic conflict with Connie and to set up the action that follows.

- *Paragraph 14:* McKnight describes the surfer catching and riding a wave, intensifying the action until it reaches its most dramatic moment when the surfer disappears under the wave's curl.

- *Paragraphs 15–18:* This dialogue sequence re-emphasizes the danger and reveals the narrator's state of mind.

- *Paragraphs 19–20:* McKnight resolves the story—the surfer reaches safety— and makes a final observation that implies a message.

McKnight's effective use of narrative techniques helps guide the reader through the action. At no point do they seem obtrusive. In fact, they blend with the flow of events.

WRITING AN ESSAY DEVELOPED BY NARRATION

Narration and *description* are closely related. But unlike description, which pictures experience, narration presents a connected succession of events. Pure description often seems static, whereas narration moves through a series of events, often ending in a payoff.

Create a Narrative Effect

The payoff in narration is called the *narrative effect,* which is the feeling or meaning the writer wants the reader to experience. The narrative effect might be a simple surprise, an insight, a message, a moral, or a belly laugh—something that makes the narrative worth reading.

Writers arrange the events in their narratives to achieve the narrative effect. For example, read W. Somerset Maugham's retelling of a brief Arabian story, "The Appointment in Samarra." In this tale, Death is the storyteller:

Death speaks: There was a merchant in Baghdad who sent his servant to market to buy provisions and in a little while the servant came back, white and trembling, and said, Master, just now when I was in the marketplace I was jostled by a woman in the crowd and when I turned I saw it was Death that jostled me. She looked at me and made a threatening gesture; now, lend me your horse, and I will ride away from this city and avoid my fate. I will go to Samarra and there Death will not find me. The merchant lent him his horse, and the servant mounted it, and he dug his spurs in its flanks and as fast as the horse could gallop he went. Then the merchant went down to the marketplace and he saw me standing in the crowd and he came to me and said, Why did you make a threatening gesture to my servant when you saw him this morning? That was not a threatening gesture, I said, it was only a start of surprise. I was astonished to see him in Baghdad, for I had an appointment with him tonight in Samarra.

This brief story presents a succession of three connected events:

1. The servant reports his fear of Death and desire to escape.
2. The servant escapes to Samarra.
3. The master talks to Death.

These three events, presented with very little description, create the narrative effect—in this case, the idea that one cannot escape a fated appointment with Death.

Not all narratives have such dramatic purposes. The following narrative, for example, "Dead on the Road," from Bailey White's *Mama Makes up Her Mind*, seems to have a different purpose in mind—to entertain:

> My mother eats things she finds dead on the road. Her standards are high. She claims she won't eat anything that's not a fresh kill. But I don't trust her. I require documentation. I won't eat it unless she can tell me the model and tag number of the car that struck it.
>
> Mama is an adventurous and excellent cook, and we have feasted on not only doves, turkeys, and quail, but robins, squirrels, and, only once, a possum. I draw the line at snakes. "But it was still wiggling when I got there," she argues. "Let's try it just this once. I have a white sauce with dill and mustard."
>
> "No snakes," I say.
>
> And she won't even slow down for armadillos, although they are the most common dead animal on the road these days. "They look too stupid to eat," she says.
>
> We have a prissy aunt Eleanor who comes to dinner every third Friday. We always get out the linen and polish the silver when she comes. She expects it. Last month we sat her down to an elegant meal, complete with the Spode china and Camellias in a crystal bowl.
>
> "The quail are delicious," my aunt sighed. "And I haven't found a single piece of buckshot. How do you manage it?"
>
> "Intersection of 93 and Baggs Road," recites Mama. "Green late model pickup, Florida tag. Have another one. And some rice, El."

A smile, a chuckle, or an "I don't believe it!"—any of these responses seems appropriate for the narrative effect White wants to achieve.

Richard McKnight's essay, "The Last Ride," is longer than Maugham's or White's tales; nevertheless, McKnight builds the narrative effect throughout the essay. He wants his readers to get the message that elderly people don't have to give up physical challenges. Each detail in McKnight's essay builds to this insight, which becomes clear in the last paragraph.

Follow a Narrative Structure

To create a narrative effect, writers carefully select the significant events of the story. (They only include minor events in a sketchy fashion to keep the story flowing.) Then they arrange the events for dramatic effect, building it as they go. Remember, a narrative is essentially concerned with action, with moving the story along. The typical narrative, whether brief or long, has three distinct parts:

1. The *opening* may be composed of a few sentences in a short narrative essay or several paragraphs in a long one. The opening orients the reader and may suggest the purpose of the narrative without revealing its outcome. Writers shape openings with one intent: to create suspense by arousing reader interest.

2. The *complication*, the body of the narrative, presents the significant events in dramatic form. The complication increases the suspense and ends with a climax, the most dramatic moment in the experience. An effective complication should increase in tension, each significant event becoming more dramatic than the last.

3. The *resolution*, which should be no longer than a sentence or two, closes the narration. In the resolution, the suspense ends and the dramatic effect should become clear or be felt, though not necessarily stated. An effective resolution creates the impression that the narrative is complete and final—nothing more need be said.

Few writers view this structure as a rigid formula for writing narrative essays. Even so, it does create a sense of rising intensity as readers move from event to event to the final effect.

You can also usually count on writers to establish a narrative situation in the opening by directly providing or suggesting the answers to these questions:

Who are the people involved?
What is the situation?
Where and when does it happen?

Conflict is another important element in narrative arrangement. It can be subtle or overt. It can be external—reflecting a clash between individuals, society, or elements in nature—or it can be internal—involving warring impulses within one person. But no matter what form conflict takes, it fuels most narratives.

With the questions Who? What? Where? and When? in mind and with an eye for whatever conflict is suggested, read the opening passage from Art Harris's "Trapped in Another Life":

> She stares out the window past twin 12-foot fences topped with razor wire, watchtowers manned by armed guards, steel electronic gates, past the stand of hardwoods, the nearby men's prison and up the road.
> It's dusting snow, cold, bleak. Just over the hill, a 10-minute drive if she could just drive out of here, and she would be home in her split-level house with a devoted but baffled brood: her husband, Ray, two teenage sons.

Kay Smith was the very model of a Severn, Md., housewife and working mother, so perfect that no one around here can believe she was once a hard-drinking, pill-popping criminal with a gun.

First, consider the questions:

- *Who?* A woman named Kay Smith, who's serving a prison sentence, appears to be the center of this narrative.
- *What?* The opening suggests Harris will deal with the criminal past that caught up with Smith.
- *Where?* From these details, we know the action will take place in Maryland.
- *When?* Though not stated directly, the passage suggests a contemporary setting.

And the *conflict?* Harris suggests the conflict will be between the current Kay Smith, who is a model housewife and working mother, and the former Kay Smith, who was a criminal.

McKnight establishes the narrative situation in the first paragraph of "The Last Ride":

- *Who?* McKnight himself and a lifeguard named Connie
- *What?* A dangerous situation
- *Where?* A surfing spot
- *When?* In the recent past

As a reader, any assumptions you make from reading a narrative opening are tentative. But as a writer, you must be in charge of your opening by providing the reader important information and arousing his or her interest.

Use Scene and Summary

Narrative writers use two techniques to move their stories along: *scene* and *summary,* or, as these techniques are sometimes described, *showing* and *telling.* Of the two, scene is the most vivid and dramatic because it directly portrays events on the page. In contrast, summary presents a synopsis of events, usually relating only the high points and leaving out much of the specific detail that a scene might include.

In most effective narratives, scene and summary work together. Writers present the most significant events in scenes and less significant events, such as background information necessary to establish the situation, in summaries.

For example, examine the following passage from Edward Rivera's *Family Installments: Memories of Growing Up Hispanic.* The passage deals with Rivera being late for a college sociology final. He opens with a summary that helps establish the situation and then moves to a scene to dramatize the classroom setting, as if his readers were seeing it themselves. Then he returns to a summary to report a verbal exchange with his instructor. Read this brief summary passage, which *tells* you about the situation and sets up the class-room scene below:

> I took a cab up to school, but I was still late. On the way there, I reviewed the "material" in my head: almost total confusion, a jumble of jargon, ordinary things passed off as profundities with the aid of "abstractionitis."

In this summary passage, Rivera could have included a great deal of detail—about the weather, the heavy traffic, a surly cab driver—but instead, he only presents the high points, concentrating on establishing the situation.

Now read the following scene, which *shows* the classroom and his meeting with his professor:

> The classroom was packed for the first time since the opening day of classes, and filled with smoke. Over forty students were bent over their examination booklets, most of them looking confused by the questions. The professor, puffing on an immense pipe, was at his desk (manufactured by Vulcan), reading Riesman's *The Lonely Crowd*, casually, as if it were a murder mystery whose ending he had figured out back on page one. He didn't look pleased when I stepped up to his desk: another pair of lungs in a roomful of carbon dioxide and cigarette smoke.
> "Yes?"
> I asked him for a question sheet and an examination booklet. They were on the desk, weighted down with the eighth edition of his anthology.
> "Are you registered in this course?" he asked.

When you compare the two passages, the difference in technique is striking. This scene is much more vivid and dramatic than the opening summary passage, indicating its importance. Rivera returns to summary in the next passage, presenting the thrust of a professorial interrogation and an ironic observation:

> Yes, I was. He wanted to know my name. I told him. He looked me up in his roll book. Had I been coming to class regularly? Every time. How come I never spoke up in class? Because I sat in the back. It was hard to be heard from back there. I might try sitting up front, he said. I said I would. He said it was a little late for that. For a moment I'd forgotten what day it was. *Dies irae*, according to my paperback dictionary of foreign phrases. Do-or-die day.

Rivera effectively interweaves scene and summary—that is, showing and telling—throughout his entire narrative. Notice also how he uses *dialogue*. In a narrative, dialogue creates a sense of immediacy, the feeling that the scene is unfolding before the reader's eyes. But when dialogue is overused—as when a writer records an entire conversation, word for word—it can slow the narrative pace. Effective dialogue gives the *impression* of a conversation, not a literal transcription of a conversation. In the scene passage, Rivera uses dialogue effectively. In the final summary paragraph, he wisely gives an overview of the conversation, thus avoiding the risk of stalling the story.

In the following passage from "The Last Ride," McKnight makes effective use of scene, summary, and dialogue. The passage intensifies the potential danger in the situation and the subtle verbal conflict with the lifeguard. Notice, in particular, how McKnight moves from dialogue to summary and then back to dialogue to pick up the conversation and advance the action. Worried that the surfer will have an accident, the narrator says:

> "Better call him in," I said. "He's going to get hurt."
>
> "He won't come in," Connie said.
>
> "You're in charge of the beach."
>
> "Don't you know who he is?" she asked.
>
> I said I didn't. She asked if I had ever seen <u>Slippery When Wet</u>. The film was made by an amateur photographer 30 years earlier and had become a surfing classic in the late 1950s. I told her I had. She said that when he was a young man, the old surfer had been featured in it. She said he was shown riding long boards on waves over 25 feet high at Sunset Beach in Hawaii and that he was even shown riding shore break at this beach. I vaguely remembered him, but there were many surfers in the film agilely maneuvering their boards as they rode waves.
>
> "He's a living legend," Connie said.
>
> "A living legend should know when to quit."
>
> "If it's in your blood, you don't quit."
>
> "Look," I said, "the living legend's going to need an ambulance."

Note how the first four lines of dialogue advance the action. And then the question asked in line 4 leads into a summary of the rest of the conversation and background information. If McKnight had not summarized the background information about the surfer, the story's movement would have stalled. Also note how McKnight uses the last line of the summary passage to lead back into dialogue.

Like Rivera and McKnight, most writers present dialogue in short sentences and simple words, avoiding the annoying characteristics of actual speech—that is, verbal ticks, such as *well, hmmm, uh,* and *like, you know.* Also, to indicate when different people are speaking, writers usually begin new paragraphs.

Establish Point of View

Point of view refers to the perspective from which events are told. Narratives use one of two possible points of view: first person or third person. In a *first-person* narrative, a participant in the events tells the story. In a *third-person* narrative, a nonparticipant tells the story.

In a first-person narrative, the events have usually directly affected the storyteller in some emotional or intellectual way, which is characteristic of autobiographical or personal experience essays. You can identify a first-person narrative quite easily because the writer must use first-person pronouns, such as *I, me, my, we,* and *ours.* Usually, a writer will establish a first-person point of view in the opening paragraph. For example, read the opening paragraph from Robert Stone's "A Higher Horror of the Whiteness: Cocaine's Coloring of the American Psyche":

> One day in New York last summer I had a vision near Saint Paul's Chapel of Trinity Church. I had walked a lot of the length of Manhattan, and it seemed to me that a large part of my time had been spent stepping around men who stood in the gutter snapping imaginary whips. Strangers had approached me trying to sell Elavil, an antidepressant. As I stood on Broadway I reflected that although I had grown up to middle age seeing strange sights, I had never thought to see people selling Elavil on the street. Street Elavil, I would have exclaimed, that must be a joke!

Stone establishes the first-person point of view very quickly, thus letting readers know they will be hearing the story from a participant. Notice also that Stone's subjective attitude about this experience is very clear. "That must be a joke," he writes, indicating that what was taking place before his eyes seemed impossible. Subjectivity—writers revealing their attitudes—is characteristic of first-person narratives. After all, the story is being told by someone the events have affected.

In a third-person narrative, the storyteller has seldom experienced the events directly, which is characteristic of news reporting and biographical essays. As a nonparticipant, the third-person narrator will have developed the story from reports of others, much like a journalist collects information for a story, and will present the events as accurately as possible. In third-person narratives, you will find third-person pronouns, such as *he, she, him, her, they,* and *them.* (The only first-person pronouns that might appear will be in dialogue.) Again, the point of view will be established early in the essay. For example, read the opening of Martin Gansberg's "Thirty-Eight Who Saw Murder Didn't Call the Police":

> For more than half an hour thirty-eight respectable, law abiding citizens in Queens watched a killer stalk and stab a woman in three separate attacks in Kew Gardens.
>
> Twice their chatter and the sudden glow of their bedroom lights interrupted him and frightened him off. Each time he returned, sought her out, and stabbed her again. Not one person telephoned the police during the assault; one witness called after the woman was dead.
>
> That was two weeks ago today.

Gansberg is clearly a nonparticipant in this tragic event, and as such, he remains objective—or at least, he doesn't directly insert his attitude about the event he describes the way Stone does in the preceding example.

Follow Chronological or Psychological Time

The classic opening "Once upon a time . . ." emphasizes an important element of storytelling: *time.* Stories unfold in time. Thus, the order in which events are portrayed is critical in narrative development.

Basically, there are two ways to arrange significant narrative events:

1. By *chronological time,* which presents the events as they happened, step by step
2. By *psychological time,* which presents the events as they might be connected in memory, shifting back and forth in time while keeping the forward movement toward the narrative effect

For example, a historical essay, such as a narrative of a political campaign or battle, usually marches along in chronological time. A personal experience essay, however, such as a recollection of the importance of a significant event on the writer's life, can unfold in chronological or psychological time, depending on which is more appropriate.

Sometimes in a chronology, the writer will use a *flashback* as a device to reveal a scene in a character's memory. A flashback is usually brief, no longer than a paragraph, but reveals an important element in the narrative. For example, McKnight uses a flashback near the end of "The Last Ride," when he remembers a scene from a surfing film that featured the surfer when he was young. McKnight sets up the flashback by associating it with an action in present time:

Still bent low on the front of the board, the surfer shot out of the curl, well ahead of the white water.

The image triggers a memory. He then indirectly announces that a flashback will follow before presenting the actual flashback:

And then an image from the film came back to me: A young man, over 30 years younger than this man, riding waves at this same beach. He, too, was shot out of the curl and cleared the reef with a massive wave, bigger than this one, crashing behind him. In the film, the beach was crowded with cheering spectators. They had seen a ride beyond their belief, but that was when surfing was new and still viewed as an astounding feat.

McKnight is careful to make this flashback relevant to the ongoing action. He also carefully guides readers with key words and phrases to clarify the relationship of the present and the past. Even though this event happens in the past, McKnight adds some vivid detail to help readers visualize the event. (Keep in mind that although a flashback goes back in time, it doesn't necessarily indicate that a narrative essay is arranged psychologically.)

Psychologically arranged narratives usually begin in *medias res*, which means "in the middle of things"—that is, with an event that comes near the end of the story but before the climax. The opening event should be highly dramatic, designed to keep readers in suspense. Following the dramatic opening, the writer moves back to the story's beginning to present the events that led to the opening scene. Then the writer presents the climax and closes the essay.

Use Transitions

Whether writers arrange their narratives chronologically or psychologically, they use *transitions* to show shifts in time. The simplest transitions are
single words that indicate when something happened: *now, then, before, today,
yesterday, tomorrow,* and so on. Brief phrases can serve the same purpose: *two
weeks later, one year ago, soon I was to learn, three years after his death.* Transitions can also comprise complete sentences:

> His behavior didn't become suspicious until the day he came home with a
> ferocious Doberman pinscher to patrol the yard.

And sometimes writers use transitional paragraphs, as McKnight does in paragraph 4 of "The Last Ride":

> Now, the old man was in that kind of danger but with one difference--he was
> well past his prime, much too old to be riding in dangerous waters.

Transitions that show time shifts are absolutely necessary for readers to
follow most narratives.

REVISING NARRATIVE PARAGRAPHS

When you revise a narrative, look for the places that seem flat and then try
to invigorate them. For example, McKnight's essay had been polished and ready
to turn in. It had been lying on his desk for two days when he decided to read
it one more time. When he did, he noticed that paragraph 14 lacked drama. He
was merely *telling* about the surfer catching and riding the wave, not *showing*
in a step-by-step fashion. He made these line edits:

The old surfer was ~~trying~~ [paddling] to catch a wave, the largest since I had been
watching. ~~He swiftly stroked his arms in~~ [His arms dug three, four times into] the water before ~~he caught the wave.~~ [the wave swept him up,]
~~He was~~ [the reef rising] dangerously close ~~to the reef.~~ He ~~stood up~~ [sprang to his feet, arched his back,] and turned the board left
as he raced down the wave's face. The wave broke behind him and crashed over
the reef. ~~He~~ [Taking short, choppy steps, he] inched his way to the board's nose to gain more speed and
crouched low, avoiding the curl, [as it cracked behind him.] ~~And then I thought he was gone. The~~
~~curl caught up with him and had the power to toss him off his board~~
~~and wash him over the rocks.~~ Suddenly, he was out of sight, [The wave had tossed forward, and the curl folded over his crouching body.] ~~the curl~~
~~folding over him.~~

McKnight increased the dramatic impact of this paragraph by adding specific detail and by using strong verbs. With the changes integrated into the text, McKnight's final draft of this paragraph reads as follows:

> The old surfer was paddling to catch a wave, the largest since I had been watching. His arms dug three, four times into the water before the wave swept him up, the reef rising dangerously close. He sprang to his feet, arched his back, and turned the board left as he raced down the wave's face. The wave broke behind him and crashed over the reef. Taking short, choppy steps, he inched his way to the board's nose to gain more speed and crouched low, avoiding the curl as it cracked behind him. Suddenly, he was out of sight. The wave had tossed forward, and the curl folded over his crouching body.

Guidelines for Writing Narrative Essays

1. Select an experience that lends itself to narrative development, and identify the narrative effect you would like to achieve.

2. Determine which point of view to use: first person for a personal experience and third person for a narrative based on outside information.

3. In prewriting, limit the events in your narrative. Pick out the highlights, and then enrich them with detail. Remember, not every event is worth narrating. By presenting the dramatic peaks, you will sustain your reader's interest.

4. Compose your first draft:
   a. Write an opening that orients your reader, suggests the conflict, and generates suspense.
   b. Structure the complication section by arranging events in climatic order, with the most dramatic and revealing event serving as the climax.
   c. Create a resolution that reveals, directly or indirectly, the narrative's purpose—that is, the payoff.

5. Revise your first draft with an eye for scene and summary. If you use dialogue, examine it to see if you should present it in scene or summary. Be sure that your narrative has a strong forward movement with enough descriptive detail to engage the reader's senses.

Suggestions for Narrative Essays

1. Write a personal narrative about one of the following experiences:
   a. A traumatic childhood event that taught you a lesson about human nature
   b. An event that exposed you to serious injury

c. An event that taught you not to follow the crowd

d. A dramatic experience that came during a competition

e. An event that helped establish your sense of individuality

Begin by developing a list of memorable experiences related to any or all of these suggestions. Doing so will help release your memories. Each item on the list should be no longer than a line or two. For example:

- I remember the thump of a fist hitting the volleyball and seeing the ball rocket toward my face. Then blackness.
- When I was 16, I recall John swigging from the whiskey bottle then passing it around the car as he sped down the road at ninety. Born to be wild!
- The first sailfish I caught burst from the sea and caught the sunlight. It was magnificent. But I felt guilty.

Once you have compiled such a list, select one subject that you can narrate effectively. Then begin prewriting by adding more detail. Finally, using the principles for writing a successful narrative, write your essay.

2. Write an objective narrative based on one of the following suggestions:

a. A dramatic experience you witnessed but were not actually part of

b. An incident about a family member that a relative has told you

c. A story that a friend has conveyed to you

d. The dramatic rise and fall of a character in a film or television show

e. A series of events that led to a significant change in someone's life

3. Responding to a photograph: *The Storyteller*

Ancient cultures viewed storytellers as being touched with divine madness. They told tales that explained life's mysteries.

But times have changed.

Astronauts have soared through space. The deepest rainforests and highest mountain peaks have been photographed. What mysteries still need to be explained? What lessons need to be taught? What is the role of the storyteller in an age when movie and television production companies create visual stories by formula?

Is the photograph *The Storyteller* commenting on the role of storytellers today? Look at its details:

The storyteller's outfit suggests he indeed might be touched by divine madness. He wears ribbons, balloons, and streamers; a whimsical laurel around his head; and a banner that identifies him.

Displayed on a wall are hundreds of photographs, many of African American and Native American leaders, perhaps each embodying a story of its own. Behind his head, slightly obscured, are the words of Martin Luther King, Jr., "I have a dream."

This storyteller stands in the classroom, but where are the students who might be eager to hear a meaningful story? He is looking and pointing outside the photographic frame, but at what or whom? From the viewer's perspective he is alone—or is he?

In a unified narrative, respond to one of the following writing tasks. Before you begin the first draft, review Guidelines for Writing Narrative Essays (p. 193) to review the conventions of effective narratives.

a. Create your own tale about the storyteller in this photograph. Begin by studying the photograph. Imagine how the storyteller feels in his attire. Imagine how he feels during his performance. Imagine what his life is like when he is not being a storyteller: What does he do? Where does he live? What do his friends think of his storytelling? Is he a fulfilled person? A happy person? A sad person?

As you imagine the storyteller, list your observations. Once you have completed this exploratory phase of the assignment, review your observations and determine what dominant impression you wish to create.

Finally, to start your first draft, you might begin this way: *Once upon a time, an ordinary man who lived in our city decided to become a storyteller.* Throughout your draft, integrate physical details from the photograph.

b. Imagine that the storyteller in the photograph is fully aware that ancient mysteries have been clarified scientifically. However, he is still compelled to tell tales—meaningful tales designed to give people insight into a society that some see as growing more and more chaotic.

For this task, tell how the storyteller became successful. Include in your narrative a summary of one tale that gave his listeners insight into contemporary life.

Examples:
Illustrating Experience

THE METHOD

Imagine, for a moment, that you are sitting in a stuffy lecture hall. The professor's gaze drops to a notepad and he says, "Often associated only with combat veterans"—his voice flat, monotonous, hypnotic—"posttraumatic stress may actually affect anyone who undergoes continuous emotional upheaval and social disruption."

Post-traumatic stress, emotional upheaval, social disruption. These words seem to float above your head toward the back of the lecture hall.

The student next to you nods into sleep, and your own eyelids begin to sag when suddenly you hear your professor say, "For example." You become alert. Your neighbor is startled from sleep.

The professor stares at the class and says, "Consider the case of an elderly victim of the recent floods in the Midwest, Francesca Johnson. Two months after the flood, she was found dazed and wandering along the river, trying to recall her address so she could go home. She did not remember that the flood had taken the riverfront house she had moved into 46 years earlier, the antique table linens her mother had sent from Italy, or even the cemetery where she had buried her husband. Suffering from deep posttraumatic stress, she could not remember the flood. The river that had broken her heart took a piece of her memory, too."

The use of this example has brought the general and abstract back to earth. You begin taking notes. You are engaged in the topic.

An example is single experience that embodies the characteristics of many experiences. In fact, the word *example* is derived from *exemplum*, a Latin word that refers to "one thing selected from the many." Writers use examples with the same intentions as speakers: to clarify a point, to make a general assertion specific, or to electrify an audience.

In fact, the use of examples is the most common development method in writing as well as speaking. Examples give readers something concrete to think about. Like sandbags that stabilize a hot air balloon, examples anchor generalizations and abstractions from drifting beyond intellectual reach. For instance, it might be difficult for a reader to understand what social critic Jonathan Kozol means by this statement:

> Illiterates live, in more than literal ways, an uninsured existence.

To be clear, Kozol follows the statement with vivid examples to illustrate his point:

> They cannot understand written details on a health insurance form. They cannot read the waivers that they sign preceding surgical procedures. Several women I have known in Boston have entered a slum hospital with the intention of obtaining a tubal ligation and have emerged a few days later after having been subjected to a hysterectomy. Unaware of their rights, incognizant of jargon, intimidated by the unfamiliar air of fear and atmosphere of ether that so many of us find oppressive in the confines even of the most attractive and expensive medical facilities, they have signed their names to documents they could not read and which nobody, in the hectic situation that prevails so often in those overcrowded hospitals that serve the urban poor, had even bothered to explain.

These examples bring to life Kozol's observation that people who cannot read lead a precarious existence, even when professionals are caring for their health. Without vivid examples, the reader might misunderstand Kozol's generalization about these people.

A STUDENT ESSAY DEVELOPED BY EXAMPLES

Daniela Taylor wrote a personal experience essay about common behavior in response to the following freshman composition assignment:

Examples Essay Assignment

In an 800- to 1,000-word essay, identify and discuss a common behavior that suggests changing social attitudes. Consider the following general subject areas as possibilities:

Dress	Speech
Manners	Dating practices
Public displays	Possessions
A sport	Games
Service	Charity

Use examples as the dominant development mode, and base your discussion on personal experiences and observations.

Taylor decided to concentrate on the general subject of *manners*, which she narrowed to a more specific subject: *the increasing level of discourtesy in public places.* She developed examples from three sources: firsthand experience, a film she had seen on television, and a news article:

Taylor's title suggests we must recognize other people's rights to be in public spaces.

We Are Not Alone

Opening question sets up discussion of public discourtesy. Taylor makes it clear essay is based on personal experience.

Acts of public discourtesy concretely illustrate Taylor's position.

Example leads Taylor to ask series of rhetorical questions that point out this woman's insensitivity.

By this point, Taylor has set up readers for thesis statement: *Discourteous behavior seems to be increasing.*

First topic sentence sets up discussion of discourtesy among drivers.

Taylor provides background to show how she first viewed driving before shifting to present, eliciting common experience with discourteous drivers. Word *typically* announces composite example will follow.

Another recent trend announces another example will follow.

1

Whatever happened to courtesy? I am referring to the everyday, run-of-the-mill courtesies people used to show each other, which now seem to have gone the way of helping the aged across busy intersections and keeping quiet in libraries. For example, last week as I came out of a grocery store, I saw a woman moving her groceries from a shopping cart to her trunk. That task completed, she shoved her shopping cart directly behind the car parked next to her. What was she thinking? Did she know that the driver of the other car would hit it if he failed to see it? Did she realize he would have to return her cart if he did see it? Did she care? The woman's behavior in the supermarket parking lot momentarily angered me and puzzled me. Sadly, however, experience soon showed that this woman's discourteous behavior was not an isolated event. It seems that basic courtesy is rapidly being replaced by basic discourtesy. Everywhere I spend time in public--at school, at work, at shopping malls, in parks, in theaters, at sports events, at movies, and even on the highway--discourteous behavior seems to be increasing.

2

Nowhere has public discourtesy become more common than in traffic. I recall my early driving experience as being pleasurable. Other drivers would follow right-of-way guidelines, waiting their turn to make a left turn or cross through an intersection. Now, this courteous attitude seems to be changing. Like me, you have probably experienced angry drivers in a rush, shouting and shaking their fists at you. Typically, these drivers may be well-mannered people, but they often go berserk behind the wheel of a car. Near campus lately, I have noticed something new taking place. After a left turn signal turns red, three, four, five, or even six drivers still rush through the intersection, delaying the cars that now have a green light. These drivers seem to share the same discourteous attitude: "I waited long enough for this left turn light to turn green, and now I'm going through, even if it turns red again." Another recent trend is the spontaneous creation of an illegal left turn lane to the right of the legal left turn lane. Of course, dangerous drivers have always been on the road, but now others are compounding the danger because of their discourteous impatience. Sometimes, discourtesy even erupts into anger. A recent survey of Southern California drivers, a place where commuters often spend two to three grueling hours a day in their cars, revealed that nearly 60 percent of those surveyed admitted giving chase to other motorists who had offended them. Usually, these chases are abandoned as tempers cool, but sometimes, the offended driver overtakes the offender and a battle of words, gestures, and even weapons ensues.

Last week, I began to notice discourteous behavior that seems to have recently developed. Rollerbladers apparently find a challenge in weaving in and out of pedestrians strolling on public walkways. They seem to lack common courtesy, failing to keep in mind that a pedestrian walking at a much slower pace than their skating pace cannot always predict their movements. Their discourteous behavior can turn a relaxing afternoon stroll into a nerve-racking game of Dodge the Rollerblader. The increased use of cellular phones has given rise to another kind of public discourtesy. People must no longer retreat to enclosed public phone booths to make private phone calls. They can now phone friends, loved ones, and business associates while standing in a crowd. Often, their voices rise well above normal speaking range, thus disrupting the casual conversations of people who share the public space.

A recent Home Box Office showing of director Barry Levinson's <u>Good Morning, Vietnam</u>, a 1987 film about the exploits of an Armed Forces Radio disc jockey in Saigon at the height of the Vietnam War, reminded me of how our culture freely and discourteously uses obscenity. A disc jockey Adrian Cronauer (played by Robin Williams) is teaching a group of Vietnamese how to use English in everyday situations. Cronauer bypasses all the conventional socially acceptable phrases and gets right to the nitty-gritty of American obscenity, teaching the Vietnamese which obscenities to use for which occasions. Political implications aside, I at first thought the scene was hilarious, perhaps the film's most memorable scene. But then I realized that beneath the obscene words and phrases, so incongruous and humorous in the mouths of non-English speakers, lies the very attitude that disturbs me, an attitude that seems to be saying, "I have a right to be as discourteous as I want, Mister!"

Taylor continues discussion of verbal discourtesy, again drawing on direct experience to develop specific example.

Now, over a decade later, I find the "Cronauer" attitude to be 5 increasing. In almost any public setting, people appear to be determined to pepper their conversations with common obscenities that used to be reserved for lockerroom conversations, scribbling on restroom walls, or moments of great frustration and anger. Recently, for example, a friend and I were standing in line to buy tickets for a popular movie. Several people behind us were speaking loudly and punctuating their observations with gutter language and uproarious laughter. The epithets in their rambling conversation, delivered by both young men and women, were directed toward actors, musical groups, members of the opposite sex, teachers, and each other when they disagreed. Behind me, an older couple waited in line with their two children. They were clearly embarrassed, their faces turning red and their expressions pained, but the speakers seemed to be unaware of their embarrassment. I think such public use of generally unacceptable language reveals an aggressive, disrespectful attitude--perhaps the most extreme form of public discourtesy. It implicitly suggests that these people feel free to say whatever they please without being sensitive to common social constraints. Should freedom of speech include the right to be publicly discourteous by spouting four-letter words, no matter how uncomfortable it makes others who share the public space?

Taylor directly expresses attitude toward such behavior, offering interpretation of what behavior means.

Taylor ends paragraph with clincher written as question.

Taylor begins conclusion with question that echoes that in introduction. She offers general observation in response to question and closes by rewording key phrase from introduction.

Why is public discourtesy increasing? I guess that more and more 6 people are focusing on themselves and forgetting that their behavior might affect others around them. I know at times I have, and you probably have, too. Yet by merely remembering that we share public spaces with others, we might help replace basic discourtesy with basic courtesy.

Taylor has met the assignment's general requirements. She shows that public discourtesy is increasing, thus suggesting a change in social attitudes. Since the assignment called for a personal essay, the examples she uses come from both direct and indirect experience. Those from direct experience come from things that happened in front of the writer, such as Taylor's example of a woman leaving a shopping cart behind a parked car. Examples from indirect experience come from things that did occur but not in front of the writer, such as Taylor's examples from *Good Morning, Vietnam* and a newspaper article.

Taylor's first paragraph serves as the introduction. She includes an example in the introduction to help make her general assertion about public discourtesy more concrete. She closes the introduction with the thesis statement, which in this simplified form asserts that *Discourteous behavior seems to be increasing*.

Taylor develops the essay's discussion around four dominant points:

1. Drivers are discourteous to other drivers (paragraph 2).
2. Rollerbladers are discourteous to pedestrians (paragraph 3).
3. Cellular phone users are discourteous in crowds (paragraph 3).
4. Profane people are discourteous to everyone around them (paragraph 5).

She then develops each separate point with one or more examples.

Taylor ends the essay swiftly by using a rhetorical question to remind readers of the thesis. She asks, *Why is public discourtesy increasing?* She answers her own question with a general observation: because people are self-centered. She then finishes the conclusion with a bit of advice, reversing a phrase that first appears in the introduction: *By merely remembering that we share public spaces with others, we might help replace basic discourtesy with basic courtesy.*

WRITING AN ESSAY DEVELOPED BY EXAMPLES

Examples should be simple and direct—even dramatic, if possible. You will seldom need to compose a complicated example. In fact, to write a complicated example would defeat the primary purpose examples serve: to clarify a point or to make a general assertion specific. Your examples, therefore, should lean toward simplicity, not complexity.

Use a Variety of Examples

In essay-length assignments, use a variety of examples in terms of both content and length. A quick review of Daniela Taylor's "We Are Not Alone" shows that she uses anecdotes, personal observations of behavior, a scene from a film, and information from a newspaper article. By using this broad range of examples, Taylor creates variety while lending credibility to her observations. The examples based on direct experience give personal authority to the discussion, and the examples from indirect experience add an additional perspective, which is especially convincing when combined with direct experience.

Taylor also varied the length of her examples. For instance, in paragraph 1, she uses a single example and follows it with questions and observations. In paragraph 2, she uses three examples—one brief example that separates two medium-length examples. In paragraph 3, she uses two medium-length examples, and in each of paragraphs 4 and 5, she uses one very long, highly detailed example.

By varying the length and complexity of examples, you, like Taylor, will be adding variety to your essays, which will help keep your readers interested in the discussion.

Select Examples with Care

Selecting examples takes particular skill. Inexperienced writers tend to use the first example that comes to mind, which might not be the best one—or even a good one. To avoid making this mistake, examine your examples by asking three questions:

1. *Are they relevant?* Examples must have direct bearing on the point you're trying to make.
2. *Are they accurate?* This question is especially important when applied to statistics and quotations, but also remember this: If your examples are far-fetched, you might sound more like a tabloid reporter than a serious writer.
3. *Are they representative?* It is always a mistake to pick a one-in-a-million event to illustrate a general assertion. The presence of unexplained barren strips of land in the Amazon jungles does not mean that spacecraft from other planets have landed on Earth.

So, remember: Don't grab the first example that comes to mind. Instead, examine examples using these questions. They will keep you on track.

Use Examples with Purpose

To make your examples vivid and dramatic, you should arrange them with care, use specific language, and create an indelible picture in the reader's mind. Of course, all your examples will not be dramatic, but strive to dramatize as many as you can. In order to control the structure of the examples you compose, think of them as falling into three categories: specific, typical, and hypothetical examples.

Specific Examples.   *Specific examples* include single events or behaviors that may come from personal observations or research. For example, in "On Natural Death," essayist Lewis Thomas uses a specific example from his World War II experience to illustrate how even violent death can be quite painless:

> The worst accident I've ever seen was on Okinawa, in the early days of the invasion, when a jeep ran into a troop carrier and was crushed nearly flat. Inside were two young MPs, trapped in bent steel, both mortally hurt, with only their heads and shoulders visible. We had a conversation while people with the right tools were prying them free. Sorry about the accident, they said. No, they said, they felt fine. Is everyone else okay, one of them said. Well, the other one said, no hurry now. And then they died.

Thomas's specific example is an *anecdote*, which is a brief narrative that illustrates a point. Often, the point of a narrative example will be stated implicitly, rather than explicitly. As you might have noticed, Thomas presents a dramatic, though understated, accident scene. The details speak for themselves by showing how the two military police officers seem to be removed from the experience, unaware of the fact that their bodies are crushed and their deaths are imminent.

Taylor develops several paragraphs with single examples, too, such as the following one excerpted from paragraph 5, in which she illustrates the assertion that the discourteous use of profanity is becoming more common in public. The example is embedded in commentary, which is why she uses a clear transitional phrase—*for example*—to announce to the reader that an example will follow. Also note that Taylor presents the example in summary form, paring away extraneous detail. She hopes the example will trigger similar experiences in the reader's memory. Does the example work?

> Recently, for example, a friend and I were standing in line to buy tickets for a popular movie. Several people behind us were speaking loudly and punctuating their observations with gutter language and uproarious laughter. The epithets in their rambling conversation, delivered by both young men and women, were directed toward actors, musical groups, members of the opposite sex, teachers, and each other when they disagreed. Behind me, an older couple waited in line with their two children. They were clearly embarrassed, their faces turning red and their expressions pained, but the speakers seemed to be unaware of their embarrassment.

Thomas and Taylor devote entire paragraphs to one example. Thomas lets his paragraph speak for itself, but Taylor embellishes hers with commentary. Each technique works because it effectively serves the writer's purpose.

Often, you will find that a single extended example won't be enough to support a broad assertion in the topic sentence of a paragraph. When faced with this situation, experienced writers present several brief, specific examples in a single paragraph. For instance, in the following paragraph from *Human Beginnings*, naturalist Olivia Vlahos offers four brief examples of animal and human behavior to illustrate that all living creatures communicate nonverbally:

> Nearly all living creatures manage some form of communication. The dance patterns of bees in their hive help to point the way to distant flower fields or announce successful foraging. Male stickleback fish regularly swim upside-down to indicate outrage in a courtship contest. Male deer and lemurs mark territorial ownership by rubbing their own body secretions on boundary stones or trees. Everyone has seen a frightened dog put his tail between his legs and run in panic. We, too, use gestures, expressions, postures, and movement to give our words point.

Bees, stickleback fish, male deer and lemurs, dogs, and even humans—all serve as examples to support Vlahos's contention. Why does she keep her examples so brief? These behaviors are widely known. To make her point, Vlahos only needs to reference them.

Another effective paragraph structure for an example is a *catalog,* which is similar to a list of specific details. Catalog paragraphs are quite straightforward. The writer usually opens with several sentences that provide background for the reader, and then writes a brief sentence followed by a colon or dash that leads into the list. For example, in "Cosby Knows Best," Mark Crispin Miller uses a catalog to emphasize the point that *The Cosby Show,* a 1980s situation comedy featuring the Huxtable family, provided viewers with a lavish display of material consumption:

> On the surface of it, the Huxtables' milieu is as upbeat and well stocked as a window display at Bloomingdale's, or any of those visions of domestic happiness that graced the billboards during the Great Depression. Everything within this spacious brownstone is luminously clean and new, as if it had all been set up by the state to make a good impression on a group of visiting foreign dignitaries. Here are all the right commodities—lots of bright sportswear, plants and paintings, gorgeous bedding, plenty of copper ware, portable tape players, thick carpeting, innumerable knickknacks, and, throughout the house, big, burnished dressers, tables, couches, chairs, and cabinets (Early American yet looking factory-new). Each week, the happy Huxtables nearly vanish amid the porcelain, stainless steel, mahogany, and fabric of their lives. In every scene, each character appears in some fresh designer outfit that positively glows with newness, never to be seen a second time.

The effectiveness of a catalog comes from immersing readers in specific detail— verbally plunging them into an experience.

Sometimes, a catalog is tucked within a sentence, usually separated by dashes. Daniela Taylor uses this method in the last sentence of her introduction, where she wants to establish the locations of her observations:

> Everywhere I spend time in public--at school, at work, at shopping malls, in
> parks, in theaters, at sports events, at movies, and even on the highway--
> discourteous behavior seems to be increasing.

You can also mix a catalog with other examples. Keep in mind, though, that if a catalog follows a colon or dash, a complete sentence should precede it (unless, of course, it is tucked into the middle of a sentence).

In the preceding paragraphs, Taylor, Thomas, Vlahos, and Miller develop their specific examples from experiences and observations. A quotation, especially when followed by a brief analysis, can also serve as an effective example. Haig Bosmajian, a professor of speech communication, uses this method in the following paragraph from "Dehumanizing People and Euphemizing War." Bosmajian has been discussing the effect of dehumanizing metaphors on thought. In this paragraph, he links this form of belligerent verbal behavior to former president Ronald Reagan's aggressive joking, which has a similar dehumanizing effect:

> Dehumanizing metaphors carry some plausibility, for they allow the expression
> of aggressive sentiments and attitudes. Belligerent metaphors' functions and effects

can readily be understood when one compares their use to that of Reagan's "aggressive" jokes. When during the microphone testing episode in August 1984, the president declared, "My fellow Americans, I'm pleased to tell you today that I've signed legislation that will outlaw Russia forever. We begin bombing in five minutes," this "joke" allowed him to express in an acceptable way the unacceptable view that millions of human beings—Russian children, women and men—ought to be killed and their nation destroyed. The metaphors and jokes permit the speaker to imply brutally hostile sentiments and thoughts which, if stated directly, would be considered coarse and inhumane.

Here's where being accurate is crucial. Whenever you write an example paragraph with a quotation, be sure to double-check the language to be sure you have recorded it correctly.

Typical Examples.   Whereas specific examples are single instances from direct or indirect experience, *typical examples* are generalized from many specific experiences. Consider this paragraph from Alice Walker's "The Black Writer's Experience." Walker, who won a Pulitzer Prize for *The Color Purple,* uses a typical example to illustrate the sense of community black writers have inherited from the South:

> What the black Southern writer inherits as a natural right is a sense of *community,* something simple but surprisingly hard, especially these days, to come by. My mother, who is a walking history of our community, tells me that when each of her children was born the midwife accepted as payment such home-grown or home-made items as a pig, a quilt, jars of canned fruits and vegetables. But there was never any question the midwife would come when she was needed, whatever the eventual payment for her services. I consider this each time I hear of a hospital that refuses to admit a woman in labor unless she can hand over a substantial sum of money, cash.

Unlike Thomas's specific example of the deaths of two MPs, which we looked at earlier, Walker's example is a composite of many experiences. That is, it's typical of the southern black community, as her mother described it to her.

In a paragraph from *Writingcraft,* Sheila Y. Graham uses a series of typical examples to illustrate the lengths some people will go for public recognition:

> Some people will do the strangest things to gain fame. For example, there are those who go in for various kinds of marathons, dancing or kissing or blowing bubble gum for days at a time, to get their names in the paper or in a record book of some kind. Then there are people who sit on flagpoles or who perch on the ledges of skyscrapers for a week or more, apparently enjoying the attention they receive from the crowd below. There are people who hope to be remembered by someone because they ate the most cream pies or because they collected the most bottle tops. And there are even people who seek public notice by way of setting a record for the number of articles of clothing they can put on at one time or the number they can take off. Of course, there are a few mentally twisted individuals who seek fame at the expense of other people's property or even lives, but fortunately the great majority of people satisfy their urge to be remembered in ways that produce little more than tired lips or a bad case of indigestion.

All these examples—marathon dancers, kissers, bubble-gum chewers, and the like—typify people who have done odd things to gain quick fame or even immortality. Notice that each example is a typical, not a specific, representation of experience.

In "We Are Not Alone," Taylor makes effective use of two typical examples in paragraph 3. Notice that she announces in the topic sentence that more examples of discourteous behavior are coming:

> Last week, I began to notice discourteous behavior that seems to have recently developed. Rollerbladers apparently find a challenge in weaving in and out of pedestrians strolling on public walkways. They seem to lack common courtesy, failing to keep in mind that a pedestrian walking at a much slower pace than their skating pace cannot always predict their movements. Their discourteous behavior can turn a relaxing afternoon stroll into a nerve-racking game of Dodge the Rollerblader. The increased use of cellular phones has given rise to a new kind of public discourtesy. People must no longer retreat to enclosed public phone booths to make private phone calls. They can now phone friends, loved ones, and business associates while standing in a crowd. Often, their voices rise well above normal speaking range, thus disrupting the casual conversations of people who share the public space.

Taylor isn't suggesting that all Rollerbladers and cellular phone users behave discourteously, but she is suggesting that enough do to make their behavior typical.

One error beginning writers make when composing typical examples is to use general language. When writing typical examples, you should follow the same general guidelines you use when writing specific examples: Make them vivid and dramatic, arrange them effectively, use specific language, and create an indelible picture in the reader's mind.

Hypothetical Examples.   *Hypothetical examples* are similar to typical examples in that they are usually composed from bits and pieces of experience or information. But unlike typical examples, writers create hypothetical examples from their imaginations. Their purpose is quite simple: to clarify an abstraction or generalization when no actual examples are available.

In the following paragraph from *Mediaspeak*, media critic Donna Woolfolk Cross creates a hypothetical example to illustrate the general role children have played in soap operas:

> Children on soap operas are secondary. Because they serve largely as foils for the adult characters, their development does not follow the slow, steady pattern of the rest of the action. Their growth is marked by a series of sudden and unsettling metamorphoses as new and older juvenile actors assume the role. On Tuesday, little

Terence is cooing in his cradle. On Monday next, he is the terror of the Little League. By Thursday, his voice begins to change. Friday night is his first date. He wakes up on Monday a drug-crazed teenager, ready to be put to use creating heartbreak and grief for his devoted mother and her new husband. He stays fifteen years old for about two to five years (more if he managed to get into lots of scrapes), and then one day he again emerges from the off-camera cocoon transformed into a full-fledged adult, with all the rights, privileges, pain, and perfidy of that elite corps. And so the cycle continues.

"Little Terence" springs from Cross's imagination, not from the television screen. Clearly, though, she makes her point that children are secondary to adult soap opera characters.

When you use a hypothetical example, don't present it as an *actual example*. Too many politicians, journalists, and advertisers have contrived examples to support their views without revealing that they are mere fabrications. The purpose of a hypothetical example is to clarify, not to provide evidence in a discussion. Toward that end, you should always make the fact that you are using a fictional example clear to your reader. You might even use the word *imagine* or *suppose* to introduce a hypothetical example.

Use Transitions

Writers commonly use overt transitions in paragraphs that have more than one example—that is, guiding words and phrases, such as *for example, for instance, first, second, another example suggests,* and so on. But a series of *for examples* and *for instances* can become repetitive, and the sequence *first, second,* and so on may be confusing because it can incorrectly indicate the chronological order of the events, instead of the order in which the writer wishes to present them.

Thus, a word of caution: When you revise example paragraphs, examine the transitions that link examples. If they seem repetitive, change them. Or drop the transition altogether, if the shift from one example to another will be clear to a reasonable reader. Note that Olivia Vlahos does this in an earlier paragraph.

REVISING EXAMPLES PARAGRAPHS

While revising an examples essay, be sure that each example paragraph relates directly to its topic sentence and that all the topic sentences relate directly to the thesis. Also check each example to make sure it is clearly a specific, typical, or hypothetical example. The function of every example should be clear to the reader. Finally, be sure the type of example is appropriate. Ask yourself: Is it too specific or too general? Is it accurate, vivid, dramatic? Is it written in concrete language?

When revising "We Are Not Alone," Daniela Taylor decided that a specific example of a Rollerblader weaving dangerously through a crowd would be more effective as a typical example. Since she had frequently seen Rollerbladers dodging pedestrians, she felt justified in generalizing from her own observations. She also reviewed her use of transitions and decided they were unnecessary. Finally, she added a phrase to help make the example more vivid. Here are her edits:

> Last week, I began to notice discourteous behavior that seems to have recently developed. ~~First, a~~ Rollerblader(s) apparently ~~found~~ find a challenge in weaving in and out of pedestrians strolling on public walkways. ~~He didn't~~ They seem to ~~care~~ lack common courtesy, failing to keep in mind that a pedestrian walking at a much slower pace than ~~his~~ their skating pace cannot always predict ~~a blader's~~ their movements. ~~His~~ Their discourteous behavior ~~turned~~ can turn a relaxing afternoon stroll into a nerve-racking experience. ~~Second, the~~ The increased use of cellular phones has given rise to ~~a new~~ another kind of public discourtesy. People must no longer retreat to enclosed public phone booths to make private phone calls. They can now phone friends, loved ones, and business associates while standing in a crowd. Often, their voices rise well above normal speaking range, thus disrupting the casual conversations of people who share the public space.

After Taylor integrated the corrections into the text, her paragraph read as follows:

> Last week, I began to notice discourteous behavior that seems to have recently developed. Rollerbladers apparently find a challenge in weaving in and out of pedestrians strolling on public walkways. They seem to lack common courtesy, failing to keep in mind that a pedestrian walking at a much slower pace than their skating pace cannot always predict their movements. Their discourteous behavior can turn a relaxing afternoon stroll into a nerve-racking game of Dodge the Rollerblader. The increased use of cellular phones has given rise to another kind of public discourtesy. People must no longer retreat to enclosed public phone booths to make private phone calls. They can now phone friends, loved ones, and business associates while standing in a crowd. Often, their voices rise well above normal speaking range, thus disrupting the casual conversations of people who share the public space.

Remember, like Daniela Taylor, you should revise your essay with care—sharpening the examples, checking the transitions, adding vivid details, and dramatizing the events.

Guidelines for Writing Examples Essays

1. Pick a subject that lends itself to development by examples.

2. Write a clear purpose statement that directs you to select examples and compile a list of examples that relate to your purpose.

3. Write a clear, limited thesis statement that indicates you will be supporting it with examples.

4. Evaluate your examples to see if they support the thesis statement, and offer a wide enough range of examples to convince the reader that you have adequately developed the discussion.

5. Write the essay, making sure that your examples are effectively structured.

Suggestions for Examples Essays

1. Write an essay on one of the prompts listed below. First, develop a thesis statement, and then plan your subpoints and organize the examples you will use. Your discussion should include a mixture of specific and typical examples.

   a. Films serve as a window to the world.
   b. Reading fiction teaches lessons about life.
   c. What people drive reveals their character.
   d. Games teach children important lessons about independence and cooperation.
   e. Exercise can be detrimental to health.
   f. A half hour of the evening news reveals a disrupted United States.
   g. Graffiti carries psychological messages.
   h. Public places are disrupted by piped-in music.
   i. Some music lyrics promote violence.
   j. Some media celebrities symbolize more than success.
   k. Americans are wasteful people.
   l. Intelligent people often lack common sense.
   m. Street crime is affecting public life.
   n. Parents are often overinvolved in their children's education.
   o. Anything worth doing is worth doing badly.
   p. There are several alternatives to public schools.

2. Write a full examples essay based on one of these situations:

   a. Streets in many communities have become extremely hazardous for pedestrians, especially for children and people who are elderly or disabled. In fact, one-sixth of those who die in traffic accidents are pedestrians; approximately 7,000 Americans were killed last year. Take a walk through a busy street in or near your neighborhood. Identify the dangers. Using examples as the primary method of development, write an essay illustrating the dangers.

b. Over the last few years, college courses of study have changed to reflect the concerns of women and minorities. Examine your college's programs and courses of study. Determine how successfully or unsuccessfully they address the concerns of women and ethnic minorities. Write an essay using examples that illustrates what you discovered.

c. People in the 1990s seem to yearn for the simple life. Perhaps this desire is fueled by the perception that there's never enough time to get everything done. People are obsessed with time. They wear digital watches that beep on the quarter hour and clutch their day organizers like life preservers. For this assignment, examine your life for examples of the impact that this focus on time has on you and the people you know. Then write an examples essay that warns others to give up the rat race and seek a simplified existence.

d. Magazine advertisers seldom only praise their products. They also associate them with pleasing images to attract consumers—images such as physically attractive men and women, working in prestigious professions or living lives of leisure. Write an essay using magazine advertisements as examples to illustrate that advertisers entice consumers to buy products for the wrong reasons—that is, not because of product quality but because of pleasing associations.

3. Responding to a photograph: *Style Is the Man*

What is *style*? If we say a certain person has style, what exactly do we mean? Is it behavior? Clothing? Speech? Posture? Grooming? All of these? Some other things? Does everyone have style or only a few?

Style may be hard to define precisely, but we know it when we see it, right? And most people would undoubtedly agree that the young man in the photograph *Style Is the Man* has it.

Style communicates. Before interacting with a person, we form impressions based on at least some elements of his or her personal style. We may be able to trace this impression to very specific things, or we may say we just have a feeling but are unable to specify particulars. A style may be created consciously and purposefully (perhaps to deceive), or it may simply grow out of the true values and accumulated experiences of the individual.

After reviewing Guidelines for Writing Examples Essays (p. 209), complete one of the following writing tasks.

a. Using specific examples from the photograph as your method of development, write a paper that characterizes the style portrayed by the young man. Begin with a short physical description of the man and lead to a generalization about his style and the attitude and values it communicates to you. Then examine various items and aspects of his appearance and discuss each as a specific example that led you to your interpretation of his message.

b. Write a paper combining typical and specific examples. Find three photographs of humans, each showing a different sense of style. These need not be as dramatic as the style illustrated in *Style Is the Man*, though they may be. As in the previous assignment, begin with a short description of each of the three photographs and lead to a generalization about each style and what it communicates to you. In the discussion section of your paper, point to specific examples in each photograph that support your generalization, and then relate typical examples of the expected behavior, dress, and attitudes of a member of each style group. Include the photographs when you submit your final draft.

Comparison: Showing Similarities and Differences

THE METHOD

If you listen carefully to casual conversations, you'll hear *comparison* at work in daily decision making:

He says, "I'll bike, you can have jogging. Biking 1 hour, I cover 15 miles, but I can only jog 20 minutes and cover 2 miles. Besides, biking doesn't hurt my body. Jogging makes my knees ache."

She says, "Give me step aerobics; you keep biking. An hour of step burns; I'm breathing hard. My body heats up, and I work my legs and swing my arms. It's a hard workout. Biking, I hardly sweat, and only my legs get a workout."

Sound familiar? Probably. Conversations such as this take place each day in classrooms, around dinner tables, and at work. We decide between alternatives by figuring out their similarities and differences.

To identify similarities is to *compare;* to identify differences is to *contrast.* Showing similarities and differences—that is, *comparison*—is not only common in daily decision making but in all forms of writing—essays, research papers, reports, and written examinations.

A STUDENT ESSAY DEVELOPED BY COMPARISON

Martina Flint wrote the following comparison essay in response to a world literature class assignment. She was asked to do the following:

Comparison Essay Assignment

In an 800- to 900-word essay, compare two myths, legends, tales, poems, or plays from different cultures and time periods to show how they are similar and/or different.

Flint decided to concentrate on heroes in myth and legend. She choose King Oedipus from ancient Greece and King Arthur from medieval Britain. She developed her comparison from a close reading of the tales and from her class notes. Here's her essay:

The Hero: Transcending Time and Culture

Flint opens by concentrating on general subjects she will address: Greek myths and British legends.

Using point-by-point arrangement, Flint points out obvious differences between subjects.

Thesis statement reverses Flint's direction: Shifts from showing obvious differences and promises to show similarities by concentrating on two mythic heroes: Oedipus and Arthur.

Topic sentence announces first similarity: Oedipus and Arthur had similarly mysterious births.

Flint uses subject-by-subject arrangement. Notice how smoothly transition sentence moves from Oedipus to Arthur.

The myths of ancient Greece and the legends of medieval Britain   1
seem to have more differences than similarities. For instance, Greek myths feature warriors who serve a variety of pagan deities living within eyeshot on a mountain top, whereas British legends feature warriors who serve a single Christian God living in the heavens. The Greek pagan gods were fallible, often making mistakes that needed correcting; the British Christian God was all knowing and all powerful, apparently unable to make mistakes. Greek warriors subscribed to a masculine battle ethic; British warriors were influenced by a feminine ethic. But even though myths and legends differ in these general ways, they share similar underlying elements that span the cultures and ages. The myth of Oedipus from ancient Greece and the tale of King Arthur from medieval Britain are two such stories. They are separated by culture, religion, and nearly 2,000 years, yet the Oedipus myth from 1500 BC and the Arthurian tale from AD 500 share striking similarities.

Oedipus and Arthur were both born under mysterious circumstances.   2
When Oedipus was born to King Laius and Queen Jocasta of Thebes, the Oracle at Delphi prophesied that the child would someday kill his father and marry his mother. Attempting to avoid the Oracle's prophesy, Laius and Jocasta set the newborn child on a hillside to perish. A shepherd took pity on the child and saved him. Arthur, like Oedipus, was born under mysterious circumstances. The Wizard Merlin used his magical powers to transform Arthur's predestined father, Uther Pendragon, into an image of his enemy identified as the Duke of Tintagel. Uther then seduced the Duke's wife, Igraine, who then gave birth to Arthur. Merlin, according to his pact with Uther, seized baby Arthur and gave him to foster parents for protection. Both Oedipus and Arthur, unaware of their actual ancestry, were then raised by surrogate parents who also were unaware that their foster children were of royal blood.

Estranged from their kingdoms and birthrights throughout their   3
youth, as young men Oedipus and Arthur returned to their origins and

Topic sentence an-
nounces second simi-
larity: Miraculous
events led both Oedi-
pus and Arthur to
their thrones. Flint
develops point using
subject-by-subject
arrangement.

ascended to their rightful places by what could be considered miraculous
events. Oedipus, after hearing the prediction that he would kill his
father and marry his mother, leaves what he believes to be his birthplace
and parents to avoid such a dire fate. On his journey, he kills a stranger
in response to an insult and then travels to Thebes, his actual
birthplace, where he confronts a monster--the Sphinx--which is
terrorizing the city. Oedipus defeats the Sphinx, frees Thebes, and as a
conquering hero is made king because the former king, Oedipus's true
father, Laius, has disappeared.

This paragraph is con-
tinuation of last. Be-
cause she had great
deal of information
related to miraculous
events leading two
kings to their thrones,
Flint devoted one
paragraph to Oedipus
and another to Arthur.
She opens with tran-
sitional sentence that
clearly shows discus-
sion continues from
previous paragraph.

The events that gave Arthur his rightful throne are equally   4
miraculous. Before dying in battle, Uther Pendragon, Arthur's true
father, stabbed his magical sword, Excalibur, into a stone and declared
that the man who could extract the sword would be the rightful heir to
the British throne. When it was time to reveal the young Arthur as the
heir, Merlin organized a New Year's Day tournament. Knights from
throughout the kingdom attempted to withdraw Excalibur from the
stone. All failed. Finally, young Arthur stepped forward and withdrew
the magical weapon. Clearly, this feat showed he was Uther Pendragon's
son and was declared King of Britain, which in the absence of leadership
had become a disunited and warring domain.

Topic sentence sets
up third similarity:
Marriages of both
heroes are doomed.

Both Oedipus and Arthur, after restoring their kingdoms, then unite   5
the populace through marriage. But the marriage of each of these two
legendary heroes is doomed, foreshadowing even more disruption by
plague and famine for their kingdoms. Oedipus, as prophesied, had
actually killed his true father, Laius, the stranger who insulted him on
the road. Moreover, he did marry his true mother, Jocasta, the queen of
Thebes whose husband had vanished, thus committing incest. Although
the details of Arthur's situation are different, the underlying elements

Another effective
transitional sentence
guides readers from
one subject to
another.

are similar. Arthur marries Guinevere, but both fall into adultery,
violating their sacred marriage vows. Guinevere commits adultery with
Arthur's champion knight, Lancelot. Arthur unknowingly commits incest
when Morgana LeFay, his half-sister and a sorceress, seduces him. As a
result of these transgressions, Arthur's Britain, like Oedipus's Thebes,
becomes ravaged by plague and famine.

Because both Oedipus and Arthur violated a cultural taboo against   6
incest, no matter how inadvertently, they must atone to restore their

Topic sentence sets up fourth similarity: Oedipus's and Arthur's violations of cultural taboo lead to their downfalls.

ravaged lands. Tragically, without knowing the truth of his actual origin, King Oedipus unwittingly sentences himself to an existence as a blind, wandering beggar. When the truth of his acts are revealed, he accepts the punishment without question, and his suffering lifts the plague from Thebes. King Arthur heroically sacrifices himself in combat during the Battle of Camlan. He challenges Mordred, his evil bastard son, to a dual. They slay one another, but by slaying the product of his unholy incest, King Arthur restores Britain. In their human suffering, both Oedipus and Arthur exemplify the sacrificial demands placed on tragic heroes.

Flint points out that at first glance, there are obvious differences between subjects, but closer examination shows several similarities.

Even though the content of the tales may be very different, such myths and legends as those of Oedipus and Arthur share many underlying elements. They transcend cultural, religious, and historic differences to become universal sagas.

7

Flint's purpose is clarification, rather than evaluation. She concentrates on the similarities between King Oedipus and King Arthur, asserting in a clearly stated thesis that these two mythic heroes—though separated in time, culture, and religion—share similar experiences. She organizes her discussion around four dominant points:

1. Being born under mysterious circumstances (paragraph 2)
2. Having miraculous ascents to their thrones (paragraphs 3 and 4)
3. Uniting their kingdoms through doomed marriages (paragraph 5)
4. Atoning for violating the incest taboo (paragraph 6)

Flint uses subject-by-subject arrangement to present her material, which is usually the case when writers concentrate on similarities. In the introduction, she establishes her subjects and her basis for comparison: the underlying elements of myths and legends that transcend time, culture, and religion. She effectively concludes by drawing attention to her thesis.

WRITING AN ESSAY DEVELOPED BY COMPARISON

Dealing with two subjects in close relationship can be a difficult task. Yet this difficulty gives you an advantage: By being aware of the pitfalls, you can carefully compose your essay by keeping in mind the following guidelines:

- Select subjects that are appropriate for comparison.
- Establish the comparison early.
- Decide on the appropriate arrangement.
- Use transitions to guide your reader as you shift from subject to subject.

Select Appropriate Subjects for Comparison

Writers should compare subjects that share some common ground, otherwise there may be no valid basis for comparison. For example, it would be appropriate to compare two basketball centers on ball handling, mobility, quickness, and individual style or two western films on their portrayal of gender, violence, and historical accuracy. Each of these pairs of subjects has a valid basis for comparison because the subjects belong to the same category: basketball centers and western films. In contrast, it would probably be inappropriate to compare a basketball center to a baseball pitcher or a western film to a comedy. Except in the broadest sense—athletes and films—there is no clear valid basis for comparison.

In the following paragraph from "What Do You Mean, You Don't Like My Style?" John S. Felden compares the tone in business writing to the tone in literary writing:

> In the business environment, tone is especially important. Business writing is not literary writing. Literary artists use unique styles to "express" themselves to a general audience. Business people write to particular persons in particular situations, not so much to express themselves as to accomplish particular purposes, "to get a job done." If a reader does not like a novelist's tone, nothing much can happen to the writer short of failing to sell some books. In the business situation, however, an offensive style may not only prevent a sale but may also turn away a customer, work against a promotion, or even cost you a job.

Clearly, business writing and literary writing share a basis for comparison—tone—which Felden establishes.

In her essay "The Hero: Transcending Time and Culture," Martina Flint followed this advice. She selected two appropriate subjects for comparison: King Oedipus and King Arthur. Both were rulers and central figures of myths. As Flint's essay points out in detail, they shared many similarities.

Analogy.   An *analogy* is a special form of comparison. It is an exception to the principle that the subjects should share some common ground in order for the comparison to be valid. An analogy is a figurative comparison that a writer may use to explain an unfamiliar subject by describing it in terms of something familiar. For example, a writer might describe watching televised quiz shows as being similar to eating junk food or suggest that growing old is like a hiker climbing a long, tedious slope. The emphasis in an analogy is always on using one familiar subject to clarify another, less familiar one.

For example, in order to clarify the relationship between fat and glucose burning, Covert Bailey uses the following analogy in *Fit or Fat:*

> The relationship between fat and glucose burning might best be explained by an analogy. Imagine building a fire in your fireplace. If you put in a big log and light a match to it, what happens? Nothing! The match just goes out. So you put some twigs of kindling wood under the log and light the kindling, which easily ignites. Well, glucose is like kindling; it is easy to burn. Fat, on the other hand, is like a log;

it is hard to get started and won't burn well unless some kindling is added once in a while. But it burns for a long time, giving off lots of heat.

Bailey's analogy is quite clear. He isn't saying that glucose and kindling or fat and logs have both similarities and differences. He's saying that if you understand the difference between lighting kindling and lighting a log, you will understand how glucose and fat work in the body.

When you write an analogy, keep in mind that you are using one subject to *clarify* another, not to spell out all the similarities and differences of two subjects.

Establish the Comparison Early

The opening of any essay or paragraph is important, but the opening of a comparison essay is especially important. Since a comparison deals with two subjects, the writers must immediately establish those subjects and the grounds for their comparison, rather than risk confusing the reader.

For instance, read the introduction to Jack Newfield's 1986 essay "Stallone vs. Springsteen." At first glance, Sylvester Stallone and Bruce Springsteen seem to be unlikely subjects for comparison: One is an actor; the other, a singer. Newfield, of course, knows he has two subjects that seem to lack a basis for valid comparison. As a consequence, he quickly establishes the ground for his comparison: Stallone and Springsteen are working-class heroes who symbolize competing visions of America's future. Here's an excerpt from Newfield's essay:

> Bruce Springsteen and Sylvester Stallone are the two great working-class heroes of American mass culture. Springsteen had the best-selling album of 1985 and Stallone has the second most successful movie. On the surface, they share stunning similarities of biceps, bandannas, American flags, Vietnam themes, praise from President Reagan and uplifting feelings of national pride. Bumper stickers proclaim, BRUCE—THE RAMBO OF ROCK.
>
> But beneath the surface—and between the lines—these two American heroes of the eighties are sending opposite messages. They are subtly pulling the 18-to-35-year-old generation toward two competing visions of the American future.

Newfield immediately reveals the subjects he will compare and the common ground they share: Springsteen and Stallone represent *two competing visions of the American future.*

In her essay, Martina Flint uses a slightly different tactic. She begins by contrasting myths and legends in general, establishing a comparison pattern. She then shifts her focus to two mythic heroes—Oedipus and King Arthur. In her thesis, which is the last line of the opening paragraph, she states she will be writing about their similarities:

> They are separated by culture, religion, and nearly 2,000 years, yet the Oedipus myth from 1500 BC and the Arthurian tale from AD 500 share striking similarities.

After reading the opening and the thesis statement, you know where Flint is headed. The pattern for her discussion is clearly established.

Decide on the Appropriate Arrangement

Writers may use two organizational strategies to arrange their comparisons: *subject-by-subject* arrangement and *point-by-point* arrangement.

Subject-by-Subject Arrangement.   A subject-by-subject paragraph is arranged in two parts: First, the details of one subject are presented, and then the details of the other subject are presented. For example, Edward T. Hall uses subject-by-subject arrangement in the following paragraph from *The Hidden Dimension*. Hall contrasts Arab and American attitudes toward *olfaction*, or "breath":

> Olfaction occupies a prominent place in Arab life. Not only is it one of the distance-setting mechanisms, but it is a vital part of a complex system of behavior. Arabs consistently breathe on people when they talk. However, this habit is more than a matter of different manners. To the Arab good smells are pleasing and a way of being involved with each other. To smell one's friend is not only nice but desirable, for to deny him your breath is to act ashamed. Americans, on the other hand, trained as they are not to breathe in people's faces, automatically communicate shame in trying to be polite. Who would expect that when our highest diplomats are putting on their best manners they are also communicating shame? Yet this is what occurs constantly, because diplomacy is not only "eyeball to eyeball" but breath to breath.

When a subject-by-subject paragraph grows too lengthy, the writer will usually break it into two paragraphs, each devoted to a single subject. As an example, study Otto Friedrich's comparison of a news story and a newsmagazine story from "There Are No Trees in Russia":

> There is an essential difference between a news story, as understood by a newspaperman or a wire-service writer, and a newsmagazine story. The chief purpose of the conventional news story is to tell what happened. It starts with the most important information and continues into increasingly inconsequential details, not only because the reader may not read beyond the first paragraph, but because an editor working on galley proofs a few minutes before press time likes to be able to cut freely from the end of the story.
>
> A newsmagazine is very different. It is written to be read consecutively from beginning to end, and each of its stories is designed, following the critical theories of Edgar Allan Poe, to create one emotional effect. The news, what happened that week, may be told in the beginning, the middle, or the end; for the purpose is not to throw information at the reader but to seduce him into reading the whole story, and into accepting the dramatic (and often political) point being made.

Notice that in the first sentence, Friedrich identifies the two subjects: news stories and newsmagazine stories. In the first sentence of the second paragraph, he clearly indicates that he is shifting from one subject to the other.

Martina Flint uses a similar strategy in her third and fourth paragraphs. The material is too lengthy for a single paragraph, so she arranges it in two paragraphs:

Estranged from their kingdoms and birthrights throughout their youth, as young men Oedipus and Arthur returned to their origins and ascended to their rightful places by what could be considered miraculous events. Oedipus, after hearing the prediction that he would kill his father and marry his mother, leaves what he believes to be his birthplace and parents to avoid such a dire fate. On his journey he kills a stranger in response to an insult and then travels to Thebes, his actual birthplace, where he confronts a monster--the Sphinx-- which is terrorizing the city. Oedipus defeats the Sphinx, frees Thebes, and as a conquering hero is made king because the former king, Oedipus's true father, Laius, has disappeared.

The events that gave Arthur his rightful throne are equally miraculous. Before dying in battle, Uther Pendragon, Arthur's true father, stabbed his magical sword, Excalibur, into a stone and declared that the man who could extract the sword would be the rightful heir to the British throne. When it was time to reveal the young Arthur as the heir, Merlin organized a New Year's Day tournament. Knights from throughout the kingdom attempted to withdraw Excalibur from the stone. All failed. Finally, young Arthur stepped forward and withdrew the magical weapon. Clearly, this feat showed he was Uther Pendragon's son and was declared King of Britain, which in the absence of leadership had become a disunited and warring domain.

Like Friedrich in the earlier paragraphs, Flint makes clear the connection between the two paragraphs in the opening sentences—that is, the miraculous events that led to Oedipus and King Arthur each assuming the throne.

Point-by-Point Arrangement. For short essays, subject-by-subject arrangement is usually effective, but when an essay is longer, the reader may not be able to remember the points of the comparison and their relationship. In this case, it is more effective to use point-by-point arrangement or a combination of point-by-point and subject by subject arrangement.

Point-by-point arrangement makes a point about one subject and then immediately follows up with a corresponding point about the other subject, thus alternating from one subject to the other. Consider, for example, the following paragraph from linguist Peter Farb's *Man at the Mercy of His Language*, which is arranged point by point:

The way culture affects language becomes clear by comparing how the English and Hopi languages refer to H_2O in its liquid state. English, like most other European languages, has only one word—"water"—and it pays no attention to what the substance is used for or its quantity. The Hopi of Arizona, on the other hand, use "pahe" to mean the large amounts of water present in natural lakes or rivers, and "kevi" for the small amounts in domestic jugs and canteens. English, though, makes other distinctions that Hopi does not. The speaker of English is careful to distinguish between a lake and a stream, between a waterfall and a geyser; but "pahe" makes no distinction among lakes, ponds, rivers, streams, waterfalls, and springs.

In the opening sentence, Farb establishes the basis for comparison: the difference between English and Hopi in identifying water. He then makes several contrasting observations.

Although Flint's dominant method of development is subject by subject, she does open "The Hero: Transcending Time and Culture" with a point-by-point comparison:

> The myths of ancient Greece and the legends of medieval Britain seem to
> have more differences than similarities. For instance, Greek myths feature
> warriors who serve a variety of pagan deities living within eyeshot on a
> mountain top, whereas British legends feature warriors who serve a single
> Christian God living in the heavens. The Greek pagan gods were fallible, often
> making mistakes that needed correcting; the British Christian God was all
> knowing and all powerful, apparently unable to make mistakes. Greek warriors
> subscribed to a masculine battle ethic; British warriors were influenced by a
> feminine ethic. But even though myths and legends differ in these general
> ways, they share similar underlying elements that span the cultures and ages.
> The myth of Oedipus from ancient Greece and the tale of King Arthur from
> medieval Britain are two such stories. They are separated by culture, religion,
> and nearly 2,000 years, yet the Oedipus myth from 1500 BC and the Arthurian
> tale from AD 500 share striking similarities.

Like Farb in the earlier example, Flint places her contrasting points one after the other. She writes them in a parallel fashion and separates the first contrasting point with a *whereas*. She continues with the same tactic, but she drops *whereas* while creating the same balanced effect with semicolons. Notice, also, that in the first sentence, Flint establishes that she will be exploring differences, but the word *seems* prepares you to shift to similarities later on.

Use Transitions

Since a comparison deals with two subjects, careful writers of comparisons concentrate on keeping their readers on track. Sometimes, they use balanced main clauses joined by a semicolon, as Flint does in her opening paragraph. Other times, they use parallel sentences. But usually, writers are more direct in guiding their readers; they use overt transitions to show the shift from one subject to the other or from one point to another. (For more on parallel structure and transitions, see Chapter 9, pp. 145–146 and Chapter 11, p. 172.)

You must, of course, use transitions that specify the relationship between your points. If you are comparing, use transitions such as *similarly, likewise,* and *also* to show the likeness of subjects. If you are contrasting, use words and phrases such as *however, yet, whereas, on the one hand/on the other hand, in contrast,* and *on the contrary* to show the differences between subjects.

REVISING COMPARISON PARAGRAPHS

Once you've completed your essay, revise it one final time so that the thesis and topic sentences clearly announce a comparison and so that each paragraph is clearly structured by subject-by-subject or point-by-point arrangement.

When completing the final revision of "The Hero: Transcending Time and Culture," Martina Flint revised several of her paragraphs to more accurately reflect comparison. For example, the following is an early draft of paragraph 6, showing Flint's line edits. She felt the topic sentence lacked a specific focus and did not announce a comparison. Also, the details were arranged point by point, but because there was only one dominant point for comparison and because the points weren't parallel, Flint rearranged the paragraph subject by subject, which also allowed to add more detail. Here's what she did:

> *Because both Oedipus and Aurthur violated* ~~The mythic hero often violates~~ a cultural taboo *against incest, no matter how inadvertently, they* ~~and~~ must atone to restore their ravaged lands. Tragically, without knowing the truth of his actual origin, King Oedipus unwittingly sentences himself to an existence as a blind, wandering beggar. *When the truth of his acts are revealed, he accepts the punishment without question, and his suffering lifts the plague from Thebes.* King Arthur heroically sacrifices himself in combat during the battle of Camlan *He challenges* ~~by challenging~~ Mordred, his evil bastard son, *to a duel* ~~and killing him. When the truth of their acts are revealed, they accept punishment without question, and their suffering lifts the plague from Thebes and Britain.~~ In their human suffering, both Oedipus and Arthur exemplify the sacrificial *They slay one another, but by slaying the product of his unholy incest, King Arthur restores Britain.* demands placed on tragic heroes.

After Flint incorporated these edits, her revised paragraph 6 read as follows:

> Because both Oedipus and Arthur violated a cultural taboo against incest, no matter how inadvertently, they must atone to restore their ravaged lands. Tragically, without knowing the truth of his actual origin, King Oedipus unwittingly sentences himself to an existence as a blind, wandering beggar. When the truth of his acts are revealed, he accepts the punishment without question, and his suffering lifts the plague from Thebes. King Arthur heroically sacrifices himself in combat during the Battle of Camlan. He challenges

Mordred, his evil bastard son, to a duel. They slay one another, but by slaying the product of his unholy incest, King Arthur restores Britain. In their human suffering, both Oedipus and Arthur exemplify the sacrificial demands placed on tragic heroes.

Remember, like Martina Flint in this essay, you, too, should carefully revise your essay to clearly indicate comparison and to accurately reflect either subject-by-subject or point-by-point arrangement in discussion paragraphs.

Guidelines for Writing Comparison Essays

1. Pick two subjects with a clear basis for comparison, and decide on a purpose for comparing them—that is, to clarify or to evaluate.
2. Develop a detailed list of similarities and differences for the two subjects.
3. Decide whether to use subject-by-subject or point-by-point arrangement or a combination of both.
4. Write a thesis statement that clearly announces a comparison follows; use it to evaluate your points to see if they support your position yet offer a wide enough range for comparison.
5. Write your essay. Be sure to establish your two subjects and your basis for comparison in the opening. Develop your points into clear topic sentences that clearly indicate a comparison will follow in each discussion paragraph.

Suggestions for Comparison Essays

1. Write a fully developed essay that compares and/or contrasts the subjects in any of the following topics. Keep in mind that you will probably need to alter the topic you choose to fit your interests and knowledge.
   a. Two groups that have contrasting values, such as smokers and non-smokers, vegetarians and meat eaters, drinkers and nondrinkers, or athletes and couch potatoes
   b. Two campus groups who hold opposing values on a particular issue
   c. Two contrasting characters in a film (If appropriate, compare their physical appearance, their psychological makeup, and their actions. Conclude with an observation about what each represents.)
   d. Two ways of losing weight
   e. Shopping styles of males and females (Develop your comparison by identifying specific people as types.)
   f. Coverage of a certain event in a newspaper versus on television
   g. Two classic films from the same category, such as westerns, science fiction, thrillers, romances, or supernatural tales
   h. Two situation comedies

    i. Watching a sports event live versus on television

    j. Children's games from the past with children's games of today

    k. A film with the novel from which it was made

    l. Two talk-radio commentators

    m. The pros and cons of two controversial points of view

    n. Two approaches to raising children

    o. How two people from different economic conditions, cultures, or age groups view the same experience

2. Use one of the following suggestions to develop a one- or two-paragraph analogy that explains an abstract idea, a process, an experience, or the odd behavior of someone you know:

    a. A poker hand   **g.** Walking through a forest

    b. A flood   **h.** A game of solitaire

    c. A merry-go-round   **i.** A flowering tree

    d. Crashing waves   **j.** Dancing

    e. Gardening   **k.** A leaky faucet

    f. A spider web   **l.** A soaring bird

3. Responding to a photograph: *The New Warriors*

For general purposes, think of photography as having two main uses: to record private experiences and to record public experiences. A photograph of a private experience—a snapshot of a family outing, a portrait of a father, a candid photo of a child—is appreciated within a private context by those who have some direct connection with the recorded event or person. A photograph that records a public experience usually has nothing directly to do with us, its viewers, but we nevertheless bring meaning to it based on our experiences.

Both private and public photographs can evoke infinite associations from the viewer's own experience. But most public photographs have a second dimension: They create social or political associations that many people share. Often, they suggest discontinuity in our common social experience. As an organizing principle, photographers create discontinuity through *juxtaposition*—that is, they oppose contrasting elements in their photographs.

Select one of the following writing assignments to explore the use of contrasting elements in photographs. Before you begin, reread Guidelines for Writing Comparison Essays (p. 222) to review strategies for developing contrasts.

a. *The New Warriors* is a photograph of a public experience that ironically explores the ideas on which the United States is predicated. By referring to details in *The New Warriors*, examine its contrasting elements and determine what social or political message it embodies. Remember, you must select details from the photograph to support your contention, presenting them to readers as if they have not seen the image.

b. Select a photograph of a private experience from your or your family's collection. Be sure to find one that embodies contrasting elements. In a brief essay, examine the contrasting elements in the photograph. Keep in mind that since your readers have not been part of your family history, you must supply background information to create a context for the photograph.

CHAPTER 15

Cause and Effect: Exploring Reasons and Results

THE METHOD

As if driven by some deep curiosity, humans relentlessly ask questions and prowl for answers. Sometimes, the questions are philosophical and don't have clearcut answers. But more often, the questions are practical and often social—the kind that probe the commonplace mysteries we encounter daily. For instance:

- Why do criminals keep committing crimes?
- Why doesn't the government ban handgun sales?
- Why can't the common cold be cured?
- What will happen if the national debt increases?
- What would happen if illegal drugs were legalized?
- What happens to farmland after a flood?

Questions such as these lead to *cause and effect* analysis, a process for exploring relationships among events or conditions.

If you think of causes as *reasons* and effects as *results,* you will better understand cause and effect patterns. A *Why?* question leads you to seek reasons, and a *What?* question leads you to seek results. For example, if you were to ask *Why did homelessness dramatically increase during the 1980s?* you would search for the reasons—that is, the causes. But if you were to ask *What was government's response to homelessness?* you would search for the results—that is, the effects. Finally, if you were to ask this compound question—*Why did homelessness dramatically increase in the 1980s, and what was the government's response?*—you would analyze both the reasons and results—the causes and the effects.

A STUDENT ESSAY
DEVELOPED BY CAUSE AND EFFECT

Tom Kim wrote a cause and effect analysis in response to a sociology assignment that asked him to identify and analyze a campus problem:

Cause and Effect Essay Assignment

In a 900- to 1,000-word essay, identify a campuswide problem and explain why it is taking place and what will result from it. Consider these possible subjects:

- Services needed by returning students
- Inadequate library support
- Lack of health professionals on campus
- Increase in student cheating
- Sexual harassment
- Tension among ethnic groups
- Lack of competitive sports
- Increase in part-time faculty

Begin by establishing the problem; then analyze both its causes and its effects. To gain background information and perspective, I suggest you discuss the problem you select with the appropriate school officials, professors, and students.

Kim decided to write on the *increase in student cheating*. It had become widespread and school officials, professors, and students were concerned about it. Here's his essay:

Kim's title clearly announces subject.   Cheating: A Growing Campus Problem

Introduction provides background to establish that cheating is problem and to orient readers.

    Five years ago, according to student government records, four students were officially charged with cheating. Each incident took place in a large lecture class: two in Psychology 100, one in Art History, and one in Economics. All four incidents seemed to be spontaneous acts that involved copying answers from another student's answer sheet and were committed "because the opportunity presented itself." Last year, 206 cheating incidents were officially reported, a dramatic increase. Although most of these incidents took place in large lecture courses, many of them took place in smaller classes that require individual work.

Series of cheating incidents helps make problem specific.

For example, a biology instructor reported two students from different classes who turned in remarkably similar projects. Two advanced psychology professors reported several students for turning in case studies done by other students during previous semesters. Four English

1

professors reported students who plagiarized material from professional sources or submitted essays someone else had written. Perhaps a way to approach the problem is to ask, Why do students cheat? and What are the effects? Although the reasons for cheating are not easy to identify, the effects of cheating are clear.

By last sentence—
thesis sentence—
Kim's purpose is
clear.

The rise in cheating is often attributed to two immediate causes. First, in these difficult economic times, more and more students are working more hours a week but not cutting back on their course load. Currently, according to the campus records office, over 90 percent of our student body works at least 25 hours a week, but the average course load has not decreased. This fact suggests that students are trying to cram too much into their schedules. Once the semester is underway, they discover they must take shortcuts or drop classes. Cheating is an easy shortcut. A second reason students cheat may be because of pressure to attend graduate school. Although most students can pass their courses through their own efforts, a few believe they must earn A's to qualify for graduate programs. These students feel that cheating will give them the grade boost they need.

Topic sentence keeps readers on track; they should expect discussion of causes. Kim devotes this paragraph and next to causes.

Kim sets off causes with clear transitions.

A third reason is more remote and thus much less obvious to a casual observer. Cheating may have increased because a subculture of cheating has developed. When a student's friends cheat, then it is easier for him or her to cheat. Students in this subculture exchange test information, science projects, essays, and research papers. This material gets reworked and recycled from semester to semester. Rather than keeping their exploits as cheaters secret, they celebrate them, often bragging about their prowess and thus fueling the process from semester to semester.

First sentence clearly indicates emphasis will be on one cause. Notice that language becomes more vivid, emphasizing importance of cause.

Although the causes of cheating are difficult to identify, its immediate effects can be seen around campus. Large lecture class professors are taking new precautions. First, they are scrambling the questions on their tests, perhaps creating as many as five different tests for one class. Second, they are using more proctors to monitor the class during the examination. One professor had 10 proctors roaming the lecture hall while students took the test. Finally, professors are requiring students to check in to get copies of the test booklet. The proctors check their driver's licenses against the roster to be sure the enrolled student is actually taking the test. The ultimate result of this

Kim wants to keep readers focused, so he announces shift to effects. Notice that second sentence narrows emphasis to large lecture courses.

Kim presents three effects in climactic order—the most dramatic last.

2

3

4

intense security could be the creation of a "Big Brother" atmosphere in some classes--yet it all seems necessary.

Topic sentence shifts emphasis to composition courses. Kim makes sure readers know he's still revealing effects.

Extended example makes Kim's point.

The effect of cheating in composition classes is less dramatic but   5
equally significant. Many composition professors are assigning more inclass writing. Once the instructor becomes familiar with a student's writing ability, then spotting plagiarized or cribbed essays is easier. For instance, if a student consistently writes C papers in class and then begins to write A papers out of class, the instructor becomes suspicious. At this point, the instructor will usually meet in conference with the student to discuss the essay's subject and content. This discussion helps the instructor determine if the student actually wrote the essay or had someone else write it. One English professor said she had not uncovered any cheating but believed her diligence deterred it.

Topic sentence announces Kim will reveal two long-term effects of cheating.

Two other effects of cheating may ultimately damage students.   6
The first is obvious: Students who cheat will eventually reach a point where they are unable to cheat and will lack the fundamental skills for success in upper-division classes. Some people might say their failure is just retribution. How sad. Most students can be successful if they accept the challenge of education; those who cheat are hobbling themselves unnecessarily. A second effect could possibly make serious students victims of cheaters. Students who actually struggle with course content may receive lower grades than those who cheat. This fact is discouraging, especially for those who know that some students achieve higher grades dishonestly. As a result, some students have quietly reported cheaters. This, of course, may make honest students feel as if they are betraying their classmates, thus disrupting their sense of collegiality.

Also suggests that second effect will become cause in causal chain: Noncheaters will get angry and report cheaters, which will then make them feel guilty.

Kim begins conclusion by putting problem into perspective.

The number of students reported to be cheating is a mere fraction   7
of the 15,673 enrolled students. But campus officials believe a great deal of unreported cheating takes place. As a consequence, a committee composed of students, faculty, and campus administration is investigating cheating to develop campus guidelines to combat it. Aside from creating a more formal process to determine if a student has actually cheated, the committee is also developing a strategy to educate the entire student body about cheating and its effects on campus life. The strategy will include information that all students will receive and a detailed honor system that all professors will present the first day of classes. What will

Kim reveals campus-wide result: outcome of concern over cheating.

Kim closes on positive note: More members of college community are aware of cheating.

be the result of the committee's work? That is hard to predict, but the effort has already heightened student and faculty awareness.

Before writing, Kim discussed the problem of cheating with college officials, professors, and students. From those discussions, he developed his essay. He conceived an *objective* cause and effect analysis. Therefore, he didn't insert his own opinions or write from the first-person point of view, which he would have done in an essay based on personal experience.

Kim has arranged his essay effectively. Paragraph 1, the introduction, clearly identifies the problem. It first states the dramatic increase in the number of reported cheating incidents over the preceding two years. Moreover, Kim uses specific examples to support his observation. He ends the introduction with a clear statement of purpose that embodies his thesis. Summarized, the thesis states that Kim will explain the causes and effects of cheating on his campus.

Kim develops the discussion in paragraphs 2 through 6, exploring the causes in two of these paragraphs and the effects in three:

- *Paragraph 2* presents two causes: (1) Students working too many hours become desperate, and (2) students feel pressure to get high grades.

- *Paragraph 3* presents a third, less obvious cause: A subculture that supports cheating has developed.

- *Paragraph 4* shifts to the effects of cheating on large lecture courses: Professors are (1) scrambling tests, (2) using more proctors to monitor tests, and (3) having proctors check students' identities.

- *Paragraph 5* presents the effects on composition classes: (1) more in-class writing and more individual student/teacher conferences.

- *Paragraph 6* presents two long-term effects: (1) Students will reach a point where they can't cheat, and (2) students will report cheaters.

Paragraph 7, the conclusion, concentrates on what's being done—that is, on one more effect. A campuswide committee of officials, professors, and students is being formed. It will develop guidelines and disseminate information to the entire student body.

WRITING AN ESSAY
DEVELOPED BY CAUSE AND EFFECT

Revealing cause and effect relationships can be difficult because they are usually complex. For you to write a meaningful cause and effect analysis, you must go deeper than the obvious. Sometimes, you'll find that a cause will have many effects—ones that a quick glance will fail to reveal. Other times, you will find that cause and effect relationships occur in a sequence, such that each event contributes to the following event in what is often referred to as a *causal chain*.

A casual chain begins with a cause that triggers an event which in turn becomes the cause of another event. Writers often use a causal chain to arrange cause and effect paragraphs or entire essays, explaining both the causes and effects of a certain event.

In the following paragraph, Laura Topolte reveals the causal chain working behind the violent teenage encounters in her hometown:

> An adolescent ritual of manhood in Lakeview, my hometown of about 75,000 people, centers on Friday night violence among teenage boys. Parents usually explain the underlying cause of the violence by saying "boys will be boys," suggesting that their children are motivated by mysterious hormonal explosions beyond anyone's understanding. Though the actual details of these violent encounters may vary from one Friday night to another Friday night, the general pattern is always predictable. Typically, an encounter is set in motion during a sports event in which a team from Northwood High School opposes a team from South Hills High School. Since the competition between the two schools is strong both on and off the playing field, the sports event usually ends with the winners taunting the losers and the losers vowing revenge. The rowdier students often withdraw to beer parties where they continue to brag about the victory or threaten their arch rivals. As the parties become rowdy, the neighbors complain, and about midnight the police disperse the teenagers, ordering them to go home. Many do, but others gather at their favorite hangouts, Northwood's Taco Bell and South Hills' Denny's. Eventually, a boisterous group, usually the winners, will cruise the opposition's hangout and shout obscenities from their cars. The losers will typically respond with obscene gestures, climb into their cars and give chase. Eventually the two sides will meet up in a parking lot or community park where they call each other's manhood into question. The final result is several broken noses, skinned knuckles, and expensive dental bills--after all, "boys will be boys."

Note that Topolte's opening sentences provide background information and establish the paragraph's direction. Then, beginning with the word *Typically*, she outlines the chain of events that results in violence:

- Strong competition between the schools leads to verbal taunting.
- Emboldened by the taunting and fueled by beer, the boys' behavior grows rowdy.
- The rowdy behavior forces the police to break up the parties.
- Sent to the streets, a few boys invade their opponents' territory, and the night ends in a fight.

When revealing a causal chain, you must be aware of the *immediate* causes or effects, which are the ones occurring soon after an event, and the *remote* causes or effects, which are the ones occurring much later. In Topolte's paragraph, for example, the rivalry between Northwood and South Hills is the remote cause of Friday night violence, and the verbal and physical confrontations are the immediate effects. Topolte is also aware that a much more remote cause for the rivalry might be at work: unknown developmental or psychological forces that the parents dismiss by saying "boys will be boys."

Avoid Reasoning Errors

When revealing a cause and effect relationship, you should try to avoid a common fallacy called *false cause* or *post hoc*, short for the Latin phrase *post hoc, ergo propter hoc*, which means "after this, therefore because of this." A writer commits the false cause fallacy by offering the wrong reasons as the cause of an event. For example, it would be poor reasoning to claim that films and television crime shows cause the social violence that seems to be sweeping the United States. A deeper analysis would reveal several possible causes:

- Americans have easy access to guns.
- The high rate of domestic violence in the United States contributes to children's violent behavior.
- The rise of inner-city gangs generates violence, which some would say is the result of a grim economic future for minorities.

Moreover, there may be even deeper causes for the rise in violence:

- The American institutions that have provided social stability—such as courts, schools, and marriage—are breaking down.
- The United States has a history that condones violence, beginning with the destruction of the Native American culture during the westward expansion and continuing in more recent conflicts, such as the Vietnam War, the invasions of Granada and Panama, and Operation Desert Storm.

Clearly, the issue of social violence is much too complex to attribute to a single cause.

In a variation of the false cause fallacy, inexperienced writers sometimes confuse *chronology* with *causation*—that is, because one event takes place before another, the first event must cause the subsequent event. An obvious example of this kind of reasoning is superstition: A black cat crosses a superstitious mail carrier's path. Later that afternoon, the mail carrier loses his wallet. Conclusion: The black cat brought bad luck, which caused the loss. This is bad reasoning, but it does provide a simple explanation.

Now consider a more sophisticated example, one writers and filmmakers have taken seriously: President John Kennedy was assassinated in 1963. The Vietnam War, which some people claim Kennedy wanted to end, subsequently escalated under Lyndon Johnson's presidency. Kennedy's death therefore cleared the way for expansion of the war. In fact, many events and changes in government policy followed Kennedy's death. Were they all connected? Most likely, not.

You should keep in mind, though, that one event may indeed trigger subsequent events. For example, most political historians agree that the Watergate burglary ultimately led to President Richard Nixon's resignation. And while the burglary is a single cause, its connection to subsequent events is clear. Think of a sort of "domino" effect. You must be cautious, however, when linking chronological events in a causation pattern. If you doubt that one event actually caused another but wish to explore it, then offer it as a possibility, not a probability.

Another reasoning error some writers make is to confuse *process analysis* with *cause and effect analysis*. Process analysis usually stems from the question *How?* not *Why?* or *What?* For example, *How can the content of music lyrics be classified the way the content of films is classified?* leads to process analysis. *Why should music lyrics be classified by content?* leads to a discussion of causes, or reasons. *What are the consequences of classifying music lyrics by content?* leads to a discussion of effects, or results.

Distinguish Causes and Effects

While being careful to avoid committing an error in reasoning, you must also make clear distinctions between causes and effects. Experienced writers tend to distinguish them clearly in their essays, usually by concentrating on causes and effects in separate paragraphs.

Concentrating on Causes.   When an effect is obvious, the writer will concentrate on presenting the causes that led to it. For example, in 1996, Bill Clinton defeated Bob Dole for the presidency. A year earlier, political pundits were predicting a victory for the Republican Party candidate, who would be riding into office by exploiting Clinton's so-called character flaws. But the pundits were wrong—Clinton held the oval office, or as some would say, the Republicans lost it. Regardless, the question is *Why?* To answer the question *Why did the Republican Party lose the 1996 presidential election?* a writer would only examine the causes of the event (since the effect is clear—Dole's loss):

- Was it the nomination of a weak candidate, Bob Dole?
- His weak performance in the televised debates?
- His caustic humor?
- His age?
- His inability to create a viable agenda for America's future?
- Was it caused by billionaire Ross Perot's second maverick candidacy that distracted voters from Dole's candidacy?

These questions probing causes—and others like them—would have to be thoroughly explored. More than likely, the writer would discover a combination of causes on which to concentrate.

In the following paragraph from *The American Past,* historian Joseph Conlin concentrates only on the *causes* for the dollar becoming the basis of U.S. currency:

> Why did the dollar, a Spanish monetary unit, become the basis of American currency rather than the British pound sterling, to which the Americans were accustomed? In part, it was a reaction against all things British. More important, there was more Spanish than British coin circulating in the colonies and states in the late eighteenth century. The British paid in trade goods for the American products they purchased, and they preferred British coin for what they sold to the colonies. Pounds tended to flow back to Great Britain. But the colonists had a favorable balance of trade with Spanish America—selling more than they bought—so Spanish coin was comparatively abundant.

Study how Conlin structures this paragraph to make it easy for the reader to follow. In the first sentence, he establishes that he will explore the causes for the United State's adoption of the dollar, a Spanish monetary unit, rather than the British pound. He then presents three dominant reasons: (1) Early Americans disliked the British; (2) more Spanish money was circulating in the colonies; and (3) the colonies had a favorable balance of trade with Spanish America.

For complex subjects, writers may examine both *immediate causes* and *remote causes*—the causes that are most apparent and those that underlie them. To explore remote causes of an event or condition, you must first establish the effect to be explored; then, you must present the immediate cause, followed by the remote causes, thus deepening the analysis.

In the following paragraph from "Freedom, Control, and Success: Asia and America," James Fallows presents the remote causes for the general success of schools in industrialized Asian nations:

> The best-educated American children are a match for the best in Asia, but the average student in Japan, Korea, Singapore, or Taiwan does better in school than the average American. The fundamental reason, I think, is that average students in these countries come from families with two parents, one of whom concentrates most of her time and effort on helping her children through school. Limits on individual satisfaction undergird this educational achievement in two ways: The mother is discouraged from pursuing a career outside the house, and she and the father are discouraged from even thinking about divorce. The typical Asian marriage is not very romantic. In most countries arranged marriages are still common, and while extramarital affairs are at least as frequent as they are in the United States, they seem to cause less guilt. But because most husbands and wives expect less emotional fulfillment from marriage, very few marriages end in divorce. Individual satisfaction from marriage may be lower, but the society enjoys the advantages of having families that are intact.

First, Fallows establishes the condition: *Average Asian students do better in school than average American students.* He then presents the immediate cause of their success: *They come from two-parent households, in which the mother concentrates on the children's education.* Next, he explains the remote cause: *Asian couples expect less from their marriages, which keeps the divorce rate low.*

In his essay, Tom Kim devotes two paragraphs to revealing two immediate causes and one remote cause. As you reread these paragraphs, notice how Kim carefully guides the reader's attention. First, he announces that he will reveal two immediate causes in the first paragraph, and then, he distinguishes each cause with a clear transition. Finally, he announces that he will reveal a remote cause in the topic sentence of the second paragraph. Here are the paragraphs:

The rise in cheating is often attributed to two immediate causes. First, in these difficult economic times, more and more students are working more hours a week but not cutting back on their course load. Currently, according to the campus records office, over 90 percent of our student body works at least 25 hours a week, but the average course load has not decreased. This fact suggests that students are trying to cram too much into their schedules. Once the semester is underway, they discover they must take shortcuts or drop classes. Cheating is an easy shortcut. A second reason students cheat may be because of pressure to attend graduate school. Although most students can pass their courses through their own efforts, a few believe they must earn A's to qualify for graduate programs. These students feel that cheating will give them the grade boost they need.

A third reason is more remote and thus much less obvious to a casual observer. Cheating may have increased because a subculture of cheating has developed. When a student's friends cheat, then it is easier for him or her to cheat. Students in this subculture exchange test information, science projects, essays, and research papers. This material gets reworked and recycled from semester to semester. Rather than keeping their exploits as cheaters secret, they celebrate them, often bragging about their prowess and thus fueling the process from semester to semester.

By examining the immediate causes and the remote causes in separate paragraphs, Kim helps his readers keep them separate in their minds.

In sum, to concentrate on causes, structure your essay as follows:

- *Introduction:* Establish the obvious effect, and announce that you will be presenting its causes. Clearly state your thesis.
- *Discussion:* Discuss the causes in several paragraphs, using clear transitions to distinguish them:
  — Cause 1
  — Cause 2
  — Cause 3
- *Conclusion*

Concentrating on Effects.   When the causes of an event or circumstance are obvious, you should concentrate on the effects. For instance, some early rap artists glorified violence and female abuse. This fact is not hard to substantiate. It has been written about in newspapers and magazines and can easily be verified by looking at some rap lyrics. Rap lyrics are clearly a cause that must have some consequences.

If you were to explore rap, you could begin by asking *What are the consequences of violent and abusive rap music?* thus concentrating on the effects. You might narrow the analysis to the effects on young men living in inner cities, on whom rap seems to have the strongest influence. What is the effect of rap on their identity? On their attitude toward crime? On their attitude toward law enforcement? On their attitude toward women? No matter what direction the analysis might take, you would be concentrating on *effects*.

In the following paragraph, John Brooks concentrates on another aspect of modern life: the effects of the telephone. Notice that Brooks clearly announces that he will reveal the immediate effects of the telephone:

> What has the telephone done to us, or for us, in the hundred years of its existence? A few effects suggest themselves at once. It has saved lives by getting rapid word of illness, injury, or famine from remote places. By joining with the elevator to make possible the multistory residence or office building, it has made possible—for better or worse—the modern city. By bringing about a quantum leap in the speed and ease with which information moves from place to place, it has greatly accelerated the rate of scientific and technological change and growth in industry. Beyond doubt it has crippled if not killed the ancient art of letter writing. It has made living alone possible for persons with normal social impulses; by so doing, it has played a role in the greatest social changes of this century, the breakup of the multi-generational household. It has made waging war chillingly more efficient than formally. Perhaps (though not probably) it has prevented wars that might have arisen out of international misunderstanding caused by written communication. Or perhaps—again not probably—by magnifying and extending irrational personal conflicts based on voice contact, it has caused wars. Certainly it has extended the scope of human conflicts, since it impartially disseminates the useful knowledge of scientists and the babble of bores, the affection of the affectionate and the malice of the malicious.

After announcing he will reveal immediate effects in the opening sentence—*What has the telephone done to us, or for us, in the hundred years of its existence?*—Brooks then devotes most of the paragraph to a catalog of those effects. (See Chapter 13, p. 204, on catalogs.) And although most of the effects he presents would be generally accepted, he is quick to point out when he is speculating about a possible effect.

Tom Kim uses a similar approach when revealing the effects of cheating. The topic sentence of the following paragraph makes a connection to the previous paragraph and then announces that it will address the immediate effects of cheating. The second sentence then narrows the focus to the effects of cheating in large lecture classes. Look again at paragraph 4 of Kim's essay:

> Although the causes of cheating are difficult to identify, its immediate effects can be seen around campus. Large lecture-class professors are taking new precautions. First, they are scrambling the questions on their tests, perhaps creating as many as five different tests for one class. Second, they are

using more proctors to monitor the class during the examination. One professor had ten proctors roaming the lecture hall while students took the test. Finally, they are requiring students to "check in" to get copies of the test booklet. The proctors check their driver's licenses against the roster to be sure the enrolled student is actually taking the test. The ultimate result of this intense security could be the creation of a "Big Brother" atmosphere in some classes--yet it all seems necessary.

Kim clearly distinguishes one effect from another by using the transitions *first, second,* and *finally.* The paragraph gains intensity as it reveals one effect after the other—the last effect being the most vivid as well as a possible cause. Kim ends with a clincher: "yet it all seems necessary."

Most subjects require more than a catalog of effects. For complex subjects, writers must often present more detailed explanations. For example, in the following paragraph from "Acid Rain," Kelly Shea details the destructive effects of polluted rainfall:

> What are these effects? What do acids do to lakes, streams, and other substances? Acids have different effects on different materials. In the case of statues, monuments, and stone buildings, acids simply break down the composition of minerals—slowly, for certain, but there is a definite breakdown. If you pour soda onto a hard crust of bread, the crust will hold up for a while, but soon it will start to melt away and will eventually fall apart. Of course, the presence of buffers combats the destruction but if, somehow, the acids become stronger (or the buffers weaker), the defense will be less powerful. More immediately noticeable effects can be seen in aquatic and terrestrial environments. Acids can leach essential nutrients from lakes, streams, and soils. They can also increase the ability of toxic metals (lead and mercury, for example) to dissolve into a medium. When these metals are released into water, for example, they can cause pipes to corrode faster, fish to become contaminated and die, and plants to be destroyed. Whole habitats can be wiped out and have been. There are lakes in the Adirondacks which have become completely barren of all life due to the devastation of acid rain.

Shea creates a disturbing picture in describing the effects of acids on nature. Stone flaking away like bread crust in soda water and rivers, streams, and soils contaminated by toxic gunk—all the effects of toxic rain.

In sum, to concentrate on effects:

- *Introduction:* Establish the obvious cause, and announce that you will be presenting effects. Clearly state your thesis.
- *Discussion:* Discuss the effects in several paragraphs, using clear transitions to distinguish them:
  — Effect 1
  — Effect 2
  — Effect 3
- *Conclusion*

Concentrating on Causes and Effects. Sometimes, you'll discover that the causes and effects of an event or condition aren't clear. When this is the case, you must reveal *both* the causes and effects, either combining them in a single paragraph or separating them into two or more paragraphs.

In "Are the Homeless Crazy?" social critic Jonathan Kozol refutes the common misconception that people live on the streets because they are mentally unstable. In the following paragraph, he analyzes both causes and effects to support his contention that homelessness might actually cause mental instability:

> Even in those cases where mental instability is apparent, homelessness itself is often the precipitating factor. For example, many pregnant women without homes are denied prenatal care because they constantly travel from one shelter to another. Many are anemic. Many are denied essential dietary supplements by recent federal cuts. As a consequence, some of their children do not live to see their second year of life. Do these mothers sometimes show signs of stress? Do they appear disorganized, depressed, disordered? Frequently. They are immobilized by pain, traumatized by fear. So it is no surprise that when researchers enter the scene to ask them how they "feel," the resulting reports tell us that the homeless are emotionally unwell. The reports do not tell us that we have *made* these people ill. They do not tell us that illness is a natural response to intolerable conditions. Nor do they tell us of the strength and the resilience that so many of these people retain despite the miseries they must endure.

Kozol immediately establishes that the cause of homelessness is not always mental instability but homelessness itself. He then uses a typical example: pregnant women who lack medical care, which he establishes as a cause. Next, he presents the effects of that cause: anemia, poor diet, and the death of children. He concludes by presenting what he believes may be the actual cause of their illness: *a natural response to intolerable conditions.* Kozol's brief analysis is complex and passionate, challenging conventional conceptions by going beyond superficial analysis to an ultimate cause and its effects.

In sum, to concentrate on both causes and effects:

- *Introduction:* Establish that you will be discussing causes and effects. Clearly state your thesis.
- *Discussion:* Discuss the causes followed by the effects in several paragraphs with clear transitions to distinguish them:
  — Cause 1 and its effects
  — Cause 2 and its effects
  — Cause 3 and its effects
- *Conclusion*

Use Transitions

Readers can often lose their way in a cause and effect analysis. It is important, therefore, to use clear transitions when shifting from one cause to another, from one effect to another, and from causes to effects. Don't use only transitional words and phrases to guide your reader, but also identify whether you are revealing immediate or remote causes or effects. Of course, the more complicated your subject, the more you need such guiding words and phrases.

REVISING CAUSE AND EFFECT PARAGRAPHS

After Tom Kim completed a final draft of his essay, he set it aside for a day before rereading it. When he picked it up again, he could see paragraph 6 lacked clear transitions. He had not distinguished one effect from another. Moreover, he saw an opportunity to reveal a causal chain that possibly could develop from the second effect. Take a look at his revisions:

Two other effects of cheating may ultimately damage students. The first is obvious: Students who cheat will eventually reach a point where they are unable to

cheat and will lack the fundamental skills for success in upper-division classes.

Some people might say their failure is just retribution. How sad. Most students

can be successful if they accept the challenge of education; those who cheat

A second effect could possibly make serious students the victims of cheaters. are hobbling themselves unnecessarily. Students who actually struggle with

course content may receive lower grades than those who cheat. This fact is

discouraging, especially for those who know that some students achieve higher

grades dishonestly. *As a result, some students have quietly reported cheaters. This, of course, may make honest students feel as if they are betraying their classmates, thus disrupting their sense of collegiality.*

Kim rewrote the paragraph, carefully integrating these changes. When rereading it, notice how the opening sentence and two additional transitional sentences keep the reader oriented. They are small but important improvements. Also notice how Kim uses *could possibly make* and *may make* to qualify his observations:

Two other effects of cheating may ultimately damage students. The first is obvious: Students who cheat will eventually reach a point where they are unable to cheat and will lack the fundamental skills for success in upper-division classes. Some people might say their failure is just retribution. How sad. Most students can be successful if they accept the challenge of education; those who cheat are hobbling themselves unnecessarily. A second effect could possibly make serious students the victims of cheaters. Students who actually struggle with course content may receive lower grades than those who cheat. This fact is discouraging, especially for those who know that some students achieve higher grades dishonestly. As a result, some students have quietly reported cheaters. This, of course, may make honest students feel as if they are betraying their classmates, thus disrupting their sense of collegiality.

Guidelines for Writing Cause and Effect Essays

1. Select a subject that lends itself to cause and effect analysis. Use prewriting techniques to develop a list of causes, effects, or both.

2. Group the causes and effects identified in your prewritten material by importance. If appropriate, separate immediate causes from remote causes.

3. Decide on your approach to the subject. If the causes are clear, then concentrate on the effects; if the effects are clear, then concentrate on the causes; or concentrate on both the causes and effects.

4. With the general purpose of the essay in mind, write a tentative thesis that signals whether you will mainly emphasize causes, effects, or causes and effects. Determine which causes or effects should be developed in single paragraphs and which should be developed in two paragraphs. Then write the first draft.

5. Revise your essay, avoiding common errors in reasoning and clearly distinguishing between causes and effects.

Suggestions for Cause and Effect Essays

1. Respond to one of the following questions, concentrating on causes (reasons), effects (results), or both. If necessary, narrow the focus of the question so that it can be discussed within an essay of reasonable length. With your professor's agreement, you may also rewrite any of these questions or create your own subject to reflect your particular interests:

    a. Is relying on intuition an effective way to solve problems?
    b. What indirect effects has a historical figure had on your life—someone such as a political leader, an artist, or a philosopher?
    c. What effects has a significant public event had on your life?
    d. Why do some artistic works affect you?
    e. Why is a particular television show, song, or film popular or successful?
    f. What are the causes of a social phenomena such as homelessness, child abuse, or gang violence?
    g. What are the causes of a family, institutional, or social custom?
    h. Should children be treated like adults?
    i. Why does the burning of the American flag enrage many Americans?
    j. What effects does a particular advertisement attempt to create in the minds of consumers?

2. Discuss one of the following subjects in an essay using cause and effect analysis (or one of the two) as the dominant pattern:

a. Violence has always been a major element in action-oriented entertainment, featuring characters from Flash Gordon to Indiana Jones. In recent years, however, action-oriented children's television cartoons, such as *G.I. Joe* and *Rambo,* have been stripped of worthwhile storylines and characterizations. Now, the shows present unrelenting karate chopping and related mayhem and "us versus them" worlds with little or no complexity. Some experts and a growing number of parents are beginning to worry about the possible harmful effects these shows might have upon children.

In a cause and effect (or cause or effect) essay, reveal the possible influence of action-oriented cartoons on children.

b. Social observer and art critic Robert Hughes has written the following:

Since our newfound sensitivity decrees that only the victim shall be the hero, Americans start bawling for victim status. Hence the rise of cult therapies teaching that we are all the victims of our parents, that whatever our folly, venality or outright thuggishness, we are not to be blamed for it, since we come from "dysfunctional families." The airwaves are jammed with confessional shows in which a parade of citizens and their role models, from LaToya Jackson to Roseanne Arnold, rise to denounce the sins of their parents. The cult of the abused Inner Child has a very important use in modern America: it tells you that nothing is your fault, that personal grievance transcends political utterance.

Based on your experience, is Hughes's theory of a victim syndrome and the prevalence of dysfunctional families valid? Write an essay on one of the following:

- Assume that someone you know has chosen to see himself or herself as the victim of a dysfunctional family. Reveal the results of that assumption.
- Explain what you perceive Hughes means by *cult therapies.* Then reveal your perception of the effects of such therapies on patients.
- Hughes suggests that guests on confessional talk shows are becoming models for behavior. Reveal what you believe to be the causes of this phenomenon, and predict its effects.

c. Many people feel frustrated by the ongoing destruction of the earth's ecological system, which they see as being beyond their individual influence. For example, tropical rainforests—all located in a narrow range near the equator in Central and South America, Africa, and Asia—are being destroyed so fast that by this century's end, 80 percent will be gone. According to scientific estimates, in a typical 4 square miles of rainforest, there are over 750 species of trees, 1,500 different kinds of flowering plants, 125 different mammals, 400 kinds of birds, 100 kinds of reptiles, 60 different kinds of amphibians, and countless insects. Moreover, only 1 percent of these species will have been studied before they are lost forever. What can any single person do to resist this destruction?

Select one threat to the earth's ecological system. In an essay, describe the scope of that threat and reveal its projected effects. Then suggest actions that individuals can take to reverse the threat, although they may be far removed from the actual problem. Remember, concentrate on a single threat: Describe it; point out its effects; and suggest actions to reverse it.

d. American poet e. e. cummings has written, "To be nobody-but-yourself in a world which is doing its best, night and day, to make you everybody else—means to fight the hardest battle which any human being can fight."

Write an essay based on personal experience that reveals the causes of conformity and its effect on an individual.

e. Social critic Mark Kram uses the marble as a symbol of games children used to play. In the following excerpt, he laments the fact that today's children have lost touch with simple games that require more direct, tactile experience than present-day games:

> All of this brings us down to marbles, not the argot for brains but the real thing: perfectly round; so smooth; brilliantly colored; as precious to generations of children as any diamond. Has anyone seen a marble lately? Has anyone seen a marble in the hand of a kid? Most likely the answer is no, for the only things kids carry these days are transistor radios, slices of pizza and tickets to rock concerts. The marble belongs to a time that now seems otherworldly, when trees lined big city blocks as far as the eye could see, when barley soup was supper three times a week, when children had secret places.
>
> Schoolchildren used to survive the year by moving mysteriously through a cycle of ill-defined seasons—marble season, jacks season, mumblety-peg season, bottle-cap season—all without the aid of any adult direction or organization. Now, even the very young, boys and girls alike, get involved in soccer season, football season, basketball season, baseball season, camping organizations, and lessons of all kinds. Old-timers will tell you that something valuable has been lost because of all this organization, carried out under constant adult supervision.

Write an essay that reveals the effects specific games might have on a person's psyche. Contrast the effects of games children play today with those played in the past. Ask your parents or grandparents to describe the games they played. Can they identify any effects from playing them?

f. Education critic John Holt criticizes schools for humiliating children. He writes:

> From the very beginning of school we make books and reading a constant source of possible failure and public humiliation. When children are little, we make them read aloud, before the teacher and other children, so

that we can be sure they "know" all the words they are reading. This means that when they don't know a word, they are going to make a mistake, right in front of everyone. Instantly they are made to realize that they have done something wrong. Perhaps some of the other children will begin to wave their hands and say, "Ooooh! O-o-o-o!" Perhaps they will just giggle or nudge each other, or make a face. Perhaps the teacher will say, "Are you sure?" or ask someone else what he thinks. Or perhaps, if the teacher is kindly, she will just smile a sweet, sad smile—often one of the most painful punishments a child can suffer in school. In any case, the child who has made the mistake knows he has made it, and feels foolish, stupid, and ashamed, just as any of us would in his shoes.

Have you ever felt humiliated in a classroom? By a teacher? By classmates? Can you recall details of the experience and how you felt? Have incidents of this nature influenced how you feel about being in classrooms even now? How do you feel? Comfortable? Uneasy? If allowed your choice, where do you sit? Why? Do you prefer an active or passive role as a student in a classroom?

Write an essay based on personal experience that reveals the result of being humiliated in school. What were the causes of the humiliation and its effects, both immediate and remote?

3. Responding to a photograph: *A Woman*

Noted author Sharon Curtain has criticized American attitudes toward people who are growing old. In the following quotation, she expresses her own feeling about aging and projects those feelings to others:

I am afraid to grow old—we're all afraid. In fact, the fear of growing old is so great that every aged person is an insult and a threat to society. They remind us of our own death, that our body won't always remain smooth and responsive, but will someday betray us by aging, wrinkling, faltering, failing. The ideal way to age would be to grow slowly invisible, gradually disappearing, without causing worry or discomfort to the young. In some ways that does happen. Sitting in a small park across from a nursing home one day, I noticed that the young mothers and their children gathered on one side, and the old people from the home on the other. Whenever a youngster would run over to the "wrong" side, chasing a ball or just trying to cover all the available space, the old people would lean forward and smile. But before any communication could be established, the mother would come over, murmuring embarrassed apologies, and take her child to the "young" side.

Curtin's reflections on aging find a haunting expression in *A Woman*, which features an older woman with a photograph of herself when she was young. Drawing on Curtin's observations and elements in the photograph, compose an essay with cause and/or effect as the dominant development pattern. Before starting your project, review Guidelines for Writing Cause and Effect Essays (p. 239). Then select one of the following writing tasks as the basis for your essay:

a. Begin with the assertion that aging is the subject of *A Woman*. Review Curtin's reflection on aging and also study the photograph, allowing its imagery to work on your imagination. Identify an emotion the photograph creates. Then discuss the reasons the photograph has this effect.

b. Imagine you are a psychologist who shares Curtin's belief about growing old in our society. The young woman in *A Woman* is your client. She is beautiful, and because of her beauty, she has a deep fear of growing old. She asks what you believe the physical and social effects of growing old will be for her. You decide to be blunt and state your feelings as directly as possible, but you decide to do so in writing. First, describe her current beauty and relate the effects of her beauty on others. Then, describe her as she will appear 50 years in the future and what will result from growing old. Then give her positive advice on how to deal with the aging process, and predict the effects the advice will have on her twilight years, if she follows it.

CHAPTER 16

Process Analysis: Explaining Step by Step

THE METHOD

Are you, like many people, fascinated by how things work? Are you attracted to writing that explains how to organize your life and time? Perhaps you would like to understand how the stock market works or how Colombian drug producers smuggle cocaine into the United States. Perhaps your interests have to do with the human mind; if so, you might want to learn how psychotherapy works. Or maybe you just need to know how to use or fix something—say, your car or computer.

Authors of essays and books that explain how things work use *process analysis*. They help us better understand something by breaking it down into its component steps or parts.

Writers sometimes use a sentence or two of process analysis to develop a passage dominated by another purpose. For example, in *Psycho-Cybernetics*, Maxwell Maltz briefly mentions the scarring process—and how plastic surgeons avoid it—to set up an analogy on *emotional scarring*, which he develops after the following passage:

> I once had a patient ask me: "If the forming of scar tissue is a natural and automatic thing, why doesn't scar tissue form when a plastic surgeon makes an incision?"
>
> The answer is that if you cut your face and it "heals naturally," scar tissue will form, because there is a certain amount of tension in the wound and just underneath the wound which pulls the surface of the skin back, creating a "gap" so to speak, which is filled in by scar tissue. When a plastic surgeon operates, he not only pulls the skin together by sutures, he also cuts out a small amount of flesh underneath the skin so that there is no tension present. The incision heals smoothly, evenly and with no distorting surface scar.

Although such snippets of process analysis appear frequently in writing, it's more likely that process analysis will be used to develop an entire work. Take a look at the number of "how to" books in most bookstores, and you'll get a good idea of how common process analysis is.

A STUDENT ESSAY
DEVELOPED BY PROCESS ANALYSIS

Careful writers distinguish between two kinds of process analysis: directive and informative:

1. *Directive process* analysis explains how to do something. It's based on the assumption that someone will follow the directions step by step. Informative process analysis explains how something works, rather than how to do something.

2. *Informative process* analysis might explain how the brain functions, how gravity holds human beings to the face of the earth, or how food is grown, processed, and sold.

Process analysis is an important development pattern in the physical sciences and social sciences. In laboratory sciences, for instance, directive process analysis is often used to write reports that communicate the procedure in an experiment or research project. In courses such as geology, biology, cultural anthropology, and social psychology, informative process analysis is used to describe such subjects as the formation of mountains, photosynthesis, initiation ceremonies, and socialization.

John Barton was asked to write a process analysis essay in response to this assignment in psychology:

Process Analysis Essay Assignment

In 550 to 750 words, write an overview of a supplemental analytic practice that attempts to show family relationships. Your essay should give a clear impression of what is involved in the process and how it proceeds. Select one of the following:

a. Transactional analysis

b. Photoanalysis

c. Encounter sessions

d. Psychodrama

e. Hypnotherapy

f. Cognitive therapy

Barton selected item b, photoanalysis, a subject his lecturer covered only briefly. He immediately knew he would write an informative analysis, since therapists don't follow specific steps, only general procedures. Here's Barton's essay:

Friendly Smile, Clenched Fist

In first two sen-
tences, Barton estab-
lishes *photoanalysis*
as subject.

Although many critics of psychotherapy claim that the field is slow   1
to change, some new techniques are developing. One is photoanalysis.
No doubt you have heard that "A picture is worth a thousand words."

Well, photoanalysts would agree, but with a slight revision: "A family photo album is worth a thousand words." For example, a person might be aware that he has difficulty showing affection and expressing himself. After a session with a photoanalyst, usually a certified psychiatrist or psychologist, he could become aware that the difficulty is rooted in his family history. Instead of spending hours verbally exploring his family relationships, a client working with a photoanalyst would examine a family photo album, where the patterns of restraint might be documented in photographs.

Besides being trained as a therapist, a photoanalyst should also be sensitive to visual images and the nonverbal expressions they embody. But analyzing photographs to uncover family themes is not simple. The analyst should use group photographs taken over a number of years. A single photograph may whet curiosity but is no more helpful in unearthing patterns of family relationship than a crystal ball.

Most analysts begin by spreading the photographs on a table. Then the analyst will study the faces to determine the general tone of the relationships. Are the subjects looking at each other or at the camera? Are their expressions happy? Or severe? Or angry? Often a child's first impression of the world comes from his or her parents. Their expressions, captured in a series of photographs, may reveal their general perceptions.

Next, the analyst will study the body language of family members. Do they seem to interact with each other, or do they seem emotionally isolated from each other? Are they touching? Perhaps one has an arm around another's shoulder or a hand on another's leg. Is the hand open or clenched?

Finally, the analyst will also examine family members' proximity to each other. If they are close enough to rub elbows, they probably enjoy a warm relationship. If they put distance between themselves to avoid touching, they may shun intimacy with each other. What if males and females are clearly separated? Does this distance suggest that men and women play traditional roles within the family? An analyst will notice who takes the dominant place in the photographs. Mother? Father? A grandparent? Perhaps the children? Whoever takes a dominant place in a series of photographs probably takes the dominant role at home, as well. A parent who consistently gravitates toward one child in photographs

Marginal notes:

Barton gives example to show how photoanalysis can help in therapeutic situations.

By end of introduction, reader knows Barton will describe process of photoanalysis.

In this paragraph, Barton emphasizes what photographs are appropriate for analysis.

Barton begins to describe process. Notice how he works in related information.

Barton uses clear transition to show he has moved on to another phase of process.

In final phase, Barton gives plenty of related information to show kinds of questions photoanalysis might raise.

Paragraph numbers: 2, 3, 4, 5

might play favorites in family relationships. A person who always chooses to stand at the outside of the group might feel like an outsider.

In conclusion, Barton cautions readers about relying merely on interpretations of photographs. They are supplemental to patient's observations.

Throughout a photoanalysis session, the analyst should avoid narrow interpretations of the photographs but should offer observations for the client's response. After all, the client is the one with the direct experience and therefore should have the last word in interpreting any photograph. The photoanalyst must, however, point out that a friendly smile might be masking the tension revealed by a clenched fist half hidden in a lap.

6

In this brief informative analysis, Barton gives a great deal of information. He certainly meets the assignment's requirements. In less than 600 words, he shows what's involved in photoanalysis and how a therapist might proceed using the process. Moreover, Barton uses specific examples and details as opposed to abstract theory, which would have taken him away from his assigned task.

Barton's development strategy is straightforward. He launches into the subject with an introduction that presents the subject and establishes the purpose, though indirectly. He involves the reader by using an example that illustrates how photoanalysis might save time in uncovering personality problems.

Next, in paragraph 2, Barton specifies the training a photoanalyst should have and the materials necessary to conduct a photoanalysis session—mainly family photographs taken over a long period.

Paragraph 3 begins the description of the steps involved in the process. Since this is an informative process analysis, the steps reflect the chronological unfolding of the process. Paragraphs 4 and 5 continue discussing the steps. Throughout this sequence, Barton enriches his discussion by relating information, raising questions and supplying possible answers. He concludes the essay (paragraph 6) by informing the reader about mistakes photoanalysts might make.

In summary, Barton's strategy is to be direct and to the point. He doesn't get sidetracked by presenting the theory underlying photoanalysis; rather, he sticks to the task at hand. He arranges the information simply and presents it in plain language.

WRITING AN ESSAY DEVELOPED BY PROCESS ANALYSIS

In some ways, process analysis is similar to narration and cause and effect analysis in that it looks at a sequence of related events. However, narration is meant to tell a story, and cause and effect deals with the reasons for and results of an event or experience. Process analysis examines how something works. In short, remember that narration concentrates on *what* happens; cause and effect, on *why* it happens; and process analysis, on *how* it happens.

Determine the Appropriate Type of Analysis

Directive Process Analysis.   Directive process analysis can range from a brief instruction on a soup can label to a complicated plan for putting an astronaut on another planet. Keep in mind that directive process analysis has one clear purpose: to guide the reader to a predetermined goal by breaking down the steps required to get there.

Consider this paragraph from Tom Cuthberton's *Anybody's Bike Book,* which gives simple directions for checking bike tire pressure:

> There's a great *curb-edge test* you can do to make sure your tires are inflated just right. Rest the wheel on the edge of a curb or a stair so the bike sticks out into the street or path, perpendicular to the curb or stair edge. Get the wheel so you can push down on it at about a 45 degree angle from above the bike. Push hard on the handlebars or seat, depending on which wheel you're testing. The curb should flare the tire a bit but shouldn't push right through the tire and clunk against the rim. You want the tire to have a little give when you ride over chuckholes and rocks, in other words, but you don't want it so soft that you bottom out. If you are a hotshot who wants tires so hard that they don't have any give, you'll have to stick to riding on cleanswept Velodrome tracks, or watch very carefully for little sharp objects on the road. Or you'll have to get used to that sudden riding-on-the-rim feeling that follows the blowout of an overblown tire.

Cuthbertson's paragraph illustrates several characteristics of directive process analysis, whether a paragraph or essay:

1. He clearly establishes his purpose: *to explain how to test bike tires for proper inflation.*
2. He breaks down the process into simple steps and explains the final result: *The curb should flare the tire.*
3. Cuthbertson addresses the reader directly by using the second-person pronoun *you,* a practice that many writers adopt in directive process analysis: *There's a great curb-edge test* you *can do to make sure* your *tires are inflated just right.*
4. He alerts the reader to possible mistakes and their consequences. Notice that Cuthbertson states the consequences of having overinflated bike tires.

Now, consider this passage from *The New York Times Complete Manual of Home Repair,* in which Bernard Gladstone gives directions for building a fire. Notice that Gladstone's passage embodies most of the common characteristics of directive process analysis, but he chooses not to address the reader as *you.* Instead, he writes in the more impersonal passive voice, which seems to create a distance between the reader and the subject. See what you think:

> Though "experts" differ as to the best techniques to follow when building a fire, one generally accepted method consists of first laying a generous amount of crumpled newspaper on the hearth between the andirons. Kindling wood is then spread generously over this layer of newspaper and one of the thickest logs is placed across the back of the andirons. This should be as close to the back of the fireplace

as possible, but not quite touching it. A second log is then placed on top to form a sort of pyramid with air space between all logs so that flames can lick freely up between them.

A mistake frequently made is in building the fire too far forward so that the rear wall of the fireplace does not get properly heated. A heated back wall helps increase the draft and tends to suck smoke and flames rearward with less chance of sparks or smoke spurting out into the room.

Another common mistake often made by the inexperienced firetender is to try to build a fire with only one or two logs, instead of using at least three. A single log is difficult to ignite properly, and even two logs do not provide an efficient bed with adequate fuel-burning capacity.

Use of too many logs, on the other hand, is also a common fault and can prove hazardous. Building too big a fire can create more smoke and draft than the chimney can safely handle, increasing the possibility of sparks or smoke being thrown out into the room. For best results, the homeowner should start with three medium-size logs as described above, then add additional logs as needed if the fire is to be kept burning.

Like Cuthbertson, Gladstone opens by stating his purpose—that is, *to explain the steps necessary to build a fire in a fireplace.* He then follows with a series of steps—six in all—that are clearly written and easy to follow. After devoting one paragraph to directions for building a fire, he presents three common mistakes people make when building fires and their consequences—with one brief paragraph devoted to each mistake.

Although Gladstone's directions are longer than Cuthbertson's, both follow the same general pattern: They begin with a statement of purpose, then present the steps necessary to complete the process, and, as is often done in directive process analysis, they identify the common mistakes people make when following the procedure.

Informative Process Analysis.   Instead of guiding a reader through a series of directions to complete a task, as directive process analysis does, informative process analysis explains how something happens or how it works. In this paragraph from *How Do They Do That?* Caroline Sutton explains how stripes are put into striped toothpaste:

> Although it's intriguing to imagine the peppermint stripes neatly wound inside the tube, actually stripes don't go into the paste until it's on its way out. A small hollow tube, with slots running lengthwise, extends from the neck of the toothpaste tube back into the interior a short distance. When the toothpaste tube is filled, red paste—the striping material—is inserted first, thus filling the conical area around the hollow tube at the front. (It must not, however, reach beyond the point to which the hollow tube extends into the toothpaste tube.) The remainder of the dispenser is filled with the familiar white stuff. When you squeeze the toothpaste tube, pressure is applied to the white paste which in turn presses on the red paste at the head of the tube. The red then passes through the slots and onto the white, which is moving through the inserted tube—and which emerges with five red stripes.

Sutton doesn't expect any of her readers to make a tube of striped toothpaste, but she does answer a common question, one that might have aroused your curiosity, too: *How do they get the stripes into the tube?*

An informative process analysis is usually arranged in chronological order and makes careful use of transitional techniques to guide the reader through the process. Sometimes, the procedure is quite simple and easily organized in a step-by-step sequence. Often, however, the process is complex—such as a chemical reaction or human digestion—and challenges a writer's organizational skills, especially when the writer wishes to interrupt the explanation to add additional information or description.

For example, in *Oranges*, John McPhee devotes a paragraph to describing the process oranges undergo when made into concentrated juice. As you read McPhee's paragraph, notice that he interrupts his process analysis to bring in related information—first, to explain that oranges culled from the crop were once dumped in fields and eaten by cattle (thus accounting for the orangeade flavor of Florida milk), and second, to describe two kinds of juicing machines. He makes good use of clear transitional techniques, especially phrases that create a sense of movement, such as *As the fruit starts to move, Moving up a conveyor belt, When an orange tumbles in,* and finally, *As the jaws crush the outside.* Note these phrases as you read McPhee's paragraph:

> As the fruit starts to move along a concentrate plant's assembly line, it is first culled. In what some citrus people remember as "the old fresh-fruit days," before the Second World War, about forty per cent of all oranges grown in Florida were eliminated at packinghouses and dumped in fields. Florida milk tasted like orangeade. Now, with the exception of the split and rotten fruit, all of Florida's orange crop is used. Moving up a conveyor belt, oranges are scrubbed with detergent before they roll on into juicing machines. There are several kinds of juicing machines, and they are something to see. One is called the Brown Seven Hundred. Seven hundred oranges a minute go into it and are split and reamed on the same kind of rosettes that are in the centers of ordinary kitchen reamers. The rinds that come pelting out the bottom are integral halves, just like the rinds of oranges squeezed in a kitchen. Another machine is the Food Machinery Corporation's FMC In-line Extractor. It has a shining row of aluminum jaws, upper and lower, with shining aluminum teeth. When an orange tumbles in, the upper jaw comes crunching down on it while at the same time the orange is penetrated from below by a perforated steel tube. As the jaws crush the outside, the juice goes through the perforations in the tube and down into the plumbing of the concentrate plant. All in a second, the juice has been removed and the rind has been crushed and shredded beyond recognition.

Some processes defy chronological explanation because one or more of their stages take place simultaneously. In such a case, a writer must present the material in parallel stages, as McPhee does in the last three sentences of his paragraph, where he describes juicing. His use of transitional phrases clearly indicates that two or more interlocked events are taking place at once.

In a paragraph from "The Spider and the Wasp," zoologist Alexander Petrunkevitch presents the procedure a female *Pepsis* wasp follows when paralyzing a tarantula before burying it with a wasp egg attached to its belly. The challenge Petrunkevitch faced was to show the wasp's and the spider's simultaneous behavior:

> When the grave is finished, the wasp returns to the tarantula to complete her ghastly enterprise. First, she feels it all over once more with her antennae. Then her behavior becomes more aggressive. She bends her abdomen, protruding her stinger, and searches for the soft membrane at the point where the spider's legs join its body—the only spot where she can penetrate the horny skeleton. From time to time, as the exasperated spider slowly shifts ground, the wasp turns her back and slides along with the aid of her wings, trying to get under the tarantula for a shot at the vital spot. During all this maneuvering, which can last for several minutes, the tarantula makes no move to save itself. Finally the wasp corners it against some obstruction and grasps one of its legs in her powerful jaws. Now at last the harassed spider tries a desperate but vain defense. The two contestants roll over and over on the ground. It is a terrifying sight and the outcome is always the same. The wasp finally manages to thrust her sting into the soft spot and holds it there for a few seconds while she pumps in the poison. Almost immediately the tarantula falls paralyzed on its back. Its legs stop twitching; its heart stops beating. Yet it is not dead, as shown by the fact that if taken from the wasp it can be restored to some sensitivity by being kept in a moist chamber for several months.

Consider the Reader's Level of Knowledge

The success of a process analysis essay often rests on the writer's having clear information about the reader. Specifically, the writer must estimate how much knowledge about the process the reader may already have and how much additional information must be included in the essay. If the writer's guess is wildly inaccurate, then he or she will include too much information, which may send the reader into a fit of yawning, or too little, which may send the reader into an intellectual fog bank. Petrunkevitch seems to hit the mark, relying on common knowledge about wasps and tarantulas while weaving together the process of their deadly encounter.

Use Transitions

Transitional words that signal sequences are particularly important when writing a process analysis. They include such words as *first, second, third, next, then, finally, afterward, before, soon, later, meanwhile, subsequently, immediately, eventually,* and *now.* Of equal importance are words that signal clauses that show simultaneous processes, such as *as, while, during,* and *meanwhile.* When writing process analysis, you are guiding readers through a chronological sequence. Carefully using transitions is the most effective way to keep them on track.

REVISING PROCESS ANALYSIS PARAGRAPHS

When revising a process analysis essay, keep in mind that you should establish a purpose early and distinguish the steps in the process clearly.

In the first draft of "Friendly Smile, Clenched Fist," John Barton discovered he didn't mention his specific subject—*photoanalysis*—until the final sentence. Moreover, he decided his reader wouldn't need the background information in the opening paragraph. In fact, the information was misleading, perhaps indicating that a discussion of various psychological therapies would follow.

After studying the logical flow of the essay, Barton decided the best way to fix his essay was to delete most of the opening paragraph and move the purpose statement to the opening of paragraph 2, which he would join to paragraph 1 to create a new introductory paragraph. First, examine Barton's edits of his original opening paragraph:

~~Besides the major psychological therapies, such as psychoanalysis, analytical analysis, behaviorism, gestalt therapy, there are several supplemental practices therapists use that are effective in exploring certain aspects of character. For example, transactional analysis analyses psychological game playing, encounter sessions pit group members against each other and lets them confront one another. Psychodrama allows patients to act out their personal difficulties, and hypno therapy uses hypnotism to reveal a patient's concerns. A new supplemental therapy is currently proving to be very effective: photoanalysis, which follows a few simple procedures.~~

No doubt you have heard that "A picture is worth a thousand words." Well, photoanalysts would agree, but with a slight revision: "A family photo album is worth a thousand words." (Run in next ¶)

Although many critics of psychotherapy claim that the field is slow to change, some new techniques are developing. One is photoanalysis.

After these changes were incorporated, Barton's new introduction paragraph read as follows:

Although many critics of psychotherapy claim that the field is slow to change, some new techniques are developing. One is photoanalysis. No doubt you have heard that "A picture is worth a thousand words." Well, photoanalysts would agree, but with a slight revision: "A family photo album is worth a thousand words." For example, a person might be aware that he has difficulty showing affection and expressing himself. After a session with a photoanalyst, usually a certified psychiatrist or psychologist, he could become aware that the difficulty is rooted in his family history. Instead of spending hours verbally exploring his family relationships, a client working with a photoanalyst would examine a family photo album, where the patterns of restraint might be documented in photographs.

Remember, when writing a process analysis, keep your eye on the task: to describe how to do something or how something works. Don't include information that doesn't advance your purpose.

Guidelines for Writing Process Analysis Essays

1. Select a subject that lends itself to process analysis. Be sure your subject is fresh; in particular, avoid such common subjects as how to cook something, how to put together something, or how to find some place. Instead, look for something unusual—something from your own experience or research.

2. Decide if your analysis will be primarily directive, informative, or a little of each. Develop a list of steps necessary to complete the process, or develop a list of key elements necessary to explain the process.

3. Use prewriting techniques to generate information necessary to understand and follow each element of the analysis. Then arrange the information in the proper order: sequentially for directive analysis and chronologically for informative analysis.

4. Write your analysis. Carefully work in related information as necessary to explain each step. Remember that the reader will be expected to follow the procedure in directive analysis and understand the process in informative analysis.

5. Revise your analysis. Be sure your purpose is clear. Pay particular attention to the transitions; they should accurately guide the reader, showing connections to related information and delineating simultaneous events.

Suggestions for Process Analysis Essays

1. Use directive process analysis to develop one of these subjects (or one you create for yourself). Try to keep the focus on your experience. Explain the process one step at a time, and be sure to provide your reader with enough detail to make each step clear.

    a. How you have prepared a garden
    b. How you have lived without an automobile
    c. How you would domesticate a wild creature, such as a falcon or rabbit
    d. How you would get rid of pests without using poisons

   e. How you would prepare for an acting role

   f. How you show appreciation for others

   g. How you deal with telemarketers

   h. How you toss a Frisbee, football, baseball

   i. How you skateboard, Rollerblade, iceskate, or surf

   j. How you bluff at cards

   k. How you survive "muzak"

   l. How you complain effectively, get a grade changed, or get into a closed class

   m. How you overcome shyness

   n. How you write an effective essay or take effective notes

   o. How you use meditation

   p. How you outsmart a video game

   q. How you might survive a natural disaster, such as an earthquake or tornado

   r. How you cope with crowds

   s. How you ride a roller coaster

   t. How you attend a concert

   u. How you would campaign for political office

   v. How you win others to your point of view

   w. How you buy a used motorcycle or car

2. Use informative process analysis to develop one of these subjects (or one you create yourself). Remember that this technique doesn't explain how to do something but rather how something happens; it informs, often using narrative and descriptive techniques.

   a. How psychoanalysis works

   b. How secret codes are broken

   c. How detective, espionage, or suspense fiction creates involvement

   d. How past experience teaches life's lessons

   e. How a stroke, heart attack, or any such malady damages the body

   f. How Alzheimer's disease develops

   g. How dreams work

   h. How intuition works

   i. How good wine is tasted

   j. How classical music stimulates intellectual activity

   k. How frightening or suspenseful film scenes engage viewers

   l. How to collect art objects or rare books

   m. How lies are detected

   n. How guilt works

   o. How community thinking can be changed

   p. How being rejected changes people

   q. How being loved changes people

   r. How ideas become accepted

   s. How voodoo works

   t. How poems are interpreted

3. Responding to a photograph: *Scribbles*

For some writers, the act of writing can be so painful they go to remarkable lengths to postpone the labor. They travel to the farthest stationery store for the "right" pencil, the one with the exact texture of lead that works best with the amount of pressure they apply to the paper. When they return, they may discover that they are short of the right kind of paper—you know, the yellow pads with the blue lines. Again, back to the stationery store. Home once again, all those new pencils must be sharpened to a fine, very, very fine, point.

What's the solution to this kind of procrastination? There probably isn't one, for writing is a deeply personal process, one full of mystery. Probably no two people go about it exactly the same way. We all use devices to get ourselves started and to keep ourselves on task. Nevertheless, something must get written. We must get the images and thoughts out of our heads, translate them to words, and put them on paper. Then, of course, a new process begins—the revision process.

Clearly, the photograph *Scribbles* captures a moment in the writing process. For this essay, explore the writing process by completing one of the following writing tasks. Before beginning the task, reread Guidelines for Writing Process Analysis Essays (p. 253), to remind yourself of process analysis strategies.

a. Come up with another title for the photograph that you feel captures some part of the writing process. In your essay, account for all the elements in the photograph that relate to the writing process—manuscript, pencils, coffee, calendar, stapler, glasses, desk or table, even the writer's posture.

b. Document your own writing process with photographs of its various stages. Then use the photographs to compose a photoessay that concentrates on your own writing process. Use at least five photographs, each one capturing a stage in the process, and explain what the photographs signify. Keep in mind that writing is a highly personal process, so be sure your photographs and essay embody your personal writing quirks.

Classification and Division: Analyzing and Arranging Experience

THE METHOD

Pause for a moment. Imagine you have stepped into the Twilight Zone, that mysterious land where Rod Serling is host to those who journey into the macabre.

In this zone, you find yourself standing on Main Street in Small Town America somewhere in the Midwest, maybe Kansas or Nebraska. People from all walks of life are scurrying along the street. They smile and nod. They stop to chat. They pause to gaze at toasters and such in store windows. At first glance, you feel life here is normal. "People have typical pursuits," you decide, "just like at home."

But then you find that these twilight people have a strange quirk: They organize things in unfamiliar ways. Twilight supermarkets, for instance, group products within categories titled *appetizers, main courses, desserts, beverages, snacks,* and *clean up,* not by product type, like the supermarkets in your hometown. Twilight libraries group books by size, not subject. Twilight hospitals group patients by height, not illness. And twilight newspapers group stories by time, not significance.

You feel disoriented. "This is absolute madness," you think. "Although there might be a method to it, it's madness, nevertheless." You desperately seek an escape from the Twilight Zone. But how? There is no category labeled *exit*.

Farfetched? Of course. Even so, the tale illustrates an important point: Grouping things into predictable categories is fundamental to human thinking. If we didn't set up categories into which we can sort our experiences, the logical relationships that underlie critical thinking would break down, and, as a consequence, the world wouldn't make much sense. *Division* and *classification* are the mental processes we use to help make sense of our complex world.

Although classification and division are intellectual companions, they are not the same. When you *classify,* your thinking moves from the particular to the general. When you *divide,* your thinking begins with the general and moves to the particular. Is this still a little too abstract? Let's take a closer look from the perspective of everyday life.

Suppose you're walking your dog Muppy around your neighborhood. It's a dark night and late, much later than the time you usually walk Muppy. To make matters worse, you realize the streets are deserted when you hear a car approach from behind. You feel tense, so you pause to glance over your shoulder. You see a black and white sedan with lights on top. A police cruiser. You relax. But at that moment, another car makes a left at the corner. It's a station wagon—clearly, a family car. Next, a four-wheel drive pickup with oversize tires, chrome rims, and a roll bar speeds down the street, the engine echoing throughout the neighborhood. A teenager's car, you decide. Then slowly, out of the darkness, an ancient van drives your way. It's gray, mud speckled, and dented. There are no side windows, and the front windows are tinted very dark, as if the owner doesn't want anyone to see inside. You feel a little creepy. The last van you saw like this one was when you watched *Silence of the Lambs.* At this point you might wish that Muppy were bigger and had a loud bark instead of a yap.

By distinguishing the dominant characteristics of each vehicle, you were informally classifying them into categories: police, family, teen, and who knows what! Although writing an essay is more formal than random thinking, the conscious act of classifying experience is similar in the two. For example, in a paragraph from *How to Mark a Book,* philosopher Mortimer Adler identifies the distinguishing characteristics of book owners in order to sort them into three categories. While reading, notice that Adler includes the distinguishing characteristics of each category:

> There are three kinds of book owners. The first has all the standard sets of best-sellers—unread, untouched. (This deluded individual owns woodpulp and ink, not books.) The second has a great many books—a few of them read through, most of them dipped into, but all of them as clean and shiny as the day they were bought. (This person would probably like to make books his own, but is restrained by false respect for their physical appearance.) The third has a few books or many—every one of them dog-eared and dilapidated, shaken and loosened by continual use, marked and scribbled in from front to back. (This man owns books.)

Although Adler chooses not to, he could have named his categories, perhaps identifying *deluded, timid,* and *aggressive* book owners.

In contrast to classification, division (at least one kind of division) involves the opposite process—and this is a significant difference. To divide, you start with a general subject and then divide it into categories. For instance, you can easily divide the general subject *ways to travel* into three categories: *air, sea,* and *land.* Or you can divide the subject *ways to travel* by means of transportation: *plane, ship, train, automobile, foot,* and *beast of burden.* In addition, each of these categories can serve as a general category that you can subdivide in several different ways. For instance, you can divide *automobiles* into categories by *size, price, use, manufacturer,* and even *color.* You can divide the subcategory *beast of burden* into *horses, camels, elephants, donkeys,* and *mules.*

In the following paragraph from "Fans," sportswriter Paul Gallico divides the subject *sports crowd* into categories based on the sports events they attend:

> The fight crowd is the beast that lurks in the darkness behind the fringe of white light shed over the first six rows by the incandescents atop the ring, and is not trusted with pop bottles or other hardware. The tennis crowd is the pansy of all the great sports mobs and is always preening and shushing itself. The golf crowd is the most unwieldy and most sympathetic, and is the only horde given to mass production of that absurd noise written generally as "tsk, tsk, tsk, tsk," and made between tongue and teeth with head waggings to denote extreme commiseration. The baseball crowd is the most hysterical, the football crowd the best natured and the polo crowd the most aristocratic. Racing crowds are the most restless, wrestling crowds the most tolerant and soccer crowds the most easily incitable to riot and disorder. Every sports crowd takes on the characteristics of the individuals who compose it. Each has its particular note of hysteria, its own little cruelties, mannerisms, and bad mannerisms, its own code of sportsmanship and its own method of expressing its emotions.

Like Adler, Gallico also includes a distinguishing characteristic for each category, thus helping readers imagine the fans who would be grouped into each category.

You may develop a classification and division paragraph as part of an entire essay—perhaps only one or two paragraphs—much as Adler and Gallico did in the last two examples. More frequently, however, you will devote an entire essay to classification and division.

A STUDENT ESSAY DEVELOPED BY CLASSIFICATION AND DIVISION

For an assignment in cultural anthropology, Mark Freeman wrote a classification essay on the general topic of *people who collect artifacts from popular culture.* Here's the assignment:

Classification and Division Essay Assignment

From your own experience and observation, write a 500- to 600-word essay that classifies *collectors*—that is, people who collect such popular culture artifacts as baseball cards, garage sale paintings, bottles, magazines, movie posters, bottle caps, tourist novelties, campaign buttons, and celebrity autographs.

Concentrate on vertical as opposed to horizontal collectors—that is, those who collect one kind of artifact, rather than several different kinds.

Freeman selected the general subject *magazines* and quickly narrowed it to the more specific subject *comic books.* Since he was once an avid comic book collector, he had plenty of material to work with, which is clear from his essay:

In Search of the Comic

Freeman opens with sentence that immediately identifies subject: *comic book collectors.* Follows with generalized physical description of collectors.

Freeman's thesis statement identifies four categories of comic book collectors, which gives readers idea of how discussion will unfold.

Discussion is divided into four paragraphs, one devoted to each category. Each paragraph begins with opening that names category and identifies collector's outstanding characteristic.

Freeman also uses key word *searches* in each opening, which suggests quality they all share and unifies discussion paragraphs.

Notice how Freeman includes details throughout discussion that separate one group of collectors from others, impressing upon reader their distinguishing behaviors.

1   Comic book collectors represent every economic strata and often fit the stereotype of the computer nerd; that is, whether young or old, they tend to be pale, disheveled males who wear glasses and speak a language the uninitiated seldom understand. They can be found rummaging through pile after pile of unsorted, secondhand comics in magazine marts across the country. These collectors, the serious ones, can be classified into four major groups: Antiquarians, Mercenaries, Idolaters, and Compulsive Completers.

2   The Antiquarian searches for classic comics only; subject matter is of no concern. He is looking for a 1933 Funnies on Parade or Famous Funnies, the first publications that are recognizable as comic books and initially used as giveaways in advertising promotions. Driven by a desire to connect with the past, the Antiquarian will travel the country's backroads to find 1933 editions of The Spider, which was reintroduced as the Spiderman series in 1962.

3   The Mercenary searches for value. Certain numbers and titles ring a bell in his cash register brain and start him checking through a half-dozen price sheets. A pristine first edition of Action Comics (value $12,000) would suit him just fine. He would also hunt down early editions of Marvel Comics, especially the first publications featuring early superheroes, such as Captain America, the Punisher, and the Human Torch. The Mercenary would, no doubt, love to have first editions of Batman and Superman, but being a realist, he knows they are locked in vaults.

4   The Idolater has little interest in age or value. He searches for favorites: a Sheena, a Flash Gordon, or an Incredible Hulk. With little money to spend, the Idolater will usually be hiding in the corner of a comic mart, reading the comic books he cannot afford to buy. He will freely announce his dream of creating his own hero figure and is always eager to display his sketches to anyone willing to listen to his heroic tales and future visions. The Idolater will be the last one out of the mart at night and the first one back in the morning.

The most frustrated of the group is the Compulsive Completer. This   5
obsessed collector will examine and reject thousands of comics in a
search for a badly needed <u>Felix the Cat</u> to complete a year's set. The
Completer is usually a specialist, perhaps concentrating on comic books
featuring animals, such as Mighty Mouse, a pint-sized superior who
became famous when featured in cartoons shown between movies in
theaters across America, or Super Rabbit, a long-eared protector of the
innocent who became known during WWII for fighting Nazis in the pages
of Marvel Comics. Compulsive Completers often become so desperate to
acquire every issue published in one year they will seek bank loans to
cover their costs.

Although driven by different motivations, the Antiquarian,   6
Mercenary, Idolater, and Compulsive Completer share a common trait:
They love the thrill of the hunt.

Conclusion is brief but effectively ends essay. Freeman renames categories and characteristic that serves as underlying theme and unites them.

Freeman's essay clearly emphasizes classification. Although he divided the subject *comic book collectors* into four categories, he did so during the composing process by examining specific collectors to determine their distinguishing characteristics. Once he identified the distinguishing characteristics, he used them to create the categories into which *all* comic collectors could be sorted and grouped. In other words, his thinking moved from the specific to the general, thus emphasizing classification over division.

Freeman's development strategy is straightforward. It follows basic college essay structure:

- He uses the *introduction*—in fact, the opening sentences—to announce his subject: *comic book collectors*. He follows with background information by creating a stereotypical portrait of them—male, nerdish, and speaking a private language—and indicates where they hang out. He closes the introduction by making it absolutely clear that he is going to classify comic book collectors. Finally, for emphasis, he names the four categories.

- In the *discussion*—paragraphs 2 through 5—Freeman keeps his readers on track by using topic sentences that name the categories and identify the groups' distinguishing characteristics. He also uses a key word, *searches* or *search*, to unify the discussion paragraphs. He ends the discussion section by keeping to the principle that a discussion should end strong. Thus, he presents the most dramatic category last: the Compulsive Completer, the collector who is willing to plunge himself into debt to complete a comic book series.

- Freeman finishes with a brief *conclusion*—only one sentence. Here, he renames the categories and identifies a powerful motivation all comic book collectors share: *the thrill of the hunt*. Freeman's strategy in the conclusion is quite simple. Since this essay is short, he concludes it quickly, rather than risk tiring readers with a restatement of his main points.

WRITING AN ESSAY DEVELOPED BY CLASSIFICATION AND DIVISION

The simplest form of classification is two-part, often called *binary*, classification. This pattern divides a subject in half, usually into positive and negative or opposing categories, such as vegetarians and nonvegetarians, smokers and nonsmokers, television viewers and nontelevision viewers, deaf people and hearing people, and runners and nonrunners.

Because of its simplicity, two-part classification is often inexact and skirts the edge of comparison and contrast. When you divide a subject, you will usually have several categories that are mutually exclusive.

Create Categories

Most subjects can be divided in a number of ways, depending on the writer's purpose. For example, consider the subject *college students*. For statistical purposes, a college registrar might group college students by their demographic profile: *age, sex, race,* and *region*. An art teacher, might group students by their talent: *painter, sculptor, ceramist, illustrator,* and *print maker*. A political science teacher might group students by their politics: *reactionary, conservative, liberal,* or *radical*.

The actual categories themselves should meet two criteria: They must be consistent and complete. For example, Mark Freeman created four separate categories of comic book collectors: *Antiquarian, Mercenary, Idolater,* and *Compulsive Completer*. At times, however, it seems that collectors might spill from one category into another, thus creating the problem of inconsistency. For instance, why couldn't people who collect for investment reasons (Mercenaries) also pursue their favorites (Idolaters)? In fact, they could. Freeman avoids inconsistency, however, by classifying his collectors according to one dominant characteristic and then identifies specific behaviors that result.

Do Freeman's categories provide for *everyone* who might collect comic books—that is, are they complete? What about another category, such as *Explorers*, the kids who buy comics on impulse, read them once, and then toss them aside or pass them on to friends? But Explorers are not collectors; they're browsers. And even though browsing might be the first step toward collecting, it should not comprise a separate category for collectors.

Like Freeman, you must analyze your subject for qualities that components share and don't share. Using these qualities, you can create categories and then sort through the various components to place each in the appropriate category. You must be logical, sorting and grouping items in a consistent manner. You must also make sure your categories don't overlap. For example, to classify a group of congresswomen as *Republicans, Democrats,* and *politicians* wouldn't make much sense; they're all *politicians.*

Arrange and Label Categories

Careful writers arrange their classifications in a straightforward division, usually in blocks and according to the order that seems most appropriate. Each block is a subclass and will usually be identified by a name or phrase to keep the reader on track.

In the following paragraph, anthropologist Ruth Benedict divides the ceremonial societies of the Zuni. She clearly identifies each society—the priestly societies, the masked-god societies, and the medicine societies—before describing them:

> This ceremonial life that preoccupies Zuni attention is organized like a series of interlocking wheels. The priesthoods have their sacred objects, their retreats, their dances, their prayers; and their year-long program is annually initiated by the great winter solstice ceremony that makes use of all the different groups and sacred things and focuses all their functions. The tribal masked-god society has similar possessions and calendric observances, and these culminate in the great winter tribal masked god ceremony, the Shalkado. In like fashion the medicine societies, with their special relation to curing, function throughout the year and have their annual culminating ceremony for tribal health.

These three major cults of Zuni ceremonial life are not mutually exclusive. That is, a man may be—and often is, for the greater part of his life—a member of all three. These cults each give the individual sacred possessions to live by and demand of him exacting ceremonial knowledge.

Writers may identify their categories by using ready-made labels or by creating their own. In the next classification passage, from *Blood and Money,* Thomas Thompson uses subclasses to present his view of the personal characteristics that describe *surgeons:*

> Among those who train students to become doctors, it is said that surgeons find their niche in accordance with their personal characteristics. The orthopedic surgeon is medicine's carpenter—up to his elbows in plaster of Paris—and tradition holds that he is a gruff, slapdash sort of man whose labor is in a very physical area of healing. Away from the hospital, the orthopedists are often hunters, boaters, outdoorsmen.
>
> The neurosurgeon, classically, does not get too involved with his patients. Or, for that matter, with anybody. They are cool men, blunted, rarely gregarious.
>
> Heart surgeons are thundering egotists, star performers in a dazzling operating theater packed with assistants, nurses, paramedics, and a battery of futuristic equipment which could seemingly lift the room into outer space. These are men who relish drama, who live life on the edge of the precipice.
>
> And the plastic surgeon? He is, by nature, a man of art, and temperament, and sensitivity. "We are the artists who deal in beauty lost, or beauty that never was," said one plastic man at a national convention. Our stitches are hidden, and so are our emotions."

Because Thompson is working with established categories, part of his task is to make his material fresh. Most readers know the professional qualities of surgeons, and so Thompson creates a sense of the person holding the scalpel by including descriptive details of each type's dominant personality trait.

In the next paragraph, novelist Larry McMurtry uses established categories in a slightly different way. He classifies *beer bars* in the city of Houston according to their locations: *East side, West side,* and *North side:*

> The poor have beer bars, hundreds of them, seldom fancy but reliably dim and cool. Most of them are equipped, with jukeboxes, shuffleboards, jars of pigs feet and talkative drunks. There are lots of bar burlesques, where from 3 p.m. on girls gyrate at one's elbow with varying degrees of grace. On the East side there are a fair number of open-air bars—those who like to watch the traffic can sit, drink Pearl, observe the wrecks, and listen to "Hello, Vietnam" on the juke box. Louisiana is just down the road, and a lot of the men wear Cajun sideburns and leave their shirttails out. On the West side cowboys are common. Members of the cross continental hitch-hiking set congregate on Franklin Street, at places like The Breaking Point Lounge. Symbolic Latinos slip over to the Last Concert on the North side; or, if they are especially bold, go all the way to McCarthy Street, where one can view the most extraordinary example of Mexican saloon-and-whorehouse architecture north of the border.

McMurtry opens with a general description of Houston beer bars: They are dim and cool with jukeboxes, shuffleboards, jars of pig's feet, and drunks—watering holes for blue-collar men. After rendering the general qualities of these bars, McMurtry presents the geographic categories, each with a brief description that characterizes it.

Writers often classify a subject that has no ready-made categories. They must, therefore, create their own categories and the labels that identify them. In this paragraph from "Here Is New York," E. B. White divides the *population of New York* into three categories according to a person's relation to the city:

> There are roughly three New Yorks. There is, first, the New York of the man or woman who was born here, who takes the city for granted and accepts its size and its turbulence as natural and inevitable. Second, there is the New York of the commuter—the city that is devoured by locusts each day and spat out each night. Third, there is the New York of the quest of something. Of these three trembling cities the greatest is the last—the city of final destination, the city that is a goal. It is this third city that accounts for New York's high-strung disposition, its poetical deportment, its dedication to the arts, and its incomparable achievements. Commuters give the city its tidal restlessness; natives give it solidarity and continuity; but the settlers give it passion. And whether it is a farmer arriving from Italy to set up a small grocery store in a slum, or a young girl moving from a small town in Mississippi to escape the indignity of being observed by her neighbors, or a boy arriving from the Corn Belt with a manuscript in his suitcase and a pain in his heart, it makes no difference: each embraces New York with the intense excitement of first love, each absorbs New York with the fresh eyes of an adventurer, each generates heat and light to dwarf the Consolidated Edison Company.

Commuters, *natives*, and *settlers*—these are White's three categories. He uses each to present characteristics of New York City. The *commuter* gives the city a sense of restlessness; the *native* gives it solidarity; and the *settler*, the category he emphasizes, gives it passion.

Use Transitions

It's important to highlight classification categories to keep readers on track. The most effective way is to name the categories and then indicate to your reader when you have finished explaining one category and are moving on to explain another. In essays where one paragraph is devoted to a single category, the task is easy: Merely identify each category in the topic sentence. But in a single paragraph devoted to classification, you must keep readers on tract by carefully stating the number of categories you've created and by listing each one.

Maryna Mannes uses this strategy in the following paragraph, which criticizes the way television commercials distort the image of women:

> In the guise of what they consider comedy, the producers of television commercials have created a loathsome gallery of men and women patterned, presumably, on Mr. and Mrs. America. Women liberationists have a major target in the commercial image of women flashed hourly and daily to the vast majority. There are, indeed, only four kinds of females in this relentless sales procession: the gorgeous teenage swinger with bouncing locks; the young mother teaching her baby girl the right soap for skin care; the middle-aged housewife with a voice like a power saw; and the old lady with dentures and irregularity. All these women, to be sure, exist. But between the swinging sex object and the constipated granny there are millions of females never shown in commercials. There are—married or single— intelligent, sensitive women who bring charm to their homes, who work at jobs as well as lend grace to their marriage, who support themselves, who have talents or hobbies or commitments, or who are skilled at their professions.

This strategy is especially effective when the list is set up by a colon, thus announcing that the categories will follow. Note how Mannes does this in her third sentence (highlighted above).

REVISING CLASSIFICATION AND DIVISION PARAGRAPHS

When rereading an early draft, Freeman decided the essay had two weaknesses: overwritten topic sentences and not enough references to specific comics and comic book characters. For example, in an early draft, the topic sentence of paragraph 3 read as follows:

The Mercenary is a collector who wants full value for his money and will examine price sheets to be sure he gets it.

Freeman felt the Mercenary's key characteristic was lost in the loose language. As a result, the sentence might misdirect his readers. He decided to revise the topic sentence so it would be as direct as he could make it:

> The Mercenary searches for value.

Now, the sentence is clear and to the point. Freeman revised each of the topic sentences using this strategy. But then, he found that having four such direct topic sentences seemed too mechanical, so he revised them again. For example, he first revised the topic sentence of paragraph 4 to read as follows:

> The Idolater searches for favorites.

Then, for the third time, Freeman recast it. This time, he wrote two sentences: one to serve as a transition into the paragraph by referring to the preceding categories and another to identify the Idolater's chief characteristic. The second sentence also addressed Freeman's other concern, which was the lack of specific references to comic book characters. Here are the new sentences:

> The Idolater has little interest in age or value. He searches for favorites: a Sheena, a Flash Gordon, or an Incredible Hulk.

For the last phase of the revision, Freeman began to insert even more references to specific comics and characters, which he felt would give the non-collecting reader a sense of the comic book world. For example, study this edited draft of paragraph 3:

The Mercenary searches for value. Certain numbers and titles ring a bell ^in his cash register brain and start him checking through a half-dozen price sheets. A pristine first edition ^of Action Comics (value $12,000) would suit him just fine. ~~These might be first~~ editions ^He would also hunt down early editions ^especially the first publications of Marvel Comics, ~~often~~ featuring early superheroes. ~~Being a realist, the~~ ~~Mercenary would~~ ~~realize that the early published exploits of popular heroes are~~ ~~now already owned.~~ , no doubt, love to have first editions of Batman and Superman, but being a realist, he knows they are locked in vaults.

such as Captain America, the Punisher, and the Human Torch. The

Once Freeman finished editing the paragraph, he retyped the new version, polishing it as he went. Study the differences, including how adding specific detail enlivens the writing:

> The Mercenary searches for value. Certain numbers and titles ring a bell in his cash register brain and start him checking through a half-dozen price sheets. A pristine first edition of Action Comics (value $12,000) would suit him just fine. He would also hunt down early editions of Marvel Comics, especially

the first publications featuring early superheroes, such as Captain America, the Punisher, and the Human Torch. The Mercenary would, no doubt, love to have first editions of Batman and Superman, but being a realist, he knows they are locked in vaults.

Guidelines for Writing Classification and Division Essays

1. Select a subject that can be divided into at least three components. Identify the chief characteristics of each, and then use the characteristics to sort and group the components into categories.

2. Examine the categories with two questions in mind: Are they complete—that is, can all the components of your subject be grouped within them? Are the categories consistent—that is, can any of your component parts be classified in more than one category? If your categories are incomplete or inconsistent, then restructure them or move on to another subject.

3. Compose a thesis that clearly indicates you'll be classifying your subject. Whether you use ready-made categories or name your own categories, include the names as part of the thesis. Naming your categories early will prepare your readers for the shift from one category to another in the discussion.

4. Decide how to arrange your categories effectively, saving the most dramatic for last.

5. Revise your essay, making sure that each category is clearly distinguished and adequately developed.

Suggestions for Classification and Division Essays

1. Choose one of the following subjects, and write an essay using division as the dominant pattern. Describe each component in some detail, distinguishing it from the other components. Keep your readers in mind by leading them carefully from component to component.
   a. A musical performance
   b. A board game, like chess, Monopoly, Risk, or Clue
   c. The human mind
   d. A ceremonial event, such as a wedding, funeral, campaign rally, banquet, or religious service
   e. A week at a teenage vacation spot
   f. A novel
   g. A police drama, situation comedy, or national news broadcast
   h. Your monthly budget
   i. Bargaining in a foreign marketplace
   j. A meal in an expensive restaurant

2. Write an essay using classification as the dominant development method. Sort one of the following subjects into categories. Be sure the basis of your

classification is clear. To direct reader attention, make up names for each category.

   a. The books, records, and/or videotapes you own
   b. Unusual sports that are seldom televised or reported in newspapers
   c. Talk show hosts
   d. "War" toys, family-oriented toys, or intellectual toys
   e. People who like to hunt
   f. Lies
   g. Ways to read a novel or poem
   h. Ways to watch a horror movie
   i. Kinds of photography
   j. Attitudes revealed by bumper stickers
   k. Trends in dating, marriage, or divorce
   l. Kinds of terror
   m. Responses to a dramatic national or international event
   n. New ways to learn
   o. Kinds of good or bad luck

3. Responding to a photograph: *Veterans Day*

Humans are social beings. We form groups and subgroups for a variety of purposes—social, economic, vocational, political.

Some of these groups are informal and temporary: a study group for the final exam, a tour group to a vacation spot, an ad hoc committee to support a municipal bond issue. Others are more formal and longer lasting, binding the common interests of large numbers of people across geographic and generational lines.

Why do we join groups? What do we expect our membership in groups to accomplish for us or for others? Do groups provide us with a sense of identity? Self-worth? Undoubtedly, the reasons vary from one individual to another.

The photograph *Veterans Day* shows two members of a veterans group posing in uniform, with an American flag unobtrusively in the background. Their stance, legs apart and feet planted firmly, gives solidity to their figures, which is tempered by the warmth of their smiles. They look content, happy, and proud. Clearly, each has found some satisfaction in belonging to this organization.

We might wonder, though, if the satisfaction of membership or the reason for joining this organization is the same for the woman as for the man. Wearing their uniforms and standing in the noonday sun, they represent the values of the veterans organization. But as individuals, their motivations for being here are personal—products of their own backgrounds and experiences.

After reviewing Guidelines for Writing Classification and Division Essays (p. 267), complete one of the following writing tasks:

a. Write a division essay that considers the woman and the man in the photograph separately. For each, describe the physical appearance. Determine what you believe are possible motivations for joining the armed services and later, a veterans organization. What do you imagine the service experience of each person was like? What would the veterans organization represent to each? What satisfactions would each receive from membership? One caution: Since there are only the two figures prominent in the picture, this will be a binary division. Don't slip into comparison and contrast, but profile the woman and the man separately.

b. Write a classification essay that presents categories of people of similar age: children, youth, young adults, older adults, and seniors. Find at least five photographs of people of one age group in social situations. Describe the people in each photograph as representatives of their age group. Discuss the characteristics of each category. Include the pictures when submitting your final draft.

CHAPTER 18

Definition: Creating Impressions

THE METHOD

You've heard the rhyme about the oversized egg Humpty Dumpty, haven't you?

Humpty Dumpty sat on a wall
Humpty Dumpty had a great fall
All the king's horses
   and all the king's men
Couldn't put Humpty Dumpty
   back together again.

Humpty makes a brief appearance in Lewis Carroll's sequel to *Alice in Wonderland,* a nineteenth-century literary spoof on society and human logic. But he's much more than a clumsy egg who can't stay balanced on a wall; he's a cantankerous egg who challenges how humans think.

During a conversation with Alice, the child who travels through this topsy-turvy world, Humpty maintains that he can make words mean what he wants them to mean. For example, in Humpty's lexicon, the word *glory* means "there's a nice knock-down argument for you." *Impenetrability* means "that we've had enough of that subject, and it would be just as well if you'd mention what you mean to do next, as I suppose you don't mean to stop here all the rest of your life."

Behind Humpty's argument is the claim that the meanings of words are arbitrary. For example, consider the words *perro, chien,* and *sobaka. Perro* is Spanish, *chien* is French, and *sobaka* is Russian. All refer to the same thing: "a dog." But if you were to ask a Mexico City resident who doesn't speak English "Donde esta mi *dog?*" you might get a quizzical stare, but you wouldn't find your dog. There is no inherent reason Spanish speakers use *perro* to refer to what some think is "humanity's best friend." It's just what Spanish speakers do because that's the way they've learned to say *dog.*

On one level, Humpty is right: Words have no inherent meanings. They only mean what people accept as their meanings. But on another level, Humpty is wrong: If each of us created our own word meanings, separate from commonly accepted ones, then we would be grunting and groaning at each other, not communicating—at least not until everyone agreed on new meanings or reverted to the old ones.

But Humpty's argument puzzles Alice. She questions whether he "can make words mean so many different things."

Humpty replies, "The question is . . . which is to be master—that's all." His comment embodies a significant insight into words.

How many words do you hear a day. A thousand? Ten thousand? Hundreds of thousands? Spoken words are plentiful. They are easy to produce: Just open your mouth, activate your larynx, wag your tongue, and words will take flight. If you have any doubts, turn your radio dial to a talk show and listen to the relentless babble. Even though spoken words are often thoughtlessly strung together, you understand them—or do you?

For example, the meanings of such words as *dog, cat, mother, father,* and *house* are relatively clear. They refer to specific things. You can walk around your neighborhood and point to them. But the meanings of such words as *love, hate, honor, freedom, justice, right,* and *wrong* are not so clear. In fact, they are downright ambiguous. They refer to abstract concepts. You can't point to them. You can't draw them. They must be explained using other words. Abstract words are pretty slippery because their meanings seem to change from group to group and from person to person. Sometimes trying to hold onto their meanings is like trying to grip a wet trout taken from a mountain stream.

If someone says "Government is controlling people's lives," you might nod your head yes, especially if you just spent hours filling out forms for a college loan. But if you reflect for a moment, you will realize that what *government* and *control* mean to you might not be what the speaker has in mind. What government is he referring to? Perhaps city government? State government? Federal government? Moreover, what is *government?* The elected officials who serve in the House of Representatives? The Senate? The president? More than likely, the *government* the speaker refers to will become a little clearer when considered in the discussion's context—*big government.* Does *big government* actually control anyone's life? Does it even exist as a single-minded entity?

So, Humpty Dumpty is right again. Because abstract concepts are so slippery, people must become their "masters" or risk failing to communicate their thoughts accurately and honestly.

Written language is held to a higher standard of accuracy than spoken language. Serious writers select their words with care. Some words are so technical that only specially trained writers use them accurately. And some words are so rarely used that few writers know what they mean. Some, especially abstract words, have meanings so ambiguous that readers understand them differently. It is important, then, that writers nail down the meanings of key terms they use by defining them. If a word is highly abstract, its meaning might be highly personal. In these cases, writers do their best to create impressions of what words mean to them.

For example, in "Higher Education and Home Defense," essayist and poet Windell Berry creates an impression of what he means by *education*. You might disagree with Berry, but at least you know what he means when he uses this word:

> Education in the true sense, of course, is an enablement to *serve*—both the living human community in its natural household or neighborhood and the precious cultural possessions that the living community inherits or should inherit. To educate is, literally, to "bring up," to bring young people to a responsible maturity, to help them to be good caretakers of what they have been given, to help them to be charitable toward fellow creatures. Such an education is obviously pleasant and useful to have; that a sizable number of humans should have it is probably also one of the necessities of human life in this world. And if this education is to be used well, it is obvious that it must be used some where; it must be used where one lives, where one intends to continue to live; it must be brought home.

Education, for Berry, leads to selfless community service. He anticipates that readers might not think of education the way he does. So he defines it to eliminate any confusion his usage might cause. Once he's defined *education* in this way, readers know what he means each time he refers to it in his essay.

A STUDENT ESSAY
DEVELOPED BY DEFINITION

Often, a concept will be so complex writers will define it in a full essay. For example, in response to a freshman composition assignment, Chris Schneider devoted an entire essay to the definition of *myth*. Her understanding of *myth* came from a cultural studies class, where the word was being used in a new way, one that went beyond the common meaning of "story" or "tale." Here's the specific assignment:

Definition Essay Assignment

Use definition to develop any of the following topics in 500 to 600 words. You may use any number of paragraph development patterns—such as description, example, and comparison—to develop your definition.

a. Commonsense
b. Code
c. Myth
d. Symbol
e. Sign
f. Saga
g. Tale
h. Legend

Keep in mind that an effective definition does not merely restate the dictionary definition. It creates a clear impression, showing the concept behind the term from several different angles.

Schneider wrote the following essay, defining the word *myth* in several ways:

Myth Redefined

Schneider uses catalog of questions to present common social myths.

Thesis statement implies that perceptions are influenced by common *myths,* which is term to be defined.

Do you believe childhood is a time of innocence separated from the emotions and cares of the adult world? Do you count on science to solve the dangers of fossil fuel shortage, ozone depletion, and toxic pollution? Do you feel men are rational and women are intuitive? Men are active; women, passive? Men are ambitious; women, nurturing? If you do, then your perceptions have been influenced by common American <u>myths</u>, as a group of contemporary scholars and social critics known as semiologists would define these beliefs.

1

Topic sentence establishes *semiologists* as paragraph's subject. Schneider uses explanation of semiologists to begin to show what *myth* means; contrasts with *semanticists.*

<u>Semiologists</u> are interested in the study of meaning. They don't limit themselves to the meanings of words. This territory belongs to the <u>semanticist</u>--that is, to those scholars who concentrate on linguistic significance. Semiologists may examine words, but they also explore the ways that advertisements, television programs, films, clothes, toys, and other such things embody meaning, a kind of cultural meaning that semiologists sometimes refer to as <u>myth</u>.

2

Opening sentence leads into discussion of general category *myth* falls into. Notice how last sentence leads into next paragraph.

To most of us, the term <u>myth</u> might call to mind marvelous Greek stories of disguised gods cavorting with humans. We might think of heroes wielding swords against dragons or of magicians mesmerizing entire armies. We might recall the story of Johnny Appleseed planting apple trees across the American landscape or of Rip Van Winkle sleeping for 20 years or of John Henry racing against a steam-powered spike driver. These myths are different from legends because they lack historical background and shade into the supernatural. They are also different from fables because they lack an overt moral intent. Like legends and fables, they are stories, imaginative stories, that, according to one popular view, embody cultural patterns. Now semiologists are using the term <u>myth</u> in a different way.

3

Topic sentence signals Schneider will explain new use of *myth.*

To semiologists, <u>myth</u> refers to deeply rooted cultural beliefs not to ancient stories. These beliefs are held by most members of any given

4

society. Despite whatever evidence there might be to contradict the validity of a myth, semiologists do not judge it as right or wrong. They merely recognize its existence and analyze its social influence. Whether valid or invalid, a myth, therefore, is a psychological and social fact projected onto experience. We never clearly see things as they really are; we only see their reflections in our cultural beliefs.

First two sentences serve as topic sentence. Schneider then explains one purpose of cultural myths—to manipulate consumers.

Cultural myths are often used for manipulative purposes. For   5
instance, one myth embedded in cultural conscious is the myth of the rugged individual. Usually a man, the rugged individual is one who can survive on his own in environments that would be hostile to all of us acculturated folks. Advertisers frequently associate their products with the image of the rugged individual to manipulate consumers. For example, consider the Marlboro man, the lone cowboy who leads a rugged life herding steers on the open range. He calls to mind the rugged individuals cowboy actors John Wayne and Clint Eastwood play in western films, tough hombres who ride the range alone. Well, not quite alone; he has his cigarette. Of course, not everyone will respond to this myth. That's why advertisers employ many different kinds of cultural myths to sell their products.

Schneider ends by showing that we are not absolute prisoners of myth. New perceptions allow us to see experience differently.

<u>Myths</u>, as semiologists use the term, pervade every aspect of our   6
cultural experience. Sometimes, these belief systems are unrecognized and have a powerful influence on how we view experience. Other times, we become aware of them and through that awareness, change our perception of the world. Remember this myth: The husband is the breadwinner; the wife is the homemaker. The world has changed dramatically since that mythic perception dominated American thinking.

Chris Schneider had a hard time limiting her essay to 600 words, the maximum length for this writing task. She had to delete a series of examples illustrating common myths along with several more examples of myths at work in advertisements. Of all these examples, she decided to keep the reference to the "rugged individual" and the Marlboro man; she felt her readers could easily recognize them since they had been published in magazines for years. Even with the deletions, her essay is an effective response to the assignment.

In paragraph 1, Schneider opens with a series of questions to help establish the concept of cultural myth. She ends with a thesis statement that clearly indicates she will define *myth* from a semiologist's perspective.

In paragraph 2, Schneider anticipates that her readers might not know what semiologists do. For clarification, she contrasts them with semanticists, whose area of scholarship is more commonly known. This contrast helps her generally explain the difference. She avoids being side-tracked here, keeping in mind that her dominant purpose is to define *myth,* not *semiology.*

In paragraph 3, Schneider uses a common tactic in definition: She places the term in a general category and then shows how it's different from and similar to other category members. Paragraph 4 works with paragraph 3. In it, she makes a direct statement about *myth.* But rather than define the word in strict terms, which is probably impossible, she continues to create an *impression* of myth. She is also moving from the general to the specific, each paragraph revealing her subject in more detail.

Paragraph 5 is the most detailed. Schneider uses some general references and a specific example to illustrate her point. There's one danger here: The subject is so large that she really needs more than one specific example, but since space was limited and she had created a broad impression of myth in the earlier paragraphs, she felt one easily recognizable example would clarify her point.

Finally, Schneider offers a brief conclusion that makes effective use of a commonly believed myth that has been exposed. This tactic illustrates that perception can be changed through awareness.

WRITING AN ESSAY DEVELOPED BY DEFINITION

At first glance, writing a definition might seem simple: Just open your dictionary, jot down the meaning of a word and it's defined. Right?

Yes and no. It's defined, but only in a very narrow sense.

Using a narrow dictionary definition recast in your own language is often an effective strategy to open a discussion, but in an essay developed by definition, your task is to go beyond the dictionary definition. You must create a strong impression of the word, one that helps the reader understand the concept it embodies. Generally, it might he helpful to think of three kinds of definition: etymological, or lexical definition; stipulative definition; and extended definition.

Determine the Appropriate Type of Definition

Etymological Definition.   An *etymological definition* is a dictionary definition. It defines a word in a narrow way by specifying its class and its distinguishing characteristics. Consider the word *thriller.* A good college dictionary will tell you that a *thriller* is "a suspenseful work of fiction that deals with crime or detection."

Sometimes, an etymological definition includes synonyms—for instance, a *thriller* might be referred to as a *whodunit.* Rather than use a ready-made dictionary definition, writers often expand on this information to create a strong impression. For example, in the following paragraph, aspiring mystery writer Cliff Serdum recasts and expands the dictionary definition of *thriller* to show what he means by the term:

> I see a "thriller" as being an imaginative narrative—usually a novel or film—that deals with crime or detection. A good thriller is distinguished by suspense, drawing the audience deeper into the story until they are unable to put the book aside or go for a bag of popcorn. Thrillers are often confused with "mysteries." Both deal with crime and detection, but mysteries, such as Dashiell Hammett's classic *The Maltese Falcon*, which is actually a "whodunit," are preoccupied with the rational pursuit of clues that will reveal a murderer (who, by the way, is seldom the butler even in English mysteries). Thrillers, such as Thomas Harris's *The Silence of the Lambs*, are less concerned with who committed the crime than with how a killer will be stopped. To draw a comparison, mysteries are like elaborate chess games with a detective and criminal trying to outwit each other; thrillers are like roller coaster rides with a detective being whip-lashed through a series of unexpected events before stopping a murderer from killing again.

Serdum opens by placing thrillers in a general class: *imaginative narrative.* He then expands the dictionary definition by contrasting thrillers and mysteries and by adding common examples. Although readers might define *thriller* differently, at least they will know what Serdum means by the term.

Stipulative Definition. A writer sometimes uses a common word extensively in a special or limited way. He or she then usually stipulates the meaning of the word—that is, the writer explains how the word is to be understood as it appears throughout the essay. This explanation creates the *stipulative definition.* In this paragraph from *Amusing Ourselves to Death*, educator and communications critic Neil Postman stipulates the meaning of *conversation:*

> I use the word "conversation" metaphorically to refer not only to speech but to all techniques and technologies that permit people of a particular culture to exchange messages. In this sense, all culture is a conversation or, more precisely, a corporation of conversations, conducted in a variety of symbolic modes. Our attention here is on how forms of public discourse regulate and even dictate what kind of content can issue from such forms.

In another example, social critic Don Pierstorff stipulates a meaning for *suits* when examining Michael Levine's *Deep Cover*, an exposé of the Drug Enforcement Administration (DEA):

> Who are the "suits"? They are the men and women who crowd the corridors and sit behind the desks of the Drug Enforcement Administration. They are government bureaucrats and managers. According to Michael Levine, they are the people who have no first-hand experience of the drug war and are unwilling to listen to agents who do. They spend their days shuffling reports and briefing politicians.

Postman's paragraph stipulates the meaning of *conversation* by enlarging it to mean "all the methods culture uses to communicate." Pierstorff's paragraph defines the commonly understood word *suits* by presenting its uncommon slang definition, the way author Michael Levine uses it. Both Postman and Pierstorff anticipate that their readers will need to know these special definitions to understand what they are writing about.

Extended Definitions.   Etymological and stipulative definitions usually are concisely written for the sole purpose of clarification. *Extended definitions* are much more detailed, often employing various development patterns to create a full impression of a word or concept. In this paragraph from *Hog on Ice,* C. E. Funk defines *white elephant.* He uses examples to establish its class and a brief narration about the word's origin to differentiate it from others:

> That large portrait of your wealthy Aunt Jane, given by her and which you loathe but do not dare to take down from your wall; that large bookcase, too costly to discard, but which you hope will be more in keeping with your future home; these, and a thousand other like items, are "white elephants"—costly but useless possessions. The allusion takes us to Siam. In that country it was the traditional custom for many centuries that a rare albino elephant was, upon capture, the property of the emperor—who even today bears the title Lord of the White Elephant—and was thereafter sacred to him. He alone might ride or use such an animal, and none might be destroyed without his consent. Because of that latter royal prerogative, it is said that whenever it pleased his gracious majesty to bring about the ruin of a courtier who had displeased him, he would present the poor fellow with an elephant from his stables. The cost of feeding and caring for the huge animal that he might neither use nor destroy—a veritable white elephant—gave the term its present meaning.

In the following two-paragraph passage from *Alligators in Sewers and Other Urban Legends,* Jan Harold Brunvand defines *urban legend.* He first establishes the class to which *urban legend* belongs and then distinguishes it from other members of the class. His definition goes beyond the etymological category because he develops the expression in greater detail, primarily with brief comparison and contrast and examples. Here's the passage:

> Urban legends are realistic stories that are said to have happened recently. Like old legends of lost mines, buried treasure, and ghosts, they usually have an ironic or supernatural twist. They belong to a subclass of folk narratives that (unlike fairy tales) are set in the recent past, involving ordinary human beings rather than extraordinary gods and demigods.
> Unlike rumors, which are generally fragmentary or vague reports, legends have a specific narrative quality and tend to attach themselves to different local settings. Although they may explain or incorporate current rumors, legends tend to have a longer life and wider acceptance; rumors flourish and then die out rather quickly. Urban legends circulate by word of mouth, among the "folk" of modern society, but the mass media frequently help to disseminate and validate them.

While they vary in particular details from one telling to another, they preserve a central core of traditional themes. In some instances these seemingly fresh stories are merely updatings of classic folklore plots, while other urban legends spring directly from recent conditions and then develop their own traditional patterns in repeated retellings. For example, "The Vanishing Hitchhiker," which describes the disappearance of a rider picked up on a highway, has evolved from a 19th-century horse-and-buggy legend into modern variants incorporating freeway travel. A story called "Alligators in the Sewers," on the other hand, goes back no further than the 1930s and seems to be a New York City invention. Often, it begins with people who bring pet baby alligators back from Florida and eventually flush them down the drain.

Both Funk's definition of *white elephant* and Brunvand's definition of *urban legend* involve much more than merely looking up the established meanings; nevertheless, these authors do make use of a common pattern of definition by placing a term in a class and distinguishing it from other members. Funk and Brunvand can successfully use this pattern because the words they define have been in common use for some time. But the strength of an extended definition is to introduce new terms to readers—or, more accurately, to introduce concepts represented by those terms. This kind of extended definition may be highly personal, embodying a writer's values and independent observations.

In this three-paragraph passage from *Zen and the Art of Motorcycle Maintenance*, Robert M. Pirsig defines *mechanic's feel*. Clearly, his definition is based on close observation during personal experience:

> The "mechanic's feel" comes from a deep inner kinesthetic feeling for the elasticity of materials. Some materials, like ceramics, have very little, so that when you thread a porcelain fitting you're very careful not to apply great pressures. Other metals, like steel, have tremendous elasticity, more than rubber, but in a range in which, unless you're working with large mechanical forces, the elasticity isn't apparent.
>
> With nuts and bolts you're in the range of large mechanical forces and you should understand that within these ranges metals are elastic. When you take up a nut there's a point called "fingertight" where there's contact but no takeup of elasticity. Then there's "snug," in which the easy surface elasticity is taken up. Then there's the range called "tight," in which all the elasticity is taken up. The force required to reach these three points is different for each size of nut and bolt, and different for lubricated bolts and for locknuts. The forces are different for steel and cast iron and brass and aluminum and plastics and ceramics. But a person with mechanic's feel knows when something's tight and stops. A person without it goes right on past and strips the threads or breaks the assembly.
>
> A "mechanic's feel" implies not only an understanding for the elasticity of metal but for its softness. The insides of a motorcycle contain surfaces that are precise in some cases to as little as one ten-thousandth of an inch. If you drop them or get dirt on them or scratch them or bang them with a hammer, they'll lose that precision. It's important to understand that the metal "behind" the surfaces can normally take a great shock and stress but that the surfaces themselves cannot. When handling precision parts that are stuck or difficult to manipulate, a person with mechanic's

feel will avoid damaging the surfaces and work with his tools on the nonprecision surfaces of the same part whenever possible. If he must work on the surfaces themselves, he'll always use softer surfaces to work them with. Brass hammers, plastic hammers, wood hammers, rubber hammers and lead hammers are all available for this work. Use them. Vise jaws can be fitted with plastic and copper and lead faces. Use these too. Handle precision parts gently. You'll never be sorry. If you have a tendency to bang things around, take more time and try to develop a little more respect for the accomplishment that a precision part represents.

Pirsig's definition of *mechanic's feel* is unique. Readers have no resources to consult for a commonly accepted definition of such an expression. Relying primarily on descriptive techniques, Pirsig carefully delineates the qualities of *mechanic's feel*, right down to naming the degrees to which someone might tighten down a bolt: *fingertight, snug,* and *tight.* Pirsig points out that metal has elasticity and that someone with *mechanic's feel* must sense that quality or face the consequences—a broken assembly. Pirsig creates a sense of the soft, delicate surfaces of metal and names the tools someone should use when working on them—hammers of many materials varying in softness as well as vise jaws fitted with soft faces. Someone with *mechanic's feel* is precise; in fact, the need for precision seems to be the message beneath the detail.

Use Extended Definition with Other Development Patterns

Unlike other development patterns—such as example, comparison and contrast, and cause and effect—extended definition can't be explained in neat paragraph strategies. As shown by Funk, Brunvand, and Pirsig, writers orchestrate a variety of development patterns to create an impression of the word or concept they define.

Look again at Chris Schneider's essay. In two paragraphs, she uses comparison and contrast to build an impression of *myth:*

> To most of us, the term <u>myth</u> might call to mind marvelous Greek stories of disguised gods cavorting with humans. We might think of heroes wielding swords against dragons or of magicians mesmerizing entire armies. We might recall the story of Johnny Appleseed planting apple trees across the American landscape or of Rip Van Winkle sleeping for 20 years or of John Henry racing against a steam-powered spike driver. These myths are different from legends because they lack historical background and shade into the supernatural. They are also different from fables because they lack an overt moral intent. Like legends and fables, they are stories, imaginative stories, that, according to one popular view, embody cultural patterns. Now semiologists are using the term <u>myth</u> in a different way.

To semiologists, <u>myth</u> refers to deeply rooted cultural beliefs not to ancient stories. These beliefs are held by most members of any given society. Despite whatever evidence there might be to contradict the validity of a myth, semiologists do not judge it as right or wrong. They merely recognize its existence and analyze its social influence. Whether valid or invalid, a myth, therefore, is a psychological and social fact projected onto experience. We never clearly see things as they really are; we only see their reflections in our cultural beliefs.

Note how the topic sentence of the first paragraph hints that a contrast will follow. Schneider both briefly compares and contrasts a traditional concept of *myth* to legends and fables. They are all stories, but as becomes clear in the next paragraph, her definition of *myth* is much different. The last sentence in this paragraph sets up the contrast.

Schneider opens the second paragraph with a direct statement that redefines myth. She follows with an explanation of how semiologists view myth—not as being right or wrong but as cultural fact.

In the following paragraph, Schneider's opening sentence clearly announces this paragraph's purpose: to establish that cultural myths are used for manipulative purposes. She uses a brief stipulated definition of *rugged individual* and an extended example to illustrate the definition that emerged from the preceding two paragraphs:

Cultural myths are often used for manipulative purposes. For instance, one myth embedded in cultural conscious is the myth of the rugged individual. Usually a man, the rugged individual is one who can survive on his own in environments that would be hostile to all of us acculturated folks. Advertisers frequently associate their products with the image of the rugged individual to manipulate consumers. For example, consider the Marlboro man, the lone cowboy who leads a rugged life herding steers on the open range. He calls to mind the rugged individuals cowboy actors John Wayne and Clint Eastwood play in western films, tough hombres who ride the range alone. Well, not quite alone; he has his cigarette. Of course, not everyone will respond to this myth. That's why advertisers employ many different kinds of cultural myths to sell their products.

In an effort to develop a extended definition completely, writers ask themselves five groups of questions about the word or concept they want to define:

1. Is this interpretation unique, or does it resemble that of another word or concept? How are they similar and different?

2. Who perceives the word in this way? Who has another perception?
3. Under what conditions or in what situations is the word used in this fashion?
4. What does the word mean now as compared to in the past?
5. Who uses the word in this special way? How is it used? What's its purpose? What activities is it the center of?

You may not be able to answer all these questions, but if you ask them, you will generate plenty of information about your subject to write an extended definition.

Use Transitions

Whether stipulated or extended, a definition essay usually employs a variety of development patterns. For example, consider some of the excerpts we have looked at in this chapter: Pirsig's definition of *mechanic's feel* relies on process analysis, Funk's definition of *white elephant* relies on examples, and Brunvand's definition of *urban legend* relies on comparison.

To keep your writing coherent as you shift from one development pattern to another, you should use a variety of overt transitions:

- For process analysis, use transitions that show a series of steps—such as *first, second,* and *third*—or indicate the passage of time—such as *next, finally, subsequently, meanwhile, while, immediately,* and *after.*

- When presenting examples, use transitions that announce illustrations will follow, such as *for example* and *for instance.*

- For comparison and contrast, use transitions that show relationships: *on the one hand, on the other hand, in contrast, similarly, like,* and *whereas.*

Remember, your goal is to keep your reader on track. When you reread your definition, try to consider it from the reader's point of view to see how well the various parts fit together, in terms of both sense and readability. If you hit a snag, see if adding a transition will smooth over the problem.

REVISING DEFINITION PARAGRAPHS

It's important to begin an extended essay by directly stating or strongly suggesting that a definition will follow. In the first draft, Schneider's introduction presented common myths in declarative sentences but did not clearly indicate or suggest that a definition would follow. Her peer-editing group pointed out that by rephrasing the declarative sentences as questions, she would arouse curiosity about their answers. Her group also pointed out that she needed to include more specific details, especially when referring to science and men and women. Finally, they recommended that she create a sense of who semiologists are. In revision, she tried to integrate all these suggestions:

~~Some people~~ *Do you* believe ~~that~~ childhood is a time of innocence separated from the emotions and cares of the adult world~~.~~*?* ~~Some people believe that~~ science *Do you count on* ~~will~~ solve the fuel shortage ~~and environmental destruction. Some people~~ *dangers of fossil ozone depletion, and toxic pollution?* *to* ~~believe that~~ men and women ~~embody a set of opposing psychological and social~~ *Do you feel are rational are intuitive? Men are active; women, passive?* *Men are* ~~characteristics. The perceptions of these people~~ have been influenced by *ambitious; women, nurturing?* *If you do, then your perceptions* common American <u>myths</u>, as a group of semiologists would ~~claim.~~ *define these beliefs.* *contemporary scholars and social critics known as*

Now read the final draft, with the changes integrated:

Do you believe childhood is a time of innocence separated from the emotions and cares of the adult world? Do you count on science to solve the dangers of fossil fuel shortage, ozone depletion, and toxic pollution? Do you feel men are rational and women are intuitive? Men are active; women, passive? Men are ambitious; women, nurturing? If you do, then your perceptions have been influenced by common American <u>myths</u>, as a group of contemporary scholars and social critics known as semiologists would define these beliefs.

Adding specific details helps clarify Schneider's thought. And indeed, shaping the declarative statements into questions helps her to quickly involve the reader. Finally, using the phrase *would define these beliefs* indicates that a definition will follow.

Guidelines for Writing Definition Essays

1. Select a word or concept that's currently being used in a new way or for which there's no clear etymological definition, such as a slang term or a new term from technology.

2. Develop a rough working explanation of what you will be defining. Then use the five groups of questions listed earlier (pp. 280–281) as a prewriting activity to generate information. If you're writing to define a special term, generate information that explains how to use it effectively and how it's misused.

3. Evaluate your prewritten material to see what you can and can't use effectively. Develop a clear purpose for your essay, one that clearly shows you will be writing a definition.

4. Write your essay. Organize it by moving from the general to the particular; that is, first create a broad sense of your term or concept, and then

present particular examples, comparisons, and information to clarify it in more detail.

5. Revise your definition. Be sure it's clear. Check your examples and comparisons to see that they are integrated effectively into the definition. Polish the entire definition for clarity.

Suggestions for Extended Definition Essays

1. Write an essay that defines one of the following terms. Explore the subject beyond its dictionary meaning, using a variety of methods to develop your definition. As part of this or any extended definition, you can also state what the subject is *not* as a way to clarify it.

   a. Humanity
   b. Education
   c. Armageddon
   d. Terror
   e. Empathy
   f. Honesty
   g. Fad
   h. Evil
   i. Female liberation
   j. Male liberation
   k. Corruption
   l. Intuition
   m. Liberation theology
   n. Social responsibility
   o. Obsession
   p. Team player
   q. Sociopath
   r. Maverick
   s. Imagination
   t. Tragedy
   u. Confidence
   v. Luck
   w. Glamour
   x. Scorched earth
   y. Genocide
   z. Blindsided

2. From the following list of seldom-used slang terms, select one and define it in several paragraphs. After you explain the term, create a situation in which it might apply, using it in several sample sentences as a speaker might. Also include a current slang term that has a similar meaning.

   a. Hoodwink
   b. Greenhorn
   c. Whoopee
   d. Boss
   e. Raise Cain
   f. Peacenik
   g. Bamboozled
   h. Boodle
   i. Macho
   j. Bonehead

3. Suppose that as a representative of a student rights organization, you have accepted the responsibility to convince a campus grievance committee composed of students, faculty, and administrators that a sexual harassment policy should be adopted as official college policy. Your first task is to define *sexual harassment* and give at least three different illustrations of harassing behavior.

4. Parts a and b examine the same issue—*environmentalism*—from two different perspectives. Choose one and write an essay that portrays that view:

   a. You are an environmentalist living in a major metropolitan area. You have formed an action group committed to protect all the natural landscapes that still exist in your city, even to the point of taking militant action against developers. You have used the phrase *urban environmentalist* to describe people who think and act as you do. In an essay, define *urban environmentalist* and describe what developers can expect from them.

    b. A group of self-designated *urban environmentalists* are disrupting development in the city. They see themselves as saviors of natural settings that exist within the urban landscape, but you regard them as *environmental terrorists*. In an essay, define *environmental terrorists* and predict what city officials can expect from them.

5. Look up the medical explanation of a debilitating ailment such as *Alzheimer's disease, multiple sclerosis,* or *Hodgkin's disease.* Once you understand the medical terminology, write a definition essay that explains the disease to someone who has no background in medicine. Imagine and describe a person who has the disease to further explain its debilitating effects.

6. Responding to a photograph: *Touching a Snake*

    Symbols are visible objects or actions that communicate significance beyond their literal meaning. For example, the American flag might stir our patriotic feelings. A superstitious person might grow anxious if he breaks a mirror, predicting a streak of bad luck for himself. The flag and breaking a mirror are both symbols.

Often, symbols have conventional meanings. For example, a heart sent on St. Valentine's Day is an emblem of affection. A wedding ring is an emblem of eternal commitment to another person. A Christian cross is an emblem of devotion. Many objects or actions do not have conventional meanings but create significance from their context. For instance, imagine you observe the following scene. You see a woman in black standing next to a tombstone, which reads:

Harold Ross
1930–1993
May He Rest in Peace

Next to the woman, with their heads bowed, stand three young children. From a few yards away, you watch the scene, believing that this is a widow and her children in mourning. After all, the grave, the tombstone, the black dress, and the bowed heads all suggest this interpretation. But then, the woman turns from the grave and you see her face. She's smiling—joyfully smiling. The children begin to skip and sing, "Who's afraid of the big bad wolf/the big bad wolf/the big bad wolf? Who's afraid . . ." Suddenly, the significance of this symbolic scene has changed. But to what? Well, that's open to interpretation, which is characteristic of symbolic experience.

Frequently, a symbolic dimension is at work in photographs. Photographers carefully compose the elements of their images so we sense a symbolic dimension in a photograph. *Touching a Snake* is such a photograph. With definition as the dominant development pattern, complete one of the following writing tasks. Before beginning the task, reread Guidelines for Writing Definition Essays (pp. 282–283) to review the conventions involved in writing a definition.

a. Begin by looking up the definition of *symbol* in an unabridged dictionary or other resource material in the library. From the information you gather and from information you glean from the introductory comments to this assignment, develop a full definition of *symbol*, using examples from your experience and reading. Next, interpret the symbolic significance of *Touching a Snake*. Consider several elements: the snake itself, which has a rich conventional symbolic history; the teddy bear; the fact of the generational difference between the man and the boy; and the image on the man's T-shirt. In the process of developing your material, you might decide that there are several ways to interpret the photograph. Try to accommodate them in your essay.

b. Research the symbolic significance of *snake* as it has appeared throughout history and in different cultures. Integrating the various symbolic meanings your research has uncovered, define *snake* as a multidimensional symbol, integrating its various interpretations. Finally, using one or more views of the symbolic snake, interpret the meaning of *Touching a Snake*.

CHAPTER 19

Argument:
Convincing a Reader

THE METHOD

Imagine this situation: You are eating with some friends you haven't seen for awhile. One has changed dramatically. She will no longer let meat touch her lips. You remind her that she was once the Queen of Burger King.

"Not anymore," she says. "I don't eat flesh of any kind. Not Bossie, Charley Tuna, Colonel Claghorn, Lamb Chop, Porky, and certainly not Bambi or Thumper. Nothing that swims, flies, or has eyelashes."

"Why?" you ask, a little stunned by her vehemence.

"A good question," she says, and begins to explain her reasons for becoming a vegetarian—and why *you* should become one, too.

She opens rationally. First, she points out the high cost of meat compared to the low cost of grains, which provide comparable protein. Second, she argues that grains grown for animal feed, also protein rich, would be better used to feed the world's hungry people. Then, she talks about the danger that eating highly marbled meat poses to health.

These reasons all make sense to you. Who doesn't want to save money, help feed starving people, and protect themselves from having a heart attack?

Your friend pauses for a moment, as if gaining energy, and then becomes emotional. She vividly describes animals, such as calves, being raised in pens to keep their flesh tender. She relates examples of force feeding, chemical injections, and slaughterhouse procedures. By this point, you lack the strength to lift up your knife and fork to cut into the steak the waiter just placed in front of you.

So, will eating meat be in your future? Maybe or maybe not. One thing is certain, though. Your friend used some common strategies that are characteristic of most effective arguments.

A *written argument*, like a spoken one, is an attempt to change or reinforce someone's opinion or to move someone to take action. On the one hand, a written argument may be highly rational, appealing to a reader's intellect with logic.

This writing is called *argument* or *logical argument*. On the other hand, an argument may be emotionally charged, appealing to a reader's feelings with emotional detail and biased language. This writing is then called *persuasion* or *persuasive argument*. Scientific writing relies on argument, and political writing relies on persuasion. Rarely, however, does an argument appeal only to reason or only to emotion. Usually, writers appeal to both, striving to convince their readers that a certain position is valid.

To write an effective argument, you must carefully balance reason and emotion. If your essay is so self-righteous that it ignores reason or so rational that it ignores feeling, you risk alienating most readers. Consequently, writers of effective arguments usually present their opinions persuasively, but they also take pains to develop ample and strong evidence throughout their essays. This practice will impress readers. They will see you as being *ethical*—a well-informed, reasonable person committed to a position and, therefore, worthy of being believed.

A STUDENT ESSAY
DEVELOPED BY ARGUMENT

Rolonda Burris received the following assignment to write an argument essay in a mass communications course:

Essay Assignment

In an essay of 1,000 to 1,250 words, take a position for or against controlling some message that is perpetuated by popular culture that social critics perceive to be a detriment to the public welfare. Examples include violence against authority and women in music lyrics; the display and use of weapons in cartoons; and the portrayal of drinking, smoking, drugs, or sexual relations in movies or on TV.

Burris decided to convince her readers that films featuring characters who smoke should carry a warning, much like the one cigarette companies are required to place in magazine advertisements. A movie buff, Burris enjoyed reviewing the history of films to gather evidence of the role that smoking has played. As you read her essay, notice how she uses historical examples to build her case:

Burris's title is ironic twist of famous line from *Casablanca:* "Here's looking at you, Kid." Use of word *reality* cuts through romance of smoking.

Here's Looking at Reality, Kid

1

Among college students, Humphrey Bogart is a cult figure. His films, such as The Maltese Falcon, The Harder They Fall, and To Have and Have Not, are still shown at colleges across the United States. Just last Saturday, our Film Society sponsored a Bogart retrospective. I watched

Burris begins indirectly, building romantic image of Bogart, detail by detail. Then she reverses tone, giving readers peek behind make-believe Bogart. His death from lung cancer helps dramatize point. Last sentence in introduction establishes issue in form of question.

Casablanca again. It becomes more romantic each time I see it. Casablanca is set in an exotic place and time. It features mysterious supporting characters. It concentrates on a dilemma: The beautiful heroine must decide between two men who love her, a political idealist and a world-weary cynic. Bogart, the cynic, is suave. His style dominates the film. During this viewing, I saw something I had not noticed before: No actor could handle a cigarette better than Bogart. Hanging from the corner of his mouth as he talks or held between two fingers as he drinks, a smoldering cigarette is clearly associated with the stylish image Bogart will eternally project from the screen. Bogart the actual man, however, was not eternal. At 58, he died from lung cancer after a lifetime of heavy smoking. After the movie, I asked myself, How many film buffs smoke because they admired the way Bogart handled a cigarette? If Bogart's style influenced just one filmgoer to smoke, shouldn't Casablanca--in fact, all films that feature characters who smoke--carry a warning about the dangers of smoking?

In topic sentence, Burris sets up power of association and that cigarette companies exploit it. Is assumption valid, or is she misleading readers?

Apparently, cigarette manufacturers understand the power of association to influence someone's decision to smoke. In an effort to attract more smokers, Philip Morris, the company that sells Benson and Hedges ("For people who love to smoke"), Virginia Slims ("You've come a long way, Baby"), and Merit ("For those who want marital bliss"), once paid $350,000 to have secret agent 007 James Bond smoke Larks in License to Kill. Philip Morris seems to believe that many young men are too immature to make the logical connection between smoking and death yet do make the illogical connection between smoking and the adventurous life James Bond leads, even though it is not real life.

Burris offers another specific example to support her assumption. Since she's dealing mainly in supposition, it's important she rely on plenty of concrete examples.

A couple of years before License to Kill was released, Philip Morris paid a substantial amount to have Lois Lane smoke Marlboros in Superman II. One movie critic raised the question that even if Lois Lane had to smoke, why feature a particular cigarette brand so prominently? Philip Morris must have been counting on the power of association even then. Will every immature young woman who sees Lois Lane lighting up conclude that if she smokes Marlboros, her own Man of Steel will drop from the sky? Probably not consciously, but the subconscious might associate smoking with sex appeal.

2

3

Recently, cigarette companies have had to pay billions in legal   4
settlements for misleading consumers. A reasonable person might
assume they would be chastened after their lies were exposed publicly.
But selling cigarettes has little to do with reason. The industry seems to
be intensifying its effort to glamorize smoking.

Burris continues to pile up examples of smoking in films, shifting to more recent movies until she concentrates on record-setting *Titanic*. She shows how independence and style are associated with smoking.

Just the other night on the Movie Channel, I watched Die Hard.   5
There was megastar Bruce Willis, smoking Marlboros and blasting away a
band of terrorists. I recently watched the video of My Best Friend's
Wedding. There was the stunning Julia Roberts nervously puffing on a
Newport while trying to disrupt the wedding plans of a rival. But the
most shocking movie display of smoking came to the public through the
cinematic talents of director John Cameron.

In Titanic, the world's largest-grossing film to date, Cameron shows   6
every major character smoking. Teen heartthrob Leonardo DiCaprio
smokes. His love interest, Kate Winslet, also smokes. At one point,
Winslet rebelliously blows smoke in her social-climbing mother's face.
Later, she snatches a cigarette from a young man's lips in an act of
independence. Cameron portrays smoking as sexy, glamorous, and
sophisticated. To smoke, the unstated message suggests, is to have
style--maybe not Bogart's style, but style nevertheless.

Now that she's laid down evidence, Burris takes new tact. She points out that public is warned about films that feature violence and explicit sexual behavior. They should also be warned about film that features characters smoking because smoking is health hazard.

Movies are rated according to who should be allowed to see them.   7
The National Coalition on Television Violence discovered that cigarette
smoking appears in 100 percent of PG-13 films. These movies have
been approved for 13-year-olds who have parental permission to
watch. Even if they come from families who do not smoke, young
people may be influenced by powerful images that show smoking as an
accepted behavior. But where is the warning in movies that smoking is
a health hazard?

Burris devotes paragraph to counterpoint but not very strong one. She dismisses it easily and moves on.

I can hear opponents now. "One more law designed to control   8
personal freedom," they will charge. Following this logic, if government
wants to protect people, it should put warnings about cars on films with
car chases or warnings about guns on films with shootouts. But they
would be wrong. Cars and guns do not kill people; drivers and gun
owners kill people. In contrast, cigarettes do kill people, and that's a
well-documented fact. Moreover, the government has already taken
actions to control smoking.

Now Burris is gaining momentum, increasing tension and emotion. She has laid foundation for her conclusion.

Cigarette advertisements have been banned from television   9
and radio for years. When they appear in magazines, cigarette
advertisements must include the Surgeon General's warning that
smoking can result in cancer, heart disease, or fetal injury in pregnant
women. This legal requirement is sensible public health policy, but
where does such a warning appear in films that feature characters
who smoke? Clearly, cigarette companies believe that by associating
cigarettes with appealing characters, they will influence people's
decision to smoke. Why else would Philip Morris pay movie producers
to feature its products?

The practice of featuring smokers in films is disturbing enough, but   10
when cigarette companies actually <u>pay</u> to have their brands featured in
films, the practice goes beyond being disturbing to being criminal. It is
time government put a stop to this kind of indirect advertising, just as
it did with radio and television advertising. If politicians lack the
courage, at the very least, they should require that films featuring
smokers announce the dangers of smoking before the plot begins. Then
the next time someone watches Humphrey Bogart raise a glass, squint
through a cloud of cigarette smoke at Ingrid Bergman, and say, "Here's
looking at you, Kid," viewers will not be seduced by the romantic image.
Instead, they might be awakened to the excruciating pain Bogart must
have felt while dying of lung cancer.

Burris closes with final emotional nod to Bogart, using him once again to point out that smoking isn't romantic, it's deadly.

Rolonda Burris's argument is hard to resist. Not even a hostile audience
would support the secret promoting of smoking. Her goal, then, is to offer a
new perspective: that displaying cigarettes in films is indirect advertising. Burris doesn't call for a ban on smoking in films, but she does assert that films
should be treated like advertisements. This seems like a reasonable position. After all, as she points out, the precedent has already been established.

Burris mixes emotion and logical argument. She begins indirectly by creating an impression of the suave Bogart style. And in the closing sentences of paragraph 1, she intensifies the emotional appeal by revealing that Bogart, usually
portrayed with a cigarette in hand, died of lung cancer. She maintains that films
that associate stylish actors with smoking potentially influence viewers to smoke.

In paragraphs 2 and 3, Burris gives two examples that show that one cigarette company, Philip Morris, believes showing actors smoking helps increase
their business. The company actually paid movie producers to display its
cigarettes.

In paragraphs 4, 5, and 6, Burris moves to the present. First, she points out
the tobacco industry has agreed to pay billions for misleading consumers but

asserts that they are still trying to glamorize smoking. She then presents more current films—*Die Hard, My Best Friend's Wedding,* and the blockbuster *Titanic*—as examples of efforts to glamorize smoking.

In paragraph 7, Burris presents a point that goes to the heart of her argument: Through movie ratings, viewers are warned about violence and nudity, but nothing is done to warn viewers about smoking, a clear hazard to health. At the end of the paragraph, she raises a question that echoes her conclusion: *Where is the warning in movies that smoking is a health hazard?*

In paragraph 8, Burris recognizes a counterargument but then quickly dismisses it. Now she's ready to drive her position home. In paragraph 9, she reminds readers of the Surgeon General's warning about smoking. Burris's reasoning clearly leads to one conclusion, which she states specifically in the conclusion:

> It is time government put a stop to this kind of indirect advertising, . . . or at the very least, they should require that films featuring smokers announce the dangers of smoking before the plot begins.

Burris closes with an emotional reference to Bogart's painful death from lung cancer.

WRITING AN ESSAY DEVELOPED BY ARGUMENT

An argumentative essay is distinguished from other essays because it has an *argumentative edge*—that is, the writer takes a stand on a controversial issue and attempts to change a reader's opinion or move him or her to take action.

The ancient Greeks, who formulated the underlying concepts of *logic,* identified three factors crucial to the construction of an effective argument:

1. *Logos,* or the quality of arguing soundly, refers to the quality of evidence—that is, examples, facts, statistics, authority statements, and reasonable interpretations.
2. *Pathos,* or the feeling dimension of language, refers to the ability to connect with a reader's emotion—that is, his or her values, attitudes, and psychological needs.
3. *Ethos,* or credibility and honesty, refers to how writers present themselves—that is, as knowledgeable, trustworthy, and logical or ignorant, shiftless, and erratic.

An effective argument usually blends logos, pathos, and ethos—or information, emotion, and integrity. The exact mixture varies with the audience and your purpose.

Establish an Assertion and Provide Evidence

An argument is predicated on an *assertion*, which is an opinion you want a reader to accept or an action you want him or her to take. When stated in a sentence, the assertion is referred to as a *proposition* or *thesis*. Here are some examples:

The high-fashion fur industry should be curtailed.

The state should resume capital punishment.

Magazines featuring nudity—such as *Playboy, Penthouse,* and *Playgirl*— should be banned from community magazine stands.

The writer then supports the thesis with *evidence*, which is the proof behind the assertion. It's the *quality* of evidence that goes a long way to persuade a reader to agree with a writer and reject an opposing position. Keep in mind that the evidence writers use to develop an argument is the same as that any of us uses in oral arguments: our own personal experience, the experiences of others, and authoritative sources.

Personal Experience.   Suppose you assert in an argument that police are harassing college-age drivers. You have had firsthand experience. Several times, patrol cars have pulled you over while you were driving near campus. Each time, an officer initiated a search of your car. Once, one even required you to take a field sobriety test, which you passed. At none of these times did any officer issue a traffic citation. These personal experiences could serve as legitimate evidence to support your position.

Experiences of Others.   You might narrate the story of a friend who has had a similar experience—say, being harassed by local police. You might also include observations by a passenger or bystander to corroborate your friend's experience.

When using the experience of others, however, you must do all you can to verify that the information is *accurate*. You know how accurate a description of your experience is because you lived it, but when you use the experiences of others as evidence, you are, in effect, vouching for its veracity. It's wise, therefore, to include more than one account of the same event.

Authoritative Sources.   An argument gains its strength from the quality of authoritative evidence a writer can marshal. You can develop some authoritative information yourself. Once again, consider the argument supporting the proposition that police are harassing collage-age drivers. To support your opinion even more thoroughly, you might research police records. If they reveal that police stop and search a significantly larger number of college-age drivers than older drivers, then you could use the information as evidence.

Sometimes, however, you must rely on other authoritative sources, such as encyclopedias, dictionaries, handbooks, digests, journals, and scientific research as well as people who are recognized as having extensive knowledge about a subject. When citing knowledgeable people to support an argument, be sure their expertise is in the subject you are discussing. It won't do your argument much good to quote a well-known nuclear physicist's opinion on gun control; your reader won't accept that specialist's word as authoritative—at least not on this subject.

Facts and statistics from authoritative sources can lend a great deal of credibility to any argument. *Facts* are irrefutable. No matter what the source, a fact is a fact:

The earth revolves around the sun.

John F. Kennedy, the thirty-fifth president of the United States, was assassinated on November 22, 1963.

When facts are corroborated by statistics, they exert a powerful influence on the reader. For instance:

The United States has more homicides each year than Japan, Taiwan, and the combined countries of Western Europe.

But what does this statistical fact mean? Should the government execute all convicted murderers? Do we need stricter handgun laws? Should every citizen be armed for self-protection? Answering these questions involves interpretations of facts based on personal feelings and beliefs. In other words, it involves opinions (see Chapter 2, pp. 14–17).

Arrange the Argument Logically

To be convincing, evidence must be arranged so that it all makes sense to the reader. Presenting evidence logically is the most important part of argument writing.

There are two logical approaches to arranging evidence: inductive and deductive. Remember, *inductive* arrangement moves from particular details to a generalization. Whenever you begin by presenting evidence and end by drawing a logical conclusion from the evidence, you are using inductive reasoning. *Deductive* arrangement is the opposite. Whenever you begin with a generalization, consider a specific case of that generalization, and then arrive at a conclusion, you are using deductive, or *syllogistic,* reasoning. Should you ever include an actual syllogism in an argument? No, but sometimes an argument can be reduced to syllogistic form. (See Chapter 3, pp. 31–36, for more on inductive and deductive reasonings.)

Recognize the Reader

While writing and revising an argument, always keep your readers in mind. Since you can't be all things to all readers, you might find it helpful to lump them into one of three general categories and then address them appropriately:

1. *Supportive readers:* They already agree with you, so there's no need to overload your argument with dry facts and statistics. You can emphasize pathos over logos—that is, rely more on emotion and less on information. Touch the right emotional nerve, and this crowd will carry you away on its shoulders.

2. *Wavering readers:* These uncommitted or uninformed readers are the ones you want to move through both logos and ethos—that is, by presenting solid evidence and by establishing your trustworthiness and honesty. Establish the right image, and they will hop on your bandwagon.

3. *Hostile readers:* These readers are apathetic, skeptical, and may be even downright mean. Convincing them of *anything* will be like trying to pull an angry bull's tooth with a pair of pliers. Give them just the facts—simple facts, dramatic facts, any facts that will penetrate their intransigence. Ethos won't help much, since they already see you as a schemer, and pathos will be thrown back in your face. Just keep writing calmly and rely on logos. It's hard to spit in the face of truth.

Should you arrange your argument inductively or deductively? Does it matter to readers? Not much. What *does* matter, however, is having strong evidence and making clear connections between the evidence and thesis.

Examine the Argument

Philosopher Stephen Toulmin has developed a way to examine the strength of an argument, one that will help you check if you are covering everything you should. It's a simple system to use in ordinary thinking situations and reflects how most people use their minds. It's now called the *Toulmin model,* and it consists of three main elements:

1. The *claim* is the conclusion you draw from your examination of the information—the thesis.
2. The *grounds* are the pieces of information related to the issue—the evidence.
3. The *warrant* is the principle that links the evidence to the thesis—the assumption.

How does the Toulmin model work? Here's a simplified example: Someone suggests that you and your roommates would have fun camping over the upcoming weekend. You respond by saying, "We can't. We have an examination in freshman composition on Monday."

CLAIM

We can't go camping.

GROUND

We have a midterm exam.

WARRANT (UNSTATED BUT IMPLIED)

Students should stay home and study before a test.

A warrant is often left unstated because it's usually so obvious that the listener will fill it in. *Students should stay home and study before a test* is a warrant—an assumption behind the claim and grounds—that most college students would agree with. But suppose that one of your roommates has a different warrant—one that says *Students should relax before a test.* He or she would likely insist everyone should go camping. You might find this view strange or even unreasonable until you clarified the conflicting assumptions behind each other's thinking.

Notice that a warrant is similar to the generalization used in a syllogism (see Chapter 3, pp. 33–36) or the conclusion of an inductive chain. You could easily show the following:

Students who have an examination on Monday shouldn't camp the weekend before.

All of us have an examination on Monday.

Therefore, none of us should go camping Friday, Saturday, and Sunday.

Toulmin's model is especially useful in argument writing. You probably won't write in syllogisms or in pure inductive arrangements. An untrained writer will usually make a claim and offer grounds to support it. He or she will not pay much attention to the actual reasoning process that goes into the conclusion and the assumption behind the argument. By using Toulmin's model to identify the warrant, claim, and grounds, you will see whether the warrant links the claim and grounds and whether it should be stated explicitly or left implicit. The model will also help you clarify or even qualify your claim and help you determine if you have enough information to convince a reader that your claim is justified.

Rolonda Burris used the Toulmin model to clarify the elements in her argument:

CLAIM

Films that feature characters who smoke should carry warnings about the dangers of smoking.

GROUND

Films that feature characters who smoke are a form of advertisement.

WARRANT

Advertisements for cigarettes carry warnings about the dangers to health that smoking poses.

Since the law requires that cigarette companies need to post warnings on every advertisement they publish, Burris realized she didn't need to backup her warrant. She also realized, however, that she did need to show how cigarettes are displayed in films. She also needed to lead the reader to make the inductive leap that showing glamorous film characters smoking might influence some people to smoke. By reducing her argument to the bare bones (which is one of the advantages of using Toulmin's model), Burris could clearly see how all the elements related. Given this, she could easily identify what she had to do to develop her argument.

Structure Argument Paragraphs

Like all essays, an argument essay is composed of paragraphs. In fact, it usually employs a variety of paragraph modes, such as examples, comparison and contrast, cause and effect, and definition. Like all effective discussion paragraphs, these paragraphs will have a topic sentence that relates to the thesis and adequate details provided for support.

There is another paragraph structure, however, that is unique to argument: a *refutation* paragraph, which presents an opposing point and offers the author's response. For example, in the following passage from "Politics and the English Language," George Orwell recognizes and refutes a point of argument that counters his position:

> I said earlier that the decadence of our language is probably curable. Those who deny this would argue, if they produced an argument at all, that language merely reflects existing social conditions, and that we cannot influence its development by any direct tinkering with words and constructions. So far as the general tone or spirit of a language goes, this may be true, but it is not true in detail. Silly words and expressions have often disappeared, though not through any evolutionary process but owing to the conscious actions of a minority.

Orwell's refutation paragraph follows a common structure, or sequence of sentences. He begins by establishing his position. He then states a counterargument. Next, he writes a sentence that swings the direction from the counterpoint to his response. He closes with an interpretation that supports his opinion.

Keep this structure in mind as you reread Rolonda Burris's refutation paragraph:

> I can hear opponents now. "One more law designed to control personal freedom," they will charge. Following this logic, if government wants to protect people, it should put warnings about cars on films with car chases or warnings about guns on films with shootouts. But they would be wrong. Cars and guns do not kill people; drivers and gun owners kill people. In contrast, cigarettes do kill people, and that's a well-documented fact. Moreover, the government has already taken actions to control smoking.

Often, argument writers employ a particular paragraph mode in refutation paragraphs. In the following paragraph from "Scientist: I Am the Enemy,"

pediatrician Ron Karpati responds to accusations made by animal rights activists with stunning, brief examples. Notice how Karpati first summarizes the
activists' point before countering it:

> Much is made of the pain inflicted on animals in the name of medical science. The
> animal-rights activists contend that this is evidence of our malevolent and sadistic
> nature. A more reasonable argument, however, can be advanced in our defense. Life
> is often cruel, both to animals and human beings. Teenagers get thrown from the
> back of a pickup truck and suffer severe head injuries. Toddlers, barely able to walk,
> find themselves at the bottom of a swimming pool while a parent checks the mail.
> Physicians hoping to alleviate the pain and suffering these tragedies cause have but
> three choices: create an animal model of the injury or disease and use that model to
> understand the process and test new therapies; experiment on human beings—some
> experiments will succeed, most will fail—or finally, leave medical knowledge static,
> hoping that accidental discoveries will lead us to the advances.

In "The Futility of the Death Penalty," attorney Clarence Darrow uses comparison and contrast to refute a counterpoint:

> It seems to be a general impression that there are fewer homicides in Great
> Britain than in America because in England punishment is more certain, more
> prompt, and more severe. As a matter of fact, the reverse is true. In England the av-
> erage term for burglary is eighteen months; with us it is probably four or five years.
> In England, imprisonment for life means twenty years. Prison sentences in the
> United States are harder than in any country in the world that could be classed as
> civilized.

In "Letter from Birmingham Jail," Martin Luther King, Jr., uses analogy to
refute a public statement made by Alabama clergy who opposed civil rights
demonstrations:

> In your statement you assert that our actions, even though peaceful, must be
> condemned because they precipitate violence. But is this a logical assertion? Isn't
> this like condemning a robbed man because his possession of money precipitated
> the evil act of robbery? Isn't this like condemning Socrates because his unswerving
> commitment to truth and his philosophical inquiries precipitated the act by the
> misguided populace in which they made him drink hemlock? Isn't this like con-
> demning Jesus because his unique God-consciousness and never-ceasing devotion
> to God's will precipitated the evil act of crucifixion? We must come to see that, as
> federal courts have consistently affirmed, it is wrong to urge an individual to cease
> his efforts to gain his basic constitutional rights because the quest may precipitate
> violence. Society must protect the robbed and punish the robber.

Even process analysis can be effective in refuting a counterpoint. In "Concerning Abortion: An Attempt at a Rational View," Charles Harshrone analyzes
the function of a fertilized egg to refute the view that the egg in this early stage
is a human being:

> Anti-abortion advocates argue that human life begins at the moment of concep-
> tion. But this is not accurate.

The fertilized egg is an individual egg, but not an individual human being. For such a being is, in its body, a multicellular organism, a *metazoan*—to use the scientific Greek—and the egg is a single cell. The first thing the egg cell does is to begin dividing into many cells. For some weeks the fetus is not a single individual at all, but a colony of cells. During its first weeks there seems to be no ground for regarding the fetus as comparable to an individual animal. Only in possible or probable destiny is it an individual. Otherwise it is an organized society of single-celled individuals.

Although not all argument writers state an opposing point of argument in order to refute it, it's an effective technique. It shows your reader that you have thoroughly considered the issue, thus making your argument all the more convincing.

REVISING ARGUMENT PARAGRAPHS

The complex nature of argument makes careful revision all the more important. Once you've written your essay, you must evaluate it to see if the key elements are clear to the reader. Here's where the Toulmin model will help. Reread your early draft and ask yourself these questions:

- Is the claim clearly stated in thesis form?
- Are the grounds for the claim fully developed?
- Is the warrant clear, or does it need to be expressed more directly?

Next, track the logic:

- Will a reader be able to track the line of reasoning?
- Is the evidence arranged logically?
- Does the evidence justify the conclusion?

Finally, trace the emotion:

- Have I made my emotional commitment to the argument clear?
- Have I become too overtly emotional by using loaded words and phrases?
- Will my reader see me as being passionately reasonable?

In an early draft of "Here's Looking at Reality, Baby," Rolonda Burris caught herself stacking the emotional deck against cigarette companies. The draft was peppered with loaded words and phrases, such as *greedy manufacturers, legalized murder,* and *perpetuating a health holocaust.* She decided to tone down the emotion. She knew her position was so reasonable she didn't need to be emotionally shrill. Here are her changes to paragraph 10, the conclusion:

The practice of featuring smokers in films is disturbing enough, but when

~~greedy~~ cigarette companies actually <u>pay</u> to have their brands featured in films,

the practice goes beyond being disturbing to being criminal.
~~they are financing a health holocaust and should be seen as criminals.~~ It is
this kind of indirect
time government put a stop to ⌃advertising, ~~that sells death~~ just as it did with

radio and television advertising. If politicians lack the courage, at the very

least, they should require that films featuring smokers announce the ~~mortal~~

dangers of smoking before the plot begins. Then the next time someone

watches Humphrey Bogart raise a glass, squint through a cloud of cigarette

smoke at Ingrid Bergman, and say, "Here's looking at you, Kid," viewers will

not be seduced by the romantic image. Instead, they might be awakened to ⌃

~~Bogart as a victim of legalized murder.~~ the excruciating pain Bogart must
have felt while dying of lung cancer.

Now, study Burris's final draft of this paragraph. She has deleted all but one
emotionally loaded word: *criminal*. Instead of trying to fire readers' emotions
explicitly, she lets the emotionally charged details—a Hollywood icon dying a
painful death from smoking—carry the emotional appeal implicitly:

> The practice of featuring smokers in films is disturbing enough, but when
> cigarette companies actually <u>pay</u> to have their brands featured in films, the
> practice goes beyond being disturbing to being criminal. It is time government
> put a stop to this kind of indirect advertising, just as it did with radio and
> television advertising. If politicians lack the courage, at the very least, they
> should require that films featuring smokers announce the dangers of smoking
> before the plot begins. Then the next time someone watches Humphrey Bogart
> raise a glass, squint through a cloud of cigarette smoke at Ingrid Bergman,
> and say, "Here's looking at you, Kid," viewers will not be seduced by the
> romantic image. Instead, they might be awakened to the excruciating pain
> Bogart must have felt while dying of lung cancer.

Like Rolonda Burris, you should seek a balance between emotion and reason. Merely exhorting readers to action will not convince them you're right. But
strong evidence and a well-reasoned argument built on emotional bedrock will.

As you revise your essay, keep in mind that an effective argument has five
elements:

1. A clear representation of the controversial issue and the writer's position on it
2. A succinctly stated proposition or thesis
3. Ample evidence and an orderly arrangement with a refutation counterargument
4. A reasonable tone with an undercurrent of emotion
5. A compelling conclusion that emphasizes the assertion

Guidelines for Writing Argument Essays

1. Once you select a controversial subject and decide on your position, gather two kinds of evidence: that which supports your position and, if appropriate, that which opposes it.

2. Develop a plan that arranges the evidence in a logical order. Use inductive arrangement if your evidence would best be organized by moving from specifics to a general conclusion; use deductive arrangement if your evidence would best be organized by moving from a generalization to the specifics.

3. Determine who your readers are. If you perceive they are already committed to your position, then you won't have to establish your credibility or write an argument dense with facts, examples, and statistics. Your goal will be to reinforce their support.

   If you perceive your readers are uncommitted, then you must establish yourself as a reliable source and offer a detailed presentation of the evidence, one that not only informs them but also stirs their emotions. Your goal is to win their support.

   If you perceive your readers are hostile, then you must establish your authority, present compelling evidence (that is, indisputable facts and carefully reasoned arguments), and avoid emotional appeals that they might perceive as an attack on their beliefs. Your goal is to encourage them to question their position.

4. Write the essay. If the arrangement is inductive, begin with a stated or implied hypothesis and lead your reader through the evidence to a reasonable conclusion. If the arrangement is deductive, begin with an introduction that states your position and ends with a thesis that clearly indicates an argument will follow. Develop the evidence, which should address the questions your thesis raises, in an orderly, step-by-step fashion. Note, where appropriate, the opposing position. Conclude by restating your thesis and reviewing the evidence to show the reader that your position is valid and should be accepted.

5. Review the essay to catch and correct any errors in reasoning. Look for logical fallacies, such as overgeneralization, oversimplification, faulty either/or reasoning, and flawed syllogistic reasoning embedded in your discussion. (See Chapter 2, pp. 17–20, for more on how to identify logical fallacies.)

Suggestions for Argument Essays

1. Write an argument in which you express one of your own deeply felt opinions. If the subject has undergone extensive public discussion, assume that your reader is familiar with the general elements of the debate and develop specific evidence based on your own observations, reading, and experi-

ences. Use the following list to stimulate your thinking, but don't feel bound by these subjects:

  a. Fraternities
  b. Sororities
  c. Hiring quotas
  d. Euthanasia
  e. Prayer in schools
  f. Giving birth-control advice to teenagers
  g. Sex education for teenagers
  h. Legalized drugs
  i. Capital punishment
  j. Smoking in public places
  k. Public use of profanity
  l. Disruptive behavior in public
  m. Requiring people on welfare to work for the state
  n. Animal rights
  o. Student codes of conduct
  p. Violence on television
  q. Movie ratings
  r. Subliminal messages in music
  s. Emotional advertising in political campaigns
  t. Censorship

2. Plastic disposable diapers are becoming a significant pollution problem. Each year, Americans throw away approximately 18 billion diapers, containing an estimated 2.8 million tons of excrement and urine. Every one of these disposable diapers takes up to 500 years to decompose. Aside from the solid waste issue, there are also growing concerns about infectious material seeping into the soil and groundwater, wasted natural resources, the rising costs of diaper production, disposal, and increasing risks of severe rashes and toxic shock syndrome in children.

Write an argument opposing the use of disposable diapers. Direct your essay to new parents.

3. Many people find junk mail entertaining—something to thumb through during a leisure moment. You, however, believe junk mail is not only a nuisance but a hazard, as well. For example, all the junk mail you receive this year will have consumed the equivalent of 1½ trees. One year's junk mail sent in the United States involves destroying 100 million trees.

Write an argument against junk mail. Here are some commonly known facts you might want to use:

  a. Almost 2 million tons of junk mail are sent each year.
  b. Over 40 percent of all junk mail is never opened.
  c. Junk mail receives special postage rates (currently less than 14¢ per piece, if arranged in presorted batches).

    d. The average American will spend eight months of his or her life open-
ing junk mail.

    e. The junk mail sent to 1 million people means the destruction of 1.5 mil-
lion trees.

4. A radical counterculture has emerged in Germany's inner cities. Called the
autonomen, they wear masks at demonstrations and are composed of
squatters and street people. They see themselves as the last hope of revolutionary activism. They refuse to participate in any political or social system,
and their brand of activism is usually spontaneous, unorganized, and often
violent.

    The *autonomen* have no counterpart on the American social scene.
However, some social psychologists predict the U.S. government's failure to
solve the problems of homelessness, drug abuse, and street gangs will lead
to formation of groups like the *autonomen* as a means to express the anger
and alienation the inner-city underclass already feels.

    Write an essay in which you argue that inner-city life must be improved
or city governments will soon be dealing with groups like Germany's *autonomen.* You might begin by using the *Readers' Guide to Periodic Literature*
or the Internet to find background information on these groups.

5. Responding to a photograph: *Saturday Morning—USA*

    What's the impact of television violence on children? Does it cause ag-
gressive behavior. Research hasn't conclusively proven that it does or does
not teach children to use force or violence in their relationships with other

children. But most researchers agree that when children watch hours of television, they participate in *imitative learning* or *modeling*. In simple terms, watching television creates a "monkey-see, monkey-do" effect.

Research has even shown that one-time exposure to televised aggressive behavior can be repeated in children's play by as many as 88 percent of the children who have seen it. Moreover, a single experience viewing a dramatic aggressive act can be recalled and re-enacted by children six months after the viewing. Earlier studies indicate that the average child between 5 and 15 will witness during this 10-year period the violent deaths of more than 13,400 humans. Surely, the accumulated impact of television violence must influence monkey-see, monkey-do behavior. Or does it?

Saturday Morning—USA captures a moment when television generates imitative learning. Drawing on details from the photograph and from the discussion here, compose an argument based on one of the following assignments. Before beginning your first draft, reread Guidelines for Writing Argument Essays (p. 300) to review the conventions of a sound argument.

a. Compose an inductive or deductive argument that leads your reader to conclude that children should not be allowed to watch television violence. Here are a few suggestions to get you started: Include a description of *Saturday Morning—USA* that leads to the conclusion that television has a powerful modeling effect. You might also include some of your own observations of children modeling violent television behavior. You might then point out what research suggests about the effects of television violence on play, thus leading your reader to an obvious conclusion.

b. Compose an inductive or deductive essay that takes the opposing position called for in option 1; that is, children's viewing of television violence should not be curtailed because it, like all television viewing, stimulates creative play. Here are a few suggestions to get you started: Again, describe the content of *Saturday Morning—USA*, but interpret the photograph as an indication that television stimulates imaginative play, not actual violent behavior. You might also draw on your own experience modeling television violence during play but point out that you and your friends are not criminals or violent people. You might state and agree with the research alluded to in the opening discussion of the writing task, but interpret it in a way that supports your point; that is, modeling is a powerful teacher, but children have the ability to separate television behavior from real behavior.

The Research Essay

CHAPTER 20

Finding and Researching a Topic

Suppose you had to offer a convincing response to the following question: *Is there or has there ever been life on Mars?* Scientists are debating this very question as you read this page. Some say chemical compounds recently discovered in 4.5 billion-year-old rock samples from Mars represent evidence of once-living, ancient microorganisms. Other scientists argue that the compounds in question could never have combined to produce even the simplest of life forms. What's your opinion? Is there or has there ever been life on Mars?

Your first thought may be something like "How should I know?" But if you knew that you were going to be held responsible for giving an informed, detailed opinion about this question, your answer might be "Let me find out. I need to do a little research."

Let's say you then go to the library for a book on Mars or a magazine or journal about the evidence in the rock samples. Maybe you even interview a biology professor on your campus about the topic or chat with a research scientist over the Internet. Slowly but surely, you gather information, weigh the evidence, and begin to form an opinion—an informed and convincing response to the question about life on Mars.

You may not have thought of all you were doing to answer that question as being *research*, but it was. And if you had written about what you found out—stated what it amounted to and listed the sources you consulted—you would have done something else, as well: You would have put together all the ingredients of a well-considered college research paper.

WHAT IS A RESEARCH ESSAY?

You can think of a research paper as a kind of extended argumentative essay, only more objective in style and based on an investigation of sources and evidence. Like other papers you have written, a research essay presents your opinion about a subject by stating a thesis, or main idea, and supporting it with details and examples. One major difference is that the primary focus of a research essay is on the subject of the paper and the objectively gathered evidence that supports the thesis. Your own ideas about the topic are central to the paper's success; however, the evidence you use to support those ideas comes from other sources, such as books, newspapers, magazines, journals, films, laboratory reports, and even personal interviews. You acknowledge, or *document,* such sources by citing them directly in the text of the research essay and also by listing them at the end in a section called *Works Cited* or *References.*

Length

The amount of discussion needed to support your main point about the research topic should determine your paper's length. In general, you should select a research topic that can be adequately discussed in 10 to 12 typewritten pages (5,000–6,000 words), the usual length for most college research essays. Depending on your topic, the length of time you have for research, and the expectations of your instructor, your paper may be somewhat shorter or longer.

Organization

A completed research essay includes several major parts, usually arranged in this order:

Title page (optional)
Outline (optional)
Text
Notes (optional)
Works Cited
Appendix (optional)

Note the sections listed above that are identified as *optional.* To determine whether you need to include these items, check with your instructor. He or she may require that you follow a standard set of guidelines for preparing your research essay, such as those of the Modern Language Association (MLA) or American Psychological Association (APA). (We'll discuss both of these styles in Chapter 23 on documentation.) Even if that's not the case, many instructors have certain guidelines that they expect students to follow—covering everything from how to show course information to what sort of paper, typestyle, and binder to use. Find out what your instructor's requirements are and follow them—to the letter!

The largest part of the paper—the *text,* or content portion—generally consists of three major sections: the *introduction, body,* and *conclusion.* As shown in Figure 20.1, a research essay also includes *documentation*—sources cited in the text and then listed at the end of the paper in a section titled *Works Cited* or

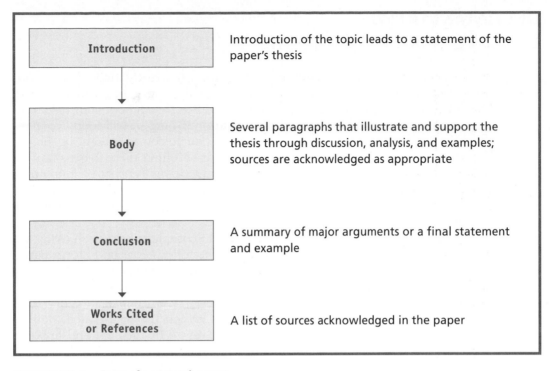

Introduction	Introduction of the topic leads to a statement of the paper's thesis
Body	Several paragraphs that illustrate and support the thesis through discussion, analysis, and examples; sources are acknowledged as appropriate
Conclusion	A summary of major arguments or a final statement and example
Works Cited or References	A list of sources acknowledged in the paper

FIGURE 20.1   Parts of a research paper

References. The content of each of these major sections of the paper will reflect the efforts of your research and thinking about the topic.

Including Your Own Ideas

If you are like some students and approaching a research essay for the first time, you may wonder how your own ideas fit into a paper that requires research and incorporates materials from outside sources. While the documentation of sources is an important, essential ingredient, keep in mind that at the heart of every effective research essay is the writer's own understanding of the topic. Your paper should analyze, compare, and evaluate information and sources to support *your position* and clarify *your thoughts* for the reader.

As you go about writing, remember that your own ideas are not only valuable but actually are, in one sense, what the paper is about. If you are writing on the subject of *homeless people in the United States,* for example, your reader not only wants to know about these people but also what the information you provide really means. Your presentation and interpretation of the facts, your analysis and comparison of other writers' opinions, and your conclusions about all this information constitute the heart of your research essay.

GETTING STARTED:
FIND AND NARROW A SUITABLE TOPIC

Getting started on a research essay begins with investigating a broad *subject* of interest and then moving to a more particular aspect of it called a *topic*. Your ongoing goal in finding such a topic, as well as throughout your research, is to refine and narrow the area of investigation. Doing so will focus your research activities and lead you to an informed conclusion to present in the paper. If you were interested, for example, in researching the subject of *space exploration*, a possible topic for research might be *the benefits of long-range space probes* like *Explorer I* or *Galileo*. Another topic for a paper on the subject of *space exploration* would be *the physiological effect on humans of spending prolonged periods of time in outer space.*

To hear firsthand what some students do to complete a research essay, we asked student Marcia Valen about the steps she followed recently for a paper she wrote in her English class. Valen explained that when she began thinking about a possible research topic, she remembered the issues surrounding the selection of a jury for the O. J. Simpson murder trial. Her English class had read about and followed the trial as it proceeded. When the trial ended, her instructor asked each student to select an issue raised by the case and to write about it as the topic of a research essay. After much consideration, Valen settled on the issue of *how juries are selected* as a potential research topic. We'll trace the steps she took in researching and writing the paper throughout the following chapters on writing a research essay. Her completed research essay, titled "Flawed Justice: Why and How the American Jury System Must Be Reformed," appears in Chapter 22 on pages 367–382.

Frame a Research Question

Once you have selected a suitable topic for research, you can begin to frame one or more potential *research questions* about it. These questions will help you focus your research and, as you begin to answer them, serve as the basis for the final form of your paper's main argument. *How beneficial are long-range space probes?* might be one question to answer on the topic of long-range space exploration, for example. *Should we continue sending long-range probes into space?* would shift the focus of your research to a different aspect of the same topic. A topic concerning the effects on humans of prolonged time in space could generate a research question such as *Are prolonged flights in space too dangerous for humans?*

Questions like these direct the investigation of sources and focus your note-taking. They ensure that your paper will raise a significant issue and provide a thoughtful discussion about the topic.

Figure 20.2 shows how Marcia Valen narrowed the focus of her research from the broad subject of *juries* to a narrower topic on *the jury selection pro-*

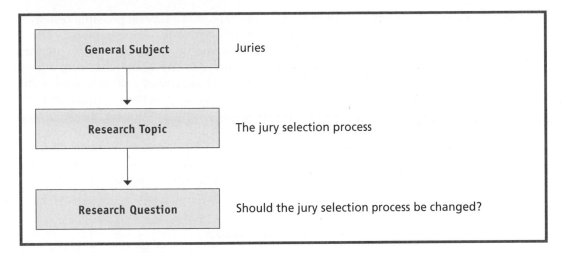

FIGURE 20.2   Moving from a general subject to a research question

cess, finally arriving at the research question *Should the jury selection process be changed?* This question directed Valen's investigation of sources and focused her notetaking. It also gave her research essay a significant issue to address and provided a thoughtful discussion for her reader.

Keep in mind that the actual progress of your research efforts may not evolve as directly as suggested here and in the following pages. You will most likely recognize several possible subjects, topics, or research questions at the same time or in a different sequence throughout your research. Remember that research is an evolving process: Expect to modify an initial topic and any related research questions as your insight about the subject itself develops.

Start with a Topic That Interests You

If there were one simple rule for selecting the right research subject, it would be this: *Work with your interests.* You will write best on a subject you care about and already have a feeling for. Your favorite section of the newspaper; the kinds of books, magazines, or films you enjoy; or a particular textbook chapter that excited your curiosity are all strong clues to your real interests. Avoid any that are not part of your general field of interest or that you may be drawn to for the wrong reasons. Although a subject like *uniform commercial code laws* may sound impressive, you won't be able to go very far with it unless you are genuinely interested in laws governing various kinds of commercial transactions. Similarly, *microwave cooking* may sound like an easy subject to write about. But unless you care enough to research and think critically about it, such a subject may generate only a tiring exercise for you and a dull paper for your instructor.

Although Marcia Valen's instructor had suggested several possible research topics—*the validity of DNA evidence, spousal abuse laws, the televising of court cases,* and others—Valen wanted to find her own. She had watched the jury selection process in the O. J. Simpson trial, and she knew that choosing a jury was a complex and often controversial process. Valen also recalled when her father, a medical doctor, was excused from serving on a jury in a medical malpractice suit because he was considered overqualified. With the Simpson jury selection and her father's earlier experience in mind, Valen began to investigate the issues surrounding how juries are chosen. After some preliminary reading in the library and further discussion with her instructor, Valen eventually decided to write about the problems posed by current jury selection processes in the United States.

Select a Topic That Allows for Discussion

To choose an appropriate research topic, you must be aware of what your paper can achieve. Most research essays attempt to add a new dimension or perspective to a body of ideas already expressed by others, so process ("how to") essays or those that merely summarize already known information (e.g., *the dangers of cocaine addiction*) are not good choices. Topics that focus on a philosophical approach to a subject or are based on personal beliefs (e.g., *the purpose of evolution* and *the immorality of popular music*) also should be avoided because they are so rooted in opinion that they don't lend themselves to research and the presentation of objective evidence. (You may be able to refocus the approach to such a topic in order to treat it more objectively, however.) Also avoid topics that are too recent or too local to have generated enough material available for research (e.g., *last month's countywide power failure*) or those issues that have been so abundantly discussed that it would be impossible to become adequately familiar with the existing research (e.g., *the John F. Kennedy assassination*).

Look instead for a topic that allows you to explore areas that still need discussion, such as an unsettled and continuing problem or a little-known situation. *An assessment of current employee drug-testing programs* might prove a suitable topic. Another, framed as a research question, may be *Why are local frog populations disappearing worldwide, and what should be done about it?* An examination of any one of the several complex problems surrounding *how juries are selected* (as in the sample research essay by Marcia Valen) could also produce an informative, researched discussion.

Use Library Resources
to Find and Narrow a Topic

You will need to make any topic you select as specific as possible. Although you may not know very much about a subject when you first begin a research essay assignment, you will find that every subject can become increasingly focused as you learn more about it through research. Your library's reference section or book collection contains excellent sources for discovering a potential subject or topic for your research essay. As a general rule, consult as many such sources as possible. Preliminary investigation of standard library materials will provide important general information as well as specific sources essential to your later research.

Locate Primary and Secondary Sources.   In order to present an informed and balanced discussion of the research topic, your research essay should reflect a comprehensive understanding of issues and points of view. For this reason, you will need to use both primary and secondary sources to give your paper's discussion of the research topic depth and originality:

▪ A *primary source* is the actual material that you write about in a research essay. Primary sources include works of literature, letters, journals, government documents, surveys, reports of experiments or research, laboratory specimens, interviews, and oral histories. You might use a primary source such as Nathaniel Hawthorne's *The Scarlet Letter* if you were writing a research essay about the author's use of symbolism in the novel. Using such primary sources allows you to make your own assessment of the raw material from which your paper will develop. Through this contact, your own analysis or reaction to such sources can become an integral part of your research essay.

▪ A *secondary source* is written *about* a topic. Secondary sources include books, magazines, newspaper articles, encyclopedia entries, pamphlets, and other works that examine, analyze, or report information. A journal article about teenage driving habits or a film documentary showing the effects of illegal hunting on certain wildlife populations are examples of secondary sources.

You should consult as many available primary and secondary sources as are relevant to your subject or required by your instructor. Avoid basing too much of your research on any one source or type of source. Consulting a variety of sources will ensure that your thinking about the topic reflects a balance of information and is fair to the complexities it presents.

Consult Encyclopedias.   No matter what subject or topic you consider investigating, it is wise to begin all your research with a study of relevant encyclopedia articles. Written by well-chosen experts who provide reliable facts and informed insights, encyclopedias provide broad, informative discussions of what's currently known about a subject. Such basic information is essential to your conducting effective research or writing on any topic.

You are probably already familiar with multivolume, comprehensive encyclopedias like *Encyclopedia Americana, Encyclopaedia Britannica,* and *Collier's*

Jury Procedures.

Selection.

The commitment of important decisions to a random group of laypersons has been moderated, particularly in the United States, by an elaborate screening, voir dire, conducted by trial counsel at the inception of a trial. The law permits counsel to challenge prospective jurors either for cause (if there is specific likelihood of bias) or, for a limited number, "peremptorily"—that is, without having to give a reason. American trial tradition attaches a great deal of significance to the strategies of juror selection, and in celebrated cases the lawyers' INDEX voir dire examination has extended for several weeks.

FIGURE 20.3   Entry on *Jury Procedures* from the CD–ROM version of *Encyclopaedia Britannica*

Source: From "Judicial and Arbitrational Systems," in *Britannica CD 97* © 1997 Encyclopaedia Britannica, Inc. Reprinted by permission.

Encyclopedia. These references cover hundreds of subjects and include maps, illustrations, and highly useful bibliographies. Entries appear alphabetically by subject, and discussions vary in length from a single paragraph to a dozen or more pages. Most public or campus libraries carry one or more complete editions of such encyclopedias as well as the yearbook supplements intended to keep them up to date. Many encyclopedias, such as *Encyclopaedia Britannica* and the *Academic American Encyclopedia,* are also available online or on CD–ROM at most libraries or through the Internet. Figure 20.3 shows an entry for *jury procedures, selection* which Marcia Valen accessed from *Britannica CD 97* for her research on juries.

Search the Card Catalog.   The best guide to the books available for research is your library's card catalog. Whether on microfilm or microfiche, on a computer screen, or in the traditional card tray, the library's catalog alphabetically lists and cross-references its holdings by subject, author, and title. Special information given with each entry can supply useful data about a book's publication date, whether it includes illustrations, and its length. You can locate books on your topic by looking under the subject, author, or title heading (see Figure 20.4). Most libraries are organized using one of two classification systems—the *Dewey decimal system* and the *Library of Congress system.* Which of the two a library uses will make no difference to your research, since the classification system merely determines the identification, or *call,* number of any book.

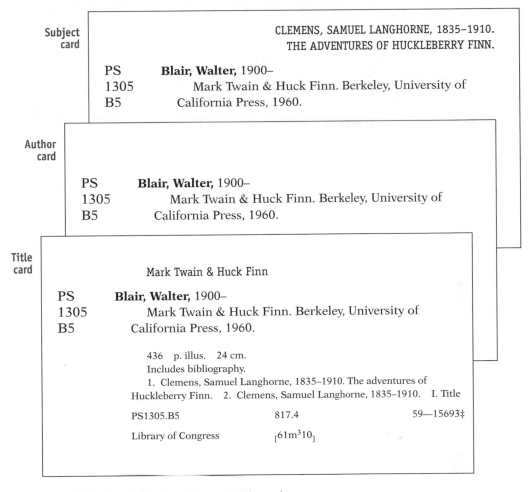

FIGURE 20.4 **Subject, author, and title cards**

***Use the* Social Issues Resources Series (SIRS).** Your library's reference section will no doubt carry several volumes of the *Social Issues Resources Series*, or *SIRS*, which is available in printed form or online. In the print version of *SIRS*, over 30 different subjects are titled and numbered on the spines of large binders containing hundreds of short, up-to-date articles on dozens of interesting subjects. A "Quick Reference Guide" lists the subject volumes and indicates which ones contain articles on various major topics.

You can use *SIRS* to find a subject or to learn about a potential topic. Looking over the "Quick Reference Guide," for example, may start you thinking about the relationship of *alcohol* and *divorce*. Perhaps you might begin to wonder about *education* or *civil rights* as possible research interests. A brief search

E

Earth, Chemical composition
See Geochemistry
Earth, Orbit, 2
Earth-friendly products
See Green products
Earth Summit
See United Nations Conference on Environment and Development
Earthwatch, 18
Ecology
See Coastal ecology: Food chains (Ecology)
Education, Environmental
See Environmental education
El Nino Current, 7, 8
Electric apparatus and appliances, 5
Emission reduction credits, 9
Emission standards, Automobile
See Automobiles, Environmental aspects
Energy efficiency, 16
Environment, Effect of man on
See Man, Influence on nature
Environmental degradation, 20
Environmental education, 20
Environmental health, 17, 20
See also Health risk assessment
Environmental impact analysis, 8
Environmental policy, 11
Environmental technology, 4
EPA
See U.S. Environmental Protection Agency (EPA)
Extinct amphibians, 10
Extinction (Biology), 20

FIGURE 20.5 Listing from the index of *SIRS Critical Issues: The Atmosphere Crisis*
Source: From the index of *SIRS Critical Issues: The Atmosphere Crisis,* Vol. 3, Articles 1–20. Reprinted from *SIRS Researcher*®. Copyright © 1998 SIRS, Inc. Reprinted with permission.

through the subject volume on *drugs* will turn up such articles as "Addicted Doctors," "The Drug Gangs," "Should Hard Drugs Be Legalized?" and "Cocaine's Children." Figure 20.5 shows some of the topics listed in the index of *SIRS Critical Issues: The Atmosphere Crisis.* After reading some of these articles, you could decide if one of the topics interests you enough to research further, or you could turn to a different volume to get ideas about another subject.

Look for a Topic Online

Computers have created entirely new and exciting ways to conduct research. If you have used a computer at your local or university library to locate sources within the library or elsewhere, you may already be familiar with some of the many information-searching programs connected to databases, the Internet, and other telecommunications sources.

Information available through databases, the Internet, and other online resources is highly organized. It's usually listed by topic and then categorized in successively narrowing, increasingly focused menus. Once online, you can use these organizational features to discover subjects of interest or to help find a related topic for research. In addition, you may also find topics online by following the *hypertext links* (see Chapter 21, pp. 337–338): colored or highlighted words that link electronically to related information sources. By using hypertext, you can identify possible topics to investigate and, at the same time, become aware of important concepts that may be relevant to your later research and discussion.

Search Databases. Most of the research information you might access by computer will be the kind stored in a *database,* which is a collection of information stored in a computer and available to other computers. Libraries and commercial Internet service providers, such as America Online or Compu-Serve, subscribe to commercial database vendors, whose systems provide access to hundreds of separate databases on a fee-for-use basis. Databases incorporate hundreds of general indexes and journal abstracts, even the complete texts of a variety of sources:

Books	Government reports
Newspapers	Dissertations
Magazines	Grants
Journals	Conference proceedings
Reviews	Financial reports

When student Marcia Valen was seeking journal articles for her research paper on the jury selection system, she used *LawCrawler,* an Internet search engine for legal resources. LawCrawler linked Valen to the website for *FindLaw,* a database listing online law journals and reviews. The menu choices listed by FindLaw are shown in Figure 20.6. After selecting *Public Law Research Institute Reports* from this menu, Valen was able to search that journal's index, where she found abstracts and full texts of several published articles related to her topic. Since Valen found these sources online, she had the choice of reading them online, printing copies, or downloading them to a disk. Like Valen, you will find that database searches are fairly simple to conduct.

Database Size. Databases exist for hundreds of subjects, ranging from agriculture and chemical compounds to the stock exchange and current Chinese technology. A single large database like *AGRICOLA,* which covers agriculture and related subjects, contains over 2.5 million records. A national database vendor such as *DIALOG,* to which many libraries subscribe, can search over 300 such separate databases, offering researchers access to more than 175 million records.

Searching a Database. To search a database, to locate an online source, you use a program called a *search engine.* Popular search programs—such as Lycos, Yahoo, Magellan, and AltaVista (see Figure 21.3, p. 343)—are often

> **Public Policy and Law Journals**
>
> - BYU Journal of Public Law (Brigham Young University)
> - Canadian Journal of Law and Society (Universite du Quebec a Montreal) Abstracts
> - Cornell Journal of Law and Public Policy (Cornell University) Full Text
> - Journal of Law and Policy (Brooklyn Law School)
> - Journal of Law and Public Policy (University of Florida) Abstracts
> - Kansas Journal of Law and Public Policy (University of Kansas) Full Text
> - Law & Contemporary Problems (Duke University) Full Text
> - LBJ Journal of Public Affairs Online addresses diverse issues including domestic policy, economics, education, environmental policy, human and social services, international affairs, legal and judicial issues, local and state government, nonprofit organizations and community development, minority and women's issues, public administration and financial management, U.S.-Mexico border issues, and more. Full Text
> - Michigan Journal of Law Reform (University of Michigan)
> - Michigan Law & Policy Review (University of Michigan)
> - New York University Journal of Legislation and Public Policy (NYU)
> - Perspectives on Law and The Public Interest (University of Richmond) Full Text
> - Public Law Research Institute Reports (University of California, Hastings) Full Text
> - Review of Law & Social Change (New York University)
> - Stanford Law & Policy Review (Stanford University) Abstracts
> - Statute Law Review (Oxford Journals Abstracts
> - Texas Review of Law & Politics (University of Texas) Full Text
> - The Urban Lawyer (University of Missouri, Kansas City and the ABA) Abstracts
> - Virginia Journal of Social Policy & the Law (University of Virginia)
> - Yale Law and Policy Review (Yale Law School)

FIGURE 20.6   Menu choices for FindLaw database
Source: Reprinted with permission of FindLaw.

available on the computers of campus libraries, or you may have access to these or other search engines on your home computer through commercial service providers such as America Online, Microsoft Network, and CompuServe.

If you use campus library facilities, you probably have access to a number of databases for free or for a minimal cost. You can have at-home access to independent commercial databases by making direct billing arrangements with commercial providers such as Northern Light and America Online. While having this access would be handy, unless it's part of the services already supplied by your provider, searching independent databases from your home can be very expensive. Plan to use these databases to supplement your research or to reach sources you can't access otherwise, possibly through your campus library or another library accessible via the Internet.

GATHER INFORMATION ON THE RESEARCH TOPIC

Once you have identified a promising, potential topic to research, you will be ready to start gathering information about it. Most of your research data will probably come from reference books, general books, and periodicals available in your college or community library. Systematically investigate each of these three major sources to establish a preliminary bibliography for your research essay.

Consult Bibliographies

One of the most useful aids to research is a *bibliography*, which is a work listing books and/or articles by an author or about a particular subject. You can use bibliographies to find a topic as well as to see what sources may be available on it. The most comprehensive bibliography is the *Bibliographical Index: A Cumulative Bibliography of Bibliographies*, which is international in scope and lists other published bibliographies by subject, including those in books and periodicals. Most other bibliographies, such as *A Selected Bibliography on the Asians in America* and *Bibliography of Mexican American History*, emphasize particular subjects. Figure 20.7 shows an entry from the all-inclusive commercial bibliography *Subject Guide to Books in Print*, which Marcia Valen used for her research on *jury selection*.

JURY
See also Grand Jury; Instructions to Juries
ABA, Committee on Jury Standards, et. al Standards
    Relating to Juror Use & Management: Tentative Draft.
    208p. 1982. 11.50 (*0-89656-603-5*, R-069) Natl Ctr St
    Courts.
Abbott, Walter F. Analytic Juror Rater. 142p. 1987. 31.00
    (*0-8318-0588-9*, B588) Am Law Inst.
—Surrogate Juries. LC 90-80485. 265p. 1990. 80.00
    (*0-8318-0607-9*, B607) Am Law Inst.
Abbott, Walter F., et. al. Jury Research: A Review &
    Bibliography. LC 90-75867. 346p. 1993. 31.00
    (*0-8318-0638-9*, B638) Am Law Inst.
The Anglo-American Jury: Keystone of Human Rights.
    1993. lib. bdg. 75.00 (*0-8490-8726-0*) Gordon Pr.
Antitrust Civil Jury Instructions (Supplement) LC 80-67740.
    88p. 1986. ring bd. 30.00 (*0-89707-215-4*, 503-0060-01)
    Amer Bar Assn.
Austin, Arthur D. Complex Litigation Confronts the Jury
    System: A Case Study. LC 84-19500. 120p. 1984. text
    ed. 55.00 (*0-313-27009-6*, U7099, Greenwood Pr)
    Greenwood.
Berger, Richie E. & Lane, Frederick S., 3rd. Vermont Jury
    Instructions. 400p. 1993. ring bd. 85.00 (*1-56257-293-8*)
    Michie Butterworth.

FIGURE 20.7   **Entries under *Jury* in the *Subject Guide to Books in Print***
Source: From the *Subject Guide to Books in Print 1995–1996*, p. 5205. Published by R. R. Bowker, 121 Chanlon Rd., New Providence, NJ 07974, © 1995 by Reed Elsevier, Inc. Reprinted by permission.

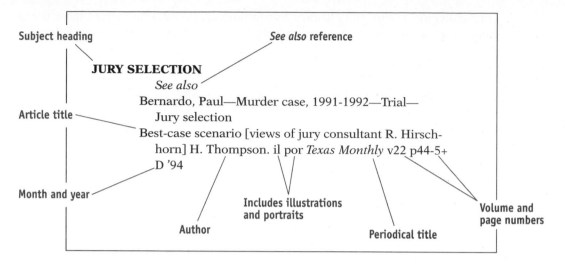

FIGURE 20.8   Entry on *Jury Selection* from the *Readers' Guide to Periodical Literature*
Source: From *Readers' Guide to Periodical Literature,* November 1995, p. 480. Published by the
H. W. Wilson Company. Reprinted by permission.

Use Book, Magazine, and Journal Indexes

As you search for a topic to narrow for research, you will need to consult
books as well as various kinds of *periodicals*—works such as magazines, journals, or newspapers that are published at regular intervals. Available in both
print and online, several kinds of *indexes* catalog books and/or periodical articles on a variety of subjects.

One of the best-known indexes is the *Readers' Guide to Periodical Literature*,
which provides a monthly, quarterly, and annual index to more than 200 of the
most popular magazines in the United States. Articles in the *Readers' Guide* are
cross-referenced under author, title, and subject; information about each entry
is listed in a condensed form, which is explained at the front of each volume.
Figure 20.8 shows an entry on *jury selection*, which identifies an article in a
journal called *Texas Monthly*.

Other useful indexes include the following:

*The MLA International Bibliography of Books and Articles on the Modern
Languages and Literatures,* an authoritative guide to books and journal articles on literature

The *Essay and General Literature Index,* a useful source listing books in
which a subject is discussed, even though it is not the main subject of that
work

The *Social Sciences Index,* a guide to journal articles in the social sciences

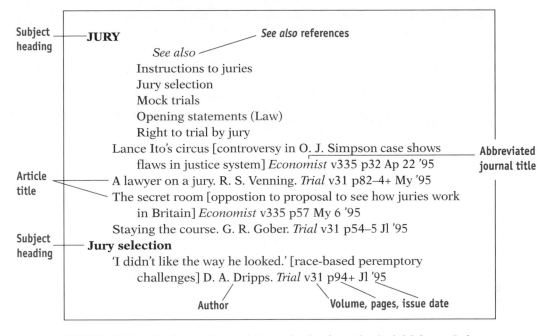

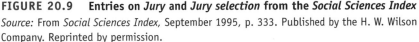

FIGURE 20.9 Entries on *Jury* and *Jury selection* from the *Social Sciences Index*
Source: From *Social Sciences Index,* September 1995, p. 333. Published by the H. W. Wilson Company. Reprinted by permission.

The *Social Sciences Index* is another of the reference sources Marcia Valen consulted for her paper on jury selection (see Figure 20.9).

In addition to these traditional types of indexes, there are multivolume *citation indexes,* such as the *Arts & Humanities Citation Index, Social Sciences Citation Index,* and *Science Citation Index.* These indexes not only cross-list information about scholarly articles and books by subject, title, and author but also tell where and when a work has been cited by another writer.

Use Newspaper Indexes

Newspaper articles are important sources for research on current as well as past topics. While most libraries can store no more than a few nationally circulated or local newspapers, most university and college libraries keep copies of several major newspapers on microfilm. Newspaper articles are usually listed in a separate index, such as *The New York Times Index,* which lists news articles, first by general subject and then in chronological sequence according to the dates they appeared in the newspaper. Like entries in the *Readers' Guide,* subject headings in *The New York Times Index* are cross-referenced by *see* and *see also* directions. An additional feature is that each entry in *The New York Times Index* describes the length of the article as either short *(S)*, medium *(M)*, or long *(L)*. This feature can help you decide whether the article is likely to yield enough information to make researching it further worthwhile.

Marcia Valen looked in *The New York Times Index* under the general subject heading *Jury System*. Although she didn't find any articles listed there, she did find a number of *see also* references to other subjects (see Figure 20.10). She found the subject *Murders and Attempted Murders—Simpson Murder Case* most useful, given the media's attention to the selection of jurors in that trial. When she looked up *Murders and Attempted Murders,* she saw many articles listed. For each, there was a summary of the article along with the date and the section and page numbers on which it appeared in *The New York Times.*

Like *The New York Times,* other major newspapers—such as the *Chicago Tribune, Christian Science Monitor, Los Angeles Times, Wall Street Journal,* and *Washington Post*—are also individually indexed. You can find and compare articles in these and several other newspapers at the same time by consulting sources such as the *National Newspaper Index, The Newspaper Index,* and *The Times Index,* each of which indexes articles from several major newspapers.

Survey your library for the reference sources most applicable to your research subject, and use them to find a topic and conduct your research.

General subject heading ——— **JURY SYSTEM. See also**

Courts, Ja 20, F 12, Mr 19, Ap 12,26, My 16,29, Je 11,14,
    24,29, Jl 25,30, Ag 6, S 10,25, N 2,4,8
Crime and Criminals, My 7, S 1, O 5,6,12, N 4,26
Inventions and Inventors, Ja 4, Ap 8, S 28
Kidnapping, Ja 7

See also reference ——— Murders and Attempted Murders—Simpson Murder Case,
    Ja 15,19,27,30, Mr 2,18, Ap 7,8,9,11,12,14,21,22,25, My 2, ——— Dates of articles
    5,21,26,27,29, Je 2,3,4,6,7,9,11,24,25, Ag 13, S 13, O 4,5
Prostitution, Ja 24, Mr 26
Robberies and Thefts, Ag 13
Smoking and Tobacco, D 13
Terrorism, S 30

FIGURE 20.10   Subject entry for *Jury System* in *The New York Times Index*

Source: The New York Times Index (1995), p. 620. Copyright © 1995 by The New York Times. Reprinted by permission.

PREPARE A WORKING BIBLIOGRAPHY

A *working bibliography* is a list of the books, articles, and other sources that might be useful in writing your research essay. You should establish such a bibliography early in the research process as a means of gauging your topic's suitability for research—that is, to see if there are enough primary and secondary materials available for you to work with on this topic. Later, you can use the preliminary bibliography as a more permanent record of the sources you actually consult and later use in writing your research essay.

Keep your working bibliography on 3" × 5" index cards. Record each source on a separate card. So you can find the source easily or for reference, in case you need the work later, record the source's library call number in the upper-righthand corner of the card.

Write down on the card the information you will need to list the source in your paper's Works Cited section:

- For a *book,* this information includes the author's name (or editor's name followed by *ed.*); the title of the book (underlined); the place of publication; the publisher's name; and the year of publication.

- For a *magazine or journal article,* list the author's name; the title of the article (in quotation marks); the title of the magazine or journal (underlined); the volume or issue number, if the source is a journal; the date of publication; and the page numbers on which the article appears.

Figure 20.11 shows the bibliography card that Marcia Valen prepared for a journal article she found. Note that she also added a brief note at the bottom of the card, reminding herself of the content. Other kinds of sources will

Weinstein, Jack B.
　　"Considering Jury 'Nullification': When, May, and
　　Should a Jury Reject the Law to Do Justice?"
　　<u>American Criminal Law Review</u> 30.2 (1993): 229–254.

　　—Says nullification may be appropriate and important
　　to maintain

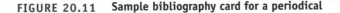

FIGURE 20.11 **Sample bibliography card for a periodical**

require slightly different information. Follow the documentation guidelines of your instructor about which information to record on your bibliography cards and what to include in your paper's Works Cited section. (See Chapter 23: Modern Language Association [MLA] guidelines appear on pp. 385–414, and American Psychological Association [APA] guidelines appear on pp. 414–430.)

TAKE NOTES ON YOUR RESEARCH

As you conduct your research and record information for your working bibliography, you should also begin taking notes about what you find. While everyone has his or her own method for taking notes, you will find that using large notecards is the most efficient form for taking down and storing research notes for several reasons:

- Cards are more durable than loose strips of paper.
- Cards are more easily organized than entries on notebook pages.
- Unlike computer-stored notes, cards can go with you and are easily available for reference anywhere you research.
- You will find large 4" × 6" index cards the most practical, since they provide plenty of space for content and are easily distinguished from the smaller 3" × 5" bibliography cards you have been keeping.

Take Notes Strategically

Make a habit of using notecards to create consistent and useful records throughout your research. Start by skimming sources, and then read closely those that appear promising. Analyze information and take notes as you proceed. What you select to read and then take notes about should correspond to the major categories of ideas listed earlier on your working outline. As you read, organize your notes by major categories, writing topic headings on the tops of notecards. Expect to create additional headings for notecards as your later reading suggests. Use a separate card for each note, even if two notes come under the same heading or from the same source.

Since you will undoubtedly need to document the source for any material included in your paper, be sure to record the name of the author and the page numbers for each piece of information that you record. The sample summary card in Figure 20.12 demonstrates a basic format for notecard information.

Take Notes with a Purpose in Mind

A good deal of your notetaking will depend on your evolving intuition about the topic and where your research is leading. If you keep your preliminary thesis in mind, your increasing sense of what you will eventually say about the topic should help you identify material for notes. Depending on your topic and

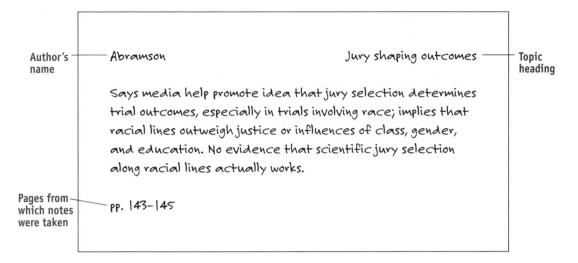

Author's name — Abramson   Jury shaping outcomes — Topic heading

Says media help promote idea that jury selection determines trial outcomes, especially in trials involving race; implies that racial lines outweigh justice or influences of class, gender, and education. No evidence that scientific jury selection along racial lines actually works.

Pages from which notes were taken — pp. 143–145

FIGURE 20.12   Summarized notes recorded on a notecard

the need to document the material you might use, the contents of your notes will include a variety of information:

1. *Take notes to record background information* that you need to understand the research topic better. Before you can write knowledgeably about *welfare fraud,* for example, you will need to know the extent of the problem, existing laws, facts about its history, and current assistance programs.

2. *Take notes to summarize general ideas* that support your preliminary thesis statement. Group major ideas and information, shifting the focus of the thesis as your notes' contents seem to suggest.

3. *Take notes on explanatory information* such as histories, definitions of terms, plot summaries, biographical data, and other material that you may need to provide to your readers. A paper on *cocaine use* would need notes for accurately defining such terms as *crack* and *freebasing,* for example.

4. *Take notes to record quotations, examples, and anecdotes* that will illustrate and support ideas in your paper. A paper on *the problems faced by new U.S. immigrants* might include an anecdote or eloquently stated comment about someone's first attempt to register for school or to apply for a job.

5. *Take notes on little-known facts or questionable and controversial ideas* that you may want to include in the paper. Selected research, for example, may suggest that people can lose weight by *thinking* themselves thin, but you will need to summarize the research or cite an authority if you expect your readers to believe you have reported such information accurately.

6. *Take notes to record statistical figures* such as percentages, weights, amounts of money, ratios, and dates not commonly known as well as the sources in which you found them. How frequently you come across such figures in your research will determine whether they are commonly known and need to be documented in the paper.

Use Effective Notetaking Methods

The information you store as research notes must not only be accurate but also useful—worth the time you spend writing it down. Using the right recording methods will allow you to tailor your notes to your expected needs for the paper and will also keep you from overrecording information or writing too little. You can ensure the value of your notes and the time you spend on them by practicing four standard techniques for recording information: summarizing, paraphrasing, using quotation, and combining quotation and paraphrase.

Summarize to Condense Source Content. *Summary* is a technique for quickly recording information in a condensed form and in your own words and style. Summarize whenever you need only a few facts or statistics from a source but not a larger, more detailed record of its content or an author's perspective. Summarizing is also useful for broadly characterizing the general contents of a source or for registering your own reactions.

Convenience and brevity are the keys to effective summarizing. Focus on recording only main points and useful facts, possibly adding a brief note to yourself when doing so seems helpful. Write the notes quickly, without too much concern for wording and style. Use synonyms and other wording or symbols to express information in your own way, but also take care not to distort the meaning of the original. Avoid simply copying words and sentences from the original, since this defeats the purpose of summarizing by taking more time. Copying like this also easily leads to *plagiarism* if you don't put the material in quotation marks and cite the source (see Avoid Plagiarism, p. 330).

To get an idea of how to summarize, look at the following paragraph, which is from one of Marcia Valen's sources about *jury selection:*

ORIGINAL

Media accounts of jury selection bear involuntary witness to our widespread belief that jury selection determines all. Race especially gains privileged status in popular accounts of why verdicts turn out as they do, as if it were obvious not only that justice does not cross racial lines but also that a juror's race always outweighs the competing or overlapping influences of class, gender, or education. . . . My conclusions about this science of jury selection will be straight forward. Empirically, there is no evidence that it works.*

Source: Jeffrey Abramson, *We, the Jury: The Jury System and the Ideal of Democracy* (New York: Basic-Harper, 1994) 143–145.

The notes Valen summarized from this paragraph appeared in Figure 20.12 (p. 325). Notice that the notecard includes a topic heading to help her locate and organize the material later. Now here's an excerpt from Valen's paper, showing how she incorporated her notes into the content of her research essay:

> While the significance of such indicators remains unclear, attorneys use peremptory challenge rights to create a jury whose members have the attitudes or education levels believed to be most promising for their case. Although there is little empirical evidence that such quasi-scientific methods of selecting juries work (Abramson 145), attorneys and the public continue to believe in their importance in shaping verdicts. Their faith in such methods is renewed each time the outcome of a trial seems to be explainable in terms of jury demographics, such as gender, education, and other factors (Abramson 144).

Paraphrase to Clarify Information. Use *paraphrase* to clarify or simplify a source's content by recasting it in your own words. Whereas a summary seeks to condense or eliminate length, a paraphrase restates the original almost line by line. The result is that a paraphrase is usually about the same length as the original, but the words are your own. Remember that proper citation of the source must always accompany a paraphrase.

You should paraphrase whenever the language or content of the original cannot be adequately summarized. This often happens with technical, scientific, and legal material in which the detailed content or language may be unsuitable for condensing to notes or using in your paper. At other times, you may paraphrase to shorten the content by combining original details and language with your own wording.

Your goal in paraphrasing is to re-create the entire original in different, *clearer language,* while accurately conveying the source's meaning as well as the author's attitude. Be sure your paraphrase reflects the less evident as well as the obvious aspects of the original author's word choices, emphases, qualifications, and overall tone. It's often helpful to the reader if you identify content as paraphrase by including a brief phrase that describes the manner in which the original is related—for instance, *Coles argues that* . . . or *Mendez concedes that. . . .*

The following examples demonstrate the differences between good and bad paraphrasing. First, consider the original source, a journal article describing research on the effectiveness of American and foreign students' notetaking habits:

ORIGINAL

There appears, in other words, to be a need to rehearse information noted down rather than just to take notes on information imparted via lecture format. Incorporating a review-of-notes condition into the present design might have yielded quite different results and might have tested the delayed effect, not just the immediate effect, of the encoding hypothesis. In sum, results of the present study suggest that note taking without opportunity for review of notes is of questionable utility for either American or international lecture attendees.*

The language and content in this excerpt may be appropriate for the authors' intentions and their respective journal audience. For the purposes of notetaking, however, and for better understanding by your paper's reader, the passage should be restated as a paraphrase.

A good paraphrase effectively recasts the original language for better clarity and readability. A poor paraphrase simply changes the words of the original or mixes the original with rephrased material. Compare the following paraphrase with the original paragraph above:

A POOR PARAPHRASE

Dunkel, Mishra, and Berliner argue that there seems, then, to be a necessity for rehearsing note content instead of just taking notes on lecture information. Including a note-review in the current plan may have given different results and tested not only the immediate effect but also the delayed effect of the encoding hypothesis. In summary, the findings of this study suggest that taking notes without the chance to review them has questionable usefulness for American or foreign lecture students ("Effects of Note Taking" 547).

This is a poor paraphrase because it merely substitutes new words for the language of the original. A good paraphrase, on the other hand, translates the *meaning* of the original by effectively recasting its language into clearer form, like this:

A GOOD PARAPHRASE

Dunkel, Mishra, and Berliner argue that students need to review lecture notes rather than simply write down information presented in lecture. If this research study had included the practice of reviewing notes, the delayed as well as the immediate effects of note taking on learning might have been tested. Overall, however, it seems that note taking alone, without the practice of reviewing notes, may have little value for any lecture student, whether native or nonnative speaking ("Effects of Note Taking" 547).

Use Quotation to Capture Exact Wording.   You should *quote,* or take down the precise words of a source, when you sense that what's said can be used to strengthen your research essay's discussion. Quote selectively and accurately,

---

Source: Patricia Dunkel, Shitala Mishra, and David Berliner, "Effects of Note Taking, Memory, and Language Proficiency on Lecture Learning for Native and Nonnative Speakers of English," *TESOL Quarterly* 23 (1989): 547.

giving your reader only enough quoted material to convey and support your ideas. Blend single words, phrases, and sentences directly into your own writing as much as possible to keep your discussion flowing and to maintain your style. Here's how Marcia Valen used quotation in her paper:

> While it is probably unfair and extreme to perceive juries as made up of "twelve prejudiced, gullible dolts incapable of understanding the evidence or the law" (Whitman vii) as some do, it is safe to say that the majority of those who actually end up serving on juries find it more than challenging.

Always remember to put quotation marks around any quotation and to document the source in both your notes and your paper. Failure to provide either of these each time you quote is another example of plagiarism (see p. 330). Also be careful not to distort the original or to quote out of context. Although you must always use the exact language of the original whenever you quote, there are acceptable methods for altering a quotation to blend with the grammar of your own writing or to suit other needs. For example, use an ellipsis—three spaced periods (. . .)—to show that you have omitted material from a quotation, and place brackets ([ ]) around your own comments when they interrupt the quotation. See the example of how to use ellipses and brackets on pages 697–699.

Keep in mind that by using a quotation in your essay, you are introducing the voice of another writer. If you use quotations excessively, it may suggest that you are depending too heavily on others for ideas and have little to say of your own. When used sparingly and accurately, however, quotations can bring variety and a sense of immediacy to a discussion.

Here are some of the most effective reasons for using quotations:

- Quote from a source to lend authority to what you say. Use the quotation to reinforce a point, not to make it for you.
- Use quotation when summary or paraphrase will sacrifice the accuracy, precision, or eloquence of the original.
- Use quotation to provide brief examples of language, as when you discuss a literary work or analyze a political speech.
- Use quotation when the original may appear extreme or of questionable veracity.

Combine Quotation and Paraphrase. You can sometimes reduce the amount of information you need to quote by combining quotation with paraphrase. The technique is simple: Use quotation when the exact wording of the original is important, and paraphrase any content whose meaning but not precise language is worth recording.

You must be careful when using quotation and paraphrase together to distinguish quoted material from paraphrased material. Use clearly written quotation marks around all quoted text. Use ellipses and brackets to alter quotations to maintain sense or to omit material, as necessary. The following example illustrates how to use quotation and paraphrase to record information on a notecard:

> Goodman feels that "the last trusted institution" of justice is being threatened by a "habitual forfeiture" of the right to be part of a jury composed of ... our peers and [the defendant's] peers (87).

Integrating quotation and paraphrase in this manner adds variety and eliminates wordiness in your writing style. As you begin writing the draft and final versions of your research paper, add vitality to the examples you offer by integrating quotation and paraphrase as often as possible.

Avoid Plagiarism

Most of your notes will be composed of words and ideas copied directly or adapted from your sources. When you later incorporate in your paper any language, opinions, facts, particular lines of reasoning, or explanations from the authors of these sources, you must acknowledge your indebtedness (see Chapter 23 on documenting sources). Failure to give credit for words or ideas you have borrowed from another source is *plagiarism*, a serious breach of academic integrity. Plagiarism occurs, for example, any time you omit quotation marks around language you borrow directly from another source or when you record or paraphrase a source's language without citing the original author or listing the source in your paper's Works Cited section. *Done consciously or not, plagiarism in any form is the same as stealing, punishable in most colleges by immediate failure or even dismissal from school.* See Figure 20.13, which outlines the steps you should follow to avoid plagiarism.

Work with a Preliminary Thesis

At some point in the initial stages of your research and notetaking, you will begin to formulate a potential answer to the research question you have framed about your topic (see pp. 310–311). For some writers, this answer comes early in the research process. For others, it develops slowly and changes as the focus of the research question shifts in response to discovering more information about the topic. Some writers resist forming even a potential answer to the research question until their investigation of sources has been completed.

Guided by a research question, however, most writers also find it helpful to have a *preliminary thesis* in mind as they work. The preliminary thesis is a one- or two-sentence statement that summarizes your *tentative* response to the research question at that particular point in your investigation. Along with the research question, a thesis statement will direct your research activities to-

You can avoid plagiarizing by taking careful, accurate notes and by using them conscientiously while writing the paper and ensuring the integrity of your documentation.

Following these steps will help:

1. Include on every notecard the name of the source's author and the page number(s) for any text you copy or adapt and for each piece of information you record. (Other necessary information about the source is already entered on the bibliography cards you have created for it.)

2. On your notecards and in your paper, put quotation marks around any language you use directly from the source—that is, quotes.

3. Whenever you include material from the notes in your final paper, cite the source in the text and in the Works Cited section.

4. Scrupulously recheck your notecards during and after the writing stage to make sure you have used and acknowledged all your sources accurately.

FIGURE 20.13   Avoiding plagiarism

ward relevant material, helping you decide which sources should receive your close attention.

For example, suppose your research topic is *the effectiveness of antiyouth gang programs in large cities*. An appropriate research question would be *What is required for a successful antigang program?* Drawing on what you know about the topic from your beginning investigation, you might formulate a potential preliminary thesis such as this:

> The most effective antigang programs include community-based education and
>
> employment assistance.

You can use key concepts such as *community-based education* and *employment assistance* to focus your reading. And defining what your paper will mean by *effective* (and its opposite, *ineffective*) can strengthen its content and add breadth to your discussion.

Remember that the preliminary thesis is *not* intended to state your final opinion on the topic. As you investigate your topic more thoroughly, you will most likely modify the thesis or change it entirely in response to your increased knowledge. You might begin with something like *The average American's diet is certain suicide* and later decide that *Americans can choose to eat better and live longer* expresses your ideas more suitably. If a preliminary thesis seems helpful at the planning stage, use it with the research question as a way of further narrowing the focus of your research.

Research Exercises

1. Rank each of the following from 1 to 8 (most to least) according to its potential suitability as the subject of a research essay. Briefly state your reasons for ranking each as you have.

   The value of a family   The death of Princess Diana

   The dangers of body art   The development of nuclear power

   Children and the Internet   Snowboarding versus skiing

   Pablo Picasso   College drinking

2. State two potential research questions about each of the following topics:

   a. Television and race
   b. Sports fan violence
   c. Sex in advertising

3. Answer each of the following questions about your campus library's reference section:

   a. What encyclopedias and newspaper indexes are available?
   b. What bibliographical indexes are available? (List three titles.)
   c. What computer-based resources and services are available?

4. Use your library's *Readers' Guide to Periodical Literature* to prepare a bibliography card for an article written in 1997 on each of the following subjects:

   a. Teenage pregnancy
   b. Bill Clinton
   c. State lotteries
   d. El Niño
   e. "Road rage"

5. Use your library's card or computer catalog to answer the following questions:

   a. What works by *Stephen Jay Gould* does your library carry?
   b. What books on the subject of *cloning* are available in your library? (List the author, title, and date of one book.)
   c. What scholarly journals are available at your library for different academic fields, such as education, literature, political science, health, medicine, history, or music? (List three titles.)

6. Using 3" × 5" or larger index cards, prepare three bibliography cards, one each for a book, a magazine or journal article, and a newspaper article on the subject *the Internet*. Use your library's catalog, magazine, and newspaper indexes to find the information you need.

7. After reading the following paragraph, complete parts a and b:

   Traffic-USA, a branch of the World Wildlife Fund that tracks the trade in contraband wildlife products, conservatively estimates the worldwide market for crocodile skins at 1.5 to two million a year. Yet according to Don Ashley, a trade consultant in Tallahassee, Fla., in 1993 only about a million of those skins had legal documentation from the country of origin. So up to half of the skins that make up those expensive handbags, wallets and belts may have been harvested from wild animals, in violation of national and international laws. The bulk of these illegal skins comes from members of the genus *Caiman.**

    a. Write a two-sentence summary of the paragraph.
    b. Paraphrase by restating the paragraph in your own words.

8. Use a computer-based search program (such a Infotrac or Yahoo) available at your library or elsewhere to find three current sources on one of the following topics:

    a. Megan's Law
    b. Life on Mars
    c. Acupuncture
    d. Pornography
    e. Bilingual education

    **Source:* Peter Brazaitis, Myrna E. Watanabe, and George Amato, "The Caiman Trade," *Scientific American* March 1998: 70.

CHAPTER 21

Researching on the Internet

Possibly the most significant resource for worldwide communication and research on the planet is the *Internet,* a global communication system composed of thousands of other networks and computers around the world. These individual networks and computers share the information and even the capabilities they have with each other, with the result that anyone using the network has access to all the information and even some of the capabilities of every computer on the Internet.

While it's not the purpose of this chapter to introduce you to everything you need to know about the Internet, being familiar with a few basic concepts will aid your understanding of discussions that follow.

ACCESSING THE INTERNET: *ONLINE* IS *ONBOARD*

If you are new to using the Internet, you will find that connecting with it can be fairly simple. Using a college's computer network to get to Internet sources, you can generally get started by following the instructions provided on the campus system or by asking a college librarian for help. If you want to access the Internet from your own computer, you will first need to have the necessary software, computer equipment, and services of a commercial Internet service provider such as America Online, Netcom, or Microsoft Network.

Using Internet Addresses

If the computer program you use is set up to connect automatically with the Internet, your research can start as soon as you click on the software link. If not, you will need to enter an Internet *address* for the location you want to contact. You need not be an expert about the Internet or computers to use most addresses comfortably, but understanding some basics about Internet address formats can save time and greatly enhance your research efforts.

Understanding Domain Names. The thousands of individual computers that make up the Internet are each identified by a unique name, called the *domain name*, consisting of letters or words separated by the symbol **.** (pronounced "dot"). For example, the domain name for Bookwire, an Internet source about books and publishing, is *www.bookwire.com.*

As with any address, each part of a domain name tells something specific about the computer it designates. In the case of *www.bookwire.com*, the domain name describes a computer that is:

- Part of the World Wide Web—the *www*
- Identified by other computers as *bookwire*
- Operated by a commercial organization—*com*

If Bookwire were not a commercial entity, the domain name for its Internet address would end in different letters, such as *gov, edu, mil, net,* or *org* (for *commercial, government, educational, military, Internet network,* or nonprofit *organization,* respectively).

Domain names are useful for identifying Internet sources, but they are not complete addresses. To connect with a particular Internet site, your computer needs to know what communication system that site uses. This is where something called a *URL* comes in.

Understanding URLs. The complete address for a computer located on the Internet is called a *URL,* for *uniform resource locator,* a term representing a particular communication format used by Internet computers. The URL for the computer at Bookwire, for example, is *http://www.bookwire.com.* This is the address your computer needs to know in order to locate and connect over the Internet with the Bookwire computer.

A URL includes the Internet computer's domain name preceded by what is called a *protocol*—that is, the symbol *://* and letters indicating a particular communication format:

URL Protocol   Domain Name

http://www.bookwire.com

The *http* protocol in this example indicates that the Bookwire computer uses *hypertext transfer protocol,* a World Wide Web communications format providing hypertext links, which you can use to jump electronically to or from different Internet locations (see pp. 337–338). A computer with another communications format would require a different URL protocol. For instance, the URL for the library at the University of Virginia is *gopher://gopher.lib.virginia.edu,* indicating that the library's computer uses a Gopher-based communications format. Using other Internet systems—such as *ftp, Telnet, or WAIS*—to contact an Internet computer would require URLs that begin with *ftp://, telnet://,* or *wais://,* respectively. (See the sections on these systems later in this chapter.)

Occasionally during your research, you may run into a complex and lengthy URL that contains more than just a protocal and domain name. Such a URL might look something like *http://www.bookwire.com/rev7?@eri3/t62ja/html.* This kind of URL usually contains additional information—such as *path* and *file* data—telling the Internet computer where specific information is stored among its files and subdirectories. Fortunately, while such data-packed URLs can be useful, you seldom need to tork with them: You can use the common, shorter form of the URL to go first to a website's main or home page; from there you can click on a link to the files or subdirectories storing the information you want.

Researching with URLs

The information included in a URL is useful to your research because of what it tells you in advance about an Internet source. As you will learn later in this chapter, sources with, let's say, *www, gopher,* or *alt* in their addresses all provide distinct kinds of information, in different formats, and with varying capabilities and limitations. Similarly, you can expect that sources whose addresses include endings such as *com, edu,* or *gov,* for example, will all provide different types of information and with varying amounts of authority or expertise. Interpreting an Internet address in these ways beforehand will save time and help you locate the variety of sources and points of view you need for effective research.

OVERVIEW OF INTERNET SYSTEMS

Researching on the Internet would be an unthinkable challenge without the technological systems responsible for its existence. The Internet is driven by a variety of utility programs with strange-sounding names like *Telnet, Gopher, ftp, WAIS,* the *World Wide Web, e-mail, listservs,* and *Usenet.* Each of these names represents a different means of accessing the hundreds of thousands of information files stored on the Internet. (We'll look at each program later in this chapter.)

You may be already familiar with the World Wide Web or e-mail, two of the most widely used communication tools included in the Internet today; however, all the systems described in this chapter can be important in helping you make use of the full range of the Internet's resources. After studying their uses, you will appreciate the extent to which each of them can play an invaluable role in helping you find information on any research topic.

The World Wide Web:
Worlds within a World

Often written as *WWW* and spoken of as *the web,* the *World Wide Web* is one of the Internet's richest resources and its most popular means of navigating the Internet. The web was launched in 1989 in CERN, the European Center for Particle Physics in Switzerland, by scientists working together to create a global computer system for exchanging research information. The evolutionary leap that made the web what it is today is credited to two scientists at the CERN laboratories, Tim Berners-Lee and Robert Cailliau. They first conceived of the idea of *hypertext,* a means of imbedding links in a document to connect computer software to related materials. Since that time, the rapid development of additional new technologies has made the web one of the world's most important resources for commerce, education, entertainment, and communication.

Researching with Hypertext. The technological power and popular appeal of the World Wide Web would never have been possible without the development of *hypertext,* the unique and seemingly magical tool that first launched the web and continues to distinguish it from all other Internet systems. Hypertext appears on a web document page as a highlighted word or phrase that, when you click on it with your mouse, takes you automatically to another section of a document or to a whole new document. Figure 21.1, for example, shows a page with hypertext that student Marcia Valen (whom we met in Chapter 20) used for her research on jury selection procedures. Clicking on one of the hypertext words would initiate a hypertext jump to an area where the selected topic is discussed at length.

Following the hypertext links in a web document lets you experience it differently than when you read traditional text—that is, by starting at the top and proceeding linearly through a sequence of paragraphs and pages. With hypertext,

A **petit jury,** which decides criminal or civil cases, has a maximum of twelve members, which is often fewer than the number of jurors on a **grand jury**. Although practices vary within each state, the most common method of jury selection is through **voir dire examination**, which includes questioning by the attorneys, the judge, or both, as to background and possible bias of prospective jurors. Attorneys can dismiss a potential jurist "for cause" or through a **peremptory challenge**. This latter method of excusing a juror requires no reason to be given to the court. . . .

FIGURE 21.1   Excerpt from a hypertext document

you read in a nonlinear fashion, skipping from one page or document to the next, and then on to the next, and so forth, clicking on various terms of interest as you proceed. In this way, hypertext can be especially useful when you are looking for a research topic or searching for additional ideas or sources.

You can, of course, simply "surf" hypertext documents by spontaneously jumping from one to the next. A better approach, however, is to focus consciously on an area of interest, following related hypertext links and keeping an eye out for relevant topics and sources as you proceed. You might, for example, begin looking for information about the beneficial effects of *forest fires* but then jump via hypertext to related topics, starting with the damaging effects of *volcanic eruptions*, going next to a link with information about the *1980 eruption of Mount St. Helens* in Oregon, and finally settling on a topic discussing *effective forest reclamation processes*. While exploring these topics, you may also have discovered a number of useful resources to take notes from and use in your research essay.

A word of caution, however: Used in this way, hypertext can be a valuable resource and aid to your research. But take care to avoid getting caught up in surfing idly from one link to the next, until you suddenly find yourself miles away from your research topic. This can result in a loss of valuable research time and possibly additional charges for the extra time online. Remember to be judicious about how far from your topic you let hypertext links take you— and for how long.

Researching with Hypermedia. Another great feature of the World Wide Web is its ability to provide what is called *hypermedia*, a combination of hypertext and multimedia. With hypermedia, you explore a subject by moving in hypertext fashion among text, graphics, sound, and video displays in any order. You might begin by reading about the life of Martin Luther King, Jr., for example, but then jump via hypertext to a short video clip of his march for civil rights in Alabama or switch to a sound file to hear his famous "I Have a Dream" speech.

Hypermedia sources such as these can enhance your research as well as your understanding of any research subject. Look for them as you research web documents, and incorporate the insights they provide into your paper whenever you can. (To list a hypermedia source in your paper's Works Cited page, refer to the guidelines for citing electronic resources in Chapter 23, pp. 404–410.)

Search Engines: Workhorses of the Web

If you know the address, or URL, for a particular website, you can access it directly through your computer's *browser*. With more than 80 million web pages and more than 30 million sites on the web, however, you can't possibly know the address of every Internet computer site or information file you may want to research. Enter the *search engine*, the workhorse of the World Wide Web.

Using a Search Engine. A *search engine* is a computer program that hunts for information sites all over the Internet. After you enter one or more *keywords* (called a *string*) about a topic, a search engine scans its own huge database or the Internet and ultimately presents you with a list of possible sources. Although all such Internet search programs are commonly referred to as *search engines,* there are actually two kinds: *directory* programs, which primarily search only their own databases of stored Internet information, and what might be termed *true search engines,* which are programs that actually search the Internet each time you make a request. Both directory and true search engines give such good results that people seldom know or care about the difference between them. But there *is* a difference, and to get the best results from your research efforts, you need some understanding of how each type of search engine works.

Directories.   A directory search engine—such as Yahoo, HotBot, and Lycos—doesn't actually search the entire Internet for information sites and files each time it is launched. Instead, a directory searches its own preestablished database—generally, a collection of several hundreds of thousands of preselected Internet files. In response to a keyword request, the directory engine searches its database and then presents successive layers of menu choices listing related topic categories. From this point, you proceed almost intuitively, selecting first one category, then the next related one, and so on—making each selection based on your sense of a category's relevance to your topic. Eventually, you will come to a specific topic and a list of sources from the directory database about it. Figure 21.2 illustrates the way a directory-based search might lead you through several layers of potential, progressively more focused subjects until you eventually arrive at a specific topic to research.

Layer 1——Government	**Politics**	Law	Health	Arts and Humanities
Layer 2——Foreign Policy	**Elections**	Interest Groups	Political Issues
Layer 3——Voter Information	**1996 Presidential Elections**	Congressional Elections
Layer 4——Party Platforms	**1996 Voter Opinions**	Campaign Issues
Layer 5——	**African American Support for Bill Clinton**
Layer 6——	**Selected Internet Resources (polls, speeches, books, articles)**

FIGURE 21.2   Menu options for a directory-based search

A directory search can be especially helpful when you first want to explore a potential research topic, discover and examine related issues, or assess the types of resources available for it. You might begin a directory search with no certain idea about a research subject but eventually find several central and related topics for research after working through the directory's layers of categories.

Another plus to a directory search is that it is fast and efficient. You will waste less time hunting for information because most directory databases are large enough to include information on nearly any topic imaginable. So, with a directory-based search, you will not only avoid having empty search results (in most cases), but you will also benefit from having had someone else already screen potential sources for their relevancy and quality.

A small drawback to a directory-based search engine is that, unlike a true search engine, it searches for and finds only items listed in its *own* database. Whatever topics and information files are stored in a directory's database have been previously defined, selected, and categorized according to criteria established by the search site personnel. Thus, if your topic requires that you connect with very recent, offbeat, amateur, or seldom-visited Internet sites, you may have better luck researching with a true search engine.

True Search Engines.　　Unlike a directory search program, a true search engine—such as AltaVista, for example—presents no menu of subject choices to follow. Instead, you simply enter a keyword string, and the search engine finds and presents a list of Internet sources. Because you can't depend on the search engine program to find and narrow a potential topic for you (as you can with a directory search), you need to use very specific keywords to define accurately what you want to investigate and what sources you want the search engine to find. Since several directory-type search engines today also provide for keyword searches of the Internet, you will find understanding such searches useful for researching with both kinds of engines.

Performing Keyword Searches.　　When you enter a keyword string in the search box of a true search engine, the program looks through all the websites it knows about to find as many matches with the string as it can. Depending on the particular search engine or the user's instructions, a search might include a comparison of the keywords with the words in a site's URL, document titles, text, a website's own summary of its contents, or all of these.

Although each search engine has its own methods for defining a search, certain conventions are fairly common. For example, search engines are *case insensitive,* meaning they don't distinguish between upper- and lowercase letters; whether you enter *California* or *california* makes no difference. Most engines also have a means of defining a keyword phrase as a group, rather than as separate words, usually by enclosing the phrase in quotation marks, as in *"Civil War."* This is an important technique, since entering the words *Civil War* alone—or even *Civil AND War*—without the quotation marks would yield literally thousands of results for the single word *Civil* and very likely the same number for the word *War*.

A number of special approaches can simplify a keyword search and make it more precise. While few search engines actually provide for *all* the methods described in the following section, acquainting yourself with the possible refinements for a search will help you decide which search engines allow the techniques most helpful to your research.

Refining a Search Engine Query. A variety of options are available to refine a search query, or keyword string. In fact, many search engines ask you to specify which options you want to use when you enter a keyword string. The following descriptions will help you become acquainted with these options and use them to aid your research:

- *Boolean and other logical operators* limit the terms of a search string to make it more exact. *Boolean operators* are capitalized words and phrases such as *AND, OR, NOT,* and *BUT NOT.* For example, *dolphins BUT NOT bottlenose* would eliminate getting unwanted sources on bottlenose dolphins, a heavily documented species. Many search engines work with a simplified version of Boolean operators or employ other punctuation or devices, such as using + or – signs in front of search terms.

- *Concept searching* occurs when a search engine runs one or more keywords through its database and then returns with a list of suggested, possibly related sources. If you entered *adolescent* as a keyword, for instance, the search engine would return potential sources using the terms *juvenile, minor,* and *teen.*

- *Date searching* is a means of limiting a search to web pages that have been posted within a specified period of time. For instance, you could use date searching to ensure getting a list of only those web pages discussing the Jerry Seinfeld show *after* the last original episode had run on television.

- *Keyword weighting* allows you to define the relative importance of each word in a string by sequencing. When entering a search string such as *Princess Diana AND paparazzi AND Paris,* for instance, you instruct the engine to pay more attention to sources containing references to *Princess Diana* and *paparazzi* than to *Paris.*

- *Location limiting* allows you to specify a particular web domain or a range of geographical locations. Thus, you could limit a search to include only those sites with *.edu* in their URL or only those located in the *United States* or *France.*

- *Media searching* allows you to specify a particular type of file, such as one formatted in Java or VRML, or to locate image, audio, or video files specifically.

- *Natural language queries* define a search in ordinary sentence form, rather than by Boolean or other logical operators or truncated language. Entering *I want to know about national drunk driving rates and insurance costs for drunk drivers,* for instance, would turn up search results regarding the query's key terms, such as *drunk driver, drunk driving,* and *insurance.*

■ *Nesting* is a way of using parentheses in a Boolean-type search to indicate the order in which a search engine should locate material. The string *(american literature AND (faulkner OR sound and fury)* directs the engine to locate first any sites using the term *american literature* and then from this list report the ones also using the terms *faulkner* and *sound and fury*.

■ *Proximity searching* locates documents in which two or more search terms appear within 10 words of each other. Thus, *civil AND war NEAR american* will turn up references to *American Civil War* as well as *An American who fought in the Civil War.*

■ *Relevancy ranking* provides for returns ranked according to how often or where in the searched document the search string appears. Sources in which a keyword appears more frequently or in a more central part of a document than in others are ranked higher.

■ *Wildcards* are symbols that tell search engines to substitute letters after a keyword root. For example, to ensure that the engine registers *electrical* and *electrified* when searching for *electric field,* you would use a wildcard such as *electr* field* as the search string.

Using a Metasearch Engine.　Rather than hunt through the Internet or even its own database for information sources, a *metasearch engine* goes to several other search engines and returns with the results from all of them listed on a single page. If you used the search engine for Highway 61, for example, it would consult the other engines at Yahoo, Lycos, WebCrawler, Infoseek, and Excite and then return with a list of sources gathered by each. Metasearch engines can be slower in returning with information than other kinds of engines, but you should use them when you can to reach a variety of sources from the Internet and databases—as well as to save time searching.

Finding a Search Engine to Use.　You will find search engines available on most campus and public library computer systems as well as on the Internet itself. Figure 21.3 lists some of the most popular search engines and their URLs.

Telnet: Borrowing a Remote Computer

Any time you need to find out which books or other sources for your research project are available at a library upstate, across the nation, or around the world, Telnet should be the access tool of choice. *Telnet* is an Internet utility that connects you with another computer at a remote Internet site and then allows you to operate that computer's systems. Using Telnet, you can search a library's catalog, take part in a live online discussion, read and print files, or access any of the other functions the other computer is running.

Accessing Telnet.　You can access an Internet Telnet computer by entering the site's URL (e.g., *telnet://fisp.emc.gov)* and letting your software program

General Search Engines

AltaVista	http://www.altavista.digital.com
DejaNews	http://www.dejanews.com
Excite	http://www.excite.com
HotBot	http://www.hotbot.com
Infoseek	http://www.infoseek.com
Inktomi	http://inktomi.berkeley.edu
Lycos	http://www.lycos.com
Netguide Live	http://www.netguide.com
Northern Light	http://www.nlsearch.com
WebCrawler	http://www.webcrawler.com
Yahoo	http://www.yahoo.com

Metasearch Engines

All-In-One	http://albany.net/allinone
Galaxy	http://galaxy.tradewave.com/galaxy.html
Highway 61	http://www.highway61.com
Metacrawler	http://www.metacrawler.com
SavySearch	http://guaraldi.cs.colostate.edu.2000
Starting Point	http://stpt.com

FIGURE 21.3   **World Wide Web search engines and their URLs**

connect you. Once you have linked with a Telnet computer, you will be asked to enter an account password; if you don't have one, you can use *anonymous* or *guest* to log in. After logging in, Telnet allows you to open files or run certain programs on the other computer as if it were the one sitting in front of you.

Researching with Telnet.   The files you can access through Telnet are textual resources—programs with files and databases such as a library's catalog listing, directories, indexes, abstracts, stock prices, and many kinds of public documents. If you were researching *privacy issues,* such as *wiretapping* or *credit reporting,* for example, you could use the Telnet address *telnet://teetot.acusd.edu/* to access fact sheets, position papers, copies of legislation, and press releases provided by the Privacy Rights Clearinghouse. Addressing *telnet://locator@ locator.nim.nih.gov* would access the National Library of Medicine Online Catalog System, with listings of over 4.9 million items relating to medicine, biomedicine, the health sciences, and the history of medicine.

In addition to resources like these, the MELVYL online library system for the entire University of California is also accessible through Telnet, as are the libraries of Cornell, Princeton, Rutgers, Michigan, Oregon, Texas A&M, Stanford, and Brown Universities and a host of other academic institutions. In addition, you can use Telnet to connect to a number of government research sites and NASA databases, to get weather reports, and to find business and entertainment information. Ongoing dialogues from several interactive Internet groups—such as bulletin board services, Usenet, and MUDs (short for "multi-user dungeons")—are also available via Telnet.

Most Telnet resources can also be accessed through Gopher or the World Wide Web. However, using Telnet for text-based documents located at busy Internet sites can help you avoid access delays or time lost to loading unneeded images. To learn which resources are available through Telnet and to find their URLs, use the World Wide Web to go to a *hytelnet* program developed by Peter Scott of the Berkeley university library. The URL is http://www.lights.com/hytelnet/.

FTP: Borrowing Remote Files

Need to download new software to aid your research? Want to copy a lengthy data file from a distant research laboratory to your own computer? *File transfer protocol (FTP)* can help, since it allows you to retrieve files from or even send files to another computer, called a *host*, at a remote distance.

Accessing an FTP Site.   Since using FTP doesn't require much knowledge of Internet protocols, it's generally easier to use and consequently more commonly known than Telnet. To access a host computer's files via FTP, you first need to log in, usually as *anonymous* or *anonymous ftp* (unless you have an account at that site), and enter your complete e-mail address as a password. Once you have logged in, you move through relevant directories and subdirectories until you find a file you want to download to your own computer. In most cases, you will need to use the basic FTP commands for the host computer you contact, but these are usually available from an online help file at the site.

Researching with FTP.   FTP allows you to download software or copy text, graphics, audio, and video files as well as application programs and software updates right to your own computer and store them for later use. For instance, you could strengthen your research on trends in radio programming by using FTP to retrieve sound files of actual radio shows from *ftp://ni.funet.fi* (path = */pub/sounds/**). To access a copy of the speech by President Bill Clinton on the occasion of the twentieth anniversary of the Apollo moon landing, you could use FTP to address *explorer.arc.nasa.gov* and retrieve a file (*apollo.ann*) with the complete text.

Most computer browsing software sold today will allow you to transfer files without using an FTP program; however, as with Telnet, a few older Internet resources may be available only through FTP and many more popular sites and resources may actually be more readily accessible through it.

Using Archie.   One drawback with FTP is that, like Telnet, it requires you to know the URL for any file you want to access. This is where a program known as *Archie* (short for "archiving utility") can be of significant help.

An Archie program finds the URLs for FTP sites and their information files by constantly scanning for such sites and building an index listing them and the files they contain. Archie is especially useful when you know either the name or part of the name of an FTP file you want to access but not the URL for the file or for the site where it's stored. Suppose, for example, that you wanted to find President Clinton's speech on the Apollo moon landing but didn't know the address for any FTP site that held the file. Going to an Archie site (usually via Telnet or another online system), you could initiate a search for a site with a file named *apollo.ann* (assuming you knew the file name). If you didn't know the file name, you could ask Archie to search for all files with the word *apollo* in their titles. The Archie system would return an indexed list of FTP site addresses and files matching your request.

Using Archie for such searches can save a great amount of time, since your other alternative is to search large numbers, perhaps hundreds, of FTP sites to find the files you want. You will find Archie searches helpful any time you want to locate text files or documents from government or private organization sources as well as graphic files, mailing lists, and Usenet archives.

Gopher: Searching a Menu

As whimsical as the name may sound, *Gopher* is a highly useful search program that locates and searches files at other Internet sites and then returns its findings as a list of successively narrower menu options. You select one topic from a Gopher menu; move to a submenu with additional related subtopics; select one of those subtopics, which brings up another submenu; and so on until you come to a source you want to use (see Figure 21.4).

Accessing a Gopher Site.   You can connect with most Internet Gopher sites by using a URL beginning with a Gopher protocol (i.e., *gopher://*) followed by the site's domain name. For example, the URL for the National Science Foundation is *gopher://stis.nsf.gov*.

Researching with Gopher.   Suppose you were interested in getting information about *nutrition* from a worldwide perspective. You could begin by accessing the Gopher server menu for the United Nations' World Health

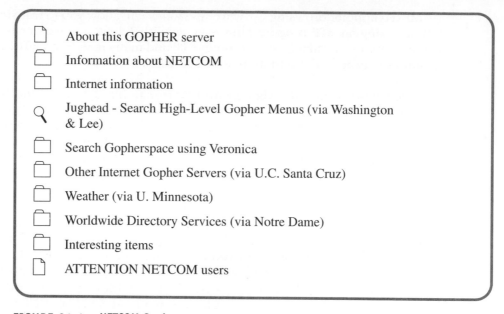

About this GOPHER server

Information about NETCOM

Internet information

Jughead - Search High-Level Gopher Menus (via Washington & Lee)

Search Gopherspace using Veronica

Other Internet Gopher Servers (via U.C. Santa Cruz)

Weather (via U. Minnesota)

Worldwide Directory Services (via Notre Dame)

Interesting items

ATTENTION NETCOM users

FIGURE 21.4   NETCOM Gopher server menu
Source: Reprinted with permission from NETCOM On-Line Communication Services, Inc.

Organization: *Gopher.who.ch.* The menu would present you with these successively more specific menu topics to select from:

Menu choice 1	WHO's Major Programmes
Menu choice 2	Food & Nutrition
Menu choice 3	Int'l Conference on Nutrition, Rome, 1993

Working from the last menu, you would be able to access information about topics presented at the Rome conference, which would lead you to other resources with an international perspective.

One drawback with Gopher is that you must search a series of menus in order to find a source that may be useful. Fortunately, a system exists for getting past immediate menus quickly and going directly to a source.

Meet Veronica.   If you know about comic books, you know that the comic book character Archie has a girlfriend named Veronica. Program developers apparently had this in mind when they created *Veronica,* a utility that works for Gopher sites much the same way an *Archie* program (discussed earlier) does for FTP sites. That is, Veronica saves you from having to search thousands of separate Gopher sites to locate the one with a particular information file. Veronica does this work for you by finding and indexing keywords in thousands of Gopher-site databases. Once you input one or more keywords describing the file you want, Veronica retrieves a list of files with those words in their titles.

Using Veronica can save you a great deal of time and frustration when you need to access any research source stored on a Gopher system.

To connect with Veronica, you must first arrive at a Gopher menu offering a selection specifically referencing it by name, such as *Search Gopherspace using Veronica* (see Figure 21.4). Once you select this option and enter a keyword or keyword string, the Veronica search system bypasses all other Gopher servers until it locates and connects you to one with a file whose title contains your keywords. Using Boolean operators (see p. 341) such as *AND* or *OR* with your keyword requests—*juries AND selection,* for example—allows you to narrow the search criteria in time-saving ways. (Another more locally focused search tool known as *Jughead* also searches titles, but it's rarely referred to by name in a system.)

Many of today's search engines automatically scan Gopher sites in their search for files through the Internet. Consequently, you don't always need to worry about performing a separate Gopher search for a source unless it's available only by that means or you know its URL and want to go to it directly. You can make an explicit search of Gopher sites by using the Galaxy metasearch engine at *http://galaxy.tradewave.com/galaxy.html.*

WAIS: Ranking Search Results

WAIS (wide area information service) searches by descriptive phrases or keywords through the indexes of other WAIS servers to find relevant sources. WAIS searches databases with a variety of sources, including text, sound, and images. Many U.S. government files are stored at WAIS sites, and America Online has recently acquired the WAIS system for use by its customers.

Researching with WAIS. Many WAIS servers rank located sources on a scale of 1,000 according to the frequency with which the search description or keywords appear in them. For example, if you entered the key phrase *plankton,* WAIS might return a list such as this:

marsys-int	1,000
USDOS	783
osea-news	528

The lefthand column contains names of databases, and the righthand column indicates the number of sources found in each database. You could select any of these database sources to find files on your topic. Keep in mind, however, that WAIS searches all terms as the same, regardless of the meaning you intend. If you enter the term *salmon,* for example, WAIS will return a list of sources including discussions of *salmon fishing, salmon biology, salmon cooking,* and so forth. For this reason, you need to be careful about the keywords you enter and use Boolean-type operators (see p. 341) such as *AND* or *NOT,* to restrict your searches appropriately.

E-Mail: Electronic Letters

"Have you checked your e-mail today?" is becoming a common question across campuses, at home, at work, and around the world. *E-mail*, a means by which you can send and receive electronic messages, is probably the most widely used feature of the Internet and one with which millions of people are already familiar.

Accessing E-Mail.   If you don't have an e-mail account, you may want to investigate getting one, both as an aid to your current research project and as a way to communicate on a daily basis with others in your community and around the globe. Many college campuses offer e-mail free to their students, or you can sign up for free e-mail service from national systems such as Juno. By paying a small monthly fee, you can also get e-mail and other Internet services from commercial providers like America Online, Prodigy, and the Microsoft Network.

Researching with E-Mail.   Besides the communication conveniences e-mail provides, the fact that so many people have e-mail today makes it a useful tool for research. You can use e-mail to find and ask questions of specialists, query libraries about sources, conduct interviews, check source authorities, send and receive files, subscribe to online magazines and newspapers, and even get help with Internet access.

If you know the name of an authority who might be willing to talk with you about your research subject but don't know how to contact him or her, you can try looking for an e-mail address through easy-to-use search systems such as *Finger* (available from most search engine sites) or a free service such as *Four11* (*http://www.four11.com/*), which lists over 1.5 million names and e-mail addresses of people who have voluntarily provided the information. If you find an e-mail address, send a polite, brief message about your research subject and the questions you would like answered. (Note that in order to use Four11, you have to list your own name and e-mail address with the service.)

Two other popular uses of e-mail—Internet mailing lists and Usenet newsgroups—can be especially helpful to your research.

Listservs and Mailing Lists: Group E-Mail

"How big is your conference table?" is a question posed by an Internet site that indexes mailing lists, worldwide addresses of thousands of people who receive and send e-mail to each other about a wide variety of subjects. A mailing-list service is commonly referred to as a *listserv* (for "list service"), a term derived from the name of the best-known mail-list program. *Listserv* has become an informally used generic term for all Internet e-mail systems, although other programs, such as *listproc* and *majordomo*, are also widely used.

Some listservs use e-mail only to disseminate information, but most use it to allow for ongoing group discussions on topics ranging from *Phen-fen* (a controversial diet medication) to *gender communication* or the music group known as *The Police.* Several thousand listservs exist already, and more are started daily. Some last no more than a week or two; others are well established. Although listserv sites are often operated by and sometimes moderated by the individuals who begin them, many are also automated, so that e-mailing takes place via a computerized program.

Joining a Mailing List.   To join a mailing list, you might start by accessing a comprehensive Internet directory called the *PAML* (publicly accessible mailing lists). You can get to the PAML directory through anonymous FTP at *rtfm. mit.edu* or use a searchable indexed version at *http://www.Neosoft.com/internet/paml/*. Once you find a mailing list that focuses on your research topic, you can subscribe to it (and later unsubscribe, if you wish) by sending an e-mail to the list's subscription address. Once you have subscribed, you will receive the e-mail address where you can begin sending messages.

Researching with Mailing Lists.   At the start of your research efforts, mailing lists can be a good way to learn about a topic and some of the major issues surrounding it. Later in your research, becoming part of a mailing list can also provide you with an informal forum for questions and an opportunity to discuss ideas and resources with others. In some cases, the list may become a means for you to conduct an interview or survey about your research topic. As you participate in a mailing list, keep in mind that your audience will range from individuals only mildly interested in and knowledgeable about your research subject to experienced or recognized experts. Avoid being judgmental, but do exercise a critical attitude about any respondents' authority on a subject and what you decide to include in your research paper. The guidelines given later in this chapter for evaluating Internet sources should help in this regard (see pp. 351–353).

Usenet/Newsgroups: Posting Information

Like mailing lists, *Usenet* groups (also known as *newsgroups*) are conferencelike, e-mail-based discussions on practically every subject you can imagine. Currently, some 9,000 to 10,000 Usenet groups around the world dialogue in a variety of languages on topics as serious as *women's rights* and *euthanasia* to some as lighthearted as *whether American cooking is as good as French cuisine.*

Understanding Usenet Postings.   Usenet differs from a mailing list in the way information is shared. Whereas a mailing-list system routinely sends each e-mail message received to every subscriber in a group, Usenet participants send messages—variously called *posts, postings,* and *articles*—to a central Internet site for others to read and respond to. The postings are listed and numbered in the order they are received, which means you need to keep up with or read several postings on a topic to follow and respond to the ongoing flow of responses (called a *thread*). Also, unlike a listserv, there are no subscribers in a Usenet group; individuals participate by simply accessing a newsgroup site and then reading and responding to what's posted there.

Given the number and variety of newsgroups, software programs called *newsreaders* are a necessity. Newsreaders can be configured to collect information only from those newsgroups that are of interest, thereby relieving you of having to keep track of existing and new groups on the Internet. Newsreaders are available commercially and included in popular browser software such as Netscape Navigator and Microsoft Explorer. Commercial providers like America Online and CompuServe offer Usenet connections, as well, and you can also reach Usenet sites through any Gopher client.

Accessing Usenet.   Addresses for Usenet groups and their postings follow a standard hierarchical naming system, which makes them similar to but not the same as Internet URLs. A typical address begins with a hierarchy category such as *alt.* (for "alternative"), *sci.* (for "science"), and *misc.* (for "miscellaneous"), followed by the various subjects discussed in a successively narrowing order. For example, *alt.rec.sport.paintball.rules* specifies a site listing discussion about the *rules of paintball.* Addresses such as *misc.writing, biz.stocks.dj,* and *sci. photosyn.orchids* indicate Usenet discussions about *miscellaneous/writing topics, business/Dow-Jones stocks,* and *science/photosynthesis in orchids,* respectively. Several search engines, such as AltaVista and Excite, link to Usenet postings; however, the most comprehensive one is DejaNews *(http://www.dejanews.com/),* which provides a searchable database where you can locate current newsgroups as well as past Usenet postings by topic.

Researching with Usenet.   The majority of information in Usenet postings is in the form of an informal opinion. Used carefully, such postings can provide you with information you may not be able to find in more usual sources. You might go to a Usenet discussion to ask for information or about sources on a particularly current topic or obscure hobby, to find someone who has experience with your research topic, or just to get a sense of people's attitudes. Following the death of Princess Diana in 1997, for example, the need to regulate news photographers, the rights of the press, and a celebrity's right to privacy were common topics for discussion among Usenet groups. You might consult similar discussions for ideas about a topic or to learn about other sources of information available through the Internet or elsewhere.

Figure 21.5 shows an excerpt from a web page listing Usenet postings that Marcia Valen examined while researching her paper on the jury selection process. After reading and evaluating several postings, Valen decided the varieties of personal opinions expressed would be most appropriately used in her paper as only a summary note that supported other research findings. (See Chapter 20, pp. 326–327, to review the use of summary.) In making this decision, Valen practiced the kind of critical judgment necessary for the effective and well-balanced use of research materials.

Search Results [Help]

Messages **1–20** of exactly **17584** for jury

	Date	Scr	Subject	Newsgroup	Author
1.	98/03/12	037	Re: Jury Duty Tomorrow	rec.arts.sf.fandom	Jamie R.
2.	98/03/12	037	Re: Jury Duty Tomorrow	rec.arts.sf.fandom	Spring
3.	98/03/10	037	Re: How to Get Out of Jury	alt.lawyers.sue.sue.	Mary L.
4.	98/03/11	036	Re: How to Get Out of Jury	alt.jury.duty	Bob BR
5.	98/03/06	036	Re: If I'm Called	alt.jury.duty	Rio
6.	98/03/08	036	Re: Jury Duty Tomorrow	rec.arts.sf.fandom	Jan Tran
7.	98/03/09	035	Re: I Got Out of Jury Duty	rec.arch.sf.glass	Kenny Davis
8.	98/02/07	035	Re: As Dilbert would say	alt.jury.duty	Erik M
9.	98/02/07	035	Re: Why juries	alt.law.ny.codes	aleaf
10.	98/02/03	035	Re: Jury compensation was	alt.jury.duty	sammy j
11.	98/01/06	034	Re: No Pay for Justice	alt.gov.law	MidPo
12.	98/01/06	034	Re: Juries are someone's	alt.jury.duty.fla	Karen Lal

FIGURE 21.5   **Web page listing of Usenet postings**

EVALUATING INTERNET RESOURCES: WHOM CAN YOU TRUST?

Many people naively believe that if something appears in print, it must be true. In fact, it might not be. As a critical reader, you should *always* consider the source of information as a primary factor in determining its value. Ask yourself these questions: What agenda does this person or group have? and How reliable are they in terms of providing complete and accurate information?

The need to be critical is particularly important in using information from the Internet. You should approach this information with a critical attitude that includes consciously evaluating authority, questioning of the origins of information, and understanding the source's assumptions and values.

The Range of Internet Content

A critical mindset is essential for anyone conducting effective research on the Internet, considering the vast number of people posting information and expressing ideas on it. You will find that much of the information available over the Internet is commercial in nature, which raises the obvious possibility that it's biased—presented to sell a product or at least emphasize certain characteristics over others. Further, because it is democratic and essentially unrestricted, Internet content often lacks the usual information-filtering mechanisms, such as competition, academic review, financial and legal concerns, and even matter-of-fact judgments about whether something is worth circulating. As a result, you can find on the Internet everyone with an idea, every group with a cause, everything and anything someone thinks is important, needed, or valuable to someone else. These conditions account for much of the Internet's great value, of course, but they also mean there's a lot of junk out there. It's *your* job to sort through it.

A Reliability Checklist for Internet Sources

None of what's said here should diminish your enjoyment of the Internet and your use of its resources for your research. Just keep in mind that you should continue to apply the same critical assessment to Internet sources and content that you would to traditional library sources but with a sense of the differences between the two. Although there are no certain criteria for evaluating Internet sources, the following checklist may guide you to think critically about your research on the Internet.

CONTENT

- *Currency:* Does the material appear to be current, and is there any indication of how often it's updated?
- *Fairness:* Does the material demonstrate not only the author's knowledge but also other viewpoints, and research that may be relevant? Is the author's tone reasonable and temperate?
- *Evidence:* Does the content provide statistics, examples, or anecdotal evidence to support the author's position? Are the examples and other evidence presented fairly? Are they current? Is there a clear separation of fact and opinion?
- *Research:* Is there evidence of credible research, such as a description of methodology or a bibliography? Are links to other sites with established credibility listed?
- *Credibility:* Would the document's content be credible in the non-Internet world? If so, why and with whom? If not, why?

AUTHORITY

- *Identity:* Does the author of the material or the person responsible for posting it include an e-mail address, URL, or other means of being contacted for comments and questions?
- *Qualifications:* Does the author include or express a willingness to provide information about his or her qualifications?
- *Reputation:* Is the author or organization responsible for the content commonly accepted as credible? What do you know about the author's education, employment, publications, awards, experience, or other verifiable qualifications?

- *Other Postings:* Has the author posted other kinds of entries on the Internet? If so, what kinds? How do they compare with the current document?

- *Credibility:* Would the author of this document be considered credible in the non-Internet world? If so, why and with whom? If not, why?

Remember to keep these criteria in mind during both the research and writing stages for your paper. Doing so can help you avoid using questionable evidence or, in some cases, remind you to support ideas more fully.

Research Activities

1. To experience the difference between using a search engine and a directory, connect with the Internet sites for AltaVista (*http://www.altavista.com/*) and Yahoo (*http://www.yahoo.com/*). Perform searches at both sites on the topics below, and make a list of the first five sources each search engine finds:
   a. Laser surgery
   b. Rap music
   c. Body building

2. Go to each of the Internet sites listed below to conduct a search using the indicated technique. Describe the results you get with each search. If you are unsure about how to conduct the search, go to the search engine site's "Help" section for directions.
   a. At Lycos (*http://www.lycos.com*), use the Boolean operator *BUT NOT* to find sources about *stars* and not about *movie stars*. List the first five results of your search.
   b. Connect to the periodical archive at Northern Light (*http://nlsearch.com*) to locate an article on *marijuana*. List the article title, author, periodical title and date, and page numbers. (Note: You don't need to download the article's text; viewing basic information about an article is available from a menu and free of charge.)
   c. Connect with WebCrawler (*http://www.webcrawler.com*), and follow the directions for a search with *relevancy ranking* for the topic *jazz*. List the five top-ranked sources and the frequency with which the search term appears in each.
   d. Go to Infoseek (*http://www.infoseek.com*) and perform a *natural language* search on the topic *the causes of divorce*. List the five top-ranked sources.

3. Identify the Telnet and FTP sites addressed by the following URLs:
   a. *Telnet address:* kraus.com
      — *Login:* gpn
   b. *Telnet address:* telnet://Locis.loc.gov.23/
      — *Login:* anonymous

    c. *FTP address:* oak.oakland.edu
      — *Path:* /pub/misc/ss-info
    d. *FTP address:* ftp://dunkin.Princeton.EDU/pub/golf/

4. The following URLs are for different Gopher and WAIS Internet sites. Connect with each site and identify it:

    a. *Gopher address:* http://mojones.com/
    b. *Gopher address:* gopher://gopher.med.und.nodak.edu/
    c. *WAIS address:* world-factbook/
    d. *WAIS address:* geo-state

5. Go to the Usenet site at *alt.rock-n-roll.classic.* After browsing the site, write a brief paragraph summarizing what you find.

6. After visiting the Usenet site at *comp.ai.alife,* write a brief summary of what you have learned there about *artificial life.*

7. Go to a search engine of your choice to find sources on any two of the topics below. Select two of the sources you find, and compare their credibility.

    a. Family violence
    b. Dreams
    c. Dyslexia
    d. The right to privacy

CHAPTER 22

Writing Your Research Essay: From Planning to Typing the Final Draft

Having come this far in the research process, you should now be ready to begin planning the organization and content of your paper in preparation for writing and typing the final draft. You should expect to plan and write the essay over several days as you organize your notes, devise a working thesis, revise drafts, and then put the finishing touches on the completed final paper.

PLANNING YOUR ESSAY

Since your research essay will probably be longer and more complex than other essays you have written, take time before writing to organize your ideas. By doing so, you will make the best use of your research material. Once you have developed a plan, you will be prepared to use it to begin writing the paper.

Use Your Research Notes

Plan your paper by first reviewing the notes you recorded from library materials and other research sources. Your goal at this point is to get an overall view of your topic, as represented in the notes. Reviewing your notes will also show what you have to work with in terms of ideas and information for the paper.

Read carefully through your notes several times, studying their contents and noting subheadings and other clusters of information. Relate the contents of each set of notes to the information in other sets as you proceed. Your purpose here is to see how your notes—all the pieces of information you have collected—fit together and exactly what picture they make in terms of answering your research question. You may find it useful to merge separate groups of notes with previously different subheadings or to arrange the notes into a particular order, such as a chronological or cause/effect sequence. The use of notecards makes such rearranging easy, as does having the notes on a computer. If you use a notebook to record notes, cut out each section so you can rearrange the notes, as needed.

Look for examples, anecdotes, quotations, and statistics that appear particularly useful or striking. Consider how these and other content relate to your research question or preliminary thesis statement.

Review Your Research Question

Although the planning stage is not the place to change to a new research topic, you may need to modify the focus of your research question (see Chapter 20, pp. 310–311) and its answer before proceeding further. After reviewing your research notes, take time to consider what research question and answer they best support. Suppose you began your research by asking *What effect does early fame have upon he adult lives of child stars?* However, a review of your notes suggests a different approach: *What factors contribute to successful adult lives for child stars?* A slight change such as this may promote fuller use of your research material and help you frame a more precise final thesis statement.

Review Your Preliminary Thesis Statement

The preliminary thesis statement you devised earlier (see Chapter 20, pp. 330–331) to guide your research may still be sufficient, or it may need to be revised to reflect the content of your notes and any modification to your original research question. Write the research question and thesis statement at the top of a notebook page or other sheet of paper. Underneath them, list the topic headings from your notecards. As you do so, include under the various headings the major ideas or examples that should be part of the paper. Here's an example done by student writer Marcia Valen in planning to write her paper on jury selection procedures:

Research question: Should the jury selection process be changed?

Possible thesis: The jury selection process is unfair and needs to be changed.

Jury selection procedure

Jury service

Attitudes about jury duty

Peremptory challenges

O. J. Simpson case

Reform efforts

Nullification laws

Faulty judgments

Cross-sectional jury requirement

Judges' orders to juries

Jury shaping

Don't worry too much whether you list information in some final order or even if it will be part of your final paper. At this stage, you simply want to see how major ideas relate and how accurately your thesis statement matches your note material. As you compare the research question, note material, and preliminary thesis, consider the extent to which they relate. Modify your preliminary thesis as needed to match your research question, as well as the ideas and information on your notecards.

Devise a Final (Working) Thesis Statement

The *thesis statement* asserts the main idea controlling your paper's content and organization. In turn, every part of the paper's content supports the thesis statement by explaining it further or offering evidence and examples that show it's accurate. Your thesis will grow out of the thinking you do about your research topic and from focusing on the information you have collected from sources.

A good thesis statement isn't devised quickly. In fact, it's often revised several times before and during the writing of the paper to make it conform to the evolving content. You may also need to add or delete content during the writing stage in order to support the thesis statement more closely. Good planning of the thesis *before you write* can help you avoid making too many alterations later. Review Chapter 6 (pp. 75–79) about developing a thesis statement, and refer to it as necessary during the planning and writing stages of your research essay.

Develop an Outline

An *outline* is a tool to assist you in organizing and writing your essay. Some writers work best by drafting an informal outline before they write and then making changes to it as the paper develops; others prefer to work from a more formal outline.

You may want to use both types of outlines. Marcia Valen did in planning and writing her paper. Here's her informal outline:

Thesis Statement: The United States must reform the process by which jurors are selected to render justice in the courtroom.

Background to the Problem

The trials of the Menendez brothers and O. J. Simpson have resulted in people becoming outraged over the system of justice in this country.

Trials cost a lot of money, but they don't always seem to bring justice.

Problems with the Jury Selection Process

People don't even want to serve on juries.

1968 civil rights laws intended to make juries represent a cross-section of the community.

Jury notices reach only about 50–70% of the people they are sent to.

Abramson thinks cross-sectional jury is not good; leaves only the weaker types available to serve.

$5.00 a day is nationwide average for jurors; no incentive there.

Attorneys don't usually want highly educated people on a jury.

One man was actually denied the chance to serve because he was a judge.

In addition, as a means of checking the organization and support for the thesis, Valen—like many writers—created a formal outline after she finished writing her essay. Your instructor may require that you use an outline for the planning and writing stages or that you to turn one in with the final paper. Valen's final outline is included with her essay later in this chapter (p. 368).

Both informal and formal outlines, as well as how you can use them to plan and write an essay, are discussed in Chapters 5 and 6 (pp. 70–72 and 80–83). After reviewing this discussion, use either type of outline—or both types, if you prefer—to plan and write your essay.

Use Other Planning Strategies, as Needed

Given the length and complexity of a research essay, any kind of outline is an especially practical tool for organizing and writing. You may also find it helpful to use other planning and prewriting strategies, such as listing, freewriting, and clustering. Chapter 5 (pp. 54–74) discusses several additional ways to plan and get started writing an essay.

WRITING YOUR ESSAY

Once you have completed a carefully planned outline, writing your essay should proceed fairly smoothly. Plan to write the essay over a period of at least two or three days. This will give you time for revising the drafts, checking the documentation, and typing and proofreading the final version. Keep your research question, thesis statement, outline, and notecards nearby as you work to help generate ideas and keep you organized as you write.

Write an Effective Introduction

Write an *introduction* that announces your paper's topic in an interesting and informative way and that includes an effectively placed thesis statement. There are no rules about how long or short an introduction should be. An overly lengthy introduction, however, can lose the paper's focus and eventually cause the reader to wonder what you are getting at. An introduction that is too abrupt, on the other hand, may omit necessary information or lack enough focus for the reader to grasp what your essay is about.

How you introduce the essay's topic and thesis will depend on your own writing preferences and the material you need to present before moving to the body of the paper. You can use any of the following strategies to introduce your essay's topic and thesis statement:

- Begin with an anecdote.
- Offer statistics.
- Summarize the literature.
- Define a key term or concept.
- Point out the topic's significance.
- Review a controversy.
- Provide background information.
- Pose a significant question.

These and other useful strategies for writing an introduction are discussed in Chapter 7 (pp. 87–89).

Develop a Discussion of the Topic

You might think of the *discussion* section of a research essay as the "meat and potatoes" of what you offer the reader. This section—the longest and most complex in the paper—develops the thesis statement according to the sequence of ideas planned in the outline. You should write the discussion portion as though it were an unfolding argument, advancing one major idea at a time. Your goal is to examine your topic thoroughly while using your research material to support and develop the thesis statement.

Develop your essay's discussion through a series of logically arranged paragraphs, each with a clearly stated topic sentence that supports the thesis. Use relevant details and examples drawn from your research to develop each paragraph's discussion and to illustrate your own ideas. (See Chapter 4, pp. 90–100, for more on discussion paragraphs.)

Integrate Source Material and Your Own Thinking. One of the greatest challenges in writing a research essay is to make sure the research material doesn't dominate to the point of excluding or obscuring your own thinking. Using too many quotations, depending too much on one or two particular works, and merely presenting series after series of unexamined examples will give your reader the impression that you have not developed your own thinking about the topic.

To avoid this problem, write clearly stated topic sentences in paragraphs that develop the thesis, and use your research material to support and illustrate your own well-developed ideas. Observing the following guidelines can help you make the most of your research material while keeping your own ideas prominent throughout the paper:

- Understand your sources before you begin to write by using *analysis* and *synthesis,* first separating the research material into parts and then studying the parts to see relationships and make connections among them. Your goal here is to come up with original ideas and insights about the topic and the issues it contains.

■ Use *quotations* to support and illustrate your ideas, not to present them for you. Quote only when summarizing would lose important qualities of the original. Use only the relevant, necessary part of an original quotation, and use brackets and ellipsis to blend quoted material smoothly into your own writing (see Chapter 20, pp. 329–330).

■ Avoid an *overreliance* on one or two particular sources. Repeated citations of the same authorities throughout the discussion can make your paper's content appear biased and suggest you have not consulted other opinions. Worse yet, relying too much on one or two sources may suggest that you have not integrated other opinions into your own thinking or that you have few ideas of your own to offer.

Develop the essay by arguing your thesis, which means supporting each paragraph topic sentence with examples, quotations, and other relevant information. The following paragraph is from Marcia Valen's research essay on jury selection reform. Notice how she incorporates examples, quotations, and documentation of her sources to illustrate and support the paragraph's topic sentence (which is highlighted):

> An important factor that further distorts the pool of jurors, and consequently skews the resulting jury, is the practice of peremptory challenges. Such challenges "require no justification, no spoken word of explanation, no reason at all beyond a hunch, an intuition" (Abramson 170). They allow attorneys on either side to dismiss prospective jurors whom they believe might be hostile to their case or simply too independent minded to be swayed by the attorney's presentation of evidence. Thus, about 30 percent of the 80 million Americans who have been called for jury duty have been sent home because of an attorney's judgment, and "many of those who are removed appear to be more alert and unbiased than many who are seated" (Adler 221). Although a 1986 US Supreme Court decision forbids the elimination of jurors because of race or gender (Greenburg), the decision says nothing about attorneys eliminating jurors on the basis of education or experience. The result is that, used in this fashion, peremptory challenges actually seem to oppose the very purposes for which they are intended: that is, to ensure an unbiased and broadly representative jury from the community as a whole.

(Intext citations for Valen's sources follow the MLA guidelines in Chapter 23, pp. 385–392.)

Write a Concluding Paragraph

The *conclusion* of your research essay should be a final paragraph that signals the reader the discussion is coming to a logical close. Avoid simply restating the thesis or starting a new discussion that's not pertinent to the paper's thesis. Instead, use the conclusion to summarize important points, evaluate results, re-emphasize the thesis, and place the topic in a larger perspective. This is also the place to use any material you think will make a lasting impression on the reader.

There are a number of ways to achieve these purposes in writing a conclusion. The following paragraph, for example, begins with a summary of preceding examples and re-emphasizes the paper's thesis—*that international treaties are inadequate protection for the wetlands of Third World countries:*

Re-emphasis of thesis

As the preceding cases demonstrate, international treaties alone cannot overcome the enormous worldwide threats to fragile ecosystems and endangered species. The Third World countries in which threatened species and environments reside are simply too often too poor to enforce agreements, so that they end up preserving what are referred to as "paper parks" (Globos 39), sanctuaries that exist only in writing. Written agreements, in fact, will never be enough to protect endangered species and wetlands until people everywhere recognize that protecting nature's diversity is essential to all life on this planet. Unfortunately, without such recognition, human beings may some day find that they themselves have become one of the most endangered species on the planet.

States possible future consequences

This paragraph concludes by pointing out the possible consequences to humans of depending too much on treaties to protect endangered species and environments. You can use any of the following methods to bring closure to your research essay and re-emphasize the thesis:

- Summarize the main points of the essay.
- Evaluate results.
- Point out future consequences.
- Call for action or increased awareness.
- Provide direction or offer solutions.
- Use an effective quotation.
- Offer a memorable example.

(Also review Chapter 7, pp. 103–104, for more discussion about writing a conclusion.)

REVISE, EDIT, AND PROOFREAD

Plan to devote a good deal of your total writing time to rereading the rough draft of your research essay several times to improve the content and readability. Some writers prefer to reread and make changes to a draft as they write; some revise and edit during separate stages of the writing process; and others like to hold off on revising, editing, and proofreading until the paper is in a nearly final form. Each of these approaches has its merits, so you should practice any that suit your method of writing. The important rule to keep in mind is that *you can never do too much revision, editing, and proofreading* to strengthen your essay's overall effectiveness.

Revise to Improve Global Qualities

The goal of revision is to strengthen major areas—such as the content, organization, and thesis—while the essay is still in the draft stage. Revise from the reader's perspective by considering the content and following the discussion with an objective point of view. Check to see that the content supports the paper's thesis statement and that the discussion unfolds smoothly, developing logically in a straightforward manner. Add examples or revise topic sentences if any paragraphs seem weak or underdeveloped. If necessary, revise the thesis to better match the content and organization. If your discussion seems one sided, rebalance the discussion by including material from any sources you may have omitted or underutilized and perhaps eliminating material from sources you have used too much.

Attention to matters such as these will strengthen the paper's content and make full use of all the research you have done. Use the revision checklist in Figure 22.1 to make sure you address all these issues. (Also review Chapter 9, pp. 115–146, on revising a rough draft.)

Edit for Clarity and Correctness

Also edit your essay by checking grammar, punctuation, mechanics, and spelling. Pay particular attention to sentence forms, verb tenses, pronoun references, and adjective and adverb forms (see Chapter 9, pp. 125–146). You can use your computer's spellcheck function to catch misspelled words, but remember that it won't identify incorrect word choices, such as *there* versus *their,* or incorrect spellings, like *from* versus *form.* You can catch these kinds of errors only by reading the paper carefully and finding them yourself.

In addition to editing for grammar, punctuation, and spelling errors, also look closely at how you have handled long and short quotations, and carefully review each text citation and entry in the Works Cited for accuracy of form and content. (See Chapter 23 on documentation.) Use the checklist in Figure 22.2 to edit your essay for these purposes.

Ask yourself the following questions and make any necessary changes as you reread the draft of your essay:

■ Is enough introductory information provided?

■ Is the thesis clearly stated and consistently emphasized?

■ Do the topic sentences adequately support the thesis?

■ Are opposing points of view adequately and fairly represented in the discussion?

■ Has source material been adequately integrated in the text?

■ Are sources correctly documented throughout the paper?

■ Are examples and other evidence sufficient and relevant?

■ Does the content demonstrate that the writer sufficiently understands the topic?

■ Are unfamiliar terms and processes adequately described?

■ Does the conclusion effectively close the essay?

FIGURE 22.1   Revision checklist

Use the following questions to guide your editing of your essay:

■ Have you avoided common writing errors in grammar involving subject and verb agreement, pronoun use, capitalization, and word order?

■ Have you checked the spellings of unfamiliar terms, important words and phrases used throughout the paper, and your own personal spelling demons?

■ Have you checked punctuation, paying extra attention to the uses of commas, quotation marks, and other special marks?

■ Are all sources cited parenthetically in the text and also included in the Works Cited pages in correct form?

FIGURE 22.2   Editing checklist

Proofread to Make Minor Corrections

Even the most careful typing and editing cannot eliminate minor mistakes in the final version of a lengthy and complex paper such as a research essay. Once you have typed the final version of your paper, proofread it several times to catch any omitted or misplaced words and content. Read the paper slowly *several times* to be sure you are reading what's actually written and

Plan to proofread the final draft of your paper several times, using these questions as a guide:

- Have you used your computer's spellcheck function to catch misspelled or mistyped words?

- Have you read the paper carefully to check for repeated or omitted words or other words the spellcheck will have overlooked?

- Are periods, commas, and quotation marks placed correctly, especially around quoted text?

- Are the pages correctly ordered and numbered?

- Do any pages need to be retyped or reprinted because of too many corrections?

- Is the final draft stapled, paper-clipped, or otherwise bound as requested by your instructor?

FIGURE 22.3   Proofreading checklist

not unintentionally missing any possible errors. Perhaps read it aloud to make sure you see and hear every word. Be alert to any typing mistakes and uncorrected spelling mistakes. In most cases, you can make one or two necessary corrections to the final draft by hand in ink, but you should retype any page that requires many corrections or appears messy. Use the checklist in Figure 22.3 to do a thorough proofread of your essay.

GUIDELINES FOR TYPING YOUR RESEARCH ESSAY

Although formats for research essays vary, the following guidelines reflect the most common practices for typing the title page, outline, quotations, citations, and Works Cited. Unless otherwise noted, all typing should be double spaced.

As noted in Chapter 20 in discussing the parts of a research essay, you should check with your instructor regarding his or her preferences for how your final essay should be prepared. He or she may require that you follow a standard set of guidelines, such as those of the Modern Language Association (MLA) or American Psychological Association (APA) (see Chapter 23). Or your instructor may have his or her own guidelines for any or all of the following:

- *Title page*: Center and type the title about one-third of the way down the page. Don't underline it or put quotation marks around it, unless some words are also underlined or quoted in the paper's text (e.g., include a title or special term). Ten lines down from the title, center and type your name. Below your name, double space and type the course number, the instructor's name, and the date, each on a separate line and centered. See Marcia Valen's title page on page 367. Also see page 366 on how to prepare a paper without a title page or outline.

- *Outline:* On a separate page, center the word *Outline* 1" from the top. Two lines below, type the thesis statement, followed by the outline itself. Use standard outline form, such that the various topic levels are successively indented and numbered with roman or arabic numerals or lowercase or uppercase letters, as required. See the outline included in Marcia Valen's paper on page 368.

- *Quotations:* Indent each quotation that will run more than four typed lines 10 spaces from the left margin (or 1"), double-spacing throughout. Don't put quotation marks around an indented quotation. When quoting two or more paragraphs, indent the first line of each paragraph 3 additional spaces (or ¼"). Add the parenthetical source citation at the end of the indented quotation, following the period or other end mark. Shorter quotations, which are run into text and not indented, should be enclosed in double quotation marks. For examples of Valen's use of quotations, see pages 369 (short, run-in quotation) and 372–373 (long, indented quotation).

- *Notes:* Starting on a new page, center the word *Notes* 1" from the top; type the first entry two lines below this title. Indent the note number 5 spaces from the left margin, and type it raised, about ½ line above other type. Leave 1 space between the raised number and the first word of the note. All subsequent lines of the note begin at the left margin. Double-space within each note and between notes. See Valen's Notes section on page 380.

- *Works Cited:* Type the words *Works Cited* on a new page, centered and 1" from the top. Begin the first alphabetized entry at the left margin two lines below the title. Remember to cite each author with the last name first; indent each subsequent line of an entry 5 spaces for MLA-style papers and 5–7 spaces for APA-style papers (see Chapter 23 on documentation styles). When you have more than one work by the same author, don't repeat the name; instead, type three unspaced hyphens followed by a period. Double-space throughout. Marcia Valen's Works Cited section is on pages 381–382.

- *Page numbers:* Except for the title page, number all pages preceding the first page of actual text consecutively with lowercase roman numerals: *i, ii, iii,* and so on. Count but don't put a number on the title page, if it appears as a separate page. If the title page is also the first page of text (as for a short paper), number it as *page 1.* Number the first page of text and all other pages consecutively using arabic numerals: *1, 2, 3,* and so on. Include your last name, followed by a space, before each page number: *Valen 1.* Count and number every page, including the first page of the text. Type each page number ½" down from the top of the paper and 1" in from the right edge. See examples of Valen's page numbers on pages 368 (lowercase roman numeral) and 369–382 (arabic numeral).

A STUDENT'S RESEARCH ESSAY

Marcia Valen's research essay about the need to reform the jury selection process appears on the following pages. You should read and study the essay to note how Valen organized her research material and integrated it into her discussion of the topic. Use her essay's intext citations and Notes and Works Cited pages as examples to follow in writing your own paper.

Again, be sure to check with your instructor regarding his or her preferences for how your final essay should be prepared. In particular, if your instructor doesn't require that you submit an outline with your essay, you likely won't need a title page, either. In that case, follow the style illustrated below: In the upper-lefthand corner (1" from the top and 1" from the left margin), type your full name, your instructor's name, the course number, and the date, all double spaced. Double-space again to the title, which should be centered, and then again to the first line of text, which begins on a 5-space indent.

Valen 1

Marcia Valen

Professor Stevenson

English 101

May 4, 1996

Flawed Justice: Why and How
the American Jury System Must Be Reformed

The recent trials and resulting verdicts in complex cases such as that of O. J. Simpson or the Menendez brothers[1] have raised national concern about whether the courts and jury selection system in this country can work effectively for justice. According to writer and journalist, Ellen Goodman, "The last trusted institution is being doubted. . . ."

Include title page
if paper has outline
and/or instructor
requires.

Center title about
one-third down
page.

Flawed Justice: Why and How
the American Jury System Must Be Reformed

Center and double-
space your name,
course information,
and date.

Marcia Valen

English 101

Professor Stevenson

May 4, 1997

Valen ii

Outline

Thesis: The United States must reform the process
by which jurors are selected to render justice in the
courtroom.

  I. Introduction: The lack of confidence in the
American jury system

 II. Problems with the jury selection process

    A. Intention of cross-sectional juries

    B. Homogeniety of jury pools and juries

      1. Resistance to serving

      2. Exemption practices

    C. Peremptory challenges

      1. Jury consultants

      2. Jury-shaping practices and results

    D. Effects of limited jury composition

      1. Bias and nullification

      2. Misunderstanding by the jury

III. Corrective measures

    A. Elimination of exemptions

    B. Addressing needs of jurors

    C. Limitations on peremptory challenges

Repeat paper's title, centered on first page. Double-space between lines of title and text and title.

Valen 1

1

Flawed Justice: Why and How
the American Jury System Must Be Reformed

Valen introduces topic with reference to two highly publicized trials.

The recent trials and resulting verdicts in complex cases such as that of O. J. Simpson and the Menendez brothers[1] have raised national concern about whether the courts and jury selection system in the United States can work effectively for justice. According to writer and journalist Ellen Goodman, "The last trusted institution is being doubted. . . . In the public mind, there is an emerging suspicion that a verdict represents nothing more than the idiosyncratic views of 12 individuals." Mirroring an attitude shared across the nation, a recent California poll reported that some 55 percent of those surveyed had "only some or very little" confidence in the ability of juries to decide criminal cases (Dolan A1). Like Goodman and others, critics point to a generally standard process of jury selection that in too many instances results in overly homogenous juries: groups of citizens with the same experience, education levels, and general socioeconomic standing who increasingly ignore or grossly misunderstand evidence (Abramson 99-143; DiPerna 227-37). If we are to restore the public's confidence in jury decisions and in the justice system as a whole, the United States must begin by reforming the processes by which jurors are selected to render justice in the courtroom.

Advocates of jury reform say it is precisely the question of who gets chosen to serve on juries that lies at the heart of the current problems with the jury process. Although the US Supreme Court has ruled that juries, once selected from a representational pool, need not necessarily represent a cross-section of the general population (Nolan), the overall intent in selecting a jury remains that

Raised numeral refers reader to explanatory information in Notes.

Ellipsis indicates irrelevant content has been omitted from quotation.

First paragraph concludes with thesis statement.

2

Source's author is named in text rather than cited parenthetically.

Cite sources parenthetically in text, with author's name before page number.

Use semicolon to separate multiple sources.

Cite single-paged source by author's name only.

Valen 2

Separate continuous page numbers with hyphen; abbreviate successive numbers, as shown.

of finding one representing the diverse perspectives of race, religion, gender, ethnic, and educational backgrounds found in the community (Abramson 100-01).

Unfortunately, current jury selection practices fall considerably short of this goal. Depending upon the location, for example, today's jury notices reach only about 75 percent of the adult population, and in some jurisdictions up to two-thirds of the people who receive jury notices simply ignore them (Adler 219). Nationally, only 20 to 30 percent of those who even respond to jury summonses ever end up serving on a jury, while in some areas, such as Los Angeles, that figure can be as low as 10 to 15 percent (Adler 243). Indeed, with the average juror pay nationwide at roughly $5 per day, it is no wonder that the jury pool often becomes limited to government workers, retired persons, and low-paid workers. While it may be argued that there is nothing inherently wrong with such individuals serving on juries, the consistent homogeneity represented in their availability, education, and social and economic status defeats the need for greater diversity and the presence of more educated professionals among members of the jury pool.

That educated professionals are usually missing on juries results partly from a general resistance among all potential jurists to the possibility of being sequestered for long periods of time. Most jurors, including professionals, simply want to avoid the stress of confinement and isolation. Thus, one survey found that up to 59 percent of potential jurors said they "would resist serving on a jury if they had to be isolated from family and friends. A majority also said they would try to get out of a trial that lasted more than two weeks" (Dolan A18).[2]

Consistently spell out or use numerals for percentages.

3

Statistical examples support thesis.

Valen analyzes preceding examples and summarizes point.

4

Integrate quoted material into sentences.

Valen 3

5

Topic sentence states main idea of paragraph. Series of specific examples support topic sentence and thesis.

Other potential jurors, especially educated professionals, avoid jury duty out of economic and professional interests. In most cases, selection processes tend to accommodate them. Most states do not grant automatic exemptions from jury duty to lawyers, doctors, teachers, and other professionals; however, the general unwillingness on the part of such professionals to be away from their careers, added to their roles in serving the community, often prompts their dismissal from jury duty (Meyer A2). In New York, nearly anyone with a professional title--including physicians, clergy, optometrists, podiatrists, registered and practical nurses, embalmers, Christian Science practitioners, sole business proprietors, police and fire personnel, licensed physical therapists, and others--are automatically exempt from service on a jury. As a result of practices like these, "The jury system has lost access to [such] people's special perspectives, their education and expertise, [and] their contribution to the community profile" (Adler 219).

Use brackets in quotation to show enclosed wording not part of original.

6

Author and source are named in text instead of parenthetically.

In most court cases, eligible jurors who do show up to serve are often less likely to be educated, involved citizens with varieties of expertise and insight. A 1994 survey found, for example, that fewer than 20 percent of jurors serving nationwide had education beyond high school, and many (30 percent of those who served) had not completed a high school education (Meyer A2). That finding supports jury reformists who, like well-known Chicago Tribune columnist Mike Royko, have concluded that "jury selection is often a demonstration in the dumbing down of the legal system. Anyone with an impressive education, a high IQ or a professional job is usually given the boot."

Valen 4

7

An important factor that further distorts the pool of jurors, and consequently skews the resulting jury, is the practice of peremptory challenges. Such challenges "require no justification, no spoken word of explanation, no reason at all beyond a hunch, an intuition" (Abramson 170). They allow attorneys on either side to dismiss prospective jurors whom they believe might be hostile to their case or simply too independent minded to be swayed by the attorney's presentation of evidence. Thus, about 30 percent of the 80 million Americans who have been called for jury duty have been sent home because of an attorney's judgment, and "many of those who are removed appear to be more alert and unbiased than many who are seated" (Adler 221). Although a 1986 US Supreme Court decision forbids the elimination of jurors because of race or gender, the decision says nothing about attorneys eliminating jurors on the basis of education or experience. The result is that, used in this fashion, peremptory challenges actually defeat the very purposes for which they are intended: that is, to ensure an unbiased and broadly representative jury from the community as a whole.

Examples develop topic sentence and support paper's thesis.

Attorneys, however, view peremptory challenges as necessary to their roles in achieving the fairest trial possible. One experienced trial attorney expresses the matter this way:

8

Use colon to introduce indented quotation.

> All potential jurors . . . inevitably bring with them the views and biases built into their race, religion, age, and gender. These preconceptions supposedly influence the eventual verdict as much, if not more than, the evidence presented at trial. The task of the lawyer, therefore, is to outsmart the system--to figure out the demographics of justice

Indent long quotations 10 spaces from left margin.

Valen 5

Cite source for indented quotation at end, following final period.

and manipulate it during jury selection by eliminating jurors with the so-called wrong personal characteristics. (Abramson 143)

To determine during jury selection precisely whom they want and do not want on a jury, attorneys frequently hire high-priced jury consultants, professional analysts who offer charts, focus groups, surveys and psychological profiles that try to predict how potential jurors will vote by using "everything from race, income, and gender to personal history and what kind of car they drive" (Gleick, "Rich"). While the significance of such factors remains unclear, attorneys use their peremptory challenge rights to create a jury whose members have the attitudes or education levels they want. Some consultants suggest that clergymen, school teachers, and lawyers do not make desirable jurors because they are too often sought out for advice and tend to be too opinionated. Attorneys are also usually advised to avoid bank employees or management employees because they "are trained to give or take orders [and] they expect others to conform as well" (Simon 262). Although there is little empirical evidence that such quasi-scientific methods of selecting juries work, attorneys and the public continue to believe in their importance in shaping verdicts. Their faith in such methods, in fact, seems to be renewed each time the outcome of a trial seems to be explainable in terms of jury demographics such as gender, education, and other factors.

The extent to which such faith in jury-shaping matters, perhaps not to the outcome but to the handling of a case, can be extremely significant. For example, studies show that a woman juror is more likely to be intolerant of the complaints of her own sex and thus return

For multiple works by same author, include relevant title in citation.

Bracket words added to quotation to make it blend with own writing.

9

10

Valen 6

a verdict unfavorable to another female. In the 1992 trial of William Kennedy Smith, a nephew of John F. Kennedy, jury research showed that conservative women over 40 were the types of jurors most likely to acquit Smith. According to defense attorney Roy Black, "They were most skeptical of claims made by younger women who would go out all night in bars," and the defense counted on this bias in making its case to the jury (Lacayo).[3]

Not surprisingly, race and education are also major factors for attorneys to consider in molding an acceptable jury. The 1979 Washington, DC, trial of Mayor Marion Barry, who was charged with 14 felony counts after the FBI and police videotaped him using cocaine, is an example. After Barry was acquitted of the charges, jury consultants attributed the votes of older, poorer, black jurors to their racial identification with him as someone like themselves, an underdog or victim of the establishment (Adler 265).

Though such analyses may amount to little more than posttrial hindsight, the advice of jury consultants in the O. J. Simpson case appears to have been more credible. Decision Quest, Inc., a consulting firm for the defense, guaranteed a jury with a low educational level by advising Simpson's attorneys to reject anyone who read a newspaper regularly. One juror said that she read nothing at all "except the horse sheet" (Miller 39). The majority of jurors selected said they derived their information about national and world events from tabloid TV, "a factor Decision Quest found correlated directly with the belief that Simpson was not guilty" (Miller 39). So effective was the defense strategy in using peremptory challenges to eliminate better-educated jurors that, according to Paul Lisneck, a

Valen uses appositive to identify William Kennedy Smith for reader.

11

Example discusses impact of race and education in jury decisions.

12

Valen continues to integrate quoted material within own sentences.

Valen 7

Chicago-based trial consultant, the O. J. Simpson case "was over with the jury pick" (Greenburg).

In the Simpson case and others in which peremptory challenges have been used to create a jury easily influenced and perhaps simply outsmarted by defense attorneys, it has seemed to observers that some juries' verdicts have clearly ignored the evidence because of racial bias or other causes. In many cases, and especially those with largely minority juries, critics have charged that jurors were exercising nullification, a practice in which juries "disregard a law if they feel that its strict application would result in an unjust verdict" (Kerwin and Shaffer 140).[4]

Apparent nullification in such cases often grows out of jurors' misunderstanding of the law or of the evidence brought forward in a case--or both. No one would argue that jurors need to be experts themselves to hear a case or that they must hold a PhD degree to serve effectively on a jury. For jurors to make informed decisions, however, they need to be able to understand the testimony of witnesses, many of whom are experts testifying about complex and sophisticated subjects. At the same time, they must also be able to interpret facts and follow the instructions of a judge when he or she explains the law. Such is not always the case, however. After studying several juries in action, one legal expert described them as "lots of sincere, serious people who--for a variety of reasons--were missing key points, focusing on irrelevant issues, succumbing to barely recognized prejudices, failing to see through the cheapest appeals to sympathy or hate, and generally botching the job" (Adler 220).

Indeed, while it is probably extreme to describe the average jury as made up of "twelve prejudiced, gullible

13

14

15

Appositive here defines term *nullification.*

Dash signals emphatic addition or qualification.

Separate two authors' names with *and.*

Valen effectively states own ideas, supported by quotation from authority.

Valen 8

Use roman
numerals for
page numbers
of preface or
introduction

dolts incapable of understanding the evidence or the law"
(Wishman vii), as some have, it is safe to say that the
majority of those who actually end up serving on juries
find it more than challenging. Studies show that most
jurors cannot interact effectively with other jurors or
judges and attorneys, nor can they usually understand
the huge amounts of complex information and evidence
presented to them in a trial (Meyer A2). While many
judges discourage jurors from taking notes while they
listen to a trial, over one-third of judges nationally
explicitly forbid jurors to take any notes all (Adler 239).
Thus, it should, be no surprise that juries "sometimes
come down on the wrong side of the law" (Meyer A2).

Examples con-
tinue to develop
topic sentence
and support
thesis.

    Unfortunately, lack of understanding and the failure
of jurors to clarify information often leads to unjust or
overturned verdicts. A 1992 death sentence case in
Chicago, for example, was thrown out on the basis of a
court study that showed that "75 percent of jurors in the
local courts didn't understand parts of the instructions"
(Adler 231). In another case involving an unfair
competition lawsuit filed by Brown & Williamson against
a rival tobacco company, jurors were given 81 pages of
instructions by the judge and had to rely on memory alone
to recall testimony that filled 108 volumes. Although the
jury ultimately awarded $49.6 million in damages to
Brown & Williamson, the Supreme Court later ruled that
no "reasonable jury" with adequate understanding of the
evidence could have concluded that the other company's
actions were illegal or that Brown & Williamson were
entitled to any damages (Lacayo).

    An underlying factor in all of the weaknesses described
so far has been the lack of genuinely diverse pools of

16

17

Valen 9

Section of paper presents the *how* of Valen's title.

potential jurors, especially pools that include educated professionals. To remedy this problem, we must find ways to increase the scope of jury pools and broaden their community representation. Although jurisdictions in some states continue to excuse those who have traditionally been seen as too indispensable to serve as jurors, many others have begun to eliminate laws granting automatic exemptions for certain classes of individuals, including doctors, lawyers, teachers, and even judges (Abramson 249). Every citizen needs to understand that his or her participation in jury service is essential to its very existence and that "no one can have the right to be tried before a jury unless we all feel an obligation to accept jury duty in turn" (Abramson 248). In California, Los Angeles District Attorney Gil Garcetti has called for "mandatory jury service--no excuses allowed" (Kaplan 59) as a means of increasing broader participation in juries. Praiseworthy as such a goal may be, however, it misses the reason people try to avoid jury duty in the first place. States must simply do more to ensure people's willingness to serve on juries and also take steps to make doing so is less burdensome.

18

Paragraph is developed with examples of current changes in jury selection process.

Some states have already made progress in this direction. Florida and Colorado, as well as many counties in California, require jurors to serve only one day or for the length of one trial. This option has attracted more professionals and others who have traditionally found ways to avoid taking part in jury duty. Massachusetts, Colorado, and Connecticut require employers to cover an employee's wages for the first few days of service, after which the court pays $50 a day. The court rate is also paid to unemployed individuals who serve. In Minnesota, state and local courts provide daycare in order to allow parents

Valen 10

with children to meet their responsibilities as citizens available for jury duty. Finally, some states have considered holding court during evening hours to encourage more professionals to sit on juries (Meyer A2).

Other progress is being made through recommendations coming from special-focus national groups such as the Fully Informed Jury Association, which promotes juror rights (Adler 241), and the National Center for State Courts' Center for Jury Studies near Washington, DC, which has recently unveiled a 56-point reform plan for strengthening jury selection and jury procedures within the courtroom. The Center's plan calls for child care and other supportive measures for jurors, including time limits on trials, more use of technology such as computers and video recordings of the trial, as well as a bill of rights guaranteeing juror respect from attorneys and judges and defining each citizen's right to serve, rather than to be dismissed without cause, on a jury (Meyer A10). Such efforts to review the jury system and propose reforms, controversial as they sometimes become, need to be encouraged nationwide if we are to address the roots of the problems afflicting current juror selection processes.

In addition, states must also undertake steps to eliminate attorneys' rights to peremptory challenges. Such challenges restrict and homogenize juries in ways that undermine the full participation of the citizenry and deprive juries of their necessary diversity in perspectives, experiences, and education. Although attorney groups in several states are currently considering proposals that would limit the number of peremptory challenges in a case, it may ultimately prove more effective to eliminate the procedure altogether from the American courtroom.

19

20

Repetition of word *progress* relates this paragraph to preceding one.

Valen continues to argue for ways jury selection system could be changed.

Paragraph argues for eliminating peremptory challenges as means of improving juries.

Valen 11

The British eliminated peremptory challenging in 1988 and thereafter instituted a process wherein jurors are selected randomly from voter lists and not addressed by attorneys until they have been sworn in and the trial has actually begun. Such a process greatly reduces the amount of time and frustration that jury selection now involves in the United States, while at the same time validating the democratic and representative nature of the jury selection process (Adler 223-24). The United States would do well to institute a similar system.

Valen concludes with summary of main ideas, implications for future, and re-emphasis of thesis statement.

Loss of faith in the effectiveness of juries has resulted in a worldwide decline in their use in this century (Nolan). If the practice of trial by jury is to continue in the United States, steps must be taken to improve the jury selection process and to ensure that citizens of all backgrounds and abilities have the opportunity to serve on a jury. Broadening the jury pool, eliminating most juror exclusions, and abolishing peremptory challenges would greatly improve many of the serious problems now undermining Americans' confidence in this nation's jury system. The public and its leaders must become actively concerned about the erosions already underway in the jury system itself. If not, we assume the great and serious risk that juries and the duties they perform will become mere fruitless and pathetic imitations of justice.

21

Notes

[1] A jury acquitted O. J. Simpson after a highly publicized, one-year trial in which he was charged with the double murder of his wife Nicole Brown Simpson and Ron Goldman in June 1994. In the 1991 trials of Lyle and Eric Menendez, the defendants admitted to having murdered both their parents but claimed they did so out of fear of being further abused by them. Although the Menendez brothers were acquitted by their juries, they were convicted when their cases were retried.

[2] The reluctance most Americans have about serving on a jury can be seen in the numerous discussions on the Internet concerning jury service. The majority of Usenet postings listed over a two-month period from February through March 1998, by Excite and Dejanews, for example, concerned ways to avoid jury duty.

[3] This is not to imply, however, that attorneys in the case used peremptory challenges to exclude jurors on the basis of gender alone or to systematically shape the jury along gender lines. The Supreme Court forbid such uses of peremptory challenges in 1994. See Abramson 137.

[4] Although highly controversial, nullification is explicitly legal in 3 states but only an implied or assumed jury right in the other 47. For discussions of nullification, see Kerwin and Shaffer 140-46.

Valen 13

Works Cited

Abramson, Jeffrey. We, the Jury: The Jury System and the Ideal of Democracy. New York: Basic-Harper, 1994.

Adler, Stephen J. The Jury: Trial and Error in the American Courtroom. New York: Times Books, 1994.

DiPerna, Paula. Juries on Trial: Faces of American Justice. New York: Dember, 1984.

Dolan, Maura. "Jury System Is Held in Low Regard by Most." Los Angeles Times 27 Sept. 1994: A1+.

Gleick, Elizabeth. "Rich Justice, Poor Justice." Time 19 June 1995: 40-47.

---. "Disorder in the Court." Time 12 June 1995: 65.

Goodman, Ellen. " Today's Juror Must Carry the Baggage of Evolving Values." Boston Globe 21 March 1994. 5 April 1997. <http://www.boston.com/news/nation>.

Greenburg, Jan Crawford. "Jury System Goes under the Microscope after Simpson Verdict, Some Specialists Argue for Big Overhaul." Chicago Tribune Online 9 April 1997. 13 Oct. 1995. <http://www.chicagotribune.com/archives>.

Kaplan, David A. "Disorder in the Court." Newsweek 16 Oct. 1995: 58-61.

Kerwin, Jeffrey, and David R. Shaffer. 'The Effects of Jury Dogmatism on Reactions to Jury Nullification Instructions." Personality and Social Psychology Bulletin 17.2 (1991): 140-46.

Lacayo, Richard. "Jury System in Trouble: Questionable Judgment." Time 13 Oct. 1994: 45.

Meyer, Josh. "Small Vanguard Presses Its Case for Jury Reforms." Los Angeles Times 28 Sept. 1994: A1+.

Miller, Mark. "How the Jury Saw It." Newsweek 16 Oct. 1995: 37-39.

Alphabetize entries by authors' last names.

Center title *Works Cited* at top of page.

Form for book.

Form for newspaper article.

Use 3 unspaced hyphens to represent author's name for multiple works by same author.

Form for online newspaper article.

Form for work with two authors.

Use + to show discontinuous pages.

Valen 14

Form for online encyclopedia article.

Nolan, Kenneth P. "Jury." Academic American Encyclopedia
  11 April 1997. <http://www.compuserve.com/iquest.
  telebase.com/>.

Royko, Mike. "Jury System Often Blind about Justice."
  Chicago Tribune Online 2 Mar. 1995. 13 April 1997.
  <http://www.chicagotribune.com>.

Form for online sources without page numbers given.

Form for article in journal.

Simon, Rita J. "Jury Nullification, or Prejudice and
  Ignorance in the Marion Barry Trial." Journal of
  Criminal Justice 20.3 (May-June 1992): 261-66.

Wishman, Seymour. Anatomy of a Jury: The System on
  Trial. New York: Times, 1986.

Research Exercises

1. In a brief paragraph, describe the relationship among your research question, your working or final thesis, and the subject headings from your research notes. What modifications to each will you need to make before you begin to write your research essay?

2. Following the guidelines on pages 70–72 and 80–83, develop an informal or formal outline for your paper. Be sure to place the working thesis at the top of the page.

3. Write a draft of your paper's introductory paragraph. Position the thesis statement at the end of the paragraph, so that it serves to introduce the rest of the paper's discussion.

4. Write a discussion paragraph that develops your paper's working or final thesis. Include a clearly stated topic sentence, supporting examples, and at least one quotation. Cite sources parenthetically in the text, as necessary.

5. After completing a draft of your research essay, review the organization and content with the intent of revising any parts needing improvement. Check to see that the paper's thesis is logically developed and well supported. Paragraphs should contain topic sentences that advance the discussion and develop the paper's thesis. Make sure you have used your sources fairly and effectively and that your own thinking is apparent throughout the paper. Submit a copy of the original draft to your instructor for comments or to answer any questions before you complete the final draft.

Documenting Sources
in Your Research Essay

Acknowledging the sources you use in writing your research essay lends it authority and provides readers with information to locate the sources for themselves. To a large extent, the value of your essay's content and your own integrity as a writer depend on how accurately and fairly you make use of and credit those ideas you borrow from other writers. (See the section on plagiarism in Chapter 20, p. 330.) As you integrate information from your sources into your research essay, follow standard documentation practices to ensure you do so accurately.

This chapter presents two of the most commonly used sets of guidelines for documenting sources in research essays: those of the Modern Language Association (MLA) and the American Psychological Association (APA). The MLA guidelines (pp. 385–414) are based on the style guide for that organization, *MLA Style Manual,* 2nd edition (New York: MLA, 1998). Similarly, the APA guidelines (pp. 414–430) are based on the *Publication Manual of the American Psychological Association,* 4th edition (Washington, DC: APA, 1994).

As you read this chapter and review the examples provided, you may conclude that MLA style and APA style aren't really all that different. You're right. Each style addresses the two basic elements of documentation: how to cite sources within the text (called *parenthetical citation*) and how to list those sources at the end of the essay in a *Works Cited* or *References* section. The primary differences between MLA and APA styles have to do with the order in which source information is presented and how it's punctuated to separate the details. But for the most part, both styles use the same information and serve the same purpose: to let readers know what sources have been used in writing the essay.

MLA-STYLE DOCUMENTATION

Parenthetical Citation

Research essays following MLA-style documentation use parenthetical citation to acknowledge sources directly in the paper's text. Such acknowledgement includes the author's (or editor's) name and the page or pages where the information cited appears in the source. Whether the author is named in the text or given parenthetically depends on whether your purpose is to emphasize the authority or the information being cited. Consider these examples:

AUTHOR NAMED IN TEXT; PAGE NUMBER CITED IN PARENTHESES

Research completed by Richard R. Berman and others as far back as the 1940s has shown that adopted children have a strong, conscious desire to be connected with a past heritage or a genealogical history (119).

AUTHOR AND PAGE NUMBER CITED PARENTHETICALLY

City employees such as police and fire-fighting personnel report exceptionally high rates of marital disharmony and stress (Hoag 20).

Note that you *do not put a comma between the author's name and the page number* when they appear together parenthetically, as in the second example above.

Each source cited in the research essay is also listed and described bibliographically in the Works Cited (see pp. 392–414). Numbered endnotes, although not always necessary, may appear at the end of the essay and serve to identify supplementary or explanatory comments (see pp. 391–392).

Using Parenthetical Citation. Use parenthetical citation to acknowledge quotations (except for common sayings and well-known quotations), summaries, paraphrases, opinions, lines of thinking, and statistics. In short, use parenthetical citation whenever you borrow information that is not commonly known or believed, especially by people generally acquainted with your subject. Do not provide parenthetical citations for facts or common knowledge, such as that hydrocyanic acid is a colorless, poisonous liquid or that Abraham Lincoln was the sixteenth president of the United States.

Citation Content. Because a parenthetical citation must always identify a specific entry listed alphabetically in the Works Cited, the information in the citation must clearly direct a reader to that entry. Usually, but not always (see examples that follow), the author's last name and a page reference are enough to identify the source and the specific location from which you have borrowed material:

> Asians and Europeans do not necessarily consider all US exports inferior,
> however. American-made clothing--especially denim jeans--and Hollywood
> films, for example, are still top-rated imports everywhere (Holloway 34).

Page citations should never include *p.* or *pp.* If you are referring to several consecutive pages, join the page numbers with a hyphen—for example:

> (Holloway 74-78).

For consecutive page numbers over 100, abbreviate the second number—for example:

> (Holloway 129-38).

> (Holloway 216-18).

When referring to two or more individual pages in one citation, use commas to separate them—for example:

> (Holloway 23, 34, 50).

If the work consists of only one page, list the page number only in the Works Cited entry; do not include it in the parenthetical citation, for example:

> (Carter).

Citation Style.   To keep interruptions in your text at a minimum, make parenthetical citations as concise as possible. Give only enough information to guide your reader to the specific source you have fully identified in the Works Cited. If you have integrated any information into your text that could be included in the parenthetical citation, such as the author's name, don't include it in the citation:

> Donald R. Griffin points out that many scientists have interpreted the
> movements and sounds of sleeping dogs as evidence that they dream (258).

To keep your research essay as readable as possible, insert each parenthetical citation before a period or comma and as close to the borrowed material as possible. Place the citation outside the quotation marks if you are directly quoting a source:

> Although Darwin was careful in the 1859 edition of <u>Origin of Species</u> in
> referring to apes and chimpanzees only as "man's nearest allies" (210), his

later works boldly assert the evolutionary linkages implicit in his theory (Leakey 4).

If the borrowed material is set off from the text (usually by a colon or other punctuation), the parenthetical citation should follow the final punctuation:

> Heaton and Wilson describe the openness of the television talk show host as necessary to the program's success:
>
> > A sense of camaraderie with the host is crucial to developing a loyal following. The shows depend on the willingness of some people to tell their secrets and others to listen attentively. In fact, the success or failure of shows is often a matter of whether or not viewers like the host. So the shows work hard to foster a sense of "friendship" and all that entails--trust, loyalty, consistency, sharing of secrets, and a willingness to overlook flaws. (43)

To acquire skill in accurately acknowledging your sources in parenthetic citations, review the following guidelines, paying close attention to the details of form and punctuation. Also study their use in Marcia Valen's research essay (Chapter 22, pp. 367–382).

Citing an Author.   When citing one or more authors parenthetically, treat individuals, editors, corporate authors, and others responsible for producing a work as its author. Don't include any designation (e.g., *ed.* for "editor") with an individual's name; specific roles will be identified in the Works Cited. You may list one, two, or three authors as needed in a citation, but more than three requires giving only the first author's last name followed by *et al.* ("and others"). Depending on your emphasis and considering the readability of the parenthetical citation, you may name an author in your text or include the name in parentheses with the page number(s).

The following examples demonstrate alternative techniques for the placement of author names:

SINGLE AUTHOR
Warren argues that students who cannot afford test tutors are being treated unfairly and denied access to the better colleges (83).

TWO AUTHORS
We are approaching the day when "virtually all women will work except for a few months or years when they are raising children full-time" (Naisbitt and Aburdene 7).

THREE AUTHORS

Whitman was initially scorned or simply ignored by the Imagist poets of the early twentieth century. It was not until Ezra Pound and T. S. Eliot finally acknowledged his contribution that Whitman was seen as anything more than a quaint mid-nineteenth-century eccentric (Hall, Taylor, and Morgan 245).

FOUR OR MORE AUTHORS

Hyperspace theory holds that matter can also be viewed as vibrations rippling through space and time, a concept that may ultimately prove central to any attempt to explain the forces of nature (Shato et al. 11).

Citing a Corporate Author.   Because the names of corporate authors are often long, identify them in your text and cite the specific page reference in the parenthetical citation:

CORPORATE AUTHOR NAMED IN TEXT

A recent survey by the American Public Opinion Association shows that more than 50 percent of Americans surveyed dislike or distrust the current jury system in the United States (66).

When necessary, you may offer a shortened version of a corporate author in the parenthetical citation:

SHORTENED CORPORATE AUTHOR CITED PARENTHETICALLY

A recent nationwide survey shows that more than 50 percent of Americans surveyed dislike or distrust the current jury system in the United States (American 66).

Citing a Source with No Author Given.   If a source has no author identified, describe its origin in your text, and use a shortened version of the title (underlined or in quotes, as appropriate) to cite the source parenthetically:

One scientific journal has reported the development of genetically engineered mice with "powerhouse" hearts. These lucky creatures have up to 100 times more protein receptors--which contribute to the heart's pumping of blood--than ordinary mice ("New Gene" 113).

Citing Part of an Article or Book.   When you summarize ideas or information, refer to specific passages, or quote directly from a work, give the relevant information in the parenthetical reference:

The US Department of Safety reports that deaths from ATVs (all terrain vehicles) have increased by over 15 percent a year since 1987 (74).

It is precisely because Macbeth's final battle scene with McDuff (<u>Mac.</u> 5.3.50-119) is so expected that it lacks the element of high tragedy we find in <u>King Lear.</u>

Citing an Entire Work.   At times, you may wish to acknowledge an entire work, rather than a specific part. In this case, include the author's name and the title of the work in the text, rather than in a parenthetical citation. Since the reference is to a work in general, you are not required to cite a page number:

Alice Walker's <u>The Color Purple</u> attracts a wide audience because of its sensitive treatment of universal hopes and desires.

Citing a Single Volume or Multivolume Source.   In the parenthetical citation for a work composed of multiple volumes, begin by giving the author's name (unless you include it in the text) and then the number of the volume you are acknowledging, followed by a colon and a space and the page number(s):

(Davis 2: 234-40)

If you refer to an entire volume, rather than to specific pages, place a comma after the author's name and include *vol*:

(Shire, vol. 1).

When you place the information in your text, write out the word *volume*, followed by the numeral:

Shire's volume 1 covers the first . . .

Use arabic numbers, rather than roman, to indicate volume numbers:

A letter dated 16 May 1934 shows that Einstein was thinking even then about the negative consequences of traveling through time, but he also understood that no one would ever turn down the opportunity to do so (2: 146).

Citing Multiple Works in a Single Parenthetic Citation.   To acknowledge more than one source in a single citation, include both sources within a single parentheses. Follow the form you normally would use for each, but separate the sources with a semicolon and a space:

Social researchers and defenders of television talk shows say that these programs provide a valuable outlet for individuals who would otherwise remain silent or misunderstood (Priest 73-91; Cabot 20).

Citing Classical Works of Literature and the Bible.   When citing the Bible and other classical literature—that is, works published in different editions and therefore varying in page and chapter numbers—include the appropriate unit of information: namely, the chapter, book, scene, or line. In general, use arabic numerals, rather than roman numerals, in citing volumes and divisions of works. You may, however, use roman numerals in citing the acts and scenes of plays.

To cite a passage from a novel, mention the author and title in text. Then, in parentheses, give the page number first, followed by a semicolon and space, and then the divisions, using appropriate abbreviations with periods:

The main character in Dostoyevsky's Crime and Punishment tries to convince himself that he has "killed a principle" rather than another human being (271; pt. 3, sec 6).

For extended works of poetry, give the division first, followed by the line reference. Use a period with no space to separate the two. Do not give a page reference:

Milton's Satan exhibits "monarchal pride/Conscious of highest worth" (PL 2.428-29) when speaking early in the poem. Later, however, he is described as "Squat like a toad, close at the ear of Eve" (4.799).

If the poem is short or not divided into books or cantos, give only the line reference. When acknowledging only line numbers, use *line* or *lines* (not abbreviated) in the citation, but after you have established that the numbers designate lines, use only numbers:

The pervasive grimness of the speaker's vision in "The Second Coming" is announced in the poem's opening lines: "Things fall apart; the center cannot hold;/Mere anarchy is loosed upon the world" (Yeats, lines 3-4). Despite the hope that a "revelation is at hand" (8), the dreadful vision of the emerging future remains relentlessly ominous.

For a play, give the act, scene, and line references, using periods without spaces to separate the divisions:

The imagery of futile battle is also found in the "To be or not to be" soliloquy in Hamlet (Shakespeare 3.1.56-89).

If your instructor prefers, you may also use roman numerals in citing acts and scenes:

(Shakespeare III.i.56-89)

To cite a source from the Bible, give the book, chapter, and verse, using periods to separate the divisions. Within the parenthetical citation (but not in the text itself), you may abbreviate a book title, using a period to end the abbreviation—for example, *Gen.* for *Genesis* and *Rev.* for *Revelations:*

Many early pioneers accepted the Bible's advice to "Be fruitful, multiply, fill the earth and conquer" (Gen. 1.28) as a literal mandate.

Citing Indirect Sources. Though it's always best to consult a source directly for any material you adapt from it, you may not always be able to do so. In a case in which you can't locate the original source of a quotation, cite the source you have, preceding it with *qtd. in* ("quoted in"):

As two ex-secretaries of State, Henry Kissinger and Cyrus Vance, warned in a recent Foreign Affairs article, "America's ability to influence events abroad . . . will be determined in a large part by how rapidly we get our economic house in order" (qtd. in "Fitting" 80).

Content Notes

Use *explanatory* or *content notes* to offer definitions, provide translations, make comparisons between sources, and otherwise furnish information not strictly pertinent to the immediate discussion in the text. In general, include such notes sparingly so as not to add unnecessarily to the paper's length.

Identify notes in your text by numbering them consecutively throughout with superscript, or raised, arabic numerals. Each numeral corresponds to a note appearing on a page titled *Notes* at the end of the essay (before the Works Cited).

Following is an excerpt from Marcia Valen's research essay. Notice that the superscript number in the text signals the reader to consult the correspondingly numbered section in her paper's Notes:

TEXT REFERENCE

In many cases, and especially those with largely minority juries, critics have charged that jurors were exercising nullification, a practice in which juries "disregard a law if they feel that its strict application would result in an unjust verdict" (Kerwin and Shaffer 140).[4]

NOTE

[4] Although highly controversial, nullification is explicitly legal in 3 states but only an implied or assumed jury right in the other 47. For discussions of nullification, see Kerwin and Shafer 140-46.

Remember that any source mentioned as part of a note must also appear with complete documentation in the Works Cited.

Preparing the Works Cited Page

The rest of this section on MLA style discusses standard forms for source listings in the Works Cited section of the research essay. Use the list that follows as a quick index to these forms when compiling and editing your paper:

INDEX TO WORKS CITED FORMS

Books

1. A Book by One Author
2. Two or More Books by the Same Author
3. A Book by Two or Three Authors
4. A Book by Four or More Authors
5. A Book with an Editor
6. A Book with Two or Three Editors
7. A Book with Four or More Editors
8. A Book by a Corporation, Committee, Institution, or Other Group
9. An Entry from an Encyclopedia or Other Reference Work
10. A Work That Is Included in an Anthology or Collection
11. A Book That Is a Later Edition, a Revision, or a Reprint
12. A Book That Has Been Printed by a Division of a Publisher
13. A Book That Has Been Translated
14. A Dissertation
15. A Government Publication

Periodicals: Magazines and Journals

16. An Article in a Journal with Continuous Yearly Pagination
17. An Article in a Journal with Discontinuous Yearly Pagination
18. An Article with No Author Named
19. An Article in a Magazine
20. A Published Interview
21. An Article That Includes Another Title
22. A Letter or Comment in a Journal or Magazine
23. A Dissertation or Article in an Abstract Journal

Newspapers

24. Citing the Edition of a Newspaper
25. Citing the Pagination of a Newspaper

Electronic, Computer-Based, and Online Sources and Materials

26. Material on CD–ROM

  a. CD–ROM Sources from Newspaper, Magazine, Journal, and Other Periodically Published Databases
  b. CD–ROM Material Not Indicated As Appearing in a Newspaper, Magazine, Journal, or Other Periodically Published Database
  c. CD–ROM Material That Is Not Periodically Updated after Its Original Publication

27. Material in Multiple Electronic Publication Forms
28. Material Accessed through an Online Newspaper, Magazine, Journal, or Other Database

  a. Sources Also Available in Printed Versions
  b. Sources Not Indicated As Appearing in Printed Versions

29. Sources from Electronic Journals, Electronic Newsletters, and Electronic Conferences
30. Published Material Received As Electronic Text
31. E-Mail, Discussion Lists, and Online Postings (Usenet, Listserv, BBS)

  a. An E-Mail Communication
  b. A Public Online Posting

32. Websites and Web Pages

  a. Scholarly Project Websites
  b. Personal Websites and Home Pages
  c. Professional Websites

Other Sources

33. An Interview
34. A Public Address, Speech, or Lecture
35. A Letter or Memo
36. A Pamphlet
37. An Advertisement
38. A Work of Art or a Photograph
39. An Illustration, Table, Chart, or Map
40. A Cartoon
41. A Film, Videotape, Videodisc, or Slide Program
42. A Television or Radio Program
43. A Sound Recording

Notes about Formatting.   As you review the sample citations in the sections that follow, you will see two formats followed consistently:

1. Underlining is traditionally used to identify the titles of books, journals, and magazines and to highlight certain words and phrases. You may have noticed, however, that many publications, including this one, use *italic type* for the same purposes. To avoid misreading, both MLA and APA guidelines recommend the use of underlining as preferable to italic type for indicating titles and highlighting terms. Both styles allow the use of italics, however, as long as it's in accordance with your instructor's preferences. Find out what your instructor requires—underlining or italicizing—and use one or the other exclusively in your paper. Note that the same guidelines (as explained throughout this chapter) apply to both underlining and italicizing.

2. Note from the examples provided that they all follow what's called a *hanging indentation style,* in which each first line is flush left and each subsequent, or *turnover,* line is indented five spaces. Also note that none of the entries are hyphenated; that is, none of the words at the ends of lines are broken into syllables and split across lines, except those words that already include hyphens. Again, you should follow your instructor's preferences in formatting your paper.

Books

1. A BOOK BY ONE AUTHOR

Stanley, Steven M. <u>Children of the Ice Age: How a Global Catastrophe Allowed Humans to Evolve</u>. New York: Harmony, 1996.

2. TWO OR MORE BOOKS BY THE SAME AUTHOR

Following the author's name, list multiple works by the same author (or editor) in alphabetical order by title (ignoring the words *A, An,* and *The* at the beginnings of titles). After listing the first work, substitute three unspaced hyphens and a period in place of the author's name. But if that author is an editor or writes a work with another person, list such works as different entries:

Daiches, David. <u>The Novel and the Modern World</u>. Chicago: U of Chicago P, 1984.

---. <u>Two Worlds: An Edinburgh Jewish Childhood</u>. Tuscaloosa: U of Alabama P, 1989.

Daiches, David, and John Flower. <u>Literary Landscape of the British Isles: A Narrative Atlas</u>. New York: Penguin, 1981.

3. A BOOK BY TWO OR THREE AUTHORS

Invert the first author's name, followed by a comma and a space, followed by the word *and.* List the names of other authors in regular order:

Heaton, Jeanne Albronda, and Nona Leigh Wilson. <u>Tuning in Trouble: Talk TV's Destructive Impact on Mental Health</u>. San Francisco: Jossey-Bass, 1995.

Roueche, John E., Susanne D. Roueche, and Mark D. Milliron. <u>Strangers in Their Own Land: Part-Time Faculty in American Community Colleges</u>. Washington, DC: American Association of Community Colleges, 1995.

4. A BOOK BY FOUR OR MORE AUTHORS

To avoid lengthy parenthetical citations for sources with four or more authors, list only the first author's name, followed by a comma and the abbreviation *et al.* (meaning "and others"):

Merit, Linda A., et al. <u>Families and Family Violence: A Report on the Effects of Intervention Counseling</u>. New York: Altran, 1994.

If you choose to cite all authors in the order they are listed on the source's title page, invert the first author's name, followed by a comma and the other authors' names in usual order:

Merit, Linda A., Carl H. Danz, Robert Ulrich, Janice Pohl, and Daniel M. Vance. <u>Families and Family Violence: A Report on the Effects of Intervention Counseling</u>. New York: Altran, 1994.

5. A BOOK WITH AN EDITOR

List the editor whose work you are citing as you would the single author of a book (see item 1, above), but follow the name with a comma and the abbreviation *ed.* or *eds.* (for "editor" or "editors"):

Morton, Andrew, ed. <u>Selected Poems of Thomas Hardy</u>. By Thomas Hardy. London: Dent, 1994.

If you are focusing on an author and work included in the edited source, cite that author and the work's title first. Then list the title of the edited source, followed by the capitalized abbreviation *Ed.* and the name of the editor:

Hardy, Thomas. "Channel Firing." <u>Selected Poems of Thomas Hardy</u>. Ed. Andrew Morton. London: Dent, 1994. 75-76.

6. A BOOK WITH TWO OR THREE EDITORS

Rees, A. L., and Frances Bozello, eds. <u>The New History of Art</u>. Atlantic Highlands, NJ: Humanities, 1992.

Danziger, Sheldon H., Gary D. Sandefur, and Daniel W. Weinberg, eds. <u>Confronting Poverty: Prescriptions for Change</u>. Cambridge, MA: Harvard UP, 1994.

7. A BOOK WITH FOUR OR MORE EDITORS

You may choose to list all the editors' names as they appear on the work's title page:

> Hum, S. Randall, Beate Anna Ort, Martin Mazen Anbari, Wendy S. Lader, and William Scott Biel, eds. Child, Parent, and State: Law and Policy Reader. Philadelphia: Temple UP, 1994.

To maintain a brief parenthetical citation form, you should generally use *et al.* ("and others") after the first editor's name and omit the names of the other editors:

> Mandel, Richard E., et al., eds. Casebook on Poverty: American Families at Risk. New York: Bass, 1995.

8. A BOOK BY A CORPORATION, COMMITTEE, INSTITUTION, OR OTHER GROUP

> American Psychiatric Association. Diagnostic and Statistical Manual of Mental Disorders. 4th ed. Washington, DC: American Psychiatric Association, 1994.

9. AN ENTRY FROM AN ENCYCLOPEDIA OR OTHER REFERENCE WORK

If an article from an encyclopedia or other reference work carries the author's name or is signed with the author's initials (usually identified elsewhere in the source), list the article by that name, followed by the title. If no author's name or initials are given, list the title of the reference article first in quotation marks. If the entries in an encyclopedia or dictionary appear alphabetically, omit the volume and page numbers. Also, for generally well-known reference works, list only the edition (if given) and the year published, omitting editors' names and publication information:

> "Alcohol." Encyclopaedia Britannica: Macropaedia. 1991 ed.

For lesser-known reference works, list full publication information:

> Barnhart, Robert K. "Protein." The American Heritage Dictionary of Science. Boston: Houghton, 1986.

10. A WORK THAT IS INCLUDED IN AN ANTHOLOGY OR COLLECTION

Give the name of the author of the work you are citing, followed by that work's title in quotation marks or underlined, depending on how it is regularly indicated. Next, give the title of the anthology or collection, followed, if appropriate, by the editor's or translator's name in normal order, preceded by *Ed.* or *Trans.* After the publication information, give the page numbers on which the work appears:

Chopin, Kate. "A Pair of Silk Stockings." The Oxford Book of Women's Writing in the United States. Eds. Linda Wagner-Martin and Cathy N. Davidson. Oxford, Eng.: Oxford UP, 1995. 63-67.

Miller, Arthur. Death of a Salesman. Literature: An Introduction to Reading and Writing. Eds. Edgar V. Roberts and Henry E. Jacobs. Englewood Cliffs, NJ: Prentice-Hall, 1986. 1294-1363.

11. A BOOK THAT IS A LATER EDITION, A REVISION, OR A REPRINT

Following the information on the title page or copyright page, indicate that a book is a later, revised, or reprinted edition by giving an edition number (*2nd ed.* or *3rd ed.*), a description (*Rev. ed.* for "Revised edition" or *Abr. ed.* for "Abridged edition"; *rpt* for "reprinted"), or a year (*1972 ed.*). For a work that has been revised by someone other than the original author, give the name of the reviser after the title (see the *Fowler* entry below):

Christians, Clifford G., Mark Fackler, and Kevin B. Rotzall. Media Ethics: Cases and Moral Reasoning. 4th ed. White Plains, NY: Longman, 1995.

Fowler, H. W. Modern English Usage. Rev. Ernest Gowers. 2nd ed. New York: Oxford UP, 1965.

Taylor, Michael J. H., ed. Jayne's Encyclopedia of Aviation. Rev. ed. New York: Crescent, 1995.

12. A BOOK THAT HAS BEEN PRINTED BY A DIVISION OF A PUBLISHER

Paperback versions of hardcover editions are often reprinted by divisions of the main publishers. If the title or copyright page indicates this is the case, list the division first, joined by a hyphen to the name of the main publisher:

Abramson, Jeffrey. We, the Jury: The Jury System and the Ideal of Democracy. New York: Basic-Harper, 1994.

13. A BOOK THAT HAS BEEN TRANSLATED

To focus on the original author of a translated work, cite that author first, followed by the title of the work. Next, list the name of the translator, preceded by the abbreviation *Trans.* for "Translator":

Sace, Henri. Paris Notebooks. Trans. Robert Hanna. Paris, France: Cassel, 1996.

When focusing on the work of the translator, list that individual's name first, followed by a comma and the abbreviation *trans.*, not capitalized. Next, give the title of the work, followed by the word *By* and the name of the original author:

> Hanna, Robert, trans. <u>Paris Notebooks</u>. By Henri Sace. Paris, France: Cassel,
>   1996.

14. A DISSERTATION

Use the abbreviation *Diss.* for "Dissertation" after the title of the work and before the name of the degree institution. Include the year in which the degree was granted after the institution's name. For an unpublished dissertation, put the title in quotation marks:

> Allen, Annette Marie. "AIDS and the Aging: Are the Elderly Becoming the New
>   At-Risk Population?" Diss. U of North Texas, 1994.

For a published dissertation, underline the title and include standard publication information (place, publisher, date). For works published by University Microfilms International (UMI), you may include the order number as supplementary material, if you wish:

> Ramsey, Arnold G. <u>On the Significance of Success Attitudes among Elite College</u>
>   <u>Athletes</u>. Diss. U of Virginia, 1994. Ann Arbor: UMI, 1994. 6239772

15. A GOVERNMENT PUBLICATION

In most cases, treat the major agency as the author, followed successively by any named subagencies:

> United States. Dept. of Justice. Bureau of Investigation

For U.S. government documents, it helps to remember that *departments* (e.g., Department of Health and Human Welfare, Department of Justice) oversee *bureaus, administrations, offices,* and the like.

Also note the standard abbreviations for certain items when citing U.S. government publications. For instance, the *Congressional Record* is abbreviated *Cong. Rec.;* its page numbers begin with an *H* or *S* to stand for the *House* or the *Senate* sections of the publication. Also, most U.S. government materials are printed by the *Government Printing Office,* which is abbreviated *GPO.*

Here are some examples:

> <u>Cong. Rec.</u> 17 Mar. 1989. S2966. Florida State. Joint Committee on Language
>   Education. <u>Standards for Elementary Grades Language Instruction</u>. Tampa:
>   Greydon, 1988.

United Nations. General Assembly. <u>Resolutions and Decisions</u>. 42nd sess. 15-21 Dec. 1987. New York: United Nations, 1988.

United States. Dept. of Commerce. Bureau of the Census. <u>1987 Census of Retail Trade: Pennsylvania</u>. Geographic Area Ser. Washington: GPO, 1989.

Note: Although you may cite the author of a government publication parenthetically—for example, (*United Nations, General Assembly 65–81*)—it's best to avoid interrupting the reader with a lengthy parenthetic citation (see pp. 386–387). Whenever possible, name the author in the text and cite page numbers in parentheses:

The report from the United Nations General Assembly shows worldwide crop yields have changed dramatically in the last seven years (225).

Periodicals: Magazines and Journals

Magazines, journals, and newspapers are *periodicals*—that is, publications that are published at regular intervals. They each differ, however, not only in their contents and intended audiences but also in the information needed to locate them and to document their use in your paper.

Volume and Issue Numbers.   Volume and issue numbers are important for documenting journal articles. Each *issue* of a journal is usually numbered, and all the issues published in a single year make up one *volume* of the particular journal. Thus, the cover or title page of a particular journal may indicate that its contents make up *Vol. 2, number 2,* or the second issue of volume two of that journal. This information may be all you have to locate the journal in a library or to document its contents in your paper.

Although magazines also have volume and issue numbers, their more specific dates of publication make that information unnecessary for documentation purposes. (Newspapers are discussed on pp. 402–404.)

Dates.   Magazines are generally published either monthly or weekly, but journals appear less frequently and often irregularly. For this reason, publication information for a magazine and a journal differ significantly. Whereas a magazine will carry a weekly or monthly date of publication—say, *May 24, 1994,* or *August 1995*—a journal will have a publication date indicating a more general time period—say, *Winter 1995* or *Vol. 4, number 3, 1996.*

Page Numbers.   Another difference in documentation information between magazines and journals is the way issues are paginated. Magazines use *discontinuous* pagination, whereby each issue starts with page 1 and ends at any given page number. The next issue then starts numbering pages all over again—beginning with page 1 and so on. Some scholarly journals also use discontinuous pagination, but some appear with *continuous* pagination, in which each issue continues the numbering of pages from wherever the previous issue stopped. Thus, a single continuously paginated journal issue may begin on page 1 and end on page 260; the next issue would begin numbering with page 261, and so forth. Each successive issue would continue pagination from where the previous issue stopped.

These differences between the information needed to document sources from magazines and journals will become increasingly clearer to you once you begin working with such periodicals and follow the guidelines below.

16. AN ARTICLE IN A JOURNAL WITH CONTINUOUS YEARLY PAGINATION

For an article in a journal with continuous pagination, give the author's name first, followed by the article title in quotation marks. Next, give the journal title (underlined) and the volume number, the publication year in parentheses, followed by a colon and a space. Then list the page numbers of the article, followed by a period. Since the volume number and sequential pagination are all that are needed to locate the source, do not include the issue number for a continuously paginated journal:

Bracher, Mark. "Doctor-Assisted Suicide: Psychoanalysis of Mass Anxiety."
Psychoanalytic Review 82 (1995): 657-58.

17. AN ARTICLE IN A JOURNAL WITH DISCONTINUOUS YEARLY PAGINATION

For a journal with separate, discontinuous pagination for every issue, begin with the author's name, the article title, and the journal title (formatted as described in item 16 for continuously paginated journals). Then, give the volume number and issue number, separated by a period (e.g., *9.3*). Use a hyphen to show combined issues (e.g., *44.2–3*). Do not include the word *volume* or any abbreviation for it, such as *vol.* or *vols.* Following the volume and issue numbers, add a space and the date in parentheses, followed by a colon, a space, and the page numbers:

Moore, Kevin Z. "Eclipsing the Commonplace: The Logic of Alienation in
Antonioni." Film Quarterly 48.4 (1995): 22-34.

18. AN ARTICLE WITH NO AUTHOR NAMED

Begin the entry with the article title, and follow the format for a magazine or journal, as appropriate (see items 16, 17, and 19). List the article alphabetically by its title, but ignore the words *A, An,* and *The* as the first words in the title:

"The Rush to Save Antarctica." Hemisphere Quarterly 16.4 (1995): 34-40.

19. AN ARTICLE IN A MAGAZINE

To list an article in a magazine appearing weekly or every two weeks, give the author's name, the article title in quotation marks, and the magazine title underlined, in that order. Next, list the full date—day, month (abbreviated), and year—with no intervening punctuation, followed by a colon and the article page numbers. If the article did not appear on consecutive pages, give only the first page number, followed by a plus sign (+):

Cowen, Ron. "Coloring the Cosmos." <u>Science News</u> 21 Dec. 1996: 392-94.

Gleick, Elizabeth. "Sex, Betrayal and Murder." <u>Time</u> 17 July 1995: 32+.

For an article published in a magazine appearing every month or two months, follow the form for a weekly magazine, but list only the month and year for the date:

Trefil, James. "Dark Matter." <u>Smithsonian</u> July 1993: 27-35.

20. A PUBLISHED INTERVIEW

Begin the entry with the name of the person interviewed, followed by a period. Add the descriptive phrase *Interview,* and include the name of the interviewer, if pertinent; end with a period. For the rest of the entry, include the information and follow the format used for a magazine or journal article, as appropriate:

Clinton, Hillary Rodham. Interview. "'We've Had Some Good Times.'" <u>Time</u> 10
   May 1993: 37.

Gerbner, George. Interview with Sara Kelly. "To Free the World." <u>Utne Reader</u>
   Jan.-Feb. 1997: 80-81.

Note: The title of the Clinton example has both single and double quotation marks around it because the original article used double quotes to indicate that the title is a quotation. (For listing other sources of interviews, see item 33.)

21. AN ARTICLE THAT INCLUDES ANOTHER TITLE

Put the title of the article you are citing in double quotation marks, and underline or italicize, as appropriate, any titles of whole works within it:

Cosgrove, Peter. "Snapshots of the Absolute: Mediamachia in <u>Let Us Now Praise</u>
   <u>Famous Men</u>." <u>American Literature</u> 67 (1995): 329-58.

22. A LETTER OR COMMENT IN A JOURNAL OR MAGAZINE

Give the author's name, followed by a period and the word *Letter* or another appropriate descriptive term. Follow with the periodical title and other standard information:

Harris, Angela. Letter. <u>Harper's</u> May 1994: 9.

23. A DISSERTATION OR ARTICLE IN AN ABSTRACT JOURNAL

Abstract journals publish condensed versions of scholarly and professional works such as articles and dissertations. When you list an abstract in the Works Cited portion of your research essay, give the original publication information about the abstracted work first; follow this information with the underlined title of the abstract journal; then give the volume number, year (in parentheses), and item number or page number of the abstract. Whether you list an item or page number will depend on the journal source. Some journals, such as *Psychological Abstracts* and *Current Index to Journals in Education*, use an item number with each abstract entry; others, such as *Dissertation Abstracts* and *Dissertation Abstracts International*, use a page number.

If the title of the journal does not indicate that the item you are citing is an abstract, include the word *Abstract* (capitalized but not underlined or in quotation marks) immediately after the original publication information (see the entry for *Keely* below).

Use the abbreviation *DA* for *Dissertation Abstracts* and *DAI* for *Dissertation Abstracts International*, followed by the volume number and then the date in parentheses. Give the page number on which the abstract appears, including the series letter (*A* denotes "humanities and social sciences"; *B*, "the sciences"; *C*, "European dissertations"):

Haldeman, Melissa Anne. "The Effects of Motivation, Anxiety, and Visualization on Creative Behavior." Diss. U of California, Los Angeles, 1992. DAI 52 (1992): 1846A.

Keely, Robert A. "Economic Reward as Educational Motivation: Factors in College Students' Perseverance and Success." Research in Higher Education 36 (1995): 432-39. Abstract. Current Index to Journals in Education 37 (1996): item LR275964.

Robbins, Michael T. "Hiding in Cyberspace: Inhibition and Online Addiction." Journal of Psychology and Technology 20 (1995): 17-26. Psychological Abstracts 43: item 10B5854.

Newspapers

For each newspaper article, provide the name of the author, the article title (in quotation marks), and the newspaper title (underlined), as well as the publication date, section (if appropriate), and page number(s). If the place of publication is not part of the title, supply it in square brackets after the newspaper name (but not underlined or italicized; see the entry for *Rollins* below). When the pages on which an article appears are not continuous, give only the first page number and a plus (+) sign, with no intervening space:

Rollins, Fred. "Teachers Say Yes to Parents in the Classroom." Newsday [Garden City, NY] 9 July 1994: 2+.

Schmitt, Eric. "Admiral's Remark Puts Navy on Hot Seat Again." San Diego Union Tribune 9 Nov. 1995: A1.

Wildermuth, John. "Elections Bad Bets for Card Parlors." San Francisco Chronicle 10 Nov. 1995: A1+.

Note that when a newspaper article is only one page, just the author's name should be included in the parenthetic citation (see *Schmitt*, above). When a newspaper article does not indicate the author's name, list the article alphabetically by its title:

"X-Generation Tells It Like It Is." Boston Globe 17 Sept. 1993: A2.

24. CITING THE EDITION OF A NEWSPAPER

The front page, or *masthead,* of a newspaper indicates if the issue is a particular edition, such as the *national, final,* or *Barton County* edition. Because such newspapers contain different information than the same issues distributed in other areas or other times of day, it's important that you list the edition, when one is given. When it is, designate the edition after the date:

Rohter, Larry. "A Witness Says He Lied, but the Execution Is On." New York Times 8 Oct. 1995, natl. ed.: 9.

25. CITING THE PAGINATION OF A NEWSPAPER

Newspapers vary in pagination practices, and some even change the paginating format for different editions of the publication. A few have continuous pagination (see the entry for *Washington,* below), while many others have paginations that combine section letters or numbers with the page numbers (e.g., *B3* or *4-2*; see *Bannon,* below). If no section letter or number is included in the pagination, you must add the abbreviation *sec.* to show the "section" of the indicated page (see *Franklin,* below). As explained elsewhere, cite the first page number, followed by a plus (+) sign for an article that doesn't appear in full consecutive pages:

Bannon, Lisa. "Is the Debonair 007 Too Old to Charm Grunge Generation?" Wall Street Journal 7 Nov. 1995: B1+.

Franklin, Stephen. "Colorblind Hiring Brightens Up Small Firms." Chicago Tribune 18 Sept. 1995, sports final ed.: sec. 4: 1.

Washington, David. "Courts Assailed As Ineffective." <u>New York Times</u> 4 Mar.
    1995: 32-33.

Electronic, Computer-Based, and Online Sources and Materials

Electronic sources include materials ranging from information on a
CD–ROM disk to data on a diskette to an e-mail or other communication you
might receive over the Internet. While many such sources are available only electronically—that is, via computer—many also appear as printed material or in another medium such as videotape. Because electronic sources are fairly new in
their widespread use, diverse in form, and not always uniform in their formatting, they can sometimes be difficult to document properly in a research essay.

As you begin to include electronic sources in your research, study the relevant guidelines and examples in this section. You will find that in addition to
helping you document a particular electronic source, they will also help you understand electronic materials generally and make better use of them.

26. MATERIAL ON CD–ROM

a. CD–ROM Sources from Newspaper, Magazine, Journal, and Other Periodically Published Databases

In most cases, the sources listed on a CD–ROM are derived from the databases of published periodicals (i.e., newspapers, magazines, and journals) and
so are also available in print or microfilm versions. When a CD–ROM source
you need to list in your Works Cited section has also appeared in one of these
other forms (such as a magazine or journal article), you will need to provide all
the information you would normally include for such a work along with information about the CD–ROM source.

To list CD–ROM material that also appears in another version, give the author's name (if provided), followed by the publication information for the other
form of the material. Then, provide the underlined title of the database in
which the other form of the source is listed, followed by the publication
medium, vendor, and publication date of the CD–ROM, in that order and separated by periods:

Hastie, Reid. "Is Attorney-Conducted <u>Voire Dire</u> an Effective Procedure for the
    Selection of Impartial Juries?" <u>The American University Law Review</u> 40
    (1991): 703-726. <u>InfoTrac: Magazine Index Plus</u>. CD-ROM. Information
    Access. Nov. 1995.

"Number of Hospitals in Decline." <u>New York Times</u> 8 Mar. 1994: B2+. <u>New York</u>
    <u>Times Ondisc</u>. CD-ROM. UMI-Proquest. Sept. 1994.

Silby, Caroline Jane. "Differences in Sport Confidence among Elite Athletes with
    Different Perceived Parenting Styles." <u>DAI</u> 54 (1995): 3145A. U of Virginia,
    1994. <u>Dissertation Abstracts Ondisc</u>. CD-ROM. UMI-Proquest. Dec. 1995.

If the CD–ROM doesn't give all of the information needed for entries such as the above (such as a vendor name), cite what's available:

Crane, Graham T., ed. The Complete Works of William Shakespeare. New York: Cleo, 1990. CD-ROM. 1994.

b. CD–ROM Material Not Indicated As Appearing in a Newspaper, Magazine, Journal, or Other Periodically Published Database

If the CD–ROM bears no information stating that its contents are also available in a printed form (e.g., a newspaper, magazine, or journal), provide only the necessary information about the CD–ROM itself. First, give the author's name (if provided), followed by the title of the material accessed in quotation marks, the date of the material, the title of the database (underlined), the publication medium, the vendor name (if relevant), and the CD–ROM's publication date, in that order:

Michelucci, James L. "Market Trend Analysis: Bookstar Inc." 18 Feb. 1993. Business Database Plus. CD-ROM. Information Access. Oct. 1993.

Wells, Henry R. "North American Indian Legends." 1996. Access One. CD-ROM. Sounds-On. 1996.

If you can't find some of the information needed for a complete entry, list what's available:

Wells, Henry R. "North American Indian Legends." 1996. CD-ROM. Sounds-On. 1996.

c. CD–ROM Material That Is Not Periodically Updated after Its Original Publication

Some information on CD–ROM isn't intended to appear periodically or be updated regularly. Cite such sources as you would a book, but include the publication medium after the title:

The Best of the Mayans. CD-ROM. Research International, 1995.

The Oxford English Dictionary. 2nd ed. CD-ROM. Oxford: Oxford UP, 1992.

If you are citing only part of a work, give the name of that part first:

"Leopards." Animals of the World. CD-ROM. New York: Chestnut, 1994.

27. MATERIAL IN MULTIPLE ELECTRONIC PUBLICATION FORMS

When electronic publications are issued together as a single product, include each medium in the Works Cited listing:

Smolan, Rick, and Jennifer Erwitt. Passage to Vietnam: Seven Days through the Eyes of Seventy Photographers. Sausalito, CA: Eight Days, 1994. CD-ROM, videodisc. International Research. 1995.

28. MATERIAL ACCESSED THROUGH AN ONLINE NEWSPAPER, MAGAZINE, JOURNAL, OR OTHER DATABASE

a. Sources Also Available in Printed Versions

When the source you retrieve through a database has also appeared in another form (e.g., a magazine or journal article), provide all the information normally included for such a work as well as information about the database. Begin by giving the author's name (if available), followed by the article title, periodical name (underlined), volume or issue number, date of publication, range of page numbers or total paragraphs, date of access, and Internet address (URL) in angle brackets, in that order:

"Number of Hospitals in Decline." New York Times on the Web 8 Mar. 1994. 27 Feb. 1997 <http://www.nytimes.com/ns94mar/dis9/front/html>.

Priest, Patricia Joyner. "Self-Disclosure on Television: The Counter-Hegemonic Struggle of Marginalized Groups on Donahue." DAI 53 (1993): 2147A. U of Georgia, 1992. Dissertation Abstracts Online. 10 April 1997 <http://www.acmot.com/h4/8y23/html>.

Van Ness, Daniel. "Preserving a Community Voice: The Case for Half-and-Half Juries in Racially-Charged Criminal Cases." John Marshall Law Review 28.1 (1994): 1-56. 16 Nov. 1995 <http://www.lri.ctsid.com/uy40s09f. html>.

If you can't find all of the information about the source, provide as much information as you can:

"Number of Hospitals in Decline." New York Times on the Web 8 Mar. 1994. 27 Feb. 1997 <http://www.nytimes.com>.

b. Sources Not Indicated As Appearing in Printed Versions

Some material appears only in an online form via the Internet or other computer-based systems. If the material you retrieve from a database does not indicate that it's also available in a printed version, give only the information required for the database source. Give the author's name (if provided), followed by the title of the material accessed (in quotation marks), the date of the material, the title of the database (underlined), the date of your access to the material, and the Internet address (URL), in that order:

> College Board. "1995-96 Test Dates." College Board Online 7 Nov. 1995
>   <http://www.cbo.cs.com/62so8/ts/html>.
>
> "Jury." Academic American Encyclopedia 20 Sept. 1995 <http://
>   prodigy.enc.com>.
>
> "Microsoft Corporation: Patent Applications Summary." Disclosure 25 Jan. 1993
>   <gopher:mcs.fisc.pat.com/3fg/html>.

29. SOURCES FROM ELECTRONIC JOURNALS, ELECTRONIC NEWSLETTERS, AND ELECTRONIC CONFERENCES

Treat material from an electronic journal, newsletter, serial, or conference as you would its printed counterpart. The only difference is that you must also include information about the electronic format of the material and your access to it.

Begin by giving the author's name (if provided), followed by the document title (in quotation marks) and then the title of the journal, newsletter, or other type of source in which the document appeared (underlined). Next, state the volume and issue number, followed by the publication date in parentheses. Note that because electronic sources sometimes appear without dates, volume and issue numbers, and the usual pagination of printed articles, you may need to indicate "no date" with *n.d.* or show the pagination by the number of paragraphs (abbreviated *par.* or *pars.*). Following the date, state your date of access and the Internet address (URL).

> Childs, Margo T. "Battered Wives Deserve Attention." ReaLines 2 (April 1994):
>   3 pp. 3 Oct. 1995 <gopher://gopher.real.com>.
>
> "Lone Star Equity: State Asks Court to Give Law a Chance." Daily Report Card
>   3.19 (1993): n. pag. 27 Mar. 1995 <http://www.drc.com>.
>
> Sapontzis, S. F. "The Nature of the Value of Nature." Electronic Journal of
>   Applied Philosophy 3 (1995): 39 pars. 17 July 1995 <http://ejap.com/
>   sem/html>.
>
> Tidmus, Michael, comp. "AIDS Front: Medical Briefs." AIDSwire Digest 1 Nov.
>   1993: 1 par. 9 May 1994 <http://www.aidswire.com/3f.lma/47/html>.

30. PUBLISHED MATERIAL RECEIVED AS ELECTRONIC TEXT

A great number of complete printed works, especially literary and historical texts, are now available as electronic text on the Internet or through commercial computer networks. The full texts of Shakespeare's plays, for example, are available free over the Internet, as are Aesop's tales and copies of the Declaration of Independence and the Constitution of the United States. Since such electronic texts may vary in their reliability, you need to assess each for its sufficiency for your research and study purposes. At the very least, check to see that an electronic text bears a title, an editor's name, and edition information.

To cite electronic texts that are also available in printed, published forms, begin by giving the author's name (if provided), followed by the title of the text (underlined) and the publication information (if available). Complete the entry with your date of access, and the Internet address, in that order:

Dante. La Divina Commedia. Ed. Riccardo Scateni. 24 June 1995 <http://www. crs4.it/~riccardo/DivinaCommedia/DivinaCommedia.html>.

Hawthorne, Nathaniel. The Scarlet Letter. Ed. Thomas Rowley. New York: Harper, 1970. 10 Aug. 1995 <http://www.umin.lib.edu/haw.jt67/htm>.

United States. National Institute on Alcohol. Research Summary, 1993–94: A Report to the Chairman, Health and Welfare Committee, U.S. Senate. 28 Jan. 1994. 12 Sept. 1995 <gopher://infopath.ucsd.edu>.

31. E-MAIL, DISCUSSION LISTS, AND ONLINE POSTINGS (USENET, LISTSERV, BBS)

a. An E-Mail Communication

For an e-mail communication, list the writer's name, followed by the title of the message (if there is one) in quotation marks, a description of the message (including to whom it was sent), followed by the date it was sent:

Uribe, Terry. "Re: Lost Bank Card." E-mail to US Bank. 14 Mar. 1996.

Hartz, John. E-mail to author. 24 June 1997.

b. A Public Online Posting

You may find information that appears reliable among the public messages on commercial online services such as America Online and CompuServe, Usenet and Internet newsgroups, and online bulletin board services. To cite such a source, begin with the author's name, followed by the title of the document (in quotation marks), the description *Online posting*, the date the material was posted, the name of the forum (if known), the date of access, and the address of the Internet site:

Jamieson, Carol. "About Princess Diana." Online posting. 10 Sept. 1997. T_NetListserv. 5 Feb. 1997 <http://teltalk.cte.edu/Virtual/Listserve_HN/ T_Net/1997/34/92.html>.

Hunt, Laney. "Sleep Disorders." Online posting. 3 Oct. 1997. U_News. 20 Nov.
1997 <sci.health.sleep>.

Miner, Herald. "Waco." Online posting. 12 July 1997. Usenet. 19 Nov. 1997
<talk.politics.militia>.

32. WEBSITES AND WEB PAGES

Much of the information on the World Wide Web is available at sites host-
ing scholarly projects (such as the Gutenberg Project for publishing books on
the Internet) and individual web, or *home*, pages. The sample entries below
demonstrate the forms recommended by the MLA for including such sources
in the Works Cited list.

a. Scholarly Project Websites

List as much information as is available, starting with the title of the project (underlined), the author or editor of the source material (if given), followed
by the electronic publication information, including the version number (if
any), the release date, and the name of the sponsoring institution. End with the
date of your access and the Internet address (URL):

Renaissance Poetry Project. Ed. Janice Altram. Mar. 1997. Indiana U. 3 June
1998 <http://www.indiana.edu/~ren/p57/>.

b. Personal Websites and Home Pages

In general, follow the format described in item 32a for a scholarly project
website, giving as much information as is available. Unless the site or page
bears a specific title, begin with the individual's name and use *Home page* to
describe it:

Holly, Barbara. Home page. 18 April 1988 <http://www.unewhaven.ca:8283/
~log/index.html>.

c. Professional Websites

Some websites are created and maintained by professionals for public service or commercial purposes. In general, list such sites as you would a scholarly project website:

Yung, Seymour. Chinese Written Characters. Asian Studies Page. U of Chicago.
12 Nov. 1996 <http://humanities.uchicago.edu/asian/port/>.

Other Sources

33. AN INTERVIEW

For an interview you have conducted yourself, first list the name of the interviewee. Indicate the type of interview, and give the date on which it was conducted:

Nguyen, Phan. Personal interview. 10 Nov. 1996.

Tomlinson, David. Telephone interview. 7 Jan. 1997.

Treat a real-time interview conducted through an Internet connection the same way, but add the Internet address:

Chay, Sharon. Online interview. 12 May 1997 <http://www.livtalk.com.prs/html>.

To list a published or recorded interview, start with the name of the interviewee, followed by *Interview* (unless the title makes it obvious). If the interview has a title, include it in quotation marks:

Edwards, Robbie. "An Interview with Robbie Edwards." Profile 12 July 1996: 34-35.

Gore, Al. Interview. "Gore CompuServe Conference." On the Info Highway 11
  Jan. 1994. 10 April 1994 <http://netfind.aol.com/aol.reviews/politics>.

34. A PUBLIC ADDRESS, SPEECH, OR LECTURE

Begin with the speaker's name, followed by the title of the presentation (in quotation marks), the occasion or sponsoring organization, the place, and the date of the presentation. If the presentation doesn't have a title, provide a descriptive phrase after the speaker's name (without quotes):

Whitson, Carol. Address. City Council Meeting. Branning, MI. 24 Feb. 1996.

Yamada, Mitsuye. "The Current Trend to Silence Artists: A Call to Action."
  English Council of California Two-Year Colleges Annual Statewide
  Conference. Newport Beach, CA. 21 Oct. 1995.

35. A LETTER OR MEMO

To cite a letter published in another work, begin with the name of who wrote the letter, followed by a descriptive title of the letter in quotation marks. Next, add the date of the letter and, if the editor has assigned one, its number.

After including information about the source in which the letter appears, include the page numbers on which the letter appears:

T. S. Eliot. "To John Quinn." 13 Nov. 1918. Letter 16 of <u>The Letters of</u>
    <u>T. S. Eliot</u>. Ed. Valerie Eliot. Vol. 1. San Diego: Harcourt, 1990.
    254-55.

To cite an unpublished letter, first list the author, followed by a description of the letter (no quotes), the date on which it was written, the collection in which it was found (if any), and the place in which it is now located:

Eliot, T. S. Letter to Bertrand Russell. 4 Jan. 1916. Mills Memorial Library.
    McMaster U, OH.

A citation for a letter written to you begins with the author's name, followed by a description and the date:

Cheney, Sharon. Letter to the author. 4 Feb. 1996.

36. A PAMPHLET
List a pamphlet the same as you would an entry for a book:

<u>Cats and More Cats</u> . . . . Millpark, MI: Newsway, 1996.

Nolan, Kenneth C. <u>Gangs in Your Neighborhood</u>. Sante Fe, NM: Trend,
    1995.

US Public Health Service. <u>Have You Seen This Virus</u>? Washington, DC: GPO,
    1996.

37. AN ADVERTISEMENT
Begin with the name of the product or company that is the subject of the advertisement, followed by a period. Then add the word *Advertisement*, without underlining or quotation marks, and another period. End with the remaining information about where and when the ad appeared:

Ford Aerostat. Advertisement. NBC. 6 June 1994.

Dell Computers. Advertisement. <u>Yahoo</u>! May 1998: 43.

38. A WORK OF ART OR A PHOTOGRAPH
Give the name of the artist, when known, followed by a period and then the title of the work (underlined if the work is a painting or sculpture), also

followed by a period. For any art you view personally, list the proprietary institution and, if not indicated in the institution's title, the city:

Duchamp, Marcel. <u>Nude Descending a Staircase</u>. Philadelphia Museum of Art.

Refer to such a work of art in your text, rather than in a parenthetical citation:

Duchamp's <u>Nude Descending a Staircase</u> shows . . .

Cite photographs or other reproductions of works of art the same way, but also add publication information about the source of the reproduction:

Moore, Henry. <u>Recumbent Figure</u>. <u>History of Art</u>. By H. W. Janson. 2nd ed.
    Engelwood Cliffs, NJ: Prentice-Hall, 1977. Illus. 842.

Van Gogh, Vincent. <u>Self-Portrait</u>. The Louvre, Paris. <u>Vincent by Himself</u>. Ed.
    Bruce Bernard. Boston: Little, Brown, 1985. 279.

Again, try to avoid parenthetical citations of artworks by naming the artist and work in the text.

39. AN ILLUSTRATION, TABLE, CHART, OR MAP

In most cases, treat illustrations like anonymous books: List the work by its title (underlined), followed by a descriptive label (e.g., *Chart* or *Map*); then provide other identifying information, as available. Use the abbreviation *n.p.* to indicate when there is "no place" or "no publisher" information available; use *n.d.* to indicate that "no date" is given:

<u>Birds of California</u>. Chart. San Diego: Walson, n.d.

<u>Mexico</u>. Map. Chicago: Rand, 1995.

40. A CARTOON

Maslin, Michael. Cartoon. <u>New Yorker</u> 21 and 28 Aug. 1995: 87.

41. A FILM, VIDEOTAPE, VIDEODISC, OR SLIDE PROGRAM

For a film, list the title (underlined), followed by the name of the director, the distributor, and the year of release, in that order. Add other information you feel is relevant to your purpose. To focus on one person's involvement, cite him or her first, followed by a description of his or her role:

<u>Forrest Gump</u>. Dir. Robert Zemeckis. Perf. Tom Hanks. Paramount, 1995.

Reiner, Rob, dir. and prod. <u>The American President</u>. Perf. Michael Douglas and
Annette Benning. Columbia/Castle Rock, 1995.

For a videocassette, videodisc, slide program, or filmstrip, begin with the
title (underlined), followed by the medium, the distributor, and the release date
(if available). You can specify individual performances or roles as for a film entry (see above):

<u>Building a Successful Medical Transcription Business</u>. Videocassette. Health
Profession Institute, 1996.

<u>Climbing the Rockies</u>. Sound filmstrip. Colorado Environments, 1995.

Shakespeare, William. <u>All's Well That Ends Well</u>. Prod. Johnathan Miller.
Videocassette. Time-Life, 1981.

42. A TELEVISION OR RADIO PROGRAM

First, list the name of the episode or segment (in quotation marks), followed by the title of the program (underlined). Next, give the title of the series
(if any), the name of the network on which the program appeared, the call letters and city of the local station (if any), and the broadcast date, in that order.
Cite the names of individuals and their roles after the program title, or list them
first, if your focus is primarily on their work:

Springer, Jerry, host. "Wild Teens." <u>Jerry Springer</u>. ABC. KCAL, Los Angeles. 28
Oct. 1995.

"Superabled." <u>Dateline NBC</u>. Rpt. John Larson. NBC. KNBC, Los Angeles. 27 Dec.
1995.

43. A SOUND RECORDING

List a sound recording the same as a film, videotape, or other performance
(see items 41 and 42), identifying roles as relevant to your purpose:

Hillerman, Tony. <u>Talking God</u>. Audiotape. Read by Hillerman. Caedmon, 1989.

Tchaikovsky [Peter Ilyich]. <u>The Nutcracker</u>. St. Louis Symphony Orchestra.
Cond. Leonard Slatkin. RCA, 1985.

The example for *Tchaikovsky* uses square brackets to show that the composer's
first and middle names were not included in the source and have been added
by the entry's author.

Sample Works Cited Page

For an example of an MLA-style Works Cited page, see Marcia Valen's research essay at the end of Chapter 22 (pp. 381–382). Refer to it as you prepare your own Works Cited page.

APA-STYLE DOCUMENTATION

Research essays written for most college English courses follow the Modern Language Association (MLA) documentation style, which names the source's author and page number(s) in the text—for example, *(Miller 230)*. Another common form of documentation is recommended by the American Psychological Association (APA) and is called *author/date* style because it calls for naming the author and publication year in the text.

APA-style documentation predominates in papers for the social sciences and several other disciplines, including anthropology, biology, business, education, economics, political science, psychology, and sociology. You should follow the guidelines given on pages 414–429 if your instructor prefers that you document sources for your research essay according to author/date, or APA, documentation style.

Abstracts and Headings

In addition to the documentation practices described on the following pages, APA-style papers differ from those done according to MLA and certain other formats by usually including an abstract and using headings. An *abstract* is a short summary of the paper that announces the topic and briefly describes the content. *Headings* function like brief subtitles to emphasize certain content and to indicate the main sections of the paper. Since including an abstract and using headings are optional for college research essays, you should include them in your paper only if your instructor requires.

Parenthetical Citation

As stated earlier, APA-style documentation calls for citing the source author's last name, along with the work's publication date, parenthetically in the text:

The slight changes that Kilner (1963) traced continue to demonstrate increased patterns of erosion and decreased vegetation (Shore, 1990).

Intext citations such as these direct the reader to more complete descriptions of the named authors' works in the paper's References section. Placed at the end of the essay, the References lists each source cited in the text alphabetically by the author's last name (or by a work's title, when no author is given). In addition to the author's name, each entry also provides the work's title and publication information.

Using Parenthetical Citation. Like MLA style, APA style documents the sources used in the paper by citing each in the text and describing it bibliographically in the paper's References list. As noted earlier, APA style includes the source's publication date (instead of the page number, as in MLA style) in parentheses when the author of the source is named in the text:

> Ramirez (1989) has pointed out the disadvantages of postponing counseling until depression begins to curtail normal activities.

When the author is not named in the text, the name is also cited parenthetically, followed by a comma and the year of publication:

> Decorative items found at the Sungir burial sites demonstrate the early existence of social hierarchies (Harlan, 1989).

(Note that APA style differs from MLA style in placing a comma after the author's name.)

The following method of citing an entire work is also acceptable in APA style:

> Sark's 1988 study has shown that early humans switched to meat eating much earlier than previously thought.

Citation Style. As the above examples demonstrate, parenthetical citation allows acknowledging sources with the least interruption of the reader's attention to the paper's content. You should give immediate credit to a source whose work you have drawn upon and support your own arguments in doing so. Including the source's publication date in the citation is also important because information changes rapidly in some disciplines. The date allows the reader to assess the relevancy of data and to make comparisons.

Citing an Author, Editor, or Corporate Author. Treat individuals, editors, corporate authors (e.g., associations, committees, departments), and others who would normally be considered responsible for producing a work as its author. Cite personal authors or editors in text by their surnames only:

INDIVIDUAL AUTHOR
According to Butler (1994), active group participation is another effective route to indirect self-assessment.

EDITOR

The list of recognized AIDS-related infections has grown every year since the disease was first identified (Rossman, 1997).

Spell out the name of each group or corporate author the first time you cite it parenthetically. For subsequent citations, you may cite the name in full or use a shortened version, depending on whether the name will be readily recognizable to the reader and whether the source can be easily located in the References section. For a recognizable, easily located source, give an abbreviated form of the name in brackets within the first parenthetical citation (see the following example, *World Health Organization*). But if the name is short or would not be easily understood as an abbreviation, spell out the full name each time you cite the source (see *Red Cross*, below):

GROUP OR CORPORATE AUTHOR

It has been estimated that diarrheal diseases cause the deaths of more than 3.2 million children before they reach their fifth birthday (World Health Organization [WHO], 1991). The cost of antibiotics to fight the diseases has led to rationing in some countries (Red Cross, 1995).

GROUP OR CORPORATE AUTHOR (SUBSEQUENT CITATION)

These outbreaks continued even after prolonged attempts to eradicate all known causes of the virus (WHO, 1991). . . . Not until five years later did the missing serum arrive, and most of it was too contaminated to use (Red Cross, 1995).

Citing a Source with Two Authors.   Cite both names each time the source is mentioned in the text. Use an ampersand *(&)* between the names:

FIRST CITATION

Fuller and Morrison (1995) have interpreted these incidents as memory lapses.

Other researchers (Fuller & Morrison, 1995) have interpreted these incidents . . .

SUBSEQUENT CITATIONS

. . . although Fuller and Morrison (1995) had different results.

. . . although others (Fuller & Morrison, 1995) have had different results.

Citing a Source with Three to Five Authors.   Name each author the first time the work is cited, but in subsequent citations, give only the first author's last name, followed by a comma and *et al.:*

FIRST CITATION

Arita, Fenner, Osborn, Purtilo, and Sigal (1995) found no evidence that the drug was harmful.

SUBSEQUENT CITATION

These results were less reliable than those found by Arita et al. (1995).

Note: The phrase *et al.* comes from *et alii,* Latin for "and others." Since *al.* is an abbreviation for *alii,* it must always be written with a period after it. Don't underline *et al.* or put quotation marks around it in your paper.

Citing a Source with Six or More Authors.   Give only the first author's name, followed by a comma and *et al.* Include the date in parentheses:

SOURCE

Brunnell, Lemoy, Massey, Freeman, Noser, Siegele, and White (1995)

ALL TEXT CITATIONS

According to Brunnell et al. (1995), such recovery does not last.

If two of your sources with six or more authors happen to have the same first author (or several authors), include as many other names as needed to distinguish between the sources:

TWO SOURCES

1. Brunnell, Lemoy, Massey, Freeman, Noser, Siegele, and White (1995)
2. Brunnell, Lemoy, Ramirez, Noser, Kelly, and White (1995)

TEXT CITATIONS

Research findings vary: Brunnell, Lemoy, and Massey et al. (1995) found that . . . , whereas Brunnell, Lemoy, and Ramirez et al. (1995) found that . . .

Be sure to spell out the names of all authors, regardless of number, when listing a source in the References section of your paper.

Citing Two Authors with the Same Last Name.   Differentiate two authors with the same last name by including their initials in the running text or in the parenthetical citation. Cite the authors in alphabetical order by their initials:

M. Street (1994) and W. R. Street (1996) identify major lunar provinces yet to be explored by satellite.

At least two experts (M. Street, 1994; W. R. Street, 1996) identify major lunar provinces yet to be explored by satellite.

Citing Sources by the Same Author(s) That Were Published the Same Year.
Proceeding alphabetically by title, assign each individual work by the same author and published in the same year a lowercase letter (*a*, *b*, *c*, and so on) after the publication date:

(Navarro, 1994a)

(Navarro, 1994a, 1994b)

Also add the assigned letter to the publication date of each work as it appears alphabetically by title in the References section of the paper (see item 3, p. 423).

Citing a Source with No Author.   Cite the work by its title, using the first two or three keywords in place of an author's name:

FULL TITLE

A Study of Adults Exhibiting Stable Behavioral Patterns over a Twenty-Year Period (1996)

TITLE CITED IN TEXT

One 20-year study found a significant correlation between the way individuals behaved in high school and later as adults (Study of Adults, 1996).

List such works alphabetically by full title in the paper's References section.
    Cite a work's author parenthetically as *Anonymous* only if that's how the author is named in the source. The intext citation will look like this:

The cost of such programs (Anonymous, 1997) may account for . . .

If you do cite an anonymous source, also list the work alphabetically—with *Anonymous* as author—in the References.

Citing a Source with More Than One Author.   Separate multiple authors' names with *and* when the names are part of the running text. When you cite names parenthetically, separate them with an ampersand sign *(&)*:

NAMES CITED IN RUNNING TEXT

Wing and Gould (1996) have shown a correlation between autism and low scores on intelligence tests.

Gourdet, Ringly, Howland, and Lin (1997) found that picture dependency decreases as children improve their reading skills.

NAMES CITED PARENTHETICALLY

Other studies (Wing & Gould, 1996) have shown a correlation between autism and low scores on intelligence tests.

Picture dependency decreases as children improve their reading skills (Gourdet, Ringly, Howland, & Lin, 1997).

Citing Authors of Two or More Separate Sources Together. 　Cite such works only parenthetically, beginning in alphabetical order with the first author's last name. Separate the citations with semicolons:

The privileged classes, for instance, have the luxury of time for long-term education and career planning (Breit, 1993; Lovett & Anderson, 1990; Wertham, 1994).

Citing Legal Sources. 　Underline the names of court cases; separate the names of the parties with the abbreviation *v.* (for "versus"). If the case is mentioned in the text, put the date in parentheses immediately after the case name. Or cite both the case name and date in parentheses:

Fletcher v. Peck (1810) established the right of the U.S. Supreme Court to declare a state law unconstitutional more than 100 years ago.

The U.S. Supreme Court established its right to declare a state law unconstitutional more than 100 years ago (Fletcher v. Peck, 1810).

Note that the names of court cases are underlined when cited in text but not when listed in the References section.

To cite a statute, give the name and year. Do not underline the name in either the text or the References section:

The Securities Exchange Act (1934) was designed to protect the public from fraud or manipulation in the sale of securities.

Federal law requires the regulation and registration of securities exchanges (Securities Exchange Act, 1934).

Personal Communications. 　Unpublished letters, memos, telephone conversations, interviews, and the like are personal communications. Since they are not available to other researchers, cite such information sources *only in the text*, not in the References list for your paper. Give the last name and initials of your personal source as well as the date on which the communication took place:

The institute's chairperson, Dr. A. M. Reyes (personal communication, September 4, 1990), thinks American society celebrates childhood almost effortlessly but has difficulty dealing with the changes that appear in adolescence.

Some forestry personnel are now beginning to regret all the media attention given to the new park proposal (Charles May, personal communication, November 4, 1995).

Citing Quotations and Specific Parts of Sources.   APA-style documentation uses the abbreviations *p.* and *pp.* for "page" and "pages," *ch.* for "chapter," and *sec.* for "section." Use these or other standard abbreviations when citing specific parts of a work and whenever you use a direct quotation or paraphrase. The following examples demonstrate common practice:

Shepard and Chipman (1996) found that people can rotate mental images but only at a limited rate (see also Ferguson, 1987, pp. 827-836).

According to Beach (1995, ch. 3), perceptual distortions can be both psychological and cognitive.

Horne (1994) concludes that one primary function of sleep may be "to repair the cerebral cortex from the wear and tear of consciousness" (p. 41).

If we interpret dreaming as "an analogue to our artistic yearnings" (Sheah, 1996, p. 207), we are still left with no explanation of its physiological importance beyond the cases made by Randall (1990, sec. 1) and Horne (1994).

Note that in APA style, consecutive page numbers are cited in full, not abbreviated.

Citing Sources of Long Quotations.   Quotations of 40 words or more should be typed double spaced and indented five spaces from the left margin. Don't indent the first line of the first quoted paragraph, but indent the first line of any subsequent paragraphs five additional spaces. Cite the author's name and publication date (in parentheses) in the lead-in to the quote. Place the page number of the source in parentheses after the period ending the quotation:

Gregory (1992) explains these effects as follows:

> Sleep-deprivation causes sleepiness. It is difficult to keep awake someone who has been deprived of sleep for 60 hours. Such a person has frequent "microsleeps" and recurrently fails to notice, being unable to sustain a high level of attention. Sometimes visual illusions or hallucinations are experienced or the individual becomes paranoid. (p. 719)

Preparing the References Page

Except for personal communications (e.g., letters, personal interviews, and the like), the References list includes all of the sources cited in the paper's text. It should not include any other works, however, no matter how useful they may have been to you in providing background information or common knowledge to your research. You may have consulted 50 sources during your research and ended up paraphrasing, quoting, or naming only 10 of them in your paper. If that's the case, list only those 10 in your References.

List all works alphabetically by the author's last name, corporate or committee author name, or by title, if no author is given in the source. Also include the basic publication information a reader will need to locate the source.

The rest of this section on APA style provides guidelines and sample entries for listings in the References section of the research essay. As with MLA style, note that these entries follow hanging indentation style, in which the first line begins flush left and subsequent lines are indented five to seven spaces. If your instructor prefers, you may also use an alternate form, in which each first line is indented but not those following:

> Hatton, F. (1996). Thinking and imagination in children's dreams: An introduction for parents. New York: Lammon, 1996.

INDEX TO REFERENCES FORMS

Authors' Names

1. Authors, Editors, and Corporate Authors
2. A Source with No Author
3. Sources Published by the Same Author(s) in the Same Year
4. Multiple Sources by the Same Author(s)
5. Multiple Sources by Single and Joint Authors

Dates of Publication

Titles

6. Books
7. Periodicals

Periodical Volume and Issue Numbers

Page Numbers

Special Types of Books

8. An Edition or Revision of a Book
9. A Volume in a Multivolume Work
10. A Work Published in an Edited Book
11. A Book in a Series
12. A Technical or Research Report

Other Sources

13. Proceedings of a Meeting
14. Legal Sources
   a. A Federal District Court Opinion
   b. A Case Appealed to the U.S. Supreme Court
   c. A Federal Law
15. Nonprint Sources
   a. A Film or Video
   b. A Cassette Recording

Authors' Names

1. AUTHORS, EDITORS, AND CORPORATE AUTHORS

Treat the names of editors and corporate authors (i.e., associations, committees, corporations, councils) and editors the same as authors' names. Cite corporate authors by name, alphabetically. List personal authors and editors alphabetically by surname, followed by the initials of their first and (if given) middle names. For editors, use *Ed.* or *Eds.* in parentheses after the name, followed by a period. Use the ampersand sign *(&)* between names of joint authors. Follow these examples:

SINGLE AUTHOR

Atkinson, W. W. (1991). Memory culture: Remembering and recalling. Sante Fe, NM: Sun.

SINGLE EDITOR

Bell, W. R. (Ed.). (1993). Hemotologic and oncologic emergencies. New York: Churchill.

JOINT EDITORS

Hume, C. A., & Pullen, I. (Eds.). (1993). Rehabilitation for mental health problems: An introduction handbook (2nd ed.). New York: Churchill.

TWO AUTHORS

Selnow, G. W., & Gilbert, R. R. (1993). Society's impact on television: How the viewing public shaped television programming. Westport, CT: Greenwood.

CORPORATE AUTHOR

Washington State Rehabilitation Board. (1994). Guidelines for mental health facilities funding: 1993–94. Spokane: Author.

Note in the last example that the corporate author is also the publisher. In such a case, use the word *Author* in place of the publisher's name.

2. A SOURCE WITH NO AUTHOR

Cite a work with no author alphabetically by title. Include the articles *a*, *an* and *the* at the beginning of a title, but ignore them when ordering titles alphabetically:

BOOK CITED BY TITLE

A course for the 90's. (1990). Austin, TX: Four Square.

NEWSPAPER ARTICLE CITED BY TITLE

Higher health costs hit all sectors, U.S. says. (1991, January 10). The Wall Street Journal, p. A2.

When a source provides no author's name, do not use *Anonymous* as the author *unless that term is actually given* in the source. If the author *is* named as *Anonymous*, list the work alphabetically under that term.

3. SOURCES PUBLISHED BY THE SAME AUTHOR(S) IN THE SAME YEAR

Proceed alphabetically by title to assign lowercase letters (*a*, *b*, *c*, and so on) after the publication date. List works in the alphabetical order of the letters assigned:

Searle, J. R. (1990a). Consciousness, explanatory inversion, and cognitive science. Behavioral Brain Science, 13, 385-442.

Searle, J. R. (1990b). Is the brain's mind a computer? Scientific American, 262, 26-31.

4. MULTIPLE SOURCES BY THE SAME AUTHOR(S)

List the works in chronological order of publication, oldest to newest. Include each author's last name(s) and first and (if given) middle initial in each entry:

SINGLE AUTHOR

Neiderman, S. (1993). Taking charge of your life: A guide for women. Boston: Avery.

Neiderman, S. (1995). How to stay married: Ten simple rules. New York: Engleman.

JOINT AUTHORS

Leakey, R., & Lewin, R. (1977). Origins: The emergence and evolution of our species and its possible future. New York: Dutton.

Leakey, R., & Lewin, R. (1979). People of the lake: Mankind and its beginnings. New York: Avon.

Leakey, R., & Lewin, R. (1992). Origins reconsidered: In search of what makes us human. New York: Anchor-Doubleday.

5. MULTIPLE SOURCES BY SINGLE AND JOINT AUTHORS

Give the name of the first author in each entry. List personal works before edited works and single-author entries before joint-author entries. Put joint-author entries in alphabetical order by the second and succeeding authors' names:

SINGLE AUTHOR
Lave, L. B. (1981). The strategy of social regulation: Decision frameworks for policy. Washington, DC: Brookings Institute.

SINGLE EDITOR
Lave, L. B. (Ed.). (1983). Quantitative risk assessment regulation. Washington, DC: Brookings Institute.

JOINT AUTHOR
Lave, L. B., & Omenn, G. S. (1981). Clearing the air: Reforming the Clean Air Act. Washington, DC: Brookings Institute.

JOINT EDITOR
Lave, L. B., & Upton, A. C. (Eds.). (1987). Toxic chemicals, health and the environment. Baltimore, MD: Johns Hopkins University Press.

For ordering multiple works published under the same name(s), follow the guidelines above.

Dates of Publication

Place the work's publication date in parentheses, followed by a period, after the author's name. For a magazine or newspaper article, give the month and day of publication in parentheses after the year, separated by a comma. Do not abbreviate the month. Follow these examples:

JOURNAL ARTICLE
Merson, M. H. (1993). Slowing the spread of HIV: An agenda for the 1990s. Science, 206, 1266-1268.

NEWSPAPER ARTICLE
Hoff, G. (1995, November 14). Fat genes may change your life. Los Angeles Times, p. A3.

MAGAZINE ARTICLE

Raloff, J. (1994, May 7). Cigarettes: Are they doubly addictive? Science News, 14, 294.

BOOK

Priest, P. J. (1995). Public intimacies: Talk show participants and tell-all TV. Cresskill, NJ: Hampton.

Titles

6. BOOKS

Capitalize only the first word of a work's title, the first word of a subtitle, and all proper nouns. Underline the complete title:

Hermstein, R. J., & Murray, C. (1994). The bell curve: Intelligence and class struggle in American life. New York: Free Press.

7. PERIODICALS

As with a book title, capitalize only the first word, the first word of a subtitle, and all proper nouns in the title of a magazine article. Do not underline the article title or put it in quotation marks. Type the full name of the journal, magazine, or newspaper in which the article appears in upper- and lowercase letters; underline the title and the comma that follows:

Angrist, J. D. (1991). Does compulsory school attendance affect schooling and earnings? Quarterly Journal of Economics, 106, 979-1014.

Taubes, G. (1994, December). Surgery in cyberspace. Discover, 15, 85-94.

Periodical Volume and Issue Numbers

For a journal, give the volume number, *underlined*, after a comma following the journal title. Indicate the issue number in parentheses immediately (no space) after the volume number whenever each issue of the journal begins with page 1. Follow the punctuation and spacing shown in these examples:

JOURNAL WITH VOLUME NUMBER ONLY

Zollo, P. (1995, November). Talking to teens. American Demographics, 17, 22-28.

JOURNAL WITH VOLUME AND ISSUE NUMBERS

Moore, K. Z. (1995). Eclipsing the commonplace: The logic of alienation on Antonioni. Film Quarterly, 48(4), 22-34.

MAGAZINE ARTICLE WITH VOLUME NUMBER ONLY

Shreeve, J. (1995, September). The Neanderthal peace. Discover, 16, 70-81.

Page Numbers

Use *p.* or *pp.* before the page number(s) to cite parts of books and articles in newspapers but not to cite the pages of journal, magazine, and newsletter articles. Add the page numbers for part of a book (such as a chapter) in parentheses following the book's title (see *Heaton & Wilson* example, below). Add the page numbers for a newspaper article after the title of the newspaper (see examples below). Add the page numbers for an article in a periodical at the end of the entry, following the volume and issue numbers. Give inclusive page numbers in full: *361–382*. Separate discontinuous page numbers with a comma: *pp. A5, A12*. Follow these examples:

MAGAZINE ARTICLE

Bartusiak, M. (1990, August). Mapping the particle universe. Discover, 7, 60-63.

JOURNAL ARTICLE

Simon, R. J. (1992). Jury nullification. Journal of Criminal Justice, 20(3), 261-266.

CHAPTER IN A BOOK WITH SEVERAL VOLUMES

Burke, R. E. (1979). Election of 1940. In A. M. Schlesinger, Jr. (Ed.), History of presidential elections, 1798-1968 (Vol. 4, pp. 2917-3006). New York: McGraw-Hill.

CHAPTER IN A BOOK

Heaton, J. A., & Wilson, N. L. (1994). Problems for viewers. In Tuning in trouble: Talk TV's destructive impact on mental health (pp. 127-173). San Francisco: Jossey-Bass.

SIGNED NEWSPAPER ARTICLE

Kelly, J. (1995, April 12). Lawyers ready for battle. Los Angeles Times, pp. A1, A6.

UNSIGNED NEWSPAPER ARTICLE

Christmas cancelled for these juvenile offenders. (1995, November 19). San Diego Union-Tribune, p. A-24.

Special Types of Books

8. AN EDITION OR REVISION OF A BOOK

Indicate an edition or revision of a book in parentheses after its title:

Herzfield, E. E. (1988). Iran in the ancient East (Rev. ed.). New York: Hacker.

Hess, B. B., & Markson, E. W. (Eds.). (1985). Growing old in America (3rd ed.). New Brunswick, NJ: Transaction.

Wilson, M. (1983). Managing a work force (2nd ed.). Brookfield, VT: Gower.

9. A VOLUME IN A MULTIVOLUME WORK

Give the number of the volume(s) you consulted in parentheses after the title. Use *Vol.* or *Vols.* before the volume number:

> Grouws, D. A., & Cooney, T. (1989). Perspectives on research on effective mathematics teaching (Vol. 1). Hillsdale, NJ: Erlbaum.

If particular volumes are published over more than a one-year period, indicate the dates:

> Scammon, R. M., & McGillivary, A. V. (Eds.). (1972-1979). America votes: A handbook of contemporary American election statistics (Vols. 9-13). Washington, DC: Elections Research Center.

10. A WORK PUBLISHED IN AN EDITED BOOK

List the work by its author's last name, followed by first and (if given) middle initial(s). Then, cite the title, followed by the editor's initials and last name, in that order. Include the volume number (if applicable), followed by a comma and the page number(s) for the included piece in parentheses:

> Burke, R. E. (1979). Election of 1940. In A. M. Schlesinger, Jr. (Ed.), History of presidential elections, 1789-1968 (Vol. 4, pp. 2917-3006). New York: McGraw-Hill.

11. A BOOK IN A SERIES

Give the name or number of the series, including the page number(s), if you are citing a particular section of the work:

> Crump, D. J. (Ed.). (1995). Into the wilderness (Special Publications Series 13, No. 2). Washington, DC: National Geographic Society.

> Population Reference Bureau. (1995). Family size and the Black American. Population Bulletin (No. 4. p. 11). Washington, DC: Author.

12. A TECHNICAL OR RESEARCH REPORT

List a published report the same as a book. If the issuing agency has assigned a number to the report, include it in parentheses after the title, with no punctuation preceding it:

> Briggs, D. E. G. (1981). Relationship of arthropods from the Burgess Shale and other Cambrian sequences (Open File Report 81-743). Washington, DC: U.S. Geological Survey.

Olivas, M. (1982). The condition of education for Hispanics. In La Red [The Net] (Report No. 56). Ann Arbor, MI: University of Michigan, Institute for Social Science.

U.S. Congress, Office of Technology Assessment. (1988). Electronic delivery of public assistance benefits: Technology options and policy issues (S/N 052-003-01121-2). Washington, DC: U.S. Government Printing Office.

Other Sources

13. PROCEEDINGS OF A MEETING

List the work the same as a book; include the date and location, if they are part of the title:

World Food Conference. (1994, May). Proceedings of the Carmichael conference on health and technology. Lexington: University of Kentucky.

14. LEGAL SOURCES

Give the information needed for a reader to locate a source. Using the source itself or a referent to it as your guide, give the information indicated in the following examples. If your typewriter or computer doesn't have keys for typing the symbol for *section* (§), use the abbreviation *Sec.* Underline names of court cases when citing them in the text but not in the References. Also, do not underline the names of laws, acts, codes, or documents (such as the *U.S. Constitution*) in either the text or the References.

a. A Federal District Court Opinion

Name   Volume   Source   Page   Region   Date

Harper v. Kinola, 554 F. Supp. 927 (S. W. Ark. 1994).

[This 1994 case was tried in federal district court for the Southwestern District of Arkansas. It appears in volume 554, page 927, of the *Federal Supplement.*]

b. A Case Appealed to the U.S. Supreme Court

Name   Source   Volume   Page   Date

Baker v. Carr, 369 U.S. 186 (1985).

[This case was tried in 1985 before the U.S. Supreme Court. It appears in volume 369 of the *United States Reports*, page 186.]

c. A Federal Law

```
                  Title number    Section
                        |            |        Date
           Name         |   Source   |          |
            |           |     |      |          |
Voting Rights Act, 42 U.S.C. Sec. 1973 (1965).
```

[Passed into law in 1965, this act appears in title 42, Section 1973, of the *United States Code.*]

Many federal laws are often cited by title number, rather than by name. Note that the *United States Code* (cited above) may be abbreviated as *U.S.C.:*

> 15 U.S.C. Sec. 221 (1978).

For more information about the forms of legal references, see *A Uniform System of Citation* (Cambridge, MA: Harvard Law Review Association, 1991).

15. NONPRINT SOURCES

a. A Film or Video

Give the principal contributors' names, followed by their function(s) in parentheses. Specify the medium in brackets after the title, followed by the location and name of the distributor:

> Choate, H. R. (Producer), & Kimbel, M. M. (Director). (1993). <u>Marriage and commitment</u> [Film]. Chicago: Academy Productions.

> IRA [Intercultural Relations Institute]. (1992). <u>Take Two</u> [Video]. Palo Alto, CA: Intercultural Relations Institute.

b. A Cassette Recording

Give the principal contributors' names, followed by their function(s) in parentheses. Specify the medium in brackets after the title. If a recording number is given on the source, include that information with the medium specification—for example, *(Cassette Recording No. 71)*. List the publisher's location and name last:

> Peterson, R. T. (Ed.), & Walton, R. K. (Narrator). (1990). <u>Birding by ear</u> [Cassette Recording]. Columbus, OH: Ohio State University.

Sample References Page

Figure 23.1 shows the APA-style References page for a research essay on public health issues, which conforms to the guidelines discussed on pages 414–429. Use it as a model to follow in creating your own References list.

Public Therapy 19

References

Group author/ publisher — American Psychiatric Association. (1994). <u>Diagnostic and statistical manual of mental disorders</u> (4th ed.). Washington, DC: Author.

Banks, J. (1990). Listening to Dr. Ruth: The new sexual primer. In G. Gumpert & S. L. Fish (Eds.), <u>Talking to strangers: Mediated therapeutic communication</u> (pp. 73-86). Norwood, NJ: Ablex. — Selection included in another work

Journal article — Carbaugh, D. (1993). "Soul" and "self": Soviet and American cultures in conversation. <u>Quarterly Journal of Speech, 79</u>(5), 182-200.

Didion, J. (1992, July 26). Trouble in Lakewood. <u>New Yorker, 68,</u> 46-50, 60, 62-65. — Magazine article

Book/ single author — Holmes, D. (1994). <u>Abnormal psychology.</u> New York: HarperCollins.

McGuire, W. J. (1993). Social psychology. In <u>Academic American Encyclopedia</u> [On-line]. Available: http://www.academiconline. socpsych.html — Encyclopedia article/online source

Morris, A. D., & Mueller, C. M. (Eds.). (1992). <u>Frontiers in social movement theory.</u> New Haven, CT: Yale University Press. — Book/joint editors

Unsigned newspaper article — "People." (1994, September 30). <u>USA Today,</u> p. D-2.

Prout, N. A. (n.d.). Is confession really good for the soul? <u>Psych Web</u> [On-line]. Available: http://www.elsu.edu/psychweb/ confgood.html — Online journal article

Report/ corporate author — Psychiatry and the Community Committee. (1995). <u>A family affair: Helping families cope with mental illness</u> (GAP Report: No. 119). New York: Bruner-Mazel.

Stocking, B. (1994, October 1) Confession may be costly. <u>The News and Observer,</u> pp. 1A, 10A. — Newspaper article

FIGURE 23.1 **Sample APA-style References page**

Research Exercises

1. Using the sources you examined during your research and recorded on your notecards, create a Works Cited or References page for your own research essay. Your instructor's requirements will determine whether you should follow MLA or APA style.

2. According to your instructor's preference, use MLA or APA guidelines to create a Works Cited or References page for the following sources:

   a. A book entitled *Theories of Everything;* published by Ballantine Books in 1991; written by John D. Barrow; the subtitle is *The Quest for Ultimate Explanation.*

   b. A chapter entitled "Preparing for the Expedition"; on pages 80–92 in a book by Stephen E. Ambrose; the title is *Undaunted Courage: Meriwether Lewis, Thomas Jefferson, and the Opening of the American West;* published in New York by Simon and Schuster in 1996.

   c. "The English Dialect Society," an entry on page 121 in *The Linguistics Encyclopedia;* edited by Kirsten Malmkjær; published in 1991 in London by Routledge.

   d. An anonymous article on page 20 of the March 1998 issue of *Discovery* magazine; the title is "A New Breed of Star."

   e. An article from a CD–ROM entitled "Some Smoke Is Good for You," written by Martin Scholes; first appeared in *Science Digest* on August 7, 1995; the article came from a database called *Proquest Resource One;* the CD–ROM was published by UMI in January 1995.

   f. An article in the Orange County edition of the *Los Angeles Times* newspaper for September 12, 1997, written by Jane Fowley; it appears on pages 2A and 7A; the title is "And Now Back to Bach. . . ."

   g. A magazine article by Alex Madera; viewed online March 2, 1998; the title is "Practice Teachers"; posted online at <http://classroom.com/HELM/dec97/report.htm> on November 14, 1997; no page numbers.

   h. A telephone interview with Sandra Anton on April 5, 1997.

   i. A book entitled *Science as History: Scientific and Human Events in Time,* published in London by Beacon House in 1988; the editors are Consuela Adante, Gordon R. Judd, Paul Kimbal, and Janice Reid.

   j. An article in a journal with discontinuous pagination; written by Katherine Wills and entitled "Education as a Grail"; published in volume 53, issue 4, of *Western Educator,* September 29, 1996, on pages 78–82.

3. Using the sources described in exercise 2, write the correct parenthetical, intext citation form for each. Based on the examples, make up any page numbers you need for a complete citation. Follow either MLA or APA style, as your instructor requires.

Writing for Other Purposes

Writing about Literature

Writing about literature provides you the opportunity to revisit a work and involve yourself more completely with it. Simply put, you begin by carefully rereading a short story, poem, or work of drama, analyzing its various parts, and then focus your attention on a single part or quality to write about. Your objective in writing about literature is to discover your own sense of the work's meaning and then to write an essay that reflects an accurate, sensitive understanding and presents valid conclusions.

READ TO RESPOND TO THE WORK

Although you may have read a particular piece of literature for personal enjoyment or as an assignment in a course, your first step in *writing* about the work is to reread it with a new purpose in mind. Carefully reread the entire text at least once. As you do so, pay particular attention to details such as style, structure, and plot and how they combine to make meaning or create a particular effect in the work. (See the Glossary of Literary Terms and Concepts on pp. 447–448.) Make note of patterns and relationships among elements and consider how they work together to create the whole. Once your ideas about the work begin to develop and your paper begins to take shape, return as often as necessary to reread any difficult or significant parts that may be central to your discussion.

Take Notes As You Read

Many writers find it helpful to annotate a literary text by recording their reactions directly on the page as they read. Annotating a text in this way involves writing marginal notes and underlining, circling, and otherwise marking parts of the text that seem significant in some way. If you were writing about Flannery O'Connor's short story "Revelation," you might annotate the text like this:

Until the sun slipped finally behind the tree line, Mrs. Turpin remained there

with her gaze bent to them as if she were absorbing some abysmal life-giving

Her vision =
knowledge

knowledge. At last she lifted her head. There was only a purple streak in the sky,

cutting through a field of crimson and leading, like an extension of the highway,

Like a
priest...

into the ascending dusk. She raised her hands from the side of the pen in(a gesture

hieratic and profound.)A(visionary)light settled in her eyes. . . .

Note how this reader has marked specific words and phrases in the text and also jotted down notes in the margin. Do whatever will help increase your understanding of the work.

List Your Ideas As You Read

If you prefer not to annotate a work by marking the text, you can also list elements that appear important on a separate sheet of paper and then analyze relationships and look for patterns among them later. To determine the significance of the title of O'Connor's story "Revelation," you could list your responses in this way:

"Revelations" in the story

—Title a reference to Revelations chapter in the Bible?

—Mrs. Turpin expects the girl to give her a "revelation" (149).

—At the pig parlor, she gazes "through the very heart of the mystery" (154)—another kind of "revelation"?

Making annotations and lists, such as those above, can help you clarify and organize your thoughts about a literary work. Use these and other prewriting strategies, such as clustering and freewriting (see Chapter 5, pp. 60–64), to stimulate your thinking and develop a preliminary thesis about the work.

FORMULATE A THESIS STATEMENT ABOUT THE WORK

Once you have carefully reviewed the text several times and examined its details for patterns of meaning, you are ready to formulate a thesis statement that sets forth your understanding of the work. An effective thesis statement will state a point about the literary work and express your attitude about it. Note how each of the following thesis statements focuses on a particular aspect of a work and presents a claim that could serve as the basis of a discussion:

SHORT STORY

In Flannery O'Connor's "Revelation," Mrs. Turpin's self-confidence about her relationship with God undergoes significant change as a result of her vision at the end of the story.

POEM

The speaker's attitude about the death of the young man addressed in A. E. Housman's "To an Athlete Dying Young" is actually more complex than his words suggest.

PLAY

Shakespeare's imagery throughout <u>Macbeth</u> reflects the play's emphasis on the tragic results of unnatural and excessive ambition.

Remember to avoid thesis statements that merely summarize a work (e.g., *Flannery O'Connor's "Revelation" describes a day in the life of the main character*) or imply that you have knowledge of the author's intentions or personal views (e.g., *"To an Athlete Dying Young" shows A. E. Housman's respect for athletic achievement*). Instead, keep your thesis and your paper's discussion clearly focused on the work itself and the ideas expressed in your thesis statement.

Once you have devised an appropriate thesis about the literary work, organize the evidence you have gathered by rereading the text and developing a plan, as you would for any essay (see Chapter 6).

WRITE AN EFFECTIVE INTRODUCTION TO YOUR ESSAY

The introduction to a discussion of a literary work should include the work's full title and the name of the author, any necessary background information, and a clear thesis statement. Although you should assume throughout the paper that your reader is familiar with the work you are writing about, include in the introduction relevant background information, such as an explanation of a historical event, a summary of recent criticism, or your definition of a key term related to your thesis. You should also include a brief summary of the work to focus the discussion on the central issues addressed in your essay. Most important, make sure the introduction includes a thesis statement that clearly presents the point you are making about the work.

As the introduction to an essay on "The Horse Dealer's Daughter," a short story by D. H. Lawrence, one student wrote the following:

> D. H. Lawrence's "The Horse Dealer's Daughter" portrays falling in love as unexpected and therefore somewhat frightening. This is the lesson Mabel Pervin and the young doctor Fred Fergusson learn when he rescues her after she has tried to drown herself. When she asks if he loves her, Fergusson inwardly resists the idea of falling in love with anyone. Struggling to respond to her question, however, he suddenly discovers that he indeed loves Mabel and tells her so, with a "terrible intonation" (256) that echoes the desperation they both feel. In this way, the story demonstrates that people fall in love for different purposes and for reasons beyond their control.

This introduction includes a summary that focuses on the story's theme and its development through the actions of the main characters. Although you may begin your own literary discussion in others ways, always be sure to include the author's name, the title of the work, and a clear thesis statement in your introduction.

DEVELOP YOUR DISCUSSION OF THE LITERARY WORK

Your discussion of the literary work should be guided by the argument presented in your thesis statement. Rather than follow the structure of the story, novel, poem, or play you are writing about, organize your discussion according to significant ideas about the work. Develop the essay through a logical series of paragraphs, each supporting an idea implied in the thesis statement and unified by a fully developed topic sentence.

Notice how another writer develops a discussion of Robert Frost's short poem "Stopping by Woods on a Snowy Evening" by supporting a topic sentence with examples and quotations:

> The tension between the speaker's desire to linger in the woods and the obligation he feels to leave is echoed by several contrasting elements in the poem. The speaker's isolation in the woods is balanced against the images of people and society suggested by his mention of a distant "house" and "village." Similarly, the "easy sweep" of the wind and overall quietness of the woods contrast with the horse's abrupt shaking of the harness bells, and the speaker describes the woods themselves as being both "lovely" as well as

"dark and deep." The effect of such contrasts is subtle but pervasive in the poem. They reinforce the reader's sense of the speaker's internal tension, a conflict between surrendering to the dark beauty of the woods or to the responsibilities of life.

This paragraph presents one part of the writer's analysis of the speaker's character. The essay's discussion of the poem is developed further through a succession of paragraphs, each developing a related aspect of the thesis statement.

WRITE AN EFFECTIVE CONCLUSION TO YOUR ESSAY

An effective conclusion briefly summarizes the thesis statement and the major ideas in the essay. It should end with a general view of the work. Here is an effective conclusion from a paper discussing Arthur Miller's famous drama *Death of a Salesman:*

> Willy Loman's fate results from his desperate striving to achieve dignity in a world that denies respect to dreamers like himself. Although Willy envies the success of others, his desire for recognition is not rooted in greed or personal ambition. He is clearly naive and self-deluded but in ways all of us recognize in ourselves. The play demonstrates that a person's struggle and failed attempt to gain a sense of personal dignity is not only tragic but tragically human. That is why, as Linda insists, "attention must be paid" even to a life like Willy Loman's.

IDENTIFY YOUR SOURCES

If you are writing about a literary work that's included in a class text, your instructor may not require that you cite the edition or page numbers for that particular work in your essay. On the other hand, if you are required to give information about the text you are using for your discussion or if you refer to or quote from other sources, you will need to cite those works the same as you would sources in a research paper. Likewise, you should include a Works Cited page at the end of your essay, listing the appropriate bibliographical information for the literary text and any other sources you refer to in the paper. Here are some examples of Works Cited entries:

Housman, A. E. "To an Athlete Dying Young." Literature: Reading Fiction, Poetry, Drama, and the Essay. Ed. Robert DiYanni. Boston: McGraw, 1997. 739.

Leggett, B. J. The Poetic Art of A. E Housman: Theory and Practice. Lincoln: U
of Nebraska P, 1978.

(Chapter 23 provides additional guidelines for including works of literature
and other kinds of sources in the Works Cited.)

Use Parenthetical Citation

You don't need to cite page or line numbers when you quote or refer to the
content of a single-page source, such as a brief essay or poem. For longer
works, however, you should identify the location of each quotation and any
specific references you make.

Follow a quotation or reference citation with its original page or line number enclosed in parentheses. If the quoted or referenced material appears at the
end of a sentence in your essay, end the sentence with a final punctuation mark
after the last parenthesis. Here are some examples:

> Mrs. Turpin is convinced that the girl knows her "in some intense and personal
> way" (149) that both frightens and angers her. The girl's words so haunt Mrs.
> Turpin the rest of the day that she angrily tries to refute them in an imagined
> conversation with God (153).

Because some literary works exist in several different editions, it's helpful to follow a page number for such a source with a semicolon and the appropriate abbreviation for the divisions of the work: for example, *(118; ch. 4); (237; bk. 2.
ch. 1)*.

When you cite page numbers for poems longer than a page, give the line
number(s) parenthetically, using the word *line* or *lines* in your first reference
but including only the line numbers thereafter:

> The speaker in Plath's "Daddy" says she is "finally through" (line 67) with her
> father's domination. She boasts that "If I've killed one man, I've killed two--/
> The vampire who said he was you" (70-71).

For a drama written in verse (such as the plays of Shakespeare), give the
act, scene, and line numbers, separated by periods, rather than page numbers.
Unless your instructor prefers that you use roman numerals for citing acts and
scenes, use arabic numerals:

> Hamlet speaks compassionately of "poor Ophelia/Divided from herself and her
> fair judgement/Without the which we are pictures, or mere beasts" (1.4.84-86).

Note in these last two examples that a slash is used to indicate line breaks
when quoting three or fewer lines of poetry. When you quote more than three

lines, type the quotation double spaced, indented 10 spaces from the left margin, and omit slash marks as well as any quotation marks that are not part of the original.

If you refer to or quote from other sources, cite them parenthetically also, giving the author's name and relevant page numbers, as appropriate:

> This interpretation reflects not only Mrs. Turpin's belief in an ordered universe in which all events have meaning (Kramer 76) but also her desire to relate events to herself. According to Robert Booth, Mrs. Turpin "believes in the vision because she assumes that she is the kind of person to whom visions are granted" (34).

(Refer to Chapter 23 for additional guidelines on citing literary works and other sources parenthetically in your essay.)

FOLLOW OTHER STANDARD PRACTICES FOR WRITING ABOUT LITERATURE

By now, you are no doubt aware that discussing a literary work sometimes requires slightly different practices from those used in writing other kinds of essays. In addition to those practices already discussed, you should observe the following conventions when you write about literature.

Mention Authors' Names

It's customary in literary discussions to refer to authors by their last names after the first complete mention. Doing so avoids awkward repetition of the full name throughout the discussion and keeps the tone of the essay more objective. So, the first time you mention an author in your paper, give his or her full name, but use only the last name in subsequent references:

> John Steinbeck's short story "The Chrysanthemums" is a study of values and how they are revealed by people's actions. Steinbeck creates two contrasting scenes to define the story's characters and the values they represent.

Remember that you should not refer to an author by his or her first name in a literary essay. Referring to the author as *John* when you are discussing Steinbeck's work, for instance, would make your writing sound casual and imply a personal familiarity that doesn't exist. You should also avoid using *Mr., Mrs., Miss,* and other titles with an author's last name, since they can sound condescending and are, in fact, irrelevant to your paper's purpose.

Write in the Present Tense

In one sense, the action in a novel, short story, poem, or play never really ends. Instead, it's considered as continuously occurring and present within the imaginary, ever-existing world of the text. For these reasons, you should use the present tense to describe both the literary work and the actions that occur within it:

In "Stopping by Woods on a Snowy Evening," Frost contrasts the speaker's reaction to the beauty of the woods with those of his horse, who cannot understand why they are stopping at all. Their different reactions suggest that the speaker's conflict over stopping among the woods or going on is an essentially human dilemma.

Avoid Using Excessive Summary

Don't make the mistake of oversummarizing in your essay. Use summary to introduce your essay topic and to clarify or illustrate a point. By doing so, you will keep your discussion focused on clearly expressing content in support of the paper's thesis statement. Keep any summary brief and use it only when it serves a clear purpose. The same advice applies to using examples and quotations, too.

Create an Accurate Title

The title of your literary essay should be brief and accurately express the focus of your discussion. Don't underline (or italicize) or put quotation marks around the essay's title. If you include the name of a literary work in your title, only the title of the literary work should be underlined or put between quotation marks, as appropriate:

Tone in A. E. Housman's "To an Athlete Dying Young"

The Imagery of War in Shakespeare's Macbeth

Thurber's Use of Irony

As noted in Chapter 23, the guidelines of the Modern Language Association (MLA) recommend the use of underlining as preferable to italic type for indicating titles and highlighting terms. You should find out what your instructor prefers—underlining or italicizing—and use one or the other exclusively throughout your essay. The same guidelines apply to both underlining and italicizing.

A SAMPLE ESSAY ON A LITERARY WORK

The following sample essay discusses the importance of tone in A. E. Housman's poem "To an Athlete Dying Young." The poem is printed below for your convenience, and the sample essay follows. Read the essay carefully and note how its author, Laura Rice, has developed the discussion of the paper's thesis statement. Use the essay as a guide in developing and writing your own discussion of a literary work.

TO AN ATHLETE DYING YOUNG
by A. E. Housman (1859–1936)

The time you won your town the race
We chaired you through the market-place;
Man and boy stood cheering by,
And home we brought you shoulder-high.

To-day, the road all runners come,   5
Shoulder-high we bring you home,
And set you at your threshold down,
Townsman of a stiller town.

Smart lad, to slip betimes away
From fields where glory does not stay;   10
And early though the laurel grows
It withers quicker than the rose.

Eyes the shady night has shut
Cannot see the record cut,
And silence sounds no worse than cheers   15
After earth has stopped the ears:

Now you will not swell the rout
Of lads that wore their honours out,
Runners whom renown outran
And the name died before the man.   20

So set, before its echoes fade,
The fleet foot on the sill of shade,
And hold to the low lintel up
The still-defended challenge-cup.

And round that early-laurelled head   25
Will flock to gaze the strengthless dead,
And find unwithered on its curls
The garland briefer than a girl's.

Heading should include your name, instructor's name, course number, and date—all double spaced.

Include names of author and literary work in introduction.

Summarize literary work in introduction.

Keep use of quotations to minimum and integrate into own sentences, when possible.

Rice 1

Number each page using your last name and arabic number.

Laura Rice

Professor Lawton

English 123

10 March 1998

The Speaker's Tone in

"To an Athlete Dying Young"

Title should name poem and give focus of discussion.

1

A. E. Housman's "To an Athlete Dying Young" is an eloquent seven-stanza monologue addressing a deceased youth being carried by fellow townspeople to his burial. After recalling how he and others had once before borne the young man "shoulder-high" following his victory in their town's race, the poem's speaker praises the permanence that death will bestow upon the young man's fame. By dying now, he says, the young champion will neither have to see his record broken nor outlive his fame the way others before him have. He encourages the young man to accept death and enjoy the permanence that it will provide his fame and youth. The words of the speaker thus present a practical and somewhat blunt argument in favor of the young man's early demise. Though outwardly a practical and slightly blunt the speaker's attitude toward the young man's death is a mixture of resentment and compassion that together account for the effectiveness of his address to the dead youth.

Include thesis statement that expresses ideas paper will support.

2

The speaker's somewhat paradoxical attitude about the death of the young athlete is apparent early in the poem. After the first two stanzas describe how the townspeople had earlier "chaired" the youth through the market-place in victory and today are bearing him "shoulder-high" in death, the reader is prepared for a traditional lament for the death of a young hero. This expectation is enhanced

Rice 2

by the speaker's familiar, warm tone as he addresses the youth directly as "you," calls him by the colloquial term "lad," and refers to himself and others as simply "we." The conversational yet solemn rhythm of the poem's rhymed iambic tetrameter lines reinforces the reader's sense that the speaker is addressing someone with whom he is familiar, even closely associated, and whose early death he will openly mourn.

Use topic sentences to organize essay's discussion.

An unexpected shift occurs in the speaker's tone in the third stanza, however. Rather than lament the youth's death, the speaker welcomes it, expressing a somewhat bitter, cynical attitude about the impermanence of fame and, by extension, the brevity of life itself. He calls the youth a "Smart lad" for having "slip[ped] . . . away" so soon from life. In life, he assures the young man, "glory does not stay" but "withers quicker than the rose." By living longer, he insists, the young man could expect only to "see the record cut" and to hear the cheering for his victory cease. Contemptuous of those who cling to life, the speaker is pleased that the young athlete will not "swell the rout" of other heroes who "wore their honours out" by living too long. In the poem's last stanza, he describes these others as "the strengthless dead," bygone heroes from whom life has stripped not only fame but youthful vigor, as well.

Quotations from single-page source do not need page number citation.

Brackets indicate change in tense from original. Ellipsis indicates words have been omitted to make quotation grammatical.

3

4

Although this slightly surprising, unsentimental, and cynical attitude dominates the speaker's address, it does not ultimately define his response to the young man's death. The personal tone and suggestion of loss established in the first two stanzas actually continue throughout the poem, subtly blending with the speaker's otherwise stoic response. This more sentimental attitude

Rice 3

on the part of the speaker is felt through his use of traditional, euphemistic metaphors that dignify and soften the effect of the youth's death. Thus, he makes no explicit references to dying or death but says instead that the youth was right to have "slip[ped] . . . away" into "shady night." Now traveling "the road all runners come," the young man is not dead but, in the speaker's words, merely the "Townsman of a stiller town." In the last stanza of the poem, he describes the dead youth's "unwithered" victory wreath as being "briefer than a girl's," a sensitive and compelling image that expresses his sense of life's ultimate fragility and the delicate, fleeting nature of the young man's youth and glory.

Such metaphors as these are important for their cumulative effect and what they imply about the speaker's unexpressed feelings about the youth's death. By softening the speaker's apparent lack of sentiment, they reveal his pervasive stoicism as the masking of a deeper and more personal sense of loss. Although he emphatically stresses the virtues of death's permanency, the speaker is actually emphasizing the unchangeable, permanent absence of the youth from life. In this way, the speaker's seemingly conflicting attitude--bitter resentment of life's impermanence and sorrow for the young man's death-- conveys an emotional tension that elevates the poem beyond a merely cynical response or sentimental lament. Rather than endorsing the young man's early death, then, the speaker's tone and highly metaphoric language reveal his compassionate sense of permanent loss, not only of the young athlete but for all that his youth and glory represent in life, as well.

Example maintains capitalization of original.

Conclusion restates major ideas of discussion and comments on literary work as a whole.

5

GLOSSARY OF LITERARY TERMS AND CONCEPTS

character: A person in a literary work. Characters in literary works are often said to be either flat or round. A *flat* character usually has a single outstanding trait and remains the same throughout the work; a *round* character may have several traits and develops or changes over the course of the work.

characterization: The means by which an author presents or develops a character in a literary work.

climax: The part of a story or play in which a crisis is reached and a resolution is usually achieved.

conflict: Tension or struggle between opposing forces or characters in a work. A story's plot often develops from a conflict that leads to a climax and resolution (see **climax** and **plot**).

diction: An author's choice of words.

figurative language: Language that uses figures of speech.

figure of speech: A nonliteral use of language to compare dissimilar things (see **simile, metaphor,** and **personification**).

foreshadowing: Arranging information or events in a story or play in such a way that they suggest or hint at later events.

image: A sensory impression—such as seeing, hearing, touching, smelling, or tasting—evoked by a writer's words.

imagery: The use of recurrent and related images to produce a certain effect in a work.

irony: A discrepancy or contradiction between what is said and what is meant or between what is expected to happen and what does happen.

metaphor: A figure of speech that states or implies a comparison between two dissimilar things, as in *He bulldozed his way through the crowd.* This metaphor compares a person's actions to the way a bulldozer pushes obstacles out of its path.

narrator: The person telling the story in a literary work. The narrator should be considered a character in the work; he or she is not necessarily the same as the author.

paradox: A statement that, at first, appears contradictory or absurd but actually contains an understandable truth.

personification: A metaphorical figure of speech in which an inanimate object is spoken of as if it were living or human—for example, *An envious moon peeked through the trees.*

plot: The pattern of events in a literary work. In most cases, plot is driven by the conflict within a character or between one or more characters (see **character** and **conflict**).

point of view: The perspective from which a work is narrated. In a work with a *first-person point of view,* a character identified in the work tells the story. In *a third-person point of view,* the author is implied as being the narrator.

protagonist: The main character in a literary work.

rhyme: Repetition of identical or similar sounds, as in *ache* and *break*.

rhythm: A pattern of recurrent qualities; usually stressed syllables, words, or sounds.

setting: The time and place in which the events of a literary work take place.

simile: A figure of speech using *like* or *as* to create a comparison between two unlike things, as in *He pushed through the crowd like a bulldozer.*

speaker: The named or imagined character or voice is speaking the words of a poem. The speaker of a poem is not the author but a persona created by the author to express the work.

stanza: A group of two or more lines in a poem.

structure: The overall design or organization of a work.

style: The manner in which an author uses language and other literary devices to tell a story.

symbol: A person, place, object, or set of events representing something beyond itself.

theme: The main or controlling idea in a literary work. A successful theme comments on the larger aspects of the human experience, not just the condition of an individual character in a literary work.

tone: The writer's attitude toward the characters, subject, and audience, as revealed through the language of his or her work.

Activities

1. Write a brief essay analyzing how the central theme of a short story or work of drama is conveyed by the actions of its main character or characters.

2. Select a short poem and write a brief essay about the relationship between the author's diction and the poem's central meaning.

3. Meet with some of your classmates and take turns reading aloud some of the poetry you admire. Discuss the strengths and weaknesses of each poem to determine if you can agree on some principles for evaluating poetry. Use those principles as the basis for a short essay in which you evaluate one of the poems you shared with the group.

4. Select a short story in which setting plays a central role. Write a brief essay in which you explain the influence of the story's setting upon the work's characters or theme.

Writing for an Essay Exam

In taking an essay examination, you face two important tasks: knowing and understanding the course content and writing clearly and effectively about it in the time allowed. The first task means that you will need to study your class notes and review the course textbook in many of the same ways you would for any other kind of exam. The second task requires that you plan your writing before the exam and then briefly plan again when you receive the exam question and prepare to answer it. Following these steps, you should be able to write an essay that demonstrates an understanding of the course content and responds effectively to the exam question.

PREPARING FOR AN ESSAY EXAM

Begin planning for an essay exam *as early as possible*. Pay attention at the start of the course to the kinds of tests mentioned in the class syllabus or by the instructor. If you know a course will require an essay exam, take notes that focus on relating key concepts and events discussed in lectures and readings. Keep all handouts and quizzes given during the course, and pay particular attention to information related to special films, fieldtrips, and presentations by guest speakers. Since you will need to study the course content as well as prepare for writing about it effectively, give yourself enough time before the exam to prepare adequately for both tasks.

Review Major Course Concepts

To begin preparing for an essay exam, use the course syllabus and the table of contents in your textbook to prepare a list of major topics to study. Be especially sure to include any topics to which a large portion of class time was devoted—such as a series of lectures, special demonstrations, guest speakers, or a class project. Beneath each topic, list significant events, examples, persons, dates, and definitions that are associated with it. As you study for the exam, relate the listed topics and supporting information to your class notes, assigned readings, handouts, and other course materials.

Use Direction Words to Write Practice Questions

An essay exam question usually includes important *direction words* that describe how you are supposed to answer. Words like *compare, define, list, show, summarize,* and *evaluate* specify how your instructor expects you to respond and indicate the scope of the answer he or she expects. (See Figure 25.1, which is a list of commonly used direction words and what they mean.) As you review major topics covered in the course, you can use such direction words to create and study for potential exam questions that you devise for yourself.

WORD	MEANING
Analyze	Separate the subject into its major parts. Describe each part, and explain the relationship of the parts to each other and to the whole.
Classify	Separate the subject into categories on the basis of their shared characteristics.
Compare/ Contrast	Show the similarities/differences between two or more subjects. You may be asked to compare, to contrast, or to do both.
Define	State the meaning of a word or phrase in a way that distinguishes it from similar words or phrases in the same category.
Describe	Use details to present a clear picture of an event, object, or procedure.
Discuss	Talk about the different issues involved in a subject.
Distinguish	Show the differences between two things to clarify the identity of each.
Enumerate	Discuss the points in a list, naming and describing each as you proceed.
Evaluate	Judge and explain the value of something according to your own criteria or others that may be specified.
Explain	Make clear what is said by interpreting or clarifying its meaning.
Identify	Name or define specified items.
Illustrate	Show by providing details and examples.
Interpret	Explain your understanding of what something means.
Justify	Offer reasons or other evidence to show that something is correct or valid.
Prove	Provide evidence or logical reasoning to establish the validity or truth of something.
Relate	Show how two or more things are connected.
Show	Demonstrate using explanations, details, and examples.
Summarize	Express something in briefer form by stating the main points.
Support	Argue or present evidence in favor of something.
Trace	Identify the steps of development or change.

FIGURE 25.1   **Direction words for essay exams**

For example, suppose that in addition to having assigned readings about *youth gangs*, your sociology course also included several lectures on that topic. You could use a variety of direction words (shown highlighted below) to devise potential essay questions like these:

Define gang membership as viewed by Peters and Walton, and show how gang activity in Central Los Angeles fits that definition.

Compare and contrast the values of two different types of youth gangs we have studied in this course.

Explain the appeal of gang membership beyond the teenage years.

Generating 6 to 10 questions like these will familiarize you with direction words that may appear on the exam as well as help you focus your preparation.

Prepare a List or Outline

After you have created a number of potential exam questions, create a brief list or informal outline of the main points to be discussed for each question. An informal outline for the last question above, for example, might look like this:

1. Explain the appeal of gang membership beyond the teenage years.
   a. Lack of maturity
   b. Desire to maintain youth
   c. Social and financial dependency
   d. Community prestige

Make an outline like this for each of the potential questions you devise. You can then use it as a study guide as well as a preliminary plan for writing a practice essay.

Write a Practice Response

Rehearsing a written response to a likely exam topic will build your confidence and prepare you to handle other questions, as well. After making up two or three potential exam questions for topics likely to appear on the test, allow yourself 30 or 40 minutes (the usual time allotted for most exam essays) to write a response to each of them. When you have finished, review what you have written for clarity, organization, and development. In particular, make sure you have a clearly stated thesis and included relevant information and examples. Make corrections to the essay as needed by adding omitted material or deleting anything that doesn't address the question directly. Practicing in this way will reinforce good essay-writing habits and help you to remember the material better.

Make a Spelling List

Your instructor will expect you to be familiar enough with key terms and concepts from the course to be able to spell them correctly. If you are a weak speller, practice writing words that you expect to use in your exam responses, especially those that are central to the course. For an exam in a psychology class, for instance, you might need to practice writing terms such as *neurosis*, *Jungian*, and *paranoid*. For an exam in biology, you may want to rehearse words like *synapse*, *protozoa*, and *cellular*. And for an exam in a history or literature course, make sure you know how to spell the names of people and places you have studied.

Make a list of any such terms that you find difficult, and practice writing them correctly before an exam. Preparing in this way will not only improve your spelling but will also increase your familiarity with the words and the concepts behind them.

Prepare Yourself for the Exam

After studying and mentally preparing all you can for an essay exam, also make sure you are *physically* ready to do your best. Get a good night's sleep before the exam and eat a healthy meal beforehand. Prepare yourself to be ready to devote all your energy and attention to the exam, not to trying to stay awake or listening to your stomach growl.

WRITING THE ESSAY EXAM

Be on time to the examination, and bring any necessary and permitted items, such as a test booklet, pen or pencil, notes, a computer disk, and so on. Once you have the exam in hand, take the time to read it carefully and to plan your response.

Read and Understand the Question

In order to write an acceptable response on an essay exam, you must first read and understand the essay question accurately. Don't make the mistake of rushing through the question to formulate a hasty and likely inaccurate response. Instead, read the entire exam carefully. Next, underline the essay question, and circle the direction words in it. For example:

In a paragraph or two, (discuss) the ways in which evolution may be correctly described as both a theory and fact.

Briefly (summarize) Jesperson's case against same-sex marriages, and (evaluate) his three major arguments.

If you are unsure about what the exam directions say or what's being asked in an exam question, ask your instructor or the exam proctor for clarification.

Plan Your Time

As you read the exam instructions, also make a point of circling the time allowed for the test. Consider the steps involved in completing the exam, and decide how long you can take for each. The majority of your time should go for writing the essay response, but you should also allow time to read and understand the essay question, plan your response, and revise and proofread your finished essay. Generally speaking, you can plan on about 45 minutes of writing time during a 1-hour essay exam, which leaves about 15 additional minutes for planning, revising, and proofreading.

Unless you are taking the exam on a computer, remember also to write legibly, adding corrections and making changes as needed. Don't plan to rewrite or copy the exam. Use the time you have for answering the exam question, and save time at the end to revise and add changes.

Plan Your Answer

Quickly plan your essay response by using the direction words (e.g., *define* or *trace*) from the exam question to guide the form of your answer. As you did in preparing for the exam, jot down in rough outline form the main points you intend to discuss, and use clustering or other techniques to generate supportive details and examples. Use the outline of your main points as a working plan for writing the essay.

Write Your Response

An essay exam doesn't allow you the time to write an introduction and accompanying thesis statement, as you would do with other essays. For this reason, you should forego an introduction and begin by directly answering the exam question. To do so, start your essay with a sentence that rephrases all or part of the exam question and turns it into a statement, as in these examples:

EXAM QUESTION
Explain why Spanish rule in the early nineteenth century did not expand into what later became the northwestern United States.

QUESTION REPHRASED AS OPENING STATEMENT
Spanish rule in the early nineteenth century did not expand into what later became the northwestern United States due to opposition from the French government and because of economic conditions within Spain.

EXAM QUESTION

Contrast the wedding rites of the Tair people of West India with traditional American wedding ceremonies.

QUESTION REPHRASED AS OPENING STATEMENT

The wedding rites of the Tair people are far simpler than traditional American ceremonies but also more legally and morally binding.

Use statements such as these to announce your answer and focus your response. Develop the rest of the essay by discussing the main points and supportive information in the order you listed them in the working outline you made earlier.

As you complete the essay, write steadily and neatly. Again, don't expect to recopy your work, as that will sacrifice valuable writing time. Instead, plan to proofread your answer and make necessary corrections neatly when it's finished.

Support Clearly Stated Main Points. State the main points of your response as clearly worded topic sentences that address the essay question and follow a logical sequence. Develop your paragraphs with specific details and examples that support the topic sentence and show how well you know the course content. Support generalizations by describing events and individuals, providing dates and statistics, and citing research. To help your reader follow your ideas, use transitional expressions—such as *in addition, also, however, finally,* and *first, second,* and *third*—to show relationships among sentences and paragraphs.

Answer the Question. Be sure that you *answer the question that's asked,* not a different one. The direction words in essay questions call for specific kinds of responses—for instance, asking you to *define* a set of terms, *trace* a development, or *identify and evaluate* a cause. If you do something other than what is asked—like offering examples instead of defining terms or identifying but not also evaluating—your instructor will most likely consider your answer incomplete and give you a lower score.

In addition, take care not to wander off the question asked into one you think you know more about. No matter how well you write on a different topic, your instructor will unlikely give you credit if you don't answer the exam question—*and only the exam question.* Keep your working outline in front of you, and refer, at times, to your thesis statement in order to stay on track.

Finally, keep in mind that not all written exams require essay-length answers. Some may ask you to respond to each question in a few sentences, while others may ask for a paragraph or two. When a question explicitly asks you to respond *in a certain length,* make sure your answer stays near the specified range. This is the approximate quantity of writing your instructor has determined is necessary to compose a satisfactory answer.

Revise and Proofread

When you have finished your essay, take a few minutes to reread it for completeness and to make minor corrections. If you have left out words or even a sentence or two, add them neatly, using a caret (∧) to show where each fits into the content. Also neatly cross out any irrelevant material, and replace it with more suitable content. Be sure your sentences are complete and that they make sense. Check for punctuation and spelling errors, paying special attention to the spellings of key terms and names of places and individuals. Before you hand in the essay, make sure your name and other necessary information appears on the test booklet cover or at the top of each page.

A SAMPLE ESSAY EXAM RESPONSE

The essay that follows was written in response to this exam question:

Summarize the evidence indicating a relationship between human emotions and the body's immune defenses, especially regarding serious disease.

Read and study the essay. As you do, note how the author turned the exam question into an opening statement and then developed main points with supporting examples. Note also how changes to some wording and spelling were made after the author revised and proofread the essay.

Rephrases exam question as thesis

First main point

Transition words connect supporting examples

A growing amount of evidence indicates that a significant relationship exists between human emotions and the body's immune defenses, especially regarding serious disease. The immune system appears to function less effectively, for example, among people who suffer from depression, loneliness, or a generally negative outlook on life. Studies of men and women who had recently lost a spouse showed that the surviving individuals had much lower immune functions than did individuals married to a living husband or wife. Similarly, stress has been linked to renewed outbreaks of herpes in people already infected with that virus, and occurrences of Epstein-Barr ∧virus and ~~menum~~ mononucleosis have been shown to be higher among people suffering from anxiety and depression. In other studies, students who felt most pessimistic or fatalistic about life while they were in college were also shown to be more prone to disease and earlier deaths later in life than students with more positive attitudes.

Second main point

In fact, a positive attitude about life and one's medical condition has been shown generally to have a beneficial effect on one's health and survival. Author Norman Cousins, for example, argued in his book Anatomy of an Illness that he cured himself of spinal arthritis by adopting a healthy mental attitude, laughing a lot, and thinking positively. Cousins's claims have been supported by other research, such as that showing longer survival rates among heart attack victims with strong social ties and a positive attitude about their recovery.

Example from class lecture

A ~~good~~ positive mental attitude was also linked to survival in studies of women with breast cancer. In these cases, women who exhibited a "fighting spirit" and freely expressed their anger or distress over having breast cancer displayed stronger immune responses and lived longer than women who were more accepting and showed signs of depression. The same kind of link between a positive mental state and longer survival rates was also found among people with AIDS who were assertive about their illness, had strong social support, and exhibited lower levels of anxiety and frustration.

Continued supporting examples

Although not all scientists agree about the extent to which our feelings affect our health, the ~~evident~~ evidence of an important relationship between human emotions and the body's immune response to serious disease appears overwhelmingly convincing. Studies done with cancer, AIDS, heart-attack patients, and others clearly indicate that an individual's mental attitude can play a significant part in lowering the body's immunity to disease as well as helping it to overcome and survive serious illness.

Conclusion re-emphasizes exam question and thesis

Activities

1. Use your class textbook and course syllabus to prepare a list of study topics for an essay exam in one of your college courses. Below each topic, list related supportive and other important information.

2. Make a spelling list of words you would have trouble with on an essay exam for one of your current college courses. Study the list and then practice writing the words several times each.

3. Using any of the direction words listed in Figure 25.1, write five practice questions for any of the topics you listed for activity 1.

4. After making an informal outline for a response to one of the questions you drafted in activity 3, write a practice essay response to the question. Allow yourself about 30 or 40 minutes to write the essay.

5. Reread your practice essay response to make any needed revisions. Analyze the strengths and weaknesses of your response. If you were the instructor reading your essay, what grade would you give it? Why?

CHAPTER 26

Writing for Business: Letters, Resumes, Memos, FAXes, and E-Mail

At various times during your college or professional life, you will need to write a business letter, send a resume and cover letter, and FAX or e-mail communication to individuals and companies. Since such correspondence will represent nearly everything recipients will know about you, you will want to write thoughtfully and ensure that what you send to others conforms to the conventions of business and professional writing.

WRITING A BUSINESS LETTER

A business letter should be brief, to the point, and representative of your best writing skills. Regardless of the subject, make the tone of a business letter courteous but also perhaps firm, depending on your purpose. As in all your writing, observe the rules of grammar, usage, and punctuation, and take extra care to proofread any letter several times before sending it. Make sure that your letter includes all necessary information and follows the basic format expected in a business letter.

Formats of Business Letters

A business letter usually follows one of three basic formats: block style, modified block style, or simplified style. Although government offices and private businesses today may use any of these, block style is by far the most common. Nonetheless, each of these basic styles has its own strengths and weaknesses. You should use the one that most suits your purpose and individual style.

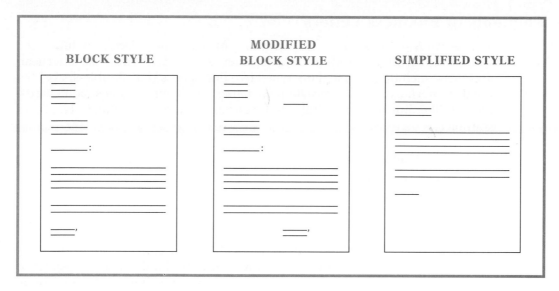

FIGURE 26.1   **Common formats for business letters**

Block Style.   *Block style* is the most formal layout for business letters and is usually written on letterhead stationery. To type a letter in block style, begin all the elements—including the date, inside address, salutation, body, and close— flush against the left margin (see Figure 26.1). If there is a second page to a block-style letter, begin the content just below the top margin; don't center it on the depth of the page.

Modified Block Style.   A business letter in *modified block style* appears less formal and, for some people, suggests more warmth than correspondence in block style. Type a modified block letter the same as one in block style, begin-ning every line at the left margin, with one major exception: The date and the signature lines must begin at the horizontal center of the page (see Figure 26.1).

Simplified Style.   Although it's not often used for personal business corre-spondence, the *simplified style* is often preferred for form letters, correspon-dence with unknown parties, and mass mailings. Type a letter in simplified style by lining up all the elements flush against the left margin, as in block style. A major difference, however, is that you include no salutation or com-plimentary close. The body of the letter begins immediately after the inside ad-dress (or after the subject line), with no salutation such as *Dear* _____. Similarly, include your name and signature right after the last line in the body, with no intervening close such as *Sincerely* or *Yours truly* (see Figure 26.1). (We will talk about these different parts of a letter in the next section.)

Elements of Business Letters

Return Address Heading.   The *heading* of a business letter includes the sender's return address and the date the letter was written. If you use letterhead stationery, include only the date, typed two line spaces (i.e., double-space) below the letterhead. Don't abbreviate the names of streets, avenues, boulevards, and the like, but do use postal abbreviations for names of states. Here's an example:

Anthony Marcos

1559 West Summer Street

Orleans, MA 02653

September 24, 1998

The address part of the heading should always be flush left on the page, regardless of which letter format you follow. The date should also be flush left if you are using block or simplified style; the date should align on the horizontal center of the page, however, if you are using modified block style (see Figure 26.1).

Inside Address.   The *inside address* includes the recipient's name, title, and complete address. If the person's title is short, include it following the name, separated with a comma, if the title is long, add the title below the name. Write the company name as it usually appears. Again, don't abbreviate the names of streets, avenues, boulevards, and the like, but do use postal abbreviations for names of states. Here's an example of an inside address:

Dr. John Stuart, Chair

Department of English

LaSalle University

2749 West Monitor Street

Collegetown, WI 71239

Type the inside address two lines below the return address heading and *always* on the lefthand side of the page.

Salutation.   The *salutation* is the greeting to the reader of the letter. If you aren't addressing a particular person, use a general salutation, such as *Dear Sir* or *Dear Madam* (but not *Dear Sir or Madam*). You may use a person's position—*Dear Director of Personnel*—or the name of the company—*Dear Microsoft Corporation*. If you know who you are writing to, use the same name listed in the inside address—*Dear Leonard Miller*. Use *Ms.* for all women, unless you know from a previous letter or another source that a female recipient prefers *Mrs.* or *Miss*.

Type the salutation two lines below the inside address and two lines above the body of the letter. End the salutation with a colon.

Subject Line. As its name suggests, a *subject line* briefly names the subject of a letter. Use the word *subject* or the abbreviation *re* (Latin for "thing"), followed by a colon, to identify your letter's content. As the following examples show, several styles are acceptable. Whichever you choose, be consistent:

Subject: Summer employment

SUBJECT: Ticket sales

Re: Employment Opportunities

RE: Retroactive salary

Place the subject line two lines below the letter's salutation.

Body. Try to keep your business letter to one page in length, using two pages only if necessary. The content of most business letters is expressed in three main parts:

1. The *introduction*, usually one paragraph, states the purpose of the letter and establishes a courteous tone.
2. One or more *body* paragraphs develop major points and provide details.
3. The *conclusion* paragraph should be short, thanking the reader and suggesting possibilities for further action.

Begin each line of the body of the letter at the left margin. Double-space between paragraphs to set them off from each other.

Close. Choose a close that reflects the tone—formal or informal—of the salutation and the rest of your letter. Typical closes include *Sincerely yours, Sincerely, Yours truly, Best regards,* and *Cordially.* Capitalize only the first letter.
Begin the close of the letter two lines below the last line of the body. Except for modified block form (see Figure 26.1), align the close with the return address heading, flush left. Follow the close with a comma.

Name and Signature. Type your name four lines below the letter's close. Add any title you hold that may be relevant to the letter's content (such as *Business Club President*) after your name. Write your signature in the space between the close and your typed name. If you have addressed your letter's recipient by his or her first name, sign your letter with your first name, also.

Enclosures. If you include other material with a letter, add an *enclosure* notation at the left margin, two lines below your typed name. You may write out or abbreviate the notation for *enclosure (encl.)* or *enclosures (encls.).* List important enclosures by name (preferable) or type, with multiple items listed and indented below the notation, or use parenthetic numerals to indicate their quantity. For example:

> Enclosure: Resume
>
> Encl.: Transcript of College Coursework
>
> Enclosures (2)
>
> Encls:
>> Argon Company Profile 1997-98
>>
>> Resume
>>
>> Letter of recommendation

Copies.   If copies of your letter are being sent to other persons, add a *carbon copy* notation *(cc)* two lines below your typed name or the enclosure notation (if there is one). Use any one of the common styles below, followed by the initials, names, or names and addresses of those who are receiving the copies:

> cc: Dr. Carol Hann
>
> CC: Mr. David Ore
>
> Copies to Peter Demming
>> 2135 Shadywood
>>
>> Los Angeles, CA 90204

If your letter contains sensitive information and you don't want the recipient to know copies are being sent to other people, as well, use a *blind carbon copy* notation on the carbon or copy sheets only, *not on the original letter:*

> bcc: Personnel Department
>
> BCC: Gladys Shuit, Attorney at Law

Postscripts.   Since a *postscript* may suggest a last-minute, casual addition, it should rarely appear in a business letter. If you do need to use a postscript to emphasize an important point not covered in the letter, use an abbreviated form—such as *P.S., PS,* or *PS:*—and type it single spaced two lines below the last notation:

> P.S. I want to emphasize my willingness to move nearer to town if I am hired
>> for this position.

Paper and Typing or Printing.   Write a business letter on good-quality, unlined paper—usually 20-pound weight, white bond. If you use letterhead stationery of your own or from a company or school, its color and design should

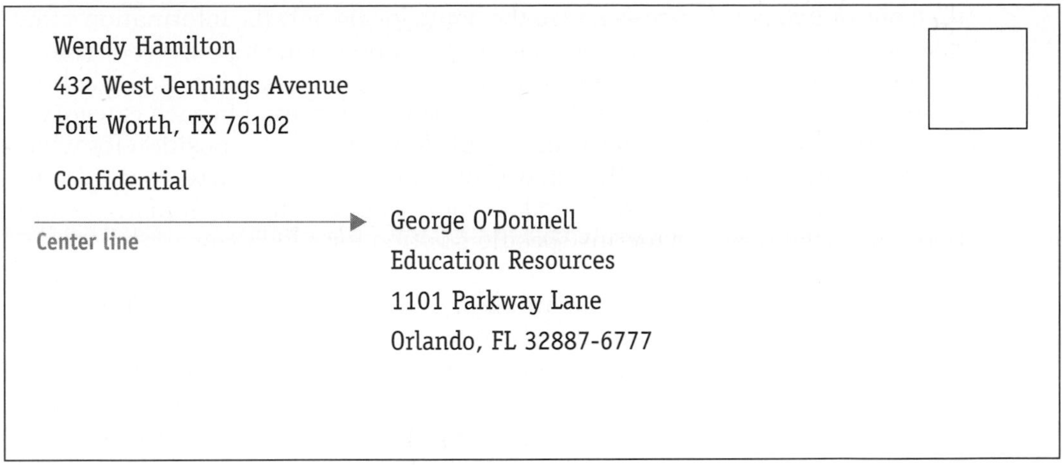

Wendy Hamilton
432 West Jennings Avenue
Fort Worth, TX 76102

Confidential

Center line ——————————→   George O'Donnell
                            Education Resources
                            1101 Parkway Lane
                            Orlando, FL 32887-6777

FIGURE 26.2   Addressed business envelope

be conservative. Write on only one side of the paper, single-spacing between lines and double-spacing between paragraphs. Allow 1" margins on the left- and righthand sides of the paper. Depending on the formality you wish to suggest, margins may be ragged (i.e., type aligns at the left margin but not at the right) or justified (i.e., type aligns evenly at both the left and right margins). Type or print the letter using black or dark blue ink.

Envelope.   Use a business-size envelope that is the same width as your letter and about one-third its height. Type your name and address in the upper-right-hand corner. Include any instructions, such as *Confidential* or *Dated material*, just below your address. To the left of vertical center, type the recipient's name, title, and address, just as you did for the inside address. See Figure 26.2, which shows a sample addressed business envelope.

WRITING A RESUME AND COVER LETTER

A *resume* should present an easy-to-read summary of your qualifications for a certain position, such as a job. It is usually accompanied by a letter of application, called a *cover letter*, which introduces you and states your interest and general abilities for a position. You may choose to send your resume and accompanying cover letter directly to employers, or you can ask them to request it from a placement service or employment agency.

Creating a Resume

Although no standard form will cover all resume writing, some general principles are useful to know. For instance, your resume should be brief—no more

than one or two typed pages—and to the point, giving only the information someone needs to decide whether you are a valuable applicant. Organize your resume
according to categories relevant to the position you are seeking, and use brief,
positive, active phrases to summarize pertinent information in each category.

As much as possible, tailor your resume to the particular position for which
you are applying. The most efficient way of doing this is to use a word-processing
program to design and regularly update your resume so that it emphasizes your
particular qualifications for any specific position for which you apply.

Personal Data.   Begin your resume by listing your name and address along
with a telephone number where you can be reached during business hours. Include a FAX number or e-mail address, if you wish. Don't include information
such as your age, marital status, race/ethnicity, religion, height, or weight. Employers are forbidden by law from using such information as a basis for inter-
viewing or hiring job applicants.

Career Objective.   As a means of further identifying an individual's suitability for a position, a resume may sometimes include a brief statement of the
person's long-range goals or specific job interests. If you include such a statement, limit it to a phrase or two, such as *Ultimately seeking a position with
managerial responsibilities. Special interests in computer sales and service.* Keep
such statements honest and direct. Don't use them to misrepresent yourself or
to flatter a prospective employer.

Education.   Describe your education by listing all the schools you have attended since high school, the most recent schools first. Include the years you
attended, the degrees or honors you received, and your area of study. If you
didn't receive a degree from a school, list the number of units you completed.
If you took courses that specifically relate to a position, mention them in your
cover letter but don't list them in your resume.

Employment History.   Indicate the jobs you have held, listing the most recent
first. Include each company's name and address, and identify the position you
held. Use short phrases and appropriate action verbs to describe your responsibilities: *Conducted public tours of the Jefferson Memorial* or *Supervised ship-
ping and receiving of small parts orders.*

Activities.   Your resume may also include a section indicating other activities,
memberships, hobbies, skills, or awards that would be of interest to a prospective employer—for instance, that you speak a foreign language or served as
treasurer of your youth group. However, only include information about yourself that suggests your suitability for a position.

References.   Depending on your personal preference or the application requirements, you can provide employers with references in any one of three

common ways. The simplest is to indicate near the bottom of your resume that *References are available upon request;* you will provide a list of references later, if an employer asks for them. Be sure that you have permission from the persons on the list to give their names as references.

Another method of including references in your resume is to list them in a section entitled *References*. Provide the names, titles, addresses, and phone numbers of three or four individuals—such as teachers, former employers, and community leaders—who can vouch for your skills and character. Again, be sure you have permission from each of the individuals you list as a reference.

Finally, if you have a current resume and cover letter on file with your school's placement office, you can indicate that references are available there. List the name of the placement office as well as the address and phone number. Before you send out your resume, contact the placement office yourself to make sure your file is complete and up to date. It's a good idea to do this each time you apply for a job.

Sample Resume.   Individual preferences, practices common to particular occupations, and the desire to address the needs of employers have resulted in a number of acceptable variations in resumes. The resume in Figure 26.3 demonstrates the most common form and follows the guidelines suggested in this chapter.

Writing a Cover Letter

Your interest in a job and request for an interview should be stated in a cover letter that refers the recipient to your enclosed resume. Since employers rely on a resume to determine an applicant's qualifications, keep your cover letter brief and avoid repeating what's stated in your resume.

Because a company may have several job openings, it's useful for you to begin the letter by identifying the job you want and telling specifically where or how you heard about it. Next, indicate one or two aspects of your resume that would be particularly relevant to the job or that an employer might find interesting or impressive. End the cover letter by stating your interest in receiving an interview for the job. In writing the cover letter, follow standard business letter guidelines, as described earlier in this chapter (pp. 458–463).

WRITING A MEMO

A *memo*, or memorandum, is a written communication used to deal with routine business matters between offices, departments, and individuals. Compared to a letter, a memo is less personal, more narrowly focused, and concerned with public matters. You might use a memo to announce or verify the date of a meeting, to make a request, to clarify a procedure, to summarize a policy, or to order supplies. You would not ordinarily use a memo to analyze, discuss, or

Cheryl Tynan
331 Oakwood Lane
Laguna Hills, CA 92676
(714) 555-7823
tynan@locus.com

Career Objective

To be employed as a research chemist for a company interested in environmental studies and products

Education

1995-present	University of California, Irvine	
	Major: Chemistry	Minor: Mathematics
	Degree: B.A., Chemistry	
1993-95	Orange Coast College	
	Major: Biology	Minor: Mathematics
	Units completed: 63	

Employment History

1997-present   Allied Chemical Corporation
738 Hampton Street
Irvine, CA 92648
    Duties: Laboratory assistant. Responsible for daily recordings of filtration data. 23 hours weekly.

1996-97   Rancho Sante Fe Market
222 Remington Boulevard
Costa Mesa, CA 92626
    Duties: Stock clerk and cashier. Responsible for ordering and stocking grocery goods and cashiering. 18 hours weekly.

1996-97   Los Amigos Environmental Volunteers
5522 Center Avenue
Laguna Hills, CA 92676
    Duties: Data collection on Newport Bay duck populations.

Activities and Interests

• President of Omega Mathematics Club, University of California, Irvine, 1996-97
• Member of Audubon Society local chapter
• Enjoy hiking and camping, tennis, skiing, and snowboarding

References

Placement Office
University of California, Irvine
Irvine, CA 92715
(714) 555-7881

FIGURE 26.3   **Sample resume**

evaluate material that would be better addressed at length through a letter, report, or personal meeting. Thus, most memos range from a few sentences to about a page in length; they rarely need to be longer. Depending on their purpose and audience, memos may be written by hand or typewritten, formal or informal.

Memo Form

Unless you are following a form indicated on preprinted company or commercial stationery, begin a memo by typing the word *MEMORANDUM* (centering, capitalization, and underlining optional) at the top of the page. Two line spaces below this heading, include a block of standard information elements—such as *TO, FROM, DATE, RE* (or *SUBJECT*)—typed double spaced in all capital letters or with only the first letter capitalized and usually in this order. Follow each element with a colon and the accompanying relevant information.

Type the body of the memo single spaced, beginning two lines below the last element of information. The content is usually typed flush with the left margin, but you may indent the first line of each paragraph, if you wish. Don't include a closing or signature element, but you may add your initials next to your name or end the memo with your signature, centered at the bottom. If the memo includes copies or enclosures, note them the same way you would in a letter (see pp. 461–462).

Although variations are common, the sample memo in Figure 26.4 demonstrates typical memo form.

WRITING A FAX AND AN E-MAIL

Electronic communications like FAXes and e-mail are common in today's business world and should be treated with the same care as traditional business correspondence. Although the newness of such communication forms often leads writers to relax their correspondence styles, make sure your FAX and e-mail transmissions represent your regard for professional standards and respect for the recipient.

Sending a FAX

Make sure any FAX you send reflects common practices regarding professional correspondence plus the special requirements of communicating electronically. Use the following guidelines to help ensure your FAXes are appropriately received and read:

- Since a FAX may be received in a mail room or other common area, consider who may receive and read it before it's delivered to the intended recipient. You may want to send personal, confidential, or sensitive material by traditional correspondence.

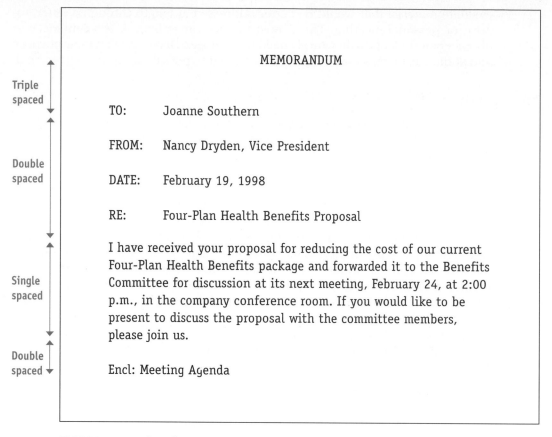

FIGURE 26.4   **Sample memo**

- Select letterhead, fonts sizes, images, and colors that will FAX clearly. To ensure readability, use 10-point or 12-point type for all contents, and remember that colors other than black may not transmit clearly. Avoid sending or retransmitting copies of a FAX with fuzzy print or hazy images.

- Include a cover sheet with your name and your company name, address, and telephone number as well as a FAX or e-mail address where you can be reached in case of transmittal problems. Also indicate the total number of pages you are sending, including the cover sheet.

- Check your FAX machine's readout to ensure proper transmission and receipt of your FAX, or follow-up the transmittal with a telephone call to verify that it was received.

Keep in mind that a FAX may not be an acceptable form of communication for all business correspondence. When it is, however, following the above guidelines will help to ensure the effectiveness of your FAX and receiving a timely response.

Sending an E-Mail

A clearly written and thoughtfully directed e-mail transmission will not only save you and the recipient time, it will also show that you are an effective communicator. Although e-mail messages are frequently informal, any written for business purposes need to be easily understood and professional in form and content. The following suggestions can help make your e-mail effective for any purpose:

- Whenever possible, compose an e-mail offline. This will allow more time for composing, revising, and editing any draft versions as well as provide you with an easily accessible file copy and backup. Once you have finished writing your e-mail, use your computer's "Copy" function to insert it into your e-mail program.

- Make sure your e-mail is easy to read and remember. Check for spelling errors and follow standard punctuation and grammar practices. Use indentation, paragraph divisions, capitalization, bullets, and headings to separate content and organize it for the reader.

- Guide the recipient to the point of your e-mail by including a clear subject line identifying your message's content or purpose.

- Reading a lengthy e-mail online can tire a reader and thus lessen the impact of the message. For this reason, limit an e-mail correspondence to no more than one full screen in length. Use your e-mail program's "Attachment" function to send additional content as an attached file.

- Sending unwanted communications takes up other people's time and appears unprofessional. Copy only those individuals directly concerned with matters treated in your e-mail.

Like a FAX, an e-mail may not be appropriate for all types of business correspondence. For instance, because e-mail programs don't always accurately transmit or reproduce formatting, the original spacing and organization of something like a resume sent by e-mail would probably be altered. In most instances, you should use e-mail for routine business matters or to communicate with individuals you have already corresponded with by traditional means.

Finally, keep in mind that e-mail isn't necessarily a confidential form of communication. Even after you have deleted an e-mail from your message center, it still exists somewhere on your computer system and perhaps on your company's and server's systems, as well. Many companies issue guidelines to employees about the appropriate uses of e-mail, warning against using it to discuss personal or potentially litigious topics.

Activities

1. Using the block, modified block, or simplified style, write a business letter to the president of your college campus. In the body of the letter, describe the need for improving a particular campus service or facility and your recommendations for doing so. Include an appropriate salutation and close.

2. Following the guidelines provided in this chapter, create a resume that you could use to apply for employment in the area of your college major or in another field of interest.

3. Write a brief cover letter to a prospective employer in the area of your college major or in another field that interests you. In the letter, describe the position or kind of employment you are seeking and your qualifications for it.

4. Write a memo to a group of your classmates to inform them of a future study session. In addition to mentioning this purpose, include the time and place of the meeting as well as any materials individuals should bring.

5. Investigate the availability of FAX or e-mail services on your campus. Using one or both of these communication forms, send a brief report of your findings to your instructor.

Readings
for Writers

We offer the essays in the following anthology as a means to help you develop a writer's mind—that is, to move consciously beyond *functional* reading to *critical* reading. When reading critically, you are not just reading for the facts, you are actively engaged in reflective and critical analysis, examining a writer's purpose, the strategies that achieve the purpose, and the style that reflects the purpose. You must use your own experience and knowledge in the analysis, making associations between your world and that of the essay. When you master reading with a writer's mind, you will bring the skill to your own writing. Specifically, you will begin to clarify your writing purpose with care, refine a strategy to achieve your purpose, and create the appropriate style to display your purpose.

Critically examining well-written essays is the most direct approach to developing a writer's mind. The *essay* is often described as a well-organized nonfiction composition in which an author concentrates on a single aspect of a subject. This kind of essay is usually written in formal English and designed to convey information. But as a group, essays cover a much broader territory. Many are impressionistic or exploratory. Often, they express personal feelings or attitudes based on a writer's experience.

Because essays are so varied, the selections that follow represent a great range—all the better, we believe, to help you sharpen your critical perspective. Included are works by such well-known essayists as George Orwell and E. B. White, as well as works by less-known, rising essayists, such as Gretel Ehrlich and Stephanie Ericsson. The essays are from varied sources: newspapers, magazines, academic and scientific journals, and nonfiction books. And they cover many subjects: crime and violence, men and women, censorship and free speech, even culture and customs. The collection embodies several styles, ranging from the newswriter's objective report to the poet's subjective expression. Some are serious; some are playful. All are written by writers who are well worth studying.

THREE TIPS FOR A FIRST READING

When reading to improve your writing, you can't sweep through an essay and then set it aside. You should be prepared to read it several times. The first reading may be quick, designed to give you a view of the content, a sense of the purpose, and a feeling for the style. When you begin the first reading, we suggest you keep three tips in mind:

1. Examine the Title

Sounds obvious, right? Well, you would be surprised how many readers mistakenly believe an essay begins with the first line. It doesn't. It begins with the title.

A title can help you anticipate what's to follow. It may announce a writer's subject, suggest a dominant rhetorical pattern, or hint at the writer's attitude. The title "A Hanging" lets you know you won't be hearing about a tea party. Instead, you will anticipate an essay about an execution, which will not be a pretty experience. The title "Cyclone! Rising to the Fall" is a little more ambiguous. Does *cyclone* refer to the destructive natural phenomenon? Or does it mean a roller coaster? Or could "Cyclone" be the name of a bronco? Regardless, you will probably expect a description of a thrilling or even frightening experience. "I Want a Wife" seems like a straightforward title. But when you find out that a woman wrote the essay, you will likely expect an ironic tone.

2. Take Quick Notes

Always read with a pencil in hand. Don't just chew on the eraser, engage the essay: star key passages, underline startling images, bracket shifts in thought, and scribble notes in the margins. Roughly write your reactions to the text, questions that come to mind, and even disagreements with the writer. And yes, circle words you don't know so that you can look them up in the dictionary before your second reading.

Why go to all this trouble for a first reading? We don't suggest that you linger on any page for very long. Rather, think of a first reading like traveling in new territory. Much like markings on a map, markings on an essay will help you explore more deeply during your return visit.

3. Record First Impressions

We urge you to record your impressions after the first reading and before going on to the second reading. Write down what you think the writer is trying to achieve—his or her purpose. Identify dominant strategies. Jot down your thoughts on style. Record any impressions you have.

To put these guidelines to use, let's look at an essay, Willard Gaylin's "What You See Is the Real You." As you read, you'll see that the essay is accompanied by marginal notes that reflect the guidelines for a first reading. Remember, the reader jotted down these observations for herself, not for an audience. Even though the notes are often incomplete, maybe even cryptic, they clearly represent the reader's encounter with a serious essay.

After the first reading, you should be familiar with the essay's content and purpose. You should also have a sense of the writer's strategies and style. And you should have jotted down general impressions and responses to the essay. In other words, make sure you've left your markings.

Enjoy your first trip through the territory!

What You See Is the Real You   1977

WILLARD GAYLIN

It was, I believe, the distinguished Nebraska financier Father Edward J. Flanagan who professed to having "never met a bad boy." Having, myself, met a remarkable number of bad boys, it might seem that either our experiences were drastically different or we were using the word "bad" differently. I suspect neither is true, but rather that the Father was appraising the "inner man," while I, in fact, do not acknowledge the existence of inner people.

Since we psychoanalysts have unwittingly contributed to this confusion, let one, at least, attempt a small rectifying effort. Psychoanalytic data—which should be viewed as supplementary information—are, unfortunately, often viewed as alternative (and superior) explanation. This has led to the prevalent tendency to think of the "inner" man as the real man and the outer man as an illusion or pretender.

While psychoanalysis supplies us with an incredibly useful tool for explaining the motives and purposes underlying human behavior, most of this has little bearing on the moral nature of that behavior.

Like roentgenology, psychoanalysis is a fascinating, but relatively new, means of illuminating the person. But few of us are prepared to substitute an X-ray of Grandfather's head for the portrait that hangs in the parlor. The inside of the man represents another view, not a truer one. A man may not always be what he appears to be, but what he appears to be is always a significant part of what he is. A man is the sum total of *all* his behavior. To probe for unconscious determinants of behavior and then define *him* in their terms exclusively, ignoring his overt behavior altogether, is a greater distortion than ignoring the unconscious completely.

Kurt Vonnegut has said, "You are what you pretend to be," which is simply another way of saying, you are what we (all of us) perceive you to be, not what you think you are.

Consider for a moment the case of the ninety-year-old man on his deathbed (surely the Talmud must deal with this?) joyous and relieved over the success of his deception. For ninety years, he has shielded his evil nature from public observation. For ninety years he has affected courtesy, kindness, and generosity—suppressing all the malice he knew was within him while he calculatedly and artificially substituted grace and charity. All his life he had been fooling the world into believing he was a good man. This "evil" man will, I predict, be welcomed into the Kingdom of Heaven.

Contrasting
example: bad
person has good
thoughts.

Similarly, I will not be told that the young man who earns his pocket money by mugging old ladies is "really" a good boy. Even my generous and expansive definition of goodness will not accommodate that particular form of self-advancement.

7

*Echoes point
of view.

It does not count that beneath the rough exterior he has a heart— or, for that matter, an entire innards—of purest gold, locked away from human perception. You are for the most part what you seem to be, not what you would wish to be, nor, indeed, what you believe yourself to be.

8

Tone: ironic,
sounds as if he
is exhausted by
hearing the same
old tales. Spare
me! A plea to stop.

Spare me, therefore, your good intentions, your inner sensitivities, your unarticulated and unexpressed love. And spare me also those tedious psychohistories which—by exposing the goodness inside the bad man, and the evil in the good—invariably establish a vulgar and perverse egalitarianism, as if the arrangement of what is outside and what inside makes no moral difference.

9

Alludes to
1. Saint—Francis
2. Conqueror—
Attilla

Saint Francis may, in his unconscious, indeed have been compensating for, and denying, destructive, unconscious Oedipal impulses identical to those which Attilla projected and acted on. But the similarity of the unconscious constellations in the two men matters precious little, if it does not distinguish between them.

10

3. Nazi—Hitler
only behavior
can be judged.

I do not care to learn that Hitler's heart was in the right place. A knowledge of the unconscious life of the man may be an adjunct to understanding his behavior. It is *not* a substitute for his behavior in describing him.

11

Only behavior
causes joy or
suffering.

The inner man is a fantasy. If it helps you to identify with one, by all means, do so; preserve it, cherish it, embrace it, but do not present it to others for evaluation or consideration, for excuse or exculpation, or, for that matter, for punishment or disapproval.

12

Restates key
idea/central point.

Like any fantasy, it serves your purposes alone. It has no standing in the real world which we share with each other. Those character traits, those attitudes, that behavior—that strange and alien stuff sticking out all over you—*that's the real you!*

13

Echoes the title.

Final Notes—

Purpose: To show that people should be judged by what they do, not by what they think.

Strategy: Argues the point, sets up opposites, good vs bad; inner vs outer. Problem—no shades of grey between black and white.

Style: Tone is ironic at times and authoritative. He seems to be shaking a finger at the reader. Sexist use of pronouns & "man".

FIVE TIPS FOR REREADING

Before rereading the Gaylin essay, review your notes and reconsider the title:

- Did it accurately reflect the purpose of the essay?

- Did it have an overall strategy?
- What did the style reveal to you?

Once you have become familiar with the essay in general, you're ready to reread. Once again, read with pencil in hand, ready to explore the discussion in more depth and revise or expand your first observations. Remember, too, you're attempting to read like a writer examining another writer's techniques—that is, you're reading from a critical perspective. Follow these five guidelines:

1. Review the Beginning and End

The beginning and the end are critical sections. Directly or indirectly, the opening paragraphs usually establish the purpose of the essay. Sometimes, the purpose will be immediately clear, as in Gaylin's "What You See Is the Real You." Clearly, his purpose is to argue that people should be judged by the sum total of their behavior, not by their unconscious determinants. The end will often restate the purpose—or in a narrative, dramatize it. Gaylin's essay ends by restating the purpose, thus making his intent unmistakable.

2. Reread with the Purpose in Mind

The purpose can serve as a beacon that will guide you as you reread the essay. And knowing the purpose will clarify the strategies the writer uses to achieve that purpose. For example, two of Gaylin's examples become clear on rereading—the X-ray of Grandfather's head and the anecdote about a man who suppressed his evil nature and lived a good life.

3. Examine the Style

You should already have a sense of style from the first reading. On rereading, try to to pin it down. Notice the selection of words. Pay close attention to the shapes and rhythms of sentences. Underline phrases that embody the tone. Gaylin has the tone of a highly educated and authoritative writer. He sometimes uses erudite vocabulary, which might be difficult for the average reader—for instance, *roentgenology,* referring to the use of film in X-rays; *overt behavior,* referring to action; and *exculpation,* referring to having been declared innocent of a crime. He also makes several literary allusions, which demonstrate his wide knowledge and which he expects his reader to know—Father Edward J. Flanagan, founder of a home for wayward boys he called "Boys Town"; Kurt Vonnegut, the author of such satiric novels as *Cat's Cradle* and *Slaughterhouse-Five;* the Talmud, the Jewish book of spiritual laws; and Francis of Assisi, who renounced his wealth and founded the Franciscan religious order of monks, which earned him sainthood in 1228.

4. Linger on Interesting Passages

Pause while rereading to examine passages that catch your attention. What's an interesting passage? The answer to that question, of course, is a judgment call. Perhaps you will be interested in a passage that's a well-structured paragraph or series of paragraphs. Later, you might want to use it as a model to emulate in your own writing.

For example, in one interesting paragraph, Gaylin makes a point through *metaphor*, which is a brief comparison between dissimilar subjects to clarify a point:

> Like roentgenology, psychoanalysis is a fascinating, but relatively new, means of illuminating the person. But few of us are prepared to substitute an X-ray of Grandfather's head for the portrait that hangs in the parlor. The inside of the man represents another view, not a truer one. A man may not always be what he appears to be, but what he appears to be is a significant part of what he is. A man is the sum total of *all* his behavior. To probe for unconscious determinants of behavior and then define *him* in their terms exclusively, ignoring his overt behavior altogether, is a grater distortion than ignoring the unconscious completely.

The metaphor comparing an X-ray and a portrait to the concept of the inner and outer person makes the abstract discussion concrete—something readers can visualize and that reflects Gaylin's point.

5. Record Your Closing Impressions

Your impressions may be analytical observations related to purpose, strategy, and style. They may also be reflective observations related to your personal experience:

- Does the essay bring to mind any experiences you've had?
- Do you associate it with something you've learned or something you've seen or heard about?
- Does it stir a specific meaning in you?
- And perhaps most important, does it call to mind any ideas you might like to explore in writing?

SELECTED READINGS

The guidelines for a first reading and for rereading give you procedures to follow when studying each of the following essays or any written work that deserves your attention. We've also added individual and group activities at the end of each essay to direct your encounter with it and help you develop a writer's mind. Your goal is to read like a writer!

Finishing School   *1969*

MAYA ANGELOU

Recently a white woman from Texas, who would quickly describe herself   1
as a liberal, asked me about my hometown. When I told her that in Stamps my
grandmother had owned the only Negro general merchandise store since the
turn of the century, she exclaimed, "Why, you were a debutante." Ridiculous
and even ludicrous. But Negro girls in small Southern towns, whether poverty-
stricken or just munching along on a few of life's necessities, were given as extensive and irrelevant preparations for adulthood as rich white girls shown in
magazines. Admittedly the training was not the same. While white girls learned
to waltz and sit gracefully with a tea cup balanced on their knees, we were lag-
ging behind, learning the mid-Victorian values with very little money to indulge
them. . . .

We were required to embroider and I had trunkfuls of colorful dishtowels,   2
pillowcases, runners and handkerchiefs to my credit. I mastered the art of cro-
cheting and tatting, and there was a lifetime's supply of dainty doilies that
would never be used in sacheted dresser drawers. It went without saying that
all girls could iron and wash, but the finer touches around the home, like setting a table with real silver, baking roasts and cooking vegetables without meat,
had to be learned elsewhere. Usually at the source of those habits. During my
tenth year, a white woman's kitchen became my finishing school.

Mrs. Viola Cullinan was a plump woman who lived in a three-bedroom house   3
somewhere behind the post office. She was singularly unattractive until she
smiled, and then the lines around her eyes and mouth which made her look per-
petually dirty disappeared, and her face looked like the mask of an impish elf. She
usually rested her smile until late afternoon when her women friends dropped
in and Miss Glory, the cook, served them cold drinks on the closed-in porch.

The exactness of her house was inhuman. This glass went here and only   4
here. That cup had its place and it was an act of impudent rebellion to place it
anywhere else. At twelve o'clock the table was set. At 12:15 Mrs. Cullinan sat
down to dinner (whether her husband had arrived or not). At 12:16 Miss Glory
brought out the food.

It took me a week to learn the difference between a salad plate, a bread   5
plate and a dessert plate.

Mrs. Cullinan kept up the tradition of her wealthy parents. She was from   6
Virginia. Miss Glory, who was a descendant of slaves that had worked for the
Cullinans, told me her history. She had married beneath her (according to Miss
Glory). Her husband's family hadn't had their money very long and what they
had "didn't 'mount to much."

As ugly as she was, I thought privately, she was lucky to get a husband   7
above or beneath her station. But Miss Glory wouldn't let me say a thing against

her mistress. She was very patient with me, however, over the housework. She explained the dishware, silverware and servants' bells. The large round bowl in which soup was served wasn't a soup bowl, it was a tureen. There were goblets, sherbet glasses, ice-cream glasses, wine glasses, green glass coffee cups with matching saucers, and water glasses. I had a glass to drink from, and it sat with Miss Glory's on a separate shelf from the others. Soup spoons, gravy boat, butter knives, salad forks and carving platter were additions to my vocabulary and in fact almost represented a new language. I was fascinated with the novelty, with the fluttering Mrs. Cullinan and her Alice-in-Wonderland house.

Her husband remains, in my memory, undefined. I lumped him with all the other white men that I had ever seen and tried not to see. 8

On our way home one evening, Miss Glory told me that Mrs. Cullinan couldn't have children. She said that she was too delicate-boned. It was hard to imagine bones at all under those layers of fat. Miss Glory went on to say that the doctor had taken out all her lady organs. I reasoned that a pig's organs included the lungs, heart, and liver, so if Mrs. Cullinan was walking around without those essentials, it explained why she drank alcohol out of unmarked bottles. She was keeping herself embalmed. 9

When I spoke to Bailey about it, he agreed that I was right, but he also informed me that Mr. Cullinan had two daughters by a colored lady and that I knew them very well. He added that the girls were the spitting image of their father. I was unable to remember what he looked like, although I had just left him a few hours before, but I thought of the Coleman girls. They were very light-skinned and certainly didn't look very much like their mother (no one ever mentioned Mr. Coleman). 10

My pity for Mrs. Cullinan preceded me the next morning like the Cheshire cat's smile. Those girls, who could have been her daughters, were beautiful. They didn't have to straighten their hair. Even when they were caught in the rain, their braids still hung down straight like tamed snakes. Their mouths were pouty little cupid's bows. Mrs. Cullinan didn't know what she missed. Or maybe she did. Poor Mrs. Cullinan. 11

For weeks after, I arrived early, left late and tried very hard to make up for her barrenness. If she had her own children, she wouldn't have had to ask me to run a thousand errands from her back door to the back door of her friends. Poor old Mrs. Cullinan. 12

Then one evening Miss Glory told me to serve the ladies on the porch. After I set the tray down and turned toward the kitchen, one of the women asked, "What's your name, girl?" It was the speckled-faced one. Mrs. Cullinan said, "She doesn't talk much. Her name's Margaret." 13

"Is she dumb?" 14

"No. As I understand it, she can talk when she wants to but she's usually quiet as a little mouse. Aren't you, Margaret?" 15

I smiled at her. Poor thing. No organs and couldn't even pronounce my name correctly. 16

"She's a sweet little thing, though."   17

"Well, that may be, but the name's too long. I'd never bother myself. I'd call   18
her Mary if I was you."

I fumed into the kitchen. That horrible woman would never have the   19
chance to call me Mary because if I was starving I'd never work for her. . . .

That evening I decided to write a poem on being white, fat, old and with-   20
out children. It was going to be a tragic ballad. I would have to watch her carefully to capture the essence of her loneliness and pain.

The very next day, she called me by the wrong name. Miss Glory and I were   21
washing up the lunch dishes when Mrs. Cullinan came to the doorway. "Mary?"

Miss Glory asked, "Who?"   22

Mrs. Cullinan, sagging a little, knew and I knew. "I want Mary to go down   23
to Mrs. Randall's and take her some soup. She's not been feeling well for a few
days."

Miss Glory's face was a wonder to see. "You mean Margaret, ma'am. Her   24
name's Margaret."

"That's too long, She's Mary from now on. Heat that soup from last night   25
and put it in the china tureen and, Mary, I want you to carry it carefully."

Every person I knew had a hellish horror of being "called out of his name."   26
It was a dangerous practice to call a Negro anything that could be loosely construed as insulting because of the centuries of their having been called niggers,
jigs, dinges, blackbirds, crows, boots and spooks.

Miss Glory had a fleeting second of feeling sorry for me. Then as she   27
handed me the hot tureen she said, "Don't mind, don't pay that no mind. Sticks
and stones may break your bones, but words . . . You know, I been working for
her for twenty years."

She held the back door open for me. "Twenty years. I wasn't much older   28
than you. My name used to be Hallelujah. That's what Ma named me, but my
mistress give me 'Glory,' and it stuck. I likes it better too."

I was in the little path that ran behind the houses when Miss Glory shouted,   29
"It's shorter too."

For a few seconds it was a tossup over whether I would laugh (imagine be-   30
ing named Hallelujah) or cry (imagine letting some white woman rename you
for her convenience). My anger saved me from either outburst. I had to quit the
job, but the problem was going to be how to do it. Momma wouldn't allow me
to quit for just any reason.

"She's a peach. That woman is a real peach." Mrs. Randall's maid was talk-   31
ing as she took the soup from me, and I wondered what her name used to be
and what she answered to now.

For a week I looked into Mrs. Cullinan's face as she called me Mary. She ig-   32
nored my coming late and leaving early. Miss Glory was a little annoyed because I had begun to leave egg yolk on the dishes and wasn't putting much
heart in polishing the silver. I hoped that she would complain to our boss, but
she didn't.

Then Bailey solved my dilemma. He had me describe the contents of the 33
cupboard and the particular plates she liked best. Her favorite piece was a
casserole shaped like a fish and the green glass coffee cups. I kept his instructions in mind, so on the next day when Miss Glory was hanging out clothes and
I had again been told to serve the old biddies on the porch, I dropped the empty
serving tray. When I heard Mrs. Cullinan scream, "Mary!" I picked up the casserole and two of the green glass cups in readiness. As she rounded the kitchen
door I let them fall on the tiled floor.

I could never absolutely describe to Bailey what happened next, because 34
each time I got to the part where she fell on the floor and screwed up her ugly
face to cry, we burst out laughing. She actually wobbled around on the floor
and picked up shards of the cups and cried, "Oh, Momma. Oh, dear Gawd. It's
Mamma's china from Virginia. Oh, Momma, I sorry."

Miss Glory came running in from the yard and the women from the porch 35
crowded around. Miss Glory was almost as broken up as her mistress. "You
mean to say she broke our Virginia dishes? What we gone do?"

Mrs. Cullinan cried louder. "That clumsy nigger. Clumsy little black nigger." 36

Old speckled-face leaned down and asked, "Who did it, Viola? Was it Mary? 37
Who did it?"

Everything was happening so fast, I can't remember whether her action 38
preceded her words, but I know that Mrs. Cullinan said, "Her name's Margaret,
goddamn it, her name's Margaret." And she threw a wedge of broken plate at
me. It could have been the hysteria which put her aim off, but the flying crockery caught Miss Glory right over her ear and she started screaming.

I left the front door wide open so all the neighbors could hear. 39

Mrs. Cullinan was right about one thing. My name wasn't Mary. 40

RECORDING REFLECTIONS

Angelou's name is important to her, so important that if it were arbitrarily
changed, she would lose a sense of self-identity and a portion of her humanity.
How do you feel about your name? List experiences in which someone used
your name in a peculiar or even hurtful way.

Choose one experience from that list, and write about it for 10 minutes, exploring your feelings about your own name.

ACTIVITIES FOR REREADING

1. One of the ways Angelou develops her narrative is through contrasts. Race
   is the most obvious contrast: black versus white. When you reread "Finishing School," identify other contrasts and list them. How does each help
   develop the essay's meaning?
2. What are Margaret's feelings toward Mrs. Cullinan before Mrs. Cullinan
   calls her *Mary?* And after? List the incidents that illustrate those feelings.

3. The tone of Angelou's essay changes after Mrs. Cullinan starts calling her *Mary* instead of *Margaret*. How is that change of tone reflected in Angelou's diction? List words that reflect the difference.

GROUP WORK

Personal Responses: To launch the discussion, refer to your Reflection Log entries and discuss two or three incidences about how your names have been used peculiarly, misused, or forgotten. Describe your reactions to those incidences, and compare your reactions to Angelou's. How are they similar? Different? How do you account for the differences?

Objective Responses: Compare the contrasting incidences each of you noticed, the incidences that illustrate the narrator's change in feeling toward Mrs. Cullinan, and Angelou's change of diction. Discuss the significance of each of these contrasts and changes.

Discuss how Angelou repeats the adjective *poor* to describe Mrs. Cullinan in paragraphs 11 and 12. In the context of the essay, how many meanings and feelings does this word hold?

What is Angelou's primary point in the essay—her moral or message?

WRITING ASSIGNMENTS

1. Using Angelou's essay as a model, write a narrative essay that demonstrates how you or someone else was misinterpreted, misunderstood, or mistreated by an authority figure. Use significant incidences that lead to and away from your central scene. Your reaction could be internal, external, or both. Make sure your essay is controlled by a central purpose—a *moral,* or payoff for the reader.

2. Closely examine all the differences implicit in Glory's accepting and Margaret's rebelling against their imposed name changes. Then write an essay in which you examine similar situations in which one person rebelled and another conformed in the same situation. Examine family, school, and work experiences for examples. What do the situations have in common? How are they different? Make sure to compose an explicitly stated thesis that ties all of your examples together.

I Want a Wife

1971

JUDY BRADY

I belong to that classification of people known as wives. I am A Wife. And, not altogether incidentally, I am a mother.

Not too long ago a male friend of mine appeared on the scene fresh from a recent divorce. He had one child, who is, of course, with his ex-wife. He is looking for another wife. As I thought about him while I was ironing one evening, it suddenly occurred to me that I, too, would like to have a wife. Why do I want a wife?

I would like to go back to school so that I can become economically inde-   3
pendent, support myself, and, if need be, support those dependent upon me. I want a wife who will work and send me to school. And while I am going to school I want a wife to take care of my children. I want a wife to keep track of the children's doctor and dentist appointments. And to keep track of mine, too. I want a wife to make sure my children eat properly and are kept clean. I want a wife who will wash the children's clothes and keep them mended. I want a wife who is a good nurturant attendant to my children, who arranges for their schooling, makes sure that they have an adequate social life with their peers, takes them to the park, the zoo, etc. I want a wife who takes care of the children when they are sick, a wife who arranges to be around when the children need special care, because, of course, I cannot miss classes at school. My wife must arrange to lose time at work and not lose the job. It may mean a small cut in my wife's income from time to time, but I guess I can tolerate that. Needless to say, my wife will arrange and pay for the care of the children while my wife is working.

I want a wife who will take care of *my* physical needs. I want a wife who   4
will keep my house clean. A wife who will pick up after my children, a wife who will pick up after me. I want a wife who will keep my clothes clean, ironed, mended, replaced when need be, and who will see to it that my personal things are kept in their proper place so that I can find what I need the minute I need it. I want a wife who cooks the meals, a wife who is a *good* cook. I want a wife who will plan the menus, do the necessary grocery shopping, prepare the meals, serve them pleasantly, and then do the cleaning up while I do my study-ing. I want a wife who will care for me when I am sick and sympathize with my pain and loss of time from school. I want a wife to go along when our family takes a vacation so that someone can continue to care for me and my children when I need a rest and change of scene.

I want a wife who will not bother me with rambling complaints about a   5
wife's duties. But I want a wife who will listen to me when I feel the need to ex-plain a rather difficult point I have come across in my course of studies. And I want a wife who will type my papers for me when I have written them.

I want a wife who will take care of the details of my social life. When my   6
wife and I are invited out by my friends, I want a wife who will take care of the babysitting arrangements. When I meet people at school that I like and want to entertain, I want a wife who will have the house clean, will prepare a special meal, serve it to me and my friends, and not interrupt when I talk about things that interest me and my friends. I want a wife who will have arranged that the children are fed and ready for bed before my guests arrive so that the children do not bother us. I want a wife who takes care of the needs of my guests so that they feel comfortable, who makes sure that they have an ashtray, that they are passed the hors d'oeuvres, that they are offered a second helping of the food,

that their wine glasses are replenished when necessary, that their coffee is served to them as they like it. And I want a wife who knows that sometimes I need a night out by myself.

I want a wife who is sensitive to my sexual needs, a wife who makes love 7 passionately and eagerly when I feel like it, a wife who makes sure that I am satisfied. And, of course, I want a wife who will not demand sexual attention when I am not in the mood for it. I want a wife who assumes the complete responsibility for birth control, because I do not want more children. I want a wife who will remain sexually faithful to me so that I do not have to clutter up my intellectual life with jealousies. And I want a wife who understands that *my* sexual needs may entail more than strict adherence to monogamy. I must, after all, be able to relate to people as fully as possible.

If, by chance, I find another person more suitable as a wife than the wife I 8 already have, I want the liberty to replace my present wife with another one. Naturally, I will expect a fresh, new life; my wife will take the children and be solely responsible for them so that I am left free.

When I am through with school and have a job, I want my wife to quit 9 working and remain at home so that my wife can more fully and completely take care of a wife's duties.

My God, who *wouldn't* want a wife? 10

▦ RECORDING REFLECTIONS

Brady defines a *wife* by listing all those things a traditional wife and mother does. As you read, make your own list of characteristics a wife and mother should have.

After listing the characteristics, write for 10 minutes, exploring how and why your list is different or similar to Brady's.

▦ ACTIVITIES FOR REREADING

1. As you reread, look for Brady's thesis. When you've finished rereading, write down her thesis in your own words.
2. In paragraphs 3–7, Brady defines a *wife* by listing her expected duties and behaviors. She organizes these into groups of related items. Mark the groups, and assign them appropriate labels.
3. When Brady lists a wife's duties toward her husband, she is also implicitly identifying a husband's needs. Write down those needs. In no more than three or four sentences, explain why you think Brady is or isn't fair to the husband.

▦ GROUP WORK

Personal Responses: Refer to your Reflection Logs to discuss your own lists of a wife's/mother's duties. Discuss how your lists differ and whether those differences are significant.

Objective Responses: See if you can agree on Brady's thesis. Discuss the groups of duties you've identified and the appropriateness of your labels for them. See if you can agree on the most appropriate labels.

Discuss Brady's implied list of a husband's needs and the fairness of that list. Refer to the notes from your rereading, as well as the text itself, to validate your observations.

Discuss the reason Brady capitalizes *A Wife* in the first paragraph.

What effect is Brady after by repeating *I want a wife* so many times in the essay? Does she get the effect she wants? Why or why not?

WRITING ASSIGNMENTS

1. Brady defines an ideal wife by describing the various duties and behaviors she must have to please a self-centered husband. Define your own ideal person—perhaps a wife, husband, mother, father, girlfriend, waiter, teacher, aerobics instructor, boss, or roommate—by describing his or her behavior in a variety of situations.

2. Answer Brady's essay by writing your own, but from a *man's* point of view. Define the ideal husband/father in an essay called "I Want a Husband." Try to create a sarcastic tone similar to Brady's.

Why Don't We Complain?   *1960*

WILLIAM F. BUCKLEY, JR.

It was the very last coach and the only empty seat on the entire train, so   1
there was no turning back. The problem was to breathe. Outside, the temperature was below freezing. Inside the railroad car the temperature must have been about 85 degrees. I took off my overcoat, and a few minutes later my jacket, and noticed that the car was flecked with the white shirts of the passengers. I soon found my hand moving to loosen my tie. From one end of the car to the other, as we rattled through Westchester County, we sweated; but we did not moan.

I watched the train conductor appear at the head of the car. "Tickets, all   2
tickets, please!" In a more virile age, I thought, the passengers would seize the conductor and strap him down on a seat over the radiator to share the fate of his patrons. He shuffled down the aisle, picking up tickets, punching commutation cards. *No one addressed a word to him.* He approached my seat, and I drew a deep breath of resolution. "Conductor," I began with a considerable edge to my voice. . . . Instantly the doleful eyes of my seatmate turned tiredly from his newspaper to fix me with a resentful stare: What question could be so important as to justify my sibilant intrusion into his stupor? I was shaken by

those eyes. I am incapable of making a discreet fuss, so I mumbled a question about what time we were due in Stamford (I didn't even ask whether it would be before or after dehydration could be expected to set in), got my reply, and went back to my newspaper and to wiping my brow.

The conductor had nonchalantly walked down the gauntlet of eighty sweating American freemen, and not one of them had asked him to explain why the passengers in that car had been consigned to suffer. There is nothing to be done when the temperature *outdoors* is 85 degrees, and indoors the air conditioner has broken down; obviously when that happens there is nothing to do, except perhaps curse the day that one was born. But when the temperature outdoors is below freezing, it takes a positive act of will on somebody's part to set the temperature *indoors* at 85. Somewhere a valve was turned too far, a furnace overstocked, a thermostat maladjusted: something that could easily be remedied by turning off the heat and allowing the great outdoors to come indoors. All this is so obvious. What is not obvious is what has happened to the American people.

It isn't just the commuters, whom we have come to visualize as a supine breed who have got on to the trick of suspending their sensory faculties twice a day while they submit to the creeping dissolution of the railroad industry. It isn't just they who have given up trying to rectify irrational vexations. It is the American people everywhere.

A few weeks ago at a large movie theatre I turned to my wife and said, "The picture is out of focus." "Be quiet," she answered. I obeyed. But a few minutes later I raised the point again, with mounting impatience. "It will be all right in a minute," she said apprehensively. (She would rather lose her eyesight than be around when I make one of my infrequent scenes.) I waited. It was *just* out of focus—not glaringly out, but out. My vision is 20–20, and I assume that is the vision, adjusted, of most people in the movie house. So, after hectoring my wife throughout the first reel, I finally prevailed upon her to admit that it *was* off, and very annoying. We then settled down, coming to rest on the presumption that: (a) someone connected with the management of the theatre must soon notice the blur and make the correction; or (b) that someone seated near the rear of the house would make the complaint in behalf of those of us up front; or (c) that—any minute now—the entire house would explode into catcalls and foot stamping, calling dramatic attention to the irksome distortion.

What happened was nothing. The movie ended, as it had begun *just* out of focus, and as we trooped out, we stretched our faces in a variety of contortions to accustom the eye to the shock of normal focus.

I think it is safe to say that everybody suffered on that occasion. And I think it is safe to assume that everyone was expecting someone else to take the initiative in going back to speak to the manager. And it is probably true even that if we had supposed the movie would run right through the blurred image, someone surely would have summoned up the purposive indignation to get up out of his seat and file his complaint.

But notice that no one did. And the reason no one did is because we are all   8
increasingly anxious in America to be unobtrusive, we are reluctant to make
our voices heard, hesitant about claiming our rights; we are afraid that our
cause is unjust, or that if it is not unjust, that it is ambiguous; or if not even that,
that it is too trivial to justify the horrors of a confrontation with Authority; we
will sit in an oven or endure a racking headache before undertaking a head-on,
I'm-here-to-tell-you complaint. That tendency to passive compliance, to a heed-
less endurance, is something to keep one's eyes on—in sharp focus.

I myself can occasionally summon the courage to complain, but I cannot,   9
as I have intimated, complain softly. My own instinct is so strong to let the
thing ride, to forget about it—to expect that someone will take the matter up,
when the grievance is collective, in my behalf—that it is only when the provo-
cation is at a very special key, whose vibrations touch simultaneously a com-
plexus of nerves, allergies, and passions, that I catch fire and find the reserves
of courage and assertiveness to speak up. When that happens, I get quite carried away. My blood gets hot, my brow wet, I become unbearably and uncon-
scionably sarcastic and bellicose; I am girded for a total showdown.

Why should that be? Why could not I (or anyone else) on that railroad   10
coach have said simply to the conductor, "Sir"—I take that back: that sounds
sarcastic—"Conductor, would you be good enough to turn down the heat? I am
extremely hot. In fact, I tend to get hot every time the temperature reaches 85
degr—" Strike that last sentence. Just end it with the simple statement that you
are extremely hot, and let the conductor infer the cause.

Every New Year's Eve I resolve to do something about the Milquetoast in   11
me and vow to speak up, calmly, for my rights, and for the betterment of our
society, on every appropriate occasion. Entering last New Year's Eve I was for-
tified in my resolve because that morning at breakfast I had had to ask the
waitress three times for a glass of milk. She finally brought it—after I had finished my eggs, which is when I don't want it any more. I did not have the manliness to order her to take the milk back, but settled instead for a cowardly sulk,
and ostentatiously refused to drink the milk—though I later paid for it—rather
than state plainly to the hostess, as I should have, why I had not drunk it, and
would not pay for it.

So by the time the New Year ushered out the Old, riding in on my morn-   12
ing's indignation and stimulated by the gastric juices of resolution that flow so
faithfully on New Year's Eve, I rendered my vow. Henceforward I would conquer my shyness, my despicable disposition to supineness. I would speak out
like a man against the unnecessary annoyances of our time.

Forty-eight hours later, I was standing in line at the ski repair store in Pico   13
Peak, Vermont. All I needed, to get on with my skiing, was the loan, for one
minute, of a small screwdriver, to tighten a loose binding. Behind the counter
in the workshop were two men. One was industriously engaged in servicing the
complicated requirements of a young lady at the head of the line, and obviously
he would be tied up for quite a while. The other—"Jiggs," his workmate called
him—was a middle-aged man, who sat in a chair puffing a pipe, exchanging

small talk with his working partner. My pulse began its telltale acceleration. The minutes ticked on. I stared at the idle shopkeeper, hoping to shame him into action, but he was impervious to my telepathic reproof and continued his small talk with his friend, brazenly insensitive to the nervous demands of six good men who were raring to ski.

Suddenly my New Year's Eve resolution struck me. It was now or never. I broke from my place in line and marched to the counter. I was going to control myself. I dug my nails into my palms. My effort was only partially successful. 14

"If you are not too busy," I said icily, "would you mind handing me a screw-driver?" 15

Work stopped and everyone turned his eyes on me, and I experienced that mortification I always feel when I am the center of centripetal shafts of curiosity, resentment, perplexity. 16

But the worst was yet to come. "I am sorry, sir," said Jiggs deferentially, moving the pipe from his mouth. "I am not supposed to move. I have just had a heart attack." That was the signal for a great whirring noise that descended from heaven. We looked, stricken, out the window, and it appeared as though a cyclone had suddenly focused on the snowy courtyard between the shop and the ski lift. Suddenly a gigantic army helicopter materialized, and hovered down to a landing. Two men jumped out of the plane carrying a stretcher, tore into the ski shop, and lifted the shopkeeper onto the stretcher. Jiggs bade his companion goodbye, was whisked out the door, into the plane, up to the heavens, down—we learned—to a near-by army hospital. I looked up manfully—into a score of man-eating eyes. I put the experience down as a reversal. 17

As I write this, on an airplane, I have run out of paper and need to reach into my briefcase under my legs for more. I cannot do this until my empty lunch tray is removed from my lap. I arrested the stewardess as she passed empty-handed down the aisle on the way to the kitchen to fetch the lunch trays for the passengers up forward who haven't been served yet. "Would you please take my tray?" "Just a *moment*, sir!" she said, and marched on sternly. Shall I tell her that since she is headed for the kitchen *anyway*, it could not delay the feeding of the other passengers by more than two seconds necessary to stash away my empty tray? Or remind her that not fifteen minutes ago she spoke unctuously into the loudspeaker the words undoubtedly devised by the airline's highly paid public relations counselor: "If there is anything I or Miss French can do for you to make your trip more enjoyable, *please* let us—" I have run out of paper. 18

I think the observable reluctance of the majority of Americans to assert themselves in minor matters is related to our increased sense of helplessness in an age of technology and centralized political and economic power. For generations, Americans who were too hot, or too cold, got up and did something about it. Now we call the plumber, or the electrician, or the furnace man. The habit of looking after our own needs obviously had something to do with the assertiveness that characterized the American family familiar to readers of American literature. With the technification of life goes our direct responsibility for our material environment, and we are conditioned to adopt a position 19 of helplessness not only as regards the broken air conditioner, but as regards the overheated train. It takes an expert to fix the former, but not the latter; yet these distinctions, as we withdraw into helplessness, tend to fade away.

Our notorious political apathy is a related phenomenon. Every year, 20 whether the Republican or the Democratic Party is in office, more and more power drains away from the individual to feed vast reservoirs in far-off places; and we have less and less say about the shape of events which shape our future. From this alienation of personal power comes the sense of resignation with which we accept the political dispensations of a powerful government whose hold upon us continues to increase.

An editor of a national weekly news magazine told me a few years ago that 21 as few as a dozen letters of protest against an editorial stance of his magazine was enough to convene a plenipotentiary meeting of the board of editors to review policy. "So few people complain, or make their voices heard," he explained to me, "that we assume a dozen letters represent the inarticulated views of thousands of readers." In the past ten years, he said, the volume of mail has noticeably decreased, even though the circulation of his magazine has risen.

When our voices are finally mute, when we have finally suppressed the natural instinct to complain, whether the vexation is trivial or grave, we shall have become automatons, incapable of feeling. When Premier Khrushchev first came to this country late in 1959 he was primed, we are informed, to experience the bitter resentment of the American people against his tyranny, against his persecutions, against the movement which is responsible for the great numbers of American deaths in Korea, for billions in taxes every year, and for life everlasting on the brink of disaster; but Khrushchev was pleasantly surprised, and reported back to the Russian people that he had been met with overwhelming cordiality (read: apathy), except, to be sure, for "a few fascists who followed me around with their wretched posters, and should be horsewhipped."

I may be crazy, but I say there would have been lots more posters in a society where train temperatures in the dead of winter are not allowed to climb to 85 degrees without complaint.

■ RECORDING REFLECTIONS

Buckley offers several anecdotes to demonstrate that Americans often don't complain about the flaws in official systems that irritate and frustrate them. As you read, jot down experiences that have irritated and frustrated you, especially the ones you've remained silent about.

From your list, choose one of those incidents and write about it for 10 minutes.

■ ACTIVITIES FOR REREADING

1. Examine in particular the first and last paragraphs of the essay. What do they have in common? Write a brief answer.

2. What is Buckley's thesis? Highlight those places where he states it. Comment briefly in writing why you think he places his thesis where he does.

3. Pay close attention to paragraphs 19 and 20 as you reread. How do they differ from the other examples Buckley has given? Briefly explain in writing.

GROUP WORK

Personal Responses: Use your Reflection Logs as sources to discuss your irritating or frustrating experiences with "the system." What are your various reasons for not complaining? What would have happened had you taken a stand?

Objective Responses: Discuss the relationship between and functions of the first and last paragraphs. What is Buckley's strategy? How effective is it?

Discuss Buckley's thesis. How accurate is it? How well does he support it? Discuss the reasons he places the thesis in two places and in different forms. How effective is this strategy? Why?

Discuss paragraphs 19 and 20 in relation to the rest of the essay. Why does Buckley change the kind of evidence he uses to support his thesis? Jot down your answers.

WRITING ASSIGNMENTS

1. Write an essay that concentrates on a personal encounter with impersonal technology. Emphasize the complexity and difficulty of the situation. Include your emotional and intellectual responses. Be specific. Concentrate on moving from the particular situation to a more general assertion.

2. Buckley's thesis is that Americans have been so browbeaten by the complexities of technology that they no longer complain when a situation demands that they should. Their reluctance to complain is based on the feeling that "our cause is unjust, or if it is not unjust, that it is ambiguous; or, if not that, that it is too trivial to justify the horrors of a confrontation with Authority" (paragraph 8). Write an essay in which you either agree or disagree. Show whether or not Buckley's evidence adequately supports his thesis.

Entropy   *1982*

K. C. COLE

It was about two months ago when I realized that entropy was getting the   1
better of me. On the same day my car broke down (again), my refrigerator
conked out and I learned that I needed root-canal work in my right rear tooth.
The windows in the bedroom were still leaking every time it rained and my
son's baby sitter was still failing to show up every time I really needed her. My
hair was turning gray and my typewriter was wearing out. The house needed
paint and I needed glasses. My son's sneakers were developing holes and I was
developing a deep sense of futility.

After all, what was the point of spending half of Saturday at the Laundromat if the clothes were dirty all over again the following Friday? 2

Disorder, alas, is the natural order of things in the universe. There is even 3 a precise measure of the amount of disorder, called entropy. Unlike almost every other physical property (motion, gravity, energy), entropy does not work both ways. It can only increase. Once it's created it can never be destroyed. The road to disorder is a one-way street.

Because of its unnerving irreversibility, entropy has been called the arrow 4 of time. We all understand this instinctively. Children's rooms, left on their own, tend to get messy, not neat. Wood rots, metal rusts, people wrinkle and flowers wither. Even mountains wear down; even the nuclei of atoms decay. In the city we see entropy in the rundown subways and worn-out sidewalks and torn-down buildings, in the increasing disorder of our lives. We know, without asking, what is old. If we were suddenly to see the paint jump back on an old building, we would know that something was wrong. If we saw an egg unscramble itself and jump back into its shell, we would laugh in the same way we laugh at a movie run backward.

Entropy is no laughing matter, however, because with every increase in en- 5 tropy energy is wasted and opportunity is lost. Water flowing down a mountainside can be made to do some useful work on its way. But once all the water is at the same level it can work no more. That is entropy. When my refrigerator was working, it kept all the cold air ordered in one part of the kitchen and warmer air in another. Once it broke down the warm and cold mixed into a lukewarm mess that allowed my butter to melt, my milk to rot and my frozen vegetables to decay.

Of course the energy is not really lost, but it has defused and dissipated into 6 a chaotic caldron of randomness that can do us no possible good. Entropy is chaos. It is loss of purpose.

People are often upset by the entropy they seem to see in the haphazard- 7 ness of their own lives. Buffeted about like so many molecules in my tepid kitchen, they feel that they have lost their sense of direction, that they are wasting youth and opportunity at every turn. It is easy to see entropy in marriages, when the partners are too preoccupied to patch small things up, almost guaranteeing that they will fall apart. There is much entropy in the state of our country, in the relationships between nations—lost opportunities to stop the avalanche of disorders that seems ready to swallow us all.

Entropy is not inevitable everywhere, however. Crystals and snowflakes and 8 galaxies are islands of incredibly ordered beauty in the midst of random events. If it was not for exceptions to entropy, the sky would be black and we would be able to see where the stars spend their days; it is only because air molecules in the atmosphere cluster in ordered groups that the sky is blue.

The most profound exception to entropy is the creation of life. A seed soaks 9 up some soil and some carbon and some sunshine and some water and arranges it into a rose. A seed in the womb takes some oxygen and pizza and milk and transforms it into a baby.

The catch is that it takes a lot of energy to produce a baby. It also takes en- 10
ergy to make a tree. The road to disorder is all downhill but the road to creation
takes work. Though combating entropy is possible, it also has its price. That's
why it seems so hard to get ourselves together, so easy to let ourselves fall apart.

Worse, creating order in one corner of the universe always creates more 11
disorder somewhere else. We create ordered energy from oil and coal at the
price of the entropy of smog.

I recently took up playing the flute again after an absence of several 12
months. As the uneven vibrations screeched through the house, my son covered
his ears and said, "Mom, what's wrong with your flute?" Nothing was wrong
with my flute, of course. It was my ability to play it that had atrophied, or en-
tropied, as the case may be. The only way to stop that process was to practice
every day, and sure enough my tone improved, though only at the price of constant work. Like anything else, abilities deteriorate when we stop applying our
energies to them.

That's why entropy is depressing. It seems as if just breaking even is an up- 13
hill fight. There's a good reason that this should be so. The mechanics of entropy are a matter of chance. Take any ice-cold air molecule milling around my
kitchen. The chances that it will wander in the direction of my refrigerator at
any point are exactly 50–50. The chances that it will wander away from my refrigerator are also 50–50. But take billions of warm and cold molecules mixed
together, and the chances that all the cold ones will wander toward the refrigerator and all the warm ones will wander away from it are virtually nil.

Entropy wins not because order is impossible but because there are always 14
so many more paths toward disorder than toward order. There are so many more
different ways to do a sloppy job than a good one, so many more ways to make
a mess than to clean it up. The obstacles and accidents in our lives almost guarantee that constant collisions will bounce us on to random paths, get us off the
track. Disorder is the path of least resistance, the easy but not the inevitable road.

Like so many others, I am distressed by the entropy I see around me today. 15
I am afraid of the randomness of international events, of the lack of common
purpose in the world; I am terrified that it will lead into the ultimate entropy
of nuclear war. I am upset that I could not in the city where I live send my child
to a public school; that people are unemployed and inflation is out of control;
that tensions between sexes and races seem to be increasing again; that relationships everywhere seem to be falling apart.

Social institutions—like atoms and stars—decay if energy is not added to 16
keep them ordered. Friendships and families and economies all fall apart unless we constantly make an effort to keep them working and well oiled. And far
too few people, it seems to me, are willing to contribute consistently to those
efforts.

Of course, the more complex things are, the harder it is. If there were only 17
a dozen or so air molecules in my kitchen, it would be likely—if I waited a year
or so—that at some point the six coldest ones would congregate inside the
freezer. But the more factors in the equation—the more players in the game—

the less likely it is that their paths will coincide in an orderly way. The more pieces in the puzzle, the harder it is to put back together once order is disturbed. "Irreversibility," said a physicist, "is the price we pay for complexity."

RECORDING REFLECTIONS

Cole uses multiple examples to define *entropy*. What examples of entropy in your own life do you feel strongly about? List them as you read.

Choose one example from your list, briefly describe it, and explain in writing why you feel strongly about it.

ACTIVITIES FOR REREADING

1. The essay defines the term *entropy*. As you reread, pay close attention to paragraphs 7, 15, and 16. How do these paragraphs extend Cole's definition?
2. Cole defines *entropy* by giving numerous examples. How does she organize her examples? Highlight the text at points where the kinds of examples change.
3. Notice how Cole maintains coherence. Highlight the transitional expressions and words in each paragraph.

GROUP WORK

Personal Responses: Referring to your Reflection Logs, discuss your own experiences with entropy and how you deal with them. What are your attitudes toward the experiences individually? Are your feelings different when you consider entropy as a whole as opposed to when you look at individual cases? Why or why not?

Objective Responses: Discuss the effectiveness of Cole's examples, how she arranges them, and how she ties them all together. Refer to your notes and textual highlighting from your rereading activities to remind yourself of specific observations.

Cole says that the fact of "entropy is no laughing matter" (paragraph 5). In context, what is the tone of that comment? Of the entire essay? What particulars can you cite that demonstrate that tone?

WRITING ASSIGNMENTS

1. Write an essay about something—an object, possession, or relationship—that you feel strongly about and that requires a good deal of your energy to maintain. Concentrate on the natural entropy of the thing, and use examples and specific instances to develop your argument.
2. Write an essay about the process and effort required to maintain one particular social institution—say, a school, place of worship, government service, or volunteer organization. Write the essay inductively; that is, begin with specific instances and move to a general conclusion you can logically draw from your specifics.

Toxins in the Mother Tongue   *1994*

DAVID JAMES DUNCAN

1. Censored

I was invited, a few years back, to speak to 60 or so high school English stu-   1
dents in a small town neither geographically nor demographically far from
Sweet Home, Oregon—from whence the Oregon Citizens Alliance and its now
nationally famous, selective-Leviticus-quoting anti-homosexual agenda sprang
into the national headlines. I was buried in work at the time, but I chose to visit
anyhow, when the English teacher who'd invited me mentioned that her students were being forced to read a version of my first novel, "The River Why,"
from which hundreds of words had been purged by a team of parents armed
with indelible black felt pens.

My novel had already been assigned, the teacher explained, and her class   2
was halfway through it, when the mother of a student happened to pick the
book up and discover my protagonist's use of language. By no stretch of the
imagination or Bible could that language be considered "obscene." Using
the Hollywood rating, I believe my novel would receive a PG-13—and I'm embarrassed to add that a G would be more likely than an R. The passages this
mother nevertheless proceeded to underline, Xerox and distribute to all com-
ers at a PTA meeting nearly caused the book to be banned outright. But at this
same meeting, a couple of brave English teachers stood up and tenaciously defended the morality of my novel's overall aims, and a compromise—which of
course satisfied neither side—was reached. The book was called back from the
students, duly purged by the parents, reassigned and, as some sort of finale
(and, I think, a small act of teacherly revenge upon the vigilantes), I was invited
to visit.

The first thing I did upon arriving at the school was paw through an excised   3
copy to see just how black my prose had been deemed to be—and more than a
few pages, it turned out, looked rather as if Cajuns had cooked them. But what
interested me far more than the quantity of black marks was the unexpected difficulty of the whole censorship endeavor. Hard as these parents had tried to
Clorox my prose, a myopic focus on "nasty words" at the expense of attention to
narrative flow had resulted in a remarkably self-defeating arbitrariness. They'd
taken care, for instance, to spare their big, strapping logging-town teenagers my
protagonist's dislike of the Army Corps of Engineers by converting the phrase
"God damn dams" to "God ■■ dams." Yet when the same protagonist, one Gus
Orviston, told a story about an inch-and-a-half-long scorpion his kid brother lost
inside his fly-fishing-crazed family's house, not a word was blackened out of Gus'
surmise that the lonely creature had ultimately "found and fallen in love with one
of my father's mayfly imitations and died of lover's nuts trying to figure out how
to screw the thing." Along similar lines, Gus was allowed, in a scene when his
lady-love rejected him, to describe himself as a "blubbering Sasquatch . . . my

beard full of lint, my teeth yellow, my fly open and undershorts showing there the same color as my teeth, and thick green boogers clogging both my nostrils." Yet when he attempted moments later to describe the bottom of a river as "the place where the slime and mudsuckers and fish-shit live," student innocence had to be protected by the prophylactic "fish-███."

The pattern grew obvious: While my protagonist had been allowed to piss,   4
puke and fornicate, to insult door-to-door evangelists and even to misread and reject the Bible with impunity, every time he tried to use an old-fashioned four-letter word—even the innocuous likes of "hell," "damn" or "ass"—down came the indelible markers. Some kind of "suitable-for-mixed-company" politeness was, then, what my censors were out to impose. It always seems to dumbfound and offend the promulgators of such cleanlinesses when the makers and defenders of literature declare even purges like theirs to be not just ineffective but dangerous.

The students' reactions to being censored in this way were mild compared   5
to the teachers' reactions and to my own. Most of them considered it an embarrassment—but less of an embarrassment, probably, than a dozen other inescapable facets of high school, small-town and family life. When I read to them the single most censored scene—an exposé of the greed and stupidity of two drunken fishermen—with the missing words restored, the students, on a show of hands, unanimously preferred their drunks to sound like drunks, not Sunday-school teachers. They also agreed unanimously that the purge had been utterly ineffective. But most of them, I felt, were no more able than the parent-censors themselves to perceive any genuine danger in the laundering of their curriculum or literature.

A parable on the danger: 6

When I was a kid and picked raspberries for pocket money, some of the   7
teen-age boys in the fields used to defy the heat, boredom and row-bosses (most of whom were staid Christian housewives) by regaling us with a series of formulaic, ad-libbed yarns they called "The Adventures of One-Eyed Dirk." To a casual listener, One-Eyed Dirk's were some of the dullest adventures ever endured. We pickers listened with bated breath, though, knowing that it was actually our teen raconteurs, not Dirk, who were having the adventure. The trick to a One-Eyed Dirk story was to juxtapose strategic verbs and modifiers with names of common objects in a way that enabled you, through the magic of metaphor, to spout pure analogical pornography within the hearing of everyone, yet to proclaim your literal innocence if confronted by an offended adult. An example might go: "Stunned by the size of the musk melons she'd offered him, One-Eyed Dirk groped through his own meager harvest, found the bent green zucchini, sighed at the wormhole in the end, but, with a shy smile, drew it out and thrust it slowly toward her. . . ."

Silly as this kind of thing may be, it underscores the fact that there is vir-   8
tually nothing a would-be censor can do to guarantee the purity of language, because it is not just words that render language impure. Even "dirty" words tend to be morality neutral until placed in a context—and it is the individual

human imagination, more than individual words, that gives a context its moral or immoral twist. One-Eyed Dirk's G-rated zucchinis and wing nuts and valve jobs drive home the point that a bored kid out to tell an off-color yarn can do it with geometry symbols, nautical flags or two rocks and a stick if he wants. The human imagination was designed (by its Designer, if you like) to make rapid-fire, free-form, often-preposterous connections between shapes, words, colors, ideas, desires, sounds. This is its weakness, but also its wondrous strength. The nature of the imagination itself is, at bottom, why organized censorship never works. And it is also why every ferociously determined censorship effort sooner or later escalates into fascistic political agendas, burnings at the stake, dunking-chairs, gulags, pogroms and other literal forms of purge. Obviously, the only failsafe way to eliminate impurities from human tongues, minds and cultures is to eliminate human life itself.

2. A Liberal Inconsistency

The censors of my novel achieved a laughable inconsistency by zeroing in on "four-letter words" and letting the narrative imagery ride. But there seems to me to be a culturally accepted yet comparable inconsistency practiced by some of our most respected publications. Scores of nationally important newspapers and magazines refuse to print some of the very words purged from my novel by small-town parents belonging to the Oregon Citizens Alliance. The national publications characterize their own refusal as "editorial policy." The same publications characterize the Alliance parents' refusal as "religious fanaticism" or "fascism." [9]

How to work it out? [10]

We must begin, I think, by admitting that an editorial policy is, in fact, a kind of fascism. In the litigious context of today's censorship wars, the admirable editorial gentility of, say, a William Shawn is, unfortunately, an indefensible inconsistency. I'm reminded of Austrian novelist Heimito von Doderer's lines: "Weapons that we have not loaded are forced into our hands. And still we fire the shot." Anyone who believes that censorship tends toward fascism is logically forced to admit that the urbane Mr. Shawn used to unwittingly duplicate the small-town vigilantes' "fascistic tendencies" by refusing to print the "s" or "f" words. And those who can't accept this—those who choose to believe that such a word in Shawn's New Yorker would have served no compelling purpose, would have offended many readers and would have cost the publication subscription money—must also admit that there is no compelling reason for small-town parents not to wade through their children's school libraries eliminating "offensive" words and "non-compelling" books. [11]

I am not suggesting that all periodicals and newspapers must print such words. I am suggesting that the average citizen's desire to improve the quality of language or art is born, in rural Oregon as it is in Manhattan, of an increasingly desperate concern for the health of the culture; that, given the rampant decay of the quality of American life, this concern is not about to leave us: that big-city editors, small-town parents, gay artists, unemployed loggers, Baptist preachers [12] and working novelists express their desperation in different ways; and that we are united—and should, I think, be humbled—by our own inconsistencies.

But, as Krishna tells the reluctant archer, Arjuna, in the Bhagavad Gita, we 13 also have our own individual dharmas to follow. Loggers need trees to remain loggers; preachers need full pews and offering plates; and writers need unexpurgated bookstores, libraries and lexicons. When Arjuna balked on the eve of battle, seeing that the opposing army included beloved old teachers, relatives and friends, Krishna told him that our hopes are vain and our labours futile till we see ourselves one with the Maker of the million faces. But Krishna also advised that, with this Oneness at heart, Arjuna should go forth and play his archer's role to the best of his devastating ability. That said, I feel that I—as a novelist engaged in the ongoing fight for every writer's and reader's freedom— must now do my best to destroy, in argument, even a few beloved old teachers, relatives and friends.

3. The Morality of Literature

Ever since the advent of the printing press, there have been readers who 14 slip from enthusiasm for a favorite text into the belief that the words in that text embody truth: do not just symbolize it, but literally embody it. Not till the past few decades, though, has an alliance of American "conservative Christians" declared that this slip is, in fact, the true Christian religion, that a single bookful of words is Truth, and that this Truth should become the sole basis of the nation's political, legal and cultural life. The growing clout of this faction does not change the theological aberrance of its stance: Fundamentalists defy the written word in a way that—in light of every Scripture-based Wisdom Tradition in the world, including Christianity's 2,000-year-old own—is not just naive. It is idolatrous. Words in books can remind us of truth, and occasionally help awaken us to it. But in themselves words are just paint, and writers are just painters—Old Testament and Gospel writers, bhakti and Sufi saints, Tibetan lamas and Zen masters included. There are, of course, crucial differences between Scripture and belles-lettres, and between inspired and merely inventive prose. But the authors of both write with human hands, and in human tongues. Let's not overestimate the power of literature.

Let's not underestimate it either. As readers we are asked on Page One to 15 lay our hand upon the back of an author's as he or she begins to paint a world. If the author's strokes somehow repel or betray our trust, if our concentration is lax or if we're biased or closed in some way, then no hand-in-hand magic can occur. But when a great word-painter is read with reciprocally great concentration and trust, an incredible thing happens. First, the painter's hand disappears. Then so does our own. Till there is only the living world of the painting.

This disappearance, the way we lose ourselves in the life of a story, is, I be- 16 lieve, the greatest truth in any literature, be it discursive or dramatic, sacred or secular. It is at any rate the greatest describable truth, because for the duration of the disappearance we possess no *I* with which to describe anything outside the text in which we're lost. Like all great truths, it is simultaneously a sacrifice (of the reader's ego) and a resurrection (of the world, the characters and the ideas in the text). And like all great truths, it is not brought about by any kind of mental computations upon literal meanings or sentences or words. All that's required is a willing immersion of imagination and mind in the dynamic pulse and flow of written language.

In light of this great truth, the most valid form of censorship is that prac- 17
ticed by authors themselves. It is the duty of all writers to scrupulously destroy or revise any or all writing that fails to let them vanish into the life of their own language. What authors are morally obligated to censor from their work is their own incompetence. Nothing more, nothing less. Simple as it sounds, it keeps most of us more than busy. Ezra Pound was quoted as saying, "Fundamental accuracy of statement is the one sole morality of literature." If, in other words, a story requires that its writer create a mountain and further requires that this mountain be imposing, the immoral mountain is not the one with the pair of unmarried hikers copulating on a remote slope. It is the mountain that fails to be imposing. The "sole morality of literature" demands that an author con-template his peak till frozen clouds begin to swirl round its summit; till the bones of lost climbers and mountain goats appear deep in its crevasses; till its ice and stone mass haunts and daunts us like a cold moon rising not in some safe distance but from the scree at our very feet.

And the same goes—with all due apologies to literary inquisitors every- 18
where—for the imposing penis. This is not to say that all penises are, according to Pound's dictum, moral. Indeed, a gratuitously shocking penis, an extraneous-to-our-story penis, a hey-look-at-me-for-the-sake-of-nothing-but-me penis, how-ever imposing, is literarily immoral (that is, incompetent), because by jarring the reader from the narrative or argumentative flow into a mood of "What's this stu-pid penis doing here?" the author has undermined the greatest truth of his tale: i.e., our ability to immerse ourselves in it. But once the dramatic demands of the story itself have requested of its author an imposing penis, it is the one-pointed, apoplectic-veined archetype, the one that has us crossing imaginary legs before we know it (or opening them, as the literary case may be), that is the moral pe-nis, and it is the church, quasi-religious political cult or government agency that seeks to zip a zipper over it that is immoral.

"But how could the decision of male members, filthy language, perversion, 19
sadomasochism, sexual violence and so on ever be wrong? Why, in God's name, shouldn't we censor literature, art and human behavior itself in order to safe-guard the purity of our children and our culture?" These are the fundamental-ist questions—the Helms, Falwell and Robertson questions. Those who ask them seem to some of us to pride themselves on their amnesia, considering how recently the likes of Stalin, Hitler, McCarthy and Khomeini have asked the same sort of questions. But it's a widespread amnesia. So here are two more an-swers to the questions—one civil and American, one literary and Christian. First the civil:

All citizens of this country possess a constitutional right to detest the work 20
of any writer or artist they choose to detest—and to criticize that writer or

artist, in public and in private, in the most filthy language they are able to devise. I, to cite the handiest possible example, found the few pages of Bret Easton Ellis' "American Psycho" that I was able to read to be as crassly sensationalistic and literarily incompetent, despite a glib facility with sentence-making, as anything I've ever read. But to say that much satisfies me. And it's all the fun the Constitution allows: To carry my disgust further, to try to summon the courage, compose the propaganda, induce the paranoia and generate the political clout that would let me and my ideological clones ban or purge one overpaid hack is simply not the way that people in this tenuously free country long ago agreed to do things.

The old Irish bards, when asked to recite certain stories, would sometimes say to their audience: "'Tis an evil tale for telling. I canna' make it." And hearing this, their listeners would request a different tale. I believe Ellis, and Americans in general, are dying for a dose of this bardic wisdom. Yet sickening stories are an unavoidable byproduct of a sick culture, and a crucial diagnostic tool for anyone who seeks a cure. Writers need the freedom to invoke body parts, mayhem and twisted visions for many profound reasons, among them (jumping metaphors) the same reason that chefs need the freedom to invoke curry, garlic, extreme heat and many other things we can't tolerate in straight doses. There is no mention of jalopeño peppers in the Christian Scriptures, and neither the average child nor the average televangelist can handle them. That's no reason to legislate them clean out of our *huevos rancheros.*

Now the literary and Christian argument: In the slender classic, "An Experiment in Criticism," the non-literalistic but indefatigably Christian professor of literature, C. S. Lewis, wrote that our access to a diverse and uncensored literature is spiritually crucial because "We demand windows. [And] literature . . . is a series of windows, even of doors. . . . Good reading . . . can be described either as an enlargement or as a temporary annihilation of the self. But that is an old paradox: 'he that loseth his life shall save it.' We therefore delight to enter into other men's beliefs . . . even though we think them untrue. And into their passions, though we think them depraved. . . . Literary experience heals the wound, without undermining the privilege, of individuality. . . . In reading great literature I become a thousand men and yet remain myself. . . . Here, as in worship, in love, in moral action, and in knowing, I transcend myself; and am never more myself than when I do."

4. Why No Argument Against Fundamental Censorship Works

My home state, Oregon, according to its Library Association was third in the nation in 1992 in the number of challenges to the printed word in schools, libraries and bookstores. The vast majority of these challenges were made by people who consider themselves fundamentalist Christians. I've just provided two arguments against such challenges. But I don't for a minute believe that either of my arguments—nor any conceivable argument resembling them in category—will persuade a single committed fundamentalist that censorship is an ineffective or negative or potentially deadly cultural strategy. The only way to convince a fundamentalist of such a thing would be with a fundamentalist argument. And there are none. Fundamentalism and censorship have always gone hand in hand.

My aim here is literary, not theological. But for literary reasons I am com- 24 pelled to point out that a theologically motivated, politically powerful cult is out to simplify and "improve" our literature, art, science, sexual choices, Constitution and souls. And I see no effective choice, in defending all of the above, but to confront the theological basis of the cult itself. When I see poets and authors capable of making crowds weep at the beauty of their words reduced to explaining to some half-sentient TV news hound that they are trying to defend freedom of expression, not the freedom of pedophiles, I feel that some huge strategic error is being committed.

Literary people, being comparatively deep, are often mystified and stymied 25 by the relentless shallowness of the fundamentalist attacks. But the belligerent mind-set and self-insulating dogmas that enable this cult to thrive are neither complicated nor invulnerable to criticism. To treat the earth as disposable and the Bible as God, turn that God into a political action committee, equate effrontery with "evangelism," disingenuous televised prattle with "prayer" and call the result "Christianity" is hardly an invincible position. Evangelists such as Pat Robertson subsidize their organizations by manufacturing a series of carefully designed "moral emergencies" that threaten "us," or better yet "our children." Rather than defending various scapegoats over the din of fundamentalist alarms and media sirens, I'd like to take a brief look at the manufacturers themselves.

5. American Fundamentalism

All of the famous televangelists, all the leaders of the contemporary Bible- 26 based political alliances and most of the recent censors of school libraries, crusaders against homosexuality and politically active fundamentalists in general share a conviction that their political and social causes and agendas are approved of, if not inspired, by no less a being than God. This enviable conviction is less enviably arrived at by accepting on faith, hence as fact, that the Christian Bible, pared down into American TV English is God's "word" to mankind, that this same Bible is "His" only word to mankind, and that the fundamentalist's unprecedentedly literalistic slant on this Bible is the one true slant.

The position is remarkably self-insulating. Possessing little knowledge of 27 and no respect for the world's many rich spiritual, literary and cultural traditions, these people have no conceptions or models of love and compassion but their own and can therefore honestly, even good-heartedly, say that it is out of "Christian" compassion and a sort of "tough love" for others that they seek to impose on all others their God, Bible, and slant.

The position is also far from unprecedented. Well-known variations on the 28 theme include the Inquisitor's tough love for heretics, the conquistador's tough love for Incans, Aztecs and Mayans, the Puritan's tough love for witches, the white Western settler's tough love for Native Americans, and so on. Every Biblereifying crusader group from the European prototype to my home state's Citizens Alliance has seen itself as fighting to make its own or some other community more "Christian." The result, among contemporary non-fundamentalists, has been a growing revulsion toward anything that chooses to call itself "Christian." Yet to this day, I see no more crucial text, in defusing fundamentalist crusades, than the four books of the Gospels, and no more important question to keep asking all such crusaders than whether there is anything truly Christian—that is, anything compassionate, self-abnegating, empathetic and enemy-loving—about their various crusades.

This being a literary essay, it's only fair to point out that fundamentalists are book lovers, too. They just happen to have invested so much brittle love in the first three (Genesis, Exodus, Leviticus) and final (Revelations) books of the one black-covered volume that their ability to enjoy, comprehend or even tolerate other volumes has been drastically curtailed. But another question—again, both literary and theological—that needs to be asked is: How brittle can one's love become before it ceases to be love at all?   29

The ex-Dominican priest and writer Matthew Fox answers this question by calling contemporary evangelical fundamentalism "Christofascism." But when I've tried to deploy this term, it has felt noxious upon my tongue. What's the difference between Fox or me shouting "Christofascist!" at fundamentalists and Rush Limbaugh shouting "feminazi!" at feminists? Both coinages are a calculated descent into the realm of name-calling. Of course, in the escalating verbal and political warfare between fundamentalism and arts and letters, name-calling has become so difficult to avoid that even actual names have become a form of name-calling. If you want to attack conservative Christianity, for instance, you describe the shenanigans of the Jimmys Bakker and Swaggart; and if you want to demonstrate the decadence of literature and art, you describe the imaginative abominations of Bret Easton Ellis and rectal bullwhips of Robert Mapplethorpe. But with "Christofascism" supposedly lurking to the right of us, and "feminazism" to the left, I am inclined to place Mahatma Gandhi front and center, warning: "Be careful of the means you use to fight the fascist, lest you become fascists yourselves."   30

The fundamentalist right is outspoken in its desire to simplify and control my vocabulary, my profession and my spirituality. What I feel compelled to do in response is insist upon a distinction. There is a complex 2,000-year-old religious and cultural tradition that calls itself Christianity. There is a plethora of comparatively new factions of Bible-idolizing literalists who call themselves by the same name. But they are not the same. To refer to Origen, Oral Roberts, Dante, Billy Graham, St. Francis, Jerry Falwell, Pat Robertson and Lady Julian of Norwich all as "Christians" stretches the meaning clear out of the term. The word "humanoid" is as helpful. The gulf between traditional Christianity and American fundamentalism is vast. A Francis Schaeffer text used to instruct Baptist seminarians all over the United States on the world's supposed cults, doctrinal blunders and "other religions" defines and illustrates the concept and history of what it calls "mysticism" by analyzing the writings of Henry Miller.   31

To teach that mysticism equals Henry Miller is not teaching at all. It's an attempt to churn out ideological clones who want no "windows," no insight into others, no enlargement or effacement of self—clones content to read and idolatrize their one book, willfully misread all others and deliberately use the resulting curtailment of comprehension, pleasure and tolerance as a unifying principle.

6. Shame and Reverence

That fly-fishing protagonist of my censored novel, Gus, voiced some serious reservations about the being fundamentalists so possessively refer to as "God." But a literary morality problem that Gus (and I) ran into in telling his story was that, after a climactic all-night adventure with a river and a huge chinook salmon, he had a sudden, transrational (or, in the old Christian lexicon, "mystical") experience that left him too overwhelmed to speak with Pound's "fundamental accuracy of statement," yet too grateful to speak not at all. The paradox this presented my protagonist was, and is, autobiographical. As the recipient of several such detonations, I felt bound by gratitude to speak. But as a lifelong victim of the pollution of the Christian lexicon, I felt compelled to speak in non-Christian terms. Gus' account of his ineffable experience did not once invoke the word *God*. But it did speak of transcendent love, and of a being so God-like that in the end he dubbed it "the Ancient One." [32]

Reader reactions to this climax have been neatly divided. Those who have experienced analogous detonations have sometimes been so moved by the scene that their eyes filled as they thanked me for writing it; and those who have experienced no such detonation have as often asked why I ruined a dang good fishin' yarn with mystical mumbo jumbo. Odd as it may sound, I agree with both reactions. Both are perfectly honest. What more should a writer want from a reader? What more, for that matter, can mortals—be they skeptic or mystic—offer the Absolute? A French novelist/philosopher, Rene Daumal, describes the paradox I faced perfectly. He wrote: [33]

"I swear to you that I have to force myself to write or to pronounce this word: God. It is a noise I make with my mouth or a movement of the fingers that hold my pen. To pronounce or to write this word makes me ashamed. What is real here is that shame. . . . Must I never speak of the Unknowable because it would be a lie? Must I speak of the Unknowable because I know that I proceed from it and am bound to bear witness to it? This contradiction is the prime mover of my best thoughts." [34]

Another word for this shame, in my opinion, is reverence. And American fundamentalists, speaking of the Unknowable, too often lack this quality. Their preachers proudly pronounce the word "God," define it, worship their own definition, impose it upon all adherents, offer an eternal reward for this arrogance, promise eternal torment to all who fail to agree. What an abyss between this and the self-giving Christianity of a Francis, an Eckhart, a Martin Luther King, Jr. What a gulf, too, between this and the contemporary Amish—who practice no evangelism, who tease those who quote the Bible too often (calling [35] them "Scripture smart") and who consider it laughable to pronounce oneself "saved," since God alone is capable of making such weighty decisions.

And what a gulf between fundamentalism and American literature. If the latter arrives at any general theological conclusion as to what we owe to a divinity, it is probably this: Better to be honest to God—even if that means stating one's complete lack of belief in any such being—than to force one's imagination and mind into the mold of a ready-made dogma. In literature, as in life, there are ways of disbelieving in God that are more compassionate, and in that sense more "Christian," than many forms of orthodox belief. There are atheists, for example, who believe as they do because the general state of the world and of humanity makes it impossible for them to conceive of a creator who is anything but compassionless, remiss or cruel. Rather than consider God cruel, they choose disbelief. To my mind this is a backhanded form of reverence; a beautiful kind of "shame." 36

It seems to upset many fundamentalists that literature's answer to the God question is virtually the same as the Constitution's. There is also no doubt that the openness that our literature and form of government encourage results in a theological cacophony and mood of irritable independence that bear no resemblance to the unison docility that reigns in the average church. But America is a country, and America's a literature that stakes its life on the belief that this cacophony and independence are not only legal, but essential to our ultimate health. 37

Edward Abbey remains welcome in our libraries, as he will never be in our churches, to say, "God is Love? Not bloody likely!" Goethe remains welcome to reply to him: "As a man is, so is his God; therefore God is often an object of mockery." And readers remain welcome to draw their own conclusions. 38

My mother tongue, the language my parents and grandparents used to draw me from virtual non-being into the naming of and engagement with life, is English. And there are only so many English words with which to describe the eternal verities and the journey of the soul. One of the irreplaceable words in this language is *God*. Yet the God of organized fundamentalism, as advertised daily through a variety of mass media, is a supramundane Caucasian male as furious with humanity's failure to live by a few arbitrarily chosen lines from the Book of Leviticus as He is oblivious to His spokespersons' failure to live by the militant compassion of the Gospels. 39

As surely as I feel love and need for my wife and children, I feel love and need for a God. But this feeling has nothing whatever to do with supramundane Caucasian males. And I am not troubled by this. If the fundamentalists' God were indeed the One and Only, the likes of Gandhi and Mother Teresa, Tolstoy and Dostoyevsky, Jung and Merton, Black Elk and Chief Joseph, Thoreau and John Muir, Rumi and Hafiz, John of the Cross and Julian of Norwich, Lao-tzu and Bodhidharma, Kabir and Mira Bai, Shunryu and D. T. Suzuki, Valmiki and Socrates, Dogen and Dante, would all be heretics, atheists and infidels—because the Absolute they all worship is an infinitely different being. 40

I suspect the situation to be rather different. I suspect the odd "evangelical" truth of the matter to be that fundamentalists need non-fundamentalists of all 41 stripes—be they mystics, agnostics, Amish, artists, writers, scientists, believers, nonbelievers—in such a big way that it may not be going too far to say they need us for their salvation. As Mark Twain pointed out a century ago, the only really prominent Christian community that fundamentalists have ever managed to establish in any of the worlds is hell.

RECORDING REFLECTIONS

In this erudite, carefully reasoned attack on censorship, Duncan describes the frustrations he felt—and feels—arguing against people who seem incapable of understanding him or the issue involved.

After you've read "Toxins in the Mother Tongue," use your Reflection Log to describe an incident in your own life when you have felt a similar frustration. Write for 10 minutes.

ACTIVITIES FOR REREADING

1. Toward the end of this essay, in paragraph 39, Duncan says that one of the irreplaceable words in his mother tongue is *God*. In your own words, briefly describe how Duncan goes on (paragraphs 39–41) to distinguish between his concept of *God* and the censors' idea of *God*.
2. This essay begins with a personal anecdote. How would you describe its tone? Highlight the words and phrases that indicate that tone.
3. Duncan cites many religious and philosophical thinkers, distinguishing them from his censors. What are those differences? How effective is this tactic? Pay particular attention to paragraphs 32, 36, and 41. Jot down your answers.

GROUP WORK

Personal Responses: Share your experiences of meeting complete and unyielding resistance on occasions when you knew you were right. Have group members had similar experiences? How have they been alike or different?

Objective Responses: Discuss Duncan's concept of *God* as opposed to the censors' view. In what ways does Duncan claim their vision is lacking?

Duncan's personal anecdote at the beginning of this essay is important in establishing his credibility. Explain why this is so. Use the notes in your Reflection Logs and the text itself to support your discussion.

Discuss Duncan's strategy of alluding to so many religious and philosophical thinkers. How effective is that strategy? Why?

WRITING ASSIGNMENTS

1. Duncan's essay is full of provocative statements. While reading the essay, you must have vigorously agreed or disagreed with him several times. Choose one such statement and write an argumentative paper that either refutes or supports it. Make sure that you convincingly counter any opposing arguments and use concrete examples to support your own position.

2. One of Duncan's subjects is *censorship*. Write an argumentative essay in which you either condemn any form of censorship or argue that some forms are not only acceptable but necessary. Whatever position you take, make sure to use parts of Duncan's argument to support your point of view.

Marginal Men   *1990*

BARBARA EHRENREICH

Crime seems to change character when it crosses a bridge or a tunnel. In the city, crime is taken as emblematic of the vast injustices of class and race. In the suburbs, though, it's intimate and psychological—resistant to generation, a mystery of the individual soul. Recall the roar of commentary that followed the murderous assault on a twenty-eight-year-old woman jogging in Central Park. Every detail of the assailants' lives was sifted for sociological significance: Were they poor? How poor? Students or dropouts? From families with two parents or one? And so on, until the awful singularity of the event was lost behind the impersonal grid of Class, Race, and Sex.

Now take the Midtown Tunnel east to the Long Island Expressway, out past the clutter of Queens to deepest suburbia, where almost every neighborhood is "good" and "social pathology" is something you learn about in school. Weeks before the East Harlem youths attacked a jogger, Long Islanders were shaken by two murders which were, if anything, even more inexplicably vicious than the assault in Central Park. In early March, the body of thirteen-year-old Kelly Tinyes was found in the basement of a house just down the block from her own. She had been stabbed, strangled, and hit with a blunt instrument before being mutilated with a bayonet. A few weeks later, fourteen-year-old Jessica Manners was discovered along the side of a road in East Setauket, strangled to death, apparently with her own bra, and raped.

Suspects have been apprehended. Their high-school friends, parents, and relatives have been interviewed. Their homes and cars have been searched; their photos published. We know who they hung out with and what they did in their spare time. But on the scale of large social meanings, these crimes don't rate. No one is demanding that we understand—or condemn—the white communities that nourished the killers. No one is debating the roots of violence in the land of malls and tract homes. Only in the city, apparently, is crime construed as something "socioeconomic." Out here it's merely "sick."

But East Setauket is not really all that far from East Harlem. If something is festering in the ghetto, something very similar is gnawing away at Levittown and East Meadow. A "way of life," as the cliché goes, is coming to an end, and in its place a mean streak is opening up and swallowing everything in its path. Economists talk about "deindustrialization" and "class polarization." I think of

1

2

3

4

it as the problem of *marginal men:* they are black and white, Catholic and Pen-tecostal, rap fans and admirers of technopop. What they have in common is that they are going nowhere—nowhere legal, that is.

Consider the suspects in the Long Island murders. Twenty-one-year-old   5
Robert Golub, in whose basement Kelly Tinyes was killed, is described in *Newsday* as an "unemployed bodybuilder." When his high-school friends went off to college, he stayed behind in his parents' home in Valley Stream. For a while, he drove a truck for a cosmetics firm, but he lost that job, in part be-cause of his driving record: his license has been suspended twelve times since 1985. At the time of the murder, he had been out of work for several months, constructing a life around his weight-lifting routine and his dream of becom-ing an entrepreneur.

Christopher Loliscio, the suspect in the Manners case, is nineteen, and, like   6
Golub, lives with his parents. He has been in trouble before, and is charged with third-degree assault and "menacing" in an altercation that took place on the campus of the State University at Stony Brook last December. Loliscio does not attend college himself. He is employed as a landscaper.

The suburbs are full of young white men like Golub and Loliscio. If they   7
had been born twenty years earlier, they might have found steady work in de-cent-paying union jobs, married early, joined the volunteer fire department, and devoted their leisure to lawn maintenance. But the good blue-collar jobs are getting sparser, thanks to "deindustrialization"—which takes the form, in Long Island, of cutbacks in the defense and aerospace industries. Much of what's left is likely to be marginal, low-paid work. Nationwide, the earnings of young white men dropped 18 percent between 1973 and 1986, according to the Census Bureau, and the earnings of male high-school dropouts plunged 42 percent.

Landscaping, for example—a glamorous term for raking and mowing—   8
pays four to five dollars an hour; truck driving for a small firm is in the same range: not enough to pay for a house, a college education, or even a mid-size wedding reception at the VFW hall.

And even those modest perquisites of life in the subyuppie class have be-   9
come, in some sense, "not enough." On Long Island, the culture that once sus-tained men in blue-collar occupations is crumbling as more affluent settlers move in, filling the vacant lots with their new, schooner-shaped, $750,000 homes. In my town, for example, the last five years saw the bowling alley close and the blue-collar bar turn into a pricey dining spot. Even the volunteer fire department is having trouble recruiting. The prestigious thing to join is a $500-a-year racquet-ball club; there's just not much respect anymore for putting out fires.

So the marginal man lives between two worlds—one that he aspires to   10
and one that is dying, and neither of which he can afford. Take "Rick," the twenty-two-year-old son of family friends. His father is a machinist in an aerospace plant which hasn't been hiring anyone above the floor-sweeping level for years now. Not that Rick has ever shown any interest in his father's trade. For one thing, he takes too much pride in his appearance to put on the

dark green company-supplied work clothes his father has worn for the past twenty years. Rick has his kind of uniform: pleated slacks, high-tops, Italian knit cardigans, and a $300 leather jacket, accessorized with a gold chain and earring stud.

To his parents, Rick is a hard-working boy for whom things just don't seem   11
to work out. For almost a year after high school, he worked behind a counter at Crazy Eddie's, where the pay is low but at least you can listen to rock and roll all day. Now he has a gig doing valet parking at a country club. The tips are good and he loves racing around the lot in the Porsches and Lamborghinis of the stockbroker class. But the linchpin of his economic strategy is living at home, with his parents and sisters, in the same room he's occupied since third grade. Rick is a long way from being able to afford even a cramped, three-bedroom house like his family home; and, given the choice, he'd rather have a new Camaro anyway.

If this were the seventies, Rick might have taken up marijuana, the Grate-   12
ful Dead, and vague visions of a better world. But like so many of his contemporaries in the eighties, Rick has no problem with "the system," which, in his mind, embraces every conceivable hustle, legal or illegal. Two years ago, he made a tidy bundle dealing coke in a local dance club, bought a $20,000 car, and smashed it up. Now he spends his evenings as a bouncer in an illegal gambling joint—his parents still think he's out "dancing"—and is proud of the handgun he's got stowed in his glove compartment.

Someday Rick will use that gun, and I'll probably be the first to say—like   13
Robert Golub's friends—"but he isn't the kind of person who would hurt *anyone*." Except that even now I can sense the danger in him. He's smart enough to know he's only a cutrate copy of the upscale young men in *GQ* ads and MTV commercials. Viewed from Wall Street or Southampton, he's a peon, a member of the invisible underclass that parks cars, waits on tables, and is satisfied with a five-dollar tip and a remark about the weather.

He's also proud. And there's nowhere for him to put that pride except into   14
the politics of gesture: the macho stance, the seventy-five-mile-per-hour takeoff down the expressway, and eventually maybe, the drawn gun. Jobs are the liberal solution; conservatives would throw in "traditional values." But what the marginal men—from Valley Stream to Bedford-Stuyvesant—need most of all is *respect*. If they can't find that in work, or in a working-class life-style that is no longer honored, they'll extract it from someone weaker—a girlfriend, a random jogger, a neighbor, perhaps just any girl. They'll find a victim.

■ RECORDING REFLECTIONS

Ehrenreich gives three accounts of young men who are *marginal*—hanging between two social worlds without much hope of ever belonging to either. In your Reflection Log, list experiences you have had on the margin—times you wanted to belong to something but couldn't.

After you've drawn up your list, choose one experience and write about it for 10 minutes.

■ ACTIVITIES FOR REREADING

1. Ehrenreich sketches examples of three young men who live in suburban New York. As you reread, note those things they have in common. Then jot down how the third man differs from the first two.

2. In the first four paragraphs, Ehrenreich compares and contrasts an urban crime with two crimes committed in the suburbs. How are the crimes similar? How are they different? Write down your answers.

3. What is Ehrenreich's thesis? Highlight the text where she states it. Briefly explain in writing whether she adequately proves that thesis.

■ GROUP WORK

Personal Responses: Use your Reflection Logs as memory guides and compare your experiences of being on the margin. Try to recall your feelings at the time. Were group members' feelings at all similar? Were they at all similar to those of the young men Ehrenreich describes? How so?

Objective Responses: Compare what you think the three suburbanites have in common and how the third is different from the first two. Ehrenreich makes a prediction about the third young man. Does her prediction seem plausible to you? Why or why not?

Discuss the differences and similarities among the three crimes Ehrenreich describes in the first four paragraphs. What accounts for the different ways people react to the crimes?

See if you can agree about Ehrenreich's thesis and where she states it. Discuss how convincingly she proves it. Jot down why you think she was or wasn't convincing.

Ehrenreich portrays a kind of despair at the core of the lives of the young men she describes. What causes that despair? How is it manifested in their lives?

Discuss what you think Ehrenreich means by the phrase "the politics of gesture" (paragraph 14). Use examples from your own experiences to demonstrate the meaning of the phrase.

■ WRITING ASSIGNMENTS

1. Choose one or more experiences you have had on the margin—wanting to belong to something but being unable to—and write an essay about it (them). What caused the situation(s)? How did you react, feel, and think?

2. Write an essay in which you describe and explain Ehrenreich's phrase "the politics of gesture" (paragraph 14). Use examples from your own experience, as well as from the popular news media, to demonstrate your point. Make sure to analyze the significance of what you describe: its causes, effects, and meaning.

About Men   *1985*

GRETEL EHRLICH

When I'm in New York but feeling lonely for Wyoming I look for the Marl-   1
boro ads in the subway. What I'm aching to see is horseflesh, the glint of a spur,
a line of distant mountains, brimming creeks, and a reminder of the ranchers
and cowboys I've ridden with for the last eight years. But the men I see in those
posters with their stern, humorless looks remind me of no one I know here. In
our hellbent earnestness to romanticize the cowboy we've ironically dises-
teemed his true character. If he's "strong and silent" it's because there's probably no one to talk to. If he "rides away into the sunset" it's because he's been on
horseback since four in the morning moving cattle and he's trying, fifteen hours
later, to get home to his family. If he's "a rugged individualist" he's also part of
a team: ranch work is teamwork and even the glorified open-range cowboys of
the 1880s rode up and down the Chisholm Trail in the company of twenty or
thirty other riders. Instead of the macho, trigger-happy man our culture has
perversely wanted him to be, the cowboy is more apt to be convivial, quirky,
and softhearted. To be "tough" on a ranch has nothing to do with conquests and
displays of power. More often than not, circumstances—like the colt he's riding
or an unexpected blizzard—are overpowering him. It's not toughness but
"toughing it out" that counts. In other words, this macho, cultural artifact the
cowboy has become is simply a man who possesses resilience, patience, and an
instinct for survival. "Cowboys are just like a pile of rocks—everything happens
to them. They get climbed on, kicked, rained and snowed on, scuffed up by
wind. Their job is 'just to take it,' " one old-timer told me.

A cowboy is someone who loves his work. Since the hours are long—ten to   2
fifteen hours a day—and the pay is $30, he has to. What's required of him is an
odd mixture of physical vigor and maternalism. His part of the beef-raising industry is to birth and nurture calves and take care of their mothers. For the
most part his work is done on horseback and in a lifetime he sees and comes
to know more animals than people. The iconic myth surrounding him is built
on American notions of heroism: the index of a man's value as measured in
physical courage. Such ideas have perverted manliness into a self-absorbed
race for cheap thrills. In a rancher's world, courage has less to do with facing
danger than with acting spontaneously—usually on behalf of an animal or another rider. If a cow is stuck in a boghole he throws a loop around her neck,
takes his dally (a half hitch around the saddle horn), and pulls her out with
horsepower. If a calf is born sick, he may take her home, warm her in front of
the kitchen fire, and massage her legs until dawn. One friend, whose favorite
horse was trying to swim a lake with hobbles on, dove under water and cut her
legs loose with a knife, then swam her to shore, his arm around her neck life-
guard-style, and saved her from drowning. Because these incidents are usually
linked to someone or something outside himself, the westerner's courage is selfless, a form of compassion.

The physical punishment that goes with cowboying is greatly underplayed. 3 Once fear is dispensed with, the threshold of pain rises to meet the demands of the job. When Jane Fonda asked Robert Redford (in the film *Electric Horseman*) if he was sick as he struggled to his feet one morning, he replied, "No, just bent." For once the movies had it right. The cowboys I was sitting with laughed in agreement. Cowboys are rarely complainers; they show their stoicism by laughing at themselves.

If a rancher or cowboy has been thought of as a "man's man"—laconic, hard- 4 drinking, inscrutable—there's almost no place in which the balancing act between male and female, manliness and femininity, can be more natural. If he's gruff, handsome, and physically fit on the outside, he's androgynous at the core. Ranchers are midwives, hunters, nurturers, providers, and conservationists all at once. What we've interpreted as toughness—weathered skin, calloused hands, a squint in the eye and a growl in the voice—only masks the tenderness inside. "Now don't go telling me these lambs are cute," one rancher warned me the first day I walked into the football-field-sized lambing sheds. The next thing I knew he was holding a black lamb. "Ain't this little rat good-lookin'?"

So many of the men who came to the West were southerners—men look- 5 ing for work and a new life after the Civil War—that chivalrousness and strict codes of honor were soon thought of as western traits. There were very few women in Wyoming during territorial days, so when they did arrive (some as mail-order brides from places like Philadelphia) there was a stand-offishness between the sexes and a formality that persists now. Ranchers still tip their hats and say, "Howdy, ma'am" instead of shaking hands with me.

Even young cowboys are often evasive with women. It's not that they're 6 Jekyll and Hyde creatures—gentle with animals and rough on women—but rather, that they don't know how to bring their tenderness into the house and lack the vocabulary to express the complexity of what they feel. Dancing wildly all night becomes a metaphor for the explosive emotions pent up inside, and when these are, on occasion, released, they're so battery-charged and potent that one caress of the face or one "I love you" will peal for a long while.

The geographical vastness and the social isolation here make emotional 7 evolution seem impossible. Those contradictions of the heart between respectability, logic, and convention on the one hand, and impulse, passion, and intuition on the other, played out wordlessly against the paradisical beauty of the West, give cowboys a wide-eyed but drawn look. Their lips pucker up, not with kisses but with immutability. They may want to break out, staying up all night with a lover just to talk, but they don't know how and can't imagine what the consequences will be. Those rare occasions when they do bare themselves result in confusion. "I feel as if I'd sprained my heart," one friend told me a month after such a meeting.

My friend Ted Hoagland wrote, "No one is as fragile as a woman but no one 8 is as fragile as a man." For all the women here who use "fragileness" to avoid work or as a sexual ploy, there are men who try to hide theirs, all the while clinging to an adolescent dependency on women to cook their meals, wash their clothes, and keep the ranch house warm in winter. But there is true vulnerability in evidence here. Because these men work with animals, not machines or numbers, because they live outside in landscapes of torrential beauty, because they are confined to a place and a routine embellished with awesome variables, because calves die in the arms that pulled others into life, because they go to the mountains as if on a pilgrimage to find out what makes a herd of elk tick, their strength is also a softness, their toughness, a rare delicacy.

RECORDING REFLECTIONS

In "About Men," Gretel Ehrlich debunks the popular stereotype of the American cowboy. As you read, make two lists: In the first, list the individual characteristics of the cowboy stereotype; in the second, list the typical characteristics of a real cowboy.

After reading the essay, look carefully at your lists and write for 10 minutes, explaining which list more accurately portrays your idea of a real-life cowboy.

ACTIVITIES FOR REREADING

1. Ehrlich uses contrast as one of her strategies of development. Highlight paragraphs where she uses contrast, and note what the contrasts are.
2. Take particular note of paragraphs 5, 6, and 7 as you reread. Exactly how do they explain what Ehrlich claims to be the true nature of the cowboy?
3. What does Ehrlich mean when she says that notions about the myth of the hero have "perverted manliness" (paragraph 2)?
4. Does any information in the essay surprise you? If so, what? Where does your image of a cowboy come from? Be specific.

GROUP WORK

Personal Responses: Compare the lists of contrasts you noted in your Reflection Logs. Discuss and record which list is more accurate and why. Note the particular reasons you chose to justify your choices.

Objective Responses: Using your notes from rereading, discuss Ehrlich's use of contrasts. Is her use of these contrasts effective? Why or why not?

Again, using your notes, what are the functions of paragraphs 5, 6, and 7? Discuss.

What does Ehrlich mean by the term "perverted manliness" (paragraph 2)? Does she use it effectively? Why or why not?

Discuss the particular sources that formed your stereotype of the American cowboy—movies? TV shows? books? cigarette ads? If your particular sources were different, did this seem to influence the opinions you formed? How so?

WRITING ASSIGNMENTS

1. Think of a time in your life when you were threatened by a male authority figure—perhaps a policeman, doctor, or teacher. On reflection, how much

of your fear was rooted in the stereotype you held of that person? Write an essay in which you distinguish between the stereotype you reacted to and the real person behind the image.

2. Choose a stereotype that's portrayed in the popular media—for instance, pop singers, cowboys, twenty-somethings, Asians, African Americans, Hispanics, or white-middle-class families. Contrast the stereotype of this group with the real people that comprise it.

Shameless Talk Shows   *1995*

C. EUGENE EMERY, JR.

I dated Siamese twins.
I slept with Bigfoot, too.
Get me on Sally Jessy.
Put me on Donahue.
'Cause I wanna tell the world about it
Right now.*

Vicki Abt vividly recalls the first time she tuned in to the "Sally Jessy Raphael" talk show. Abt found the hostess warning viewers that her program that day was not for the squeamish. Abt, a not-so-squeamish social psychologist at Penn State University, stuck around.

"As I'm watching, she's showing a videotape of a murder," said Abt. "The kid was taped to a pole, they were shooting him, they tortured him, and they shot him to death. The second time they shot him, he moaned and I knew it was real. I freaked out. I was screaming. I was crying. I said, 'I can't believe that she's showing this. What is the point of this?'"

The more Abt thought about it—not just the violent images but the absence of a constructive motive for showing the tape—the angrier she became. "It gets people upset, but it doesn't tell them what to do prosocially afterwards, except to turn to a commercial for Nutri/System so you can worry about your diet," said Abt.

She tried to do something. Abt wrote a two-page letter to Raphael "outlining exactly what was wrong with what she was doing and how dangerous it was." Abt never got a response.

Talk-show hosts like to say they get viewers interested in important issues facing society. Raphael's show did exactly that. Abt, who studies how moral principals are shaped by society and the media, got interested in Raphael and her ilk.

---

*Lyrics from the song "Talk Soup," written by Al Yankovic. Reprinted by permission.

My dog's a narcoleptic.
My mom's a circus freak.
I gotta get a spot on Geraldo's show this week.
'Cause I wanna tell the world about it
Right now.

Using that two-page letter to Raphael as an outline, Abt began a content 6
analysis of 60 hours of television talk shows. The result was "The Shameless
World of Phil, Sally and Oprah: Television Talk Shows and the Deconstructing
of Society," an essay written with Penn State colleague Mel Seeholtz and now
published in the *Journal of Popular Culture*, 28 (no. 1), Summer 1994.

"I thought maybe this (the Raphael show) was a fluke," said Abt, who also 7
looked at how such hosts manipulate their audiences and how they make the
shows work.

She discovered it was no fluke. She concluded that talk shows: 8

- Consistently play up the freakish nature of human existence, giving it national prominence and desensitizing viewers to its social implications. As
long as they are willing to talk, child molesters, people with sexual quirks,
folks with criminal records become recast on these shows as "victims," who
can instantly amend for their sins by publicly confessing and apologizing
to their victims.

- Provide a voyeuristic look at the deepest personal secrets of dysfunctional
relationships or criminal acts, often without giving viewers the opportunity
or a feeling of obligation to help. While some talk-show hosts passionately
argue that they improve society by forcing the public to confront uncomfortable issues that should be tackled, Abt says the argument is shallow and
self-serving. Real-life problems are solved when flesh-and-blood people
(who can't escape a problem by changing channels) get involved in the solution. "The abstract concept of altruism is grounded either in experiences
that evoke empathy or in real physical consequences. Television talk shows
create an ersatz community, without any of the social and personal responsibilities that are attached to real life."

- Provide little or no reliable information to help viewers put what they are
seeing into a rational, intellectually honest context. In a program featuring
"skinheads," she wrote, "No one seriously attempted to correct their inaccurate rendering of historical events, or challenge their reliance on pseudo-
biology during their diatribes against Jews and other, unrelated minority
groups."

Thus, Abt warned, talk shows are helping to misshape our culture by mis- 9
leading viewers.

"Television talk shows create audiences by breaking cultural rules, by man- 10
aged shocks, by shifting our conceptions of what is acceptable, by transform-
ing our ideas about what is possible, by undermining the bases for cultural
judgment, by redefining deviance and appropriate reactions to it, by eroding
social barriers, inhibitions and cultural distinctions," she said in the opening
paragraph of her essay.

It was a powerful, topical, controversial attack on some of the nation's best-   11
known celebrities and the role they play in society. It wasn't surprising that Abt
would be invited to get a first-hand look at life on a talk show.

> My wife ran off with Elvis.
> My boss shaved off my hair.
> I've got a thing for poodles
> And rubber underwear.
> And I wanna tell the world about it
> Right now.

Abt knew better than to expect a reserved, thoughtful debate of the issues   12
between the experts when she agreed to discuss the points she raised on "The
Oprah Winfrey Show." She wasn't mistaken.

Instead of an intellectual dialogue, Oprah turned the program into the typ-   13
ical talk-show spectacle, with too many guests and too little time for them to
provide anything more than soundbites.

Joining Abt for the two-hour show, aired September 12 and 13, 1994, were   14
Washington Post TV critic Tom Shales (who called talk shows "the new pornography of our time" because they turn the audience into voyeurs), *People* magazine TV critic David Hiltbrand (who called Abt's conclusions "preposterous"
and argued that "people watch TV with a built-in moral sense"), and groups of
viewers from San Francisco, Atlanta, and Boston. Members of Oprah's Chicago
audience alone had collectively watched 647 hours of talk shows in one week.

Some audience members said they simply watch such shows to be enter-   15
tained. Others said they liked the programs because they believe the shows provide important information.

One teenager who expressed the latter view went on to criticize how the   16
shows portray teenagers as "all drug addicts, dropouts, pregnant, or what have
you." It didn't seem to dawn on her that if talk shows distort reality in an area
where she has some personal experience, the genre might be giving unreliable
information in other areas as well.

With Abt pressing for talk shows to feature more debates among experts   17
who actually know what they're talking about, and Shales saying he'd "like to
see more smart people on TV, fewer ordinary people and more extraordinary
people," Winfrey closed the show by lamenting that "a lot of times when it
comes down to what people actually watch, the very programs they criticize are
the ones that get the highest ratings."

> I had a close encounter.
> I never chew my food.
> I got eleven nose jobs.
> I yodel in the nude.
> And I wanna tell the world about it
> Right now.

Abt has not been alone in her criticisms.   18

When "20/20" took a behind-the-scenes look at talk shows, the ABC-TV   19
news magazine (aired September 16, 1994) revealed how one couple, Jennifer

and Uriel Soto, managed to get on three different shows with three different stories in a matter of weeks. On "The Ricki Lake Show," they lied by billing themselves as married cousins. Jennifer Soto said the show's producers never asked any questions.

The "20/20" show also featured three men who had pretended to be a gay   20
love triangle during a different Lake show. They alleged that a producer fed them titillating lines to use on the program, a claim the show denies.

Even when the shows have reason to suspect that a guest is lying, it doesn't   21
matter. On "The Montel Williams Show," Jerome Stanfield, a man who later claimed that a producer for the show had encouraged him to lie, told Williams that he was a serial rapist. Although police were unable to confirm Stanfield's story, Williams aired the show anyway. He billed it as an "exclusive," explaining to his audience that, although questions had been raised about the honesty of the guest, "we have no information at this time that leads us to believe he is *not* telling the truth. And because of that we feel it is our duty and our responsibility to broadcast the program out of concern for public safety."

> I have no genitalia.
> I sold my kids for cheese.
> I love my blow-up doll so
> Bring out those cameras, please.
> 'Cause I wanna tell the world about it
> Right now.

Despite the criticisms and the exposés of the way these programs stretch   22
the truth, there's little evidence that things have changed in the trashy world of TV talk shows.

Self-proclaimed psychics, promoters of quacky medical treatments, mira-   23
cle mongers, and UFO enthusiasts usually get to tell their stories on these shows with a minimum of criticism.

For example, hostess and fitness guru Susan Powter spent part of Febru-   24
ary fawning over the "psychic" Char, showing how a box of burning herbs placed on the abdomen can help premenstrual syndrome sufferers, and trying to scare parents away from getting their children vaccinated.

In another case, talkmeister Jerry Springer brought a woman named Shan-   25
non onto his show so her husband could shock her on national TV with the news that he had a long-standing affair with the baby-sitter of the couple's two children. Then, with Shannon already weeping, Springer brought on Cindy, the baby-sitter, who went into further detail about her ongoing relationship with Shannon's husband.

But Shannon, her husband, and the babysitter turned out to be three   26
Toronto-based comedians who reported that "The Jerry Springer Show" had misled Shannon in an effort to humiliate her on national television. Then a Springer spokeswoman had the nerve to threaten to sue the comics for breaking a written promise to tell the truth on the program.

"If I had really been this woman," Suzanne "Shannon" Muir told the *Toronto*   27
Star, "they would have ruined my life."

And in a case that brought haunting echoes of the video that originally   28
prompted Abt to examine what talk shows do to society, police in Michigan
charged Jonathan Schmitz with murder after "The Jenny Jones Show" brought
Schmitz, 24, on the program and told him he would get the chance to meet a
secret admirer on national TV.

The secret admirer of Schmitz, a heterosexual, turned out to be a man—   29
32-year-old Scott Amedure. As the show was being taped, Schmitz was stunned
to learn that he was the object of a homosexual crush.

Three days later, after also reportedly receiving an anonymous sexually sug-   30
gestive note, Schmitz bought a shotgun, went to Amedure's house, and shot
him twice, according to police. Jones and her organization have denied any responsibility for Amedure's death. The program never aired.

The murder may make talk-show hosts and their producers reexamine   31
what they're doing, but probably not for long.

Jones's program began getting good ratings only after she began trying to   32
shock viewers and guests. The lesson isn't lost on the industry, which seems
ready to do almost anything to raise the level of sensationalism in hopes of attracting a bigger share of the audience.

With 15 talk shows already on the air, television executives hawking new   33
programs are promising even more sensational fare when the new season begins in September.

"There are going to be 20 or so new shows that are worse than the ones I   34
was criticizing," says Abt. "These days, saying you had sex with your father gets
almost no reaction. Now you have to have had sex with three fathers. I think
the public thinks these shows are telling them something relevant, but the audience has been so brutalized, they need more and more to get outraged."

"The reason these talk shows are so popular is you don't have to educate   35
people to be voyeurs, you don't have to educate people to love gossip, to like
freak shows," comments Abt, adding that the same thing holds true for programs featuring psychics, UFO abductees, and the like.

In the end, it's more than the fault of the producers and hosts. The problem   36
lies with the people who choose to watch and believe such shows.

"Oprah's argument to me was that every time she does a public-interest   37
show, her ratings go down the toilet. She's certainly right. But that doesn't excuse it," says Abt. "You can also make a lot of money selling crack cocaine, but
I don't do it."

> I'm just a cross-dressin'
> alcoholic neo-Nazi
> Porno star, as you may have guessed.
> And I'm really gonna feel
> a whole lot better
> if you let me get this thing off my chest.
> Talk Soup. Talk Soup.
> Listen to me, listen to me, listen to me.

▓ RECORDING REFLECTIONS

Throughout his essay, Emery gives one example after another of sleazy and fraudulent TV talk shows. In your Reflection Log, list examples of talk shows you have seen that left an impression on you, for whatever reason.

When you've finished your list, select one of the examples and write for 10 minutes, exploring your thoughts and feelings about the show. If you seldom or never watch talk shows, write about why.

▓ ACTIVITIES FOR REREADING

1. Paragraphs 1–4 serve as Emery's introduction. As you reread, pay attention to how the paragraphs progress and the particular ways they relate to each other. Write down your observations.
2. Pay close attention to how Emery backs up his points. Does he make a convincing case? Why or why not? Jot down specific reasons that you find his argument convincing or not so convincing.
3. As you reread paragraphs 22–32, think about the functions they serve in the larger scheme of the essay. Also consider what effect Emery creates by using these paragraphs as he does. Write down your brief observations.

▓ GROUP WORK

Personal Responses: Discuss and compare both your general responses to TV talk shows and your specific responses to the examples you cited in your Reflection Logs. What's your opinion about Emery's conclusions? Are they valid? Why or why not?

Objective Responses: Discuss the functions of paragraphs 1–4 and 22–32 as well as the effects these paragraphs have on the reader. Discuss, too, the kinds of evidence Emery uses to back up his points and whether, or to what degree, that evidence is convincing.

Discuss the justifications that the defenders of TV talk shows use to validate them. How does Emery contradict these justifications? Pay particular attention to paragraph 5 and bulleted item 1 in paragraph 8; paragraph 9 and bulleted item 3; and paragraphs 15 and 16.

▓ WRITING ASSIGNMENTS

1. Write an essay in which you compare and contrast two different talk shows that have similar subject matter. How else are the shows similar? How are they different? Do the personalities of the hosts make the shows similar or different? Were your reactions to the shows similar or different? How so?
2. Emery takes a rather dim view of TV talk shows, as do his main source, Vicki Abt, and TV critic Tom Shales, who labels the shows "the new pornography of our time" (paragraph 14). But David Hiltbrand, another TV critic, defends the shows, arguing that people watch them with a morally critical eye (14). Write an essay in which you support one of those points of view. Use specific examples to back up your points, and acknowledge the opposing point of view by showing how it's wrong.

The Ways We Lie   *1992*

STEPHANIE ERICSSON

The bank called today and I told them my deposit was in the mail, even   1
though I hadn't written a check yet. It'd been a rough day. The baby I'm pregnant with decided to do aerobics on my lungs for two hours, our three-year-old
daughter painted the living-room couch with lipstick, the IRS put me on hold
for an hour, and I was late to a business meeting because I was tired.

I told my client that traffic had been bad. When my partner came home, his   2
haggard face told me his day hadn't gone any better than mine, so when he asked,
"How was your day?" I said, "Oh, fine," knowing that one more straw might break
his back. A friend called and wanted to take me to lunch. I said I was busy. Four
lies in the course of a day, none of which I felt the least bit guilty about.

We lie. We all do. We exaggerate, we minimize, we avoid confrontation, we   3
spare people's feelings, we conveniently forget, we keep secrets, we justify lying to the big-guy institutions. Like most people, I indulge in small falsehoods
and still think of myself as an honest person. Sure I lie, but it doesn't hurt anything. Or does it?

I once tried going a whole week without telling a lie, and it was paralyzing.   4
I discovered that telling the truth all the time is nearly impossible. It means living with some serious consequences: The bank charges me $60 in overdraft
fees, my partner keels over when I tell him about my travails, my client fires me
for telling her I didn't feel like being on time, and my friend takes it personally
when I say I'm not hungry. There must be some merit to lying.

But if I justify lying, what makes me any different from slick politicians or   5
the corporate robbers who raided the S&L industry? Saying it's okay to lie one
way and not another is hedging. I cannot seem to escape the voice deep inside
me that tells me: When someone lies, someone loses.

What far-reaching consequences will I, or others, pay as a result of my lie?   6
Will someone's trust be destroyed? Will someone else pay *my* penance because
I ducked out? We must consider the *meaning of our actions*. Deception, lies,
capital crimes, and misdemeanors all carry meanings. *Webster's* definition of *lie*
is specific:

> 1: a false statement or action especially made with the intent to deceive; 2: any-
> thing that gives or is meant to give a false impression.

A definition like this implies that there are many, many ways to tell a lie.   7
Here are just a few.

The White Lie

A man who won't lie to a woman has very little consideration for her feelings.
                                                              —Bergen Evans

The white lie assumes that the truth will cause more damage than a sim-   8
ple, harmless untruth. Telling a friend he looks great when he looks like hell can

be based on a decision that the friend needs a compliment more than a frank opinion. But, in effect, it is the liar deciding what is best for the lied to. Ultimately, it is a vote of no confidence. It is an act of subtle arrogance for anyone to decide what is best for someone else.

Yet not all circumstances are quite so cut-and-dried. Take, for instance, the   9
sergeant in Vietnam who knew one of his men was killed in action but listed him as missing so that the man's family would receive indefinite compensation instead of the lump-sum pittance the military gives widows and children. His intent was honorable. Yet for twenty years this family kept their hopes alive, unable to move on to a new life.

Façades

Et tu, Brute?
    —Caesar

We all put up façades to one degree or another. When I put on a suit to go   10
to see a client, I feel as though I am putting on another face, obeying the expectation that serious businesspeople wear suits rather than sweatpants. But I'm a writer. Normally, I get up, get the kid off to school, and sit at my computer in my pajamas until four in the afternoon. When I answer the phone, the caller thinks I'm wearing a suit (though the UPS man knows better).

But façades can be destructive because they are used to seduce others into   11
an illusion. For instance, I recently realized that a former friend was a liar. He presented himself with all the right looks and the right words and offered lots of new consciousness theories, fabulous books to read, and fascinating insights. Then I did some business with him, and the time came for him to pay me. He turned out to be all talk and no walk. I heard a plethora of reasonable excuses, including in-depth descriptions of the big break around the corner. In six months of work, I saw less than a hundred bucks. When I confronted him, he raised both eyebrows and tried to convince me that I'd heard him wrong, that he'd made no commitment to me. A simple investigation into his past revealed a crowded graveyard of disenchanted former friends.

Ignoring the Plain Facts

Well, you must understand that Father Porter is only human. . . .
                    —A Massachusetts priest

In the '60s, the Catholic Church in Massachusetts began hearing com-   12
plaints that Father James Porter was sexually molesting children. Rather than relieving him of his duties, the ecclesiastical authorities simply moved him from one parish to another between 1960 and 1967, actually providing him with a fresh supply of unsuspecting families and innocent children to abuse. After treatment in 1967 for pedophilia, he went back to work, this time in Minnesota. The new diocese was aware of Father Porter's obsession with children, but they needed priests and recklessly believed treatment had cured him. More children were abused until he was relieved of his duties a year

later. By his own admission, Porter may have abused as many as a hundred children.

Ignoring the facts may not in and of itself be a form of lying, but consider   13
the context of this situation. If a lie is *a false action done with the intent to deceive,* then the Catholic Church's conscious covering for Porter created irreparable consequences. The church became a co-perpetrator with Porter.

Deflecting

When you have no basis for an argument, abuse the plaintiff.
> —Cicero

I've discovered that I can keep anyone from seeing the true me by being se-   14
lectively blatant. I set a precedent of being up-front about intimate issues, but I never bring up the things I truly want to hide; I just let people assume I'm revealing everything. It's an effective way of hiding.

Any good liar knows that the way to perpetuate an untruth is to deflect at-   15
tention from it. When Clarence Thomas exploded with accusations that the Senate hearings were a "high-tech lynching," he simply switched the focus from a highly charged subject to a radioactive subject. Rather than defending himself, he took the offensive and accused the country of racism. It was a brilliant maneuver. Racism is now politically incorrect in official circles—unlike sexual harassment, which still rewards those who can get away with it.

Some of the most skillful deflectors are passive-aggressive people who,   16
when accused of inappropriate behavior, refuse to respond to the accusations. This you-don't-exist stance infuriates the accuser, who, understandably, screams something obscene out of frustration. The trap is sprung and the act of deflection successful, because now the passive-aggressive person can indignantly say, "Who can talk to someone as unreasonable as you?" The real issue is forgotten and the sins of the original victim become the focus. Feeling guilty of namecalling, the victim is fully tamed and crawls into a hole, ashamed. I have watched this fighting technique work thousands of times in disputes between men and women, and what I've learned is that the real culprit is not necessarily the one who swears the loudest.

Omission

The cruelest lies are often told in silence.
> —R. L. Stevenson

Omission involves telling most of the truth minus one or two key facts   17
whose absence changes the story completely. You break a pair of glasses that are guaranteed under normal use and get a new pair, without mentioning that the first pair broke during a rowdy game of basketball. Who hasn't tried something like that? But what about omission of information that could make a difference in how a person lives his or her life?

For instance, one day I found out that rabbinical legends tell of another   18
woman in the Garden of Eden before Eve. I was stunned. The omission of the

Sumerian goddess Lilith from Genesis—as well as her demonization by ancient misogynists as an embodiment of female evil—felt like spiritual robbery. I felt like I'd just found out my mother was really my stepmother. To take seriously the tradition that Adam was created out of the same mud as his equal counterpart, Lilith, redefines all of Judeo-Christian history.

Some renegade Catholic feminists introduced me to a view of Lilith that   19
had been suppressed during the many centuries when this strong goddess was seen only as a spirit of evil. Lilith was a proud goddess who defied Adam's need to control her, attempted negotiations, and when this failed, said adios and left the Garden of Eden.

This omission of Lilith from the Bible was a patriarchal strategy to keep   20
women weak. Omitting the strong-woman archetype of Lilith from Western religions and starting the story with Eve the Rib has helped keep Christian and Jewish women believing they were the lesser sex for thousands of years.

Stereotypes and Clichés

Where opinion does not exist, the status quo becomes stereotyped and all originality is discouraged.

—Bertrand Russell

Stereotype and cliché serve a purpose as a form of shorthand. Our need for   21
vast amounts of information in nanoseconds has made the stereotype vital to modern communication. Unfortunately, it often shuts down original thinking, giving those hungry for the truth a candy bar of misinformation instead of a balanced meal. The stereotype explains a situation with just enough truth to seem unquestionable.

All the "isms"—racism, sexism, ageism, et al.—are founded on and fueled   22
by the stereotype and the cliché, which are lies of exaggeration, omission, and ignorance. They are always dangerous. They take a single tree and make it a landscape. They destroy curiosity. They close minds and separate people. The single mother on welfare is assumed to be cheating. Any black male could tell you how much of his identity is obliterated daily by stereotypes. Fat people, ugly people, beautiful people, old people, large-breasted women, short men, the mentally ill, and the homeless all could tell you how much more they are like us than we want to think. I once admitted to a group of people that I had a mouth like a truck driver. Much to my surprise, a man stood up and said, "I'm a truck driver, and I never cuss." Needless to say, I was humbled.

Groupthink

Who is more foolish, the child afraid of the dark, or the man afraid of the flight?
—Maurice Freehill

Irving Janis, in *Victims of Group Think*, defines this sort of lie as a psycho-   23
logical phenomenon within decision-making groups in which loyalty to the group has become more important than any other value, with the result that

dissent and the appraisal of alternatives are suppressed. If you've ever worked on a committee or in a corporation, you've encountered groupthink. It requires a combination of other forms of lying—ignoring facts, selective memory, omission, and denial, to name a few.

The textbook example of goupthink came on December 7, 1941. From as early as the fall of 1941, the warnings came in, one after another, that Japan was preparing for a massive military operation. The Navy command in Hawaii assumed Pearl Harbor was invulnerable—the Japanese weren't stupid enough to attack the United States' most important base. On the other hand, racist stereotypes said the Japanese weren't smart enough to invent a torpedo effective in less than 60 feet of water (the fleet was docked in 30 feet); after all, U.S. technology hadn't been able to do it.   24

On Friday, December 5, normal weekend leave was granted to all the commanders at Pearl Harbor, even though the Japanese consulate in Hawaii was busy burning papers. Within the tight, good-ole-boy cohesiveness of the U.S. command in Hawaii, the myth of invulnerability stayed well entrenched. No one in the group considered the alternatives. The rest is history.   25

Out-and-Out Lies

The only form of lying that is beyond reproach is lying for its own sake.
—Oscar Wilde

Of all the ways to lie, I like this one the best, probably because I get tired of trying to figure out the real meanings behind things. At least I can trust the bald-faced lie. I once asked my five-year-old nephew, "Who broke the fence?" (I had seen him do it.) He answered, "The murderers." Who could argue?   26

At least when this sort of lie is told it can be easily confronted. As the person who is lied to, I know where I stand. The bald-faced lie doesn't toy with my perceptions—it argues with them. It doesn't try to refashion reality, it tries to refute it. *Read my lips* . . . No sleight of hand. No guessing. If this were the only form of lying, there would be no such things as floating anxiety or the adult, children-of-alcoholics movement.   27

Dismissal

Pay no attention to that man behind the curtain! I am the Great Oz!
—The Wizard of Oz

Dismissal is perhaps the slipperiest of all lies. Dismissing feelings, perceptions, or even the raw facts of a situation ranks as a kind of lie that can do as much damage to a person as any other kind of lie.   28

The roots of many mental disorders can be traced back to the dismissal of reality. Imagine that a person is told from the time she is a tot that her perceptions are inaccurate. *"Mommy, I'm scared."* "No you're not, darling." *"I don't like that man next door, he makes me feel icky."* "Johnny, that's a terrible thing to say, of course you like him. You go over there right now and be nice to him."   29

I've often mused over the idea that madness is actually a sane reaction to an   30
insane world. Psychologist R. D. Laing supports this hypothesis in *Sanity, Madness and the Family,* an account of his investigations into the families of schizophrenics. The common thread that ran through all of the families he studied was a deliberate, staunch dismissal of the patient's perceptions from a very early age. Each of the patients started out with an accurate grasp of reality, which, through meticulous and methodical dismissal, was demolished until the only reality the patient could trust was catatonia.

Dismissal runs the gamut. Mild dismissal can be quite handy for forgiving   31
the foibles of others in our day-to-day lives. Toddlers who have just learned to manipulate their parents' attention sometimes are dismissed out of necessity. Absolute attention from the parents would require so much energy that no one would get to eat dinner. But we must be careful and attentive about how far we take our "necessary" dismissals. Dismissal is a dangerous tool, because it's nothing less than a lie.

Delusion

We lie loudest when we lie to ourselves.
> —Eric Hoffer

I could write the book on this one. Delusion, a cousin of dismissal, is the ten-   32
dency to see excuses as facts. It's a powerful lying tool because it filters out information that contradicts what we want to believe. Alcoholics who believe that the problems in their lives are legitimate reasons for drinking rather than results of the drinking offer the classic example of deluded thinking. Delusion uses the mind's ability to see things in myriad ways to support what it wants to be the truth.

But delusion is also a survival mechanism we all use. If we were to fully con-   33
template the consequences of our stockpiles of nuclear weapons or global warming, we could hardly function on a day-to-day level. We don't want to incorporate that much reality into our lives because to do so would be paralyzing.

Delusion acts as an adhesive to keep the status quo intact. It shamelessly   34
employs dismissal, omission, and amnesia, among other sorts of lies. Its most cunning defense is that it cannot see itself.

● ● ●

The liar's punishment . . . is that he cannot believe anyone else.
> —George Bernard Shaw

These are only a few of the ways we lie. Or are lied to. As I said earlier, it's   35
not easy to entirely eliminate lies from our lives. No matter how pious we may try to be, we will still embellish, hedge, and omit to lubricate the daily machinery of living. But there is a world of difference between telling functional lies and living a lie. Martin Buber once said, "The lie is the spirit committing treason against itself." Our acceptance of lies becomes a cultural cancer that eventually shrouds and reorders reality until moral garbage becomes as invisible to us as water is to a fish.

How much do we tolerate before we become sick and tired of being sick   36
and tired? When will we stand up and declare our *right* to trust? When do we
stop accepting that the real truth is in the fine print? Whose lips do we read this
year when we vote for president? When will we stop being so reticent about
making judgments? When do we stop turning over our personal power and responsibility to liars?

Maybe if I don't tell the bank the check's in the mail I'll be less tolerant of   37
the lies told me every day. A country song I once heard said it all for me: "You've
got to stand for something or you'll fall for anything."

RECORDING REFLECTIONS

In her essay, Ericsson defines 10 different kinds of lies. Briefly note in your
Reflection Log a single experience you have had with each kind of lie.

Choose one experience from your log, and write about it for 10 minutes.

ACTIVITIES FOR REREADING

1. As you reread, notice how Ericsson orders her list of lies. What is her strategy? What effect does she seek by ordering the lies in this particular way?
   Briefly explain your answers.
2. Notice that for each category of lie, Ericsson describes a reason such a lie
   may be told and then shows its negative consequences. For you, what is
   more compelling in each case: the rationale for lying or the rationale for
   telling the truth? Explain your opinion briefly in writing.
3. What is Ericsson's primary method of defining each kind of lie? Highlight
   each time she uses this method.

GROUP WORK

Personal Responses: Using your Reflection Logs as guides, have members
describe their own experiences with each kind of lie. Discuss both the rationale
that seemed to justify each lie at the time and the negative consequences the lie
could or did cause.

Objective Responses: Discuss Ericsson's strategy for ordering her essay. If
group members have come to different conclusions about her strategy, discuss
the differences. Discuss, too, the effect Ericsson creates by ordering the categories the way she does.

Using your notes, discuss which is stronger: the rationale for lying or the
rationale for telling the truth. Does the strength of each rationale change, depending on the type of lie or the particular circumstance? Discuss.

Discuss Ericsson's main method of definition. Are any of her illustrations
more illuminating or more convincing than others? If so, which ones? Why?
Discuss your answers.

◼ **WRITING ASSIGNMENTS**

  1. Write an essay in which you describe one or more experiences in which you lied or were lied to. In your discussion, describe each kind of lie, the reason for it, and its consequences, both positive and negative. Use as many specific examples as you can to illustrate your points.

  2. Write an essay in which you argue either that lying is sometimes necessary, no matter what the negative consequences, or that lying can never be justified, under any circumstances. Use practical examples so that your argument is not merely theoretical.

How Urban Myths Reveal Society's Fears   *1995*

NEAL GABLER

The story goes like this: During dinner at an opulent wedding reception, the groom rises from the head table and shushes the crowd. Everyone naturally assumes he is about to toast his bride and thank his guests. Instead, he solemnly announces that there has been a change of plan. He and his bride will be taking separate honeymoons and, when they return, the marriage will be annulled. The reason for this sudden turn of events, he says, is taped to the bottom of everyone's plate. The stunned guests quickly flip their dinnerware to discover a photo—of the bride *in flagrante* with the best man.

At least that is the story that has been recently making the rounds up and down the Eastern seaboard and as far west as Chicago. Did this really happen? A Washington Post reporter who tracked the story was told by one source that it happened at a New Hampshire hotel. But then another source swears it happened in Medford, Mass. Then again another suggests a banquet hall outside Schenectady, N.Y. Meanwhile, a sophisticated couple in Manhattan has heard it happened at the Pierre.

In short, the whole thing appears to be another urban myth, one of those weird tales that periodically catch the public imagination. Alligators swarming the sewers after people have flushed the baby reptiles down the toilet. The baby-sitter who gets threatening phone calls that turn out to be coming from inside the house. The woman who turns out to have a nest of black-widow spiders in her beehive hairdo. The man who falls asleep and awakens to find his kidney has been removed. The rat that gets deep-fried and served by a fast-food outlet. Or, in a variation, the mouse that has somehow drowned in a closed Coca-Cola bottle.

These tales are preposterous, but in a mass society like ours, where stories   4
are usually manufactured by Hollywood, they just may be the most genuine
form of folklore we have. Like traditional folklore, they are narratives crafted
by the collective consciousness. Like traditional folklore, they give expression
to the national mind. And like traditional folklore, they blend the fantastic with
the routine, if only to demonstrate, in the words of University of Utah folklorist
Jan Harold Brunvand, the nation's leading expert on urban legends, "that the
prosaic contemporary scene is capable of producing shocking or amazing
occurrences."

Shocking and amazing, yes. But in these stories, anything can happen not   5
because the world is a magical place rich with wonder—as in folk tales of
yore—but because our world is so utterly terrifying. Here, nothing is reliable
and no laws of morality govern. The alligators in the sewers presents an image
of an urban hell inhabited by beasts—an image that might have come directly
from Hades and the River Styx in Greek mythology. The baby-sitter and the
man upstairs exploits fears that we are not even safe in our own homes these
days. The spider in the hairdo says that even on our own persons, dangers lurk.
The man who loses his kidney plays to our fears of the night and the real bo-
gymen who prowl them. The mouse in the soda warns us of the perils of an impersonal mass-production society.

As for the wedding-reception tale, which one hacker on the Internet has   6
dubbed "Wedding Revenge," it may address the greatest terror of all: that love
and commitment are chimerical and even friendship is meaningless. These are
timeless issues, but the sudden promulgation of the tale suggests its special relevance in the age of AIDS, when commitment means even more than it used
to, and in the age of feminism, when some men are feeling increasingly threatened by women's freedom. Thus, the groom not only suffers betrayal and humiliation; his plight carries the hint of danger and emasculation, too. Surely, a
legend for our time.

Of course, folklore and fairy tales have long subsisted on terror, and even   7
the treacly cartoons of Walt Disney are actually, when you parse them, dark and
complex expressions of fear—from Snow White racing through the treacherous
forest to Pinnochio gobbled by the whale to Dumbo being separated from his
mother. But these crystallize the fears of childhood, the fears one must overcome to make the difficult transition to adulthood. Thus, the haunted forest of
the fairy tales is a trope for haunted adolescence; the witch or crone, a trope
for the spent generation one must vanquish to claim one's place in the world,
and the prince who comes to the rescue, a trope for the adult responsibilities
that the heroine must now assume.

Though urban legends frequently originate with college students about to   8
enter the real world, they are different from traditional fairy tales because their
terrors are not really obstacles on the road to understanding, and they are different from folklore because they cannot even be interpreted as cautionary. In urban legends, obstacles aren't overcome, perhaps can't be overcome, and there is

nothing we can do differently to avoid the consequences. The woman, not know-ing any better, eats the fried rat. The baby-sitter is terrorized by the stranger hid-ing in the house. The black widow bites the woman with the beehive hairdo. The alligators prowl the sewers. The marriage in Wedding Revenge breaks up.

It is not just our fears, then, that these stories exploit. Like so much else in   9
modern life—tabloids, exploitalk programs, real-life crime best-sellers—urban legends testify to an overwhelming condition of fear and to a sense of our own impotence within it. That is why there is no accommodation in these stories, no lesson or wisdom imparted. What there is, is the stark impression that our world is anomic. We live in a haunted forest of skyscrapers or of suburban lawns and ranch houses, but there is no one to exorcise the evil and no prince to break the spell.

Given the pressures of modern life, it isn't surprising that we have created   10
myths to express our malaise. But what is surprising is how many people seem committed to these myths. The Post reporter found people insisting they per-sonally knew someone who had attended the doomed wedding reception. Oth-ers went further: They maintained they had actually attended the reception—though no such reception ever took place. Yet even those who didn't claim to have been personally involved seemed to feel duty bound to assert the tale's plausibility.

Why this insistence? Perhaps the short answer is that people want to be-   11
lieve in a cosmology of dysfunction because it is the best way of explaining the inexplicable in our lives. A world in which alligators roam sewers and wedding receptions end in shock is at once terrifying and soothing—terrifying because these things happen, soothing because we are absolved of any responsibility for them. It is just the way it is.

But there may be an additional reason why some people seem so willing to   12
suspend their disbelief in the face of logic. This one has less to do with the con-tent of these tales than with their creation. However they start, urban legends rapidly enter a national conversation in which they are embellished, height-ened, reconfigured. Everyone can participate—from the people who spread the tale on talk radio to the people who discuss it on the Internet to the people who tell it to their neighbors. In effect, these legends are the product of a giant campfire around which we trade tales of terror.

If this makes each of us a co-creator of the tales, it also provides us with a   13
certain pride of authorship. Like all authors, we don't want to see the spell of our creation broken—especially when we have formed a little community around it. It doesn't matter whether these tales are true or not. What matters is that they plausibly reflect our world, that they have been generated from the grass roots and that we can pass them along.

In a way, then, these tales of powerlessness ultimately assert a kind of au-   14
thority. Urban legends permit us to become our own Stephen Kings, terroriz-ing ourselves to confirm one of the few powers we still possess: the power to tell stories about our world.

▓ **RECORDING REFLECTIONS**

In this essay, Gabler concludes that many of the preposterous stories we hear are urban myths, "the most genuine form of folklore we have." Think about that for a bit. Then, in your Reflection Log, list two or three unusual "true stories" that people have told you at one time or another.

Select one of those stories and write about it for 10 minutes, noting whether you believe it's true. Include two or three reasons for your opinion.

▓ **ACTIVITIES FOR REREADING**

1. Gabler compares and contrasts the fairy tales of our youth with the urban myths of our adulthood. As you reread this essay, list the major differences that you see between fairy tales and urban myths.
2. According to Gabler, people insist that urban myths are true for three primary reasons. List the reasons.
3. Traditional myths and urban myths share one feature: terror. In two or three sentences, describe the central difference between traditional myths and urban myths.

▓ **GROUP WORK**

Personal Responses: Using your Reflection Logs for reference, discuss the supposedly true stories that people have told you. During your discussion, try to determine if these stories are more like traditional fairy tales or urban myths.

Objective Responses: Discuss the differences that Gabler offers between fairy tales and urban myths. Pay particular attention to the age at which most people hear or read fairy tales versus urban myths. Would young children be more affected by urban myths than by fairy tales?

In paragraph 11, Gabler says, "It is just the way it is," meaning in this context that we have no responsibility for the inexplicable events in our lives. Discuss this notion in terms of the purposes of urban myths. Do you agree with Gabler that urban myths are the best way to explain the inexplicable?

Gabler says in the final paragraph that we still have "the power to tell stories about our world." Why would Gabler consider the ability to tell stories about our world a power? Do you agree with him?

▓ **WRITING ASSIGNMENTS**

1. Write an essay in which you explore in personal detail the comments that Gabler makes in paragraph 7, where he discusses the fears of childhood. What were your childhood fears? Describe three of those fears, and then tell how you overcame them.
2. Write an essay that discusses in detail what Gabler calls "the pressures of modern life" (paragraph 10). Note three pressures that modern life has put upon you, and explain how you are dealing with them. Offer enough detail to help the reader to understand the real effects of these pressures in *your life.*

The Revolt of the Black Bourgeoisie   *1994*

LEONCE GAITER

At a television network where I once worked, one of my bosses told me I al-   1
most didn't get hired because his superior had "reservations" about me. The job
had been offered under the network's Minority Advancement Program. I applied for the position because I knew I was exceptionally qualified. I would
have applied for the position regardless of how it was advertised.

After my interview, the head of the department told my boss I wasn't really   2
what he had in mind for a Minority Advancement Program job. To the department head, hiring a minority applicant meant hiring someone unqualified. He
wanted to hire some semiliterate, hoop-shooting former prison inmate. That, in
his view, was a "real" black person. That was someone worthy of the program.

I had previously been confronted by questions of black authenticity. At Har-   3
vard, where I graduated in 1980, a white classmate once said to me, "Oh, you're
not really a black person." I asked her to explain. She could not. She had known
few black people before college, but a lifetime of seeing black people depicted
in the American media had taught her that real black people talked a certain
way and were raised in certain places. In her world, black people did not attend
elite colleges. They could not stand as her intellectual equals or superiors. Any
African-American who shared her knowledge of Austen and Balzac—while having to explain to her who Douglass and Du Bois were—had to be *willed* away
for her to salvage her sense of superiority as a white person. Hence the accusation that I was "not really black."

But worse than the white majority harboring a one-dimensional vision of   4
blackness are the many blacks who embrace this stereotype as our true nature.
At the junior high school I attended in the mostly white Washington suburb of
Silver Spring, Md., a black girl once stopped me in the hallway and asked bel-
ligerently, "How come you talk so proper?" Astonished, I could only reply, "It's
proper*ly*," and walk on. This girl was asking why I spoke without the so-called
black accent pervasive in the lower socioeconomic strata of black society,
where exposure to mainstream society is limited. This girl was asking, Why
wasn't I impoverished and alienated? In her world view, a black male like me
couldn't exist.

Within the past year, however, there have been signs that blacks are openly   5
beginning to acknowledge the complex nature of our culture. Cornel West, a
professor of religion and the director of Afro-American Studies at Princeton
University, discusses the growing gulf between the black underclass and the
rest of black society in his book "Race Matters"; black voices have finally been
raised against the violence, misogyny and vulgarity marketed to black youth in
the form of gangsta rap; Ellis Cose's book "The Rage of a Privileged Class,"
which concentrates on the problems of middle- and upper-income blacks, was
excerpted as part of a Newsweek magazine cover story; Bill Cosby has become

a vocal crusader against the insulting depiction of African-Americans in "hip-hop generation" TV shows.

Yes, there are the beginnings of a new candor about our culture, but the question remains, How did one segment of the African-American community come to represent the whole? First, black society itself placed emphasis on that lower caste. This made sense because historically that's where the vast majority of us were placed; it's where American society and its laws were designed to keep us. Yet although doors have opened to us over the past 20 years, it is still commonplace for black leaders to insist on our community's uniform need for social welfare programs, inner-city services, job skills training, etc. Through such calls, what has passed for a black political agenda has been furthered only superficially; while affirmative action measures have forced an otherwise unwilling majority to open some doors for the black middle class, social welfare and Great Society-style programs aimed at the black lower class have shown few positive results.

According to 1990 census figures, between 1970 and 1990 the number of black families with incomes under $15,000 rose from 34.6 percent of the black population to 37 percent, while the number of black families with incomes of $35,000 to $50,000 rose from 13.9 percent to 15 percent of the population, and those with incomes of more than $50,000 rose from 9.9 percent to 14.5 percent of the black population.

Another reason the myth of an all-encompassing black underclass survives—despite the higher number of upper-income black families—is that it fits with a prevalent form of white liberalism, which is just as informed by racism as white conservatism. Since the early 70's, good guilt-liberal journalists and others warmed to the picture of black downtrodden masses in need of their help. Through the agency of good white people, blacks would rise. This image of African-Americans maintained the lifeline of white superiority that whites in this culture cling to, and therefore this image of blacks stuck. A strange tango was begun. Blacks seeking advancement opportunities allied themselves with whites eager to "help" them. However, those whites continued to see blacks as inferiors, victims, cases, and not as equals, individuals or, heaven forbid, competitors.

It was hammered into the African-American psyche by media-appointed black leaders and the white media that it was essential to our political progress to stay or seem to stay economically and socially deprived. To be recognized and recognize oneself as middle or upper class was to threaten the political progress of black people. That girl who asked why I spoke so "proper" was accusing me of political sins—of thwarting the progress of our race.

Despite progress toward a more balanced picture of black America, the image of black society as an underclass remains strong. Look at local news coverage of the trial of Damian Williams and Henry Watson, charged with beating the white truck driver Reginald Denny during the 1992 South-Central L.A. riots. The press showed us an African-print-wearing cadre of Williams and Watson supporters trailing Edi M. O. Faal, Williams's defense attorney, like a Greek chorus. This chorus made a point of standing in the camera's range. They presented themselves as the voice of South-Central L.A., the voice of the oppressed, the voice of the downtrodden, the voice of the city's black people.

To anyone watching TV coverage of the trial, all blacks agreed with Faal's contention that his clients were prosecuted so aggressively because they are black. Period. Reporters made no effort to show opposing black viewpoints. (In fact, the media portrait of the Los Angeles riot as blacks vs. whites and Koreans was a misrepresentation. According to the Rand Corporation, a research institute in Santa Monica, blacks made up 36 percent of those arrested during the riot; Latinos made up 51 percent.) The black bourgeoisie and intelligentsia remained largely silent. We had too long believed that to express disagreement with the "official line" was to be a traitor.   11

TV networks and cable companies gain media raves for programs like "Laurel Avenue," an HBO melodrama about a working-class black family lauded for its realism, a real black family complete with drug dealers, drug users, gun toters and basketball players. It is akin to the media presenting "Valley of the Dolls" as a realistic portrayal of the ways of white women.   12

The Fox network offers a differing but equally misleading portrait of black Americans, with "Martin." While blue humor has long been a staple of black audiences, it was relegated to clubs and records for *mature* black audiences. It was not peddled to kids or to the masses.   13

Now the blue humor tradition is piped to principally white audiences. If TV was as black as it is white—if there was a fair share of black love stories, black dramas, black detective heroes—these blue humor images would not be a problem. Right now, however, they stand as images to which whites can condescend.   14

Imagine being told by your peers, the records you hear, the programs you watch, the "leaders" you see on TV, classmates, prospective employers—imagine being told by virtually everyone that in order to be your true self you must be ignorant and poor, or at least seem so.   15

Blacks must now see to it that our children face no such burden. We must see to it that the white majority, along with vocal minorities within the black community (generally those with a self-serving political agenda), do not perpetuate the notion that African-Americans are invariably doomed to the underclass.   16

African-Americans are moving toward seeing ourselves—and demanding that others see us—as individuals, not as shards of a degraded monolith. The American ideal places primacy on the rights of the individual, yet historically African-Americans have been denied those rights. We blacks can effectively demand those rights, effectively demand justice only when each of us sees him or herself as an individual with the right to any of the opinions, idiosyncrasies and talents accorded any other American.   17

RECORDING REFLECTIONS

In this essay, Gaiter recounts various times he was nearly rejected or discounted because he didn't fit the popular stereotype of an African American. In your Reflection Log, list experiences you have had in which you have been unfairly judged or misunderstood.

Then, choose one experience from your list and explore it in writing for 10 minutes.

ACTIVITIES FOR REREADING

1. Among other things, Gaiter attempts in his essay to explain why the stereotype of the African American as illiterate and impoverished is so insistent and pervasive in American culture—among blacks and whites. As you read, list what Gaiter offers as causes for this phenomenon. Then, after you have finished reading, consider which causes are short term and immediate versus long term and ingrained.

2. Consider the evidence that Gaiter uses to back up his points. As you read, highlight his evidence. When you have finished, write about whether or not you find his evidence convincing, and why.

3. Stop and reread—several times, if necessary—paragraph 7. What impression do you get from these statistics during your first reading? How about during your second reading? Does your opinion of this evidence change on subsequent readings? Why or why not? Jot down your observations.

GROUP WORK

Personal Responses: Compare and discuss your experiences of being misunderstood or misjudged. Did any of your experiences result from your not fulfilling someone's preconceived notion of you? Can you extend the meaning of your personal experiences to a larger issue, like Gaiter does in the essay?

Objective Responses: According to Gaiter, what perpetuates the black stereotype? Using your Reflection Logs as guides, see if you can agree on and then list the short-term and long-term causes of the stereotype.

Discuss the evidence Gaiter presents and how well it supports his argument. Do you think he's convincing? Why or why not? List your reasons.

Discuss your reading of paragraph 7. Do the statistics Gaiter offers sufficiently support his point? Why or why not? List your reasons.

Discuss stereotypes of other racial/ethnic groups seen in the popular media. Are any as pervasive and distorting as those of blacks? Is it more dangerous or offensive to stereotype one group than another? Why or why not? Discuss.

Consider Gaiter's conclusion. Does he offer any realistic hope or practical solution to the problem he has posed? Explain.

WRITING ASSIGNMENTS

1. Write an essay in which you describe one or more incidences in your life when you were misjudged or misunderstood because you didn't match someone's preconceived notion of you. How did you react, feel, and think? In retrospect, what were the larger issues? Why?

2. Choose any stereotype—perhaps racial, sexual, or professional—and examine how it is portrayed by various TV shows. How are the portrayals

alike? How are they different? How is each of them biased and therefore degrading? What are the dangers of this particular stereotype? Is there anything positive about how the stereotype oversimplifies the matter? Make sure to write a clear thesis and provide ample evidence.

Why Men Marry   *1986*

GEORGE GILDER

Men marry for love. But what does this mean beyond what they got in their lives as single men: the flash of a new face, new flesh across a room. The glimpse of breasts shifting softly in a silken blouse. The open sesame of a missing ring. The excited pursuit, the misunderstood meanings, the charged meetings. The telling touch of hands. The eyes welling open to the gaze. The scent of surrender. The pillowed splash of unbound hair. The ecstatic slipping between new sheets. The race. The winning. The chase and the conquest . . . and back on the road. Definitely back on the road. Free again. Strong again. For new women, new pursuit. What more is there in life—in love—than this?

Marriage means giving it all up. Giving up love? That is how it seems to the single man, and that is why he fears it. He must give up his hunter's heart, forgo the getaway Honda growl, shear off his shaggy hair, restrict his random eye, hang up his handgun, bow down and enter the cage. At bottom, what he is is hunter. No way he will be hubby.

And yet, he will. For years he lunges at women's surfaces, but as time passes he learns of a deeper promise. For years he may not know the reasons or believe them or care. The heart, it is said, has its reasons. They spring from the primal predicament of man throughout the history of the race: the need to choose a particular woman and stay by her and provide for her if he is to know his children and they are to love him and call him father.

In procreative love, both partners consciously or unconsciously glimpse a future infant—precarious in the womb, vulnerable in the world, and in need of nurture and protection. In the swelter of their bodies together, in the shape and softnesses of the woman, in the protective support of the man, the couple senses the outlines of a realm that can endure and perpetuate their union: a pattern of differences and complements that goes beyond the momentary pleasures of reciprocal sex.

Marriage asks men to give up their essential sexuality only as part of a clear scheme for replacing it with new, far more important, and ultimately far more sexual roles: husband and father. Without these roles, a woman can bear a child, but the man is able only to screw. He can do it a lot, but after his first years it will only get him unthreaded, and in the end he is disconnected and alone. In his shallow heats and frustrations, he all too often becomes a menace to himself and his community.

There are millions of single men, unlinked to any promising reality, dissipating their lives by the years, moving from job to job, woman to woman, illusion to embitterment. Yet they are not hopeless. Many more millions have passed through the same sloughs, incurred the same boozy dreams, marijuana highs, cocaine crashes, sex diseases, job vapors, legal scrapes, wanderings. They follow the entire syndrome and then break out of it. Normally they do not escape through psychiatrists' offices, sex-education courses, VISTA or Peace Corps programs, reformatories, or guidance-counseling uplift. What happens, most of the time—the only effective thing that happens, the only process that reaches the sources of motivation and character—is falling in love.

Love is effective because it works at a deeper, more instinctual level than the other modes of education and change. Love does not teach or persuade. It possesses and transforms. . . .

It is not just an intelligent appraisal of his circumstances that transforms the single man. It is not merely a desire for companionship or "growth." It is a deeper alchemy of change, flowing from a primal source. It seeps slowly into the flesh, the memory, the spirit; it rises through a life, until it can ignite. It is a perilous process, full of chances for misfire and mistake—or for an ever more mildewed middle age. It is not entirely understood. But we have seen it work, and so have we seen love. Love infuses reason and experience with the power to change a man caught in a morbid present into a man passionately engaged with the future.

The change that leads to love often comes slowly. Many of the girls a man finds will not help. They tend to go along with him and affirm his single life. But one morning he turns to the stranger sleeping next to him, who came to him as easily as a whiskey too many, and left him as heavy-headed, and decides he must seek a better way to live. One day he looks across the room over a pile of dirty dishes and cigarette butts and beer cans and sex magazines and bills and filthy laundry, and he does not see the evidence of happy carousing and bachelor freedom; he sees a trap closing in upon him more grimly than any marriage. One day while joking with friends about the latest of his acquaintances to be caught and caged, he silently wonders, for a moment, whether he really wishes it were he.

Suddenly he has a new glimpse of himself. His body is beginning to decline, grow weaker and slower, even if he keeps it fit. His body, which once measured out his few advantages over females, is beginning to intimate its terrible plan to become as weak as an older woman's. His aggressiveness, which burst in fitful storms throughout his young life but never seemed to cleanse him—his aggression for which he could so rarely find the adequate battle, the harmonious chase—is souring now. His job, so below his measure as a man, so out of tune with his body and his inspiration, now stretches ahead without joy or relief.

His sex, the force that drove the flower of his youth, drives still, drives again and again the same hard bargain—for which there are fewer and fewer takers, in a sexual arena with no final achievement for the single man, in which sex it-self becomes work that is never done.

The single man is caught on a reef and the tide is running out. He is being biologically stranded and he has a hopeless dream. Studs Terkel's book *Working* registers again and again men's desire to be remembered. Yet who in this world is much remembered for his job?   12

Stuck with what he may sense as a choice between being trapped and being stranded, he still may respond by trying one more fling. The biological predicament can be warded off for a time, like Hemingway's hyena. Death often appears in the guise of eternal youth, at the ever-infatuating fountains: alcohol, drugs, hallucinogenic sex. For a while he may believe in the disguise. But the hyena returns and there is mortality in the air—diseases, accidents, concealed suicides, the whole range of the single man's aggression, turned at last against himself.   13

But where there is death, there is hope. For the man who is in touch with his mortality, but not in the grips of it, is also in touch with the sources of his love. He is in contact with the elements—the natural fires and storms so often used as metaphors for his passions. He is a man who can be deeply and effectively changed. He can find his age, his relation to the world, his maturity, his future. He can burn his signature into the covenant of a specific life.   14

The man has found a vital energy and a possibility of durable change. It has assumed the shape of a woman. It is the same form that has caught his eye and roiled his body all these years. But now there will be depths below the pleasing surfaces, meanings beyond the momentary ruttings. There will be a sense that this vessel contains the secrets of new life, that the womb and breasts bear a message of immortality. There will be a knowledge that to treat this treasure as an object—mere flesh like his own, a mere matrix of his pleasure—is to defile life itself. It is this recognition that she offers a higher possibility—it is this consciousness that he has to struggle to be worthy of her—that finally issues the spark. And then arises the fire that purges and changes him as it consumes his own death. His children . . . they will remember. It is the only hope.   15

The man's love begins in a knowledge of inferiority, but it offers a promise of dignity and purpose. For he then has to create, by dint of his own effort, and without the miracle of a womb, a life that a woman could choose. Thus are released and formed the energies of civilized society. He provides, and he does it for a lifetime, for a life.   16

RECORDING REFLECTIONS

In this essay, Gilder represents a man's transition from the single to the married state as transformational and civilizing. As you read, list the transitional events in your own life that have proved significant.

Choose one of those events and write for 10 minutes, exploring the ways you have changed because of that transitional event.

■ **ACTIVITIES FOR REREADING**

1. According to Gilder, what forces pull men from single to married life? List them as you reread.
2. Gilder compares a single man to a hunter. Highlight the words and phrases he uses to make this comparison. In two or three sentences, comment on how this language reinforces the idea that a bachelor is a savage waiting to be domesticated.
3. Reread paragraphs 9 and 10 extra carefully. How accurate is Gilder's portrayal of the bachelor's life? How much does he rely on clichés?

■ **GROUP WORK**

Personal Responses: Using your Reflection Logs to jog your memories, discuss some of your own transitional life experiences. Can they be analyzed as neatly as Gilder has explained the transformation of the swinging bachelor?

Objective Responses: Determine the forces that compel many men to get married. Discuss the validity and effectiveness of Gilder's comparing a bachelor to a hunter. Discuss how accurately Gilder portrays a single man's life.

What is the effect of Gilder's use of the word *hubby* at the end of paragraph 2?

What, precisely, does Gilder mean by the last sentence in paragraph 5: "In his shallow heats and frustrations, he all too often becomes a menace to himself and his community"? Does Gilder offer any examples to explain this statement?

What, if anything, does Gilder imply about marriages that don't result in children?

■ **WRITING ASSIGNMENTS**

1. Write an essay that describes a transformational experience in your own life. Describe what events led up to and helped cause the experience. Reflect on the significance of the transformation.
2. Write an essay in which you agree with or refute either Gilder's portrayal of a man's single life or his idea that marriage is a civilizing force. Use specific examples to back up your contentions.

Becoming Desensitized to Hate Words   *1995*

ELLEN GOODMAN

The ceremonies are over, but I would like to suggest one last way to commemorate the golden anniversary of the defeat of the Nazis. How about a moratorium on the current abuse of terms like storm trooper, swastika, Holocaust, Gestapo, Hitler? How about putting the language of the Third Reich into mothballs?

The further we are removed from the defeat of the Nazis, the more this vocabulary seems to be taking over our own. It's become part of the casual, ubiquitous, inflammatory speech Americans use to turn each other into monsters. Which, if I recall correctly, was a tactic favored by Goebbels himself. 2

The NRA attacked federal agents as "jackbooted government thugs" who wear "Nazi bucket helmets and black storm trooper uniforms." In the ratcheting up of the rhetorical wars, it wasn't enough for the NRA to complain that the agents had overstepped their bounds; they had to call them Nazis. 3

Twice more in recent days, Republican congressmen have compared environmentalist agencies with Hitler's troops. On May 16, Pennsylvania's Bud Shuster talked about EPA officials as an "environmental Gestapo." Before that, Missouri's Bill Emerson warned about the establishment of an "eco-Gestapo force." 4

On the Democratic side, Sen. John Kerry recently suggested that a proposed new kind of tax audit, on "lifestyles," would produce an "IRS Gestapo-like entity." And John Lewis and Charles Rangel compared silence in the face of the new conservative agenda to silence in the early days of the Third Reich. They didn't just disagree with conservatives; they Nazified them. 5

Then there are the perennial entries on the Hitler log. Anti-abortion groups talk about the abortion holocaust—comparing the fetuses to Jews and the doctors to Mengele. 6

Much of the time, the hurling of "Nazi" names is just plain dumb. As dumb as the behavior of punk groups, who think they can illustrate their devotion to anarchism with symbols of fascism. Singers like Sid Vicious, groups like the Dead Boys once sported swastikas without realizing that in Hitler's time and place, they would have been rounded up as enemies of the Reich. 7

As for pinning the Nazi label on the supporters of abortion rights, the propagandists surely know that Hitler was a hardline opponent of abortion. (Did that make him pro-life?) In "Mein Kampf" he wrote, "We must also do away with the conception that the treatment of the body is the affair of every individual." A woman's body wasn't hers; it belonged to the state. 8

Even when Nazi-speak is not historically dumb, it's rhetorically dumb. The Hitlerian language has become an indiscriminate shorthand for every petty tyranny. 9

In this vocabulary, every two-bit boss becomes a "little Hitler." Every domineering high school principal is accused of running a "concentration camp." Every overbearing piece of behavior becomes a "Gestapo" tactic. And every political disagreement becomes a fight against evil. 10

Crying Hitler in our time is like crying wolf. The charge immediately escalates the argument, adding verbal fuel to fires of any dimension, however minor. But eventually, yelling Nazi at environmentalists and Gestapo at federal agents diminishes the emotional power of these words should we need them. 11

In time, these epithets even downgrade the horror of the Third Reich and the immensity of World War II. They cheapen history and insult memory, especially the memory of the survivors. 12

It's one reason George Bush was so quick to take offense at the NRA's Nazi- 13
isms. As a veteran of World War II, he still knows a Nazi when he sees one and
knows the difference between the Gestapo and a federal agent.

Exactly 50 years ago this spring, his generation liberated the concentration 14
camps. Americans learned then, with a fresh sense of horror, about the crema-
toriums, about man's inhumanity, about the trains that ran on time to the gas
chambers.

This was Nazism. This was the Gestapo. This was the Holocaust. This was 15
Hitler. If you please, save the real words for the real thing.

■ RECORDING REFLECTIONS

In this essay, Goodman strongly protests against using words and phrases
that have historical meanings many current users are unaware of. In your Reflection Log, list words and phrases you have heard others use to describe people in critical or negative ways.

After making your list, pick three terms and use each in a sentence that
clearly illustrates its meaning.

■ ACTIVITIES FOR REREADING

1. Goodman's main strategy in this essay is comparison/contrast; that is,
   she compares how a word or phrase was used historically with how it is
   used today. As you reread "Becoming Desensitized to Hate Words," list
   her comparisons. For example, she notes that some people have compared Gestapo troops and federal agents. How does her strategy of comparing help readers understand the essay? Answer in no more than three
   sentences.
2. It's been said that this essay moves back and forth in time—from the past
   to the present and then back to the past. Highlight elements of the essay
   that show whether this statement is true.
3. Goodman's tone in this essay can be described in several ways. What attitude does she have toward her topic? Copy three sentences from the essay
   that illustrate her tone. Is she concerned about how people misuse these
   words and phrases?

■ GROUP WORK

Personal Responses: Using information from your Reflection Logs, discuss
your own experiences with namecalling, not including profanity. What names
have you been called? What names have you called others? Discuss what effects namecalling has on the people who are labeled. What effects is it expected to have?

Objective Responses: Discuss Goodman's awareness of history as it pertains
to the essay. Referring to your notes, share examples from the essay that illustrate Goodman's knowledge of her topic.

In paragraph 8, Goodman mentions Hitler's views on abortion and women's control over their own bodies. Why did she choose this particular example to illustrate her main point?

Goodman wants people to stop using Nazi-related language because she believes it sets a dangerous precedent. What concerns her the most about using such language? What evidence supports your conclusion?

WRITING ASSIGNMENTS

1. More than likely, you have had the regrettable experience of losing your temper and making statements that you later wished you could take back. In an essay, describe the experience and the statements that you made. Then offer evidence as to why your comments were really deserved or not deserved.

2. In an essay containing at least three examples from movies, radio, or television, show how the media affects our use of language. To do some quick research, listen or read carefully to find examples of how words and phrases are used in ways that reduce or destroy their meanings.

Crack and the Box   *1996*

PETE HAMILL

One sad rainy morning last winter, I talked to a woman who was addicted   1
to crack cocaine. She was twenty-two, stiletto-thin, with eyes as old as tombs. She was living in two rooms in a welfare hotel with her children, who were two, three, and five years of age. Her story was the usual tangle of human woe: early pregnancy, dropping out of school, vanished men, smack and then crack, tricks with johns in parked cars to pay for the dope. I asked her why she did drugs. She shrugged in an empty way and couldn't really answer beyond "makes me feel good." While we talked and she told her tale of squalor, the children ignored us. They were watching television.

Walking back to my office in the rain, I brooded about the woman, her   2
zombielike children, and my own callous indifference. I'd heard so many versions of the same story that I almost never wrote them anymore; the sons of similar women, glimpsed a dozen years ago, are now in Dannemora or Soledad or Joliet; in a hundred cities, their daughters are moving into the same loveless rooms. As I walked, a series of homeless men approached me for change, most of them junkies. Others sat in doorways, staring at nothing. They were additional casualties of our time of plague, demoralized reminders that although this country holds only 2 percent of the world's population, it consumes 65 percent of the world's supply of hard drugs.

Why, for God's sake? Why do so many millions of Americans of all ages, races, and classes choose to spend all or part of their lives stupefied? I've talked to hundreds of addicts over the years; some were my friends. But none could give sensible answers. They stutter about the pain of the world, about despair or boredom, the urgent need for magic or pleasure in a society empty of both. But then they just shrug. Americans have the money to buy drugs; the supply is plentiful. But almost nobody in power asks, *Why?* . . .

And then, on that rainy morning in New York, I saw another one of those ragged men staring out at the rain from a doorway. I suddenly remembered the inert postures of the children in that welfare hotel, and I thought: *television.*

Ah, no, I muttered to myself: too simple. Something as complicated as drug addiction can't be blamed on television. Come on. . . . but I remembered all those desperate places I'd visited as a reporter, where there were no books and a TV set was always playing and the older kids had gone off somewhere to shoot smack, except for the kid who was at the mortuary in a coffin. I also remembered when I was a boy in the forties and early fifties, and drugs were a minor sideshow, a kind of dark little rumor. And there was one major difference between that time and this: television.

We had unemployment then; illiteracy, poor living conditions, racism, governmental stupidity, a gap between rich and poor. We didn't have the all-consuming presence of television in our lives. Now two generations of Americans have grown up with television from their earliest moments of consciousness. Those same American generations are afflicted by the pox of drug addiction.

Only thirty-five years ago, drug addiction was not a major problem in this country. There were drug addicts. We had some at the end of the nineteenth century, hooked on the cocaine in patent medicines. During the placid fifties, Commissioner Harry Anslinger pumped up the budget of the old Bureau of Narcotics with fantasies of reefer madness. Heroin was sold and used in most major American cities, while the bebop generation of jazz musicians got jammed up with horse.

But until the early sixties, narcotics were still marginal to American life; they weren't the $120-billion market they make up today. If anything, those years have an eerie innocence. In 1955 there were 31,700,000 TV sets in use in the country (the number is now past 184 million). But the majority of the audience had grown up without the dazzling new medium. They embraced it, were diverted by it, perhaps even loved it, but they weren't *formed* by it. That year, the New York police made a mere 1,234 felony drug arrests; in 1988 it was 43,901. They confiscated ninety-seven *ounces* of cocaine for the entire year; last year it was hundreds of pounds. During each year of the fifties in New York, there were only about a hundred narcotics-related deaths. But by the end of the sixties, when the first generation of children *formed* by television had come to maturity (and thus to the marketplace), the number of such deaths had risen to 1,200. The same phenomenon was true in every major American city.

In the last Nielsen survey of American viewers, the average family was   9
watching television seven hours a day. This has never happened before in history. No people has ever been entertained for seven hours a *day*. The Eliza-
bethans didn't go to the theater seven hours a day. The pre-TV generation did
not go to the movies seven hours a day. Common sense tells us that this all-
pervasive diet of instant imagery, sustained now for forty years, must have
changed us in profound ways.

Television, like drugs, dominates the lives of its addicts. And though some   10
lonely Americans leave their sets on without watching them, using them as
electronic companions, television usually absorbs its viewers the way drugs ab-
sorb their users. Viewers can't work or play while watching television; they can't
read; they can't be out on the streets, falling in love with the wrong people,
learning how to quarrel and compromise with other human beings. In short
they are asocial. So are drug addicts.

One Michigan State University study in the early eighties offered a group   11
of four- and five-year-olds the choice of giving up television or giving up their
fathers. Fully one third said they would give up Daddy. Given a similar choice
(between cocaine or heroin and father, mother, brother, sister, wife, husband,
children, job), almost every stoned junkie would do the same.

There are other disturbing similarities. Television itself is a consciousness-   12
altering instrument. With the touch of a button, it takes you out of the "real"
world in which you reside and can place you at a basketball game, the back alleys of Miami, the streets of Bucharest, or the cartoony living rooms of Sitcom
Land. Each move from channel to channel alters mood, usually with music or
a laugh track. On any given evening, you can laugh, be frightened, feel tension,
thump with excitement. You can even tune in *MacNeil/Lehrer* and feel sober.

But none of these abrupt shifts in mood is *earned*. They are attained as eas-   13
ily as popping a pill. Getting news from television, for example, is simply not
the same experience as reading it in a newspaper. Reading is *active*. The reader
must decode little symbols called words, then create images or ideas and make
them connect; at its most basic level, reading is an act of the imagination. But
the television viewer doesn't go through that process. The words are spoken to
him by Dan Rather or Tom Brokaw or Peter Jennings. There isn't much de-
coding to do when watching television, no time to think or ponder before the
next set of images and spoken words appears to displace the present one. The
reader, being active, works at his or her own pace; the viewer, being passive,
proceeds at a pace determined by the show. Except at the highest levels, television never demands that its audience take part in an act of imagination. Reading always does.

In short, television works on the same imaginative and intellectual level as   14
psychoactive drugs. If prolonged television viewing makes the young passive
(dozens of studies indicate that it does), then moving to drugs has a certain coherence. Drugs provide an unearned high (in contrast to the earned rush that
comes from a feat accomplished, a human breakthrough earned by sweat or
thought or love).

And because the television addict and the drug addict are alienated from the hard and scary world, they also feel they make no difference in its complicated events. For the junkie, the world is reduced to him and the needle, pipe, or vial; the self is absolutely isolated, with no desire for choice. The television addict lives the same way. Many Americans who fail to vote in presidential elections must believe they have no more control over such a choice than they do over the casting of *L.A. Law*. 15

The drug plague also coincides with the unspoken assumption of most television shows: Life should be *easy*. The most complicated events are summarized on TV news in a minute or less. Cops confront murder, chase the criminals, and bring them to justice (usually violently) within an hour. In commercials, you drink the right beer and you get the girl. *Easy!* So why should real life be a grind? Why should any American have to spend years mastering a skill or a craft, or work eight hours a day at an unpleasant job, or endure the compromises and crises of a marriage? Nobody *works* on television (except cops, doctors, and lawyers). Love stories on television are about falling in love or breaking up; the long, steady growth of a marriage—its essential *dailiness*—is seldom explored, except as comedy. Life on television is almost always simple: good guys and bad, nice girls and whores, smart guys and dumb. And if life in the real world isn't that simple, well, hey, man, have some dope, man, be happy, feel good. 16

The doper always whines about how he *feels;* drugs are used to enhance his feelings or obliterate them, and in this the doper is very American. No other people on earth spend so much time talking about their feelings; hundreds of thousands go to shrinks, they buy self-help books by the millions, they pour out intimate confessions to virtual strangers in bars or discos. Our political campaigns are about emotional issues now, stated in the simplicities of adolescence. Even alleged statesmen can start a sentence, "I feel that the Sandinistas should . . . " when they once might have said, "I *think*. . . . " I'm convinced that this exaltation of cheap emotions over logic and reason is one by-product of hundreds of thousands of hours of television. 17

Most Americans under the age of fifty have now spent their lives absorbing television; that is, they've had the structures of drama pounded into them. Drama is always about conflict. So news shows, politics, and advertising are now all shaped by those structures. Nobody will pay attention to anything as complicated as the part played by Third World debt in the expanding production of cocaine; it's much easier to focus on Manuel Noriega, a character right out of *Miami Vice,* and believe that even in real life there's a Mister Big. 18

What is to be done? Television is certainly not going away, but its addictive qualities can be controlled. It's a lot easier to "just say no" to television than to heroin or crack. As a beginning, parents must take immediate control of the sets, teaching children to watch specific television *programs*, not "television," to get out of the house and play with other kids. Elementary and high schools must begin teaching television as a subject, the way literature is taught, showing children how shows are made, how to distinguish between the true and the 19 false, how to recognize cheap emotional manipulation. All Americans should spend more time reading. And thinking.

For years, the defenders of television have argued that the networks are only giving the people what they want. That might be true. But so is the Medellín cartel.

20

RECORDING REFLECTIONS

In one section of his essay, Hamill describes the differences between television viewing and reading. As you read the essay, mark those passages.

After reading the essay, go back to those passages, reread them, and then write for 10 minutes about your own thoughts on reading versus watching television. Be as specific as you can.

ACTIVITIES FOR REREADING

1. As you reread, circle the slang that Hamill uses. What effect does he create by using street language in what is otherwise a formal essay? Jot down your answers.
2. Pay close attention to paragraphs 14–18 as you reread. Note whether you think each of Hamill's comparisons between watching television and doing drugs is valid and why.
3. After rereading the entire essay, write down the reasons you think Hamill's conclusion (paragraphs 19–20) is strong or weak.

GROUP WORK

Personal Responses: Refer to your Reflection Logs and discuss your personal thoughts on reading versus watching television. If your views differ, discuss the reasons for the differences.

Objective Responses: Compare your lists of the slang terms Hamill uses. How does he use slang? What does he refer to, in most cases? Discuss why you think Hamill uses slang and what effect he strives for. Does he achieve his intended effect? Discuss.

Discuss your opinions about the comparisons Hamill makes between television watching and drug taking in paragraphs 15–19. If your opinions differ, discuss why. Jot down the reasons for these differences of opinion.

Discuss the effectiveness of Hamill's conclusion. How strong a case does he make in the body of the essay that television watching is the cause of the U.S. drug plague?

WRITING ASSIGNMENTS

1. Use one or more of Hamill's distinctions between reading and television viewing (paragraph 13) to construct an essay in which you compare the two for yourself. Compare and contrast the contents of two different media presentations of one story or event—say, a newspaper story versus a report on

the television news or a novel or short story versus a television portrayal of that story. Also compare and contrast the experiences of reading about something versus having it portrayed for you.

2. Write an essay in which you examine your own television-viewing habits. What do you watch and why? How engaged or stimulated is your mind while you watch? In terms of the mental activity involved, is television viewing different from reading a book, news article, or textbook? How? Why? Be sure to control your essay with a strong thesis statement.

Why One Peaceful Woman Carries a Pistol   *1991*

LINDA M. HASSELSTROM

I'm a peace-loving woman. I also carry a pistol. For years, I've written about my decision in an effort to help other women make intelligent choices about gun ownership, but editors rejected the articles. Between 1983 and 1986, however, when gun sales to men held steady, gun ownership among women rose fifty-three percent, to more than twelve million. We learned that any female over the age of twelve can expect to be criminally assaulted some time in her life, that women aged thirty have a fifty-fifty chance of being raped, robbed, or attacked, and that many police officials say flatly that they cannot protect citizens from crime. During the same period, the number of women considering gun ownership quadrupled to nearly two million. Manufacturers began showing lightweight weapons with small grips, and purses with built-in holsters. A new magazine is called *Guns and Women,* and more than eight thousand copies of the video *A Woman's Guide to Firearms* were sold by 1988. Experts say female gun buyers are not limited to any particular age group, profession, social class, or area of the country, and most are buying guns to protect themselves. Shooting instructors say women view guns with more caution than do men, and may make better shots. 1

I decided to buy a handgun for several reasons. During one four-year period, I drove more than a hundred thousand miles alone, giving speeches, readings, and workshops. A woman is advised, usually by men, to protect herself by avoiding bars, by approaching her car like an Indian scout, by locking doors and windows. But these precautions aren't always enough. And the logic angers me: *Because* I am female, it is my responsibility to be extra careful. 2

As a responsible environmentalist, I choose to recycle, avoid chemicals on my land, minimize waste. As an informed woman alone, I choose to be as responsible for my own safety as possible: I keep my car running well, use caution in where I go and what I do. And I learned about self-protection—not an easy or quick decision. I developed a strategy of protection that includes 3 handgun possession. The following incidents, chosen from a larger number because I think they could happen to anyone, helped make up my mind.

When I camped with another woman for several weeks, she didn't want to carry a pistol, and police told us Mace was illegal. We tucked spray deodorant into our sleeping bags, theorizing that any man crawling into our tent at night would be nervous anyway; anything sprayed in his face would slow him down until we could hit him with a frying pan, or escape. We never used our improvised weapon, because we were lucky enough to camp beside people who came to our aid when we needed them. I returned from that trip determined to reconsider.   4

At that time, I lived alone and taught night classes in town. Along a city street I often traveled, a woman had a flat tire, called for help on her CB, and got a rapist; he didn't fix the tire either. She was afraid to call for help again and stayed in her car until morning. Also, CBs work best along line-of-sight; I ruled them out.   5

As I drove home one night, a car followed me, lights bright. It passed on a narrow bridge, while a passenger flashed a spotlight in my face, blinding me. I braked sharply. The car stopped, angled across the bridge, and four men jumped out. I realized the locked doors were useless if they broke my car windows. I started forward, hoping to knock their car aside so I could pass. Just then, another car appeared, and the men got back in their car, but continued to follow me, passing and repassing. I dared not go home. I passed no lighted houses. Finally, they pulled to the roadside, and I decided to use their tactic: fear. I roared past them inches away, horn blaring. It worked; they turned off the highway. But it was desperate and foolish, and I was frightened and angry. Even in my vehicle I was too vulnerable.   6

Other incidents followed. One day I saw a man in the field near my house, carrying a shotgun and heading for a pond full of ducks. I drove to meet him, and politely explained that the land was posted. He stared at me, and the muzzle of his shotgun rose. I realized that if he simply shot me and drove away, I would be a statistic. The moment passed; the man left.   7

One night, I returned home from class to find deep tire ruts on the lawn, a large gas tank empty, garbage in the driveway. A light shone in the house; I couldn't remember leaving it on. I was too embarrassed to wake the neighbors. An hour of cautious exploration convinced me the house was safe, but once inside, with the doors locked, I was still afraid. I put a .22 rifle by my bed, but I kept thinking of how naked I felt, prowling around my own house in the dark.   8

It was time to consider self-defense. I took a kung fu class and learned to define the distance to maintain between myself and a stranger. Once someone enters that space without permission, kung fu teaches appropriate evasive or protective action. I learned to move confidently, scanning for possible attack. I learned how to assess danger, and techniques for avoiding it without combat.   9

I also learned that one must practice several hours every day to be good at kung fu. By that time I had married George; when I practiced with him, I learned how *close* you must be to your attacker to use martial arts, and decided   10 a 120-pound woman dare not let a six-foot, 220-pound attacker get that close unless she is very, very good at self-defense. Some women who are well trained in martial arts have been raped and beaten anyway.

Reluctantly I decided to carry a pistol. George helped me practice with his   11
.357 and .22. I disliked the .357's recoil, though I later became comfortable with it. I bought a .22 at a pawn shop. A standard .22 bullet, fired at close range, can kill, but news reports tell of attackers advancing with five such bullets in them. I bought magnum shells, with more power, and practiced until I could hit someone close enough to endanger me. Then I bought a license making it legal for me to carry the gun concealed.

George taught me that the most important preparation was mental: con-   12
vincing myself I could shoot someone. Few of us really wish to hurt or kill an-other human being. But there is no point in having a gun—in fact, gun posses-sion might increase your danger—unless you know you can use it against another human being. A good training course includes mental preparation, as well as training in safety. As I drive or walk, I often rehearse the conditions which would cause me to shoot. Men grow up handling firearms, and learn controlled violence in contact sports, but women grow up learning to be sub-servient and vulnerable. To make ourselves comfortable with the idea that we are capable of protecting ourselves requires effort. But it need not turn us into macho, gun-fighting broads. We must simply learn to do as men do from an early age: believe in, and rely on, *ourselves* for protection. The pistol only adds an extra edge, an attention-getter; it is a weapon of last resort.

Because shooting at another person means shooting to kill. It's impossible   13
even for seasoned police officers to be sure of only wounding an assailant. If I shot an attacking man, I would aim at the largest target, the chest. This is not an easy choice, but for me it would be better than rape.

In my car, my pistol is within instant reach. When I enter a deserted rest   14
stop at night, it's in my purse, my hand on the grip. When I walk from a dark parking lot into a motel, it's in my hand, under a coat. When I walk my dog in the deserted lots around most motels, the pistol is in a shoulder holster, and I am always aware of my surroundings. In my motel room, it lies on the bedside table. At home, it's on the headboard.

Just carrying a pistol is not protection. Avoidance is still the best approach   15
to trouble; watch for danger signs, and practice avoiding them. Develop your instinct for danger.

One day while driving to the highway mailbox, I saw a vehicle parked about   16
halfway to the house. Several men were standing in the ditch, relieving them-selves. I have no objection to emergency urination; we always need moisture. But they'd also dumped several dozen beer cans, which blow into pastures and can slash a cow's legs or stomach.

As I slowly drove closer, the men zipped their trousers ostentatiously while   17
walking toward me. Four men gathered around my small foreign car, making remarks they wouldn't make to their mothers, and one of them demanded what the hell I wanted.

"This is private land; I'd like you to pick up the beer cans."   18

"What beer cans?" said the belligerent one, putting both hands on the car   19
door, and leaning in my window. His face was inches from mine, the beer
fumes were strong, and he looked angry. The others laughed. One tried the
passenger door, locked; another put his foot on the hood and rocked the car.
They circled, lightly thumping the roof, discussing my good fortune in meeting them, and the benefits they were likely to bestow upon me. I felt small and
trapped; they knew it.

"The ones you just threw out," I said politely.   20

"I don't see no beer cans. Why don't you get out here and show them to me,   21
honey?" said the belligerent one, reaching for the handle inside my door.

"Right over there," I said, still being polite, "there and over there." I pointed   22
with the pistol, which had been under my thigh. Within one minute the cans
and the men were back in the car, and headed down the road.

I believe this small incident illustrates several principles. The men were   23
trespassing and knew it; their judgment may have been impaired by alcohol.
Their response to the polite request of a woman alone was to use their size and
numbers to inspire fear. The pistol was a response in the same language. Politeness didn't work; I couldn't intimidate them. Out of the car, I'd have been
more vulnerable. The pistol just changed the balance of power.

My husband, George, asked one question when I told him. "'What would   24
you have done if he'd grabbed for the pistol?"

"I had the car in reverse; I'd have hit the accelerator, and backed up; if he'd   25
kept coming, I'd have fired straight at him." He nodded.

In fact, the sight of the pistol made the man straighten up; he cracked his   26
head on the door frame. He and the two in front of the car stepped backward,
catching the attention of the fourth, who joined them. They were all in front of
me then, and as the car was still running and in reverse gear, my options had
multiplied. If they'd advanced again, I'd have backed away, turning to keep the
open window toward them. Given time, I'd have put the first shot into the
ground in front of them, the second into the belligerent leader. It might have
been better to wait until they were gone, pick up the beer cans, and avoid confrontation, but I believed it was reasonable and my right to make a polite request to strangers littering my property. Showing the pistol worked on another
occasion when I was driving in a desolate part of Wyoming. A man played cat-
and-mouse with me for thirty miles, ultimately trying to run my car off the
road. When his car was only two inches from mine, I pointed my pistol at him,
and he disappeared.

I believe that a handgun is like a car; both are tools for specific purposes;   27
both can be lethal if used improperly. Both require a license, training, and alert-
ness. Both require you to be aware of what is happening before and behind you.
Driving becomes almost instinctive; so does handgun use. When I've drawn my
gun for protection, I simply found it in my hand. Instinct told me a situation
was dangerous before my conscious mind reacted; I've felt the same while driving. Most good drivers react to emergencies by instinct.

Knives are another useful tool often misunderstood and misused; some   28
people acquire knives mostly for display, either on a wall or on a belt, and such
knives are often so large as to serve no useful purpose. My pocket knives are always razor sharp, because a small, sharp knife will do most jobs. Skinning
blades serve for cutting meat and splitting small kindling in camp. A *sgian
dubh,* a four-inch flat blade in a wooden sheath, was easily concealed inside a
Scotsman's high socks, and slips into my dress or work boots as well. Some
buckskinners keep what they call a "grace knife" on a thong around their necks;
the name may derive from *coup de grâce,* the welcome throat-slash a wounded
knight asked from his closest friend, to keep him from falling alive into the
hands of his enemies. I also have a push dagger, with a blade only three inches
long, attached to a handle that fits into the fist so well that the knife would be
hard to lose even in hand-to-hand combat. When I first showed it, without explanation, to an older woman who would never consider carrying a knife, she
took one look and said, "Why, you could push that right into someone's stomach," and demonstrated with a flourish. That's what it's for. I wear it for decoration, because it was handmade by Jerry and fits my hand perfectly, but I am
intently aware of its purpose. I like my knives, not because they are weapons,
but because they are well designed, and beautiful, and because each is a tool
with a specific purpose.

Women didn't always have jobs, or drive cars or heavy equipment, though   29
western women did many of those things almost as soon as they arrived here.
Men in authority argued that their attempt to do so would unravel the fabric of
society. Women, they said, would become less feminine; they hadn't the intelligence to cope with the mechanics of a car, or the judgment to cope with emergencies. Since these ideas were so wrong, perhaps it is time women brought a
new dimension to the wise use of handguns as well.

We can and should educate ourselves in how to travel safely, take self-   30
defense courses, reason, plead, or avoid trouble in other ways. But some men
cannot be stopped by those methods; they understand only power. A man who
is committing an attack already knows he's breaking laws; he has no concern
for someone else's rights. A pistol is a woman's answer to his greater power. It
makes her equally frightening. I have thought of revising the old Colt slogan:
"God made man, but Sam Colt made them equal" to read "God made men *and
women* but Sam Colt made them equal." Recently I have seen an ad for a popular gunmaker with a similar sentiment; perhaps this is an idea whose time has
come, though the pacifist inside me will be saddened if the only way women
can achieve equality is by carrying a weapon.

As a society, we were shocked in early 1989 when a female jogger in New   31
York's Central Park was beaten and raped savagely and left in a coma. I was
even more shocked when reporters interviewed children who lived near the victim and quoted a twelve-year-old as saying, "She had nothing to guard herself;
she didn't have no man with her; she didn't have no Mace." And another sixth-
grader said, "It is like she committed suicide." Surely this is not a majority
opinion, but I think it is not so unusual, either, even in this liberated age. Yet

there is no city or county in the nation where law officers can relax because all the criminals are in jail. Some authorities say citizens armed with handguns stop almost as many crimes annually as armed criminals succeed in committing, and that people defending themselves kill three times more attackers and robbers than police do. I don't suggest all criminals should be killed, but some can be stopped only by death or permanent incarceration. Law enforcement officials can't prevent crimes; later punishment may be of little comfort to the victim. A society so controlled that no crime existed would probably be too confined for most of us, and is not likely to exist any time soon. Therefore, many of us should be ready and able to protect ourselves, and the intelligent use of firearms is one way.

We must treat a firearm's power with caution. "Power tends to corrupt, and   32
absolute power corrupts absolutely," as a man (Lord Acton) once said. A pistol is not the only way to avoid being raped or murdered in today's world, but a firearm, intelligently wielded, can shift the balance and provide a measure of safety.

▪ RECORDING REFLECTIONS

Hasselstrom recounts in her essay a number of dangerous incidences that led her to purchase and carry a gun. She then recounts several similar situations she found herself in after she began to carry the pistol. As you read, list some dangerous (or at least some uncomfortable) situations you have been in and how you reacted—immediately and also after the fact.

Choose one of your examples and write about it for 10 minutes, focusing on why you reacted like you did.

▪ ACTIVITIES FOR REREADING

1. As you reread, pay particular attention to paragraphs 4–8. Hasselstrom uses examples to demonstrate why she eventually decided to carry a pistol. Comment in writing whether you think her examples are effective and why.
2. After rereading paragraphs 28 and 29, think about whether they do or do not effectively contribute to the thrust of Hasselstrom's argument. List the reasons for your opinion.

▪ GROUP WORK

Personal Responses: Using your Reflection Logs to spur your memories, discuss your experiences with danger or discomfort and what resulted from them. Discuss, too, your feelings about those experiences—both at the time they occurred and now, after reflection.

Objective Responses: Discuss the effectiveness of Hasselstrom's examples in paragraphs 4–8. See if you can reach a consensus about whether these examples are effective in supporting her point. Jot down your reasons.

Discuss the effectiveness of paragraphs 28 and 29 in furthering Hasselstrom's argument. Is the information itself interesting? How do the information and opinions contribute to supporting her thesis?

■ **WRITING ASSIGNMENTS**

1. Write an essay in which you closely examine the circumstances that led you to make an important, perhaps life-altering decision. Describe the circumstances in detail to clarify the reasons for your decision. What have been the results of your decision?

2. Choose one or more incidences in which you have found yourself in danger or discomfort. Write an essay about them and how they have led you to behave or think in a particular way.

Why We Crave Horror Movies   *1987*

STEPHEN KING

I think that we're all mentally ill; those of us outside the asylums only hide it a little better—and maybe not all that much better, after all. We've all known people who talk to themselves, people who sometimes squinch their faces into horrible grimaces when they believe no one is watching, people who have some hysterical fear—of snakes, the dark, the tight place, the long drop . . . and, of course, those final worms and grubs that are waiting so patiently underground. 1

When we pay our four or five bucks and seat ourselves at tenth-row center in a theater showing a horror movie, we are daring the nightmare. 2

Why? Some of the reasons are simple and obvious. To show that we can, that we are not afraid, that we can ride this roller coaster. Which is not to say that a really good horror movie may not surprise a scream out of us at some point, the way we may scream when the roller coaster twists through a complete 360 or plows through a lake at the bottom of the drop. And horror movies, like roller coasters, have always been the special province of the young; by the time one turns 40 or 50, one's appetite for double twists or 360-degree loops may be considerably depleted. 3

We also go to re-establish our feelings of essential normality; the horror movie is innately conservative, even reactionary. Freda Jackson as the horrible melting woman in *Die, Monster, Die!* confirms for us that no matter how far we may be removed from the beauty of a Robert Redford or a Diana Ross, we are still light-years from true ugliness. 4

And we go to have fun. 5

Ah, but this is where the ground starts to slope away, isn't it? Because this is a very peculiar sort of fun, indeed. The fun comes from seeing others menaced—sometimes killed. One critic has suggested that if pro football has 6 become the voyeur's version of combat, then the horror film has become the modern version of the public lynching.

It is true that the mythic, "fairy-tale" horror film intends to take away the shades of gray. . . . It urges us to put away our more civilized and adult penchant for analysis and to become children again, seeing things in pure blacks and whites. It may be that horror movies provide psychic relief on this level because this invitation to lapse into simplicity, irrationality and even outright madness is extended so rarely. We are told we may allow our emotions a free rein . . . or no rein at all. 7

If we are all insane, then sanity becomes a matter of degree. If your insanity leads you to carve up women like Jack the Ripper or the Cleveland Torso Murderer, we clap you away in the funny farm (but neither of those two amateur-night surgeons was ever caught, heh-heh-heh); if, on the other hand, your insanity leads you only to talk to yourself when you're under stress or to pick your nose on your morning bus, then you are left alone to go about your business . . . though it is doubtful that you will ever be invited to the best parties. 8

The potential lyncher is in almost all of us (excluding saints, past and present; but then, most saints have been crazy in their own ways), and every now and then, he has to be let loose to scream and roll around in the grass. Our emotions and our fears form their own body, and we recognize that it demands its own exercise to maintain proper muscle tone. Certain of these emotional muscles are accepted—even exalted—in civilized society; they are, of course, the emotions that tend to maintain the status quo of civilization itself. Love, friendship, loyalty, kindness—these are all the emotions that we applaud, emotions that have been immortalized in the couplets of Hallmark cards and in the verses (I don't dare call it poetry) of Leonard Nimoy. 9

When we exhibit these emotions, society showers us with positive reinforcement; we learn this even before we get out of diapers. When, as children, we hug our rotten little puke of a sister and give her a kiss, all the aunts and uncles smile and twit and cry, "Isn't he the sweetest little thing?" Such coveted treats as chocolate-covered graham crackers often follow. But if we deliberately slam the rotten little puke of a sister's fingers in the door, sanctions follow—angry remonstrance from parents, aunts and uncles; instead of a chocolate-covered graham cracker, a spanking. 10

But anticivilization emotions don't go away, and they demand periodic exercise. We have such "sick" jokes as, "What's the difference between a truckload of bowling balls and a truckload of dead babies? (You can't unload a truckload of bowling balls with a pitchfork . . . a joke, by the way, that I heard originally from a ten-year-old). Such a joke may surprise a laugh or a grin out of us even as we recoil, a possibility that confirms the thesis: If we share a brotherhood of man, then we also share an insanity of man. None of which is intended as a defense of either the sick joke or insanity but merely as an explanation of why the best horror films, like the best fairy tales, manage to be reactionary, anarchistic, and revolutionary all at the same time. 11

The mythic horror movie, like the sick joke, has a dirty job to do. It deliberately appeals to all that is worst in us. It is morbidity unchained, our most base instincts let free, our nastiest fantasies realized . . . and it all happens, fittingly enough, in the dark. For those reasons, good liberals often shy away from horror films. For myself, I like to see the most aggressive of them—*Dawn of the Dead*, for instance—as lifting a trap door in the civilized forebrain and throwing a basket of raw meat to the hungry alligators swimming around in that subterranean river beneath.

Why bother? Because it keeps them from getting out, man. It keeps them down there and me up here. It was Lennon and McCartney who said that all you need is love, and I would agree with that.

As long as you keep the gators fed.

RECORDING REFLECTIONS

King cites a number of reasons he believes horror films have been and continue to be popular. Highlight each of his reasons as you read.

After reading the essay, review King's reasons and record in your Reflection Log your own responses to horror films. Do they seem to be caused by what King describes? Explain.

ACTIVITIES FOR REREADING

1. The title of King's essay implies his thesis. As you reread, determine what that thesis is and then write it out using your own words.
2. King claims that horror movies serve both psychological and social purposes. Determine what those purposes are as you reread, and determine whether you think King's claims are valid. Write down your reasons.
3. As you reread the essay, think about the evidence King cites to support his claims. Is his argument convincing? Why or why not? Write down a brief response.
4. Highlight the words and phrases that establish King's tone; then briefly describe that tone.

GROUP WORK

Personal Responses: Using your Reflection Logs as your sources, discuss your various reactions to horror films and the possible causes of those reactions. Refer to specific films as examples. In order to keep focused, refer to the reasons King gives for the popularity of horror films.

Objective Responses: Discuss what you think King's thesis is, the evidence he cites to prove it, how convincing his argument is, and whether his point of view (i.e., that horror films serve positive psychological and social purposes) is valid. Always refer to your rereading notes and specifics from the essay itself to back up your observations.

Consider the effectiveness of the essay's opening sentence. Consider, too, the specific way the sentence relates to the essay's thesis.

Discuss how King's roller-coaster analogy in paragraph 3 helps develop his argument.

WRITING ASSIGNMENTS

1. Write an essay in which you outline the reasons you like or dislike a particular horror film. Make sure you deal in specifics, always showing how the film causes your reactions.
2. Write an essay in which you either agree or disagree with King's point of view that horror films serve important functions. Cite ideas from his essay as well as specific films as evidence to prove your thesis.

The Shrieking of the Lambs   *1994*

ANDREW KLAVAN

I love the sound of people screaming. Women screaming—with their   1
clothes torn—as they run down endless hallways with some bogeyman in hot pursuit. Men, in their priapic cars, screaming as the road ends, as the fender plummets towards fiery oblivion under their wild eyes. Children? I'm a little squeamish about children, but okay, sure. I'll take screaming children too. And I get off on gunshots—machine gun shots goading a corpse into a posthumous jitterbug; and the coital jerk and plunge of a butcher knife; and axes; even claws, if you happen to have them.

Yes, yes, yes, only in stories. Of course; in fictions only: novels, TV shows,   2
films. I've loved the scary, gooey stuff since I was a child. I've loved monsters, shootouts, bluddy murther; Women In Jeopardy (as they say in Hollywood); the slasher in the closet; the intruder's shadow that spreads up the bedroom wall like a stain. And now, having grown to man's estate, I make a very good living writing these things: thriller novels like *Don't Say A Word*, which begins with a nice old lady getting dusted and ends with an assault on a child, and *The Animal Hour*, which features a woman's head being severed and stuffed into a commode.

Is it vicious? Disgusting? Sexist? Sick? Tough luck, it's my imagination—   3
sometimes it is—and it's my readers' too—always, for all I know. And when they and I get together, when we dodge down that electric alleyway of the human skull where only murder is delight—well then, my friend, it's showtime.

But enough about me, let's talk about death. Cruel death, sexy death, ex-   4
citing death: death, that is, on the page and on the screen. Because this is not a defense of violence in fiction, it's a celebration of it. And not a moment too soon either.

Hard as it is for a sane man to believe, fictional violence is under attack.   5
Again. Floundering in a mean street America where bigots and enablers dither
while the malicious play catch with live ammo, where one interest group calls
a machine gun a hunting weapon and another calls a kitchen knife a form of
feminist expression, where children are stolen from their houses and killed and
tourists are executed for the crime of getting lost on their way to Disneyworld,
the folks back home have understandably panicked, and the unerring eye of political opportunism has once more found its scapegoat: those good people who
make up scary stories to help you pass the time. This year's list of would-be censors trying to shoulder their way to the trough of celebrity is hardly worth enu-
merating: their 15 minutes might be up by the time I'm done. Film critic
Michael Medved says cinematic violence is part of a pop culture "war on traditional values"; Congressman Edward Markey says television violence should
be reduced or regulated; some of our less thoughtful feminists tried to quash
the novel *American Psycho* because of its descriptions of violence toward
women and even some more thoughtful, like Catherine MacKinnon, have
fought for censorship in law, claiming that written descriptions of "penises
slamming into vaginas" deprive actual human beings of their civil rights.

It's nonsense mostly, but it has the appeal of glamour, of flash. The "issue"   6
of fictional violence lifts crime out of the impoverished, muddy-minded, rage-
filled milieus in which it usually occurs, and superimposes it on the gaudy images manufactured in Hollywood and Manhattan. Instead of trying to understand the sad, banal, ignorant souls who generally pull the trigger in our society,
we get to discuss Hannibal Lecter, Ice-T, penises, vaginas. It makes for good
sound bytes, anyway—the all-American diet of 15 second thoughts.

But Britain—where I've come to live because I loathe real guns and politi-   7
cal correctness—is far from exempt. Indeed, perhaps nowhere has there been
a more telling or emblematic attack on fictional violence than is going on here
right now. It is a textbook example of how easily pundits and politicians can
channel honest grief and rage at a true crime into a senseless assault on the innocent tellers of tales.

It began here this time with the killing of a child by two other children. On   8
12 February, Jamie Bulger, a two-year-old toddler, was led out of a Merseyside
shopping mall by two ten-year-olds—two little boys. The boys prodded and carried and tugged the increasingly distraught baby past dozens of witnesses who
did not understand what they were seeing. When they reached a deserted railroad embankment, the two boys tortured, mutilated, and finally killed their
captive for no reasons that anyone has been able to explain.

The explicit testimony at the trial last November verged on the unbearable.   9
Even the more restrained newspapers could not be read without nausea and
tears. And looking at the photographs of the killers—two sweetly mischievous
Just William faces, Lords of the Flies in their Sunday best—there arose, in me,
in everyone I spoke to, the desperate urge to understand, to grasp, to know:
What? What is it? What rough beast, its hour come round at last?

At first, the pundits did their best to answer but the answers seemed miser- 10
ably inadequate. Psychiatrists noted the fierce sibling rivalry felt by one of the
killers; sociologists noted the broken homes, the poverty, the family violence;
columnists talked about the breakdown of society; one gay writer blamed everything on the pressures of heterosexual manhood; even the usually brilliant Martin Amis weighed in with a rather sleepy piece on the dissipation of moral energy
in the west. And it wasn't just the media flailing about. At dinner parties, we dar-
ingly ventured to talk about Evil, and then let our voices trail off to nothing. At
home, we tried to be nicer to our children—until the little pests caught on and
began to run riot. And in almost any pub, you could hear it explained how the
murderers were demon freaks of nature—an opinion that seemed a lot less
ridiculous and a lot more comforting than by any rights it should've done.

But the nation's search for an answer, its grief and disgust, its sense of so- 11
cial despair, did not resolve themselves upon a single issue until the trial judge
pronounced sentence. "It is not for me to pass judgment on their upbringing,"
Mr. Justice Morland said of the boys as he sentenced them to be detained at Her
Majesty's pleasure. "But I suspect exposure to violent video films may in part
be an explanation."

No one knew why he said such a thing. There had been speculation in some 12
of the papers that *Child's Play 3*, which had been rented by one of the killers' fathers, had given the son ideas. But there was no testimony at the trial, no evidence presented showing that the boy had seen it or that it had had a
contributing effect. Detective Superintendent Albert Kirby, who headed the investigation into the murder, said "the area of videos was one we looked very
closely at" but that no link had been established by the police at all.

It didn't matter. As far as journalists were concerned, as far as public debate 13
was concerned, "video nasties," as they are called here, became the central issue of the case. Forget the subconscious, the broken home, the poverty, the
family cruelty, the breakdown of western society, even the trials of masculinity
and the moral energy stuff. For the next few days, the newspapers were splattered with stories about *Child's Play 3* as writers combed the film for tenuous
connections between the rampages of the movie's devil doll Chucky and the
savage attack perpetrated by the Merseyside rails. In the aftermath, the British
opening of the film *The Good Son*, starring Macauley Culkin as an evil child,
was canceled. The video release of *Reservoir Dogs* was indefinitely postponed.
Twenty-five doctors and academics who had previously dismissed the effects of
screen violence made front page news with a mea culpa report saying their liberal ideals had made them naive. Action was called for, and Liberal Democrat
MP David Alton answered the call on the run. With the backing of rebel Tories,
Alton nearly pushed through a proposal that even the country's chief censor
said would prevent the video release of "half the films made in the last quarter
century and some of the greatest films ever made." The Alton bill was only
tabled when Home Secretary Michael Howard reluctantly agreed to implement
some Draconian restrictions of his own. From hereon in, if you rent *My Cousin
Vinny* to an 11-year-old, you're looking at jail time, mate.

And why not? Now, thanks to Mr. Justice Morland and an eager press, we   14
finally know what we are seeing when we look upon the rampaging fire of violence in our society: we are seeing the effects of fiction on us. Got it? Our
leaders are either mindless ideologues or soulless bureaucrats. Our cultural
heritage is under attack by morons who stand on the shoulders of giants and
think that they can fly. Our moral verities are crumbling by the hour. Our families are shattering. Our gods are dead. The best lack all conviction while the
worst are full of passionate intensity.

And it's all Chucky's fault.   15

The instinct to censor is the tragic flaw of utopian minds. "Our first job,"   16
said Plato in his classic attack on the democratic system, "is to oversee the work
of the story-writers, and to accept any good stories they write, but reject the
others." Because the perfectibility of human society is a fiction itself, it comes
under threat from other, more believable fictions, especially those fictions
which document and employ the cruel, the chaotic, the Dionysian for their
thrills. It's a form of homeopathic magic really. (A point once made by the magician Teller of Penn and Teller in an op-ed piece in *The New York Times*.) The
chants and rituals of that old witchcraft are gone, but the template of belief remains in the censor's mind: if you erase the image, he tells us, you will magically erase the thing itself.

And this superstitious fallacy plays into some prevailing fallacies of acade-   17
mic and political theory: the idea that language is the way we understand the
world, that metaphor generates consciousness and imagery fashions our feelings and choices, that a work, an author, a reader are wholly constructed of the
influences they wreak upon each other. Under such theories, literature becomes
an action taken with potentially harmful or beneficial effects on the society and
politics of the age (rather than, say, a sight to be seen like a sunset or a mountain range). Again, with their isomorphic links between image and reality, such
theories can lead to a sort of homeopathic magic in materialist guise.

Yet one can understand the appeal of these intricate alchemies. With their   18
emphasis on interpretation, they allow critics to sublimate their frustration at
not being artists. With their urgent dashes for control of the shaping culture,
they allow artists to feel they are engaged in struggles of great pith and moment. In general, they allow all of us who sit in lonesome rooms fiddling with
language to feel a little bit more like Vaclav Havel and a little bit less like Bobo
the Juggling Clown. Very tempting stuff, especially in a nation which largely refuses to make martyrs of its literati and so deprives them of political heroism;
leaves them instead to splash about like trained seals in the shallow waters of
commercial failure and success.

Fortunately for our purposes, however, a seal's life is exactly the life for me.   19
I'm just a simple barefoot spinner of yarns plying my wares from town to town.
I don't know nothing about birthing a perfect society. For me to engage the lat-
terday Platos on their own materialist, political terms would be to be sucked in
to a form of dialogue that does not reflect the reality I know—and know I know.

Because personally, I understand the world not through language but through an unfathomable spirit and an infinite mind. I sit down through an urge and with a talent as basic to my personality as inborn personality itself. With language as a rude tool I try to convey a shadow of the world my imagination makes of the world at large. I do this for money and pleasure and to win the admiration of women. And when, in an uncertain hour, I crave the palliative of meaning, I remind myself that people's souls run opposite to their bodies and grow more childlike as they mature—and so I have built, in my work, little places where those souls can go to play.

The proper response to anyone who would shut these playgrounds down   20
for any reason—to anyone who confuses these playgrounds with the real world—is not the specious language of theory or logic or even the law. It's the language of the spirit, of celebration and screed, of jeremiad and hallelujah. Of this.

Now I would not say that my fictions—any fictions—have no effect on real   21
life. Or that books, movies and TV are mere regurgitations of what's going on in the society around them. These arguments, frequently advanced by violence-meisters such as *Death Wish* director Michael Winner, strike me as disingenuous and self-defeating. Rather, the relationship between fiction and humanity's unconscious is so complex, so resonant, and even stichomythic that it is impossible to isolate one from the other in terms of cause and effect. The gentle family man enjoys a day at the beach with *Red Dragon*, the assassin cuddles up with *Catcher In The Rye*. Writers in Ceausescu's murderous Roumania weren't allowed to admit that homegrown murder even existed while the civilized and liberalizing high Victorians made a bestseller out of *Dracula*, in which babies are devoured by women and women are devoured by wolves. (Interestingly, Bram Stoker made virtually the same argument in favor of censoring pornography as has Catherine MacKinnon. He feared it would incite the susceptible sex to crime: "Women are the worst offenders in this form of breach of moral law," said Bram.)

Perhaps it is true that children, sociopaths, and American academics   22
should be protected, in their emotional immaturity, from the more vicious and explicit imagery of fiction. I know I wouldn't want any of them reading my books, and would support sane and limited measures to keep them out of their hands. But for the rest of us, who can honestly say why a film like *Psycho* inspires a sort of moral mourning in me, whereas the Bible inspires David Koresh to be, well, David Koresh? The studies are always suspect and seem to change with the political winds. Last week, a new study here purported to show a relation between child violence and video nasties. This week, a new study claimed to show that criminals watched the same things as everyone else. It all depends on how you slice it, as it were.

So fiction and reality do interact, but we don't know how, not at all. And   23
since we don't understand the effect of one upon the other—or, that is, the effect seems to be so individualistic, to depend so much upon the specific work

and person at the moment they connect—whence arises this magical certainty that violence in fiction begets violence in real life like one of those old 3D films that promised to "leap off the screen?"

The answer seems to come straight out of the pages of Sigmund Freud. Or   24
St. Paul if you prefer: "Wherein thou judgest another, thou condemnest thyself." It's *Psychology 1A*, but that doesn't negate the truth of it: that pleasure which is unknowingly repressed is outwardly condemned. The censor always attacks the images that secretly appeal to him or her the most. The assault on violent fiction is not really an attempt to root out the causes of violence—no one can seriously believe that. The attempt to censor fictional violence is a guilt-ridden slap at ourselves, in the guise of a mythical *them,* for taking such pleasure in make-believe acts that, in real life, would be reprehensible. How—we seem to be asking ourselves—how, in a world in which Jamie Bulger dies so young, can we kick back with a beer at night and enjoy a couple of hours of *Child's Play 3*? How can a man who has to fear so for his wife or daughter read *American Psycho* with such a goofy simper? How can a woman who tries to teach her children to negotiate the world in peace cheer like a maniac for the marauding cruelties of *Thelma and Louise?*

How can we enjoy this stuff so much? So very much.   25

Not all of us perhaps. I'm forever being told that there are people who'd   26
rather not take violence with their fiction—although I wonder how many would say so if you included the delicate violence of an Agatha Christie or the "literary" violence of, say, Hemingway and Faulkner. But even if we accept the exceptions, even if we limit the field to real gore, it does seem to me that the numbers are incredible, the attraction truly profound.

For instance, in the years when we could not afford to go to the movies, my   27
wife and I would read aloud to each other: a mutual entertainment that could be stretched over several days. Once, I picked out what looked like a cheap horror novel by an author I'd never heard of. We began reading it right after dinner. Around nine o'clock, we hit the scene where a little boy was sacrificed and gutted by the factotum of a vampire. It was about four a.m. before we reached the part where a priest was forced to guzzle the spurting blood from the vampire's chest. Long after dawn, hoarse and wide-eyed, we reached the novel's apocalyptic conclusion. Even my wife—who generally does avoid this sort of thing—agreed that it was one of the most wonderfully ugly and frightening things we'd ever read.

For months afterward, I asked every reader I knew if they had ever heard   28
of the book, *Salem's Lot,* or its author, Stephen King. None of them had. It had been nicely published but largely unpublicized. Later, the movie *Carrie* helped launch what has to be one of the most successful novelistic careers since Dickens. But even before that, all over the country, all over the world eventually, readers like me and my wife were steadily discovering the nausea and mayhem and terror of the man's vision.

The moral, I mean, is this: To construct a bloodsoaked nightmare of unre-   29
lenting horror is not an easy thing. But if you build it, they will come.

And so the maker of violent fiction—ho, ho—he walks among us in Nietz- 30
schean glee. He has bottled the Dionysian whirlwind and is selling it as a soft
drink. Like the *hausfrau* who charmed her babes with descriptions of the dis-
membered brides in *The Robber Baron*, like deep-browed Homer, when he told
of a spear protruding from a man's head with an eyeball fixed to the point, the
violent storyteller knows that that gape of disgust on your respectable mug is
really the look of love. You may denounce him, you may even censor him. You
may just wrinkle your nose and walk away. But sooner or later, in one form or
another, he knows you'll show up to see and listen to him—and if you don't,
your children will, in droves.

Nothing can be more cruelly risible than watching experts debate a piece of 31
fictional violence on American television, always pretending that they are above
and exempt from the sweet glee that fiction provides. Is *American Psycho* an eroti-
cized attack on womankind or an exploration of modern madness? Is *Falling
Down* an incitement to murder minorities or a warning against the promptings
of urban rage? The idea seems to be that whoever can impose a meaning on the
fiction—a meaning which will support his cause or career—wins.

But fiction, like life, is not about its meanings. Like life, any good story can 32
support any number of interpretations, many of them mutually exclusive, and
many of them at odds with the author's purposes and peccadilloes. This is precisely why fiction causes single-minded political thinkers to stomp and gnash
so much. Fiction lives or dies, not on its messages, but on the depth and power
of the emotional experience it provides. And from the *gravitas* of the Aris-
totelian notion of catharsis to the pseudoscientific palaver of modern literary
theory, an enormous amount of intellectual energy seems to have been ex-
pended in a failed attempt to suppress the central, disturbing and irreducible
fact of this experience: it's fun. Like sex: it's lots of fun. We watch fictional people love and die and screw and suffer and weep for our pleasure. It gives us joy.

And we watch them kill too. And this seems to give us as much joy as 33
anything.

All right, I suppose you can talk about the catharsis of terror, or the harm- 34
less release of our violent impulses. Those are plausible excuses, I guess. It
doesn't take a genius to notice how often—practically always—it's the villain of
a successful piece of violent art who becomes its icon. Hannibal Lecter and
Leatherface, Freddy Kreuger and Dracula—these are the posters that go up on
the wall, the characters that we remember. Several commentators have been
disturbed by the fact that modern thrillers seem more and more to take the
point of view of the bad guy rather than the hero, but perhaps that's just our increasing honesty about the nature of what's repressed. Plenty of kids have built
plastic models of Frankenstein's monster, but I don't know a single one who's
ever built a model of a Tyrolean peasant with a torch.

So I suppose, if you must, you could say these creatures represent our 35
buried feelings. Whether it's Medea or Jason (from *Friday The 13th*), the character who commits acts of savage violence always has the appeal of a Caliban:

that thing of darkness that must be acknowledged as our own. Not that people are essentially violent, but that they are violent among other things and the violence has to be repressed. After all, if I could shoot my kids every time they were snotty and beat my wife every time she was right, I'd probably be St. Francis of Assisi in my spare time. But if you want to have a civilization, you've got to roll with the discontents. Some emotions must be repressed and repressed emotions return via the imagination in distorted and inflated forms: that's the law of benevolent hypocrisy, the law of civilized life. It is an unstated underpinning of utopian thought—what Nietzsche keenly called Socratic thought—that the repressed can be eliminated completely or denied or happily freed or remolded with the proper education. It can't. Forget about it. Cross it off your list of things to do. The monsters are always there in their cages. As Stephen King says, with engaging simplicity, his job is to take them out for a walk every now and then.

36 But again, this business of violent fiction as therapy—this modern-jargon version of Aristotle—it's a defense, isn't it, as if these stories needed a reason for being. In order to celebrate violent fiction—I mean, *celebrate* it—it's the joy you've got to talk about. The joy of cruelty, the thrill of terror, the adrenaline of the hunter, the heartbeat of the deer—all reproduced in the safe playground of art. A joy indeed.

37 Americans don't seem to like that word much: joy. Every day, some newspaper seems to publish some doctor's or sociologist's reasons why we should or shouldn't take our pleasure. It deadens our brain cells, it cleans our heart, it makes us live longer, it kills us. We need to know that smoke or drink or sport, sex or entertainment, is somehow medicinal before we allow it to take the edge off the miseries of existence. Even more, Americans, culturally puritanical and yet committed to the ideal of tolerance, like to tie themselves in knots trying to show that your pleasures are not good for *them*, that is, the society at large. As a culture, we seem unable to accept the words of our great philosopher, Dr. Seuss, who said—though admittedly in a wholly other context—"These things are fun, and fun is good."

38 When it comes to our messier, our somehow unseemly, pleasures, like fictional gore, we are downright embarrassed by our delight. But delight is certainly what it is. Nubile teens caught out *in flagrante* by a nutcase in a hockey mask? You bet it's erotic. Whole families tortured to death by a madman who's traced them through their vacation photos. Ee-yewwww. Goblins who jump out of the toilet to devour you ass first. Delightful stuff.

39 I remember when *The Exorcist* (still unavailable on video in the UK) first came out over 20 years ago. The hype was extensive. The film's dramatization of a neurotic Catholic view of menarche was genuinely disgusting. Excitement in the seats ran high. Toward the climax of the picture, it all got to be too much. The fellow sitting next to me suddenly started to hyperventilate and I had to carry him out into the lobby. It was like a battlefield out there: girls sobbing, guys with their heads in their hands—a funny little mustachioed theater manager hopping from

victim to victim with a stick of smelling salts. The lines to get in to the next show went around the block. I mean, we were having a *good* time now.

And we've always been that way. The myths of our ancient gods, the lives   40 of our medieval saints, the entertainments of our most civilized cultures have always included healthy doses of rape, cannibalism, evisceration, and general mayhem. Critics like Michael Medved complain that never before has it all been quite so graphic, especially on screen. We are becoming "desensitized" to bloodshed, he claims, and require more and more gore to excite our feelings. But when have human beings ever been particularly "sensitized" to fictional violence? The technology to create the illusion of bloodshed has certainly improved, but read *Titus Andronicus* with its wonderful stage direction. "Enter a messenger with two heads and a hand," read the orgasmic staking of Lucy in *Dracula*, read de Sade, for crying out loud. There were always some pretty good indications of which way we'd go once we got our hands on the machinery.

Because we love it. It makes us do a little inner dance of excitement, ten-   41 sion, and release. What pains we go to to disguise that. With a "serious" violent work, like *Time's Arrow* or *Goodfellas*, we tell ourselves it's important, we say we thought it was good but we didn't really enjoy it—whatever that means. When we read the accounts of the Jamie Bulger case, when we watch the latest victims being dragged in pieces from the marketplace of Sarajevo, when we follow the next installment of the Menendez trial or the Amy Fisher case, we say we're out for information, a spur to political action, an insight into life—it's the *news* after all; it's really happening.

But violent fiction with its graver purposes, if any, concealed—fiction un-   42 adorned with overt messages or historical significance—rubs our noses in the fact that narratives of horror, murder, and gore are a blast, a gas. When Freddy Krueger disembowels someone in a geyser of blood, when Hannibal Lecter washes down his victim with a nice Chianti, even when the vicar merely shoots the colonel in the drawing room—the only possible reason for this non-real, non-meaningful event to occur is that it's going to afford us pleasure. Which leaves that pleasure obvious, exposed. It's the exposure, not the thrill, the censors want to get rid of. Again: celebration is the only defense.

And yet—I know—while I celebrate, the new, not-very much-improved   43 Rome is burning.

Last year sometime, I had a conversation with a highly intelligent Scottish   44 filmmaker who had just returned from New York. Both of us had recently seen Sylvester Stallone's mountaineering action picture *Cliffhanger*. I'd seen it in the placid upper class neighborhood of South Kensington, he'd seen it in a theater in Times Square. I had been thrilled by the movie's special effects and found the hilariously dopey script sweetly reminiscent of the comic books I'd read as a child. My friend had found the picture grimly disturbing. The Times Square theater had been filled with rowdy youths. Every time the bad guys killed someone, the youths cheered—and when a woman was murdered, they howled with delight.

I freely confess that I would have been unable to enjoy the movie under those circumstances. Too damned noisy for one thing. And, all right, yes, as a repression fan I could only get off on the cruelty of the villains insofar as it fired my anticipation of the moment when Sly would cut those suckers down. Another audience could just as easily have been cheering the murders of Jews in *Schindler's List* or of blacks in *Mississippi Burning*. I understand that, and it would be upsetting and frightening to be surrounded by a crowd which seemed to have abandoned the non-negotiable values.

Michael Medved believes—not that one film produces one vicious act—but that a ceaseless barrage of anti-religion, anti-family, slap-happy gore films and fictions has contributed to the erosion of values so evident on 42nd Street. I don't know whether this is true or not—neither does he—but, as with the judge's remarks in the Bulger case, it strikes me as a very suspicious place to start. The postwar generation, in which these values went openly to the wall, was raised, after all, not on the films and books that are available now, but on the value-bloated pabulum of the 1950s. And Medved's old-fashioned values, to go by the interviews he gives, have not been noticeably eroded, though he's in the business of watching these things. Surely, the Scotsman's story illustrates that the problem lies not on the screen but in the seats, in the lives that have produced that audience. Fiction cannot make of people what life has not, good or evil. "Nothing ever becomes real till it is experienced," said Keats. "Even a proverb is no proverb to you till your Life has illustrated it."

But more to the point: though the Times Square crowd's reaction was scary—rude too—it was not necessarily harmful in itself, either to them or me. For all I know, it was a beneficial release of energy and hostility, good for the mental health. And in any case, it took place in the context of their experience of a fiction and so (outside of the unmannerly noise they made) was beyond my right to judge, approve, or condemn. Nobody has to explain his private pleasures to me.

Because fiction and reality are different. It seems appalling that anyone should have to say it, but it does need to be said. Fiction is not subject to the same moral restrictions as real life. It should remain absolutely free because, at whatever level, it is, like sex, a deeply personal experience engaged in by consent in the hope of anything from momentary release to satori. Like sex, it is available to fools and creeps and monsters, and that's life; that's tough. Because fiction is, like sex, at the core of our individual humanity. Stories are the basic building blocks of spiritual maturity. No one has any business messing with them. No one at all.

Reality, on the other hand, needs its limits, maintained by force if necessary, for the simple reason that there are actions that directly harm the safety and liberty of other people. They don't merely offend them; they don't just threaten their delicate sense of themselves; they *hurt* them—really painfully, a lot. Again, it seems wildly improbable that this should be forgotten, but Americans' current cultural discussions show every evidence that it has been. Just as fictions are being discussed as if they were actions (as when MacKinnon recently made the loony tune claim that she had been effectively raped in print), actual crimes and atrocities are being discussed as if they were cultural events, subject to aesthetic considerations. Trial lawyers won a lesser conviction for lady-killer Robert Chambers by claiming his victim was promiscuous; columnists defended dick-chopper Lorena Bobbit, saying it might be all right to mutilate a man in his sleep, provided he was a really nasty guy. The fellows who savaged Reginald Denny during the L.A. riots claim they were just part of the psychology of the mob. And the Menendez brothers based much of their defense on a portrayal of themselves as victims, a portrayal of their victims as abusers. These are all arguments appropriate to fiction only. Only in fiction are crimes mitigated by symbolism and individuals judged not for what they've done but because of what they represent. We can allow our sympathies with fictional characters to be excited more easily by illustrative circumstances because our sympathies depend upon the fact that *no one has really gotten hurt.*

Our thrills depend upon that as well. The woman who cheers when Louise   50
(or is it Thelma?) shoots a would-be rapist who has already put his hands up and his penis down is not the same as the columnist who supports such an act in real life, where it would be cold-blooded murder. The man who sports a hard-on after reading Bret Ellis's meticulous eviscerations is not the same as the guy who says "she asked for it," when hearing of an actual rape. To say that the reaction to fiction and the reaction to reality are on a continuum is moral nonsense. Every thought is on a continuum with every other. Reasonable distinctions along the continuum are the only moral game in town.

And fiction and real life must be distinguished from one another. The rad-   51
ical presumption of fiction is play, the radical presumption of real life is what Martin Amis called "the gentleness of human flesh." If we have lost the will to defend that gentleness, then God help us, because consigning Chucky to the flames is not going to bring it back.

One of the very best works of violent fiction to come along in the last few   52
years is Thomas Harris's novel, *The Silence of the Lambs.* The story, inspired, like *Psycho,* by the real-life case of murderer Ed Gein, concerns the hunt for the serial killer Jame Gumb, a failed transsexual, who strips his female victims' flesh in order to create a woman costume in which he can clothe himself. Expertly worked as an entertainment, the novel brings us face to face with the necessary corollaries to the century's materialist, non-spiritual approach to the human body. Gumb, in his obsession with the outline of his own body, treats other people as outlines as well, as shapes, things, that he can use and transform at his will. But more than that, the book calls up our own materialist reactions to the flesh. All the ugliest violence in the book is committed against women who are already dead. Our disgust is excited not by the taking of human life, but only by the butchery of flesh that used to be human life. Even the victims themselves only balk at obeying the killer's commands when they realize what's going to happen after they're gone. And yet, what moral difference does it make what Gumb does to people once he's shot them? The horror of it

is nightmarish, but its moral value is nil. Our reactions seem almost to confirm Gumb in his attitude, and underscore our flirtation with the rationalist cannibal Hannibal Lecter, the ultimate believer in humanity as meat.

When Harris introduces the killer's next victim—Catherine Martin—he presents us with a character whom we aren't meant to like very much. Rich, spoiled, arrogant, dissolute, Catherine is admirable only for the desperate cleverness she shows in her battle to stay alive. But for the rest of the novel—the attempt to rescue Catherine before it's too late—Harris depends on our fear for her, our identification with her, our deep desire to see her get out of this in one piece. The killer refers to Catherine as "It." But Harris has the artistic intelligence to know that we, the reader, will care and worry for her; if we don't, the story simply won't be any fun. 53

Harris allows us the forbidden kick of our identification with the *übermensch* Lecter whose intelligence, wit, and appreciation of fine music in no way prevent him from killing and feeding on the human race. At the same time, he relies on our irrational—spiritual—conviction that Catherine, irritating though she may be, must not be killed because . . . for no good reason: because she Must Not. Harris knowingly taps in to the purely emotional imperative we share with the book's heroine, Clarice Starling: like her, we won't be able to sleep until the screaming of innocent lambs is stopped. Harris makes pretty well sure of it. 54

At the end, in the only injection of auctorial opinion in the book, Harris wryly notes that the scholarly journals which include articles on the Gumb case never use the words *crazy* or *evil* in their discussions of the killer. The intellectual world is uncomfortable with the inherent Must-Not, the instinctive absolute, and the individual responsibility those words ultimately suggest. In short, though not killers themselves, these materialist thinkers share the moral blindness of their brilliant colleague Lecter, who really, in the end, has logic on his side. Harris, I think, is trying to argue that if we don't trust our mindless belief in the sanctity of human life, we produce monsters that the sleep of reason never dreamed of. *The Silence of the Lambs,* as the title suggests, is a dramatization of a world in which the spirit has lost its power to speak. 55

We live in that world, no question. "Destitute of faith, and terrified at skepticism": Carlyle's phrase still applies. With our culture atomizing, we think we can make up enough rules, impose enough restrictions, inject enough emptiness into our language to replace the shared moral conviction that's plainly gone. I think all stories—along with being fun—have the potential to humanize precisely because the richest fun of them is dependent on our identification with their characters; in order to have a really good time, we have to stretch the muscles of the I-and-Thou. But stories can't do for us what experience hasn't. They're just not that powerful. No murderous sexual psychopath is going to walk out of *The Piano* with a new-found respect for womankind; no decent bloke is going to close *The Silence of the Lambs* and start digging an oubliette—it doesn't matter how many times these experiences are repeated: the lives of the audience will out. And if some people are living lives in our society that make them unfit for even the most shallow thrills of fiction, you can't solve that 56 problem by eliminating the fiction; it doesn't even begin to make sense. By allowing politicians and pundits to turn our attention to "the problem of fictional violence," we are really allowing them to make us turn our backs on the problems of reality. We know it too, down deep, where we're in despair. After a crime like the Jamie Bulger murder, we should be asking ourselves a million questions: about our abandonment of family life, about our approach to poverty and unemployment, about the failures of our educational systems—about who and what we are and the ways we treat each other, the things we do and omit to do. These are hard, sometimes boring questions. But when instead we let our discussions devolve, as they have, into this glamour-rotten debate on whether people should be able to enjoy whatever fiction they please, then we make meaningless the taking of an individual's life. And that's no fun at all. And it's no fun to sit back and watch it happen.

RECORDING REFLECTIONS

Throughout "The Shrieking of the Lambs," Klavan argues that there is a distinct difference between *fictional* violence and *real* violence. As you read his essay, jot down instances of fictional violence that come to mind.

When you have finished your list, choose one of those instances and explore it in writing for 10 minutes. Consider both your initial encounter with the fictional violence and your reaction now, after having read Klavan's essay.

ACTIVITIES FOR REREADING

1. As you reread, highlight each time Klavan admits a point of view different from his own. For each instance, jot down the reasons Klavan dismisses it.
2. What tone does Klavan take with those who have opposing viewpoints? Highlight the words and phrases that indicate his tone.
3. On your second reading, pay particular attention to paragraphs 34–35. Briefly explain how Klavan seems to accept the argument that fictional violence is psychologically healthy yet at the same time dismisses its impact.
4. Klavan's essay is full of *allusions,* or references to literary works. Highlight each of them and briefly explain in writing how it helps or hurts his argument.

GROUP WORK

Personal Responses: Discuss the instance of fictional violence you each chose to write about. Why did you choose what you did? Describe your initial reactions to the fictional violence. Are your reactions different now? How? Why?

Objective Responses: Discuss the opposing points of view Klavan brings up, especially the reasons he dismisses them and the tone he takes with them.

Discuss the apparent contradiction in paragraphs 34–35, where Klavan argues that fictional violence is psychologically healthy but then dismisses its impact. How does this paradox contribute to his overall argument?

What allusions did you recognize? Which were unfamiliar to you? What effects did these allusions have?

Discuss the title of this essay. What does it mean? Think about the several definitions of *lamb,* found in most dictionaries: (1) a person who is easily deceived; (2) a gentle person; (3) a weak person. Using evidence from the essay, discuss the kinds of "lambs" Klavan likely had in mind when he titled his essay. Likewise, consider Klavan's use of the word *shrieking.*

Klavan quotes Plato in paragraph 16, who said that "our first job" is to accept good stories and reject the others. Discuss whom Plato is referring to: Who should do the accepting and the rejecting? The general public? Concerned parents? A censorship committee? The government? Some other agency?

WRITING ASSIGNMENTS

1. In paragraph 37, Klavan makes the striking observation that "Americans don't seem to like that word much: joy," which he goes on to support with examples. Read paragraph 37 again carefully, and then write an essay in which you show that your joy sometimes bothers others, especially those close to you. Give two examples of things that are joyful to you, and then discuss why they might not be thought of as joyful by people who know you well.

2. Klavan says that some people argue that a great deal of violence in the United States comes from people having been exposed to violent fiction—something every adult has been exposed to in movies, television programs, and books. What do you think? Is it true that problems with real violence occur because people watch or read so much fictional violence? Be sure to offer evidence for your opinion.

The Case for Torture

1982

MICHAEL LEVIN

It is generally assumed that torture is impermissible, a throwback to a more brutal age. Enlightened societies reject it outright, and regimes suspected of using it risk the wrath of the United States.

I believe this attitude is unwise. There are situations in which torture is not merely permissible but morally mandatory. Moreover, these situations are moving from the realm of imagination to fact.

Death: Suppose a terrorist has bidden an atomic bomb on Manhattan Island which will detonate at noon on July 4 unless . . . (here follow the usual demands for money and release of his friends from jail). Suppose, further, that he is caught at 10 a.m. of the fateful day, but—preferring death to failure—won't disclose where the bomb is. What do we do? If we follow due process—wait for his lawyer, arraign him—millions of people will die. If the only way to save those lives is to subject the terrorist to the most excruciating possible pain, what grounds can there be for not doing so? I suggest there are none. In any case, I ask you to face the question with an open mind.

Torturing the terrorist is unconstitutional? Probably. But millions of lives surely outweigh constitutionality. Torture is barbaric? Mass murder is far more barbaric. Indeed, letting millions of innocents die in deference to one who flaunts his guilt is moral cowardice, an unwillingness to dirty one's hands. If *you* caught the terrorist, could you sleep nights knowing that millions died because you couldn't bring yourself to apply the electrodes? 4

Once you concede that torture is justified in extreme cases, you have admitted that the decision to use torture is a matter of balancing innocent lives against the means needed to save them. You must now face more realistic cases involving more modest numbers. Someone plants a bomb on a jumbo jet. He alone can disarm it, and his demands cannot be met (or if they can, we refuse to set a precedent by yielding to his threats). Surely we can, we must, do anything to the extortionist to save the passengers. How can we tell 300, or 100, or 10 people who never asked to be put in danger, "I'm sorry, you'll have to die in agony, we just couldn't bring ourselves to. . . ." 5

Here are the results of an informal poll about a third, hypothetical, case. Suppose a terrorist group kidnapped a newborn baby from a hospital. I asked four mothers if they would approve of torturing kidnappers if that were necessary to get their own newborns back. All said yes, the most "liberal" adding that she would like to administer it herself. 6

I am not advocating torture as punishment. Punishment is addressed to deeds irrevocably past. Rather, I am advocating torture as an acceptable measure for preventing future evils. So understood, it is far less objectionable than many extant punishments. Opponents of the death penalty, for example, are forever insisting that executing a murderer will not bring back his victim (as if the purpose of capital punishment were supposed to be resurrection, not deterrence or retribution). But torture, in the cases described, is intended not to bring anyone back but to keep innocents from being dispatched. The most powerful argument against using torture as a punishment or to secure confessions is that such practices disregard the rights of the individual. Well, if the individual is all that important—and he is—it is correspondingly important to protect the rights of individuals threatened by terrorists. If life is so valuable that it must never be taken, the lives of the innocents must be saved even at the price of hurting the one who endangers them. 7

Better precedents for torture are assassination and pre-emptive attack. No Allied leader would have flinched at assassinating Hitler, had that been possible. (The Allies did assassinate Heydrich.) Americans would be angered to learn that Roosevelt could have had Hitler killed in 1943—thereby shortening the 8 war and saving millions of lives—but refused on moral grounds. Similarly, if nation A learns that nation B is about to launch an unprovoked attack, A has a right to save itself by destroying B's military capability first. In the same way, if the police can by torture save those who would otherwise die at the hands of kidnappers or terrorists, they must.

Idealism: There is an important difference between terrorists and their victims that should mute talk of the terrorists' "rights." The terrorist's victims are at risk unintentionally, not having asked to be endangered. But the terrorist knowingly initiated his actions. Unlike his victims, he volunteered for the risks of his deed. By threatening to kill for profit or idealism, he renounces civilized standards, and he can have no complaint if civilization tries to thwart him by whatever means necessary.   9

Just as torture is justified only to save lives (not extort confessions or recantations), it is justifiably administered only to those *known* to hold innocent lives in their hands. Ah, but how can the authorities ever be sure they have the right malefactor? Isn't there a danger of error and abuse? Won't We turn into Them?   10

Questions like these are disingenuous in a world in which terrorists proclaim themselves and perform for television. The name of their game is public recognition. After all, you can't very well intimidate a government into releasing your freedom fighters unless you announce that it is your group that has seized its embassy. "Clear guilt" is difficult to define, but when 40 million people see a group of masked gunmen seize an airplane on the evening news, there is not much question about who the perpetrators are. There will be hard cases where the situation is murkier. Nonetheless, a line demarcating the legitimate use of torture can be drawn. Torture only the obviously guilty, and only for the sake of saving innocents, and the line between Us and Them will remain clear.   11

There is little danger that the Western democracies will lose their way if they choose to inflict pain as one way of preserving order. Paralysis in the face of evil is the greater danger. Some day soon a terrorist will threaten tens of thousands of lives, and torture will be the only way to save them. We had better start thinking about this.   12

■ **RECORDING REFLECTIONS**

Levin makes the argument in his essay that under certain circumstances, torture should become official public policy in the United States. As you read, mark those places in the text that make you feel hardened, uneasy, or even shocked.

When you have finished reading, review the passages you have marked, and then write for 10 minutes describing how you now think and feel about Levin's proposal.

■ **ACTIVITIES FOR REREADING**

1. In order for an argument to be effective, it must somehow admit opposing points of view and then effectively dispose of them. What opposing views does Levin admit in the first four paragraphs? How effectively does he dispose of them? Explain briefly in writing.

2. At the beginning of paragraph 5, Levin asks the reader to make a logical jump. That is, if the reader concedes at this point that torture is justified in extreme cases, he or she has already agreed with the central point of Levin's argument. As a careful reader, have you conceded this premise at this early stage? Why or why not? Explain in writing, briefly.

3. What evidence does Levin cite to show that terrorist threats are so prevalent that we must adopt a state policy of torture? Explain.

■ **GROUP WORK**

Personal Responses: Use your Reflection Logs as memory guides and discuss how your responses to Levin's essay changed during your reading. Which passages affected you more than others? If your responses differ from one another, discuss why.

Objective Responses: First, identify the opposing arguments that Levin admits. Then, discuss the methods he uses to dispose of them. Does he do so effectively? Write down the reasons he is or is not effective.

Discuss whether you conceded Levin's main point by the beginning of paragraph 5. If you have differing opinions, discuss why. At this point in the essay, was your opinion determined by the persuasiveness of Levin's argument, or did you already hold that opinion before you started reading?

Discuss Levin's evidence that terroristic threats are a very real danger. Is his evidence strong enough to warrant the remedy he proposes?

Reread paragraph 8 and discuss the historical analogies Levin presents. In the context of his argument, do they provide valid support? Jot down members' points of disagreement, if any. If you all agree, briefly describe why in writing.

■ **WRITING ASSIGNMENTS**

1. Write an essay in which you defend Michael Levin's proposition that an official state policy of torture is an appropriate response to terroristic threats. Offer solid evidence. Also demonstrate why alternative plans wouldn't work. Make sure, too, that you deal with the fact that torture would violate the U.S. Constitution.

2. Write an essay in which you attack Levin's proposition. Again, consider the use of alternative measures and the unconstitutionality of torture. Try to demonstrate that Levin overreacts to the possibility of terrorism and that there are more practical means of dealing with threats.

Denial Behavior *1992*

MICHAEL MEDVED

A Cultural Nuthouse

In the wake of the horrifying riots in Los Angeles, thoughtful observers of every political persuasion began taking a fresh look at the connection between media messages and antisocial behavior.

"Now we live in a cultural nuthouse, a mad world of blood, torture and murder that surrounds us in the movies and follows us home when we turn on T.V. 'entertainment,'" editorialized A. M. Rosenthal in *The New York Times* (May 5, 1992). ". . . Violence made fashionable in the cause of a buck is unworthy of people of talent. Aren't those who do that becoming ashamed of themselves? Haven't they discovered that ketchup can become blood?"

In their most recent responses to such charges, leaders of the entertainment industry frankly acknowledge the appalling elements in the "cultural nuthouse" they have built, but they refuse to accept the idea that this ominous structure has significantly influenced society.

Instead of defending the content of their work, they simply deny its impact. . . .

The industry apologists insist that popular entertainment is by its very nature inconsequential, and that no one is seriously damaged by the fleeting images or subtle themes in a movie, TV show, or popular song. As the Hollywood establishment never tires of pointing out, several decades of research by social scientists have failed to produce conclusive, irrefutable proof that brutality and promiscuity in a product of the mass media can *cause* destructive behavior in the real world. . . .

Hollywood 4, Straw Men 0

In March 1992, I took part in a well-publicized panel discussion on the global impact of popular culture sponsored by the American Enterprise Institute in Washington. Seated to my immediate right at the long table of participants was Mr. Jack Valenti, the unfailingly articulate and courtly president of the Motion Picture Association of America, and the most prominent spokesman for the Hollywood establishment, In the course of an occasionally heated exchange of views, Mr. Valenti made an emphatic statement that neatly summed up the industry's first line of defense in all discussions of its impact on society. "I have examined the archives of people who write on socological things in this country and sociologists, and I've found that social scientists are like psychiatrists in a murder trial," Valenti declared. "The prosecution has one . . . and the defense has one. . . . *But I haven't found anybody who has said that movies cause anybody to do anything.*"

Along similar lines, Mike Medavoy, chairman of TriStar Pictures and one   7
of the most thoughtful and respected of all motion picture executives, told a
1991 meeting of Hollywood political activists that even though he personally
disliked watching violence on screen, "to make a claim that films are *responsible* for violence in society is ludicrous."

In January 1992, *Los Angeles Times* columnist Robert A. Jones offered a   8
more detailed explanation of film's allegedly limited ability to influence its audience. "The truth is this: the power of a movie tends to last only as long as the
lights are down and the screen flickers," he wrote. "While you're watching, it
owns you. But as soon as you walk out of the theater and the cold air hits your
face, the movie starts to evaporate, almost like it's leaking through your skin.
By the time you reach the parking lot, it's mostly gone."

This reassuring notion turns up time and again in the industry's efforts to   9
confound its critics. An especially eloquent and effective attack on those of us
who try to draw a connection between media violence and its real-world counterpart came from Teller, one half of the celebrated Penn and Teller magic-and-
comedy duo, who wrote an Op-Ed piece for *The New York Times* in January
1992. In it, he derided those

> who seem to think that if we stop showing rape in movies people will stop com-
> mitting it in real life. Anthropologists call this "magical thinking." It's the same im-
> pulse that makes people stick pins in voodoo dolls, hoping to cripple an enemy. It
> feels logical, but it does not take into account that rape predates home video by
> thousands of years.
>
> Zealots have long tried to prove that "evil" fiction causes wickedness in the real
> world. But the facts fail to cooperate. . . . Those who want us to give up our free-
> dom disagree. They claim people are not smart enough to tell make-believe from re-
> ality. Give us a break! When one pays seven dollars to go into a theater to see big
> pictures moving on a wall, one does not have to be a mental giant to realize you are
> watching a movie. It makes you wonder how they explain the millions of people
> who saw Psycho without stealing bankrolls or bumping off blondes.

With this elegant flourish, the magician brought off a rhetorical sleight of   10
hand, imputing to his ideological opponents opinions that they do not hold and
demolishing positions that they had never advanced.

To the best of my knowledge, none of the prominent participants in the   11
current national debate on media values has ever suggested that "if we stop
showing rape in movies people will stop committing it in real life"; nor has anyone seriously suggested that "people are not smart enough to tell make-believe
from reality."

Instead of confronting the substantive concerns of those who question   12
Hollywood's excesses, what Teller and the other commentators quoted above
have done is to set up convenient and highly vulnerable straw men. Naturally, their self-contained debate against these phantoms allows them to
achieve a magnificent victory, with a final score reading Hollywood 4, Straw
Men 0.

Essential Distinctions

In an attempt to avoid the application of such deceptive tactics, . . . I want 13
to leave no room for confusion about what I *am* saying—and what I am *not*
saying—about the popular culture's impact on society.

All future disputants in this controversy, please take note: 14

■ I do not claim that media messages *cause* destructive behavior, but I do 15
contend that they *encourage* it. I have never suggested that Hollywood is
single-handedly responsible for America's social problems, but I do believe
that the entertainment industry exacerbates them and that it has become
an important contributing factor in many of our current difficulties.

■ At the same time, I never stress the pernicious power of *one* movie, or one 16
TV show, or one hit song; what concerns me is the accumulated impact of
irresponsible messages that are repeated hour after hour, year after year.
The most significant problems of the popular culture stem from the pervasive presence of antisocial material, not from a few isolated examples of
offensiveness.

With these essential distinctions in mind, I believe that some of the most 17
outspoken critics of Hollywood's values make a serious mistake when they try
to indict the industry by emphasizing a handful of shocking episodes in which
unbalanced individuals injured themselves or others by imitating behavior they
saw on screen.

We have all read lurid press accounts of such cases, describing the tragic 18
toll of twenty-six people who killed themselves in games of Russian roulette
shortly after *The Deer Hunter* aired on national TV; or the fourteen-year-old girl
who meticulously copied the murders she saw in the movie *Heathers* (1990) by
organizing a game of croquet and a picnic in which she poisoned two of her
best friends: or the two sixteen-year-olds who put bullets through their heads
while listening again and again to Ozzy Osbourne's "Suicide Solution"; or the
four Oklahoma high school dropouts who recently gang-raped and battered
two of their classmates while repeatedly playing a tape of the rap song "Gangster of Love"—which specifically glorifies just such an assault.

These and many similar incidents are most certainly dramatic and disturb- 19
ing, but the lawsuits and public controversy surrounding them only serve to distract attention from the more significant questions about Hollywood and society.

The most profound problem with the popular culture isn't its immediate 20
impact on a few vulnerable and explosive individuals, but its long-term effect
on all the rest of us. The deepest concerns about Hollywood go beyond the industry's role in provoking a handful of specific crimes and involve its contribution to a general climate of violence and self-indulgence.

A Clear Consensus

The entertainment establishment responds to these concerns by supple- 21
menting its standard rhetorical tricks with a few laughably bald-faced lies. On

May 18, 1992, Barbara Dixon, Jack Valenti's colleague as spokesperson for the Motion Picture Association of America, told the *Los Angeles Times*: "We have dealt with this issue for a long time and have looked at a number of studies. According to the First Amendment lawyers who have handled the issue for us, none of [the studies] say that motion picture violence affects the behavior of people."

If Ms. Dixon has accurately summarized the report she received from her lawyers, then she should immediately seek more competent legal representation: in fact, more than three thousand research projects and scientific studies between 1960 and 1992 have confirmed the connection between a steady diet of violent entertainment and aggressive and antisocial behavior.

In a comprehensive 1982 report, published along with five thick volumes of social science surveys, the Surgeon General of the United States concluded that "there is a clear consensus among most researchers that television violence leads to aggressive behavior." Or, as the American Psychological Association declared in a 1991 resolution following a five-year task-force investigation: "The conclusion drawn on the basis of twenty-five years of research . . . is that viewing televised violence may lead to increases in aggressive attitudes, values, and behavior, particularly in children."

Corporate Arrogance

In a stunning display of corporate arrogance, the major entertainment conglomerates disregard the conclusions of all the leading researchers and continue to insist that their work has no harmful impact on society.

With almost ritualized regularity, their official representatives repeat the claim that scientific investigations show "mixed" results on the question of media influence. "There are so many yesses and nos in the literature that it's confusing," declared CBS vice president David Blank in one typical statement in 1978. In a striking demonstration of wishful thinking, he then added, "I'm not sure anyone will ever solve the problem."

Meanwhile, the entertainment industry greatly encourages the confusion described by Dr. Blank by spending literally millions of dollars to commission its own studies which—surprise!—usually demonstrate that the media exert no influence on anyone. CBS, ABC, and NBC have all sponsored such projects with great fanfare, and the resulting research is regularly dusted off and trotted out whenever the industry wants to demonstrate divided opinion among the experts on the question of the pop culture's impact.

The fact that such studies are taken seriously at all is itself a scandal: the industry-originated surveys deserve no more respect or consideration than we grant to all the many research reports commissioned by the tobacco industry to prove that the Surgeon General is wrong and that cigarette smoking is actually good for you.

The claims that Hollywood's messages do nothing to shape attitudes and behavior are equally ludicrous, and on occasion the truth is so obvious that not even the generous expenditure of industry funds can guarantee the research results the moguls desire. In 1978, CBS invested $290,000 on a six-year study on the effect of television on teenage boys conducted by the Survey Research Centre of the London School of Economics. William Belson, who supervised the project, concluded from his examination that "the evidence is very strongly supportive of the hypothesis that long-term exposure to violence increases the degree to which boys engage in violence of a serious kind. The same goes for violence of the less serious kind, such as swearing and the use of bad language, aggressiveness in sport or play, threatening to use violence on another boy, writing slogans on walls, and breaking windows."

Predictably enough, when confronted with these unexpected and unwelcome results, CBS managed to keep its enthusiasm firmly under control. The network's embarrassed spokesman, David Blank, did his level best to downplay the value of the findings his own company had financed, announcing that "Belson's study was interesting, but has come along after a lot of other work has been done and adds nothing of consequence from our standpoint." 29

The Height of Hypocrisy

As representatives of the television business continue to stonewall, insisting that their programming has no power whatever to influence the public, no one seems to have noticed that this utterly implausible position contradicts the most basic assumptions of their industry. 30

In 1982, ABC released a commissioned study in which the hired-gun experts declared that "the research does not support the conclusion that television significantly cultivates viewer attitudes and perceptions of social reality." 31

If the executives at ABC sincerely believe this nonsense and agree that their broadcasts fail to "cultivate viewer attitudes," then the network should prepare to refund all the billions of dollars of advertising revenue that it has collected under false pretenses. 32

The mighty mechanism of commercial television is based entirely on the premise that broadcast advertising can alter the buying behavior of a significant segment of the huge viewing audience. That is why hardheaded corporations will gladly invest millions of dollars in a few thirty-second commercials, secure in the knowledge that even this sort of fleeting exposure can make an important difference in the public's point of view. 33

It is the height of hypocrisy that the same network executives who accept—and demand—this lavish payment for the briefest moments of broadcast advertising simultaneously try to convince us that all their many hours of programming do nothing to change the attitudes of the audience. In short, they have adopted the outrageously illogical assumption that a sixty-second commercial makes a more significant impression than a sixty-minute sitcom. 34

On the one hand we're told that an hour of television programming does nothing to shape the sentiments of the public, and on the other we're asked to believe that the brief spots that interrupt this program are powerful enough to change perceptions of anything from canned goods to candidates. The under- 35 lying idea appears to be the bizarre notion that the average viewer ignores or shrugs off the televised entertainment he has chosen to watch, while sitting up in his chair and paying close attention only when the commercials come on.

The industry simply cannot have it both ways: if it claims a near magical   36
ability to sell products or politics, planting lasting images in just a few quick seconds, then it must acknowledge the long-term impact of its prime time programs, with their frequently violent and antisocial themes.

The motion picture business faces a similarly absurd internal contradiction   37
in its refusal to acknowledge the influence of the movies it makes.

In recent years, what Hollywood calls "product placement" has played an   38
increasingly prominent role in the production process, with corporate logos and brand names frequently displayed in the course of every major film. This process helps the producers defray the astronomical costs of filmmaking, as the advertiser provides props or sets or costumes, or agrees to help sell the film by mounting a tie-in promotional campaign at the time of its release. As the *Wall Street Journal* reports: "Friendly producers send scripts . . . weeks and even months before filming starts, and the company analyzes them scene by scene to see if it can place a product—or advertising material, a billboard perhaps— on, under, or behind the stars."

According to most estimates, these efforts result in several million dollars   39
in benefits to the producers of a typical major studio film. Writing in the *Atlantic Monthly,* Mark Crispin Miller reports that the 1989 James Bond entry, *License to Kill,* featured a scene in which 007 ostentatiously smokes Larks—a magical moment for which Philip Morris paid $350,000. In the Michael Keaton comedy *Mr. Mom* (1983), Miller identified plugs for McDonald's, Domino's pizza, Terminix exterminators, Folger's coffee, Lite beer, Jack Daniel's, Van Camp's chili, Ban deodorant, Windex, Tide, Spray 'n Wash, Borax, Clorox 2, and Downy fabric softener.

Corporate marketing experts invest considerable effort and expense in   40
these placements because their research indicates that they are highly effective. Even if the viewer registers the name of the product only in an unconscious manner, the association between a familiar brand and a glamorous star will make a measurable difference in future sales.

This is an established principle in the motion picture business—accepted   41
without question when it comes to taking the money of eager advertisers. At the same time that everyone agrees that a two-second glimpse of a box of Tide can help the manufacturer, there is no acknowledgment that two hours of graphic gore can hurt the audience.

Imagine a forthcoming feature film with a torrid sex scene between two   42
charismatic stars. On the night stand beside the bed is a subtle product placement—say a bottle of mouthwash, with its label turned toward the camera. The current logic of the motion picture business suggests that the typical member of the audience turns his eyes away from two naked, gorgeous bodies in transports of passion and instead focuses all attention on the bottle of mouthwash at the edge of the frame. How else can one explain the assumption that the

mouthwash label will influence the viewers' future behavior, but the vivid sex scene will not?

In short, the industry's position is both flagrantly dishonest and lavishly   43 illogical.

■ RECORDING REFLECTIONS

Medved argues that long-term exposure to media violence promotes violent behavior. As you read, highlight examples of his cause/effect reasoning.

When you have finished reading, write for 10 minutes, explaining whether you think Medved's arguments are convincing. Use examples from your own experience to justify your opinion.

■ ACTIVITIES FOR REREADING

1. Medved quotes several movie industry representatives in the "Hollywood 4, Straw Men 0" section of his essay. Why? How does that strategy enhance his own argument? Record your answers in two or three sentences.
2. Reread paragraphs 26, 27, and 28 extra carefully. How convincing is Medved's argument here? Why? Record your reasons.
3. Why does Medved place his argument about the success of commercials and product placement where he does? What hard evidence does he cite to prove his claims? Write down your reasons.

■ GROUP WORK

Personal Responses: Refer to comments in your Reflection Logs, and discuss the effectiveness of Medved's argument. Discuss, too, how convincing your own examples are.

Objective Responses: Discuss Medved's "Straw Man" argument. What is it exactly, and how does it advance his point of view? Discuss the effectiveness of his argument in paragraphs 26, 27, and 28 and whether there are any flaws in his reasoning. Also discuss the effectiveness, placement, and evidence of his final argument.

Next, look again at Medved's final argument (paragraphs 30–43). Is it presented rationally, emotionally, or both ways? Discuss and jot down the reasons for your opinions.

■ WRITING ASSIGNMENTS

1. Medved contends that antisocial material pervades the popular media. Using your knowledge of current TV programs, books, movies, pop music, and the like, write an essay refuting or supporting his assertion. Use numerous and specific examples to support your argument. If it will help your argument, refer to Medved and specifically refute or support parts of his argument.

2. Write a more extensive essay in which you compare and contrast the views of Stephen King ("Why We Crave Horror Movies"), Andrew Klavan ("The Shrieking of the Lambs"), and Medved on media violence.

Sexism in English: A 1990s Update   1990

ALLEEN PACE NILSEN

Twenty years ago I embarked on a study of the sexism inherent in American English. I had just returned to Ann Arbor, Michigan, after living for two years (1967–69) in Kabul, Afghanistan, where I had begun to look critically at the role society assigned to women. The Afghan version of the *chaderi* prescribed for Moslem women was particularly confining. Few women attended the American-built Kabul University where my husband was teaching linguistics because there were no women's dormitories, which meant that the only females who could attend were those whose families happened to live in the capital city. Afghan jokes and folklore were blatantly sexist, for example this proverb, "If you see an old man, sit down and take a lesson; if you see an old woman, throw a stone." 1

But it wasn't only the native culture that made me question women's roles; it was also the American community. Nearly six hundred Americans lived in Kabul, mostly supported by U.S. taxpayers. The single women were career secretaries, school teachers, or nurses. The three women who had jobs comparable to the American men's jobs were textbook editors with the assignment of developing reading books in Dari (Afghan Persian) for young children. They worked at the Ministry of Education, a large building in the center of the city. There were no women's restrooms, so during their two-year assignment whenever they needed to go to the bathroom they had to walk across the street and down the block to the Kabul Hotel. 2

The rest of the American women were like myself—wives and mothers whose husbands were either career diplomats, employees of USAID, or college professors who had been recruited to work on various contract teams including an education team from Teachers College, Columbia University and an agricultural team from the University of Wyoming. These were the women who were most influential in changing my way of thinking. We were suddenly bereft of our traditional roles; some of us became alcoholics; others got very good at bridge, while others searched desperately for ways to contribute either to our families or to the Afghans. The local economy provided few jobs for women and certainly none for foreigners; we were isolated from former friends and the social goals we had grown up with. Most of us had three servants (they worked for $1.00 a day) because the cook refused to wash dishes and the dishwasher refused to water the lawn or sweep the sidewalks—it was their form of unionization. Occasionally, someone would try to get along 3 without servants, but it was impossible because the houses were huge and we didn't have the mechanical aids we had at home. Drinking water had to be brought from the deep well at the American Embassy, and kerosene and wood stoves had to be stocked and lit. The servants were all males, the highest-paid one being the cook who could usually speak some English. Our days revolved around supervising these servants. One woman's husband got so tired of hearing her complain about such annoyances as the *bacha* (the housekeeper) stealing kerosene and needles and batteries, and about the cook putting chili powder instead of paprika on the deviled eggs, and about the gardener subcontracting his work and expecting her to pay all his friends that he scheduled an hour a week for listening to complaints. The rest of the time he wanted to keep his mind clear to focus on his important work with his Afghan counterparts and with the president of the university and the Minister of Education. What he was doing in this country was going to make a difference! In the great eternal scheme of things, of what possible importance could be his wife's trivial troubles with the servants?

These were the thoughts in my mind when we finished our contract and returned in the fall of 1969 to the University of Michigan in Ann Arbor. I was surprised to find that many other women were also questioning the expectations that they had grown up with. In the spring of 1970, a women's conference was announced. I hired a babysitter and attended, but I returned home more troubled than ever. Now that I knew housework was worth only a dollar a day, I couldn't take it seriously, but I wasn't angry in the same way these women were. Their militancy frightened me. Since I wasn't ready for a revolution, I decided I would have my own feminist movement. I would study the English language and see what it could tell me about sexism. I started reading a desk dictionary and making notecards on every entry that seemed to tell something about male and female. I soon had a dog-eared dictionary, along with a collection of notecards filling two shoe boxes.

Ironically, I started reading the dictionary because I wanted to avoid getting involved in social issues, but what happened was that my notecards brought me right back to looking at society. Language and society are as intertwined as a chicken and an egg. The language that a culture uses is telltale evidence of the values and beliefs of that culture. And because there is a lag in how fast a language changes—new words can easily be introduced, but it takes a long time for old words and usages to disappear—a careful look at English will reveal the attitudes that our ancestors held and that we as a culture are therefore predisposed to hold. My notecards revealed three main points. Friends have offered the opinion that I didn't need to read the dictionary to learn such obvious facts. Nevertheless, it was interesting to have linguistic evidence of sociological observations.

Women Are Sexy; Men Are Successful

First, in American culture a woman is valued for the attractiveness and sexiness of her body, while a man is valued for his physical strength and accomplishments. A woman is sexy. A man is successful.

A persuasive piece of evidence supporting this view are the eponyms—words   7
that have come from someone's name—found in English. I had a two-and-a-
half-inch stack of cards taken from men's names, but less than a half-inch stack
from women's names, and most of those came from Greek mythology. In the
words that came into American English since we separated from Britain, there
are many eponyms based on the names of famous American men: bartlett pear,
boysenberry, diesel engine, franklin stove, ferris wheel, gattling gun, mason jar,
sideburns, sousaphone, schick test, and Winchester rifle. The only common
eponyms taken from American women's names are *Alice blue* (after Alice Roosevelt Longworth), *bloomers* (after Amelia Jenks Bloomer), and *Mae West jacket*
(after the buxom actress). Two out of the three feminine eponyms relate closely
to a woman's physical anatomy, while the masculine eponyms (except for *sideburns* after General Burnsides) have nothing to do with the namesake's body, but
instead honor the man for an accomplishment of some kind.

Although in Greek mythology women played a bigger role than they did in   8
the biblical stories of the Judeo-Christian cultures and so the names of god-
desses are accepted parts of the language in such place names as Pomona from
the goddess of fruit and Athens from Athena and in such common words as *cereal* from Ceres, *psychology* from Psyche, and *arachnoid* from Arachne, the
same tendency to think of women in relation to sexuality is seen in the eponyms
aphrodisiac from Aphrodite, the Greek name for the goddess of love and beauty,
and *venereal disease,* from Venus, the Roman name for Aphrodite.

Another interesting word from Greek mythology is *Amazon.* According to   9
Greek folk etymology, the a means "without" as in *atypical,* or *amoral* while *ma-
zon* comes from *mazos,* meaning *breast* as still seen in *mastectomy.* In the Greek
legend, Amazon women cut off their right breasts so that they could better
shoot their bows. Apparently, the storytellers had a feeling that for women to
play the active, "masculine" role that the Amazons adopted for themselves, they
had to trade in part of their femininity.

This preoccupation with women's breasts is not limited to ancient stories.   10
As a volunteer for the University of Wisconsin's *Dictionary of American Regional
English (DARE),* I read a western trapper's diary from the 1830s. I was to make
notes of any unusual usages or language patterns. My most interesting finding
was that he referred to a range of mountains as *The Teats,* a metaphor based on
the similarity between the shapes of the mountains and women's breasts. Because today we use the French wording, *The Grand Tetons,* the metaphor isn't
as obvious, but I wrote to the map-makers and found the following listings:
Nippletop and *Little Nipple Top* near Mt. Marcy in the Adirondacks, *Nipple
Mountain* in Archuleta County, Colorado, *Nipple Peak* in Coke County, Texas,
Nipple Butte in Pennington, South Dakota, *Squaw Peak* in Placer County, California (and many other locations), *Maiden's Peak* and *Squaw Tit* (they're the
same mountain) in the Cascade Range in Oregon, *Mary's Nipple* near Salt Lake
City, Utah, and *Jane Russell Peaks* near Stark, New Hampshire.

Except for the movie star Jane Russell, the women being referred to are   11
anonymous—it's only a sexual part of their body that is mentioned. When topo-

graphical features are named after men, it's probably not going to be to draw attention to a sexual part of their bodies but instead to honor individuals for an accomplishment. For example, no one thinks of a part of the male body when hearing a reference to Pike's Peak, Colorado, or Jackson Hole, Wyoming.

Going back to what I learned from my dictionary cards, I was surprised to 12 realize how many pairs of words we have in which the feminine word has acquired sexual connotations while the masculine word retains a serious businesslike aura. For example, a *callboy* is the person who calls actors when it is time for them to go on stage, but a *callgirl* is a prostitute. Compare *sir* and *madam*. *Sir* is a term of respect while *madam* has acquired the specialized meaning of a brothel manager. Something similar has happened to *master* and *mistress*. Would you rather have a painting by *an old master* or an *old mistress?*

It's because the word *woman* had sexual connotations, as in "She's his 13 woman," that people began avoiding its use, hence such terminology as *ladies' room, lady of the house,* and *girls' school* or *school for young ladies.* Feminists, who ask that people use the term *woman* rather than *girl* or *lady,* are rejecting the idea that *woman* is primarily a sexual term. They have been at least partially successful in that today *woman* is commonly used to communicate gender without intending implications about sexuality.

I found two hundred pairs of words with masculine and feminine forms, e.g., 14 *heir–heiress, hero–heroine, steward–stewardess, usher–usherette,* etc. In nearly all such pairs, the masculine word is considered the base with some kind of a feminine suffix being added. The masculine form is the one from which compounds are made, e.g., from *king–queen* comes *kingdom* but not *queendom,* from *sportsman–sportslady* comes *sportsmanship* but not *sportsladyship.* There is one—and only one—semantic area in which the masculine word is not the base or more powerful word. This is in the area dealing with sex and marriage. When someone refers to a *virgin,* a listener will probably think of a female unless the speaker specifies *male* or uses a masculine pronoun. The same is true for *prostitute.*

In relation to marriage, there is much linguistic evidence showing that 15 weddings are more important to women than to men. A woman cherishes the wedding and is considered a bride for a whole year, but a man is referred to as a groom only on the day of the wedding. The word bride appears in *bridal attendant, bridal gown, bridesmaid, bridal shower,* and even *bridegroom. Groom* comes from the Middle English *grom,* meaning "man," and in this sense is seldom used outside of a wedding. With most pairs of male/female words, people habitually put the masculine word first—*Mr. and Mrs., his and hers, boys and girls, men and women, kings and queens, brothers and sisters, guys and dolls,* and *host and hostess*—but it is the *bride and groom* who are talked about, not the *groom and bride.*

The importance of marriage to a woman is also shown by the fact that when 16 a marriage ends in death, the woman gets the title of *widow.* A man gets the derived title of *widower.* This term is not used in other phrases or contexts, but *widow* is seen in *widowhood, widow's peak,* and *widow's walk.* A *widow* in a card game is an extra hand of cards, while in typesetting it is an extra line of type.

How changing cultural ideas bring changes to language is clearly visible in   17
this semantic area. The feminist movement has caused the differences between
the sexes to be downplayed, and since I did my dictionary study two decades
ago, the word *singles* has largely replaced such sex-specific and value-laden
terms as *bachelor, old maid, spinster, divorcee, widow,* and *widower.* And in 1970
I wrote that when a man is called a *professional* he is thought to be a doctor or
a lawyer, but when people hear a woman referred to as a *professional* they are
likely to think of a prostitute. That's not as true today because so many women
have become doctors and lawyers that it's no longer incongruous to think of
women in those professional roles.

Another change that has taken place is in wedding announcements. They   18
used to be sent out from the bride's parents and did not even give the name of
the groom's parents. Today, most couples choose to list either all or none of the
parents' names. Also it is now much more likely that both the bride and groom's
picture will be in the newspaper, while a decade ago only the bride's picture was
published on the "Women's" or the "Society" page. Even the traditional wording of the wedding ceremony is being changed. Many officials now pronounce
the couple "husband and wife" instead of the old "man and wife," and they ask
the bride if she promises "to love, honor, and cherish," instead of "to love,
honor, and obey."

Women Are Passive; Men Are Active

The wording of the wedding ceremony also relates to the second point that   19
my cards showed, which is that women are expected to play a passive or weak
role while men play an active or strong role. In the traditional ceremony, the
official asks, "Who gives the bride away?" and the father answers, "I do." Some
fathers answer, "Her mother and I do," but that doesn't solve the problem inherent in the question. The idea that a bride is something to be handed over
from one man to another bothers people because it goes back to the days when
a man's servants, his children and his wife were all considered to be his property. They were known by his name because they belonged to him and he was
responsible for their actions and their debts.

The grammar used in talking or writing about weddings as well as other   20
sexual relationships shows the expectation of men playing the active role. Men
wed women while women *become* brides of men. A man *possesses* a woman; he
deflowers her; he *performs;* he *scores;* he *takes away* her virginity. Although a
woman can *seduce* a man, she cannot offer him her virginity. When talking
about virginity, the only way to make the woman the actor in the sentence is to
say that "She lost her virginity," but people lose things by accident rather than
by purposeful actions, and so she's only the grammatical, not the real-life, actor.

The reason that women tried to bring the term *Ms.* into the language to re-   21
place *Miss* and *Mrs.* relates to this point. Married women resented being identified only under their husband's names. For example, when Susan Glascoe did
something newsworthy, she would be identified in the newspaper only as Mrs.

John Glascoe. The dictionary cards showed what appeared to be an attitude on the part of editors that it was almost indecent to let a respectable woman's name march unaccompanied across the pages of a dictionary. Women were listed with male names whether or not the male contributed to the woman's reason for being in the dictionary or in his own right was as famous as the woman. For example, Charlotte Brontë was identified as Mrs. Arthur B. Nicholls, Amelia Earhart as Mrs. George Palmer Putnam, Helen Hayes as Mrs. Charles MacArthur, Jenny Lind as Mme. Otto Goldschmit, Cornelia Otis Skinner as the daughter of Otis Skinner, Harriet Beecher Stowe as the sister of Henry Ward Beecher, and Edith Sitwell as the sister of Osbert and Sacheverell. A very small number of women got into the dictionary without the benefit of a masculine escort. They were rebels and crusaders: temperance leaders Frances Elizabeth Caroline Willard and Carry Nation, women's rights leaders Carrie Chapman Catt and Elizabeth Cady Stanton, birth control educator Margaret Sanger, religious leader Mary Baker Eddy, and slaves Harriet Tubman and Phyllis Wheatley.

22 Etiquette books used to teach that if a woman had *Mrs.* in front of her name then the husband's name should follow because *Mrs.* is an abbreviated form of *Mistress* and a woman couldn't be a mistress of herself. As with many arguments about "correct" language usage, this isn't very logical because *Miss* is also an abbreviation of *Mistress*. Feminists hoped to simplify matters by introducing *Ms.* as an alternative to both *Mrs.* and *Miss,* but what happened is that *Ms.* largely replaced *Miss* to become a catch-all business title for women. Many married women still prefer the title *Mrs.*, and some resent being addressed with the term *Ms.* As one frustrated newspaper reporter complained, "Before I can write about a woman, I have to know not only her marital status but also her political philosophy." The result of such complications may contribute to the demise of titles which are already being ignored by many computer programmers who find it more efficient to simply use names; for example in a business letter: "Dear Joan Garcia," instead of "Dear Mrs. Joan Garcia," "Dear Ms. Garcia," or "Dear Mrs. Louis Garcia."

23 The titles given to royalty provide an example of how males can be disadvantaged by the assumption that they are always to play the more powerful role. In British royalty, when a male holds a title, his wife is automatically given the feminine equivalent. But the reverse is not true. For example, a *count* is a high political officer with a *countess* being his wife. The same is true for a *duke* and a *duchess* and a *king* and a *queen.* But when a female holds the royal title, the man she marries does not automatically acquire the matching title. For example, Queen Elizabeth's husband has the title of *prince* rather than *king,* but if Prince Charles should become king while he is still married to Lady or Princess Diana, she will be known as the queen. The reasoning appears to be that since masculine words are stronger, they are reserved for true heirs and withheld from males coming into the royal family by marriage. If Prince Phillip were called *King Phillip,* it would be much easier for British subjects to forget where the true power lies.

The names that people give their children show the hopes and dreams they 24
have for them, and when we look at the differences between male and female
names in a culture we can see the cumulative expectations of that culture. In
our culture girls often have names taken from small, aesthetically pleasing
items, e.g., *Ruby, Jewel,* and *Pearl. Esther* and *Stella* mean "star." *Ada* means
"ornament," and *Vanessa* means "butterfly." Boys are more likely to be given
names with meanings of power and strength, e.g., *Neil* means "champion,"
Martin is from Mars, the god of war, *Raymond* means "wise protection," *Harold*
means "chief of the army," *Ira* means "vigilant," *Rex* means "king," and *Richard*
means "strong king,"

We see similar differences in food metaphors. Food is a passive substance 25
just sitting there waiting to be eaten. Many people have recognized this and so
no longer feel comfortable describing women as "delectable morsels." However, when I was a teenager, it was considered a compliment to refer to a girl
(we didn't call anyone a *woman* until she was middle-aged) as a *cute tomato, a
peach, a dish, a cookie, honey, sugar,* or *sweetie-pie.* When being affectionate,
women will occasionally call a man *honey* or *sweetie,* but in general, food
metaphors are used much less often with men than with women. If a man is
called a *fruit,* his masculinity is being questioned. But it's perfectly acceptable
to use a food metaphor if the food is heavier and more substantive than that
used for women. For example, pinup pictures of women have long been known
as *cheesecake,* but when Burt Reynolds posed for a nude centerfold, the picture
was immediately dubbed *beefcake,* c.f. *a hunk of meat.* That such sexual references to men have come into the general language is another reflection of how
society is beginning to lessen the differences between their attitudes toward
men and women. 26

Something similar to the *fruit* metaphor happens with references to plants.
We insult a man by calling him a *pansy,* but it wasn't considered particularly
insulting to talk about a girl being a *wallflower,* a *clinging vine,* or a *shrinking
violet,* or to give girls such names as *Ivy, Rose, Lily, Iris, Daisy, Camellia, Heather,*
and *Flora.* A plant metaphor can be used with a man if the plant is big and
strong, for example Andrew Jackson's nickname of *Old Hickory.* Also, the
phrases *blooming idiots* and *budding geniuses* can be used with either sex, but
notice how they are based on the most active thing a plant can do which is to
bloom or bud. 27

Animal metaphors also illustrate the different expectations for males and
females. Men are referred to as *studs, bucks,* and *wolves* while women are referred to with such metaphors as *kitten, bunny, beaver, bird, chick,* and *lamb.* In
the 1950s we said that boys went *tomcatting,* but today it's just *catting around*
and both boys and girls do it. When the term *foxy,* meaning that someone was
sexy, first became popular, it was used only for girls, but now someone of either sex can be described as a fox. Some animal metaphors that are used pre-
dominantly with men have negative connotations based on the size and/or
strength of the animals, e.g., *beast, bull-headed, jackass, rat, loanshark,* and *vul-
ture.* Negative metaphors used with women are based on smaller animals, e.g.,

social butterfly, mousy, catty, and *vixen.* The feminine terms connote action, but not the same kind of large-scale action as with the masculine terms.

Women Are Connected with Negative Connotations, Men with Positive Connotations

The final point that my notecards illustrated was how many positive con- 28 notations are associated with the concept of masculine, while there are either trivial or negative connotations connected with the corresponding feminine concept. An example from the animal metaphors makes a good illustration. The word *shrew* taken from the name of a small but especially vicious animal was defined in my dictionary as "an ill-tempered scolding woman," but the word *shrewd* taken from the same root was defined as "marked by clever, discerning awareness" and was illustrated with the phrase "a shrewd businessman."

Early in life, children are conditioned to the superiority of the masculine 29 role. As child psychologists point out, little girls have much more freedom to experiment with sex roles than do little boys. If a little girl acts like a *tomboy,* most parents have mixed feelings, being at least partially proud. But if their little boy acts like a *sissy* (derived from *sister*), they call a psychologist. It's perfectly acceptable for a little girl to sleep in the crib that was purchased for her brother, to wear his hand-me-down jeans and shirts, and to ride the bicycle that he has outgrown. But few parents would put a boy baby in a white and gold crib decorated with frills and lace, and virtually no parents would have their little boy wear his sister's hand-me-down dresses, nor would they have their son ride a girl's pink bicycle with a flower-bedecked basket. The proper names given to girls and boys show this same attitude. Girls can have "boy" names—*Cris, Craig, Jo, Kelly, Shawn, Teri, Toni,* and *Sam*—but it doesn't work the other way around. A couple of generations ago, *Beverley, Frances, Hazel, Marion,* and *Shirley* were common boys' names. As parents gave these names to more and more girls, they fell into disuse for males, and some older men who have these names prefer to go by their initials or by such abbreviated forms as *Haze* or *Shirl.*

When a little girl is told to *be a lady*, she is being told to sit with her knees 30 together and to be quiet and dainty. But when a little boy is told to *be a man*, he is being told to be noble, strong, and virtuous—to have all the qualities that the speaker looks on as desirable. The concept of manliness has such positive connotations that it used to be a compliment to call someone a *he-man,* to say that he was doubly a man. Today many people are more ambivalent about this term and respond to it much as they do to the word macho. But calling someone a *manly man* or a *virile man* is nearly always meant as a compliment. *Virile* comes from the Indo-European vir meaning "man," which is also the basis of *virtuous.* Contrast the positive connotations of both *virile and virtuous* with the negative connotations of *hysterical.* The Greeks took this latter word from their name for uterus (as still seen in *hysterectomy*). They thought that women were the only ones who experienced uncontrolled emotional outbursts and so the condition must have something to do with a part of the body that only women have.

Differences between positive male and negative female connotations can be   31
seen in several pairs of words which differ denotatively only in the matter of
sex. *Bachelor* as compared to *spinster* or *old maid* has such positive connotations that women try to adopt them by using the term *bachelor-girl* or *bache-
lorette*. *Old maid* is so negative that it's the basis for metaphors: pretentious and
fussy old men are called *old maids,* as are the leftover kernels of unpopped popcorn and the last card in a popular children's game.

Patron and *matron* (Middle English for *father* and *mother*) have such dif-   32
ferent levels of prestige that women try to borrow the more positive masculine
connotations with the word *patroness,* literally "female father." Such a peculiar
term came about because of the high prestige attached to *patron* in such
phrases as a *patron of the arts* or a *patron saint. Matron* is more apt to be used
in talking about a woman in charge of a jail or a public restroom.

When men are doing jobs that women often do, we apparently try to pay   33
the men extra by giving them fancy titles; for example, a male cook is more
likely to be called a *chef,* while a male seamstress will get the title of *tailor.* The
armed forces have a special problem in that they recruit under such slogans as
"The Marine Corps Builds Men!" and "Join the Army! Become a Man." Once the
recruits are enlisted, they find themselves doing much of the work that has
been traditionally thought of as "woman's work." The solution to getting the
work done and not insulting anyone's masculinity was to change the titles as
shown below:

waiter ⟶ orderly
nurse ⟶ medic or corpsman
secretary ⟶ clerk-typist
assistant ⟶ adjutant
dishwasher or kitchen helper ⟶ KP (kitchen police)

Compare *brave* and *squaw.* Early settlers in America truly admired Indian   34
men and hence named them with a word that carried connotations of youth,
vigor, and courage. But they used the Algonquin's name for "woman," and over
the years it developed almost opposite connotations to those of *brave. Wizard*
and *witch* contrast almost as much. The masculine *wizard* implies skill and wisdom combined with magic, while the feminine *witch* implies evil intentions
combined with magic. Part of the unattractiveness of both *witch* and *squaw* is
that they have been used so often to refer to old women, something with which
our culture is particularly uncomfortable, just as the Afghans were. Imagine my
surprise when I ran across the phrases grandfatherly advice and *old wives' tales*
and realized that the underlying implication is the same as the Afghan proverb
about old men being worth listening to while old women talk only foolishness.

Other terms which show how negatively we view old women as compared   35
to young women are *old nag* as compared to *filly, old crow* or *old bat* as compared to *bird,* and being *catty* as compared to being *kittenish.* There is no
matching set of metaphors for men. The chicken metaphor tells the whole story
of a woman's life. In her youth she is a *chick.* Then she marries and begins

feathering her nest. Soon she begins feeling *cooped up,* so she goes to *hen parties* where she *cackles* with her friends. Then she has her *brood,* begins to *henpeck* her husband, and finally turns into an *old biddy.*

I embarked on my study of the dictionary not with the intention of prescribing language change but simply to see what the language would tell me about sexism. Nevertheless I have been both surprised and pleased as I've watched the changes that have occurred over the past two decades. I'm one of those linguists who believes that new language customs will cause a new generation of speakers to grow up with different expectations. This is why I'm happy about people's efforts to use inclusive language, to say *he* or *she* or *they* when speaking about individuals whose names they do not know. I'm glad that leading publishers have developed guidelines to help writers use language that is fair to both sexes, and I'm glad that most newspapers and magazines list women by their own names instead of only by their husbands' names and that educated and thoughtful people no longer begin their business letters with "Dear Sir" or "Gentlemen," but instead use a memo form or begin with such salutations as "Dear Colleagues," "Dear Reader," or "Dear Committee Members." I'm also glad that such words as *poetess, authoress, conductress,* and *aviatrix* now sound quaint and old fashioned and that *chairman* is giving way to *chair* or *head, mailman* to *mail carrier, clergyman* to *clergy,* and *stewardess* to *flight attendant.* I was also pleased when the National Oceanic and Atmospheric Administration bowed to feminist complaints and in the late '70s began to alternate men's and women's names for hurricanes. However, I wasn't so pleased to discover that the change did not immediately erase sexist thoughts from everyone's mind as shown by a headline about Hurricane David in a 1979 New York tabloid, "David Rapes Virgin Islands." More recently a similar metaphor appeared in a headline in the *Arizona Republic* about Hurricane Charlie: "Charlie Quits Carolinas, Flirts with Virginia."

What these incidents show is that sexism is not something existing independently in American English or in the particular dictionary that I happened to read. Rather, it exists in people's minds. Language is like an x-ray in providing visible evidence of invisible thoughts. The best thing about people being interested in and discussing sexist language is that as they make conscious decisions about what pronouns they will use, what jokes they will tell or laugh at, how they will write their names, or how they will begin their letters, they are forced to think about the underlying issue of sexism. This is good, because as a problem that begins in people's assumptions and expectations, it's a problem that will be solved only when a great many people have given it a great deal of thought.

36

37

RECORDING REFLECTIONS

This essay, particularly in paragraphs 25 through 27, lists a great many slang terms that describe males and females. In your Reflection Log, list currently common slang terms that describe males and females (and that are not profane). List at least three for females and three for males.

After you have drawn up your list, pick one of the female slang terms and one of the male slang terms. Explore them both for 10 minutes in one piece of writing.

ACTIVITIES FOR REREADING

1. One of the author's strategies is to give a lot of examples to support each point that she makes. As you reread "Sexism in English," list two of the points that she makes along with three examples that support each point.
2. The tone of this essay can be described as objective, in that it's neither angry nor placid. Instead, it's calm and deliberate. Highlight three sentences that illustrate the author's tone.
3. This essay ends on a positive note. In two or three sentences, paraphrase the last paragraph, which demonstrates Nilsen's optimism.

GROUP WORK

Personal Responses: Using the examples from your Reflection Logs, discuss the slang terms that you listed. Specifically discuss each in terms of the images it conveys. Discuss attitudes toward the sexes in the 1990s. Have sexist attitudes toward men and women changed, based on the examples you and your classmates have listed?

Objective Responses: Discuss Nilsen's experiences with sexism in Afghanistan, and compare them to her experiences with sexism in the United States. How do they differ? How are they similar?

Discuss Nilsen's attitude toward her material and her reading audience. Give evidence to support the statement that Nilsen is an objective language scholar who also has a personal interest in the topic of sexist language.

Discuss Nilsen's main point and her attitude about it. For example, is she optimistic? Pessimistic? Passionate? Neutral?

WRITING ASSIGNMENTS

1. "The language that a culture uses determines its perceptions of the world." Using this quotation and Nilsen's essay as a starting point, write an essay in which you use four currently employed slang terms to show how Americans perceive significant parts of their culture.
2. Write an essay in which you explore the ordinary spoken language of your friends in terms of its clarity of meaning. For example, many people insert the word *like* in conservation—as in "This class is, like, interesting"—when, in fact, *like* has no meaning in such a sentence. Others use the word *goes* to mean *says*—as in "He goes, 'I'm tired' "—when, in fact, *he* didn't *go* anywhere. In your exploratory essay, demonstrate that you have listened carefully to the language of the people around you by giving significant examples of how they use words that mask the clarity of their statements.

A Hanging   *1950*

GEORGE ORWELL

It was in Burma, a sodden morning of the rains. A sickly light, like yellow   1
tinfoil, was slanting over the high walls into the jail yard. We were waiting outside the condemned cells, a row of sheds fronted with double bars, like small
animal cages. Each cell measured about ten feet by ten and was quite bare
within except for a plank bed and a pot for drinking water. In some of them
brown, silent men were squatting at the inner bars, with their blankets draped
round them. These were the condemned men, due to be hanged within the next
week or two.

One prisoner had been brought out of his cell. He was a Hindu, a puny   2
wisp of a man, with a shaven head and vague liquid eyes. He had a thick,
sprouting mustache, absurdly too big for his body, rather like the mustache of
a comic man on the films. Six tall Indian warders were guarding him and getting him ready for the gallows. Two of them stood by with rifles and fixed bayonets, while the others handcuffed him, passed a chain through his handcuffs
and fixed it to their belts, and lashed his arms tight to his sides. They crowded
very close about him, with their hands always on him in a careful, caressing
grip, as though all the while feeling him to make sure he was there. It was like
men handling a fish which is still alive and may jump back into the water. But
he stood quite unresisting, yielding his arms limply to the ropes, as though he
hardly noticed what was happening.

Eight o'clock struck and a bugle call, desolately thin in the wet air, floated   3
from the distant barracks. The superintendent of the jail, who was standing
apart from the rest of us, moodily prodding the gravel with his stick, raised his
head at the sound. He was an army doctor, with a grey toothbrush mustache
and a gruff voice. "For God's sake, hurry up, Francis," he said irritably. "The
man ought to have been dead by this time. Aren't you ready yet?"

Francis, the head jailer, a fat Dravidian in a white drill suit and gold spec-   4
tacles, waved his black hand. "Yes sir, yes sir," he bubbled. "All iss satisfactorily
prepared. The hangman iss waiting. We shall proceed."

"Well, quick march, then. The prisoners can't get their breakfast till this   5
job's over."

We set out for the gallows. Two warders marched on either side of the pris-   6
oner, with their rifles at the slope; two others marched close against him, gripping him by arm and shoulder, as though at once pushing and supporting him.
The rest of us, magistrates and the like, followed behind. Suddenly, when we
had gone ten yards, the procession stopped short without any order or warning. A dreadful thing had happened—a dog, come goodness knows whence,
had appeared in the yard. It came bounding among us with a loud volley of
barks and leapt around us wagging its whole body, wild with glee at finding so
many human beings together. It was a large woolly dog, half Airedale, half

pariah. For a moment it pranced around us, and then, before anyone could stop it, it had made a dash for the prisoner, and jumping up tried to lick his face. Everybody stood aghast, too taken aback even to grab the dog.

"Who let that bloody brute in here?" said the superintendent angrily. "Catch it, someone!"   7

A warder detached from the escort, charged clumsily after the dog, but it danced and gambolled just out of his reach, taking everything as part of the game. A young Eurasian jailer picked up a handful of gravel and tried to stone the dog away, but it dodged the stones and came after us again. Its yaps echoed from the jail walls. The prisoner, in the grasp of the two warders, looked on incuriously, as though this was another formality of the hanging. It was several minutes before someone managed to catch the dog. Then we put my handkerchief through its collar and moved off once more, with the dog still straining and whimpering.   8

It was about forty yards to the gallows. I watched the bare brown back of the prisoner marching in front of me. He walked clumsily with his bound arms, but quite steadily, with that bobbing gait of the Indian who never straightens his knees. At each step his muscles slid neatly into place, the lock of hair on his scalp danced up and down, his feet printed themselves on the wet gravel. And once, in spite of the men who gripped him by each shoulder, he stepped lightly aside to avoid a puddle on the path.   9

It is curious; but till that moment I had never realized what it means to de-stroy a healthy, conscious man. When I saw the prisoner step aside to avoid the puddle, I saw the mystery, the unspeakable wrongness, of cutting a life short when it is in full tide. This man was not dying, he was alive just as we are alive. All the organs of his body were working—bowels digesting food, skin renewing itself, nails growing, tissues forming—all toiling away in solemn foolery. His nails would still be growing when he stood on the drop, when he was falling through the air with a tenth-of-a-second to live. His eyes saw the yellow gravel and the grey walls, and his brain still remembered, foresaw, reasoned—even about puddles. He and we were a party of men walking together, seeing, hear-ing, feeling, understanding the same world; and in two minutes, with a sudden snap, one of us would be gone—one mind less, one world less.   10

The gallows stood in a small yard, separate from the main grounds of the prison, and overgrown with tall prickly weeds. It was a brick erection like three sides of a shed, with planking on top, and above that two beams and a cross-bar with the rope dangling. The hangman, a greyhaired convict in the white uniform of the prison, was waiting beside his machine. He greeted us with a servile crouch as we entered. At a word from Francis the two warders, gripping the prisoner more closely than ever, half led, half pushed him to the gallows and helped him clumsily up the ladder. Then the hangman climbed up and fixed the rope around the prisoner's neck.   11

We stood waiting, five yards away. The warders had formed in a rough cir-cle round the gallows. And then, when the noose was fixed, the prisoner began crying out to his god. It was a high, reiterated cry of "Ram! Ram! Ram! Ram!" not urgent and fearful like a prayer or cry for help, but steady, rhythmical, al-   12 most like the tolling of a bell. The dog answered the sound with a whine. The hangman, still standing on the gallows, produced a small cotton bag like a flour bag and drew it down over the prisoner's face. But the sound, muffled by the cloth, still persisted, over and over again: "Ram! Ram! Ram! Ram! Ram!"

The hangman climbed down and stood ready, holding the lever. Minutes 13 seemed to pass. The steady muffled crying from the prisoner went on and on, "Ram! Ram! Ram!" never faltering for an instant. The superintendent, his head on his chest, was slowly poking the ground with his stick; perhaps he was counting the cries, allowing the prisoner a fixed number—fifty, perhaps, or a hundred. Everyone had changed colour. The Indians had gone grey like bad coffee, and one or two of the bayonets were wavering. We looked at the lashed, hooded man on the drop, and listened to his cries—each cry another second of life; the same thought was in all our minds; oh, kill him quickly, get it over, stop that abominable noise!

Suddenly the superintendent made up his mind. Throwing up his head he 14 made a swift motion with his stick. "Chalo!" he shouted almost fiercely.

There was a clanking noise, and then dead silence. The prisoner had van- 15 ished, and the rope was twisting on itself. I let go of the dog, and it galloped im- mediately to the back of the gallows; but when it got there it stopped short, barked, and then retreated into a corner of the yard, where it stood among the weeds, looking timorously out at us. We went round the gallows to inspect the prisoner's body. He was dangling with his toes pointed straight downwards, very slowly revolving, as dead as a stone.

The superintendent reached out with his stick and poked the bare brown 16 body; it oscillated slightly. "*He's* all right," said the superintendent. He backed out from under the gallows, and blew out a deep breath. The moody look had gone out of his face quite suddenly. He glanced at his wrist-watch. "Eight min- utes past eight. Well, that's all for this morning, thank God."

The warders unfixed bayonets and marched away. The dog, sobered and 17 conscious of having misbehaved itself, slipped after them. We walked out of the gallows yard, past the condemned cells with their waiting prisoners, into the big central yard of the prison. The convicts, under the command of warders armed with lathis, were already receiving their breakfast. They squatted in long rows, each man holding a tin pannikin, while two warders with buckets marched around ladling out rice; it seemed quite a homely, jolly scene, after the hanging. An enormous relief had come upon us now that the job was done. One felt an impulse to sing, to break into a run, to snigger. All at once everyone be- gan chattering gaily.

The Eurasian boy walking beside me nodded towards the way we had 18 come, with a knowing smile: "Do you know, sir, our friend (he meant the dead man) when he heard his appeal had been dismissed, he pissed on the floor of his cell. From fright. Kindly take one of my cigarettes, sir. Do you not admire my new silver case, sir? From the boxwallah, two rupees eight annas. Classy European style."

Several people laughed—at what, nobody seemed certain. 19

Francis was walking by the superintendent, talking garrulously: "Well, sir, 20
all has passed off with the utmost satisfactoriness. It was all finished—flick!
Like that. It iss not always so—oah, no! I have known cases where the doctor
was obliged to go beneath the gallows and pull the prissoner's legs to ensure de-
cease. Most disagreeable!"

"Wriggling about, eh? That's bad," said the superintendent. 21

"Ach, sir, it iss worse when they become refractory! One man, I recall, clung 22
to the bars of hiss cage when we went to take him out. You will scarcely credit,
sir, that it took six warders to dislodge him, three pulling at each leg. We reasoned with him, 'My dear fellow,' we said, 'think of all the pain and trouble you
are causing to us!' But no, he would not listen! Ach, he wass very troublesome!"

I found that I was laughing quite loudly. Everyone was laughing. Even the 23
superintendent grinned in a tolerant way. "You'd better all come out and have
a drink," he said quite genially. "I've got a bottle of whisky in the car. We could
do with it."

We went through the big double gates of the prison into the road. "Pulling 24
at his legs!" exclaimed a Burmese magistrate suddenly, and burst into a loud
chuckling. We all began laughing again. At that moment Francis' anecdote
seemed extraordinarily funny. We all had a drink together, native and European alike, quite amicably. The dead man was a hundred yards away.

■ RECORDING REFLECTIONS

In this autobiographical essay, Orwell is the colonial who observes the actions of men sworn to uphold the law. They do what they believe that they must
do, not what the author might believe is the best course of action.

You, too, have likely made decisions that you believed were the *right* decisions, under the circumstances, but not necessarily the *best* decisions, upon reflection. In your Reflection Log, jot down three of these decisions, adding
enough detail so that you can recall them later in a discussion.

■ ACTIVITIES FOR REREADING

1. Note that this is a highly descriptive essay. Its author carefully describes the
   area, the people, the gallows, and the prisoner, for example. Copy from this
   essay five descriptions of no more than 10 words each that you believe are
   particularly effective.
2. Francis, the head jailer, tells a story at the end of the essay that causes
   everyone to laugh. In a few sentences, describe your own reaction to the
   end of this essay.
3. Interestingly, one of the most active characters in this story is a dog. Record
   in your Reflection Log three of the dog's activities in enough detail that you
   can later discuss their relevance to the essay.
4. Does the essay make a statement against capital punishment? Highlight
   passages that support or contradict this possibility.

■ **GROUP WORK**

Personal Responses: Using what you have recorded in your Reflection Logs, discuss the decisions that you have made that seemed the right decisions at the time but not, as you reflect upon them, the best decisions. After hearing each group member's explanation of what he or she decided and why, discuss whether you agree that each of your peers made the right decision.

Objective Responses: Discuss Orwell's use of description in this essay, identifying which descriptions affected you more strongly than others. See if most of the group can agree that one description is superior to the others.

Orwell seems to be an observer, more than a participant, in this essay. He takes the role of a recorder of actions, rather than an involved actor. In some ways, he seems emotionally removed from the hanging. Why has he taken this role? Why isn't he engaged to the point that he tries to stop the hanging, for example, or to comfort the prisoner? Where do we learn of Orwell's actual feelings? Discuss.

This essay seems to make several points, one of which is a strong argument against the colonial occupation of a country—in this case, of course, the English occupation of what was then called *Burma*. What evidence in the essay supports that claim? Discuss.

This essay also seems to argue against capital punishment. Does it? What evidence supports your opinion?

■ **WRITING ASSIGNMENTS**

1. Using evidence from Orwell's essay, discuss whether you believe that the prisoner was treated fairly. Write an essay in which you offer clear evidence to back up your opinion. Try to relate, as best you can, to the times and conditions of the situation, as portrayed in the essay.

2. In an essay, discuss the major character—the *I* in Orwell's essay—in terms of how his presence is important to the narrative. Does he play a central role? If so, what? Who, if anyone, overshadows him? Which character, in your opinion, is the most important one in the narrative? Why?

Future Shlock   *1988*

NEIL POSTMAN

Human intelligence is among the most fragile things in nature. It doesn't   1
take much to distract it, suppress it, or even annihilate it. In this century, we have had some lethal examples of how easily and quickly intelligence can be defeated by any one of its several nemeses: ignorance, superstition, moral fervor, cruelty, cowardice, neglect. In the late 1920s, for example, Germany was, by any

measure, the most literate, cultured nation in the world. Its legendary seats of learning attracted scholars from every corner. Its philosophers, social critics, and scientists were of the first rank; its humane traditions an inspiration to less favored nations. But by the mid-1930s—that is, in less than ten years—this cathedral of human reason had been transformed into a cesspool of barbaric irrationality. Many of the most intelligent products of German culture were forced to flee—for example, Einstein, Freud, Karl Jaspers, Thomas Mann, and Stefan Zweig. Even worse, those who remained were either forced to submit their minds to the sovereignty of primitive superstition, or—worse still—willingly did so: Konrad Lorenz, Werner Heisenberg, Martin Heidegger, Gerhardt Hauptmann. On May 10, 1933, a huge bonfire was kindled in Berlin and the books of Marcel Proust, André Gide, Emile Zola, Jack London, Upton Sinclair, and a hundred others were committed to the flames, amid shouts of idiot delight. By 1936, Joseph Paul Goebbels, Germany's Minister of Propaganda, was issuing a proclamation which began with the following words: "Because this year has not brought an improvement in art criticism, I forbid once and for all the continuance of art criticism in its past form, effective as of today." By 1936, there was no one left in Germany who had the brains or courage to object.

Exactly why the Germans banished intelligence is a vast and largely unanswered question. I have never been persuaded that the desperate economic depression that afflicted Germany in the 1920s adequately explains what happened. To quote Aristotle: Men do not become tyrants in order to keep warm. Neither do they become stupid—at least not *that* stupid. But the matter need not trouble us here. I offer the German case only as the most striking example of the fragility of human intelligence. My focus here is the United States in our own time, and I wish to worry you about the rapid erosion of our own intelligence. If you are confident that such a thing cannot happen, your confidence is misplaced, I believe, but it is understandable. 2

After all, the United States is one of the few countries in the world founded by intellectuals—men of wide learning, of extraordinary rhetorical powers, of deep faith in reason. And although we have had our moods of anti-intellectualism, few people have been more generous in support of intelligence and learning than Americans. It was the United States that initiated the experiment in mass education that is, even today, the envy of the world. It was America's churches that laid the foundation of our admirable system of higher education; it was the Land-Grant Act of 1862 that made possible our great state universities; and it is to America that scholars and writers have fled when freedom of the intellect became impossible in their own nations. This is why the great historian of American civilization Henry Steele Commager called America "the Empire of Reason." But Commager was referring to the United States of the eighteenth and nineteenth centuries. What term he would use for America today, I cannot say. Yet he has observed, as others have, a change, a precipitous decline in our valuation of intelligence, in our uses of language, in the disciplines of logic and reason, in our capacity to attend to complexity. Perhaps he would agree with me that the Empire of Reason is, in fact, gone, and that the most apt term for America today is the Empire of Shlock. 3

In any case, this is what I wish to call to your notice: the frightening dis-   4
placement of serious, intelligent public discourse in American culture by the
imagery and triviality of what may be called show business. I do not see the decline of intelligent discourse in America leading to the barbarisms that flour-
ished in Germany, of course. No scholars, I believe, will ever need to flee
America. There will be no bonfires to burn books. And I cannot imagine any
proclamations forbidding once and for all art criticism, or any other kind of
criticism. But this is not a cause for complacency, let alone celebration. A culture does not have to force scholars to flee to render them impotent. A culture
does not have to burn books to assure that they will not be read. And a culture
does not need a Minister of Propaganda issuing proclamations to silence criticism. There are other ways to achieve stupidity, and it appears that, as in so
many other things, there is a distinctly American way.

To explain what I am getting at, I find it helpful to refer to two films, which   5
taken together embody the main lines of my argument. The first film is of recent vintage and is called *The Gods Must Be Crazy*. It is about a tribal people
who live in the Kalahari Desert plains of southern Africa, and what happens to
their culture when it is invaded by an empty Coca-Cola bottle tossed from the
window of a small plane passing overhead. The bottle lands in the middle of the
village and is construed by these gentle people to be a gift from the gods, for
they not only have never seen a bottle before but have never seen glass either.
The people are almost immediately charmed by the gift, and not only because
of its novelty. The bottle, it turns out, has multiple uses, chief among them the
intriguing music it makes when one blows into it.

But gradually a change takes place in the tribe. The bottle becomes an ir-   6
resistible preoccupation. Looking at it, holding it, thinking of things to do with
it displace other activities once thought essential. But more than this, the Coke
bottle is the only thing these people have ever seen of which there is only one
of its kind. And so those who do not have it try to get it from the one who does.
And the one who does refuses to give it up. Jealousy, greed, and even violence
enter the scene, and come very close to destroying the harmony that has characterized their culture for a thousand years. The people begin to love their bottle more than they love themselves, and are saved only when the leader of the
tribe, convinced that the gods must be crazy, returns the bottle to the gods by
throwing it off the top of a mountain.

The film is great fun and it is also wise, mainly because it is about a sub-   7
ject as relevant to people in Chicago or Los Angeles or New York as it is to those
of the Kalahari Desert. It raises two questions of extreme importance to our situation: How does a culture change when new technologies are introduced to
it? And is it always desirable for a culture to accommodate itself to the demands of new technologies? The leader of the Kalahari tribe is forced to confront these questions in a way that Americans have refused to do. And because
his vision is not obstructed by a belief in what Americans call "technological
progress," he is able with minimal discomfort to decide that the songs of the
Coke bottle are not so alluring that they are worth admitting envy, egotism,
and greed to a serene culture.

The second film relevant to my argument was made in 1967. It is Mel   8
Brooks's first film, *The Producers*. *The Producers* is a rather raucous comedy
that has at its center a painful joke: An unscrupulous theatrical producer has
figured out that it is relatively easy to turn a buck by producing a play that
fails. All one has to do is induce dozens of backers to invest in the play by
promising them exorbitant percentages of its profits. When the play fails, there
being no profits to disperse, the producer walks away with thousands of dollars that can never be claimed. Of course, the central problem he must solve is
to make sure that his play is a disastrous failure. And so he hits upon an excellent idea: he will take the most tragic and grotesque story of our century—the
rise of Adolf Hitler—and make it into a musical.

Because the producer is only a crook and not a fool, he assumes that the   9
stupidity of making a musical on this theme will be immediately grasped by audiences and that they will leave the theater in dumbfounded rage. So he calls
his play *Springtime for Hitler*, which is also the name of its most important
song. The song begins with the words:

> *Springtime for Hitler and Germany;*
> *Winter for Poland and France.*

The melody is catchy, and when the song is sung it is accompanied by a   10
happy chorus line. (One must understand, of course, that *Springtime for Hitler*
is no spoof of Hitler, as was, for example, Charlie Chaplin's *The Great Dictator*.
The play is instead a kind of denial of Hitler in song and dance; as if to say, it
was all in fun.)

The ending of the movie is predictable. The audience loves the play and   11
leaves the theater humming *Springtime for Hitler*. The musical becomes a great
hit. The producer ends up in jail, his joke having turned back on him. But
Brooks's point is that the joke is on us. Although the film was made years before a movie actor became President of the United States, Brooks was making
a kind of prophecy about that—namely, that the producers of American culture
will increasingly turn our history, politics, religion, commerce, and education
into forms of entertainment, and that we will become as a result a trivial people, incapable of coping with complexity, ambiguity, uncertainty, perhaps even
reality. We will become, in a phrase, a people amused into stupidity.

For those readers who are not inclined to take Mel Brooks as seriously as I   12
do, let me remind you that the prophecy I attribute here to Brooks was, in fact,
made many years before by a more formidable social critic than he. I refer to Al-
dous Huxley, who wrote *Brave New World* at the time that the modern monu-
ments to intellectual stupidity were taking shape: Nazism in Germany, fascism
in Italy, communism in Russia. But Huxley was not concerned in his book with
such naked and crude forms of intellectual suicide. He saw beyond them, and
mostly, I must add, he saw America. To be more specific, he foresaw that the
greatest threat to the intelligence and humane creativity of our culture would not
come from Big Brother and Ministries of Propaganda, or gulags and concentration camps. He prophesied, if I may put it this way, that there is tyranny lurking

in a Coca-Cola bottle; that we could be ruined not by what we fear and hate but by what we welcome and love, by what we construe to be a gift from the gods.

And in case anyone missed his point in 1932, Huxley wrote *Brave New World Revisited* twenty years later. By then, George Orwell's *1984* had been published, and it was inevitable that Huxley would compare Orwell's book with his own. The difference, he said, is that in Orwell's book people are controlled by inflicting pain. In *Brave New World,* they are controlled by inflicting pleasure.   13

The Coke bottle that has fallen in our midst is a corporation of dazzling technologies whose forms turn all serious public business into a kind of *Springtime for Hitler* musical. Television is the principal instrument of this disaster, in part because it is the medium Americans most dearly love, and in part because it has become the command center of our culture. Americans turn to television not only for their light entertainment but for their news, their weather, their politics, their religion, their history—all of which may be said to be their serious entertainment. The light entertainment is not the problem. The least dangerous things on television are its junk. What I am talking about is television's preemption of our culture's most serious business. It would be merely banal to say that television presents us with entertaining subject matter. It is quite another thing to say that on television all subject matter is presented as entertaining. And that is how television brings ruin to any intelligent understanding of public affairs.   14

Political campaigns, for example, are now conducted largely in the form of television commercials. Candidates forgo precision, complexity, substance—in some cases, language itself—for the arts of show business: music, imagery, celebrities, theatrics. Indeed, political figures have become so good at this, and so accustomed to it, that they do television commercials even when they are not campaigning. Even worse, political figures appear on variety shows, soap operas, and sitcoms. *Where* is the line that one ought to be able to draw between politics and entertainment? I would suggest that television has annihilated it.   15

But politics is only one arena in which serious language has been displaced by the arts of show business. We have all seen how religion is packaged on television, as a kind of Las Vegas stage show, devoid of ritual, sacrality, and tradition. Today's electronic preachers are in no way like America's evangelicals of the past. Men like Jonathan Edwards, Charles Finney, and George Whitefield were preachers of theological depth, authentic learning, and great expository power. Electronic preachers such as Jimmy Swaggart, Jim Bakker, and Jerry Falwell are merely performers who exploit television's visual power and their own charisma for the greater glory of themselves.   16

We have also seen "Sesame Street" and other educational shows in which the demands of entertainment take precedence over the rigors of learning. And we well know how American businessmen, working under the assumption that potential customers require amusement rather than facts, use music, dance, comedy, cartoons, and celebrities to sell their products.   17

Even our daily news, which for most Americans means television news, is packaged as a kind of show, featuring handsome news readers, exciting music,   18 and dynamic film footage. Most especially, film footage. When there is no film footage, there is no story. Stranger still, commercials may appear anywhere in a news story—before, after, or in the middle. This reduces all events to trivialities, sources of public entertainment and little more. After all, how serious can a bombing in Lebanon be if it is shown to us prefaced by a happy United Airlines commercial and summarized by a Calvin Klein jeans commercial? Indeed, television newscasters have added to our grammar a new part of speech—what may be called the "Now . . . this" conjunction, a conjunction that does not connect two things, but disconnects them. When newscasters say, "Now . . . this," they mean to indicate that what you have just heard or seen has no relevance to what you are about to hear or see. There is no murder so brutal, no political blunder so costly, no bombing so devastating that it cannot be erased from our minds by a newscaster saying, "Now . . . this." He means that you have thought long enough on the matter (let us say, for forty seconds) and you must now give your attention to a commercial. Such a situation is not "the news." It is merely a daily version of *Springtime for Hitler*, and in my opinion accounts for the fact that Americans are among the most ill-informed people in the world. To be sure, we know *of* many things; but we know *about* very little.

I do not mean to say that the trivialization of American public discourse is   19
all accomplished on television. Rather, television is the paradigm for all our attempts at public communication. It conditions our minds to apprehend the world through fragmented pictures and forces other media to orient themselves in that direction. You know the standard question we put to people who have difficulty understanding even simple language: we ask them impatiently, "Do I have to draw a picture for you?" Well, it appears that, like it or not, our culture will draw pictures for us, will explain the world to us in pictures. As a medium for conducting public business, language had receded in importance; it has been moved to the periphery of culture and has been replaced at the center by the entertaining visual image.

Please understand that I am making no criticism of the visual arts in gen-   20
eral. That criticism is made by God, not by me. You will remember that in His Second Commandment, God explicitly states that "Thou shalt not make unto thee any graven image, nor any likeness of anything that is in Heaven above, or that is in the earth beneath, or the waters beneath the earth." I have always felt that God was taking a rather extreme position on this, as is His way. As for myself, I am arguing from the standpoint of a symbolic relativist. Forms of communication are neither good nor bad in themselves. They become good or bad depending on their relationship to other symbols and on the functions they are made to serve within a social order. When a culture becomes overloaded with pictures; when logic and rhetoric lose their binding authority; when historical truth becomes irrelevant; when the spoken or written word is distrusted or makes demands on our attention that we are incapable of giving; when our politics, history, education, religion, public information, and commerce are expressed largely in visual imagery rather than words, then a culture is in serious jeopardy.

Neither do I make a complaint against entertainment. As an old song has   21
it, life is not a highway strewn with flowers. The sight of a few blossoms here
and there may make our journey a trifle more endurable. But in America, the
least amusing people are our professional entertainers. In our present situation, our preachers, entrepreneurs, politicians, teachers, and journalists are
committed to entertaining us through media that do not lend themselves to serious, complex discourse. But these producers of our culture are not to be
blamed. They, like the rest of us, believe in the supremacy of technological progress. It has never occurred to us that the gods might be crazy. And even if it did,
there is no mountaintop from which we can return what is dangerous to us.

We would do well to keep in mind that there are two ways in which the   22
spirit of a culture may be degraded. In the first—the Orwellian—culture becomes a prison. This was the way of the Nazis, and it appears to be the way of
the Russians. In the second—the Huxleyan—culture becomes a burlesque. This
appears to be the way of the Americans. What Huxley teaches is that in the Age
of Advanced Technology, spiritual devastation is more likely to come from an
enemy with a smiling countenance than from one whose face exudes suspicion
and hate. In the Huxleyan prophecy, Big Brother does not watch us, by his
choice; we watch him, by ours. When a culture becomes distracted by trivia;
when political and social life are redefined as a perpetual round of entertainments; when public conversation becomes a form of baby talk; when a people
become, in short, an audience and their public business a vaudeville act, then—
Huxley argued—a nation finds itself at risk and culture-death is a clear possibility. I agree.

RECORDING REFLECTIONS

Throughout his essay, Postman claims that American intelligence has declined as a result of new technologies, especially television. During his argument, he refers to numerous historical events and figures to illustrate his
points. As you read, make a list in your Reflection Log of the references you are
not familiar with.

After you have made your list, reflect in writing for 10 minutes on your
feelings about not knowing about these things—especially considering what
Postman has to say about the decline of intelligence in the United States.

ACTIVITIES FOR REREADING

1. Identify Postman's purpose in "Future Shlock." Highlight passages that make
   his purpose clear. What is his thesis? Where in the essay does he state it?
2. Pay particular attention to the final sentence of paragraph 1. How, specifically, does Postman use this sentence? In what other paragraphs does he
   use this same strategy?
3. What prevailing mood does Postman establish in the essay? Highlight specific passages that create that mood. Describe the mood in your own words.

■ **GROUP WORK**

Personal Responses: Using your Reflection Logs as reminders, discuss the historical references you can identify as well as those you can't. Discuss how important it is to know these references in order to understand and fully appreciate Postman's argument. Discuss your personal responses to knowing and not knowing these references.

Objective Responses: Discuss what you think Postman's purpose is and where in the essay he makes it clear. See if you can come to agreement about his thesis. As a group, restate his thesis.

Discuss how Postman ends the first paragraph by examining the final sentence. Use your notes to identify other paragraphs where he uses the same strategy. Discuss the effectiveness of this strategy.

Using your notes, compare the passages you feel demonstrate the essay's prevailing mood. Discuss. Can you agree on what that mood is?

■ **WRITING ASSIGNMENTS**

1. Write an essay in which you analyze and describe your TV-watching habits. Categorize the shows you watch. How accurately do they reflect the real world? How do you react to them? Do they in any way affect how you view the world? Explain. Make sure to use plenty of examples.

2. Watch a number of TV shows in one of Postman's "serious" categories: politics, religion, education, news. How are they alike? Different? Are they designed as mere entertainment, as Postman claims? Does watching them diminish people's skills in language, logic, or problem solving, as he claims? Write an essay with a thesis that takes a clear point of view on this issue. Illustrate your points with examples.

The War Room at Bellevue

1983

GEORGE SIMPSON

Bellevue. The name conjures up images of an indoor war zone: the wounded and bleeding lining the halls, screaming for help while harried doctors in blood-stained smocks rush from stretcher to stretcher, fighting a losing battle against exhaustion and the crushing number of injured. "What's worse," says a long-time Bellevue nurse, "is that we have this image of being a hospital only for. . . ." She pauses, then lowers her voice; "for crazy people."

Though neither battlefield nor Bedlam is a valid image, there is something extraordinary about the monstrous complex that spreads for five blocks along First Avenue in Manhattan. It is said best by the head nurse in Adult Emergency Service: "If you have any chance for survival, you have it here."

Survival—that is why they come. Why do injured cops drive by a half-dozen other hospitals to be treated at Bellevue? They've seen the Bellevue emergency team in action.

9:00 P.M. It is a Friday night in the Bellevue emergency room. The after-work crush is over (those who've suffered through the day, only to come for help after the five-o'clock whistle has blown) and it is nearly silent except for the mutter of voices at the admitting desk, where administrative personnel discuss who will go for coffee. Across the spotless white-walled lobby, ten people sit quietly, passively, in pastel plastic chairs, waiting for word of relatives or to see doctors. In the past 24 hours, 300 people have come to the Bellevue Adult Emergency Service. Fewer than 10 percent were true emergencies. One man sleeps fitfully in the emergency ward while his heartbeat, respiration, and blood pressure are monitored by control consoles mounted over his bed. Each heartbeat trips a tiny bleep in the monitor, which attending nurses can hear across the ward. A half hour ago, doctors in the trauma room withdrew a six-inch stiletto blade from his back. When he is stabilized, the patient will be moved upstairs to the twelve-bed Surgical Intensive Care Unit.

9:05 P.M. An ambulance backs into the receiving bay, its red and yellow lights flashing in and out of the lobby. A split second later, the glass doors burst open as a nurse and an attendant roll a mobile stretcher into the lobby. When the nurse screams, "Emergent!" the lobby explodes with activity as the way is cleared to the trauma room. Doctors appear from nowhere and transfer the bloodied body of a black man to the treatment table. Within seconds his clothes are stripped away, revealing a tiny stab wound in his left side. Three doctors and three nurses rush around the victim, each performing a task necessary to begin treatment. Intravenous needles are inserted into his arms and groin. A doctor draws blood for the lab, in case surgery is necessary. A nurse begins inserting a catheter into the victim's penis and continues to feed in tubing until the catheter reaches the bladder. Urine flows through the tube into a plastic bag. Doctors are glad not to see blood in the urine. Another nurse records pulse and blood pressure.

The victim is in good shape. He shivers slightly, although the trauma room is exceedingly warm. His face is bloodied, but shows no major lacerations. A third nurse, her elbow propped on the treatment table, asks the man a series of questions, trying to quickly outline his medical history. He answers abruptly. He is drunk. His left side is swabbed with yellow disinfectant and a doctor injects a local anesthetic. After a few seconds another doctor inserts his finger into the wound. It sinks in all the way to the knuckle. He begins to rotate his finger like a child trying to get a marble out of a milk bottle. The patient screams bloody murder and tries to struggle free.

Meanwhile in the lobby, a security guard is ejecting a derelict who has begun to drink from a bottle hidden in his coat pocket. "He's a regular, was in here just two days ago," says a nurse. "We checked him pretty close then, so he's probably okay now. Can you believe those were clean clothes we gave him?" The old man, blackened by filth, leaves quietly.

9:15 P.M. A young Hispanic man interrupts, saying his pregnant girl friend, 7
sitting outside in his car, is bleeding heavily from her vagina. She is rushed
into an examination room, treated behind closed doors, and rolled into the observation ward, where, much later in the night, a gynecologist will treat her in
a special room—the same one used to examine rape victims. Nearby, behind
curtains, the neurologist examines an old white woman to determine if her
headaches are due to head injury. They are not.

9:45 P.M. The trauma room has been cleared and cleaned mercilessly. The 8
examination rooms are three-quarters full—another overdose, two asthmatics,
a young woman with abdominal pains. In the hallway, a derelict who has been
sleeping it off urinates all over the stretcher. He sleeps on while attendants
change his clothes. An ambulance—one of four that patrol Manhattan for Bellevue from 42nd Street to Houston, river to river—delivers a middle-aged white
woman and two cops, the three of them soaking wet. The woman has escaped
from the psychiatric floor of a nearby hospital and tried to drown herself in the
East River. The cops fished her out. She lies on a stretcher shivering beneath
white blankets. Her eyes stare at the ceiling. She speaks clearly when an administrative worker begins routine questioning. The cops are given hospital
gowns and wait to receive tetanus shots and gamma globulin—a hedge against
infection from the befouled river water. They will hang around the E.R. for another two hours, telling their story to as many as six other policemen who show
up to hear it. The woman is rolled into an examination room, where a male
nurse speaks gently: "They tell me you fell into the river." "No," says the woman,
"I jumped. I have to commit suicide." "Why?" asks the nurse. "Because I'm insane and I can't help [it]. I have to die." The nurse gradually discovers the
woman has a history of psychological problems. She is given dry bedclothes
and placed under guard in the hallway. She lies on her side, staring at the wall.

The pace continues to increase. Several more overdose victims arrive by am- 9
bulance. One, a young black woman, had done a striptease on the street just before passing out. A second black woman is semiconscious and spends the better
part of her time at Bellevue alternately cursing it and pleading with the doctors.
Attendants find a plastic bottle coated with methadone in the pocket of a Hispanic O.D. The treatment is routinely the same, and sooner or later involves
vomiting. Just after doctors begin to treat the O.D., he vomits great quantities
of wine and methadone in all directions. "Lovely business, huh?" laments one
of the doctors. A young nurse confides that if there were other true emergencies,
the overdose victims would be given lower priority. "You can't help thinking they
did it to themselves," she says, "while the others are accident victims."

10:30 P.M. A policeman who twisted his knee struggling with an "alleged 10
perpetrator" is examined and released. By 10:30, the lobby is jammed with
friends and relatives of patients in various stages of treatment and recovery.
The attendant who also functions as a translator for Hispanic patients adds
chairs to accommodate the overflow. The medical walk-in rate stays steady—
between eight and ten patients waiting. A pair of derelicts, each with battered

eyes, appear at the admitting desk. One has a dramatically swollen face laced with black stitches.

11:00 P.M. The husband of the attempted suicide arrives. He thanks the police for saving his wife's life, then talks at length with doctors about her condition. She continues to stare into the void and does not react when her husband approaches her stretcher.

11

Meanwhile, patients arrive in the lobby at a steady pace. A young G.I. on leave has lower-back pains; a Hispanic man complains of pain in his side; occasionally parents hurry through the adult E.R. carrying children into the pediatric E.R. A white woman of about 50 marches into the lobby from the walk-in entrance. Dried blood covers her right eyebrow and upper lip. She begins to perform. "I was assaulted on 28th and Lexington, I was," she says grandly, "and I don't have to take it *anymore*. I was a bride 21 years ago, and, God, I was beautiful then." She has captured the attention of all present. "I was there when the boys came home—on Memorial Day—and I don't have to take this kind of treatment."

12

As midnight approaches, the nurses prepare for the shift change. They must brief the incoming staff and make sure all reports are up-to-date. One young brunet says, "Christ, I'm gonna go home and take a shower—I smell like vomit."

13

11:50 P.M. The triage nurse is questioning an old black-man about chest pains, and a Hispanic woman is having an asthma attack, when an ambulance, its sirens screaming full tilt, roars into the receiving bay. There is a split-second pause as everyone drops what he or she is doing and looks up. Then all hell breaks loose. Doctors and nurses are suddenly sprinting full-out toward the trauma room. The glass doors burst open and the occupied stretcher is literally run past me. Cops follow. It is as if a comet has whooshed by. In the trauma room it all becomes clear. A half-dozen doctors and nurses surround the lifeless form of a Hispanic man with a shotgun hole in his neck the size of your fist. Blood pours from a second gaping wound in his chest. A respirator is slammed over his face, making his chest rise and fall as if he were breathing. "No pulse," reports one doctor. A nurse jumps on a stool and, leaning over the man, begins to pump his chest with her palms. "No blood pressure," screams another nurse. The ambulance driver appears shaken. "I never thought I'd get here in time," he stutters. More doctors from the trauma team upstairs arrive. Wrappings from syringes and gauze pads fly through the air. The victim's eyes are open yet devoid of life. His body takes on a yellow tinge. A male nurse winces at the gunshot wound. "This guy really pissed off somebody," he says. This is no ordinary shooting. It is an execution. IVs are jammed into the body in the groin and arms. One doctor has been plugging in an electrocardiograph and asks everyone to stop for a second so he can get a reading. "Forget it," shouts the doctor in charge. "No time." "Take it easy, Jimmy," someone yells at the head physician. It is apparent by now that the man is dead, but the doctors keep trying injections and finally they slit open the chest and reach inside almost up to their elbows. They feel the extent of the damage and suddenly it is

14

all over. "I told 'em he was dead," says one nurse, withdrawing. "They didn't listen." The room is very still. The doctors are momentarily disgusted, then go on about their business. The room clears quickly. Finally there is only a male nurse and the still-warm body, now waxy-yellow, with huge ribs exposed on both sides of the chest and giant holes in both sides of the neck. The nurse speculates that this is yet another murder in a Hispanic political struggle that has brought many such victims to Bellevue. He marvels at the extent of the wounds and repeats, "This guy was really blown away."

Midnight. A hysterical woman is hustled through the lobby into an examination room. It is the dead man's wife, and she is nearly delirious. "I know he's dead, I know he's dead," she screams over and over. Within moments the lobby is filled with anxious relatives of the victim, waiting for word on his condition. The police are everywhere asking questions, but most people say they saw nothing. One young woman says she heard six shots, two louder than the other four. At some point, word is passed that the man is, in fact, dead. Another woman breaks down in hysterics; everywhere young Hispanics are crying and comforting each other. Plainclothes detectives make a quick examination of the body, check on the time of pronouncement of death, and begin to ask questions, but the bereaved are too stunned to talk. The rest of the uninvolved people in the lobby stare dumbly, their injuries suddenly paling in light of a death.

12:30 A.M. A black man appears at the admission desk and says he drank poison by mistake. He is told to have a seat. The ambulance brings in a young white woman, her head wrapped in white gauze. She is wailing terribly. A girl friend stands over her, crying, and a boyfriend clutches the injured woman's hands, saying, "I'm here, don't worry, I'm here." The victim has fallen downstairs at a friend's house. Attendants park her stretcher against the wall to wait for an examination room to clear. There are eight examination rooms and only three doctors. Unless you are truly an emergency, you will wait. One doctor is stitching up the elbow of a drunk who's been punched out. The friends of the woman who fell down the stairs glance up at the doctors anxiously, wondering why their friend isn't being treated faster.

1:10 A.M. A car pulls into the bay and a young Hispanic asks if a shooting victim has been brought here. The security guard blurts out, "He's dead." The young man is stunned. He peels his tires leaving the bay.

1:20 A.M. The young woman of the stairs is getting stitches in a small gash over her left eye when the same ambulance driver who brought in the gunshot victim delivers a man who has been stabbed in the back on East 3rd Street. Once again the trauma room goes from 0 to 60 in five seconds. The patient is drunk, which helps him endure the pain of having the catheter inserted through his penis into his bladder. Still he yells, "That hurts like a bastard," then adds sheepishly, "Excuse me, ladies." But he is not prepared for what comes next. An X-ray reveals a collapsed right lung. After just a shot of local anesthetic, the doctor slices open his side and inserts a long plastic tube. Internal bleeding had kept the lung pressed down and prevented it from reinflating. The tube releases the pressure. The ambulance driver says the cops grabbed the guy who ran the eight-inch blade into the victim's back. "That's not the one," says the man. "They got the wrong guy." A nurse reports that there is not much of the victim's type blood available at the hospital. One of the doctors says that's okay, he won't need surgery. Meanwhile blood pours from the man's knife wound and the tube in his side. As the nurses work, they chat about personal matters, yet they respond immediately to orders from either doctor. "How ya doin'?" the doctor asks the patient. "Okay," he says. His blood spatters on the floor.

So it goes into the morning hours. A Valium overdose, a woman who   19
fainted, a man who went through the windshield of his car. More overdoses. More drunks with split eyebrows and chins. The doctors and nurses work without complaint. "This is nothing, about normal, I'd say," concludes the head nurse. "No big deal."

RECORDING REFLECTIONS

This essay describes an hour-by-hour series of events during one evening at the trauma center of a major hospital. In your Reflection Log, list in order a series of events that happened to you in a single experience.

After making your chronological list, write about your personal experience for 10 minutes.

ACTIVITIES FOR REREADING

1. Simpson seems to write like a journalist. Highlight three sentences in this essay that seem to be written by a newspaper reporter. How does this strategy hold the reader's interest?

2. What is Simpson's central strategy for arranging the experiences in this essay? How does that strategy give the essay a sense of realism? Briefly record your answers.

3. How does the prevailing mood of the medical staff differ from that of the patients who are being treated or waiting to be treated? Why does Simpson emphasize these moods? Highlight the words and phrases that distinguish the moods of the two groups.

GROUP WORK

Personal Responses: Referring to your Reflection Logs, discuss your step-by-step experiences among the group. Make sure that you do not confuse one another by perhaps leaving out critical steps or telling them in the wrong order. Seek advice and add or revise steps as necessary to give a clear account of your experience.

Objective Responses: Discuss Simpson's strategy of writing like a reporter, his central strategy of using time as a unifying agent, and his strategy of using concrete description. How do these strategies combine to make the essay a quality piece of writing?

■ **WRITING ASSIGNMENTS**

1. Using the strategies of chronology, concrete language, and objective reporting, discuss an important personal experience. Describe your experience in such a way that it *shows* the reader what happened, rather than simply *tells*. Work to create pictures in the reader's mind, just as Simpson does in "The War Room at Bellevue."
2. Write an essay that explores in detail the reactions of at least four of the patients in Simpson's essay. Include in your own words the evidence and events that cause these people's reactions and evaluate whether these reactions seem warranted.

Black Men and Public Space   *1987*

BRENT STAPLES

My first victim was a woman—white, well dressed, probably in her late   1
twenties. I came upon her late one evening on a deserted street in Hyde Park, a relatively affluent neighborhood in an otherwise mean, impoverished section of Chicago. As I swung onto the avenue behind her, there seemed to be a discreet, uninflammatory distance between us. Not so. She cast back a worried glance. To her, the youngish black man—a broad six feet two inches with a beard and billowing hair, both hands shoved into the pockets of a bulky military jacket—seemed menacingly close. After a few more quick glimpses, she picked up her pace and was soon running in earnest. Within seconds she disappeared into a cross street.

That was more than a decade ago. I was twenty-two years old, a graduate   2
student newly arrived at the University of Chicago. It was in the echo of that terrified woman's footfalls that I first began to know the unwieldy inheritance I'd come into—the ability to alter public space in ugly ways. It was clear that she thought herself the quarry of a mugger, a rapist, or worse. Suffering a bout of insomnia, however, I was stalking sleep, not defenseless wayfarers. As a softy who is scarcely able to take a knife to a raw chicken—let alone hold one to a person's throat—I was surprised, embarrassed, and dismayed all at once. Her flight made me feel like an accomplice in tyranny. It also made it clear that I was indistinguishable from the muggers who occasionally seeped into the area from the surrounding ghetto. That first encounter, and those that followed, signified that a vast, unnerving gulf lay between nighttime pedestrians—particularly women—and me. And I soon gathered that being perceived as dangerous is a hazard in itself. I only needed to turn a corner into a dicey situation, or crowd some frightened, armed person in a foyer somewhere, or make an errant move after being pulled over by a policeman. Where fear and weapons meet—and they often do in urban America—there is always the possibility of death.

In that first year, my first away from my hometown, I was to become thor- 3
oughly familiar with the language of fear. At dark, shadowy intersections, I
could cross in front of a car stopped at a traffic light and elicit the *thunk, thunk,
thunk, thunk* of the driver—black, white, male, or female—hammering down
the door locks. On less traveled streets after dark, I grew accustomed to but
never comfortable with people crossing to the other side of the street rather
than pass me. Then there were the standard unpleasantries with policemen,
doormen, bouncers, cabdrivers, and others whose business it is to screen out
troublesome individuals *before* there is any nastiness.

I moved to New York nearly two years ago and I have remained an avid 4
night walker. In central Manhattan, the near-constant crowd cover minimizes
tense one-on-one street encounters. Elsewhere—in SoHo, for example, where
sidewalks are narrow and tightly spaced buildings shut out the sky—things can
get very taut indeed.

After dark, on the warrenlike streets of Brooklyn where I live, I often see 5
women who fear the worst from me. They seem to have set their faces on neutral, and with their purse straps strung across their chests bandolier-style, they
forge ahead as though bracing themselves against being tackled. I understand,
of course, that the danger they perceive is not a hallucination. Women are particularly vulnerable to street violence, and young black males are drastically
overrepresented among the perpetrators of that violence. Yet these truths are
no solace against the kind of alienation that comes of being ever the suspect, a
fearsome entity with whom pedestrians avoid making eye contact.

It is not altogether clear to me how I reached the ripe old age of twenty-two 6
without being conscious of the lethality nighttime pedestrians attributed to me.
Perhaps it was because in Chester, Pennsylvania, the small, angry industrial
town where I came of age in the 1960s, I was scarcely noticeable against a back-
drop of gang warfare, street knifings, and murders. I grew up one of the good
boys, had perhaps a half-dozen fistfights. In retrospect, my shyness of combat
has clear sources.

As a boy, I saw countless tough guys locked away; I have since buried sev- 7
eral, too. They were babies, really—a teenage cousin, a brother of twenty-two,
a childhood friend in his mid-twenties—all gone down in episodes of bravado
played out in the streets. I came to doubt the virtues of intimidation early on.
I chose, perhaps unconsciously, to remain a shadow—timid, but a survivor.

The fearsomeness mistakenly attributed to me in public places often has a 8
perilous flavor. The most frightening of these confusions occurred in the late
1970s and early 1980s, when I worked as a journalist in Chicago. One day, rushing into the office of a magazine I was writing for with a deadline story in hand,
I was mistaken for a burglar. The office manager called security and, with an
ad hoc posse, pursued me through the labyrinthine halls, nearly to my editor's
door. I had no way of proving who I was. I could only move briskly toward the
company of someone who knew me.

Another time I was on assignment for a local paper and killing time before 9
an interview. I entered a jewelry store on the city's affluent Near North Side.

The proprietor excused herself and returned with an enormous red Doberman pinscher straining at the end of a leash. She stood, the dog extended toward me, silent to my questions, her eyes bulging nearly out of her head. I took a cursory look around, nodded, and bade her good night.

Relatively speaking, however, I never fared as badly as another black male journalist. He went to nearby Waukegan, Illinois, a couple of summers ago to work on a story about a murderer who was born there. Mistaking the reporter for the killer, police officers hauled him from his car at gunpoint and but for his press credentials would probably have tried to book him. Such episodes are not uncommon. Black men trade tales like this all the time. 10

Over the years, I learned to smother the rage I felt at so often being taken for a criminal. Not to do so would surely have led to madness. I now take precautions to make myself less threatening. I move about with care, particularly late in the evening. I give a wide berth to nervous people on subway platforms during the wee hours, particularly when I have exchanged business clothes for jeans. If I happen to be entering a building behind some people who appear skittish, I may walk by, letting them clear the lobby before I return, so as not to seem to be following them. I have been calm and extremely congenial on those rare occasions when I've been pulled over by the police. 11

And on late-evening constitutionals I employ what has proved to be an excellent tension-reducing measure: I whistle melodies from Beethoven and Vivaldi and the more popular classical composers. Even steely New Yorkers hunching toward nighttime destinations seem to relax, and occasionally they even join in the tune. Virtually everybody seems to sense that a mugger wouldn't be warbling bright, sunny selections from Vivaldi's *Four Seasons*. It is my equivalent of the cowbell that hikers wear when they know they are in bear country. 12

▪ RECORDING REFLECTIONS

Throughout his essay, Staples portrays himself as an outsider. In your Reflection Log, list experiences you've had as an outsider, noting whether others made you feel that way or you made yourself feel that way.

After drawing up your list, select one experience and explore it in writing for 10 minutes.

▪ ACTIVITIES FOR REREADING

1. One of Staples's strategies is to develop contrasts throughout his essay. As you reread "Black Men in Public Space," make a list of opposites—for instance, *white/black*. See how many you can find. What does the use of contrasting elements suggest?
2. Identify Staples's strategy for arranging his experiences. Highlight transitional phrases and words that connect those experiences.
3. Staples generates a prevailing mood throughout "Black Men in Public Space." In two or three sentences, describe that mood and the words that contribute to it.

■ **GROUP WORK**

Personal Responses: With your Reflection Logs before you, discuss your experiences as outsiders. Discuss how everyone has dealt with these experiences. Also consider one of Staples's anecdotes. Share how you would have handled the situation, as he describes it.

Objective Responses: Discuss Staples's use of contrasts, essay arrangement, and mood. Refer to your notes from rereading and to details from the text to support your observations.

Staples uses the phrase "the language of fear." What does he mean? Develop a list of how "the language of fear" is expressed, both symbolically and overtly, in your own neighborhoods.

Discuss the response you believe Staples wants from his readers. To what extent does he succeed in setting it? Identify the elements that account for his effectiveness.

■ **WRITING ASSIGNMENTS**

1. Using Staples's essay as a model, write your own essay illustrating your experience as an outsider. Be sure to clearly represent the situations you have encountered. Also indicate what actions you took, if any, to be accepted as one of the group.

2. Write an essay that explores what Staples calls "the language of fear." Examine the behaviors of friends, neighbors, and merchants that indicate they are afraid. Your essay should go beyond merely presenting examples. It should also include your interpretation of each situation. Has "the language of fear" always been evident in your life, or is it a relatively recent development? Do you think it will be an issue in the future?

A Modest Proposal

1729

JONATHAN SWIFT

It is a melancholy object to those who walk through this great town or travel in the country, when they see the streets, the roads, and cabin doors, crowded with beggars of the female sex, followed by three, four, or six children, all in rags and importuning every passenger for an alms. These mothers, instead of being able to work for their honest livelihood, are forced to employ all their time in strolling to beg sustenance for their helpless infants, who, as they grow up, either turn thieves for want of work, or leave their dear native country to fight for the Pretender in Spain, or sell themselves to the Barbados.

I think it is agreed by all parties that this prodigious number of children in the arms, or on the backs, or at the heels of their mothers, and frequently of their fathers, is in the present deplorable state of the kingdom a very great additional grievance; and therefore whoever could find out a fair, cheap, and easy method of making these children sound, useful members of the commonwealth would deserve so well of the public as to have his statue set up for a preserver of the nation.

But my intention is very far from being confined to provide only for the   3
children of professed beggars; it is of a much greater extent, and shall take in the whole number of infants at a certain age who are born of parents in effect as little able to support them as those who demand our charity in the streets.

As to my own part, having turned my thoughts for many years upon this im-   4
portant subject, and maturely weighed the several schemes of other projectors, I have always found them grossly mistaken in their computation. It is true, a child just dropped from its dam may be supported by her milk for a solar year, with little other nourishment; at most not above the value of two shillings, which the mother may certainly get, or the value in scraps, by her lawful occupation of begging; and it is exactly at one year old that I propose to provide for them in such a manner as instead of being a charge upon their parents or the parish, or wanting food and raiment for the rest of their lives, they shall on the contrary contribute to the feeding, and partly to the clothing, of many thousands.

There is likewise another great advantage in my scheme, that it will prevent   5
those voluntary abortions, and that horrid practice of women murdering their bastard children, alas, too frequent among us, sacrificing the poor innocent babes, I doubt, more to avoid the expense than the shame, which would move tears and pity in the most savage and inhuman breast.

The number of souls in this kingdom being usually reckoned one million   6
and a half, of these I calculate there may be about two hundred thousand couples whose wives are breeders; from which number I subtract thirty thousand couples who are able to maintain their own children, although I apprehend there cannot be so many under the present distress of the kingdom; but this being granted, there will remain an hundred and seventy thousand breeders. I again subtract fifty thousand for those women who miscarry, or whose children die by accident or disease within the year. There only remain an hundred and twenty thousand children of poor parents annually born. The question therefore is, how this number shall be reared and provided for, which, as I have already said, under the present situation of affairs, is utterly impossible by all the methods hitherto proposed. For we can neither employ them in handicraft nor agriculture; we neither build houses (I mean in the country) nor cultivate land. They can very seldom pick up a livelihood by stealing till they arrive at six years old, except where they are of towardly parts; although I confess they learn the rudiments much earlier, during which time they can however be looked upon only as probationers, as I have been informed by a principal gentleman in the county of Cavan, who protested to me that he never knew above one or two instances under the age of six, even in a part of the kingdom so renowned for the quickest proficiency in that art.

I am assured by our merchants that a boy or a girl before twelve years old   7
is no salable commodity; and even when they come to this age, they will not

yield above three pounds, or three pounds and half a crown at most on the Exchange; which cannot turn to account either to the parents or the kingdom, the charge of nutriment and rags having been at least four times that value.

I shall now therefore humbly propose my own thoughts, which I hope will not be liable to the least objection.   8

I have been assured by a very knowing American of my acquaintance in London, that a young healthy child well nursed is at a year old a most delicious, nourishing, and wholesome food, whether stewed, roasted, baked, or boiled; and I make no doubt that it will equally serve in a fricassee or a ragout.   9

I do therefore humbly offer it to public consideration that of the hundred and twenty thousand children, already computed, twenty thousand may be reserved for breed, whereof only one fourth part to be males, which is more than we allow to sheep, black cattle, or swine; and my reason is that these children are seldom the fruits of marriage, a circumstance not much regarded by our savages, therefore one male will be sufficient to serve four females. That the remaining hundred thousand may at a year old be offered in sale to the persons of quality and fortune through the kingdom, always advising the mother to let them suck plentifully in the last month, so as to render them plump and fat for a good table. A child will make two dishes at an entertainment for friends; and when the family dines alone, the fore or hind quarter will make a reasonable dish, and seasoned with a little pepper or salt will be very good boiled on the fourth day, especially in winter.   10

I have reckoned upon a medium that a child just born will weigh twelve pounds, and in a solar year if tolerably nursed increaseth to twenty-eight pounds.   11

I grant this food will be somewhat dear, and therefore very proper for landlords, who, as they have already devoured most of the parents, seem to have the best title to the children.   12

Infant's flesh will be in season throughout the year, but more plentiful in March, and a little before and after. For we are told by a grave author, an eminent French physician, that fish being a prolific diet, there are more children born in Roman Catholic countries about nine months after Lent, than at any other season; therefore, reckoning a year after Lent, the markets will be more glutted than usual, because the number of popish infants is at least three to one in this kingdom; and therefore it will have one other collateral advantage, by lessening the number of Papists among us.   13

I have already computed the charge of nursing a beggar's child (in which list I reckon all cottagers, laborers, and four fifths of the farmers) to be about two shillings per annum, rags included; and I believe no gentleman would repine to give ten shillings for the carcass of a good fat child, which, as I have said, will make four dishes of excellent nutritive meat, when he hath only some particular friend or his own family to dine with him. Thus the squire will learn to be a good landlord, and grow popular among the tenants; the mother will have eight shillings net profit, and be fit for work till she produces another child.   14

Those who are more thrifty (as I must confess the times require) may flay   15
the carcass; the skin of which artificially dressed will make admirable gloves for
ladies, and summer boots for fine gentlemen.

As to our city of Dublin, shambles may be appointed for this purpose in the   16
most convenient parts of it, and butchers we may be assured will not be wanting; although I rather recommend buying the children alive, and dressing them
hot from the knife as we do roasting pigs.

A very worthy person, a true lover of his country, and whose virtues I highly   17
esteem, was lately pleased in discoursing on this matter to offer a refinement
upon my scheme. He said that many gentlemen of his kingdom, having of late
destroyed their deer, he conceived that the want of venison might be well supplied by the bodies of young lads and maidens, not exceeding fourteen years of
age nor under twelve, so great a number of both sexes in every country being
now ready to starve for want of work and service; and these to be disposed of by
their parents, if alive, or otherwise by their nearest relations. But with due deference to so excellent a friend and so deserving a patriot, I cannot be altogether
in his sentiments; for as to the males, my American acquaintance assured me
from frequent experience that their flesh was generally tough and lean, like that
of our schoolboys, by continual exercise, and their taste disagreeable; and to
fatten them would not answer the charge. Then as to the females, it would, I
think with humble submission, be a loss to the public, because they soon would
become breeders themselves; and besides, it is not improbable that some
scrupulous people might be apt to censure such a practice (although indeed very
unjustly) as a little bordering upon cruelty; which, I confess, hath always been
with me the strongest objection against any project, how well soever intended.

But in order to justify my friend, he confessed that this expedient was put   18
into his head by the famous Psalmanazar, a native of the island Formosa, who
came from thence to London above twenty years ago, and in conversation told
my friend that in his country when any young person happened to be put to
death, the executioner sold the carcass to the persons of quality as a prime
dainty; and that in his time the body of a plump girl of fifteen, who was cruci-
fied for an attempt to poison the emperor, was sold to his Imperial Majesty's
prime minister of state, and other great mandarins of the court, in joints from
the gibbet, at four hundred crowns. Neither indeed can I deny that if the same
use were made of several plump young girls in this town, who without one single groat to their fortunes cannot stir abroad without a chair, and appear at the
playhouse and assemblies in foreign fineries which they never will pay for, the
kingdom would not be the worse.

Some persons of a desponding spirit are in great concern about that vast   19
number of poor people who are aged, diseased, or maimed, and I have been de-
sired to employ my thoughts what course may be taken to ease the nation of so
grievous an encumbrance. But I am not in the least pain upon that matter, because it is very well known that they are every day dying and rotting by cold and
famine, and filth and vermin, as fast as can be reasonably expected. And as to
the younger laborers, they are now in almost as hopeful a condition. They can-

not get work, and consequently pine away for want of nourishment to a degree that if any time they are accidentally hired to common labor, they have not strength to perform it; and thus the country and themselves are happily delivered from the evils to come.

I have too long digressed, and therefore shall return to my subject. I think 20 the advantages by the proposal which I have made are obvious and many, as well as of the highest importance.

For first, as I have already observed, it would greatly lessen the number of 21 Papists, with whom we are yearly overrun, being the principal breeders of the nation as well as our most dangerous enemies; and who stay at home on purpose to deliver the kingdom to the Pretender, hoping to take their advantage by the absence of so many good Protestants, who have chosen rather to leave their country than to stay at home and pay tithes against their conscience to an Episcopal curate.

Secondly, the poorer tenants will have something valuable of their own, 22 which by law may be made liable to distress, and help to pay their landlord's rent, their corn and cattle being already seized and money a thing unknown.

Thirdly, whereas the maintenance of an hundred thousand children, from 23 two years old and upwards, cannot be computed at less than ten shillings a piece per annum, the nation's stock will be thereby increased fifty thousand pounds per annum, besides the profit of a new dish introduced to the tables of all gentlemen of fortune in the kingdom who have any refinement in taste. And the money will circulate among ourselves, the goods being entirely of our own growth and manufacture.

Fourthly, the constant breeders, besides the gain of eight shillings sterling 24 per annum by the sale of their children, will be rid of the charge for maintaining them after the first year.

Fifthly, this food would likewise bring great custom to taverns, where the 25 vintners will certainly be so prudent as to procure the best receipts for dressing it to perfection, and consequently have their houses frequented by all the fine gentlemen, who justly value themselves upon their knowledge in good eating; and a skillful cook, who understands how to oblige his guests, will contrive to make it as expensive as they please.

Sixthly, this would be a great inducement to marriage, which all wise na- 26 tions have either encouraged by rewards or enforced by laws and penalties. It would increase the care and tenderness of mothers toward their children, when they were sure of a settlement for life to the poor babes, provided in some sort by the public, to their annual profit instead of expense. We should see an honest emulation among the married women, which of them could bring the fattest child to the market. Men would become as fond of their wives during the time of their pregnancy as they are now of their mares in foal, their cows in calf, or sows when they are ready to farrow; nor offer to beat or kick them (as is too frequent a practice) for fear of a miscarriage.

Many other advantages might be enumerated. For instance, the addition of 27 some thousand carcasses in our exportation of barreled beef, the propagation of swine's flesh, and improvements in the art of making good bacon, so much wanted among us by the great destruction of pigs, too frequent at our tables, which are no way comparable in taste or magnificence to a well-grown, fat, yearling child, which roasted whole will make a considerable figure at a lord mayor's feast or any other public entertainment. But this and many others I omit, being studious of brevity.

Supposing that one thousand families in this city would be constant cus- 28 tomers for infants' flesh, besides others who might have it at merry meetings, particularly weddings and christenings, I compute that Dublin would take off annually about twenty thousand carcasses, and the rest of the kingdom (where probably they will be sold somewhat cheaper) the remaining eighty thousand.

I can think of no one objection that will possibly be raised against this pro- 29 posal, unless it should be urged that the number of people will be thereby much lessened in the kingdom. This I freely own, and it was indeed one principal design in offering it to the world. I desire the reader will observe, that I calculate my remedy for this one individual kingdom of Ireland and for no other that ever was, is, or I think ever can be upon earth. Therefore, let no man talk to me of other expedients: of taxing our absentees at five shillings a pound: of using neither clothes nor household furniture except what is of our own growth and manufacture: of utterly rejecting the materials and instruments that promote foreign luxury: of curing the expensiveness of pride, vanity, idleness, and gaming in our women: of introducing a vein of parsimony, prudence, and temperance: of learning to love our country, in the want of which we differ even from Laplanders and the inhabitants of Topinamboo: of quitting our animosities and factions, nor acting any longer like the Jews, who were murdering one another at the very moment their city was taken: of being a little cautious not to sell our country and conscience for nothing: of teaching landlords to have at least one degree of mercy toward their tenants: lastly, of putting a spirit of honesty, industry, and skill into our shopkeepers; who, if a resolution could now be taken to buy only our native goods, would immediately unite to cheat and exact upon us in the price, the measure, and the goodness, nor could ever yet be brought to make one fair proposal of just dealing, though often and earnestly invited to it.

Therefore, I repeat, let no man talk to me of these and the like expedients, 30 till he hath at least some glimpse of hope that there will ever be some hearty and sincere attempt to put them in practice.

But as to myself, having been wearied out for many years with offering 31 vain, idle, visionary thoughts, and at length utterly despairing of success, I fortunately fell upon this proposal, which, as it is wholly new, so it hath something solid and real, of no expense and little trouble, full in our own power, and whereby we can incur no danger in disobliging England. For this kind of commodity will not bear exportation, the flesh being of too tender a consistence to admit a long continuance in salt, although perhaps I could name a country which would be glad to eat up our whole nation without it.

After all, I am not so violently bent upon my own opinion as to reject any 32 offer proposed by wise men, which shall be found equally innocent, cheap, easy, and effectual. But before something of that kind shall be advanced in contradiction to my scheme, and offering a better, I desire the author or authors will be pleased maturely to consider two points. First, as things now stand, how they will be able to find food and raiment for an hundred thousand useless mouths and backs. And secondly, there being a round million of creatures in human figure throughout this kingdom, whose sole subsistence put into a common stock would leave them in debt two millions of pounds sterling, adding those who are beggars by profession to the bulk of farmers, cottagers, and laborers, with their wives and children who are beggars in effect; I desire those politicians who dislike my overture, and may perhaps be so bold to attempt an answer, that they will first ask the parents of these mortals whether they would not at this day think it a great happiness to have been sold for food at a year old in this manner I prescribe, and thereby have avoided such a perpetual scene of misfortunes as they have since gone through by the oppression of landlords, the impossibility of paying rent without money or trade, the want of common sustenance, with neither house nor clothes to cover them from the inclemencies of the weather, and the most inevitable prospect of entailing the like or greater miseries upon their breed forever.

I profess, in the sincerity of my heart, that I have not the least personal interest in endeavoring to promote this necessary work, having no other motive than the public good of my country, by advancing our trade, providing for infants, relieving the poor, and giving some pleasure to the rich. I have no children by which I can propose to get a single penny; the youngest being nine years old, and my wife past childbearing. 33

RECORDING REFLECTIONS

Swift's tone in this essay is one of controlled fury. His anger—which is directed at uncaring absentee English landlords, primarily—decries the horrors of Irish poverty in the eighteenth century. In your Reflection Log, list what you believe are three of the most serious social problems in the United States today.

After making your list, select one of the problems and explore it in writing for 10 minutes.

ACTIVITIES FOR REREADING

1. As you reread "A Modest Proposal," you will note that an implicit plea emerges, directed to the English. What, in fact, does the essay argue that people in power should do to ease the lot of the Irish?
2. The first paragraph of this essay engages readers, making them want to continue reading. What strategy does Swift employ to do so?
3. The last two paragraphs of this essay offer strong evidence of Swift's attitude toward his eighteenth-century audience. What is that attitude? Give evidence from those paragraphs to support your answer.

■ **GROUP WORK**

Personal Responses: Using your Reflection Logs, discuss several current social problems, as you perceive them. Agree to discuss one problem in detail. Then realistically propose and discuss possible solutions to that problem.

Objective Responses: Discuss the tone of the first paragraph. Using notes from your Reflection Logs, discuss how that tone disarms the reader in the sense that it does not prepare him or her for what follows in the essay.

With your Reflection Logs before you, discuss the final paragraph of the essay, paying particular attention to the author's true attitude toward his topic. Using examples from that paragraph—and from other parts of the essay, as you see fit—discuss how you determined the author's attitude.

■ **WRITING ASSIGNMENTS**

1. Taking a lesson from Swift's "A Modest Proposal," state a real social problem in the United States and propose an absurd solution to it. Write in such a way that an inattentive or gullible reader might believe that you are serious.
2. Swift has been described as arguably the greatest yet most bitter satirist in English literature. In an essay, explicitly describe what Swift satirizes, giving three examples of how he does so. Also give two examples from the essay to support the thesis that Swift is a bitter satirist.

Mother Tongue   *1990*

AMY TAN

I am not a scholar of English or literature. I cannot give you much more than personal opinions on the English language and its variations in this country or others.

I am a writer. And by that definition, I am someone who has always loved language. I am fascinated by language in daily life. I spend a great deal of my time thinking about the power of language—the way it can evoke an emotion, a visual image, a complex idea, or a simple truth. Language is the tool of my trade. And I use them all—all the Englishes I grew up with.

Recently, I was made keenly aware of the different Englishes I do use. I was giving a talk to a large group of people, the same talk I had already given to half a dozen other groups. The nature of the talk was about my writing, my life, and my book, *The Joy Luck Club*. The talk was going along well enough, until I remembered one major difference that made the whole tale sound wrong. My mother was in the room. And it was perhaps the first time she had heard me give a lengthy speech, using the kind of English I have never used with her. I was saying things like, "The intersection of memory upon imagination" and "There is an aspect of my fiction that relates to thus-and-thus"—a speech filled with carefully wrought grammatical phrases, burdened, it suddenly seemed to me, with nominalized forms, past perfect tenses, conditional phrases, all the forms of standard English that I had learned in school and through books, the forms of English I did not use at home with my mother.

Just last week, I was walking down the street with my mother, and I again found myself conscious of the English I was using, the English I do use with her. We were talking about the price of new and used furniture and I heard myself saying this: "Not waste money that way." My husband was with us as well, and he didn't notice any switch in my English. And then I realized why. It's because over the twenty years we've been together I've often used that same kind of English with him, and sometimes he even uses it with me. It has become our language of intimacy, a different sort of English that relates to family talk, the language I grew up with.

So you'll have some idea of what this family talk I heard sounds like, I'll quote what my mother said during a recent conversation which I videotaped and then transcribed. During this conversation, my mother was talking about a political gangster in Shanghai who had the same last name as her family's, Du, and how the gangster in his early years wanted to be adopted by her family, which was rich by comparison. Later, the gangster became more powerful, far richer than my mother's family, and one day showed up at my mother's wedding to pay his respects. Here's what she said in part.

"Du Yusong having business like fruit stand. Like off the street kind. He is Du like Du Zong—but not Tsung-ming Island people. The local people call putong, the river east side, he belong to that side local people. That man want to ask Du Zong father take him in like become own family. Du Zong father wasn't look down on him, but didn't take seriously, until that man big like become a mafia. Now important person, very hard to inviting him. Chinese way, came only to show respect, don't stay for dinner. Respect for making big celebration, he shows up. Mean gives lots of respect. Chinese custom. Chinese social life that way. If too important won't have to stay too long. He come to my wedding. I didn't see, I heard it. I gone to boy's side, they have YMCA dinner. Chinese age I was nineteen."

You should know that my mother's expressive command of English belies how much she actually understands. She reads the *Forbes* report, listens to *Wall Street Week*, converses daily with her stockbroker, reads all of Shirley MacLaine's books with ease—all kinds of things I can't begin to understand. Yet some of my friends tell me they understand 50 percent of what my mother says. Some say they understand 80 to 90 percent. Some say they understand none of it, as if she were speaking pure Chinese. But to me, my mother's English is perfectly clear, perfectly natural. It's my mother tongue. Her language, as I hear it, is vivid, direct, full of observation and imagery. That was the language that helped shape the way I saw things, expressed things, made sense of the world.

Lately, I've been giving more thought to the kind of English my mother speaks. Like others, I have described it to people as "broken" or "fractured" English. But I wince when I say that. It has always bothered me that I can think of no way to describe it other than "broken," as if it were damaged and needed to be fixed, as if it lacked a certain wholeness and soundness. I've heard other terms used, "limited English," for example. But they seem just as bad, as if everything is limited, including people's perceptions of the limited English speaker.

I know this for a fact, because when I was growing up, my mother's "limited" English limited *my* perception of her. I was ashamed of her English. I believed that her English reflected the quality of what she had to say. That is, because she expressed them imperfectly her thoughts were imperfect. And I had plenty of empirical evidence to support me: the fact that people in department stores, at banks, and at restaurants did not take her seriously, did not give her good service, pretended not to understand her, or even acted as if they did not hear her.

My mother has long realized the limitations of her English as well. When I was fifteen, she used to have me call people on the phone to pretend I was she. In this guise, I was forced to ask for information or even to complain and yell at people who had been rude to her. One time it was a call to her stockbroker in New York. She had cashed out her small portfolio and it just so happened we were going to go to New York the next week, our very first trip outside California. I had to get on the phone and say in an adolescent voice that was not very convincing, "This is Mrs. Tan."

And my mother was standing in the back whispering loudly, "Why he don't send me check, already two weeks late. So mad he lie to me, losing me money."

And then I said in perfect English, "Yes, I'm getting rather concerned. You had agreed to send the check two weeks ago, but it hasn't arrived."

Then she began to talk more loudly. "What he want, I come to New York tell him front of his boss, you cheating me?" And I was trying to calm her down, make her be quiet, while telling the stockbroker, "I can't tolerate any more excuses. If I don't receive the check immediately, I am going to have to speak to your manager when I'm in New York next week." And sure enough, the following week there we were in front of this astonished stockbroker, and I was sitting there red-faced and quiet, and my mother, the real Mrs. Tan, was shouting at his boss in her impeccable broken English.

We used a similar routine just five days ago, for a situation that was far less humorous. My mother had gone to the hospital for an appointment, to find out about a benign brain tumor a CAT scan had revealed a month ago. She said she had spoken very good English, her best English, no mistakes. Still, she said, the hospital did not apologize when they said they had lost the CAT scan and she had come for nothing. She said they did not seem to have any sympathy when she told them she was anxious to know the exact diagnosis, since her husband and son had both died of brain tumors. She said they would not give her any more information until the next time and she would have to make another appointment for that. So she said she would not leave until the doctor called her daughter. She wouldn't budge. And when the doctor finally called her daughter, me, who spoke in perfect English—lo and behold—we had assurances the CAT scan would be found, promises that a conference call on Monday would be held, and apologies for any suffering my mother had gone through for a most regrettable mistake.

I think my mother's English almost had an effect on limiting my possibilities   15
in life as well. Sociologists and linguists probably will tell you that a person's developing language skills are more influenced by peers. But I do think that the language spoken in the family, especially in immigrant families which are more insular, plays a large role in shaping the language of the child. And I believe that has affected my results on achievement tests, IQ tests, and the SAT. While my English skills were never judged as poor, compared to math, English could not be considered my strong suit. In grade school I did moderately well, getting perhaps B's, sometimes B-pluses, in English and scoring perhaps in the sixtieth or seventieth percentile on achievement tests. But those scores were not good enough to override the opinion that my true abilities lay in math and science, because in those areas I achieved A's and scored in the ninetieth percentile or higher.

This was understandable. Math is precise; there is only one correct answer.   16
Whereas, for me at least, the answers on English tests were always a judgment call, a matter of opinion and personal experience. Those tests were constructed around items like fill-in-the-blank sentence completion, such as, "Even though Tom was _____, Mary thought he was _____." And the correct answer always seemed to be the most bland combinations of thoughts, for example, "Even though Tom was shy, Mary thought he was charming," with the grammatical structure "even though" limiting the correct answer to some sort of semantic opposites, so you wouldn't get answers like, "Even though Tom was foolish, Mary thought he was ridiculous." Well, according to my mother, there were very few limitations as to what Tom could have been and what Mary might have thought of him. So I never did well on tests like that.

The same was true with word analogies, pairs of words in which you were   17
supposed to find some sort of logical, semantic relationship—for example, "*Sunset* is to *nightfall* as _____ is to _____. And here you would be presented with a list of four possible pairs, one of which showed the same kind of relationship: *red* is to *stoplight, bus* is to *arrival, chills* is to *fever, yawn* is to *boring.* Well, I could never think that way. I knew what the tests were asking, but I could not block out of my mind the images already created by the first pair, "*sunset* is to *nightfall*"— and I would see a burst of colors against a darkening sky, the moon rising, the lowering of a curtain of stars. And all the other pairs of words—red, bus, stoplight, boring—just threw up a mass of confusing images, making it impossible for me to sort out something as logical as saying: "A sunset precedes nightfall" is the same as "a chill precedes a fever." The only way I would have gotten that answer right would have been to imagine an associative situation, for example, my being disobedient and staying out past sunset, catching a chill at night, which turns into feverish pneumonia as punishment, which indeed did happen to me.

I have been thinking about all this lately, about my mother's English, about   18
achievement tests. Because lately I've been asked, as a writer, why there are not more Asian Americans represented in American literature. Why are there few

Asian Americans enrolled in creative writing programs? Why do so many Chinese students go into engineering? Well, these are broad sociological questions I can't begin to answer. But I have noticed in surveys—in fact, just last week—that Asian students, as a whole, always do significantly better on math achievement tests than in English. And this makes me think that there are other Asian-American students whose English spoken in the home might also be described as "broken" or "limited." And perhaps they also have teachers who are steering them away from writing and into math and science, which is what happened to me.

Fortunately, I happen to be rebellious in nature and enjoy the challenge of   19
disproving assumptions made about me. I became an English major my first year in college, after being enrolled as premed. I started writing nonfiction as a freelancer the week after I was told by my former boss that writing was my worst skill and I should hone my talents toward account management.

But it wasn't until 1985 that I finally began to write fiction. And at first I   20
wrote using what I thought to be wittily crafted sentences, sentences that would finally prove I had mastery over the English language. Here's an example from the first draft of a story that later made its way into *The Joy Luck Club*, but without this line: "That was my mental quandary in its nascent state." A terrible line, which I can barely pronounce.

Fortunately, for reasons I won't get into today, I later decided I should en-   21
vision a reader for the stories I would write. And the reader I decided upon was my mother, because these were stories about mothers. So with this reader in mind—and in fact she did read my early drafts—I began to write stories using all the Englishes I grew up with: the English I spoke to my mother, which for lack of a better term might be described as "simple"; the English she used with me, which for lack of a better term might be described as "broken"; my translation of her Chinese, which could certainly be described as "watered down"; and what I imagined to be her translation of her Chinese if she could speak in perfect English, her internal language, and for that I sought to preserve the essence, but neither an English nor a Chinese structure. I wanted to capture what language ability tests can never reveal: her intent, her passion, her imagery, the rhythms of her speech and the nature of her thoughts.

Apart from what any critic had to say about my writing, I knew I had suc-   22
ceeded where it counted when my mother finished reading my book and gave me her verdict: "So easy to read."

■ RECORDING REFLECTIONS

Throughout her essay, Tan describes the various forms of English she uses and how each fits a given set of circumstances and relationships. In your Reflection Log, list the different Englishes—that is, types of language—you use in certain circumstances and relationships.

After drawing up your list, choose one example and write about it for 10 minutes, describing this type of language and its functions.

■ **ACTIVITIES FOR REREADING**

1. Tan narrates several anecdotes in her essay, yet the essay is not a narrative. Explain why in two or three sentences.
2. Reread paragraph 6 carefully and interpret the meaning of Tan's mother's speech. Write down your translation in standard English.
3. How many actual versions of English does Tan speak? Jot down a short description of each.

■ **GROUP WORK**

Personal Responses: Using your Reflection Logs as memory guides, discuss the various kinds of English you use. Why does each seem to work best in its own personal and social context? What advantages does each have over standard English in its own personal/social context? What about disadvantages?

Objective Responses: Discuss why Tan's essay, taken as a whole, is not a narrative. What precise functions are served by her anecdotes (themselves, forms of narrative)?

Compare your translations of Tan's mother's speech. See if you can agree on the most accurate translation; discuss the reasons for its accuracy.

Discuss the different kinds of English Tan uses and your descriptions of each.

Reconsider paragraph 7 and Tan's claim that her mother's limited ability in standard English gives people a false impression of how much she actually understands. What impact does this seem to have on Tan's mother? Have you observed this about someone you know who has limited English skills?

■ **WRITING ASSIGNMENTS**

1. Write an essay in which you describe and analyze the various ways you use English. Like Tan, use several anecdotes to illustrate your points.
2. Write an essay that analyzes in detail one of the versions of English you speak. Analyze its diction, syntax, and structure. Explain what communication functions it serves better than standard English. In what ways, if any, is it lacking?

Being a Man   *1985*

PAUL THEROUX

There is a pathetic sentence in the chapter "Fetishism" in Dr. Norman   1
Cameron's book *Personality Development and Psychopathology*. It goes, "Fetishists are nearly always men; and their commonest fetish is a woman's shoe." I cannot read that sentence without thinking that it is just one more awful thing about being a man—and perhaps it is an important thing to know about us.

I have always disliked being a man. The whole idea of manhood in America is pitiful, in my opinion. This version of masculinity is a little like having to wear an ill-fitting coat for one's entire life (by contrast, I imagine femininity to be an oppressive sense of nakedness). Even the expression "Be a man!" strikes me as insulting and abusive. It means: Be stupid, be unfeeling, obedient, soldierly and stop thinking. Man means "manly"—how can one think about men without considering the terrible ambition of manliness? And yet it is part of every man's life. It is a hideous and crippling lie; it not only insists on difference and connives at superiority, it is also by its very nature destructive—emotionally damaging and socially harmful.

The youth who is subverted, as most are, into believing in the masculine ideal is effectively separated from women and he spends the rest of his life finding women a riddle and a nuisance. Of course, there is a female version of this male affliction. It begins with mothers encouraging little girls to say (to other adults) "Do you like my new dress?" In a sense, little girls are traditionally urged to please adults with a kind of coquettishness, while boys are enjoined to behave like monkeys towards each other. The nine-year-old coquette proceeds to become womanish in a subtle power game in which she learns to be sexually indispensable, socially decorative and always alert to a man's sense of inadequacy.

Femininity—being lady-like—implies needing a man as witness and seducer; but masculinity celebrates the exclusive company of men. That is why it is so grotesque; and that is also why there is no manliness without inadequacy—because it denies men the natural friendship of women.

It is very hard to imagine any concept of manliness that does not belittle women, and it begins very early. At an age when I wanted to meet girls—let's say the treacherous years of thirteen to sixteen—I was told to take up a sport, get more fresh air, join the Boy Scouts, and I was urged not to read so much. It was the 1950s and if you asked too many questions about sex you were sent to camp—boys' camp, of course: the nightmare. Nothing is more unnatural or prison-like than a boy's camp, but if it were not for them we would have no Elks' Lodges, no pool rooms, no boxing matches, no Marines.

And perhaps no sports as we know them. Everyone is aware of how few in number are the athletes who behave like gentlemen. Just as high school basketball teaches you how to be a poor loser, the manly attitude towards sports seems to be little more than a recipe for creating bad marriages, social misfits, moral degenerates, sadists, latent rapists and just plain louts. I regard high school sports as a drug far worse than marijuana, and it is the reason that the average tennis champion, say, is a pathetic oaf.

Any objective study would find the quest for manliness essentially right-wing, puritanical, cowardly, neurotic and fueled largely by a fear of women. It is also certainly philistine. There is no book-hater like a Little League coach. But indeed all the creative arts are obnoxious to the manly ideal, because at their best the arts are pursued by uncompetitive and essentially solitary people. It makes it very hard for a creative youngster, for any boy who expresses the desire to be alone seems to be saying that there is something wrong with him.

It ought to be clear by now that I have something of an objection to the way   8
we turn boys into men. It does not surprise me that when the President of the
United States has his customary weekend off he dresses like a cowboy—it is both
a measure of his insecurity and his willingness to please. In many ways, American culture does little more for a man than prepare him for modeling clothes in
the L. L. Bean catalogue. I take this as a personal insult because for many years
I found it impossible to admit to myself that I wanted to be a writer. It was my
guilty secret, because being a writer was incompatible with being a man.

There are people who might deny this, but that is because the American   9
writer, typically, has been so at pains to prove his manliness that we have come
to see literariness and manliness as mingled qualities. But first there was a fear
that writing was not a manly profession—indeed, not a profession at all. (The
paradox in American letters is that it has always been easier for a woman to
write and for a man to be published.) Growing up, I had thought of sports as
wasteful and humiliating, and the idea of manliness was a bore. My wanting to
become a writer was not a flight from that oppressive role-playing, but I quickly
saw that it was at odds with it. Everything in stereotyped manliness goes
against the life of the mind. The Hemingway personality is too tedious to go
into here, and in any case his exertions are well-known, but certainly it was not
until this aberrant behavior was examined by feminists in the 1960s that any
male writer dared question the pugnacity in Hemingway's fiction. All the bull-
fighting and arm wrestling and elephant shooting diminished Hemingway as a
writer, but it is consistent with a prevailing attitude in American writing: one
cannot be a male writer without first proving that one is a man.

It is normal in America for a man to be dismissive or even somewhat apolo-   10
getic about being a writer. Various factors make it easier. There is a heartiness
about journalism that makes it acceptable—journalism is the manliest form of
American writing and, therefore, the profession the most independent-minded
women seek (yes, it is an illusion, but that is my point). Fiction-writing is
equated with a kind of dispirited failure and is only manly when it produces
wealth—money is masculinity. So is drinking. Being a drunkard is another assertion, if misplaced, of manliness. The American male writer is traditionally
proud of his heavy drinking. But we are also a very literal-minded people. A man
proves his manhood in America in old-fashioned ways. He kills lions, like Hemingway; or he hunts ducks, like Nathanael West; or he makes pronouncements
like, "A man should carry enough knife to defend himself with," as James Jones
once said to a *Life* interviewer. Or he says he can drink you under the table. But
even tiny drunken William Faulkner loved to mount a horse and go fox hunting,
and Jack Kerouac roistered up and down Manhattan in a lumberjack shirt (and
spent every night of *The Subterraneans* with his mother in Queens). And we are
familiar with the lengths to which Norman Mailer is prepared, in his endearing
way, to prove that he is just as much a monster as the next man.

When the novelist John Irving was revealed as a wrestler, people took him   11
to be a very serious writer; and even a bubble reputation like Erich *(Love Story)*
Segal's was enhanced by the news that he ran the marathon in a respectable

time. How surprised we would be if Joyce Carol Oates were revealed as a sumo wrestler or Joan Didion active in pumping iron. "Lives in New York City with her three children" is the typical woman writer's biographical note, for just as the male writer must prove he has achieved a sort of muscular manhood, the woman writer—or rather her publicists—must prove her motherhood.

There would be no point in saying any of this if it were not generally accepted that to be a man is somehow—even now in feminist-influenced America—a privilege. It is on the contrary an unmerciful and punishing burden. Being a man is bad enough; being manly is appalling (in this sense, women's lib has done much more for men than for women). It is the sinister silliness of men's fashions, and a clubby attitude in the arts. It is the subversion of good students. It is the so-called "Dress Code" of the Ritz-Carlton Hotel in Boston, and it is the institutionalized cheating in college sports. It is the most primitive insecurity.   12

And this is also why men often object to feminism but are afraid to explain why: of course women have a justified grievance, but most men believe—and with reason—that their lives are just as bad.   13

▪ RECORDING REFLECTIONS

As you read this essay, you will note that Theroux makes several claims about what "being a man" means in the United States. In your Reflection Log, list three of those claims—that is, assumptions that many Americans have about "being a man."

After making your list, select one claim with which you strongly agree or disagree, and explore it in writing for 10 minutes.

▪ ACTIVITIES FOR REREADING

1. One of Theroux's strategies is to state a claim about what "being a man" means and then commenting on it. As you reread the essay, list three of his claims; then, in your own words, briefly restate his comment about each of them.
2. Theroux was affected in his early life by what others meant by "being a man." In a short paragraph, tell how those opinions probably affected his early life.
3. The last words in this essay are "their lives are just as bad." In two or three sentences, describe the kind of men whose "lives are just as bad."

▪ GROUP WORK

Personal Responses: Using the notes in your Reflection Logs, discuss the claims about what "being a man" means in the United States. Try to agree on which of Theroux's claims seem true and untrue. Discuss why.

Objective Responses: Discuss in detail three of Theroux's claims and his discussions of those claims.

Theroux discusses how male children are raised to be "men." In fact, he discusses how children of both sexes are trained to grow up "properly," meaning how society expects them to act as adults. Discuss what we teach our children and what we would like to see as the result of that teaching.

WRITING ASSIGNMENTS

1. After considering Theroux's comments about both sexes, discuss your own childhood experiences and how they molded you into the person you are now. Pay particular attention to the clothes you wore, the social and athletic activities you participated in, and your parents' expectations of how you were supposed to act.
2. Write an essay in which you examine your own efforts at "being a man" or "being a woman" in your social world. What expectations do others have of you? How consciously do you try to live up to those expectations? Why?

On Natural Death   *1979*

LEWIS THOMAS

There are so many new books about dying that there are now special   1
shelves set aside for them in bookshops, along with the health-diet and home-repair paperbacks and the sex manuals. Some of them are so packed with detailed information and step-by-step instructions for performing the function that you'd think this was a new sort of skill which all of us are now required to learn. The strongest impression the casual reader gets, leafing through, is that proper dying has become an extraordinary, even an exotic experience, something only the specially trained get to do.

Also, you could be led to believe that we are the only creatures capable of   2
the awareness of death, that when all the rest of nature is being cycled through dying, one generation after another, it is a different kind of process, done automatically and trivially, more "natural," as we say.

An elm in our backyard caught the blight this summer and dropped stone   3
dead, leafless, almost overnight. One weekend it was a normal-looking elm, maybe a little bare in spots but nothing alarming, and the next weekend it was gone, passed over, departed, taken. Taken is right, for the tree surgeon came by yesterday with his crew of young helpers and their cherry picker, and took it down branch by branch and carted it off in the back of a red truck, everyone singing.

The dying of a field mouse, at the jaws of an amiable household cat, is a   4
spectacle I have beheld many times. It used to make me wince. Early in life I gave up throwing sticks at the cat to make him drop the mouse, because the dropped mouse regularly went ahead and died anyway, but I always shouted

unaffections at the cat to let him know the sort of animal he had become. Nature, I thought, was an abomination.

Recently I've done some thinking about that mouse, and I wonder if his dying is necessarily all that different from the passing of our elm. The main difference, if there is one, would be in the matter of pain. I do not believe that an elm tree has pain receptors, and even so, the blight seems to me a relatively painless way to go even if there were nerve endings in a tree, which there are not. But the mouse dangling tail-down from the teeth of a gray cat is something else again, with pain beyond bearing, you'd think, all over his small body.

There are now some plausible reasons for thinking it is not like that at all, and you can make up an entirely different story about the mouse and his dying if you like. At the instant of being trapped and penetrated by teeth, peptide hormones are released by cells in the hypothalamus and the pituitary gland; instantly these substances, called endorphins, are attached to the surface of other cells responsible for pain perception; the hormones have the pharmacologic properties of opium; there is no pain. Thus it is that the mouse seems always to dangle so languidly from the jaws, lies there so quietly when dropped, dies of his injuries without a struggle. If a mouse could shrug, he'd shrug.

I do not know if this is true or not, nor do I know how to prove it if it is true. Maybe if you could get in there quickly enough and administer naloxone, a specific morphine antagonist, you could turn off the endorphins and observe the restoration of pain, but this is not something I would care to do or see. I think I will leave it there, as a good guess about the dying of a cat-chewed mouse, perhaps about dying in general.

Montaigne had a hunch about dying, based on his own close call in a riding accident. He was so badly injured as to be believed dead by his companions, and was carried home with lamentations, "all bloody, stained all over with the blood I had thrown up." He remembers the entire episode, despite having been "dead, for two full hours," with wonderment:

> It seemed to me that my life was hanging only by the tip of my lips. I closed my eyes in order, it seemed to me, to help push it out, and took pleasure in growing languid and letting myself go. It was an idea that was only floating on the surface of my soul, as delicate and feeble as all the rest, but in truth not only free from distress but mingled with that sweet feeling that people have who have let themselves slide into sleep. I believe that this is the same state in which people find themselves whom we see fainting in the agony of death, and I maintain that we pity them without cause. . . . In order to get used to the idea of death, I find there is nothing like coming close to it.

Later, in another essay, Montaigne returns to it:

> If you know not how to die, never trouble yourself: Nature will in a moment fully and sufficiently instruct you; she will exactly do that business for you; take you no care for it.

The worst accident I've ever seen was on Okinawa, in the early days of the invasion, when a jeep ran into a troop carrier and was crushed nearly flat. Inside were two young MPs, trapped in bent steel, both mortally hurt, with only their hands and shoulders visible. We had a conversation while people with the right tools were prying them free. Sorry about the accident, they said. No, they said, they felt fine. Is everyone else okay, one of them said. Well, the other one said, no hurry now. And then they died.

Pain is useful for avoidance, for getting away when there's time to get away, 10 but when it is end game, and no way back, pain is likely to be turned off, and the mechanisms for this are wonderfully precise and quick. If I had to design an ecosystem in which creatures had to live off each other and in which dying was an indispensable part of living, I could not think of a better way to manage.

■ RECORDING REFLECTIONS

Thomas says at the beginning of his essay that people treat *human* death as if it is somehow significantly different from death in the rest of the animal kingdom. His essay shows that it is not. Moreover, it shows that death is a natural process and thus should not be feared.

While you read, list your own observations about death—fears as well as insights. When you have finished reading, write for 10 minutes on whether Thomas's observations reflect any of your own.

■ ACTIVITIES FOR REREADING

1. Notice the time and space Thomas devotes to the death of the mouse versus the soldiers' deaths. Why the discrepancy? How does he use the first instance to set up and comment on the second? Answer in no more than a single, short paragraph.
2. Describe in three or four sentences how the quotes from Montaigne in paragraph 8 refer back to the death of the mouse and forward to the soldiers' deaths.
3. As you reread, consider the essay's title in relation to each paragraph. Make a brief comment after each paragraph about the appropriateness of the title to it.

■ GROUP WORK

Personal Responses: Compare your insights and fears about death. What concerns seem the most common? The most distinctive? Use the comments in your Reflection Logs to discuss the specific ways Thomas addresses the same concerns. If he doesn't address your concerns, explain them to the group.

Objective Responses: Discuss Thomas's title, the space he allots to discussing the deaths of the mouse versus the soldiers, and the significance of the Montaigne quotes. Use both your notes from rereading as well as specifics from the text to support your ideas.

Death is a complex subject. Why do you think Thomas made his essay so brief? What effect does its brevity have on the reader?

How would you describe the essay's tone? Does it include humor? Pick out examples from the essay to back up your opinion.

■ **WRITING ASSIGNMENTS**

1. Write an essay that discusses four or five of your fears about dying. Use as many examples as you can to illustrate your fears and how you might deal with them.

2. Write an essay in which you discuss your views of death and how they relate to Thomas's views in "On Natural Death." How have your views been shaped by your personal experiences? How have your views been shaped by reading Thomas's essay?

The Damned Human Race   *1906*

MARK TWAIN

I have been studying the traits and dispositions of the "lower animals" (so-called), and contrasting them with the traits and dispositions of man. I find the result humiliating to me. For it obliges me to renounce my allegiance to the Darwinian[1] theory of the Ascent of Man from the Lower Animals; since it now seems plain to me that that theory ought to be vacated in favor of a new and truer one, this new and truer one to be named the *Des*cent of Man from the Higher Animals.   1

In proceeding toward this unpleasant conclusion I have not guessed or speculated or conjectured, but have used what is commonly called the scientific method. That is to say, I have subjected every postulate that presented itself to the crucial test of actual experiment, and have adopted it or rejected it according to the result. Thus I verified and established each step of my course in its turn before advancing to the next. These experiments were made in the London Zoological Gardens, and covered many months of painstaking and fatiguing work.   2

Before particularizing any of the experiments, I wish to state one or two things which seem to more properly belong in this place than further along. This in the interest of clearness. The massed experiments established to my satisfaction certain generalizations, to wit: 3

1. That the human race is of one distinct species. It exhibits slight variations—in color, stature, mental caliber, and so on—due to climate, environment, and so forth; but it is a species by itself, and not to be confounded with any other.   4

2. That the quadrupeds are a distinct family, also. This family exhibits variations—in color, size, food preferences and so on; but it is a family by itself.   5

3. That the other families—the birds, the fishes, the insects, the reptiles, etc.—are more or less distinct, also. They are in the procession. They are links in the chain which stretches down from the higher animals to man at the bottom.   6

---

[1]Charles Darwin (1809–1882) published *The Descent of Man* in 1871, a highly controversial book in which he argued that humankind had descended from so-called lower forms of life. —EDS.

Some of my experiments were quite curious. In the course of my reading I   7
had come across a case where, many years ago, some hunters on our Great
Plains organized a buffalo hunt for the entertainment of an English earl—that,
and to provide some fresh meat for his larder. They had charming sport. They
killed seventy-two of those great animals; and ate part of one of them and left
the seventy-one to rot. In order to determine the difference between an anaconda and an earl—if any—I caused seven young calves to be turned into the
anaconda's cage. The grateful reptile immediately crushed one of them and
swallowed it, then lay back satisfied. It showed no further interest in the calves,
and no disposition to harm them. I tried this experiment with other anacondas;
always with the same result. The fact stood proven that the difference between
an earl and an anaconda is that the earl is cruel and the anaconda isn't; and that
the earl wantonly destroys what he has no use for, but the anaconda doesn't.
This seemed to suggest that the anaconda was not descended from the earl. It
also seemed to suggest that the earl was descended from the anaconda, and had
lost a good deal in the transition.

I was aware that many men who have accumulated more millions of   8
money than they can ever use have shown a rabid hunger for more, and have
not scrupled to cheat the ignorant and the helpless out of their poor servings
in order to partially appease that appetite. I furnished a hundred different
kinds of wild and tame animals the opportunity to accumulate vast stores of
food, but none of them would do it. The squirrels and bees and certain birds
made accumulations, but stopped when they had gathered a winter's supply,
and could not be persuaded to add to it either honestly or by chicane. In order to bolster up a tottering reputation the ant pretended to store up supplies,
but I was not deceived. I know the ant. These experiments convinced me that
there is this difference between man and the higher animals: He is avaricious
and miserly, they are not.

In the course of my experiments I convinced myself that among the animals   9
man is the only one that harbors insults and injuries, broods over them, waits
till a chance offers, then takes revenge. The passion of revenge is unknown to
the higher animals.

Roosters keep harems, but it is by consent of their concubines; therefore no   10
wrong is done. Men keep harems, but it is by brute force, privileged by atrocious laws which the other sex were allowed no hand in making. In this matter man occupies a far lower place than the rooster.

Cats are loose in their morals, but not consciously so. Man, in his descent   11
from the cat, has brought the cat's looseness with him but has left the uncon-
sciousness behind—the saving grace which excuses the cat. The cat is innocent, man is not.

Indecency, vulgarity, obscenity—these are strictly confined to man; he in-   12
vented them. Among the higher animals there is no trace of them. They hide
nothing; they are not ashamed. Man, with his soiled mind, covers himself. He
will not even enter a drawing room with his breast and back naked, so alive are
he and his mates to indecent suggestion. Man is "The Animal that Laughs." But
so does the monkey, as Mr. Darwin pointed out; and so does the Australian bird

that is called the laughing jackass. No—Man is the Animal that Blushes. He is the only one that does it—or has occasion to.

At the head of this article[2] we see how "three monks were burnt to death" a few days ago, and a prior "put to death with atrocious cruelty." Do we inquire into the details? No; or we should find out that the prior was subjected to unprintable mutilations. Man—when he is a North American Indian—gouges out his prisoner's eyes; when he is King John, with a nephew to render untroublesome, he uses a red-hot iron; when he is a religious zealot dealing with heretics in the Middle Ages, he skins his captive alive and scatters salt on his back; in the first Richard's time he shuts up a multitude of Jew families in a tower and sets fire to it; in Columbus's time he captures a family of Spanish Jews and— but *that* is not printable; in our day in England a man is fined ten shillings for beating his mother nearly to death with a chair, and another man is fined forty shillings for having four pheasant eggs in his possession without being able to satisfactorily explain how he got them. Of all the animals, man is the only one that is cruel. He is the only one that inflicts pain for the pleasure of doing it. It is a trait that is not known to the higher animals. The cat plays with the frightened mouse; but she has this excuse, that she does not know that the mouse is suffering. The cat is moderate—unhumanly moderate: She only scares the mouse, she does not hurt it; she doesn't dig out its eyes, or tear off its skin, or drive splinters under its nails—man-fashion; when she is done playing with it she makes a sudden meal of it and puts it out of its trouble. Man is the Cruel Animal. He is alone in that distinction. 13

The higher animals engage in individual fights, but never in organized masses. Man is the only animal that deals in that atrocity of atrocities, War. He is the only one that gathers his brethren about him and goes forth in cold blood and with calm pulse to exterminate his kind. He is the only animal that for sordid wages will march out, as the Hessians did in our Revolution,[3] and as the boyish Prince Napoleon did in the Zulu war,[4] and help to slaughter strangers of his own species who have done him no harm and with whom he has no quarrel. 14

Man is the only animal that robs his helpless fellow of his country—takes possession of it and drives him out of it or destroys him. Man has done this in all the ages. There is not an acre of ground on the globe that is in possession of its rightful owner, or that has not been taken away from owner after owner, cycle after cycle, by force and bloodshed. 15

Man is the only Slave. And he is the only animal who enslaves. He has always been a slave in one form or another, and has always held other slaves in bondage under him in one way or another. In our day he is always some man's 16

---

[2]In his nonfiction Twain often introduced newsclippings as evidence of human atrocity. In this instance the article has been lost, but Twain is most likely referring to the religious persecutions that followed the 1897 Cretan revolt.—Eds.

[3]***Revolution:*** Approximately 17,000 mercenaries from Hesse, a part of Germany, fought for the British during the American Revolution.—Eds.

[4]***Zulu war:*** Napoleon III's son died while fighting for the British during the 1879 Zulu rebellion in what is now the Republic of South Africa. Great Britain annexed the Zulu territory shortly after, and that is the context for Twain's remarks in the next paragraph.—Eds.

slave for wages, and does that man's work; and this slave has other slaves under him for minor wages, and they do *his* work. The higher animals are the only ones who exclusively do their own work and provide their own living.

Man is the only Patriot. He sets himself apart in his own country, under his own flag, and sneers at the other nations, and keeps multitudinous uniformed assassins on hand at heavy expense to grab slices of other people's countries, and keep *them* from grabbing slices of *his.* And in the intervals between campaigns he washes the blood off his hands and works for "the universal brotherhood of man"—with his mouth.   17

Man is the Religious Animal. He is the only Religious Animal. He is the only animal that has the True Religion—several of them. He is the only animal that loves his neighbor as himself, and cuts his throat if his theology isn't straight. He has made a graveyard of the globe in trying his honest best to smooth his brother's path to happiness and heaven. He was at it in the time of the Caesars, he was at it in Mahomet's time, he was at it in the time of the Inquisition, he was at it in France a couple of centuries, he was at it in England in Mary's day,[5] he has been at it ever since he first saw the light, he is at it today in Crete—as per the telegrams quoted above—he will be at it somewhere else tomorrow. The higher animals have no religion. And we are told that they are going to be left out, in the Hereafter. I wonder why? It seems questionable taste.   18

Man is the Reasoning Animal. Such is the claim. I think it is open to dispute. Indeed, my experiments have proven to me that he is the Unreasoning Animal. Note his history, as sketched above. It seems plain to me that whatever he is he is *not* a reasoning animal. His record is the fantastic record of a maniac. I consider that the strongest count against his intelligence is the fact that with that record back of him he blandly sets himself up as the head animal of the lot: Whereas by his own standards he is the bottom one.   19

In truth, man is incurably foolish. Simple things which the other animals easily learn, he is incapable of learning. Among my experiments was this. In an hour I taught a cat and a dog to be friends. I put them in a cage. In another hour I taught them to be friends with a rabbit. In the course of two days I was able to add a fox, a goose, a squirrel and some doves. Finally a monkey. They lived together in peace; even affectionately.   20

Next, in another cage I confined an Irish Catholic from Tipperary, and as soon as he seemed tame I added a Scotch Presbyterian from Aberdeen. Next a Turk from Constantinople; a Greek Christian from Crete; an Armenian; a Methodist from the wilds of Arkansas; a Buddhist from China; a Brahman from Benares. Finally, a Salvation Army Colonel from Wapping. Then I stayed away two whole days. When I came back to note results, the cage of Higher Animals was all right, but in the other there was but a chaos of gory odds and ends of turbans and fezzes and plaids and bones and flesh—not a specimen left alive. These Reasoning Animals had disagreed on a theological detail and carried the matter to a Higher Court.   21

---

[5]*Mary's day:* In the time of Mary I, who reigned as Queen of England between 1553 and 1558; her vigorous persecution of Protestants earned her the nickname of "Bloody Mary."—Eds.

One is obliged to concede that in true loftiness of character, Man cannot claim to approach even the meanest of the Higher Animals. It is plain that he is constitutionally incapable of approaching that altitude; that he is constitutionally afflicted with a Defect which must make such approach forever impossible, for it is manifest that this defect is permanent in him, indestructible, ineradicable. 22

I find this Defect to be *the Moral Sense*. He is the only animal that has it. It is the secret of his degradation. It is the quality *which enables him to do wrong*. It has no other office. It is incapable of performing any other function. It could never have been intended to perform any other. Without it, man could do no wrong. He would rise at once to the level of the Higher Animals. 23

Since the Moral Sense has but the one office, the one capacity—to enable man to do wrong—it is plainly without value to him. It is as valueless to him as is disease. In fact, it manifestly *is* a disease. *Rabies* is bad, but it is not so bad as this disease. Rabies enables a man to do a thing which he could not do when in a healthy state: kill his neighbor with a poisonous bite. No one is the better man for having rabies. The Moral Sense enables a man to do wrong. It enables him to do wrong in a thousand ways. Rabies is an innocent disease, compared to the Moral Sense. No one, then, can be the better man for having the Moral Sense. What, now, do we find the Primal Curse to have been? Plainly what it was in the beginning: the infliction upon man of the Moral Sense; the ability to distinguish good from evil; and with it, necessarily, the ability to *do* evil; for there can be no evil act without the presence of consciousness of it in the doer of it. 24

And so I find that we have descended and degenerated, from some far ancestor—some microscopic atom wandering at its pleasure between the mighty horizons of a drop of water perchance—insect by insect, animal by animal, reptile by reptile, down the long highway of smirchless innocence, till we have reached the bottom stage of development—namable as the Human Being. Below us—nothing. Nothing but the Frenchman. 25

There is only one possible stage below the Moral Sense; that is the Immoral Sense. The Frenchman has it. Man is but little lower than the angels. This definitely locates him. He is between the angels and the French. 26

Man seems to be a rickety poor sort of a thing, any way you take him; a kind of British Museum of infirmities and inferiorities. He is always undergoing repairs. A machine that was as unreliable as he is would have no market. On top of his specialty—the Moral Sense—are plied a multitude of minor infirmities; such a multitude, indeed, that one may broadly call them countless. The higher animals get their teeth without pain or inconvenience. Man gets his through months and months of cruel torture; and at a time of life when he is but ill able to bear it. As soon as he has got them they must all be pulled out again, for they were of no value in the first place, not worth the loss of a night's rest. The second set will answer for a while, by being reinforced occasionally with rubber or plugged up with gold; but he will never get a set which can really be depended on till a dentist makes him one. This set will be called "false" teeth—as if he had ever worn any other kind. 27

In a wild state—a natural state—the Higher Animals have a few diseases; diseases of little consequence; the main one is old age. But man starts in as a 28 child and lives on diseases till the end, as a regular diet. He has mumps, measles, whooping cough, croup, tonsillitis, diphtheria, scarlet fever, almost as a matter of course. Afterward, as he goes along, his life continues to be threatened at every turn: by colds, coughs, asthma, bronchitis, itch, cholera, cancer, consumption, yellow fever, bilious fever, typhus fevers, hay fever; ague, chilblains, piles, inflammation of the entrails, indigestion, toothache, earache, deafness, dumbness, blindness, influenza, chicken pox, cowpox, smallpox, liver complaint, constipation, bloody flux, warts, pimples, boils, carbuncles, abscesses, bunions, corns, tumors, fistulas, pneumonia, softening of the brain, melancholia and fifteen other kinds of insanity; dysentery, jaundice, diseases of the heart, the bones, the skin, the scalp, the spleen, the kidneys, the nerves, the brain, the blood; scrofula, paralysis, leprosy, neuralgia, palsy, fits, headache, thirteen kinds of rheumatism, forty-six of gout, and a formidable supply of gross and unprintable disorders of one sort and another. Also—but why continue the list? The mere names of the agents appointed to keep this shackly machine out of repair would hide him from sight if printed on his body in the smallest type known to the founder's art. He is but a basket of pestilent corruption provided for the support and entertainment of swarming armies of bacilli—armies commissioned to rot him and destroy him, and each army equipped with a special detail of the work. The process of waylaying him, persecuting him, rotting him, killing him, begins with his first breath, and there is no mercy, no pity, no truce till he draws his last one.

29   Look at the workmanship of him, in certain of its particulars. What are his tonsils for? They perform no useful function; they have no value. They have no business there. They are but a trap. They have but the one office, the one industry: to provide tonsillitis and quinsy and such things for the possessor of them. And what is the vermiform appendix for? It has no value; it cannot perform any useful service. It is but an ambuscaded enemy whose sole interest in life is to lie in wait for stray grapeseeds and employ them to breed strangulated hernia. And what are the male's mammals for? For business, they are out of the question; as an ornament, they are a mistake. What is his beard for? It performs no useful function; it is a nuisance and a discomfort; all nations hate it; all nations persecute it with a razor. And because it is a nuisance and a discomfort, Nature never allows the supply of it to fall short, in any man's case, between puberty and the grave. You never see a man bald-headed on his chin, but his hair! It is a graceful ornament, it is a comfort, it is the best of all protections against certain perilous ailments, man prizes it above emeralds and rubles. And because of these things Nature puts it on, half the time, so that it won't stay. Man's sight, smell, hearing, sense of locality—how inferior they are. The condor sees a corpse at five miles; man has no telescope that can do it. The bloodhound follows a scent that is two days old. The robin hears the earthworm burrowing his course under the ground. The cat, deported in a closed basket, finds its way home again through twenty miles of country which it has never seen.

30   Certain functions lodged in the other sex perform in a lamentably inferior way as compared with the performance of the same functions in the Higher Animals. In the human being, menstruation, gestation and parturition are terms

which stand for horrors. In the Higher Animals these things are hardly even inconveniences.

For style, look at the Bengal tiger—that ideal of grace, beauty, physical perfection, majesty. And then look at Man—that poor thing. He is the Animal of the Wig, the Trepanned Skull, the Ear Trumpet, the Glass Eye, the Pasteboard Nose, the Porcelain Teeth, the Silver Windpipe, the Wooden Leg—a creature that is mended and patched all over, from top to bottom. If he can't get renewals of his bric-a-brac in the next world, what will he look like? 31

He has just one stupendous superiority. In his intellect he is supreme. The Higher Animals cannot touch him there. It is curious, it is noteworthy, that no heaven has ever been offered him wherein his one sole superiority was provided with a chance to enjoy itself. Even when he himself has imagined a heaven, he has never made provision in it for intellectual joys. It is a striking omission. It seems a tacit confession that heavens are provided for the Higher Animals alone. This is matter for thought; and for serious thought. And it is full of a grim suggestion: that we are not as important, perhaps, as we had all along supposed we were. 32

RECORDING REFLECTIONS

Throughout his essay, Twain cites numerous examples of how humans behave poorly compared to other animals. As you read, jot down your reactions to at least five of Twain's examples.

When you have finished your list of reactions, choose one and write for 10 minutes, reflecting on both the example and your reaction to it.

ACTIVITIES FOR REREADING

1. As you reread, determine Twain's thesis. Mark where you think he states it in the text.
2. As you reread, try to determine Twain's main purpose for writing the essay. Is his purpose different from his thesis? Write a brief explanation of why you think it is the same or different.
3. According to Twain, what is the central reason that makes humans inferior to other animals? Mark where in the essay he states that reason, and then comment in writing what you think about its validity.

GROUP WORK

Personal Responses: Using your Reflection Logs as guides, compare your reactions to Twain's examples of humans' moral inferiority to animals. How are your reactions similar? Different? Discuss in particular your reactions to Twain's fictional examples. Do they help or hinder his argument?

Objective Responses: See if you can agree on what Twain's thesis is and where he states it. Does he modify his thesis in the course of the essay? If so, where? Why?

Discuss Twain's main purpose and whether it is the same as his thesis. Pick out the passages that are obviously not to be taken seriously, and discuss how we can draw serious conclusions from them.

Use the notes in your Reflection Logs to help you discuss Twain's ideas about man's "moral sense," as described in paragraphs 22–26. Try to come to a consensus about the validity of Twain's observations.

WRITING ASSIGNMENTS

1. Write an essay in which you take issue with Twain's point of view. Turn his argument around to show how humans—with all their moral failings—have contributed significantly to the world. Use mainly concrete and specific examples of humans' achievements. Be careful not to get too philosophical or fall into parochialism or sectarianism, which Twain would consider a moral failure.
2. Write an essay modeled on Twain's in which you use fictional or exaggerated examples to make a serious point.

Once More to the Lake   *1941*

E. B. WHITE

One summer, along about 1904, my father rented a camp on a lake in Maine   1
and took us all there for the month of August. We all got ringworm from some kittens and had to rub Pond's Extract on our arms and legs night and morning, and my father rolled over in a canoe with all his clothes on; but outside of that the vacation was a success and from then on none of us ever thought there was any place in the world like that lake in Maine. We returned summer after summer—always on August 1 for one month. I have since become a salt-water man, but sometimes in summer there are days when the restlessness of the tides and the fearful cold of the sea water and the incessant wind that blows across the afternoon and into the evening make me wish for the placidity of a lake in the woods. A few weeks ago this feeling got so strong I bought myself a couple of bass hooks and a spinner and returned to the lake where we used to go, for a week's fishing and to revisit old haunts.

I took along my son, who had never had any fresh water up his nose and   2
who had seen lily pads only from train windows. On the journey over to the lake I began to wonder what it would be like. I wondered how time would have marred this unique, this holy spot—the coves and streams, the hills that the sun set behind, the camps and the paths behind the camps. I was sure that the tarred road would have found it out, and I wondered in what other ways it would be desolated. It is strange how much you can remember about places like that once you allow your mind to return into the grooves that lead back. You remember one thing, and that suddenly reminds you of another thing. I guess I remembered clearest of all the early mornings, when the lake was cool and motionless, remembered how the bedroom smelled of the lumber it was made of and of the wet woods whose scent entered through the screen. The partitions in the camp were thin and did not extend clear to the top of the rooms, and as I was always

the first up I would dress softly so as not to wake the others, and sneak out into the sweet outdoors and start out in the canoe, keeping close along the shore in the long shadows of the pines. I remembered being very careful never to rub my paddle against the gunwale for fear of disturbing the stillness of the cathedral.

The lake had never been what you would call a wild lake. There were cottages sprinkled around the shores, and it was in farming country although the shores of the lake were quite heavily wooded. Some of the cottages were owned by nearby farmers, and you would live at the shore and eat your meals at the farmhouse. That's what our family did. But although it wasn't wild, it was a fairly large and undisturbed lake and there were places in it that, to a child at least, seemed infinitely remote and primeval. 3

I was right about the tar; it led to within half a mile of the shore. But when I got back there, with my boy, and we settled into a camp near a farmhouse and into the kind of summertime I had known, I could tell that it was going to be pretty much the same as it had been before—I knew it, lying in bed the first morning, smelling the bedroom and hearing the boy sneak quietly out and go off along the shore in a boat. I began to sustain the illusion that he was I, and therefore, by simple transposition, that I was my father. This sensation persisted, kept cropping up all the time we were there. It was not an entirely new feeling, but in this setting it grew much stronger. I seemed to be living a dual existence. I would be in the middle of some simple act, I would be picking up a bait box or laying down a table fork, or I would be saying something, and suddenly it would be not I but my father who was saying the words or making the gesture. It gave me a creepy sensation. 4

We went fishing the first morning. I felt the same damp moss covering the worms in the bait can, and saw the dragonfly alight on the tip of my rod as it hovered a few inches from the surface of the water. It was the arrival of this fly that convinced me beyond any doubt that everything was as it always had been, that the years were a mirage and that there had been no years. The small waves were the same, chucking the rowboat under the chin as we fished at anchor, and the boat was the same boat, the same color green and the ribs broken in the same places, and under the floorboards the same fresh-water leavings and débris—the dead hellgrammite, the wisps of moss, the rusty discarded fishhook, the dried blood from yesterday's catch. We stared silently at the tips of our rods, at the dragonflies that came and went. I lowered the tip of mine into the water, tentatively, pensively dislodging the fly, which darted two feet away, poised, darted two feet back, and came to rest again a little farther up the rod. There had been no years between the ducking of this dragonfly and the other one—the one that was part of memory. I looked at the boy, who was silently watching his fly, and it was my hands that held his rod, my eyes watching. I felt dizzy and didn't know which rod I was at the end of. 5

We caught two bass, hauling them in briskly as though they were mackerel, pulling them over the side of the boat in a businesslike manner without any landing net, and stunning them with a blow on the back of the head. When we got back for a swim before lunch, the lake was exactly where we had left it, the same number of inches from the dock, and there was only the merest suggestion of a 6 breeze. This seemed an utterly enchanted sea, this lake you could leave to its own devices for a few hours and come back to, and find it had not stirred, this constant and trustworthy body of water. In the shallows, the dark, water-soaked sticks and twigs, smooth and old, were undulating in clusters on the bottom against the clean ribbed sand, and the track of the mussel was plain. A school of minnows swam by, each minnow with its small individual shadow, doubling the attendance, so clear and sharp in the sunlight. Some of the other campers were in swimming, along the shore, one of them with a cake of soap, and the water felt thin and clear and unsubstantial. Over the years there had been this person with the cake of soap, this cultist, and here he was. There had been no years.

Up to the farmhouse to dinner through the teeming, dusty field, the road 7
under our sneakers was only a two-track road. The middle track was missing, the one with the marks of the hooves and the splotches of dried, flaky manure. There had always been three tracks to choose from in choosing which track to walk in; now the choice was narrowed down to two. For a moment I missed terribly the middle alternative. But the way led past the tennis court, and something about the way it lay there in the sun reassured me; the tape had loosened along the backline, the alleys were green with plantains and other weeds, and the net (installed in June and removed in September) sagged in the dry noon, and the whole place steamed with midday heat and hunger and emptiness. There was a choice of pie for dessert, and one was blueberry and one was apple, and the waitresses were the same country girls, there having been no passage of time, only the illusion of it as in a dropped curtain—the waitresses were still fifteen; their hair had been washed, that was the only difference—they had been to the movies and seen the pretty girls with the clean hair.

Summertime, oh summertime, pattern of life indelible, the fade-proof lake, 8
the woods unshatterable, the pasture with the sweetfern and the juniper forever and ever, summer without end; this was the background, and the life along the shore was the design, their tiny docks with the flagpole and the American flag floating against the white clouds in the blue sky, the little paths over the roots of the trees leading from camp to camp and the paths leading back to the outhouses and the can of lime for sprinkling, and at the souvenir counters at the store the miniature birch-bark canoes and the postcards that showed things looking a little better than they looked. This was the American family at play, escaping the city heat, wondering whether the newcomers in the camp at the head of the cove were "common" or "nice," wondering whether it was true that the people who drove up for Sunday dinner at the farmhouse were turned away because there wasn't enough chicken.

It seemed to me, as I kept remembering all this, that those times and those 9
summers had been infinitely precious and worth saving. There had been jollity and peace and goodness. The arriving (at the beginning of August) had been so big a business in itself, at the railway station the farm wagon drawn up, the first smell of the pine-laden air, the first glimpse of the smiling farmer, and the great importance of the trunks and your father's enormous authority in such matters, and the feel of the wagon under you for the long ten-mile haul, and at the top of the last long hill catching the first view of the lake after eleven months of not

seeing this cherished body of water. The shouts and cries of the other campers when they saw you, and the trunks to be unpacked, to give up their rich burden. (Arriving was less exciting nowadays, when you sneaked up in your car and parked it under a tree near the camp and took out the bags and in five minutes it was all over, no fuss, no loud wonderful fuss about trunks.)

Peace and goodness and jollity. The only thing that was wrong now, really, was the sound of the place, an unfamiliar nervous sound of the outboard motors. This was the note that jarred, the one thing that would sometimes break the illusion and set the years moving. In those other summertimes all the motors were inboard; and when they were at a little distance, the noise they made was a sedative, an ingredient of summer sleep. They were one-cylinder and two-cylinder engines, and some were make-and-break and some were jump-spark, but they all made a sleepy sound across the lake. The one-lungers throbbed and fluttered, and the twin-cylinder ones purred and purred, and that was a quiet sound, too. But now the campers all had outboards. In the daytime, in the hot mornings, these motors made a petulant, irritable sound; at night, in the still evening when the afterglow lit the water, they whined about one's ears like mosquitoes. My boy loved our rented outboard, and his great desire was to achieve single-handed mastery over it, and authority, and he soon learned the trick of choking it a little (but not too much), and the adjustment of the needle valve. Watching him I would remember the things you could do with the old one-cylinder engine with the heavy flywheel, how you could have it eating out of your hand if you got really close to it spiritually. Motorboats in those days didn't have clutches, and you would make a landing by shutting off the motor at the proper time and coasting in with a dead rudder. But there was a way of reversing them, if you learned the trick, by cutting the switch and putting it on again exactly on the final dying revolution of the flywheel, so that it would kick back against the compression and begin reversing. Approaching a dock in a strong following breeze, it was difficult to slow up sufficiently by the ordinary coasting method, and if a boy felt he had complete mastery over his motor, he was tempted to keep it running beyond its time and then reverse it a few feet from the dock. It took a cool nerve, because if you threw the switch a twentieth of a second too soon you would catch the flywheel when it still had speed enough to go up past center, and the boat would leap ahead, charging bull-fashion at the dock.

We had a good week at camp. The bass were biting well and the sun shown endlessly, day after day. We would be tired at night and lie down in the accumulated heat of the little bedrooms after the long hot day and the breeze would stir almost imperceptibly outside and the smell of the swamp drift in through the rusty screens. Sleep would come easily and in the morning the red squirrel would be on the roof, tapping out his gay routine. I kept remembering everything, lying in bed in the mornings—the small steamboat that had a long rounded stern like the lip of a Ubangi, and how quietly she ran on the moonlight sails, when the older boys played their mandolins and the girls sang and we ate doughnuts dipped in sugar, and how sweet the music was on the water in the shining night, and what it had felt like to think about girls then. After breakfast we would go up to the store and the things were in the same place—the minnows in a bottle, the plugs and spinners disarranged and pawed over by the youngsters from the boys' camp, the Fig Newtons and the Beeman's gum. Outside, the road was tarred and cars stood in front of the store. Inside, all was just as it had always been, except there was more Coca-Cola and not so much Moxie and root beer and birch beer and sarsaparilla. We would walk out with the bottle of pop apiece and sometimes the pop would backfire up our noses and hurt. We explored the streams, quietly, where the turtles slid off the sunny logs and dug their way into the soft bottom; and we lay on the town wharf and fed worms to the tame bass. Everywhere we went I had trouble making out which I was, the one walking at my side, the one walking in my pants.

One afternoon while we were there at that lake a thunderstorm came up. 12 It was like the revival of an old melodrama that I had seen long ago with childish awe. The second-act climax of the drama of the electrical disturbance over a lake in America had not changed in any important respect. This was the big scene, still the big scene. The whole thing was so familiar, the first feeling of oppression and heat and a general air around camp of not wanting to go very far away. In mid-afternoon (it was all the same) a curious darkening of the sky, and a lull in everything that had made life tick; and then the way the boats suddenly swung the other way at their moorings with the coming of a breeze out of the new quarter, and the premonitory rumble. Then the kettle drum, then the snare, then the bass drum and cymbals, then crackling light against the dark, and the gods grinning and licking their chops in the hills. Afterward the calm, the rain steadily rustling in the calm lake, the return of light and hope and spirits, and the campers running out in joy and relief to go swimming in the rain, their bright cries perpetuating the deathless joke about how they were getting simply drenched, and the children screaming with delight at the new sensation of bathing in the rain, and the joke about getting drenched linking the generations in a strong indestructible chain. And the comedian who waded in carrying an umbrella.

When the others went swimming, my son said he was going in, too. He 13 pulled his dripping trunks from the line where they had hung all through the shower and wrung them out. Languidly, and with no thought of going in, I watched him, his hard little body, skinny and bare, saw him wince slightly as he pulled up around his vitals the small, soggy, icy garment. As he buckled the swollen belt, suddenly my groin felt the chill of death.

■ RECORDING REFLECTIONS

This essay moves back and forth in time. White couples his experiences with that of his son to the extent that he sometimes has trouble mentally separating the man from the boy.

In your Reflection Log, think back to a specific activity that you shared long ago with someone with whom you had or have a strong bond. After selecting that person, write about the activity for 10 minutes, setting down your memories of that event.

ACTIVITIES FOR REREADING

1. One of White's strategies is to move back and forth in time—from the present, with his son, to the past, with his own father. As you reread this essay, note the three strongest shifts between the present and the past. What do these shifts suggest as a writing strategy?

2. The essay closes with "the chill of death." What does this phrase refer to, and why is it important to the overall understanding of the essay?

3. If you haven't already read it, quickly skim George Simpson's essay "The War Room at Bellevue" (pp. 600–605). Compare how White and Simpson each uses time. What is the essential difference? How does the way White use time add to the meaning of his essay?

GROUP WORK

Personal Responses: Using information from your Reflection Logs, have each group member discuss the specific activity that he or she shared with someone, paying particular attention to how vivid the memory still is. Ask each member: Do you remember mostly the details of the activity, or do you remember more so your reactions to it? How do you feel about the activity now? Did it affect the bond that you had or have with the other person?

Objective Responses: Discuss the relationship that White has with his son. What did White learn about himself by taking his son to the lake? How did that affect him?

White often describes a scene or an area in two ways: how it appears now and how it appeared when White was his son's age. Why does White use that strategy so many times? What is he trying to illustrate?

What response does White seek from his readers? Is it one that many readers will have? Why or why not?

WRITING ASSIGNMENTS

1. "People do not define themselves through their actions; they define themselves through their memories." Using that quote as your guide, write an essay demonstrating how you define a significant part of yourself through your memories. Describe in detail two or three events in your past that have helped shape you into the person you are now.

2. Write an essay that explores the use of time in White's "Once More to the Lake." How does White use it to explain his feelings? To engage the reader? In what ways is time a central character in this essay? How does White feel about time? What has it taught him?

Handbook

SENTENCE ERRORS

frag	Sentence Fragments
ro	Run-On Sentences
agr	Subject/Verb Agreement
tense	Verb Tense
case	Pronoun Case
pron agr	Pronoun/Antecedent Agreement
ref	Pronoun Reference
gen	Gender-Neutral Language
ESL	Reminders for ESL Writers

PUNCTUATION

,	Commas
;	Semicolons
:	Colons
--	Dashes
'	Apostrophes
" "	Quotation Marks
...	Ellipses
( )	Parentheses
[ ]	Brackets
/	Slashes
. ? !	End Punctuation Marks

MECHANICS

cap	Capitalization
ul	Underlining
num	Numbers
ab	Abbreviations
hyph	Hyphens
sp	Spelling

Sentence Errors

SENTENCE FRAGMENTS

frag

Writing sentence fragments is unacceptable. Fragments may look like sentences, but they are not sentences. Like a sentence, a fragment will begin with a capital and end with a final punctuation mark. But for a word group to function as a sentence, it must have at least one *independent clause*—that is, a subject and a verb, usually referred to as a *predicate*, and be able to stand alone as a complete thought.

Some fragments are *dependent clauses,* which means they can't stand alone. A dependent clause has a subject and a predicate but begins with a subordinating conjunction. Other fragments are merely phrases that lack subjects, predicates, or both.

Revise a sentence fragment in one of two ways: Make the fragment part of a sentence, or rephrase the fragment so it functions as a sentence.

Dependent Clause Fragments

Dependent clauses begin with words that indicate they can't stand alone, even though they have subjects and predicates like independent clauses. All the following words can introduce dependent clauses:

after	if	until
although	so that	when
because	that	where
before	though	who
even though	unless	which

You can usually combine a dependent clause fragment with a sentence:

➤ Driving is still cheap/ ~~Even~~ ^{even} though gas prices have skyrocketed. The price of flying, in contrast, is out of reach.

643

If a dependent clause fragment can't be combined with a sentence, rewrite it as a sentence. The most direct way to do so is to eliminate the subordinating words and add any words necessary to complete the sentence:

➤ The elderly poor live each day in fear of starvation. ~~Which some~~ Some psychologists claim *it* kills more of them than disease.

Phrase Fragments

A word group without a subject or verb is called a *phrase*. When such a word group is capitalized and punctuated like a sentence, it is a *phrase fragment*. You can usually revise a phrase fragment by combining it with another sentence:

➤ We saw Marla and Joe at the Cinco de Mayo party, ~~Dancing~~ dancing the cha-cha.

➤ Start your essay now, ~~To~~ to have it ready by Friday.

➤ The newspaper carried the story, ~~About~~ about hackers changing grades.

➤ The college is looking for a new president, ~~A~~ a person with a warm personality and patience.

If you can't combine a phrase fragment with a sentence, turn it into a sentence. To do so, you may need to add a subject, a verb, or both:

➤ Fourteen thousand angry demonstrators attended the rally. ~~Waving~~ They were waving signs and marching into the night.

Stylistic Fragments

Writers sometimes use fragments for dramatic effect or emphasis.

How many middle-income families does the reduction in luxury tax help? Frankly, none. Families earning less than $40,000 a year have trouble paying for groceries, clothes, education, and medical and dental care. They do not buy half-million dollar speed boats, private jets, and German limousines.

EXERCISE   *Correcting Sentence Fragments*

Correct each of the following sentence fragments by integrating the dependent clause with the independent clause or by rewriting the dependent clause as an independent clause. Keep in mind that each corrected sentence should read smoothly and be punctuated accurately.

1. Dragons appear in a variety of roles. Symbolizing evil to some cultures, wisdom to others, and power to still others.
2. The Sumerians thought of dragons as embodiments of evil. A concept later attached to the devil.
3. The Gnostics, early religious sects of Europe and Asia, used a figure of a dragon biting its own tail. To symbolize the cyclic nature of time and the continuity of life.
4. To convince the people that their leaders had the dragonlike qualities of strength and goodness. Early Chinese emperors adopted the dragon as a symbol of imperial power.
5. Although you may not believe they ever existed, images of dragons have survived in art, fiction, stories, and dreams. In every corner of the world.

EXERCISE *Correcting Sentence Fragments*

Rewrite each of the following sentences to correct the sentence fragments. Either integrate the dependent clause or phrase with the independent clause or rewrite the fragment as an independent clause. Keep in mind that each corrected sentence should read smoothly and be punctuated accurately.

1. Belief in dragons has persisted into the twentieth century. Although no scientific evidence has been found to support the belief.
2. Dragons' teeth and dragons' bones, believed to have nearly miraculous curative powers, could be purchased in China in this century. If one had sufficient money.
3. In Europe, the demand has been less for bones and teeth than for dragons' blood. A sure-fire love potion when burned while reciting the proper incantation.
4. Sightings of dragons continue to this day. In somewhat remote areas that have a long tradition of dragon stories.
5. The Loch Ness monster is perhaps the most famous contemporary dragon. Attracting journalists and investigators in great numbers. First seen in AD 565, this aquatic monster is extremely selective about public appearances. Defying the efforts of scientists using the latest equipment to locate it.
6. Other dragons inhabit other lakes in both Scotland and Ireland. Unfortunately, like the Loch Ness monster, they seldom show themselves to more than one person at a time.
7. In the United States, a few sightings have been made in several of the Great Lakes. The location for earlier Native American stories of dragonlike beasts.
8. What explains the popular belief in dragons? In the absence of any scientific evidence that they ever existed.

9. The problem with this theory is that dinosaurs and similar animals that could have been the ancestors of dragons ceased to exist millions of years ago. Before human beings appeared on the earth.
10. Can belief in dragons be explained? At least to everyone's satisfaction? Probably not.

RUN-ON SENTENCES

ro

A *run-on sentence* is composed of two or more independent clauses that have been written incorrectly as one sentence. Remember, an *independent clause* is a word group that has a subject and a predicate—that is, the main verb—and can stand alone as a complete thought. When you write two or more independent clauses as one sentence, they must be joined in one of two ways:

1. With a comma, followed by a coordinating conjunction: *and, but, or, nor, for, so, yet*
2. With a semicolon, or, if appropriate, a colon or a dash

There are two types of run-on sentences. The first, called a *fused sentence,* occurs when two independent clauses are joined without any punctuation:

FUSED

Primitive people have myths that reflect group consciousness modern people have television.

A second type of run-on sentence is called a *comma splice.* It occurs when two or more independent clauses are joined by a comma without a coordinating conjunction:

COMMA SPLICE

Primitive people have myths that reflect group consciousness, modern people have television.

As you can see, there is very little difference between the two types of run-on sentences. Both types, moreover, can be corrected in one of four ways:

1. Use a comma and a coordinating conjunction.
2. Use a semicolon.
3. Separate the clauses.
4. Subordinate the clauses.

None of these four ways is necessarily better than the others. How you decide to revise a run-on sentence should be determined by the meaning of the passage it appears in and by the effect you wish to create:

➤ Primitive people have myths that reflect group consciousness, ^*and*^ modern people have television.

➤ Primitive people have myths that reflect group consciousness ; modern people have television.

➤ Primitive people have myths that reflect group consciousness . ~~modern~~ ^*Modern*^ people have television.

➤ ^*Although primitive*^ ~~Primitive~~ people have myths that reflect group consciousness, modern people have television.

Use a Comma and a Coordinating Conjunction

If your intent is to give ideas equal emphasis, use a comma and coordinating conjunction to revise a run-on sentence. Keep in mind that there are only seven coordinating conjunctions: *and, but, or, nor, so, for,* and *yet.*

➤ Barbara French is a rare book collector , ^*and*^ her brother Tom is a librarian.

Use a Semicolon

Use semicolons sparingly to show the meanings of the independent clauses are closely related and to achieve a stylistic balance:

➤ American adolescence ended at the Pacific ; American maturity began with a turn toward the Atlantic.

Always use a semicolon to revise a run-on sentence that contains a conjunctive adverb—such as *however, therefore, moreover,* and *furthermore*—and be sure to follow the conjunctive adverb with a comma:

➤ Portland is the largest city in Oregon ; however , Salem is the state capital.

Separate Independent Clauses into Sentences

If the run-on sentence is exceptionally long or if you don't want to give independent clauses equal emphasis, recast them as separate sentences:

➤ Every age is dramatically affected by televised violence . ~~now~~ ^*Now*^ some 9-year-olds carry guns to school.

Subordinate Clauses

Subordinate clauses to one of the dependent clauses for two reasons: if one idea is more important than the other or if you wish to create sentence variety:

➤ ~~The~~ *Because the* ultimate effect of emphysema on the body is deprivation of oxygen, it kills by suffocating.

EXERCISE   *Correcting Run-On Sentences and Comma Splices*

Correct the run-on sentences and comma splices in the following paragraph. Use the most appropriate of the four ways in each case.

It is a summer weekend you have worked all day and want to relax "Time for the movies," you decide. The nearby theater that features classic and international films has been turned into a sixplex, the old theater had good popcorn and a nice-size screen. The new sixplex has small screens with a motel-room charm at least it offers five more movies.

What are the movies? Well, there is the picture about a scowling superhero who makes caustic remarks as he kills the bad guys in the latest cop thriller it stars a generally shirtless, muscle-bound action hero and the latest international model. There is the teen comedy about a nerdy, fast-talking, 15-year-old who anxiously chews on floppy disks he wears glasses upside down and suffers from anguish he's too skinny to make the Ping-Pong team it stars the latest teen heartthrob in baggy clothes and an unknown starlet. Then there is the latest catastrophe movie, it stars everyone, muscle men, heartthrobs, and, of course, plenty of models and starlets (catastrophe movies have plenty of cameos).

The remaining theaters are rerunning the other three movies what's a film buff to do go to the nearest Blockbuster, what else?

SUBJECT/VERB AGREEMENT

agr

Remember: When a word refers to one person or thing, it is *singular* in number. When a word refers to more than one person or thing, it is *plural* in number. For instance:

SINGULAR	PLURAL
person	people
woman	women
ox	oxen
this	these
either	both
he, she, it	they

A verb must always agree with its subject in number. Singular subjects take singular verbs:

A jet lands every four minutes.

The winner was carried from the field.

Plural subjects take plural verbs:

Jets land every four minutes.

The winners were carried from the field.

If a verb immediately follows a subject, you will probably have little trouble making them agree. But sometimes, you will write a sentence that's a little more tricky. Either the subject or its number will be hard to identify.

Intervening Words

Words that come between a subject and its verb often obscure an agreement error. Usually, these words will modify a subject and include a noun that seems to be the subject but isn't. By reading the sentence without the modifying words (shown in brackets below), you will usually be able to spot the agreement error:

➤ Archery [as practiced by Zen masters] ~~take~~ *takes* concentration.

➤ A solution [for the city's many problems] ~~do~~ *does* not exist.

➤ The mayor [surrounded by hundreds of supporters] ~~were~~ *was* singing.

Expressions such as *together with, as well as, in addition to, accompanied by,* and *along with* don't make a singular noun plural:

The major [accompanied by four scouts] ~~are~~ *was* traveling west.

Compound Subjects

When two or more subjects are joined by a coordinating conjunction, such as *and* and *or,* they form a *compound subject.* Subjects joined by *and* usually take a plural verb. Compound subjects joined by *and* are usually plural:

> ➤ Spiritual growth and psychological insight among artists is not uncommon. _are_

An exception to this guideline comes when the parts of a compound subject function as a single idea or refer to a single person or thing. In these cases, the subject should take a singular verb:

> ➤ Ham and eggs, once America's traditional breakfast, are banished from lowfat diets. _is_

> ➤ The Stars and Stripes wave over the battlefield. _waves_

When a compound subject is preceded by *each* or *every*, the verb should be singular. Although these words refer to more than one, they imply consideration of one at a time. And when a compound subject is followed by *each*, the verb is singular, too:

> ➤ Every hotel, bed and breakfast, and campground are filled. _is_

> ➤ Diplomacy and threat each require skilled execution. _requires_

When a compound subject is joined by *or* or *nor*, the verb should agree with the part of the subject nearest to the verb:

> ➤ The James Boys or Billy the Kid are the Wild West's most written-about outlaws. _is_

Even though the preceding sentence is now correct, it still doesn't sound right. It's better to correct such a sentence by rearranging the order of the compound subject so it rings truer in a reader's mind:

Billy the Kid or the James Boys are the Wild West's most written-about outlaws.

Neither the atomic bomb nor space flights have influenced human events as powerfully as the Bill of Rights.

Indefinite Pronouns as Subjects

Generally, use singular verbs with indefinite pronouns. *Indefinite pronouns* refer to unspecified subjects. Most indefinite pronouns—such as *everyone, someone, no one, everything, anybody, neither,* and *something*—are singular and take singular verbs:

> ➤ Most everyone in Utah support keeping 22 million acres of wilderness. _supports_

> ➤ Neither partner, GM nor IBM, are discussing the agreement. _is_

A few indefinite pronouns—such as *all, any, none,* and *some*—may be singular or plural. Whether you use a singular or plural verb depends on the noun or the indefinite pronoun it refers to:

The judge announced that all of the jury were present.

The judge said that all of the report was helpful.

Collective Nouns and Nouns Ending in *-s* as Subjects

Collective nouns take singular or plural verbs, depending on how they are used. Collective nouns—like *army, audience, class, committee, faculty, group, herd, public,* and *team*—are singular even though they name groups of individuals. When referring to a group as a single unit, a collective noun takes a singular verb:

➤ The American public eventually ~~see~~ sees the truth.

When you wish to draw attention to individual members of the group, a collective noun should take a plural verb:

➤ The faculty ~~argue~~ argues among themselves in meetings, hallways, and offices.

Treat units of measurement like singular collective nouns when they refer to a single unit:

By midgame, one-third of the crowd was gone.

Five dollars is the cost of a ticket.

Most nouns that are plural in form but singular in meaning take singular verbs. For example, nouns like *athletics, civics, economics, mathematics, measles, mumps, news, physics,* and *species* are singular and take singular verbs:

➤ Measles ~~are~~ is irritating but relatively harmless.

Words like *trousers* and *scissors* are regarded as plural and take plural verbs, except when used after *pair:*

These socks have holes in the toes.

➤ This pair of socks ~~have~~ has holes in the toes.

Miscellaneous Subject/Verb Agreement Problems

A verb must agree with its subject, even when the subject precedes the verb. (Verbs generally *follow* subjects.) When the subject/verb word order is reversed, check to see that the subject and verb still agree:

> ►   In the back of his mind ~~is~~ the pain of abuse and the joy of recovery.
> _{are}

Don't mistake the expletives *there* and *here* for subjects. They merely signal that the subject follows the verb:

> ►   There ~~is~~ several deceptive techniques card magicians use.
> *are*

Be sure the verb following *who, which,* and *that* agrees with its subject. *Who, which,* and *that* are *relative pronouns* that refer to other words called *antecedents.* When a relative pronoun serves as a subject, the verb must agree with the pronoun's antecedent:

> ►   Wind that ~~blow~~ over the peaks ~~create~~ massive snow plumes.
> *blows*   *creates*

In a sentence that uses *one of the,* look carefully at the meaning to determine if the verb should be singular or plural:

> ►   He is one of the critics who ~~is~~ joining the argument.
> *are*

The antecedent of *who* is *critics,* not *one:*

> ►   He is the only one of the critics who ~~care.~~
> *cares*

The antecedent of *who* is *one.*

Use a singular verb when its subject is a title or words named as words:

> ►   <u>Six Days and Seven Nights</u> ~~seem~~ to last at least that long.
> *seems*

> ►   <u>Chitlins</u> ~~refer~~ to pigs' intestines used as food.
> *refers*

EXERCISE   *Correcting Subject/Verb Agreement*

Correct the errors in subject/verb agreement in each of the following sentences.

1. In baseball, slugging percentage as well as batting average is considered in judging a batter's worth.
2. The use of automatic pitching machines make batting practice more efficient.
3. Alert fielding, consistent hitting, and reliable pitching leads to success for a baseball team.

4. Neither the first baseman nor the infielders expects a bunt.
5. Many stories about the "good old days" of baseball probably exaggerate the feats of players.
6. Neither of the batters swing hard enough to belt it over the fence.
7. The team play an opponent from Nebraska on Friday.
8. The secret of our victories are efficient practices.
9. Two dollars are a small enough price to pay for admission.
10. Here in the lockerroom is the new uniforms.

VERB TENSE

Verb tense reveals when—in the past, present, or future—an action has taken place or will take place. When you begin a passage in one tense, keep using it unless you have good reason to shift:

> Economists hope the budget will continue to be balanced in the year 2002.
>
> They are projecting an even more dramatic increase in employment and foreign exports.

These sentences move logically from the present, *hope,* to the future, *will continue,* and back to the present, *are projecting* and *increase.* This shift from present to future and back to present tense is logical and thus appropriate. When you shift tense inappropriately, though, the sense of the time sequence is disrupted:

> ➤ Outside the rain stopped and the clouds opened. The truck ~~is~~ *was* reflecting sunlight from its wet surface. The driver dashed from the store to the driver's cab, ~~opens~~ *opened* the door, and ~~leaps~~ *leaped* in.

Here, the time sequence shifts from the past to the present tense inappropriately. When correcting a passage such as this, select one dominant tense—usually, the past tense—and stick to it.

Always use the present tense, often referred as the *historical present,* as the dominant tense when writing about subjects in literature, film, and art. The logic behind this convention is that even though such works were created in the past, the action or image still exists in the immediate present.

Even so, using the historical present can sometimes create difficulty. For example, when referring to an artist, you should write in the past tense; when referring to an artwork, write in the present tense:

> Shakespeare wrote Hamlet near the turn of the seventeenth century. The plot conveys an ancient message: Revenge is a powerful human motive.

Also use the present tense when writing about habitual action or beliefs:

Even today, the rule of law reflects the desire for revenge.

EXERCISE *Correcting Verb Tense*

Recast the verb sequence in the following paragraph. The first sentence is correct as it stands, but several of the subsequent sentences are incorrect.

Properly speaking, human life began with hunting. The eating of meat is at the heart of humanity's rise to world dominion. War is not with other humans but with animals, and it is waged for meat. In hunting societies, choice of mates by women depends on the capability of men to provide meat for them and their children. The amount of flesh food establishes the standard of living for hunting societies, just as it did for the modern societies descended from them. It was not essential for modern humans to eat meat as long as they made a concerted effort to compensate for it nutritionally; however, it was doubtful that a healthy nonmeat diet was possible for most people.

PRONOUN CASE

case

Pronouns take the places of nouns. In the following example, the pronoun *her* takes the place of the noun *Joan;* the pronoun *him* takes the place of the noun *grandfather;* and the pronoun *they* takes the place of the noun *family:*

Joan photographed her grandfather. When the family saw her portrait of him, they all wanted copies.

The word that a pronoun replaces is called the *antecedent* of the pronoun. *Joan* is the antecedent of *her; grandfather* is the antecedent of *him;* and *family* is the antecedent of *they.*

Generally, which pronoun to use for an antecedent won't take much thought, but in some situations, you will have to give the choice careful consideration.

I versus *Me* and *She* versus *Her*

You must select the accurate case of a personal pronoun depending on how the pronoun functions in the sentence. Pronouns functioning as subjects, or *subject complements,* function in the *subjective case.* Pronouns functioning as objects function in the *objective case.* Finally, pronouns indicating possession function in the *possessive case.*

SUBJECTIVE CASE	OBJECTIVE CASE	POSSESSIVE CASE
I	me	my
we	us	our
you	you	your
he / she / it	him / her / it	his / her / its
they	them	their

Pronouns as Subjects and Predicate Nominatives.   Always use a subjective case pronoun when the pronoun functions as the subject of a clause. You need to be especially cautious in selecting the proper case when the subject of the clause is compound:

➤ The president and ~~her~~ *she* attended the dedication ceremony.

➤ Since Roberto and ~~me~~ *I* returned from Europe, the phone hasn't stopped ringing.

Always use the subjective case pronoun when the pronoun functions as a predicate nominative. A *predicate nominative* is a noun or pronoun that follows the main verb in a clause. A predicate nominative renames or identifies the subject of the main verb, usually following *be, am, is, are, was, were, being,* or *been:*

➤ The contestants who had the most points were Raul and ~~me.~~ *I*

In speech, it's common practice to use objective case pronouns as predicate nominatives in expressions beginning with *it is* or *it's:*

It's me.

It is him.

It's them.

Such uses of the objective case are unacceptable in writing, however. Instead, use these forms:

It is I.

It is he.

It is we.

It is they.

Pronouns as Objects.   Always use the objective case pronoun when the pronoun functions as an *object*. There are three kinds of objects: direct objects, indirect objects, and objects of prepositions.

A *direct object* receives the action of a verb. (Recall that a predicate nominative renames or identifies the subject of a main verb.) For instance:

Betty hit the ball.

Ball is the direct object. It was *hit*.

In the following example, both *Dr. Naga* and *her* (not *she*) are the direct objects of *interest:*

All forms of life interest Dr. Naga and her.

An *indirect object* always precedes the direct object and usually indicates to whom or for whom the action is done:

Betty hit John the ball.

John is the indirect object. The action was done for him.

In the following example, the direct object is *good news*. The correct indirect objects are *him* and *the family,* not *he* and *the family. Him* is the objective case of the subjective pronoun *he:*

➤   The doctor gave the family and he good news.
                                              him

Always use the objective case pronoun when the pronoun functions as the *object of a preposition*. Prepositions include such words as *of, with, by, near, above, under, behind, next to, between,* and *for.* A *preposition* always begins a prepositional phrase—that is, a word group that begins with a preposition and ends with a noun or pronoun. The noun or pronoun becomes the object of the preposition:

➤   This is a secret between you and I.
                                        me

Appositives

Appositives are phrases that rename nouns and pronouns and have the same functions as the words they rename. If an appositive phrase follows a subject, then use a subjective case pronoun; if it follows an object, use an objective case pronoun:

➤   The team leaders, Dr. Fillmore and him, disagree.
                                           he

➤   The hiring committee interviewed only three candidates: John Williams, Van Zinberg, and I.
                                                                              me

Pronouns after *Than* or *As*

Because a comparison often omits the verb at the end of a sentence, choose the appropriate subject case pronoun if a verb can be added or if the appropriate objective case pronoun if a verb can't be added. Look at these examples:

➤ Soyon Lee has played cello longer than ~~me.~~ I

The completed sentence would read . . . *than I have played cello.*

➤ Le Bon devoted as much energy to the project as ~~her.~~ she

The completed sentence would read . . . *as she devoted.*

➤ Students respected no other professor on campus as much as ~~she.~~ her

A verb cannot be added to the end of this sentence.

We or *Us* before Nouns

Always choose the appropriate pronoun by first reading the sentence *without* the noun (in brackets below):

We [seniors] deserve to have early enrollment privileges.

Rising fees are threatening those of us [students] who are existing on limited incomes.

Pronouns before Gerunds

A *gerund* is the *-ing* form of a verb that functions like a noun. Use possessive case for a pronoun that comes before a gerund:

~~Me~~ running up the hill took all my energy. My

Also use the possessive case for a noun before a gerund:

Tani running up the hill took all his energy. 's

Who and *Whom*

Writers frequently confuse the use of *who* and *whom*. If you keep the following in mind, you will use them correctly: *Who* is a subjective case pronoun and can only be used for a subject or subject complement. *Whom* is an objective case pronoun and can only be used for an object. Use *who* and *whom* in dependent clauses and questions.

You can decide which word is correct by answering the stated or implied question in the *who* or *whom* part of the sentence. If a subjective case pronoun answers the question, use *who;* if an objective case pronoun answers the question, use *whom.* For instance:

Whom did you see at the crime scene?

The answer to this stated question is *I saw **him** or **her** or **them*** (all objective case pronouns) *at the crime scene.*

The police want to know who should be considered as suspects.

The answer to the implied question is ***They*** (a subjective case pronoun) *should be considered as suspects.*

EXERCISE   *Correcting Pronoun Case*

In the following paragraph, correct any errors you find in pronoun case. (Keep in mind that some pronouns are used correctly.)

Last Saturday, Dylan and Warren invited Jamie and I to go shopping with them for birthday presents for Reza. First we went to the sporting goods department to buy him some golf balls. The clerk, who we recognized from political science class, showed us all the different brands he had in stock. We bought the cheapest ones. Then Jamie wanted a Coke. Dylan and her went to the snack bar while Warren and me looked at sport shirts. The clerk showed us several racks of shirts, but them didn't look good to us. Warren and me decided to join Dylan and Jamie at the snack bar. After we finished our drinks, we decided to try a different store. The clerk in the men's department didn't want to help us, but we saw a pale-blue sweater that was just right for Reza. Jamie couldn't resist telling the clerk, "You helping us is really appreciated." I was embarrassed and said I wanted to head back to the parking lot to find our car. On the way home, we argued to see whom would wrap the presents, and, as always happens in arguments, Dylan gave in, so the task fell to him.

PRONOUN/ANTECEDENT AGREEMENT

The *antecedent* of a pronoun is the word or words the pronoun refers to. An antecedent and its pronoun must agree, whether they are singular or plural:

SINGULAR

The anthropologist took her vacation in Mexico with a group of students.

PLURAL

The students piled their suitcases on top of the anthropologist's van.

For compound antecedents joined by *and,* always use a plural pronoun:

Ramon and Rachel gave their best effort in the tango contest.

For compound plural or singular antecedents joined by *or* or *nor,* use a pronoun that agrees with the nearest antecedent:

➤ Every evening, the singers or Tracy ~~perform their~~ favorite songs.
performs her

When a sentence that follows this convention sounds awkward or puzzling, recast it:

Every evening, Tracy or the singers perform their favorite songs.

Indefinite Pronouns

Generally, use a singular pronoun to refer to an indefinite pronoun that functions as an antecedent. *Indefinite pronouns* refer to nonspecific persons or things:

anybody	either	everything	no one
anyone	everybody	neither	someone
each	everyone	none	something

Although they seem to be plural, they should be treated as singular antecedents in writing:

➤ Every one of the women canceled ~~their~~ subscription to <u>Vanity Fair.</u>
her

➤ Everybody in the president's cabinet offered ~~their~~ advice.
his or her

Traditional grammar calls for the use of the masculine pronoun *his* (*he*) to refer to a person of either sex when the gender of the antecedent is unknown. This practice, however, reflects a gender bias in English. To offset the bias, use *his or her* (*he or she*) in place of a masculine pronoun. Or rewrite the sentence in the plural to reflect the same meaning:

> Each student was expected to furnish his or her own supplies.

> Students were expected to furnish their own supplies.

(See also the section Gender-Neutral Language, pp. 663–665.)

Collective Nouns

Generally use a singular pronoun to refer to a collective noun. *Collective nouns* include words such as *army, audience, class, committee, group, herd, jury, public,* and *team.* Even though they identify classes or groups with many members, collective nouns are usually singular because the members are acting as a single unit:

> ➤ The jury of five women and seven men spoke with one voice. ~~They~~ It declared the
>
> defendant guilty as charged.

If a passage makes clear that the members of a group are acting individually, then use a plural pronoun:

> ➤ The jury members could not agree. ~~It~~ They deliberated for three days before the judge
>
> declared a mistrial.

Generic Nouns

Use a singular pronoun to refer to a generic noun. *Generic nouns* refer to typical members of groups. They are always singular:

> ➤ A law student must study hours every night if ~~they are~~ he or she is to graduate.

Such a sentence can also be recast to reflect the same meaning:

> ➤ ~~A law student~~ Law students must study hours every night if they are to graduate.

> ➤ A law student must study hours every night ~~if they are~~ to graduate.

Who, Whom, Which, and *That*

Who refers to persons and sometimes to animals that have been named in the passage:

> Fahid, who had lived in Rome, once worked as a guide to the catacombs.

Lassie was the first Hollywood dog who had a fan club.

Which refers to things or places and unnamed animals:

Death Valley, which is an austere wasteland, is located on the California/Nevada border.

Carla's German shepherd, which is highly spirited, would have been restless in the van.

Whose, the possessive form of *who*, can be used to refer to animals and things to avoid awkward constructions using *of which:*

➤ Humongous is a word the ̲whose̲ origin ~~of which~~ puzzles me.

That also refers to things or places, unnamed animals, and sometimes to persons, when they are collective or anonymous:

The hills that border Acapulco are dotted with expensive homes.

Acapulco is heaven for tourists that love tropical beaches.

EXERCISE *Correcting Pronoun/Antecedent Agreement*

Select the correct pronoun in each of the following sentences.

1. That noise must be either the radio or the coffee pot falling out of (their, its) box.
2. Claire and Bonnie forgot (their, her) homework.
3. The group is planning to rent (their, its) boat tomorrow.
4. Her canary, Sunshine, was the one (which, who) flew out the window.
5. Acapulco, (who, which) is less than 250 miles from Mexico City, offers good fishing all year.
6. Each of the women had (their, her) speech prepared.
7. Valerie's puppy, (which, who) stayed at the dog hotel, would have been unbearable on the sailboat.
8. The creek (which, that) flowed into the pasture is dry.
9. Every one of the poets read (their, his or her) best poem.
10. Sailfish, (who, which) are most plentiful in winter, are known for their swiftness.

PRONOUN REFERENCE

A pronoun must clearly refer to its antecedent—that is, the word or words it stands for. If the *reference* is unclear, revise the sentence to clarify it.

ref

Vague Pronoun Reference

Pronouns such as *this, they,* and *which* should not refer vaguely to word groups that appear earlier in the sentence:

➤ Travelers, especially to rural areas, are more and more becoming targets for crime.
Vacationers must accept this ∧ fact when making travel plans.

➤ Silence of the Lambs is a classic thriller that chronicled the pursuit of a serial
killer referred to as Buffalo Bill. ~~which~~ The film ∧ was very chilling.

Indefinite Pronoun Reference

The pronouns *they, you,* and *it* should refer to specific antecedents. Don't use *they* to refer to an antecedent that has not been clearly stated:

➤ Often, guidelines to saving money on auto repairs are discussed on The Car Show.
For example, ~~they~~ the hosts ∧ point out that having an oil change every 3,000 miles may lead to driving an extra 25,000 miles before the valves need work.

Don't use *it* indefinitely in such constructions as *It says that . . .* For example:

➤ The
~~In the~~ ∧ Preamble to the Declaration of Independence, ~~it~~ says that everyone is created equal.

Don't use the pronoun *you* unless addressing the reader directly:

➤ a writer
When beginning to write, ~~you~~ ∧ should first create a list of ideas.

The indefinite *you* is considered very informal and thus inappropriate for most writing:

➤ They
Most people do well if they are personally engaged in learning. ~~You~~ ∧ find that losing ~~yourself~~ themselves ∧ intellectually in a problem is exhilarating.

Ambiguous Pronoun Reference

Avoid writing passages in which single pronouns have two antecedents:

➤ the Bulls
When the Bulls and the Jazz meet, ~~they~~ ∧ are predicted to win by eight points.

Also avoid *implied* pronoun references. A pronoun must have a specific antecedent, not a word that's implied but not actually stated in the sentence:

➤ After General Custer circled his troops, he discovered ^it *that doing so* was a useless defense against the attack.

➤ In Deidre's Beckett biography, ~~she~~ implies that Beckett was haunted by memories of his mother.

A pronoun ending in *-self* or *-selves* is a *reflexive* pronoun that refers directly to an antecedent in the same sentence. Don't use a reflexive pronoun to replace a grammatically appropriate pronoun. Use a pronoun ending in *-self* or *-selves* only to refer to another word in the sentence:

➤ The secret is between Riley and ^~~myself~~ *me*.

EXERCISE   *Correcting Pronoun Reference*

Rewrite each of the following sentences to correct faulty pronoun references.

1. They said the sun would shine tomorrow.
2. Lena watched a television movie and ate a TV dinner. She enjoyed that.
3. The farm had a rabbit and gopher snake, but it died.
4. The council must budget to build a foundation for the city's statue of the Martin Luther King, Jr. It is crumbling.
5. I blame me for sending the wrong report.
6. When you drive on Cliff Road after dark, it can be dangerous.
7. Although Al had neither read the novel nor seen the film, he said that he didn't like it.
8. Vandals are setting fires in the park. They concern nearby neighbors.
9. After he saw the first half, he turned it off.
10. The checks must be countersigned by you and myself.

GENDER-NEUTRAL LANGUAGE

Several changes have taken place in writing to overcome the masculine bias embedded in English. Familiarize yourself with the several options available to help you avoid such bias.

Use of Pronouns

Most obviously, gender bias has appeared in the use of pronouns. Traditionally, masculine pronouns have been used to refer to both men and women when the gender of the antecedent is unknown or when it includes both men and women:

Each teacher must post his office hours.

By merely being aware of gender bias, you can keep your writing gender neutral:

Each teacher must post his or her office hours.

Teachers must post their office hours.

A possessive pronoun can often be easily eliminated by using one of the articles *a, an,* or *the* without affecting the meaning:

➤ A mystery novelist concentrates on ~~his~~ *the* plot, whereas a suspense novelist concentrates on ~~his~~ *the* characters.

➤ A mystery novelist concentrates on his plot, whereas a suspense novelist concentrates on his characters.

➤ ~~A mystery novelist concentrates~~ *Mystery novelists concentrate* on his plot, whereas ~~a suspense novelist~~ *novelists concentrate* ~~concentrates~~ on his characters.

Use of Collective Nouns

The collective noun *man* has traditionally been used to refer to both men and women. To avoid its sexist implications, substitute *humans, human beings, humankind,* or *people:*

➤ ~~Man dominates~~ *Humans dominate* the natural world.

Referring to Occupations and Positions

Using recently coined words can also help avoid gender bias when referring to occupations and positions. In the recent past, *chairman* referred to both men and women. Now, you can use *chairwoman* when a woman holds the position and *chairperson* or *chair* when the person's gender is unknown. Similarly, *police officer, congressperson, server,* and *mail carrier* are all gender-neutral terms that can refer to a man or a woman.

These examples show other ways to correct sexist language:

➤ ~~A doctor~~ *Doctors* must pass the state medical examination before ~~he~~ *they* can be licensed to practice.

➤ A doctor must pass the state medical examination before he *or she* can be licensed to practice.

➤ A doctor must pass the state medical examination before ~~he can be~~ *being* licensed to practice.

EXERCISE   *Avoiding Gender Bias*

Revise the following passage to eliminate sexually biased language. Start by changing *actor* to *actors* in the opening sentence. (You will have to change more than single words elsewhere in the passage.)

> An actor must understand the motivation behind his character's actions. He must first develop a sense of his character's psychology and a strategy for reflecting him: What does the character think about? How does he spend his free time? Who does he like and dislike? Should he treat his character subtly or should he exaggerate him? These are questions every actor must ask himself. If he doesn't, he won't develop a feel of the person he portrays.

EXERCISE   *Using Gender-Neutral Terms*

Replace each of the following sexist terms with a gender-neutral term.

1. Policeman
2. Anchorman
3. Mailman
4. Father Christmas
5. Father Time
6. Sportsmanship
7. Congressman
8. Ladylike
9. Actress
10. Poetess

REMINDERS FOR ESL WRITERS

If you are learning English as a second language (ESL), review the information in this section from time to time. It will be very useful to you as you prepare your final draft of a paper. This section includes information about the following:

1. Omitted subjects, expletives, and verbs
2. Noun markers
3. Verb forms and combinations
4. Faulty repetitions
5. Present and past participles used as adjectives

ESL

These items may still trouble you even though you have otherwise become quite fluent in English.

Omitted Subjects, Expletives, and Verbs

Some languages allow the omission of subjects, expletives, or verbs. English generally does not. The exception is the omission of a subject in an imperative sentence—that is, when *you* is understood:

Brush your teeth.

If your first language allows for these omissions, be alert to the fact that they are unacceptable in English. Study these examples:

➤ ~~Read~~ literature assignments every day. *(I read)*

➤ University attendance important. *(is)*

➤ Juan Lopez, studied electrical engineering, fixed my computer. *(who)*

An expletive, *there* or *it*, may be required in a sentence in which the subject follows the verb:

➤ ~~Are~~ scary creatures in the park. *(There are)*

➤ ~~Is~~ easy to make mistakes in English. *(It is)*

Keep the following in mind: You can't begin a sentence with *is, are, was,* or *were,* unless the sentence is a question—such as *Are you awake?*—or an exclamation—such as *Was I sick!*

EXERCISE *Correcting Omissions*

Read the following paragraph, and add the missing subjects and verbs.

Government loans to college students the lowest in 10 years. The president very concerned. Appointed a committee to investigate falling income. Will not meet until next September. The president unhappy about the slow start. Is one of the problems the president promised to solve during his campaign. Are thousands of needy students in the United States cannot afford a college education. Are unhappy about this problem. Is little hope. Seems unfair.

Noun Markers

In English, nouns frequently have *noun markers,* which are words that indicate a noun is coming (though it might not be the *next* word). Common noun markers are articles, numbers, possessive nouns, possessive pronouns, and certain other pronouns.

COMMON NOUN MARKERS

Articles	*a car; the car; an automobile*
Numbers	*12 cats; seven dogs*
Possessive nouns	*Van's stories; China's goal*
Possessive pronouns	*my, our, your, his, her, its, their*
Other pronouns	*all, every, any, each, either, neither, few, many, more, most, this, that, these, those, much, several, some, whose*

Modifiers may be placed between the noun marker and the noun:

The old, rusty car belongs to him.

Twelve black, white, and gray cats live in the neighborhood.

Van's boring stories put us all to sleep.

His demanding employer makes him work each night.

Of all the common noun markers, articles can be the most troublesome. The following explanations should answer most of your questions about the use of articles in English.

Definite Articles.   Use the definite article *the* before a noun that is specifically identified:

Wear the hat that you bought yesterday.

Clearly, Dana had the winning routine.

I'm hot. Please turn on the ceiling fan.

The moon finally came out.

A careful reading of each preceding example shows that each noun is specifically identified by the context. However, the following example is somewhat ambiguous:

I couldn't solve a homework problem no matter how hard I tried. In class the answer to the problem became clear.

The noun *problem* is unidentified at first, so the indefinite article *a* is appropriate. But *problem* has been identified when the writer mentions it the second time; it is *the problem* that the writer couldn't solve.

Because definite articles are used only with nouns that are specifically identified, they should not be used with plural or noncount nouns when the meaning conveyed is *generally* or *all*:

➤ The cost of printing the newspapers is usually borne by advertising revenue.

➤ Health magazines report studies about drinking the coffee.

Generally, don't use a definite article with a proper noun. Proper nouns name people, places, and things: *Anita Romano, France, Three Rivers Stadium.* Although proper nouns are specifically identified by their very nature, they ordinarily do not take *the.*

There are exceptions to this rule, though. Some plural proper nouns that identify places—such as *the Pyrenees, the Sierra Nevadas, the Alps, the Great Lakes*—take a definite article. Furthermore, some countries have official names that take *the* and a shorter, more commonly used name that does not:

FORMAL NAME	COMMON NAME
the Italian Republic	Italy
the Commonwealth of Australia	Australia
the Hashemite Kingdom of Jordan	Jordan
the Principality of Liechtenstein	Liechtenstein
the United States of America	America

In each of these cases, the article *the* is used with the descriptive portion of the name—*republic, commonwealth, kingdom, principality, states*—but not with the actual name.

Indefinite Articles.   Use the *indefinite article a* or *an* for singular count nouns that are not specifically identified. Most nouns refer to things that can be counted, such as *one airplane, three candidates, seven assignments,* and *twenty dollars.* Some nouns refer to things that can't be counted, such as *homework, sugar, information,* and *rain.*

If a singular count noun is not specifically identified, use *a* or *an,* whichever is appropriate:

Airlines started a revolution in data processing.

Drozd works at an interesting job.

Whether to use *a* or *an* depends on the initial sound of the word immediately following the article (whether it is the noun or not). Use *a* before a consonant sound and *an* before a vowel sound:

`a` turtle   *but*   `an` ungainly turtle

`an` umbrella   *but*   `a` blue umbrella

A word beginning with the letter *h* may have either an initial consonant sound, if it is aspirated (*hole*), or an initial vowel sound, if it is not aspirated (*heiress*):

`a` hand   *but*   `an` hour

Don't use *a* or *an* with plural nouns:

➤ Mariko borrowed money to cover ~~an~~ expenses.

➤ The exhibit consisted of ~~a~~ hastily arranged groupings of native costumes.

And generally, don't use *a* or *an* with noncount nouns (see the list at the end of this section):

Teresa wrote on pollution.

While you are shopping, please get coffee and soap.

Love can overcome poverty.

A particular amount of a noncount noun can be indicated by placing a count noun first and using the noncount noun as the object of the preposition *of:*

a sack of beans   a pile of grass
a drop of water   a piece of cake

Here is a list of commonly used noncount nouns:

FOOD AND DRINK

bacon	beef	bread	butter
cabbage	candy	cereal	cheese
chicken	chocolate	coffee	cream
fish	flour	fruit	meat
milk	pasta	rice	salt
sugar	tea	water	wine

NONFOOD

air	cement	coal	gasoline
gold	oil	paper	plastic
rain	silver	snow	soap
steel	tin	wood	wool

ABSTRACTIONS

advice	anger	beauty	courage
employment	fun	happiness	health
honesty	information	intelligence	joy
knowledge	love	poverty	sadness
satisfaction	truth	wealth	wisdom

OTHER

biology	clothing	equipment	furniture
homework	jewelry	luggage	lumber
machinery	mail	money	news
poetry	pollution	research	scenery
traffic	transportation	violence	work

EXERCISE   *Using Noun Markers*

In each of the following sentences, identify which article should be used—*a, an,* or *the*—or that no article is needed, as appropriate.

1. Most athletes drink _____ lot of _____ sports drinks.

2. _____ most widely known sports drink is Gatorade.

3. Like _____ Coke, Gatorade has plenty of _____ sugar.

4. During workouts, _____ distance runner may get as much as _____ half cup of sugar just from drinking Gatorade.

5. Drinking plenty of water is better for _____ athlete's health, but it won't provide _____ instant rush of energy.

Verb Forms and Combinations

English sentences often require combinations of helping verbs and main verbs. The discussion that follows will help you become familiar with acceptable combinations.

Helping Verbs.   *Helping verbs* always appear before main verbs. However, only correctly combined helping verbs and main verbs make sense in English. In fact, some main verbs are not complete without helping verbs:

>   will
> ➤ The car reach the curve in a few minutes.

English has 23 helping verbs. Nine of them are called *modals* and function only as helping verbs. The others—composed of forms of *do, have,* and *be*—can also function as main verbs.

HELPING VERBS

Three forms of *do*	*do, does, did*
Three forms of *have*	*have, has, had*
All forms of *be*	*be, is, was, were, are, am, been, being*
Modals	*can, could, may, might, must, shall, should, will, would*

After a modal or form of *do* (*do, does, did*), use the plain form of the verb:

may write	might go	should bring
do swim	does feel	did hurt

Look at these examples:

>   write
> ➤ She may ~~writes~~, but don't expect her to.

>   convince
> ➤ Your answer does not ~~convinces~~ me.

>   finish
> ➤ Did you ~~finished~~ your paper?

After a form of *have* (*have, has, had*), use the past participle to form one of the perfect tenses:

have driven	has contributed	had slept

For example:

>   passed
> ➤ Those students must have ~~pass~~ the test.

>   accomplished
> ➤ Amina has ~~accomplish~~ a great deal today.

>   finished
> ➤ Luis had ~~finish~~ his sculpture just in time.

After each of the helping verbs *is, was, were, are,* and *am,* use a present participle to form one of the progressive tenses:

is going	was swimming	were eating
are studying	am thinking	

For example:

➤ Jason was ~~worked~~ on his car.
       working

Be and *been* must each be preceded by another helping verb and followed by a present participle to form one of the progressive tenses:

can	*or*	could be
may, might,	*or*	must be
shall	*or*	should be
will	*or*	would be
has, have,	*or*	had been
can	*or*	could have been
may, might,	*or*	must have been
shall	*or*	should have been
will	*or*	would have been

Look at these examples:

➤ Raul be leaving soon.
   will

➤ Minh been studying late.
   has

After each of the helping verbs *is, was, were, are,* and *am,* use a past participle to form the passive voice:

is repeated	was thrown	were submitted
are appreciated	am assisted	

For instance:

➤ The magazine is ~~deliver~~ every week.
         delivered

➤ After the wind the trees were ~~bend.~~
         bent

Be, been, and *being* must each be preceded by another helping verb and followed by a past participle to form the passive voice:

is, was, were, are,	*or*	am being
can	*or*	could be
may, might,	*or*	must be
shall	*or*	should be

> will   *or*   would be
>
> can   *or*   could have been
>
> may, might,   *or*   must have been
>
> shall   *or*   should have been
>
> will   *or*   would have been

Consider these examples:

➤ My life may have been ~~save~~ *saved* by the lifeguard.

➤ The photos were being ~~mount~~ *mounted* in the albums.

Intransitive verbs, which express actions with no direct objects, cannot be used in the passive voice:

➤ The stunt artist ~~was~~ grinned broadly.

EXERCISE   *Using Helping Verbs*

Identify the correct verb form for each set of verbs in each of the following sentences.

1. Scientists (have studied, have study) the effects of exercise on people for years.
2. Information that (was release, was released) in August indicates that exercise (is contributing, is contributes) to a longer life expectancy.
3. Further research on exercise suggests that some older people (be coping, may be coping) with mental disorders better because of daily exercise.
4. Unfortunately, many residential communities for the elderly (do not offer, do not offering) enough exercise classes.
5. Now the National Health Institute (is encourage, is encouraging) more organized exercise programs across the nation.

Phrasal Verbs.   A *phrasal verb* combines a verb with a preposition or an adverb. Often, phrasal verbs carry both idiomatic and literal meaning. For example, *look up* may be used literally to mean "focus on something above you," but it may also be used idiomatically to mean "search for information." Most phrasal meanings must be learned in context. Nonetheless, you should be able to recognize some of them and know certain rules for their use.

A phrasal verb is either *separable* or *nonseparable*, depending on whether an object can be inserted between the verb and the particle. *Clean up*, for example, is a separable phrasal verb, as in *Clean the house up* and *This weekend I will clean the house up*. Phrasal verbs have been used commonly in informal writing, but now they are appearing more frequently in formal writing, too.

The following chart lists some common phrasal verbs and their approximate meanings. Nonseparable phrasal verbs are marked with an *[N]*.

COMMON PHRASAL VERBS

ask out	ask for a date
bring up	mention casually; raise a child
call off	cancel
call up	call on a telephone
come across [N]	meet or find unexpectedly
drop in or *drop by* [N]	visit unannounced
drop off	leave someone or something at a place
fill out	complete a form
get along with [N]	have a comfortable relationship
get over [N]	recover from something
give up	stop trying
go over [N]	review
hand in	submit
help out	assist
keep on	continue
leave out	omit
make up	become friendly again; do past work; invent
pass away [N]	die
point out	call attention to
put away	stop someplace
put off	postpone, avoid
run out of [N]	have no more
take off	leave; remove something
take over	control; take charge
turn down	reject
wrap up	complete

When the direct object is a pronoun, a phrasal verb must be separated:

➤ I will help ~~out~~ him _{out} with biology.

EXERCISE *Using Phrasal Verbs*

Provide a phrasal verb that is similar in meaning to the verb in parentheses in each of the following sentences.

1. Writers must (submit) their essays on Friday.
2. Most writers (postpone) writing an essay until the last minute.
3. By starting so late, they cannot (complete) the essay on time.
4. Too often, professors (reject) late assignments.
5. Writers often (invent) dramatic excuses for being late.

Verbs Followed by Gerunds and Infinitives.   Some verbs may be followed by gerunds but not infinitives; some may be followed by infinitives but not gerunds; and some may be followed by either gerunds or infinitives. A *gerund* ends in *-ing* and functions as a noun, such as *cooking, studying,* and *painting.* An *infinitive* consists of a verb's plain form usually preceded by *to: to attend, to believe, to convince.*

Here is an example of each:

VERB WITH GERUND

Did he mention running in Mason park?

VERB WITH INFINITIVE

This light is guaranteed to work 15 hours on two batteries.

VERBS FOLLOWED BY GERUNDS BUT NOT INFINITIVES

admit	discuss	mind	recall
appreciate	enjoy	miss	resent
avoid	escape	postpone	resist
consider	finish	practice	risk
delay	imagine	put off	suggest
deny	mention	quit	tolerate

For example:

Authorities will not tolerate writing on buildings.

VERBS FOLLOWED BY INFINITIVES BUT NOT GERUNDS

afford	demand	hope	pretend
agree	deserve	learn	promise
appear	endeavor	manage	refuse
ask	expect	mean (intend)	seem
are	fail	need	threaten
claim	guarantee	offer	wait
choose	happen	plan	want
decide	hesitate	prepare	wish

Some verbs followed by infinitives must have a noun or pronoun between the verb and the infinitive:

advise	condemn	forbid	require
allow	convince	invite	teach
cause	dare	permit	tell
caution	direct	persuade	warn
challenge	encourage		

For example:

I urge you to enter the race.

William advised Nona to avoid the park after dark.

Some verbs may be followed directly by infinitives or may have a noun or pronoun between them and the infinitive, such as *ask, expect, need,* and *want.* For instance:

I want to dance until midnight.

I want you to dance with me until midnight.

VERBS FOLLOWED BY GERUNDS OR INFINITIVES

bear	deserve	love	remember
begin	read	neglect	start
hate	prefer	stop	can't bear
intend	regret	try	can't stand
continue	like		

For example:

The institute will start researching the effects of laughter.

The institute has started to research the effects of laughter.

EXERCISE *Using Gerunds or Infinitives with Verbs*

Complete the following sentences with a gerund or infinitive form of each word in parentheses.

1. Counselors want students (understand) course requirements.
2. They want students (study) the course catalogue.
3. They also suggest (examine) and (memorize) college department requirements.

4. Moreover, counselors caution students not (ignore) (read) the detailed requirements for graduation.

5. The counseling office would appreciate (know) each student's graduation plans.

Faulty Repetitions

Words that unnecessarily refer to or repeat other words in a sentence should be deleted:

➤ Driving it is my favorite method of travel.

➤ The slim woman with short hair she is my doctor.

➤ Professor Park, who lectured on Korea, she used humor to make her points.

➤ That was the year when we graduated then.

➤ The party will be held in the restaurant where we held the graduation dinner there.

➤ Carl's business trip was made miserable by the clients whom he was visiting with them.

EXERCISE *Correcting Faulty Repetitions*

Draw lines through the unnecessary words in the following sentences.

1. The Statue of Liberty, which is located in New York City, it was given to the United States by France.

2. A love letter was on the front seat of Tom's Honda, where it would be easily found there.

3. The sun it was so hot the sand sizzled.

4. The game occurred on Saturday, when thousands of people were at home then.

5. Six people they were honored, and more than fifty they were mentioned.

Present and Past Participles Used as Adjectives

A *present participle*—such as *moving, running, dancing, flying*—or a *past participle*—such as *moved, ran, danced, flew*—used as an adjective may precede the noun it modifies or follow a linking verb, such as forms of *to be* (*am, are, is, was,* and *were*).

PRESENT PARTICIPLE USED AS AN ADJECTIVE

We saw an interesting movie.

The movie we saw was interesting.

PAST PARTICIPLE USED AS AN ADJECTIVE

All interested people should attend the debate.

Many people were interested in the debate.

As you can see from these examples, the present participle describes the agent causing the feeling or reaction (*movie was interesting*), and the past participle describes the person or thing having the feeling or reaction (*interested people*). In your writing, use the proper participle forms for verbs such as these:

amazing, amazed	exciting, excited
amusing, amused	exhausting, exhausted
annoying, annoyed	fascinating, fascinated
boring, bored	frightening, frightened
confusing, confused	interesting, interested
depressing, depressed	shocking, shocked
disturbing, disturbed	surprising, surprised
embarrassing, embarrassed	thrilling, thrilled

EXERCISE *Using Participles as Adjectives*

Choose the correct participle in each of the following sentences.

1. People across the country were (shocking, shocked) by the news of the explosion in Oklahoma City.
2. The news on television showed how (frightening, frightened) and (confusing, confused) everyone was.
3. The death and destruction left the residents of Oklahoma City very (depressing, depressed).
4. The rescue of victims trapped for hours was (amazing, amazed); people were (thrilling, thrilled) to learn some victims survived.
5. Even though the emotional response of people around the nation was strong, nothing could really comfort the families of victims who were (grieving, grieved) over their losses.

Punctuation

COMMAS

The *comma* is the most frequently used—and misused—punctuation mark. Learn comma use, and you will be well on your way to controlling punctuation errors. To do so, it might help to divide comma use according to two applications: commas functioning within sentences and commas functioning within conventional constructions.

Commas Functioning within Sentences

Commas function within sentences to help readers group words that belong together. For example:

➤ Although grizzly bears like to eat hikers, campers, and picnickers seldom become meals.

Without a comma separating *eat* and *hikers,* the sentence will confuse readers for a moment. Your goal is to keep readers moving through your writing by avoiding disruptions like this.

Before a Coordinating Conjunction Joining Independent Clauses. When a coordinating conjunction (*and, but, or, nor, yet, for, so*) links independent clauses—that is, word groups that can stand alone as sentences—a comma must precede the conjunction. The comma and coordinating conjunction show readers that one independent unit of thought has ended and another is beginning:

➤ The helicopter buzzed overhead and the police sirens wailed in the distance.

➤ The crowd shouted but the senator continued to speak.

If, however, the independent clauses are short and there is no chance of misreading the sentence, then you may omit the comma:

The sky is gray and the sea is rough.

Remember that not every coordinating conjunction in a sentence joins independent clauses. (See also Misuses of Commas, pp. 685–686.)

After Introductory Word Groups.   A comma after a phrase or clause that begins a sentence shows readers that the subordinate information has ended and the main information is beginning:

➤ Off the San Francisco coast Great White sharks breed.

➤ Beaten by relentless winds the caravan returned to the oasis.

➤ Whenever heavy rains hit Southern California hillside homes slide down into valleys.

If a brief word group begins a sentence, you may omit the comma, as long as doing so doesn't create misreading:

By December the plan will be complete.

Between Items in a Series.   Use commas to separate words, phrases, and clauses in a series of three or more items:

➤ George Washington Abraham Lincoln and Franklin Roosevelt are our best-known presidents.

➤ You must clarify the goal define the objectives and establish a deadline to plan successfully.

➤ He did not know who he was where he had been or what would happen next.

Although some writers omit the comma before the last item in a series, we recommend that you always include it to avoid any chance of misreading:

➤ The cabin is primitive, but it does have electricity, hot and cold running water and gas heat.

Adding the comma avoids the silly misreading that the cabin has *hot and cold running water* and *hot and cold gas heat.*

Between Coordinate Adjectives.   If two or more descriptive words describe a noun separately, they are *coordinate adjectives.* Always separate coordinate adjectives with commas:

➤ Intelligent͵sensitive͵witty films are seldom made in Hollywood.

You can tell coordinate adjectives because they can be joined by the word *and—intelligent and sensitive and witty.*

Don't use commas between *cumulative adjectives*—that is, descriptive words that don't separately modify a noun:

A flock of large colorful birds flew across the bay.

With Restrictive and Nonrestrictive Word Groups.   Never set off a restrictive word group with commas; but always set off a nonrestrictive word group with commas. A *restrictive* word group determines the meaning of the word it modifies by defining or identifying it; it is essential to the meaning of the sentence. A *nonrestrictive* word group adds information but is not essential to the meaning of a sentence:

A student who sets academic goals will graduate in four years.

In this sentence, the word group beginning with *who* is essential to the meaning: *Only* students who set academic goals will graduate in four years. Without the word group, the sentence would mean something else: *Any* student will graduate in four years.

Here's an example of a nonrestrictive word group:

Robin Crisp, who studies five hours each day, will graduate in four years.

In this sentence, the word group beginning with *who* adds information but not essential information. The basic meaning of the sentence is clear without the word group: Robin will graduate in four years. The information that he studies five hours each day is nonessential.

Look at a few more restrictive examples:

Citizens who are interested in politics should run for office.

The meaning here is that *only* those citizens who are interested in politics should run for office; no one else should run.

The mechanic working on the Volkswagen lost his temper.

In this sentence, *only* the mechanic working on the Volkswagen lost his temper; the mechanics working on other cars did not.

Now look at a few more nonrestrictive examples:

Paris, which is flooded with tourists each summer, has always embraced
American jazz musicians.

The amount of tourist traffic is nonessential to the information that Parisians
like jazz.

The right to free speech, like breathing itself, is essential to a democratic
society.

Like breathing itself adds color to the sentence but is not essential to its
meaning.

With Transitional and Parenthetical Expressions, Absolute Phrases, and Contrasting Elements

Transitional and Parenthetical Expressions.   Use commas to set off transitional and parenthetical expressions that interrupt the flow of a sentence. *Transitional expressions* include such words and phrases as *on the one hand, on the
other hand, for example, in fact, first, second,* and so on. Transitional expressions
also include conjunctive adverbs such as *however, furthermore, nevertheless,*
and *moreover.*

Here are some examples of using commas with transitional expressions:

➤ On the one hand, she liked the color; on the other hand, she hated the design.

➤ Stephen King is the undisputed master of the horror novel; soon, however, he may

   become the master of the horror film.

Parenthetical expressions often add afterthoughts or supplemental information
to sentences:

➤ If life is a bowl of cherries, as I have heard said, then why am I in the pits?

Absolute Phrases.   Use a comma to set off an *absolute phrase*—that is, a
phrase that modifies an entire sentence:

➤ The doberman leaped at Kurt's throat, teeth snapping, eyes flashing anger.

➤ Their feet aching from the climb, the four campers crawled into their sleeping

   bags.

Be sure that by adding a comma, you have not written a comma splice, mistakenly treating an absolute phrase as an independent clause:

➤ Their feet were aching from the climb, *when* the four campers crawled into their sleeping bags.

Contrasting Elements.　Use commas to set off words that signal sharp contrasts in thought in a sentence:

➤ Love, not hate, is the essence of self-renewal.

➤ Existential thought, unlike communist practice, maintains that the individual has responsibility for his or her life.

With Direct Addresses, Interrogative Tags, the Words Yes and No, Mild Interjections, and Direct Quotations with Identifying Phrases

DIRECT ADDRESSES

➤ Friends, please have patience.

INTERROGATIVE TAGS

➤ People have to accept responsibility for their own decisions, don't they?

THE WORDS *YES* AND *NO*

➤ Yes, they have bananas.

MILD INTERJECTIONS

➤ You see, films like The Mummy become cult classics.

IN DIRECT QUOTATIONS WITH IDENTIFYING PHRASES

➤ In The Island Stallion, Walter Farley writes, "Time should be reckoned by events that happen to a person, not by the lapse of hours."

➤ "We are all strong enough," a French philosopher said, "to bear the misfortunes of others."

Commas within Conventional Constructions

Dates.   In a date, the year is set off from the rest of the sentence with commas:

➤ On February 23, 1949, artist Doree Dunlap was born.

Don't use commas if the date is inverted or if only the month and the year are given:

The concert is 29 December 1999.

September 1939 was Los Angeles's hottest month.

Addresses.   Use commas to set off elements of an address or a place name. Do not, however, set off a zip code with a comma:

➤ The campus is located at 2701 Fairview Drive, Costa Mesa, California 92926.

Titles.   If a title comes after a name, set it off from the rest of the sentence with commas:

➤ Ruth Bellow, PhD, is department chairwoman.

Numbers.   Use a comma to separate long numbers into groups of three, beginning from the right:

Over 12,000 people attended the performance.

In a four-digit number, the comma is optional—*5,675* or *5675*. Never add commas, however, in numbers that indicate addresses, pages, or years:

Report to work at the warehouse on 4424 Broadway.

The assignment starts on page 1204 of your textbook.

The year 1968 was rocked with violence.

Salutations and Closes to Friendly Letters.   In a friendly letter, add commas following the salutation (or greeting) and following the close:

Dear Uncle Joe,

Yours truly,

(For the punctuation conventions of business letters, see Chapter 26.)

Misuses of Commas

The most common misuse of commas comes when writers mistake a compound element in an independent clause for an independent clause. The comma error usually takes place when a sentence has a compound predicate:

➤ Galileo wrote extensive notes, and drew detailed images.

The word group before the comma is an independent clause because it has a subject, *Galileo,* and a predicate, *wrote.* It can stand alone as a sentence. The word group following the comma has a predicate, *drew,* but shares the subject *Galileo* with the preceding independent clause. This word group can't stand alone as an independent clause. The comma separating the two word groups is incorrect.

Other common misuses of commas include the following:

BETWEEN SUBJECTS AND THEIR VERBS

➤ First contact between humans and celestial aliens, is the subject of many science fiction writers.

BETWEEN CUMULATIVE ADJECTIVES

➤ The snail has a soft, slimy body.

WITH RESTRICTIVE ELEMENTS

➤ The belief, that comets are the fiery messages of the gods, is an ancient one.

AFTER COORDINATING CONJUNCTIONS

➤ Live performances are dramatic, but, CDs can be played over and over.

AFTER *SUCH AS* AND *LIKE*

➤ Some writers, such as, Virginia Wolfe and James Joyce, were significant innovators.

BEFORE *THAN*

➤ Watching a powerful play is more moving, than watching a film of the play.

TO SET OFF PARENTHESES

➤ Suarez, (the last of the big-time gamblers), hit Vegas with $102 and a lucky charm.

WITH END PUNCTUATION IN QUOTATIONS

➤ "To be or not to be? Isn't that the question?"ᴧPhilip mused.

EXERCISE *Using Commas*

Correct comma errors in the following sentences. Keep in mind that there may be more than one error in a sentence or none at all. Identify any correct sentences, and be able to state which guideline applies to each corrected sentence.

1. Citizens of the United States refer to themselves as *American* but seldom remember that citizens from other Western countries are also *American*.
2. In spite of early Hollywood resistance stunt women are now accepted and do everything from rolling cars at 70 miles per hour to leaping from helicopters.
3. Grammarians say we are not supposed to use *ain't* yet people still do.
4. A Zen master wrote "A person should live as if he were walking on the beach at low tide."
5. Glass sparkled in the sunlight for the clouds had drifted north.
6. Chasing gangsters at break-neck speeds is a standard sequence in cop films.
7. The aging process is relentless but most people dread growing old.
8. James Fenimore Cooper an American writer created the first espionage novel.
9. Bulging biceps rippled stomach and yes even sinewy necks are the new physical features people yearn for.
10. Advertising is often no more than a deceptive dull appeal to consumers' insecurities.
11. "A writer writes out of one thing only" says James Baldwin "personal experience."
12. The new chef praises muskrat chili which is certainly not as common as Texas chili right?
13. Early colonists brought such words as *bandit robber highwayman* and *outlaw* with them from England.
14. Presidential news conferences offer more entertainment than information because reporters do not ask pointed questions.
15. Handicapped by low budgets authorities seem to be losing the battle against poachers.
16. Professional athletes begin their careers out of a love for sports and a few of them keep loving sports.
17. If you are tempted to spend $54000 for a leopard skin coat remember that each coat requires the pelts of seven animals.
18. Ernest Hemingway who had a fine art collection claimed to have learned to write description from studying Impressionist paintings.
19. Natural meat also called game (not the kind you play on ballfields) includes a variety of wildlife found in America.
20. Seals are fun to swim with, but sharks are thrilling.

SEMICOLONS

The *semicolon* can join independent clauses, but the clauses should be closely related in meaning and not be joined by a coordinating conjunction, such as *and* or *but*. You can also use a semicolon instead of a comma in a very limited number of situations. Remember, the semicolon is not as frequently used as a comma; in fact, you should only use it in formal writing.

Between Main Clauses

Use a semicolon between main clauses that are closely related in meaning and not joined by a coordinating conjunction:

➤ Some moths escape bats by not flying; ~~and~~ others confuse bat radar.

Use a semicolon to distinguish main clauses joined by conjunctive adverbs, such as *therefore, however,* and *nevertheless:*

➤ The 1950s inspired fantastic science fiction movies, however, most of them carried a realistic social message.

When a conjunctive adverb immediately follows a semicolon, as in the previous example, always follow it with a comma. When a conjunctive adverb does not immediately follow a conjunctive adverb, put commas before and after it:

➤ Bicycle touring is a healthy way to see England; riding in a constant drizzle, unfortunately, is not.

To Separate Items in a Series

Commas are typically used to separate items in a series, but not always. If any of the items themselves contain commas or if any of the items are long, then use semicolons to separate them:

➤ Effective lawyers can become first, realistic legal advisors; second, wise business consultants; and third, close friends who know their clients from a variety of perspectives.

Misuses of Semicolons

Don't use a semicolon to join a dependent clause or phrase to an independent clause:

➤ If you want to cool down a potato, cut it into smaller pieces.

Don't use a semicolon between clauses joined by *and* or *but:*

➤ There are almost two thousand kinds of ants; and all live in ant colonies.

EXERCISE   *Using Semicolons*

In the following sentences, insert and delete semicolons and commas as needed.

1. The state police improved their record of citizen complaints however the city police received more citizen complaints than ever.
2. Summit meetings are seldom more than media events they are opportunities where world leaders thump their chests and scowl.
3. Jogging increases endurance, swimming conditions the entire body.
4. For you to excel as a police officer requires hard work, long hours, and physical strength, an ability to think fast, write reports, and talk with strangers and a taste for black coffee and fast food.
5. Through hard work; we can achieve our goals, reap our rewards, and benefit humankind; but, our descendants will neither appreciate our efforts nor credit our successes.

COLONS

The *colon* should be used only after a complete sentence to clarify, illustrate, or specify detail in what follows, such as a list or long quotation.

To Indicate Lists

Use a colon at the end of a complete sentence that sets up a list:

John Fowles has written several novels that have been made into films:
The Collector, The Magus, and The French Lieutenant's Woman.

To Emphasize Sentences

Use a colon to set off a sentence that should be emphasized, such as a conclusion or general principle:

Kevin Cestra has no doubts about his future: He will attend medical school and
then train as a psychiatrist.

To Introduce Illustrations

Use a colon at the end of a complete sentence to set off a series of illustrations or examples:

Climbing in subzero temperatures is life threatening: hypothermia sets in; concentration drifts; flesh numbs.

To Specify Details

Similarly, use a colon to identify a series of details or specific points:

They stood on the bridge and watched the crowd escape: women clutching infants, men lugging suitcases, and children dragging blankets.

To Introduce Long Quotations

Use a colon to introduce a long quotation, which is broken out from the regular text:

In 1962, Rachel Carson's <u>Silent Spring</u> sounded this warning:

> The most alarming of all man's assaults upon the environment is the contamination of air, earth, rivers, and the sea with dangerous and even lethal materials. The pollution is for the most part irrecoverable.

Remember: Only use a colon after a sentence. If the lead-in to a quotation is not a complete sentence, add *as follows* and then a colon to announce the quotation:

➤ In <u>Silent Spring</u>, Rachel Carson writes: the following:

Conventional Uses of Colons

Here are some conventional uses of colons:

After formal salutations	*Dear Sir:*
Between hours and minutes	*1:20 p.m.*
In proportions	*The ratio of cats to dogs is 3:1.*
Before subtitles	*Homicide: Life on the Streets*
In bibliographic entries	*Los Angeles: Angel City Books, 1997*

A colon is traditionally used in Biblical references between the chapter and verse, as in *Matthew 4:6*. However, the Modern Language Association, in its current style guidelines, recommends using a period, as in *Matthew 4.6*.

EXERCISE *Using Colons*

Rewrite each of the following sentences or groups of sentences by using colons accurately. Sometimes, you must drop words or combine sentences to rewrite effectively.

1. Propaganda devices have catchy names. They are *glittering generalities*, *bandwagon*, *testimonial*, *plain folks*, and *poisoning the well*.
2. The sky was full of death. Jets were strafing the hills. Artillery shells were whistling overhead. Toxic fumes were drifting from the oil fields.
3. Our forests, our hills, and our prairies all have one thing in common. They will soon succumb to land development.
4. The town meeting broke up after Simpson's fiery outburst. He said, "Either clean up the streets or declare this town a health hazard!"
5. Jonathan Swift in *Gulliver's Travels* introduced the Yahoos. They are a race of brutish, degraded creatures who have the form and all the vices of humans.

DASHES

--

The dash, perhaps the most dramatic punctuation mark, gives special emphasis to whatever follows. Be frugal, though. Try not to overuse the dash and diminish its power.

To make a dash, type two hyphens--like this. Don't worry about the tiny space between them.

To Show Breaks in Sentences

Use a pair of dashes to show a break in a sentence, much like you use commas and parentheses to set off clarifying information:

The two novelists--Hemingway and Faulkner--represent the extremes in writing style.

In any struggle with nature, humankind--with all its technology--is always the loser.

For Dramatic Effect

Use a dash to set off a list or a dramatic statement:

Tigers, lions, jaguars, cougars, leopards, cheetahs, even house cats--all are part of the feline family.

Jennifer Ramirez decided to shock her friends by wearing greasy motorcycle boots, torn jeans, a "Born-to-Die" tank top, and gold earring--but no one noticed.

The dash and the colon, though used similarly at times, are subtly different. The colon is more formal; the dash is more dramatic. Look at these examples:

Chui analyzes three key effects of depression: anxiety, paranoid, and suicide.

Two fears dominate Schiff's waking hours--fear of dying and fear of living.

To Cite Authors' Names after Quotations

Use a dash before an author's name following a quotation that stands alone:

Fasten your seat belts. We're going to have a bumpy night.

--Bette Davis

EXERCISE   *Using Dashes*

Rewrite each of the following sentences by inserting dashes as needed.

1. There is no hope other than divine intervention that can stop nuclear missiles once they have been launched.
2. His goal is clear. He wants to become the world's top sprinter.
3. The dangers of being a judge both real and threatened have increased in the last several years.
4. Bianchi, Klein, Guerciotti, Raleigh, Univega these are just a few of the bicycle brands that once dominated the roads.
5. Ralph Eggers a politician who never took an honest nickel will run for Congress.

APOSTROPHES

The *apostrophe* shows possession or ownership and indicates contractions. It also has several other conventional uses.

To Show Possession

Use an apostrophe to show that a noun is in the possessive case, as in *the King's men* and *Truman's decision*. Possession is often loosely applied, however, as in *the island's inhabitants* and *the dog's bark*. An apostrophe shows possession in one of two ways: by adding an *'s* or by adding only an apostrophe.

Singular Nouns.   For a singular noun, a plural noun not ending in *-s* (such as *men, women, oxen*), and an indefinite pronoun (such as *no one, someone, and anybody*), add an *'s:*

The officer's revolver lay on the floor.

Terrorism is Israel's biggest problem.

The women's forum meets once a week.

Someone's car alarm is blaring.

Declaring war is outside the commander-in-chief's powers.

Plural Nouns and Singular Nouns Ending in **-s.**   For a plural noun ending in *-s* and a singular noun ending in *-s,* add only an apostrophe if adding an *'s* makes pronunciation difficult:

The sports announcers' banquet is Saturday night.

The circus' snake has disappeared.

The sisters' birthdays are on the same date.

When a possessive sounds awkward or is difficult to read, revise it for clarity:

A snake from the circus disappeared.

To show joint possession, make the last noun in the series possessive; to show individual possession, make each noun possessive:

Ralph, Cherie, and Rene's business is profitable.

Ralph's, Cherie's, and Rene's businesses are profitable.

When such constructions become confusing or awkward sounding, revise them:

Ralph's bicycle shop, Cherie's pizza parlor, and Renee's consulting practice are all profitable.

To Form Contractions

Use an apostrophe in a contraction to mark an omission of letters:

it is	it's	do not	don't
cannot	can't	does not	doesn't
will not	won't	are not	aren't
you will	you'll	we will	we'll

Do not confuse the contraction *it's* (*it is*) with the possessive pronoun *its.*

Conventional Uses of Apostrophes

An apostrophe may be used to make the following plurals: numbers mentioned as numbers, letters mentioned as letters, and words mentioned as words. Consider these examples:

When speaking publicly, don't use well's, huh's, and you know's.

Multiplication is a mystery, especially the 8's and 9's.

When using a year to indicate a decade, add an *-s* without an apostrophe: *the 1980s.* When omitting the first two digits of a year, mark the omission with an apostrophe: *the '80s.*

EXERCISE *Using Apostrophes*

Correct the use of apostrophes in each of the following sentences.

1. Is this Rexs final offer?
2. No matter what the circumstances, anyones tale of woe interests Zoe Ann.
3. The Mothers Crusade, founded in the early 90s, begins its peace march in June.
4. Cameron's, Rod's, and Allison's fish tank cracked last night.
5. The tire companies attempts to scuttle mass transportation ignore the citys gridlock problem.
6. Zenas strength is cunning, not muscle.
7. *Mississippi* is spelled with four ss and four is.
8. Whose classic 57 Ford is that?
9. His *what ifs* make the world sound gloomy.
10. Santa Cruzs city center is sensational.

QUOTATION MARKS

Quotation marks help readers see the beginning and the end of a direct quotation. They also identify some titles and words used in special, nonliteral ways.

" "

To Identify Direct Quotations

Whenever you directly quote spoken or written words, place quotation marks around them:

"Don't look back. Just run like the competition is gaining fast," wrote Justin Wickes.

If you include a quotation within a quotation, use single quotation marks:

Armando Ruiz attributes his success to a single source. He writes, "The thought of Ralph Waldo Emerson has helped me, especially his comment that 'A foolish consistency is the hobgoblin of little minds.' "

If you set off a long quotation by indenting every line, then you don't need to use quotation marks because the indentation tells readers where the quotation begins and ends:

In The Raptor and the Lamb, Christopher McGowan writes:

> Most animals are either eaten or eat other animals. Plants, too, are often consumed by animals. Consequently the chances of being devoured, or of eating some other organism in order to survive, are exceedingly high.

Use a colon following the formal introduction of a quotation. A formal introduction should always be an independent clause or a word group using *as follows:*

Kelly Valles sees a bright future for eagles: "The eagle population at Point Roberts has increased 200 percent in five years."

An old proverb goes as follows: "Do not climb the mountain until you reach it."

If you introduce or follow a quotation with a brief phrase—such as *he said, she remarked,* or *they claimed*—use a comma:

Snoopy said, "Maybe the sky is falling."

"What are you, crazy?" she remarked.

If you interrupt a quotation with explanatory words, use commas to set off those words:

"I don't have the benefit of your native intelligence," Franz said to Klein, "which is why I never make the same mistake twice."

If you interrupt successive sentences from a quotation with explanatory words, use a comma and a period to clarify the break:

"Faulkner's best novels are like marble sculpture," Filmore writes. "They are chiseled from raw life."

If you begin with a quotation that ends with a question mark or exclamation point and then follows with a brief phrase, include the question mark or exclamation point in the quotation:

"What is the answer to life's mysteries?" he asked, gazing at the stars.

To Identify Titles of Short Works

Use quotation marks to enclose the titles of articles, short stories, short poems, chapters and other subdivisions of books and periodicals, and episodes of radio and television programs:

"To the Man in the Yellow Terry" appeared in Alice Walker's first volume of poems.

My favorite <u>Star Trek</u> episode is "The Menagerie."

Do not use quotation marks around titles of your own works. If, however, your title includes the title of someone else's short work, then identify it with quotation marks:

Second Thoughts on Hawthorne's "Young Goodman Brown"

To Identify Words Used in Special Ways

When you use a word in an unusual, nonliteral way—say, to be ironic or sarcastic—enclose it in quotation marks:

The computer's "brain" can handle more than you can even imagine.

My "friend" has been copying my work all semester.

Be frugal in using quotation marks this way. For instance, it's not necessary to qualify words like *average* and *normal* when you are using them to mean what they really mean.

Note that in the second example above, the quotation marks could be eliminated by adding *so-called* before the word *friend:*

My so-called friend has been copying my work all semester.

Uses of Quotation Marks with Other Punctuation

Follow these standard practices when using other marks of punctuation with quotation marks:

Periods and Commas.   Always place periods and commas at the ends of quotations but within the quotation marks:

He raised his glass above his head. "The time has come," he announced, "to toast the happy couple."

This rule holds true for even single words in quotation marks:

As I told you before, the answer is "no."

Colons and Semicolons.   Always place colons and semicolons outside quotation marks:

We smiled as the child read each of the items on her list of "Things to Do Today": "feed the goldfish"; "send Valentines to Tracy, Patti, and Mildred"; "do arithmetic homework"; and "brush teeth."

Question Marks and Exclamation Points.   When a question mark or exclamation point is part of the quotation, you should place it within the quotation marks:

Kim Sonies asked an interesting question: "Does Descartes's statement 'I think therefore I am' really mean I think therefore I <u>think</u> I am?"

When a question mark or exclamation point applies to the whole sentence, place it outside the quotation marks:

Did Descartes really mean "I think therefore I <u>think</u> I am"?

Misusing Quotation Marks

Don't add end punctuation marks following quotation marks at ends of sentences:

➤ Akimitsu Takgi asks an important question: "Do tattoos carry a symbolic

significance?"̷

Don't place quotation marks around an indirect quotation—that is, a report of a person's words, rather than a direct quotation:

➤ He said ~his purpose was to break with the traditions of the past and bring new life to the film industry.~

Don't use quotation marks to highlight slang or clichés; rather, replace them with words and phrases from standard English usage:

               trusting

➤ It's really "cool" of your parents to let you take the car.

                                  make definite plans.

➤ Until you get a formal job offer, I wouldn't "count your ~~chickens before they hatch.~~"

And as noted on page 695, use quotation marks sparingly to qualify words used in nonliteral ways.

EXERCISE   *Using Quotation Marks*

Supply or delete quotation marks as appropriate in each of the following sentences. Place other punctuation marks correctly, as well.

1. Read O'Connor's short story A Good Man Is Hard to Find, said Professor Bloom.
2. Do you remember what song contains the lines You say tomato, I say tomato?
3. Let me remind you the professor said of the words of Edward R. Murrow. We cannot defend freedom abroad by deserting it at home.
4. In 1927 Harry M. Warner of Warner Bros. said Who the hell wants to hear actors talk?
5. One of Emily Dickinson's famous lines reads as follows I'm nobody! Who are you?

ELLIPSES

Use an *ellipsis,* three spaced periods, within a direct quotation to indicate that you have deleted language from it:

"All his novels reflect life . . . as it is lived in Dublin."

"It is his unyielding sense of reality . . . that draws generations of readers to his work."

When an ellipsis falls at the end of a sentence or is used to indicate that a full sentence or more has been deleted from the original, add a period before the ellipsis:

Saul Bellow said, "Art attempts to find in the universe . . . what is fundamental, enduring, and essential. . . ."

The report concluded, "If we are going to save the rainforests, we must act now. . . . They are disappearing as we speak."

If you delete words at the beginning of a sentence, don't add an ellipsis. If the quoted material isn't a complete sentence, incorporate it in one of your own sentences:

John F. Kennedy said that the arts establish "the basic human truths which must serve as the touchstone of our judgment."

If you delete words at the beginning of a quoted sentence but it is still a sentence, begin it with a capital letter but don't add an ellipsis.

PARENTHESES

( )

Use *parentheses* to enclose supplemental information, such as descriptions and comments:

Henry Kissinger (once Richard Nixon's Secretary of State) has become a high-priced Washington lobbyist.

Use parentheses to enclose a subordinate sentence between two other sentences; place the end punctuation within the parentheses:

Dr. Parma was born into a Kansas family at the height of the Depression. (What a period that was!) Bread cost nine cents a loaf and a new Ford cost about five hundred dollars. His farming family could usually afford bread, but they couldn't buy a new Ford until 1949.

If the supplemental material is imbedded within a sentence, the punctuation may follow the parenthetical information if the punctuation is part of the main sentence:

As the exhausted runners approached the finish line (over three hours after they had started), they were saluted with fireworks and whistles.

You may also use parentheses to enclose letters or numbers labeling items in a series:

The program succeeded for three reasons: (1) talented musicians, (2) enthusiastic students, and (3) mild weather.

BRACKETS

When presenting a direct quotation, always use *brackets*, not parentheses, to distinguish your comments from the person's you are quoting:

[ ]

According to Mexico's Longevity Report, "Over 10 percent of the deaths [of those under 22 years of age] will be caused by unnatural causes."

The Latin term *sic* ("thus it is") should be placed in brackets immediately after an error an author made in material you are quoting directly:

Wesley records that "the English monarchs are crowned and buried in Westminister [sic] Abbey."

Use *sic* only to indicate errors, not to indicate disagreements you may have with the author you are quoting.

SLASHES

Use a *slash* (or *solidus*) to separate two or three lines of poetry or song lyrics that are run consecutively into your text. Add a space before and after each slash:

/

Faustus is astounded at the beauty of Helen, whom Mephistopheles has summed to his room: "Was this the face that launch'd a thousand ships, / And burnt the topless towers of Illium? / Sweet Helen, make me immortal with a kiss."

You can also use a slash to indicate options, but do so sparingly because it creates the feeling of official prose:

Westhill's Board of Directors wants to end pass/fail courses. Each individual member voted his/her conscience, regardless of whether he/she had attended the school.

Don't add spaces before and after the slash when presenting options in this way.

END PUNCTUATION MARKS

Periods

Use a *period* at the end of each sentence except a direct question and exclamation. Use a period at the end of an indirect question—that is, a report of a question someone else has asked. For example:

➤ Jorge asked who was responsible for the stock market collapse.

Use periods in abbreviations such as the following:

Mr.   Oct.   Dr.   i.e.   a.m. (or A.M.)
Ms.   Jan.   Jr.   e.g.   p.m. (or P.M.)

Don't use periods in the following types of abbreviations:

- Postal abbreviations for the names of states: *CA, MN, TX,* and so on.
- Names of scholarly degrees: *BA, BS, MA, PhD, MD, JD,* and so on.
- Historical eras: *AD, BC,* and so on.

And ordinarily, you would not use periods in commonly used abbreviations:

NATO   IBM   AFL-CIO   USA (or U.S.A.)
TV   NBC   mpg   USAF
UCLA   NBA   NAACP   NFL

Whenever you are unsure if a common abbreviation should include periods, check a good college dictionary or consult another authoritative source.

Never use a period at the end of a sentence that ends in an abbreviation followed by a period or by a direct quotation that ends in a period, even though the final period is enclosed within quotation marks:

➤ Everyone was to meet again at 6:00 p.m.,

➤ Smiling, Conrad said, "If it's up, it isn't down.",

Question Marks

Use a *question mark* at the end of a direct question:

Where is Java located?

Generally, use a question mark when a request is written as a question:

Will you please send me your catalogue?

Never use a question mark to close an indirect, or reported, question:

➤ He asked where the rare books were kept.

Use a question mark in parentheses to indicate doubt about the accuracy of a date or number:

The Peloponnesian War ended in 404 BC (?) with a victory for Sparta.

Don't use a question mark in parentheses in an attempt to indicate sarcasm:

➤ I never saw such a hard-working (?) writer.

Instead, shape your words to convey your intention:

Sam is seldom accused of being hard working.

Exclamation Points

Use *exclamation points* with caution, only after statements that deserve special emphasis:

Look at that little S-car go!

Don't use an exclamation point in parentheses in an attempt to indicate sarcasm or amusement:

➤ Gail's winning (!) essay was in the Coast Report.

And don't use an exclamation point with a period or a question mark at the end of a sentence:

➤ Are you sure the ticket costs $100?!

Mechanics

CAPITALIZATION

cap

Whenever you are in doubt about capitalizing a word, refer to a good dictionary for help. For general capitalization guidelines, the following information should help.

To Identify Proper Nouns and Words Made from Proper Nouns

Proper nouns name specific persons, places, and things and should be capitalized. All other nouns are *common nouns* and should not be capitalized. For instance:

Jung ⟶ Jungian ⟶ psychoanalyst

California ⟶ Californian ⟶ state

England ⟶ English ⟶ country

Words in the following groups are usually capitalized:

Specific names	*Pat Kubis*
Places	*Atlantic Ocean*
Historic events	*World War II*
Historic periods	*Renaissance*
Historic documents	*Bill of Rights*
Days	*Monday*
Months	*September*
Holidays	*Labor Day*
Associations	*American Bar Association*
Government departments	*State Department*
Political parties	*Republican Party*
Schools	*Westbrook College*
School departments	*Department of English*

Specific courses	*Biology 100*
Degrees	*Bachelor of Arts*
Religions	*Christianity*
Religious followers	*Christians*
Religious terms	*Judgment Day*
Deities	*God*
Racial and ethnic groups	*Native American, Latino*
Tribal names	*Iroquois*
Nationalities	*Irish*
Celestial bodies	*Big Dipper*
Trade names	*Frisbee*
Radio and TV stations	*KNBC*

Don't capitalize references to centuries, as in *the eighteenth century.* You *may* capitalize pronouns referring to *God* in general writing (e.g., *He, His*), but you must in religious writing.

To Identify Titles of Works

Capitalize major words in the titles and subtitles of works such as books, articles, films, and songs. Do not capitalize articles (*the, a, an*), prepositions (*on, in, for*), or coordinating conjunctions (*and, but, or, nor, yet, for, so*), unless one begins the title or serves as the first word in the subtitle:

The Color Purple

Against the Gods: A Remarkable Story of Risk

Gone with the Wind

"Night Train"

To Identify Titles with Proper Nouns

Capitalize titles that appear with people's names:

Professor Henry Higgins

Doctor Man Pham

Stella Murphy, PhD

Jason Duca, Jr.

Do not capitalize such titles when they stand alone:

Henry Higgins is a professor of linguistics.

Man Pham worked hard to become a doctor.

To Indicate the First Word of a Sentence and a Quoted Sentence

Note that two sentences are capitalized in the following example:

In <u>Love and Will</u>, psychologist Rollo May writes, "Today, love and will have become a problem."

If you interrupt a quoted sentence, don't capitalize the first word following the interruption:

"The world is what it is," he frowned, scratching his head, "and that is truly depressing."

You may or may not capitalize the first word following a colon if it begins an independent clause. It's your decision. Keep in mind that capitalizing the next words will add emphasis:

Eyes do more than scan the physical world: They reveal the soul.

or

Eyes do more than scan the physical world: they reveal the soul.

Whatever style you choose, use it consistently.

UNDERLINING

ul

As noted in earlier chapters, underlining is traditionally used to identify titles of long works, such as novels and movies, and to emphasize special words and phrases. Italic type may be used for the same purposes (as shown in this book), *if your instructor approves of this method.* Whatever method you choose, use it consistently throughout your essay.

When underlining, be precise. To underline more than a single word, use a continuous line. When using MLA style, try not to underline punctuation marks such as periods and commas following underlined words. And don't underline the article *a, an,* or *the* unless it is part of the title. For example:

Once again, the <u>Los Angeles Times</u> carried the story a day after <u>The New York Times</u>.

To Identify Titles of Works

The following kinds of titles should be underlined:

Books	The Magus, Into Thin Air
Comics	Batman, Calvin and Hobbes
Films and plays	Citizen Kane, Death of a Salesman
Long poems	Paradise Lost
Magazines	Time
Musical works	Phantom of the Opera
Pamphlets	Drinking and Driving
Software	WordPerfect
TV and radio shows	The X-Files, The Shadow
Visual artworks	Michelangelo's David

Enclose the titles of short works, such as short stories and poems, within quotation marks.

Don't underline the word *Bible* or the titles of books in the Bible. Don't underline the titles of legal documents, but do underline the names of court cases:

Smith v. State of Arkansas

Do underline the names of ships, trains, aircraft, and spacecraft:

Apollo XI   Hindenburg   Andrea Doria

In general, underline foreign words:

Each professional criminal develops a modus operandi.

But don't underline commonly used foreign words:

Libertarians have a laissez-faire attitude toward industry.

Underline words, letters, phrases, and symbols when you refer to them as such:

Is Mississippi the only word in English with four s's?

You may underline to show emphasis, but do so only rarely:

Sherman burned the whole town.

Don't underline the titles of your own essays, but do underline a title mentioned in your own title:

Mythical themes in The Magus

NUMBERS

num

Style guidelines for treating numbers as words versus numerals vary among different disciplines. In the sciences, for instance, where numbers such as measurements and statistics are frequently used, the general rule is to spell out numbers less than 10 and use numerals for 10 and up. It is not uncommon in these cases to use numerals and symbols for exact figures, such as *98%* and *21"*.

But if you are writing about literature or another subject that uses few numbers, spell out numbers of one or two words and use numerals for those of more than one or two words:

Holly Zareel had been in a coma for three days when she won a two million dollar lottery.

If a sentence begins with a number, always spell it out or rephrase the sentence opening:

> *One hundred twenty-two*
> ➤ 122 volunteers fought the blaze for over twenty-three hours.

> *At least*
> ➤ 122 volunteers fought the blaze for over twenty-three hours.

Use figures in the following cases:

Addresses	*12 Antares, 223 West 56th Street*
Book divisions	*volume 2, chapter 6, page 111*
Dates	*May 21, 1998; 10 BC; AD 10*
Exact amounts	*$124.45*
Fractions, decimals	*⅓; 2.10*
Percentages	*22 percent* or *22%*
Play divisions	*Act 1, scene 2*
Statistics	*Average age 26*
Surveys	*2 out of 5*
Time	*11:09 p.m.*

ABBREVIATIONS

ab

As a general rule, avoid using abbreviations in your essays. In particular, don't abbreviate a word because doing so is easier than writing it out. For example:

DON'T WRITE	DO WRITE
dept.	department
yr.	year
co.	company
soc. sci.	social science
Engl.	English
gov't.	government
w/	with
prof.	professor
&	and
Edw.	Edward
lb.	pound
Mon.	Monday
Xmas	Christmas
ch.	chapter

It's acceptable to abbreviate words you see abbreviated frequently in print because they are commonly accepted:

Mr. Linder	Mrs. Linder	Ms. Pham
Dr. Johns	Ross LeMar, PhD	William Chin, MD
FBI	USA	UN
IBM	KNBC	TV
a.m. (A.M.)	p.m. (P.M.)	$200
$1 million	10 BC	AD 10

Abbreviate the name of an organization if it's long and appears throughout the essay. Write out the full name the first time it appears, followed by the abbreviation in parentheses. Then use the abbreviation in the rest of the essay:

The American Federation of Teachers (AFT) awarded over $1 million in scholarships. Most of this money came from dues of AFT members.

Don't use Latin abbreviations for English equivalents except in footnotes and parenthetical text:

DON'T USE	DO USE
etc.	and so forth, and the like
i.e.	that is
et al.	and others
e.g.	for example, for instance

HYPHENS

hyph

The *hyphen* has three main uses: (1) to link elements of compound words; (2) to divide a word at the end of a typed line; (3) to follow certain conventions.

To Form Compound Nouns and Adjectives

Compound nouns come in three forms: single words, such as *campground;* two separate words, such as *sound barrier;* and hyphenated compounds, such as *great-grandmother.*

Here are some examples:

The cure-all for most violent crime is legalizing drugs.

Clarence Darrow was an attorney-at-law with a conscience.

Every celebrity needs a hideaway for escape.

Refer to a dictionary whenever you are in doubt about how to write a particular compound word.

Most *compound adjectives* of two or more words are hyphenated:

A fun-loving attitude adds zest to living.

After years of hard work, she gained well-earned respect.

But if the compound adjective *follows* the noun, the words should not be hyphenated:

The respect was well earned.

To Divide Words

Arranging text on a page obviously requires breaking it into separate lines. To make those lines as even in length as possible, sometimes it's necessary to break words at the ends of lines. A hyphen is used to indicate such a break:

Emergency volunteers, medical workers, and aviation experts began sift-
ing through the wreckage.

You should always divide words between syllables, which means you can't divide one-syllable words. Also, don't divide a word so that a single letter ends a line or fewer than three letters begin a line. Always divide a compound word where the words join; if you can't, then move the whole word to the next line.

If you are unclear about where to break a word, refer to a dictionary. The syllable breaks are usually marked by dots: *a·vi·a·tion.*

You should also check with your instructor regarding his or her preference for hyphenation in student essays. As noted in earlier chapters on the research essay, some editorial styles (such as that of the Modern Language Association, or MLA) discourage hyphenation in student papers. It is acceptable, however, to break words that contain hyphens across lines.

Conventional Uses of Hyphens

Always use hyphens in spelling out numbers from *twenty-one* to *ninety-nine;* in fractions (*one-third*); with prefixes such as *ex-, self-,* and *all-;* and with the suffix *-elect:*

> At ninety-one Pablo Picasso died in France, where he lived three-fourths of his life. His talent was so all inclusive that art critics made him the century's master artist eleven years before it ended.

EXERCISE   *Using Hyphens*

Insert hyphens where appropriate in the following sentences.

1. Argentina won with a well developed game plan.
2. Self discipline and an all inclusive health strategy lead to a longer life.
3. The defense attorney cross examined the victim for thirty six minutes.
4. The H bomb had significantly more destructive power than the A bomb.
5. The ex convict was ill mannered but well dressed.

SPELLING

Nobody improves poor spelling without working at it. To get started, use a dictionary to check the spellings of words you are uncertain about. If you write on a word processor, use the "Spellcheck" program to check spelling in each paper you write. But be careful: A "Spellcheck" won't distinguish among words that sound the same but are spelled differently, such as *accept/except; their/there/they're; who's/whose; its/it's;* and *won/one.*

Also compile a personal list of spelling demons—words you frequently misspell, such as *occasion, separate, rhythm, negotiator,* and *strategy.* When you use a word on your demon list, double-check its spelling.

Finally, remembering basic spelling guidelines and commonly misspelled words will help you eliminate spelling errors. Try to remember the following:

1. Place *i* before *e* except after *c* or when pronounced like *ay* as in *neighbor* or *weigh*.

i BEFORE *e*

chief, grief, belief, brief, fierce, frieze, sieve

e BEFORE *i*

ceiling, conceit, receive, freight, eight

EXCEPTIONS

either, neither, foreign, forfeit, height, leisure, weird, seize, sheik

2. Usually drop the silent final *e* before a suffix that begins with a vowel. Usually keep the silent final *e* before a suffix that begins with a consonant.

DROP THE *e*

come + ing = coming   force + ible = forcible

fame + ous = famous   love + able = lovable

EXCEPTIONS

dying, singeing, mileage, noticeable, courageous

KEEP THE *e*

care + ful = careful   arrange + ment = arrangement

EXCEPTIONS

awful, ninth, truly, argument, judgment

3. When a final *y* follows a consonant, change *y* to *i* before a suffix except when the suffix begins with *i*.

y BEFORE A CONSONANT

try + ed = tried   messy + er = messier

y BEFORE A VOWEL

obey + ed = obeyed   sway + s = sways

SUFFIX BEGINNING WITH *i*

apply + ing = applying   try + ing = trying

4. Double the final consonant before a suffix beginning with a vowel if the word has only one syllable or is stressed on the last syllable.

drop + ing = dropping	stop + ed = stopped
forget + ing = forgetting	submit + ed = submitted

5. Form plurals correctly. Add an -s to form the plurals of most words. Add -es to form the plurals of words ending in -s, -sh, -ch, and -x. For most words ending in -y, change the y to i and add -es.

book, books	dress, dresses	bush, bushes
fox, foxes	fly, flies	church, churches

Form the plural of a hyphenated word by adding an -s to the main word:

son-in-law, sons-in-law   passer-by, passers-by

Form the plurals of family names ending in -y by adding -s, such as *McCurry/McCurrys*.

Form the plurals of most nouns ending in -f or -fe by adding -s. The plurals of some of these nouns are formed by changing the -f to -v and adding an -s or -es:

chief, chiefs	dwarf, dwarfs	roof, roofs
calf, calves	knife, knives	leaf, leaves

Form the plurals of words ending in -o following a vowel by adding an -s. But form the plurals of most words ending in -o following a consonant by adding -es:

radio, radios   mosquito, mosquitoes

However, form the plurals of musical terms ending in -o by adding an -s:

piano, pianos   solo, solos

The plurals of a few nouns are formed by irregular methods:

child, children	goose, geese	mouse, mice
ox, oxen	tooth, teeth	woman, women

Some nouns borrowed from French, Greek, and Latin retain the plural forms of the original languages:

alumnus, alumni	analysis, analyses
basis, bases	datum, data
medium, media	criterion, criteria

And some nouns are the same in plural and singular forms:

deer   Chinese   species   trout

EXERCISE   *Using Spelling Guidelines*

Complete each of the following words by filling in the blank with *ie* or *ei*, whichever is correct.

1. w__rd   6. l__sure
2. p__ce   7. c__ling
3. perc__ve   8. ach__ve
4. n__ce   9. for__gn
5. th__f   10. rec__pt

Add the final suffix to each word below, correcting the spelling as needed. Be able to explain the rule that applies to spelling each word. Use the dictionary to check your work.

11. unwrap + ed   16. casual + ly
12. stubborn + ness   17. move + ing
13. plant + ing   18. merry + ly
14. ski + ing   19. argue + ment
15. commit + ed   20. write + ing

Write the plural form of each of the following words. Be able to explain your spelling according to the rules for forming plurals. Refer to a dictionary when in doubt.

21. father-in-law   26. crisis
22. cameo   27. loaf
23. wife   28. alumnus
24. loss   29. Kelly
25. box   30. approach

Commonly Confused Words

Many spelling errors result from confusion over commonly used words. Learn the spellings and the meanings of the following commonly confused words:

accept	to receive
except	to exclude
advice	counsel (noun)
advise	to give advice (verb)

affect	to influence (verb)
effect	a result (noun); to accomplish (verb)
all ready	prepared
already	previously
brake	to stop
break	to smash
buy	to purchase
by	near
capital	accumulated wealth; city serving government seat
capitol	building in which legislative body meets (lowercase for state, uppercase for federal)
choose	to select
chose	past tense of *choose*
cite	to quote
sight	ability to see
site	a place
complement	something that completes
compliment	a flattering remark
conscience	moral sense (noun)
conscious	aware (adj.)
coarse	rough (adj.)
course	path, procedure, class, process (noun)
decent	moral (adj.)
descent	a way down (noun)
dissent	disagree (verb); difference of opinion (noun)
desert	barren land (noun); to abandon (verb)
dessert	last course of a meal
formally	in a formal manner
formerly	previously
forth	forward
fourth	after *third*
hear	to perceive by the ear (verb)
here	in this place
heard	past tense of *hear*
herd	a group of animals
instance	an example
instants	moments

its   possessive of *it*
it's   contraction of *it is*

lead   to show the way (verb); a metal (noun)
led   past tense of *to lead*

lessen   to make less
lesson   something learned

loose   to free from restraint (verb); not fastened (adj.)
lose   to misplace; to be deprived of

passed   past tense of *pass*
past   no longer current (adj.); an earlier time (noun); beyond in time
                     or place (prep.)

peace   the absence of strife
piece   a part of something

plain   clear (adj.); level land (noun)
plane   airplane; carpenter's tool

principal   most important (adj.); leader (noun)
principle   basic truth or law (noun)

right   correct (adj.)
rite   ceremony (noun)
write   to record (verb)

road   a driving surface
rode   past tense of *ride*

stationary   unmoving
stationery   writing paper

their   possessive of *they*
there   in that place
they're   contraction of *they are*

to   toward
too   also; excess amount
two   the number following *one*

weak   not strong
week   Sunday through Saturday

weather   condition of climate
whether   if, either

who's   contraction of *who is*
whose   possessive of *who*

your   possessive of *you*
you're   contraction of *you are*

EXERCISE *Using Commonly Confused Words*

For each of the following sentences, choose the correct word in parentheses.

1. The ancient temple was the (cite, sight, site) of mysterious rituals.
2. The coat does not (complement, compliment) the dress.
3. Her job is to (advice, advise) the board, not make its decisions.
4. You must contribute (weather, whether) you want to or not.
5. The boys were not (conscience, conscious) of the damage they did.
6. I think I know (who's, whose) thumbprint that is.
7. He stands as (stationary, stationery) as a statue.
8. There is a (principal, principle) cause for his joy—money!
9. Can you identify the (affect, effect) of the chemical?
10. (Accept, Except) for Roberta, no one was in the house last night.

Frequently Misspelled Words

Learn to spell frequently misspelled words. The following is a list of 100 commonly misspelled words:

absence	develop	maneuver	quiet
academic	dilemma	marriage	quite
accidentally	dining	mathematics	quizzes
accommodate	embarrass	misspelled	receive
achieve	emphasize	neither	reference
across	existence	ninth	referred
all right	familiar	occasion	referring
already	fascinate	occur	reminisce
apparent	February	occurrence	repetition
appearance	foreign	optimistic	rhythm
athletic	forty	parallel	ridiculous
attendance	friend	pastime	sacrifice
believe	fulfill	personnel	safety
benefited	government	precede	salary
Britain	grammar	prejudice	satellite
business	harass	prevalent	secretary
calendar	height	privilege	seize
candidate	independent	probably	separate
cemetery	intelligence	procedure	sergeant
definite	license	proceed	similar
desperate	luxury	quantity	sincerely

sophomore	succeed	tendency	vacuum
specimen	succession	thorough	vengeance
strategy	surprise	tragedy	weird
subtly	temperament	usually	writing

EXERCISE   *Correcting Frequently Misspelled Words*

Test yourself on the list of frequently misspelled words. Ask someone to read each word aloud so that you can spell it.

Author Biographies

Maya Angelou, "Finishing School"

Angelou has been a dancer, actress, script-writer, television writer and producer, poet, and civil rights activist. She is perhaps best known for her autobiography *I Know Why the Caged Bird Sings*.

Judy Brady, "I Want a Wife"

As a wife and the mother of two children, Brady has written extensively on feminist issues. She studied painting at the University of Iowa and worked as a secretary in San Francisco before traveling to Cuba to study social class relationships.

William F. Buckley, Jr., "Why Don't We Complain?"

As the founder and editor-in-chief of *National Review*, a journal of conservative politics and opinion, Buckley has been a leading voice for conservative causes for many years.

K. C. Cole, "Entropy"

Cole writes on science, especially physics, for a number of national publications, such as the *New York Times*, the *Washington Post*, and *Discover* magazine. His essays have been collected in *Sympathetic Vibrations: Reflections on Physics as a Way of Life*.

David James Duncan, "Toxins in the Mother Tongue"

An Oregon native, Duncan's first novel, *The River Why*, won the Pacific Northwest Booksellers Award for Library Excellence.

Barbara Ehrenreich, "Marginal Men"

Ehrenreich has a PhD in biology and has published nonfiction books, a novel, and extensive articles, essays, and book reviews on a wide variety of subjects.

Gretel Ehrlich, "About Men"

Ehrlich is an American poet, essayist, journalist, and filmmaker. Her best-known work is *The Solace of Open Spaces*, a collection of personal essays based on her experience as a rancher following the death of a loved one.

C. Eugene Emery, Jr., "Shameless Talk Shows"

Emery is a social commentator who writes extensively on popular media.

Stephanie Ericsson, "Why People Lie"

Ericsson writes for a variety of magazines and is the author of *Companion through the Darkness: Inner Dialogues on Grief*.

Neal Gabler, "How Urban Myths Reveal Society's Fears"

Gabler won the 1988 Theatre Library Association Award for excellence in writing about film, television, and radio for his book *An Empire of Their Own: How the Jews Invented Hollywood*.

Leonce Gaiter, "The Revolt of the Black Bourgeoisie"

Currently living in Los Angeles, Gaiter often writes on social issues.

Willard Gaylin, "What You See Is the Real You"

Gaylin is a psychiatrist and psychoanalyst who co-founded the Institute of Society, Ethics, and the Life Sciences. His published works, which reflect a wide range of interests, include *In the Service of Their Country: War Resisters in Prison, Partial Justice: A Study of Bias in Sentencing, Feelings: Our Vital Signs*, and *Rediscovering Love*.

George Gilder, "Why Men Marry"

Gilder is a sociologist who has observed, studied, and written about various social phenomena. His works include *Men and Marriage, Life after Television*, and *Visible Man: A True Story of Post-Racist America*.

Ellen Goodman, "Becoming Desensitized to Hate Words"

As a syndicated columnist for the *Boston Globe*, the *Washington Post*, and other newspapers, Goodman keeps a keen eye on social movements and postures.

Pete Hamill, "Crack and the Box"

Hamill has been a sheet metal worker, advertising designer, and journalist. He has written for such publications as the *New York Post, Newsday*, the *New York Daily News, Esquire*, and the *Village Voice*. Hamill also writes screenplays, short stories, and novels. In 1994 he published *A Drinking Life: A Memoir*.

Linda Hasselstrom

Hasselstrom is a rancher in western South Dakota as well as an environmental writer and poet. Her books of poetry include *Caught by One Wing* and *Roadkill.* Her nonfiction works include *Windbreak: A Woman Rancher on the Northern Plains*.

Stephen King, "Why We Crave Horror Movies"

King is a prolific and enormously popular writer, most notably of horror fiction. His latest novel is *Bag of Bones*.

■ **Andrew Klavan, "The Shrieking of the Lambs"**

An American writer living in England, Klavan is known for suspense novels, such as *Agnes Mallory.*

■ **Michael Levin, "The Case for Torture"**

Levin is a professor of philosophy at City College of the City University of New York.

■ **Michael Medved, "Denial Behavior"**

Medved is a film critic for the *New York Post* and the Public Broadcasting System (PBS). He is noted for his critical analysis of the film and television industries, *Hollywood versus America.*

■ **Alleen Pace Nilsen, "Sexism in English"**

Nilsen earned her doctorate from the University of Iowa, where she studied the sexism of language in children's literature. She currently teaches at Arizona State University.

■ **George Orwell, "A Hanging"**

Orwell, whose real name was Eric Arthur Blair, is most famous for his novels *Animal Farm* and *1984.* He also served in the Indian Imperial Police in Burma (now Myanmar) in 1922.

■ **Neil Postman, "Future Shlock"**

Often calling for radical educational reform, Postman has written extensively on American education. He is noted for such works as *Teaching as a Subversive Activity* and *Amusing Ourselves to Death: Public Discourse in the Age of Show Business.*

■ **Mike Royko, "Endorsements: Just a Shell Game"**

Royko, a long-time columnist for the *Chicago Tribune* who died suddenly in 1997, has been called a "journalist's journalist," "a guard dog of the common man," and a "thick-skinned curmudgeon." His writing is characterized by compassion mixed with biting satire. His early columns have been collected in *Sez Who? Sez Me: Mike Royko,* but he is more widely known for his exposé of Chicago politics, *Boss: Richard J. Daley of Chicago.*

■ **George Simpson, "The War Room at Bellevue"**

Simpson has written for such publications as the *New York Times* and *Newsweek* and *New York* magazines. He won the Sigma Delta Chi Best Feature Writing Award in 1972 for a series of articles on the football program at the University of North Carolina.

■ **Gary Soto, "Like Mexicans"**

Soto, a poet and essayist, worked as a farm laborer picking produce in California's San Joaquin Valley. He attended Fresno City College (where he encountered poetry), California State University at Fresno, and the University of California at Irvine and now teaches at the University of California at Berkeley. He is best known for his volumes of

recollections, *Living Up the Street: Narrative Recollections* and *A Summer Life.*

■ **Brent Staples, "Black Men and Public Space"**

Staples has been a science writer for the *Chicago Sun-Times* and is currently an editorial writer for the *New York Times.* In his highly acclaimed memoir, *Parallel Time: Growing Up in Black and White,* he explores the complexities of living in a multicultural world.

■ **Jonathan Swift, "A Modest Proposal"**

Born of English parents who lived in Ireland, Swift was ordained in the Church of Ireland in 1665 and eventually became dean of St. Patrick's Cathedral, Dublin. He devoted much of his life to exposing the injustices imposed by the English against the Irish.

■ **Amy Tan, "Mother Tongue"**

Tan is a popular and critically acclaimed American novelist. Her novels *The Joy Luck Club* and *The Kitchen God's Wife* have examined the immigrant experience as well as the relationships among young Chinese American women. Her latest work is *The Hundred Secret Senses.*

■ **Paul Theroux, "Being a Man"**

Born in Medford, Massachusetts, Theroux is a poet, essayist, and novelist. He has spent many years teaching abroad and is well known for his travel writing, including such works as *The Great Railway Bazaar: By Train through Asia* and *The Old Patagonian Express: By Train through the Americas.*

■ **Lewis Thomas, "On Natural Death"**

Thomas has been a pathologist, a practicing medical doctor, a biologist, a professor, and a writer. He is well known for his "occasional" essays, written for the *New England Journal of Medicine* and collected in *The Lives of a Cell: Notes of a Biology Watcher* and *The Medusa and the Snail: More Notes of a Biology Watcher.*

■ **Mark Twain, "The Damned Human Race"**

Under the pen name Mark Twain, Samuel L. Clemens became one of America's major nineteenth-century novelists, journalists, and humorists. He worked as a riverboat pilot, gold prospector, and printer. At least two of his novels— *The Adventures of Tom Sawyer* and *The Adventures of Huckleberry Finn*—are considered American classics.

■ **E. B. White, "Once More to the Lake"**

Elwyn Brooks White, one of America's foremost modern essayists, worked as an editor for *The New Yorker* for 60 years. A prolific writer of essays, letters, poetry, and children's tales, he is noted for *Essays of E. B. White* and *Letters of E. B. White* along with *Charlotte's Web,* an endearing children's classic.

Rhetorical Index

Most writers use a variety of paragraph structures to develop an idea, such as description, narration, illustration, and comparison. As a result, their essays cannot be easily categorized by rhetorical pattern. Essays do, however, usually embody *dominant* patterns.

In the list that follows, essays are grouped by dominant patterns; some essays are listed in more than one category because their authors rely heavily on other patterns to develop their thoughts. For example, the dominant pattern of Linda M. Hasselstrom's "Why One Peaceful Woman Carries a Pistol" is cause and effect, but Hasselstrom relies heavily on examples from personal experience.

Description

George Simpson, " The War Room at Bellevue," 600
Through the objective eye of a reporter, Simpson describes the events of a typical night in the Bellevue emergency room.

E. B. White, "Once More to the Lake," 635
White merges past and present in this description of a summertime retreat.

Narration

Maya Angelou, "Finishing School," 479
Angelou narrates an event from her early childhood to reveal hypocrisy and racial differences.

George Orwell, "A Hanging," 589
Told from the point of view of a military officer, Orwell recounts the brief journey from a prisoner's cell to the gallows.

Amy Tan, "Mother Tongue," 616
Although the dominant pattern in this essay is development by examples, Tan uses several narrative examples, as well.

Examples

Linda M. Hasselstrom, "Why One Peaceful Woman Carries a Pistol," 545
Hasselstrom uses a variety of examples to explain the reasons she travels armed.

Michael Levin, "The Case for Torture," 567
To develop his argument, Levin uses several hypothetical examples.

Neil Postman, "Future Shlock," 593
Using novels, films, television programming, and historical events as examples, Postman illustrates his claim that the United States is the Empire of Shlock.

Brent Staples, "Black Men and Public Space," 606
In a series of anecdotal examples, Staples illustrates his experience as an African American walking and shopping in "public space."

Amy Tan, "Mother Tongue," 616
Raised in a bilingual family, Tan gives examples of the two "Englishes" that have dominated her life.

Lewis Thomas, "On Natural Death," 625
Using examples from personal observation and reading, Thomas illustrates his contention that pain recedes as death approaches.

Comparison and Contrast

Barbara Ehrenreich, "Marginal Men," 506
Ehrenreich defines *marginal men* through implicit comparison and contrast.

Pete Hamill, "Crack and the Box," 540
Hamill compares drug addiction with television viewing.

Process Analysis

Cause and Effect

Classification

Definition

Thematic Index

General Index

Text Credits

Photo Credits